the Unofficial Guide® to England

Also available from John Wiley & Sons, Inc.:

Beyond Disney: The Unofficial Guide to Universal, SeaWorld, and the Best of Central Florida

Inside Disney: The Incredible Story of Walt Disney World and the Man Behind the Mouse

Mini Las Vegas: The Pocket-Sized Unofficial Guide to Las Vegas

Mini-Mickey: The Pocket-Sized Unofficial Guide to Walt Disney World

The Unofficial Guide to Bed & Breakfasts and Country Inns:
California Great Lakes States Mid-Atlantic
New England Northwest Rockies
Southeast Southwest

The Unofficial Guide to the Best RV and Tent Campgrounds:
California and the West Florida and the Southeast
Great Lakes Mid-Atlantic Northeast Northwest
Southwest U.S.A.

The Unofficial Guide to Branson, Missouri

The Unofficial Guide to California with Kids

The Unofficial Guide to Central Italy: Florence, Rome, Tuscany, and Umbria

The Unofficial Guide to Chicago

The Unofficial Guide to Cruises

The Unofficial Guide to Disneyland

The Unofficial Guide to Disneyland Paris

The Unofficial Guide to Florida with Kids

The Unofficial Guide to Golf Vacations in the Eastern U.S.

The Unofficial Guide to the Great Smoky and Blue Ridge Region

The Unofficial Guide to Hawai'i

The Unofficial Guide to Las Vegas

The Unofficial Guide to London

The Unofficial Guide to Maui

The Unofficial Guide to Mexico's Best Beach Resorts

The Unofficial Guide to New Orleans

The Unofficial Guide to New York City

The Unofficial Guide to Paris

The Unofficial Guide to San Francisco

The Unofficial Guide to Skiing in the West

The Unofficial Guide to the Southeast with Kids

The Unofficial Guide to South Florida, including Miami and the Keys

The Unofficial Guide to Walt Disney World

The Unofficial Guide to Walt Disney World with Kids

The Unofficial Guide to Walt Disney World for Grown-Ups

The Unofficial Guide to Walt Disney World with Kids

The Unofficial Guide to Washington, D.C.

The Unofficial Guide to the World's Best Diving Vacations

the Unofficial Guide® to England

1st Edition

Stephen Brewer

WILEY

Please note that prices fluctuate in the course of time, and travel information changes under the impact of many factors that influence the travel industry. We therefore suggest that you write or call ahead for confirmation when making your travel plans. Every effort has been made to ensure the accuracy of information throughout this book, and the contents of this publication are believed correct at the time of printing. Nevertheless, the publishers cannot accept responsibility for errors or omissions or for changes in details given in this guide or for the consequences of any reliance on the information provided by the same. Assessments of attractions and so forth are based upon the author's own experience, and therefore, descriptions given in this guide necessarily contain an element of subjective opinion, which may not reflect the publisher's opinion or dictate a reader's own experience on another occasion. Readers are invited to write the publisher with ideas, comments, and suggestions for future editions.

Published by:
John Wiley & Sons, Inc.
111 River Street
Hoboken, NJ 07030

Produced by Menasha Ridge Press
Cover design by Michael J. Freeland
Interior design by Michele Laseau

For information on our other products and services or to obtain technical support please contact our Customer Care Department within the U.S. at (800) 762-2974, outside the U.S. at (317) 572-3993 or fax (317) 572-4002.

John Wiley & Sons, Inc. also publishes its books in a variety of electronic formats. Some content that appears in print may not be available in electronic formats.

ISBN 0-7645-6719-5

ISSN 1544-0613

Manufactured in the United States of America

5 4 3 2 1

Contents

Part Four London 73

Part Five The Southeast of England 201

Part Six The South of England 239

Part Seven The Southwest of England 289

Part Eight Bath, Oxford, and the Cotswolds 325

Part Nine The Heartland and Welsh Border 375

List of Maps

Acknowledgments

I wish to acknowledge the contributions of Donald Olson, enlightened colleague and sometime traveling companion, and Lesley Logan, long-time Londoner. I dedicate this book to the late Gertrude Buckman, who over the many years of our friendship never tired of sharing her enthusiasm for her adopted country. Thanks go to Geoffrey Hollis, for his hospitality and deft driving skills, and to the staff of *Visit Britain,* for unfailing patience and objectivity. And much gratitude to editor Chris Mohney and the rest of the staff of Menasha Ridge Press, who made it possible, and such a pleasure, to write about this endlessly fascinating island.

–Stephen Brewer

Introduction

Welcome to England

So, you're going to England! We could drag out all the workhorses—you know, all those Shakespearean lines about this "blessed plot, this earth, this realm" or "sceptered isle, this royal throne of kings." We won't, because we don't necessarily think of this fascinating, complex, ever-changing island nation of 60 million souls in such highbrow terms, although pomp and ceremony are certainly a visible and much appreciated part of British culture. Besides, you will be bringing with you plenty of your own notions of what England is like. In fact, your perceptions of what England is or should be may well have inspired you to buy the ticket for the flight to Heathrow (or Gatwick or Manchester) in the first place. Your impressions may have been shaped by Puck, Oliver Twist, Miss Marple, Inspector Morse, or Bond, James Bond . . . the fact is, you'll probably come to England with some notion of what you'll find there, and you probably won't be disappointed.

Yes, many of the stereotypes are true. The British stand patiently in line (on queue), and you'd better be prepared to do the same. They really do talk about the weather (which, given the changeability of the weather systems that sweep over the country, is a fairly juicy topic of conversation), soccer hooligans are even more frightening up close than they are on TV, and you only need stand on an underground platform surrounded by blue-suited gents on their way to work in the City to understand what's meant by "stiff upper lip." Of course, you've come to England to see treasures, and you'll find them: the museum masterpieces, villages of half-timbered houses, soaring cathedrals, ruined abbeys, castles and country houses. Then, too, you'll want to see some theater, step in and out of High Street shops, hunker down with a pint (of beer) and a ploughman's lunch (cheddar, a bread roll, and pickled onions), or settle in for a four-course dinner. In *The Unofficial Guide to England,* we help you do all this.

Plan on the unexpected, too—on being a bit overwhelmed by England, on having your notions of what England is like turned upside down, on being bombarded with new sensations and impressions. In London, take a walk along the South Bank and Bankside, currently the city's "happening place"; check out the new Saatchi Gallery, filled with works by young British artists; see the *Golden Hinde,* Sir Francis Drake's flagship; marvel at a natty reconstruction of Shakespeare's Globe Theatre; and the Tate Modern, where modern art hangs in a former power plant. The point is obvious—there's layer upon layer of history in England. Mighty cathedrals are built atop Saxon and Norman churches; modern streets follow the paths of Roman roads; Georgian elegance and Victorian arrogance are in evidence in cities and small towns alike. Just as intriguing, though, is the way that England continues to evolve. Just step into those aforementioned art museums on the banks of the Thames to see how England's knack for setting a trend didn't come to a close with the end of the 1960s. No small part of the pleasure of walking through a centuries-old city like Salisbury or Winchester or York or Bath is to see the effects of successful urban planning and a pride in preserving the old while carrying on with the present day.

The Unofficial Guide to England will show you how to make the most of your trip to England, whether you're traveling on business or pleasure. We share our enthusiasm with you, and take you to our favorite hotels, museums, and patches of moorland. (For a highly selective list of our favorite places in England, see the "Not to Be Missed" lists at the beginning of each chapter.) We like to think that our advice will make your trip through England enjoyable and memorable. But follow your own travel instincts, too. Make discoveries of your own; take time out for some quiet contemplation in a cathedral or a park or in front of a painting when the mood hits; step into a pub on a rainy afternoon and enjoy a pint next to a crackling fire; wander through the back streets of a country town and follow a footpath or two across the greenest countryside you'll ever see. We'll help you with all the basics, but we leave it up to you to enjoy the sceptered isle the way you wish.

About This Guide

Why "Unofficial"?

Most travel guides to England follow the usual tracks of the typical tourist: automatically sending everyone to the well-known towns and sights without offering any information about how to tour in a way to get the most out of the visit; recommending restaurants and hotels indiscriminately; and failing to recognize the limits of human endurance in sight-seeing. This guide is different. We appreciate the fact that you'll want to be discerning about hotels and restaurants, to spend your time doing what you really want to do and seeing what you want to see.

Accordingly, we help you make the choices you need to make in order to get the most out of your trip to England. We tell you what we think of certain tourist traps, why you should spend time in one place and not in another, what rooms to ask for in hotels, what to order (and not to order) in restaurants, what the options are if you want to stay off the beaten track, and how to spend a little less money so you can splurge a little when you want to (and we give you suggestions of places worthy of a splurge). We complain about rip-offs, advise you on bargains, and steer you out of the madness of the crowds for a break now and then. We also give you the kind of details, from historical background to juicy tidbits, that will make you appreciate England all the more.

We're well aware of the fact that you probably only have a week or two to spend in England, so we've done the footwork to help you prepare and strategize to get the most out of your time. We lead you to hotels that offer the best deals and the most pleasant surroundings, good restaurants in varying price ranges, the sights you won't want to miss (and when to visit them, so you won't have to cope with crowds). In laying out our visits, we take things easy—the way we think you'll want to travel—and we have gone to considerable effort to ensure that the quality of your travels in England will be high and the irritation quotient low. We've tried to anticipate the special needs of older people, families with young children, families with teenagers, solo travelers, people with physical challenges, and those who have a particular passion for literature, sports, architecture, shopping, painting, antiques, or whatever.

Please remember that prices and admission hours change constantly; we have listed the most up-to-date information we can get, but it never hurts to double-check times in particular (if prices of attractions change, it is generally not by much). Most of all, whether you're visiting England for the first time or the twentieth time, traveling on pleasure or business, we trust we will help you better enjoy the experience.

About *Unofficial Guides*

Readers care about authors' opinions. The authors, after all, are supposed to know what they are talking about. This, coupled with the fact that the traveler wants quick answers (as opposed to endless alternatives), dictates that travel authors should be explicit, prescriptive, and above all, direct. The authors of the *Unofficial Guide* try to be just that. We spell out alternatives and recommend specific courses of action. We simplify complicated destinations and attractions to allow the traveler to feel in control in the most unfamiliar environments. Our objective is not to give the most information or all the information, but the most accessible, useful information. Of course, there are many hotels, restaurants, and attractions that are so closely woven into the fabric of England that omitting them from our guide because we can't recommend them would be a disservice to our readers. So, we've included all the famous haunts, giving our opinion and experience of them, in the hopes that you will approach (or avoid) these institutions armed with the necessary intelligence.

An *Unofficial Guide* is a critical reference work; we focus on a travel destination that appears to be especially complex. Our authors and researchers are completely independent from the attractions, restaurants, and hotels we describe. *The Unofficial Guide to England* will be especially helpful to those hopping "across the pond" for the first time. The guide is directed at value-conscious, consumer-oriented adults who seek a cost-effective but not spartan travel style.

Special Features

- Vital information about traveling abroad.
- Introductions to English towns and cities.
- Listings that are keyed to your interests, so you can pick and choose.
- Advice to sightseers on how to avoid the worst crowds; advice to business travelers on how to avoid traffic and excessive costs.
- Recommendations for lesser-known sights that are off the beaten tourist path but no less worthwhile.
- In London, a zone system and maps to make it easy to find places you want to go and avoid places you want to skip.
- Hotel and restaurant selections that help you narrow down your choices quickly, according to your needs and preferences.
- A table of contents and detailed index to help you find things fast.

What You Won't Get

- Long, useless lists where everything sounds the same.
- Information that gets you to your destination at the worst possible time.
- Information without advice on how to use it.

How This Guide Was Researched and Written

In preparing this book, we took nothing for granted. Each hotel, restaurant, shop, and attraction was visited by trained observers who conducted detailed evaluations and rated each according to formal criteria. Team members conducted interviews with tourists of all ages to determine what they enjoyed most and least during their visit to England.

Though our observers are independent and impartial, they are otherwise "ordinary" travelers. Like you, they visited England as tourists or business travelers, noting their satisfaction or dissatisfaction. The primary difference between the average tourist and the trained evaluator is the evaluator's skills in organization, preparation, and observation. A trained evaluator is responsible for more than just observing and cataloging. Observer teams use detailed checklists to analyze hotel rooms, restaurants, nightclubs, and attractions. Finally, evaluator ratings and observations are integrated with tourist reactions and the opinions of patrons for a comprehensive quality profile of each feature and service.

In compiling this guide, we recognize that a tourist's age, background, and interests will strongly influence his or her taste in England's wide array of attractions and will account for a preference for one sight or museum over another. Our sole objective is to provide the reader with sufficient description, critical evaluation, and pertinent data to make knowledgeable decisions according to individual tastes.

Letters, Comments, and Questions from Readers

We expect to learn from our mistakes, as well as from the input of our readers, and to improve with each new book and edition. Many of those who use the *Unofficial Guides* write to us asking questions, making comments, or sharing their own discoveries and lessons learned. New hotels, restaurants, and attractions are opening all the time in England, and if there's something new you'd like us to check out, let us know about it. We appreciate all such input and encourage our readers to continue writing. Readers' comments and observations will be frequently incorporated in revised editions of *The Unofficial Guide to England* and will contribute immeasurably to its improvement.

How to Write the Author

Stephen Brewer
The Unofficial Guide to England
P.O. Box 43673
Birmingham, AL 35243

When you write, be sure to put your return address on your letter as well as on the envelope—sometimes envelopes and letters get separated. Remember, our work takes us out of the office for long periods of time, so forgive us if our response is delayed.

How This Guide Is Organized: By Region and by Subject

We have organized this guide by region—not by any sort of official or government-designated regional organization, but by manageably sized geographic areas that we use to help you plan your travels through England. We then organize each region by the major (and the most appealing) cities and towns that you can use as a base. Within our coverage of each place, you'll find detailed coverage on the following:

Planning Your Visit, listing local information resources and seasonal events that may or may not help you decide when to visit.

Hotels, so you can peruse our choices and book ahead if you wish.

Arriving and Getting Oriented, where we give information on reaching the city by air (when relevant), train, car (including where to park), and bus.

Getting Around (in larger destinations where walking is not an option), with detailed descriptions of how to use the bus network, underground, or other public transportation.

Tours, with our choices for the best guided tours to help you become acquainted with a place.

Exploring, where we lead you through a town, city, or region, pointing out the sights (including those of secondary interest but still worth a quick visit), then provide detailed profiles of all the major sight-seeing attractions.

Dining, with our choices of the most pleasant places to eat.

Entertainment and Nightlife, where we lead you to theaters, concert halls, pubs, discos, and other venues.

Shopping, with a focus on items that are unique to a particular place.

Exercise and Recreation, with ideas on where to exercise—we often lead you to walking and biking trails, of which England has so many.

We discuss these categories in greater depth in Part Two, Arriving and Getting around in England; and in Part Three, Lodging, Dining, and Shopping in England. Below are the geographical regions that comprise our coverage of England.

London

Okay, we know you've heard it, but there's no harm in hauling out the famous old saw from Dr. Samuel Johnson just one more time: "When a man is tired of London, he is tired of Life, for there is in London all that Life can afford." We never tire of London, after years of residency and countless visits to the capital. You will find so much to amuse you in London, from centuries-old art to colorful buskers (street musicians), that you will probably have a hard time tearing yourself away to visit other parts of England. We guide you through all the major attractions (and many of our favorite minor ones) and provide our top choices for hotels, restaurants, shops, and clubs—all with an eye to making sure you appreciate one of the world's great cities as much as we do.

The Southeast of England

Here you'll follow twisting roads through the beautiful countryside of Kent and Sussex to two of the most delightful places in all of England: Canterbury, the famous cathedral city that has been attracting pilgrims for centuries; and Rye, a romantic town of cobbled lanes and half-timbered houses that over the years has harbored smugglers and writers (including

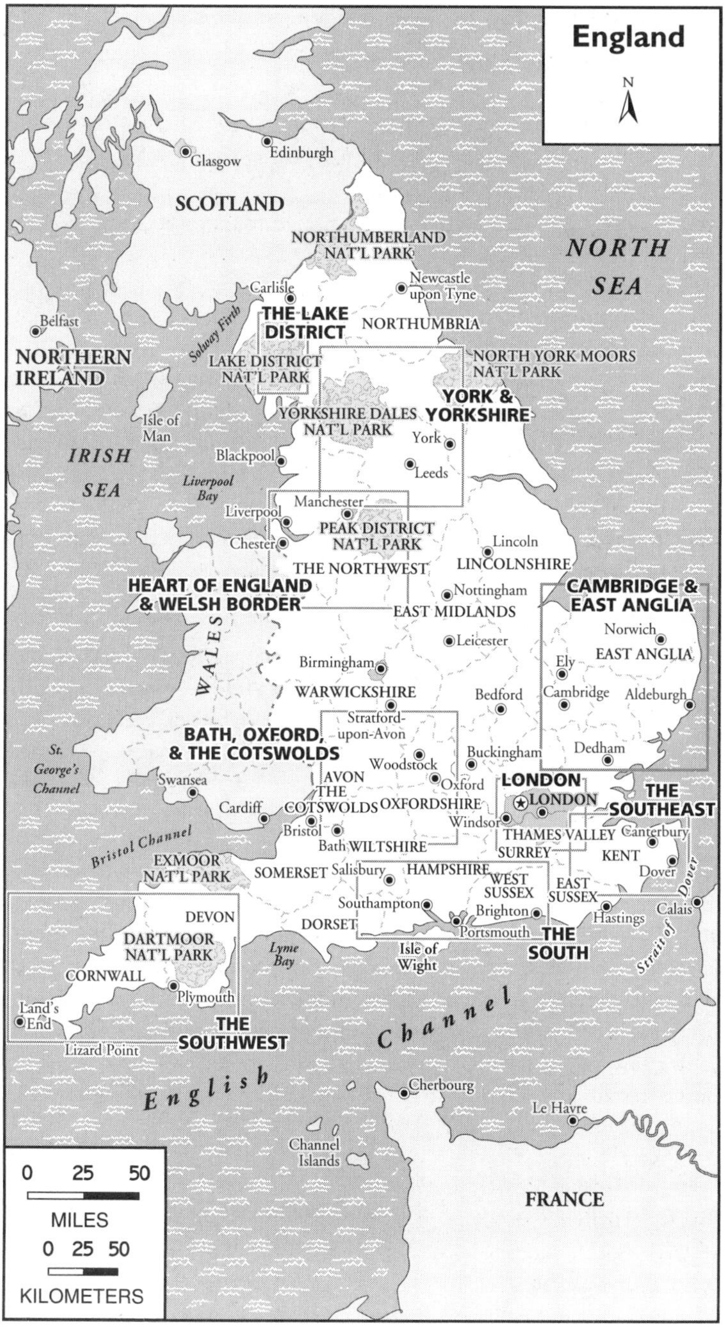
England
N
Glasgow
Edinburgh
SCOTLAND
NORTHUMBERLAND NAT'L PARK
NORTH SEA
Carlisle
Newcastle upon Tyne
THE LAKE DISTRICT
NORTHUMBRIA
Belfast
Solway Firth
NORTHERN IRELAND
LAKE DISTRICT NAT'L PARK
NORTH YORK MOORS NAT'L PARK
YORK & YORKSHIRE
YORKSHIRE DALES NAT'L PARK
Isle of Man
York
IRISH SEA
Blackpool
Leeds
Liverpool Bay
Manchester
Liverpool
PEAK DISTRICT NAT'L PARK
Chester
Lincoln
THE NORTHWEST
LINCOLNSHIRE
HEART OF ENGLAND & WELSH BORDER
Nottingham
CAMBRIDGE & EAST ANGLIA
EAST MIDLANDS
WALES
Norwich
Leicester
EAST ANGLIA
Birmingham
Ely
Cambridge
Aldeburgh
WARWICKSHIRE
Bedford
Stratford-upon-Avon
BATH, OXFORD, & THE COTSWOLDS
Dedham
Buckingham
St. George's Channel
Woodstock
AVON
Oxford
LONDON
Swansea
THE COTSWOLDS
OXFORDSHIRE
THE SOUTHEAST
Cardiff
Windsor
Bristol
THAMES VALLEY
Canterbury
Bath
WILTSHIRE
Bristol Channel
SURREY
KENT
EXMOOR NAT'L PARK
SOMERSET
Salisbury
HAMPSHIRE
WEST SUSSEX
EAST SUSSEX
Dover
Southampton
Brighton
Hastings
Calais
DEVON
DORSET
Portsmouth
THE SOUTH
Strait of Dover
DARTMOOR NAT'L PARK
Lyme Bay
Isle of Wight
CORNWALL
Plymouth
Land's End
THE SOUTHWEST
Lizard Point
English Channel
Cherbourg
Le Havre
Channel Islands
FRANCE
0 25 50
MILES
0 25 50
KILOMETERS

Henry James). Nearby are notable castles (including Leeds and Dover) and some of England's greatest country homes, manors, and gardens.

The South of England

We focus our coverage of the South on Brighton, the garish seaside playground of kings and queens (and these days, mere mortals); and Winchester and Salisbury, two appealing cathedral cities. From these cities you can cross the downs and plains to visit the homes of Jane Austen and Virginia Woolf, and to get a sense of Britain's prehistoric past at Stonehenge.

The Southwest of England

England's southwestern counties, Devon and Cornwall, occupy a long peninsula that juts into the English Channel to the south and the Atlantic Ocean on the north, coming to a breathtakingly dramatic finale at Land's End, the western edge of England. Altogether, some 650 miles of coastline skirt these counties. You can walk along jagged coastlines (including the stretch at Tintagel of Arthurian legend) as well as across the wild moors of Dartmoor National Park, swim from golden sands, stroll through Heligan and other famous gardens, and then take your sight-seeing indoors for visits to such storied places as Exeter Cathedral.

Bath, Oxford, and the Cotswolds

In the Cotswolds, a region of rolling hills and villages of golden stone, you'll find the English countryside as you expect it to be. Two of England's most beautiful and fascinating cities are at the edges of the Cotswolds: Bath, a famous 18th- and 19th-century watering hole that was founded by the Romans and is now an architectural treasure trove; and Oxford, the lively and engaging home to one of the two great British universities.

The Heartland and Welsh Border

In the so-called heart of England are three manufacturing cities: Birmingham, Manchester, and Liverpool. Business travelers may well find themselves in one of these cities, and nearby places are likely to be of interest to leisure travelers, including Shakespeare's Stratford-upon-Avon, and Shrewsbury, one of several attractive towns near England's border with Wales.

Cambridge and East Anglia

This medieval university city is a pleasure to explore, and you can follow our suggestions for visiting the colleges of the famous university. Around Cambridge are any number of appealing towns and villages, including two noted cathedral cities, Ely and Norwich, as well as Newmarket, famous not for religious monuments but for the sport of kings.

York and Yorkshire

The walled, medieval city of York is at the center of this swath of northern England that consists of the deep, luxuriant river valleys of the Yorkshire

Dales and the rugged, heather-covered Yorkshire Moors. In these landscapes are literary shrines, such as Haworth, where the Brontë sisters wrote their masterpieces; ruined abbeys at Bolton, Rievaulx, and elsewhere; isolated but lavish country houses (Castle Howard may well be the grandest private home in England); and charming towns and villages, including seaside Whitby.

The Lake District

The poet William Wordsworth rambled and climbed through almost every square mile of this region wedged into a small corner of the northwest coast near the Scottish border, and you can follow his footsteps on hundreds of miles of walking paths. In addition to ambling, as the British describe the preferred way to enjoy these landscapes of peaks, crags, meadows, valleys, and lakes, you can visit historic homes (including two where Wordsworth lived) and explore towns and small villages built of slate and stone.

ENGLISH ETIQUETTE: Some Dos and Don'ts

The English often look at their American visitors with a mixture of amusement, appreciation, and (sigh) sometimes even contempt. Here are some dos and don'ts that may help keep the contempt quotient to a minimum.

- Don't call people by their first names unless expressly asked to do so—it is considered normal not to use names when addressing people.
- Don't try to intervene in soccer arguments—this is a very serious subject, one no outsider can comprehend properly.
- Don't brag about how much sunlight you get at home; this will not endear you to anyone.
- Do be prepared to talk about the weather. The British are passionate about the extremes of inclemency that nature inflicts on their islands, and they will often go so far as to discuss it vigorously with complete strangers.
- Don't tell anyone that his or her accent is "cute." It is you who have the accent, and it is not considered remotely cute by the British.
- Don't jump the queue. To jump the queue is the height of bad manners, an invitation for tut-tutting, muttered comments, and possibly even an open challenge.
- Do be courteous—it's much more appreciated than friendliness.
- Do remember that this is a country of rules, rules, rules—and they aren't just making them up as they go along, though it sometimes seems they are.
- Do be patient in restaurants and stores; use your vacation as an opportunity to slow down.
- Do learn to enjoy being called "love" and "darling" and "sweetheart" by certain strangers.
- Do prepare for your visit by reading as much as you can on England. Make the most of your visit.

An Overview of English History

England takes on even more interesting dimensions when you know something about its past. A bit of the history of England is just as useful for the discerning visitor as a map. So, here we go.

The Earliest Record

You've no doubt heard of Stonehenge, the famous stone circle on the Wiltshire plains. What you may not realize is that England is covered with ancient stone circles, from Wiltshire and Cornwall all the way up to Cumbria (the Lake District). These circles are evidence of a Neolithic civilization that was capable of cutting enormous stones, hauling them for miles, and erecting them in such a way that they served as astronomical calendars. The earliest circles probably date to about 3000 B.C.

England's history, because of its proximity to the Continent, was initially one of invasion and conquest. Because of England's system of monarchy, her later history is one of bloody factionalism and revolving persecutions. But throughout all of it, the history of England has been the history of commerce.

When Rome Ruled Britannia

Julius Caesar's famous remark about how Britons were simply not good slave material was sour grapes; he tried to subdue England twice, in 55 and 56 B.C., and he failed both times. In A.D. 43, the Romans again sent an army to conquer the island. This time they built a bridge over the Thames at the narrowest crossing, near the present London Bridge. Soon, this Roman fort called Londinium grew into a thriving port of commerce, as luxury goods from all over the Roman Empire arrived and were exchanged for corn, iron, and—Julius Caesar notwithstanding—slaves. Roman historian Tacitus wrote that Londinium was "famed for commerce and crowded with merchants," a description that would remain accurate for the next 2,000 years (and will continue to do so, one assumes). Roadways, the most ubiquitous and long-lasting feature of Roman rule, soon headed in every direction from this trading post and were well traveled by Romans and Britons in search of adventure and wealth. After a period of Pax Romana (peace imposed by ancient Rome on its dominions), the Roman rule became increasingly unbearable to the local tribes. Queen Boudicca of the Iceni tribe led a violent revolt, invading Londinium, massacring everyone in sight, and burning the camp to the ground. The revolution was short lived, however; Londinium was rebuilt with a huge wall around it, encompassing what is presently the City and Barbican area. A piece of the wall is preserved near the Museum of London, which displays relics of the Roman past.

Roman remains are scattered throughout England. A Roman-era lighthouse still stands at Dover Castle, Roman villas have been excavated in

Dover and in the Cotswolds, and fragments of original Roman road can still be seen on the Yorkshire moors. But perhaps the most spectacular remnant of the Romans in Britannia is Hadrian's Wall, which stretches for miles across the Northumbrian border with Scotland. In 410, the sun was setting on the Roman empire and the troops were withdrawn, leaving the sprouts of the newly adopted Christian faith behind. New invaders arrived and superstitiously stayed away from the Roman ruins, which were soon buried, not to be rediscovered until centuries later.

The Saxons

After the Saxons came over the North Sea in about 450 to settle in southeast England, London again became a trading post, called Lundenwic. King Ethelbert, after presiding over a pagan society, became a Christian convert, and the first cathedral of St. Paul was built. The Saxon kings spent most of the next five centuries fighting Viking invaders and fortifying their kingdom, whose capital was at Winchester. Little remains from the Saxon period, but here and there across the country you can still find Saxon churches. The oldest, St. Martin's Church in Canterbury, dates from the 6th century—and so do the nearby ruins of St. Augustine's Abbey, which was founded in A.D. 598.

In the 11th century, the Danes finally conquered the island, and England was forced to accept the Danish King Canute as its leader. Eboracum, a former Roman settlement in the north, became Jorvik, a Viking city, and eventually York. (An attraction in York called Jorvik, the Viking City, re-creates the Viking era.) Canute put London back on the map as the capital of the kingdom, and by 1042, when Edward the Confessor took the scepter, Westminster Abbey and the Palace at Westminster gave the raucous commercial port of London a new dignity.

William the Conqueror

In 1066, at the Battle of Hastings, a Norman army led by William of Normandy conquered the Saxon armies. William decided to have his coronation in Westminster Abbey, a tradition since that time. He saw that London was perfectly placed to be a rich capital, and located the impressive stronghold of the White Tower (the tallest building at the Tower of London) on the Thames. William and his French nobles took control of Saxon estates and began erecting some of England's most famous castles, including Windsor, and its great cathedrals. Every monarch to the present day claims descent from William the Conqueror.

Magna Carta and Medieval England

In 1215, the Magna Carta, which attempted to limit the excesses and power of the king and establish personal rights and political freedom for the nobility, was signed at Rimmymede by King John, who was forced to do so by rebellious barons and the newly created lord mayor of London.

Soon Parliament and the House of Commons were created. Though the Magna Carta was designed to free the aristocracy from the despotism of a monarch, it contained the fateful word *freemen* and so signaled at least theoretical rights for the common people.

In 1348, the thriving port of London, crowded with thousands of people, experienced its first outbreak of plague. Nearly half of London's population succumbed to the Black Death, which was carried by rats.

Throughout the medieval era, religious pilgrims traveled to the great cathedral at Canterbury to worship at the shrine of Thomas à Becket. In the 1390s, Geoffrey Chaucer wrote *The Canterbury Tales,* our first literary snapshot of medieval English society. In 1476 William Caxton set up his printing press at Westminster. The numerous and wealthy monasteries—places like Rievaulx and Bolton in Yorkshire—became centers for teaching and learning, and literacy began creeping into the middle and upper classes, setting the scene for the Renaissance culture of the Tudor era.

Tudor England

The War of the Roses between factions of the House of Plantagenet—York and Lancaster—later provided William Shakespeare with a superabundance of material for his tragedies. The bloody reign of Richard III marked the end of the Plantagenet dynasty.

Next came the Tudors. Henry VIII married his brother's widow, Catherine of Aragon, but after 20 years of marriage and one daughter, Mary, Henry fell in love with Anne Boleyn and decided he had to marry again in order to have a male heir. He cast off his wife, alienating the Catholic Church in Rome, which refused to grant him an annulment. Not one to take no for an answer, Henry reformed the church in England, styling himself as its supreme ruler. Then he went on a serial marital spree that left in its wake a total of six wives; as the nursery rhyme goes, "two beheaded, two divorced, one died, and one survived."

The most radical expression of this religious overhaul was the dissolution of monasteries. Henry took for the Crown all the property of the Catholic cathedrals, churches, priories, convents, and monasteries in England. He destroyed beautiful gothic and medieval buildings, redistributing the land among the new, loyal-to-Henry aristocracy. All across England, the ruins of churches and abbeys destroyed at this time still stand. When Bloody Mary, Henry's first daughter, became queen, she put her half-sister, Elizabeth, in the Tower of London, and it was the turn of the Protestants to have their property seized and be hung or burnt alive. In another turn of the dynasty, Elizabeth returned England to its Protestant base, forestalling any Catholic overthrow by having her cousin Mary Queen of Scots executed.

The Elizabethan Flowering

In 1586, William Shakespeare arrived in London from Stratford-upon-Avon, joining Ben Jonson, Christopher Marlowe, John Donne, and others in what became the boom years of English drama and poetry. London, by this time, had a population of 200,000 people, up from 50,000 in the 1300s.

The great era of exploration was under way as the English sailed from ports such as Plymouth, Southampton, and Penzance to ply the oceans in search of riches, returning with sugar, spice, coffee, and tobacco. Sir Thomas Gresham started the Royal Exchange and made London the world's most important financial center, a position it maintained into the early 20th century.

Queen Elizabeth understood that her greatest power lay in the love of her subjects and had an instinctive gift for public relations. Perhaps the greatest gift she gave the nation was her much vaunted virginity: By not marrying a foreign prince, she kept England solidly English for 45 prosperous years. By the end of her long reign, the memories of those ugly battles of succession had faded.

Roundheads and Restoration

In 1603, James VI of Scotland, the son of Mary Queen of Scots, became King James I of England, thus uniting the crowns of England and Scotland. The Gunpowder Plot—in which a group of Catholic conspirators, including Guy Fawkes, were thwarted in their plan to blow up King James, his ministers, and Parliament at the Palace of Westminster—is remembered on November 5, Guy Fawkes Day, when bonfires are lit across the country.

James's successor, Charles I, started a civil war by his insistence on the divine right of kings, a philosophy that was anathema to the Parliament and businessmen of England. The monarchist Cavaliers were defeated by the Puritan Roundheads led by Oliver Cromwell, and Charles I was beheaded outside his Banqueting Hall, a building designed by Inigo Jones. (The king's last walk is still commemorated on the last Sunday in January.) Eighteen years of dour Puritan reign under Cromwell, during which theaters, brothels, and gambling houses were closed, left the country gasping for a breath of fresh air. In 1661, after Cromwell's death, the country welcomed the exiled Charles II back from France. Charles "made a statement" by ordering the exhumation of the three-year-old corpses of Cromwell and two cronies and hanging and beheading them publicly for the murder of his father.

London's Great Plague and Great Fire

Disaster struck London in early 1665 when the first cases of a second major round of the bubonic plague were seen. The hot summer saw the outbreak burst into an epidemic. Infected houses were painted with red crosses and shut up with a guard outside so that the inhabitants died either of the plague or starvation. The disease dispatched an estimated 100,000 people.

The capital hardly had time to recover before it was hit with another calamity. On September 2, 1666, sparks from a baker's oven in Pudding Lane ignited like tinder the dry wood of crowded houses. No measures were taken to control the conflagration until it was too late. King Charles finally stepped in and ordered his navy to blow up the houses in the way of the fire, creating a break in its path. After four grim days, the driving wind died down and the fire finally ended. In its wake lay an unrecognizable London, suffering untold losses in its architecture, treasures, books, and art. In all, 436 acres of London had been consumed by the fire: 13,200 houses, 87 parish houses and many of their churches, 44 merchants' halls, the Royal Exchange, the magnificent medieval Guildhall, and St. Paul's Cathedral. Amazingly, very few lives were lost.

Although both John Evelyn and the young Christopher Wren submitted designs for a new London with wide thoroughfares and sensible squares, the urgent need for housing and the legal problems of ownership of land assured that the rebuilding followed the original "plan" of medieval London. The main differences were that the lanes were widened to a mandatory 14 feet, and the buildings were made of stone. This was Wren's great opportunity, as he rebuilt 51 of the ruined churches, including St. Paul's Cathedral. Despite the loss of many of those edifices during World War II, Wren's name will forever be associated with the glory of that age, as London rose like a phoenix from the ashes of the fire into the magnificence of the 18th century.

Georgian England

To many Englishmen and Anglophiles, the 1700s represent the very apex of the country's greatness: in architecture, literature, theater, painting, sculpture, the building of stately homes and parks (Blenheim in Oxfordshire is one of the most extraordinary examples), philosophy and sciences. The names of the artists, thinkers, and artisans of the day have come to define their disciplines: William Hogarth, Sir Joshua Reynolds, Thomas Gainsborough (painting); Jonathan Swift, Henry Fielding, Oliver Goldsmith (literature); David Garrick (theater); Alexander Pope (poetry); John Nash, Robert Adams (architecture); Edward Gibbon (history); John Gay (opera); David Hume (philosophy); Captain James Cook (exploration); Adam Smith (economics); James Watt (technology); and the naturalized British subject, composer George Frederic Handel. This was the century of the formidable writer and lexicographer Dr. Samuel Johnson and his biographer and friend, James Boswell.

The monarchy certainly did not set the pace of intellectual and artistic activity. In 1714 came the Hanover succession from Germany. Georges I through IV presided over the acquisition of imperial lands from Canada to Australia, as well as the loss of the American colonies. They saw the rise of a new technology that revolutionized the cotton and wool trades of England. Thanks to the madness of King George and the dissolute lifestyle of the prince regent, however, the policy-making powers of the monarch were carefully whittled away by an increasingly powerful Parliament.

There was an increasing polarization—due to the incipient Industrial Revolution—of English society into owners and workers, rich and poor. Toward the end of the 18th century, Bath became one of Europe's most fashionable resorts, and Jane Austen's novels evoked a class-ridden world where financial and romantic desperation hid beneath a veneer of charm, wit, and elegance.

Victorian England

Princess Victoria was only 18 years old when she became queen in 1837. As Queen Victoria, she gave her name to an age of change and reaction, reform and wretchedness, empire and exploitation. Another name identified with 19th-century England—particularly London—is Charles Dickens. It is the London of Dickens we tend to think of when we envision the 19th century: poor Bob Cratchit freezing in Scrooge's office; the convict Magwitch and Pip fleeing on the Thames under cover of a pea-soup fog; Oliver Twist asking for more food in the orphanage. Through his deeply compassionate reporting and fiction, Dickens opened up the eyes of the middle class to the misery of the poor. He helped steer England toward a more humane course as reformers worked to abolish the slave trade, put limits on child labor, allow women to keep their own property, extend voting rights, and open the first state schools.

In England's countryside, the Industrial Revolution didn't so much flower as detonate. The gulf widened between rich and poor, the landscape and atmosphere were degraded, and as people in the country lost their self-sustainability, they trickled into cities already bursting at the seams with immigrants from the far reaches of the empire. With all that cheap labor available, London and cities like Manchester, Leeds, and Liverpool grew at an amazing rate. In mines and mills children as young as six were put to work and conditions were appalling. While the industrialized cities were growing ever more filthy and unhealthy, the Romantic poet William Wordsworth was roaming the countryside of the Lake District and extolling its beauties and the Brontë sisters of Yorkshire were penning romantic novels like *Jane Eyre* and *Wuthering Heights.*

In London, the first underground trains began operation, sewers were built, transatlantic cable was laid, the first police force was established, train tracks originating in London crisscrossed the country (you can see one of the first trains at the National Railway Museum in York), omnibuses were pulled through the streets by huge workhorses (the London Transport Museum has examples of these), streets were gas lit, and roads were laid all over the country. Museums, monuments, learned societies, and public libraries flourished. The Great Exhibition of 1851, organized by Victoria's husband, Prince Albert, showed the world that England was a country of cosmopolitan culture, firmly looking to the future. Progress was the watchword of the day.

Terrible social inequities also defined the Victorian Age. Yet it was a time in which enormous changes took place, age-old injustices were examined, new heroes and heroines were created, and unforgettable literature was penned. Florence Nightingale, Oscar Wilde, Lewis Carroll, and Mary Shelley were all citizens of 19th-century Victorian England.

World War I

Queen Victoria died in January 1901 and the 20th century dawned with the poor old prince of Wales becoming King Edward and lending his name to a new era. It was a short reign—only a decade—but it was distinctive enough to earn the title of the Edwardian Age. It turned out to be England's last age to be described in terms of the monarch.

Edwardian England was a a time of accelerated progress. Motorcars became common, corsets came off, women demonstrated for the vote, and people started to challenge a number of tired Victorian verities. Virginia Woolf's famous quote, "In or about December 1910, human character changed," underscores the leap made in thought and behavior by a new generation.

In 1914, the British Empire enjoyed the zenith of world power. The British pound sterling was as safe as gold and was the currency of international commerce all over the globe. There was peace and prosperity. But the shadow of the German zeppelins loomed above England. Despite the efforts of pacifists like George Bernard Shaw, England was plunged into a war that came close to wiping out an entire generation of young Englishmen. When it was over in 1918, the whole social order changed. It was a completely different England.

The Long Weekend: 1918–1939

There is a sense, as there is of America of the 1920s, that the period between the two World Wars was a last gasp of glamor. There is something to that, despite the ugly rumblings from the black-shirted British fascists led by Nazi sympathizer Sir Oswald Mosley; despite the economic depression that left millions unemployed; and despite the terrible losses of life, limb, and hope during World War I.

People embraced the work of humorist P. G. Wodehouse, which helped them shake off the blues of the war and depression. To this day, the country still loves Wodehouse's version of England between the wars: gin-soaked parties with bright young things, dim "right honorables," creaking lords and terrifying aunts, and, of course, the unflappable Jeeves and his young master Bertie Wooster. But nothing cooked up in the imagination could even come close to the real-life drama involving the abdication of King Edward VIII in 1936 for the American divorcée Mrs. Wallis Simpson. Although the event was billed as a grave constitutional crisis, it was clear that the monarch of England was becoming increasingly irrelevant to the citizenry, except as gossip and newsreel fodder. Before the stock market crash of 1929, England's last private castle—Castle Drogo, in Dartmoor—was built. Several grand country houses were erected in the 1920s, and many of them are today grand country-house hotels.

The Blitz: "Our Finest Hour"

World War I, the "war to end all wars," couldn't live up to that promise for long; Only two decades after the armistice was signed, England was once again anxiously watching the skies, though this time it wasn't the lumbering zeppelins but the significantly more deadly Messerschmitts, Stukas, and unpiloted "doodle-bugs" that spelled disaster. The attack started in earnest on a sunny day on September 7, 1940, when hundreds of fighter planes and bombers buzzed up the Thames and destroyed docks, gasworks, and power stations. The Luftwaffe went on to bomb London nightly for 76 consecutive nights, dropping over 27,000 high explosives and thousands more incendiaries. The Blitz was on. Children were hurriedly sent to the countryside or to America, but the royal family made a point of staying in London, even after nine bombs dropped on Buckingham Palace. Other cities, including Coventry, Exeter, and Plymouth, also suffered severe bomb damage. The way they look today is a direct result of whole sections being leveled and rebuilt.

The bombardment put the famous English stiff upper lip to the test. The country's amazing rise to the challenge earned the admiration of the rest of the world. Prime Minister Winston Churchill was the voice of the people during those dark days with exhortations such as, "Let us therefore brace ourselves to our duties, and so bear ourselves that, if the British Empire and its Commonwealth last for a thousand years, men will still say, 'This was their finest hour.'" Eden Camp, a prisoner-of-war camp the government established in Yorkshire, still exists and tells the entire story of England's brave fight.

Sunset of the Empire

In 1948, England lost the jewel of her colonial crown when India became independent, and over the next decade it continued to lose colonies around

DIVIDED BY A COMMON LANGUAGE:

For all the talk about the blending of American and British culture, we're pleased to see that natives on both sides of the Atlantic retain their particular vocabulary. So, if you want to communicate with the English, you better pick up a bit of Brit-speak.

AMERICAN	ENGLISH
At the airport	
bill	bank note
wallet	billfold/purse
telephone booth	telephone box/kiosk
On the road	
baby carriage/stroller	pram/buggy
back-up lights	reversing lights
dead-end road	cul-de-sac
delivery truck	van
divided highway	dual carriageway
detour	diversion
gas	petrol
hood (car)	bonnet
license plate	number plate
minivan	people carrier
sedan car	saloon car
subway	tube/underground
overpass	flyover
one-way ticket	single journey
pull-off	lay-by
round-trip ticket	return ticket
station wagon	estate car
truck	lorry
trunk	boot
underpass (pedestrian, under streets)	subway
windshield	windscreen

the world, as well as much of the shipping and manufacturing business that made her rich. The 1950s were spent cleaning up bomb wreckage and continuing to live under strict food rationing. The welfare state of the Labour government helped people rebuild their lives and gave them a sense of security unknown up to that time. In 1946, London's Heathrow Airport was opened, followed by Gatwick Airport three years later. The Festival of Britain in 1951, which took place on what would eventually become the site of the South Bank Arts Centre, celebrated the centennial of Prince

A British/English Glossary

AMERICAN	ENGLISH
At the hotel	
antenna	aerial
apartment hotel	service flats
apartment building	block of flats, mansion flats
baby crib	cot
baggage room	left-luggage office
bathe (verb)	bath (bathing—short "a" sound)
bathrobe	dressing gown
cot	extra bed or camp bed
call (on the telephone)	ring
call collect	reverse charges
closet	cupboard/wardrobe
comforter/quilt	eiderdown/duvet
connect (on the telephone)	put through
elevator	lift
first floor	ground floor
second floor	first floor
long-distance call	trunk call
make a reservation	book
milk in coffee/tea or not	white or black
outlet/socket	power point
rent	let
vacuum	Hoover
washcloth	face flannel
In a restaurant or food store	
buffet	sideboard
broiled	grilled
bun (hamburger)	bap
can (of food)	tin
candy	sweets
check	bill

Albert's Great Exhibition. In 1953, millions of people watched the colorful coronation of Queen Elizabeth II from the comfort of their armchairs.

The Swinging Sixties and Punk Seventies

Whatever England may have lost in her empire, London certainly tried to make up for by becoming ground zero of the 1960s' "youth quake." The quintessential 1960s figures of the Beatles and James Bond joined Twiggy and Julie Christie in making all things British very hip. Fashion

DIVIDED BY A COMMON LANGUAGE:

AMERICAN	ENGLISH
***In a restaurant or food store** (continued)*	
cookie	biscuit
cotton candy	candy floss
cracker	savoury biscuit
dessert	pudding
diaper	nappy
downtown	town center/high street
druggist/drugstore	chemist/chemist's shop
eggplant	aubergine
eraser	rubber
French fries	chips
hamburger meat	mince
hardware store	ironmonger
lima bean	broad bean
molasses	black treacle
potato chips	crisps
pit	stone
popsicle	ice lolly
raisin	sultana
smoked herring	kipper
zucchini	courgette
At the theater	
aisle	gangway
balcony	gallery/upper circle
intermission	interval

designers of Carnaby Street and the King's Road started the miniskirt and bell-bottom trends. England's bands in the 1960s were a veritable Debrett's Peerage of rock and roll: The Rolling Stones, The Kinks, Cream, The Yardbirds, Marianne Faithfull, Led Zeppelin, and The Who. In 1967, the law that made homosexuality a criminal offense subject to a two-year prison sentence was finally repealed.

No one did sex, drugs, and rock and roll better than the glam rockers and punks of the 1970s. Green mohawk hairdos, safety pins piercing cheeks, very high platform shoes, and in-your-face attitudes were the norm for the King's Road. Squatters took over entire buildings that were earmarked for renovation; the value-added tax was introduced; and a

A British/English Glossary *(continued)*

AMERICAN	ENGLISH (continued)
***At the theater** (continued)*	
mezzanine/loge	dress circle
movie theater	cinema
movie	film
In the markets and on the high street	
cigarettes	fags
liquor store	off license
newsstand	newsagent
notions	haberdashery
panties	knickers
panty hose	tights
raincoat	macintosh (or mac)/kagool
rest room	public convenience/loo/w.c./lavatory
sneakers	trainers or plimsolls
scotch tape	cellotape
shorts (underwear)	pants
sweater	jumper
undershirt	vest
vest	waistcoat
In sickness and in health	
acetaminophen (Tylenol)	paracetamol
emergency room	casualty
Band-Aids	plasters
funny bone	crazy bone
pimples	spots
rubbing alcohol	surgical spirit

Women's Year Rally coincided with the election of Margaret Thatcher as leader of the Conservative Party.

The Thatcher Years

When Margaret Thatcher was made prime minister in 1979, she announced the somewhat astonishing goal of returning to Victorian values. She began by axing 40,000 civil-service jobs, and soon the gap between rich and poor became wider, as a very Victorian economic and social Darwinism—the survival of the fittest and fattest—took shape. Everyone was a "consumer," according to Thatcher; her record on human rights was abysmal, and discrimination against gays was again written into the law. People in the City were suddenly making lots of money (as they were on Wall Street across the pond), property prices were sky-high, and the materialistic yuppie came to define the era in both England and the United States.

England in the 1980s also saw race riots in Brixton, the first cases of AIDS, strikes by tube and steel workers; and the "fairy-tale wedding" of Prince Charles and Diana Spencer. Homelessness rose, as Thatcher dismantled the socialist safety net, and the real-estate boom took its toll on government housing. In 1989, Thatcher closed out her decade by resigning, and John Major took over as another Conservative prime minister.

Cool Britannia: The 1990s and Beyond

The 1990s started with the historical joining of the French and English sides of the new tunnel beneath the English Channel, linking Paris and London with a three-hour train ride. The local fears that hordes of foreigners would breach England by rail never quite materialized, although the train surely had a part to play in the huge upsurge of tourism in the 1990s.

In 1992, the queen suffered her famous "annus horribilis": a fire at Windsor Castle caused extensive damage, two of her sons were going through horrendously public marital scandals, and she started paying taxes for the first time in her life. Not one to leave books unbalanced—this is a woman who lived through the Blitz and food rationing—the queen decided to pay for the repair of Windsor Castle by opening Buckingham Palace to the public for two months a year. The two royal divorces, between Charles and Diana and Andrew and Sarah (Fergie), as well as the mad-cow disease that rocked the British beef industry, helped to keep the international media eye on England. By the time the Britpop explosion signaled the start of "Cool Britannia," everyone in the world knew that London was again the place to be. The Spice Girls, Oasis, All Saints, and Robbie Williams put British music back at the top of the charts. London Fashion Week became one of the hottest tickets in Europe, rivaling even Milan and Paris as the event in which to showcase new collections.

In May 1997, Tony Blair of the Labour Party was voted in as prime minister, signaling an end to the Conservative Party's 18-year run. Blair ran on a platform of finding the "third way" between the policies of Tory and Labour, and he has succeeded in annoying both parties. The same year also saw the tragedy of Princess Diana's death in a car crash in Paris, followed by a spasm of national grief that had Buckingham Palace doing back flips to appease the people who found fault with how the royal family was responding. Mourners stood in line for days to sign the condolence book at St. James Palace, while a sea of flowers numbering in the millions was left at the gates of Kensington Palace.

Next up was the opening of the Millennium Dome, the much maligned and hyped exhibition to celebrate the turning of the century and the next millennium. Like Prince Albert's Great Exhibition of 1851, and the Festival of Britain in 1951, the exhibits in the Millennium Dome were meant to showcase British advances in science and technology. But to the bitter delight of its critics, the exhibition was a huge flop and failed to draw anywhere near the crowds anticipated. Plans on what to do with the structure are still up in the air. Meanwhile, the Queen raked in so much money from the yearly late-summer opening of Buckingham Palace that there was enough left over to upgrade the Queen's Gallery, letting commoners see more of the royal treasures. This was one of many events timed to coincide with her Golden Jubilee in 2002. Despite a lot of hype, the Jubilee was as big a fizzle as the Millennium Dome. A seemingly endless supply of royal scandals, including, most recently, one involving the Queen herself (when Princess Di's butler was about to go to trial for stealing some of Di's possessions, the Queen suddenly "remembered" that he'd told her he had the items and was holding onto them for safekeeping), keeps the British public both disillusioned and endlessly titillated. If the monarchy goes, and many think it should, one of England's most bankable tourist attractions will be lost.

Part One

Planning Your Visit to England

How Far in Advance Should You Plan?

There are advantages to planning your trip several weeks or even months in advance. Airline fares are generally lower if you book at least a month ahead. You may also lock into lower prices for air/hotel packages or find a super price for a hotel. Advance hotel planning is usually a must if you are traveling to London or any of England's top resort areas (Cornwall, the Cotswolds, and the Lake District among them) in the high-season months from Easter through August. We discuss Internet resources in "Websites for Further Research" (page 32), but keep in mind just how valuable the Web can be in planning your trip to England. Throughout this book, we provide websites for tourist information offices, hotels, and tour companies, and we strongly suggest you check them out when planning your trip.

On the other hand, you may come across a last-minute airline deal that saves you bundles of money but requires that you leave on short notice (see "Websites for Further Research" on page 32; many sites lower prices close to the date of departure, so if you're ready to hop on a plane, you can save a good amount). Before you act on any spur-of-the-moment airline deals, make certain that all the basic details of your trip are taken care of, especially the hotel part—we often hear of travelers who get a terrific last-minute airfare to London but end up paying a fortune for a hotel. Keep in mind, too, that airfares don't always come down. You might wait only to find out that the fares actually increased.

When to Go

If this is going to be your first trip to England and you want to visit historic castles, manor houses, and glorious gardens, the best time to travel is from April through October. All the major attractions throughout the country are open daily, or almost daily, during these months. Summer days are delightfully long, remaining light until 9 or 10 p.m. The downside is that this is also the time when crowds tend to be densest, so you may be kept waiting in line at popular attractions, or have trouble finding a hotel if you haven't booked one in advance. London, on the other hand, is a year-round destination, with so much to see and do that you can have a great time during any season. Culturally, the city is busiest from September through June—the months when opera, ballet, and symphony performances are most plentiful—but during the summer, there are outdoor festivals, and the parks are green oases that are most welcome after a day of trudging through the streets. If you're going to London for theater, any time of year will do.

Autumn is a lovely time to visit England: the crowds thin out and the cultural calendar picks up steam, but attractions close earlier. In fact, most historic properties owned by the National Trust close in early November and remain closed until sometime in March. Though the gardens and grounds of the great manor houses often remain open year-round, you have to be a dedicated gardener to appreciate the beauty of an empty flowerbed, bare trees, and sodden paths.

Winter can be a special time to visit England, too, but be prepared for early twilights (3:30 p.m.), lots of gray skies, and very unpredictable weather—that is, weather that is even more unpredictable than usual. London decks itself out in high style for Christmas, which is one of its prime tourist seasons. Throughout the country, old towns and villages spruce themselves up for the holiday season, too, with results that are sometimes positively Dickensian. Be aware, however, that the entire country basically shuts down from December 24 to December 26.

Seasonal Pricing

There's no getting around the fact that England is an expensive country to visit. London hotel and restaurant prices are on a par with New York. Hotels are somewhat less expensive outside of London, especially if you stay at a bed-and-breakfast, but eating out in a good restaurant anywhere in the country is always pricey. Admission prices for top attractions are also higher than in other European countries. There is some good news, though—thanks to an infusion of cash from the national lottery, museums administered by the national government are now free, meaning you can pop into such top attractions as the Victoria and Albert Museum in London and the National Railway Museum in York without paying a cent.

There are two high seasons in England: from Easter through August, and again for about two weeks before Christmas. You're more likely to find better deals on hotels during the shoulder seasons of January to March and mid-September to mid-December. During these periods hotel prices may drop by 20% or more and airfares are generally cheaper.

In fact, airfares to England are amazingly low in January and February, when you can often travel from New York to London for as little as $250—round trip! Winter hotel prices are especially reasonable in resort areas like the Cotswolds and the Lake District.

To give you a very rough idea of what things cost in England, here's a list of some approximate prices, given in U.S. dollars:

Transfers to and from airport in London $6–$60 one way
Medium-range hotel (top of the range is for London) $150–$250 per night
Meal for two in an upscale restaurant (without wine) $50 and up
Pub meal for two (without wine) $20–$30
Theater ticket for a show in London's West End or in a well-respected theater outside London $35–$70
Admission to top attractions throughout the country $10–$20

Weather

In England, you can't count on having good weather at any season, but the climate is *generally* mild year-round. Spring comes earliest to Cornwall in the west, where shrubs, trees, and bulbs flower as early as March. Daffodils, England's quintessential springtime flower, appear throughout the country in April. The great English gardens generally hit their peak in May and June, as do the ancient hedgerows in the countryside.

LONDON'S AVERAGE TEMPERATURES AND RAINFALL

Temperature	Fahrenheit	Celsius	Rainfall (inches)
January	40°F	4°C	2.1"
February	40°F	4°C	1.6"
March	44°F	7°C	1.5"
April	49°F	9°C	1.5"
May	55°F	13°C	1.8"
June	61°F	16°C	1.8"
July	64°F	18°C	2.2"
August	64°F	18°C	2.3"
September	59°F	15°C	1.9"
October	52°F	11°C	2.2"
November	46°F	8°C	2.5"
December	42°F	6°C	1.9"

Summer can be hot and humid, or cold and drizzly, or pleasantly warm with blue skies. It's the only time when you can reasonably expect to sit outside for a meal or a drink at a London café or a country pub. Bear in mind that most English hotels, even those in London, do not have air-conditioning. Air pollution can be a problem in London during the summer, too.

Autumn, one of the prettiest times to visit, is sometimes blessed with what Americans call "Indian summer," but again, you cannot count on this. Winter generally brings rain and sleet; if it snows, the snow does not stay on the ground for long except for the highest peaks in the Lake District.

Travel Deals and Package Tours

Start with Your Local Travel Agent

Finding a good travel agent to help with trip planning is a boon to any traveler. A travel agent can save you time and money by booking your flights, scouting out special package deals, reserving hotels, arranging car rentals, and issuing BritRail passes. If you don't already have a travel agent, ask your friends if they can recommend one. Or, contact the **American Society of Travel Agents** (1101 King Street, Suite 200, Alexandria, VA 22314; (703) 739-2782; **www.astanet.com**), or the **Association of Canadian Travel Agents** (130 Albert Street, Suite 1705, Ottawa, Ontario K1P 5G4; **www.acta.ca**). Ask the travel agent if he or she has experience with booking trips to England, or has visited the country—if the answer is no, find someone else. You are not charged for a travel agent's services—although this could change in the future, now that agents no longer receive the same kind of commissions from airlines and hotels.

Check the Travel Section of Your Local Newspaper

One of your best sources of information on package tours to England is the travel section of your local newspaper. England (especially London) is a popular destination, and there are frequently special money-saving deals that combine airfare and hotel costs. The paper may also advertise special cut-rate charter flights to London. Blackout dates and a host of restrictions generally apply to these offers. Do a little research before you book a tour. Call the tour operator and ask questions about what is and is not included in the deals they're offering.

Surf the Web

With all the information that's available on the Web, more and more travelers are acting as their own travel agents. By using the Web, you can find and book special airline fares, surf for discounted hotel rooms (see Part Three, Lodging, Dining, and Shopping in England, for specific websites), order BritRail passes, and much more. Special low prices and seasonal deals are often available only on the Web.

Many travel-related websites offer reservations and tickets for airlines, plus reservation and purchase capabilities for hotels and car-rental companies. Some to check out are **Travelocity** (**www.travelocity.com**),

Expedia Travel (**www.expedia.com**), **Yahoo! Travel** (**www.travel.yahoo.com**), **Cheap Tickets** (**www.cheaptickets.com**), Frommers (**frommers.com**), and **Orbitz** (**www.orbitz.com**). We find some of the lowest prices available on **Hotwire** (**www.hotwire.com**), but there's a catch—you provide the dates you want to travel, Hotwire comes up with a fare, and you purchase the ticket—but you don't know departure times or the airlines until you've finalized the purchase. Many other websites offer similar approaches. Likewise, you can also get some great deals on **Priceline** (**www.priceline.com**)—you provide the price you want to pay, along with your credit card info; if your price is accepted, your credit card is charged before you know departure times and airlines.

It's also useful to check out the websites for the airlines flying to England. Frequently they post special discounts that are not available except by reserving online. Some airlines will send you weekly e-newsletters and special last-minute e-fares, including specials for weekend travel from major North American hubs to London. The airlines are also one of your best sources for finding package tours to England.

There's no reason why you shouldn't call an airline directly—except for long waits on the phone and the possibility that you may get a cheaper deal by using the Web. If you call the airline, be prepared to ask questions such as "Will this flight cost less if I fly on a different day of the week, or at a different time?" and "What is the cancellation policy if I can't use the tickets I've already paid for on my credit card?" Your goal is to get the lowest fare to your destination. You can be direct and simply ask what the lowest fare is from your city to London. Chances are, the service rep will tell you; if he or she won't, hang up and try again. If you've done some comparison shopping, the airline will usually match the lowest fare you've already found for specific flights on their airline.

AIRLINE CONTACT INFORMATION FOR NORTH AMERICA

Air Canada	(888) 247-2262	**www.aircanada.ca**
American Airlines	(800) 433-7300	**www.americanair.com**
British Airways	(800) AIRWAYS	**www.british-airways.com**
Continental Airlines	(800) 231-0856	**www.flycontinental.com**
Delta Air Lines	(800) 241-4141	**www.delta-air.com**
Icelandair	(800) 223-5500	**www.icelandair.is**
Northwest Airlines	(800) 447-4747	**www.nwa.com**
United Airlines	(800) 538-2929	**www.ual.com**
Virgin Atlantic Airways	(800) 862-8621	**www.virgin.com**

Packages versus Escorted Tours

Escorted tours differ from package tours in several fundamental ways. With a package tour, you generally get your airfare and hotel and are left on your own to tour at your leisure (and expense). Escorted tours offer full-service itineraries that generally include transfers to your hotel(s), meals, sightseeing, nightlife, etc. Dozens of companies offer escorted tours to London and destinations in the rest of England. Many cater to special interests, such as theater or history; others are more general. A good travel agent can help you find a tour that suits your particular interests. It's also a good idea to scan the travel section in your local paper for tour possibilities. American Express and many of the airlines offer escorted tours.

It's important to know the basics of what is and is not offered on an escorted tour before you sign up. When and how much do you pay? Will the trip be canceled if not enough people sign up? If so, what must you do to get a refund? You'll also want to know how big the group will be, and if the daily schedule is reasonable or so jam-packed that you won't have time to breathe. Don't assume that anything not specifically spelled out is included in your fee. For example, you may have to pay to get yourself to or from the airport, or admission to attractions may not be included.

Cosmos (www.cosmos.com), Trafalgar Tours (www.trafalgartours.com), and **Maupintour (www.maupintour.com)** are some of the major companies that offer escorted tours to London and the rest of England.

Gathering Information

Visit Britain Offices

For general information about England, contact these offices or visit **www.visitbritain.com.**

In North America
Visit Britain
551 Fifth Avenue, Suite 701
New York, NY 10176-0799
(800) 462-2748; fax: (212) 986-1188

In New Zealand
Visit Britain
(0800) 700-741 (toll free)
fax: (09) 377-6965

In Australia
Visit Britain
Level 2
15 Blue Street
North Sydney, NSW 2060
(02) 9021-4400; fax: (02) 9021-4499

Regional Tourist Boards in England

For more specific information on a particular region, contact the following regional tourist boards. We strongly recommend that you visit their excellent and information-packed websites before attempting to contact the boards by mail or phone; before going to these individual sites, you may also wish to visit **www.travelengland.org.uk,** a composite site managed by the Yorkshire Tourist Board on behalf of all the regional tourist boards of England.

Cumbria (the Lake District) Tourist Board
Ashleigh
Holly Road
Windermere, Cumbria LA23 2AQ
(01539) 44444
www.cumbria-the-lake-district.co.uk

East of England Tourist Board
Toppesfield Hall
Hadleigh, Suffolk IP7 5DN
(0870) 225-4890
www.eastofenglandtouristboard.com

Heart of England Tourist Board
Woodside
Larkhill Road
Worcester WR5 2E2
(01905) 763436
www.visitheartofengland.com

North West England Tourist Board
Swan House
Swan Meadow Road
Wigan Pier, Wigan WN3 5BB
(01942) 821222
www.visitnorthwest.com

South East England Tourist Board
The Old Brew House
Warwick Park
Tunbridge Wells, Kent TN2 5TU
(01892) 540766
www.southeastengland.uk.com

Southern Tourist Board
40 Chamberlayne Road
Eastleigh, Hampshire SO50 5JH
(01703) 620006
www.southerntb.co.uk

West Country Tourist Board
60 St. David's Hill
Exeter, Devon EX4 4SY
(01392) 425426
www.westcountrynow.com

Yorkshire Tourist Board
312 Tadcaster Road
York YO24 1GS
(01904) 707961
www.ytb.org.uk

Tourist Information Centres

Your best source of up-to-date information in any city or town is the Tourist Information Centre. You'll find addresses for them in every "Planning a Visit to . . ." section in the regional chapters later on. Tourist Information Centres are always centrally located, usually in the busiest areas of a city or town. In larger cities, you'll often find a branch in the train station. What are they good for? First and foremost, they offer easy-to-use maps and guides to the city or town. These local sight-seeing maps used to be free, but nowadays you usually have to pay for them, generally £1 or less for a local map. You'll also find racks of brochures on local attractions. Something might catch your fancy, but remember that the brochures are advertisements—the fact that they are in a Tourist Information Centre doesn't automatically mean they are worth your time or money. There will often be a currency exchange window in the Tourist Information Centre, and a convenient hotel-booking service. For hotel booking there's usually a fee (10% of room cost) that is refunded when you pay for your room. Some Tourist Information Centres have a small bookstore stocked with titles of local interest, regional maps and guides, and souvenirs. Many offer free or low-cost guided walks of a city or town, and we advise joining one of these informative tours if you have the time.

Websites for Further Research

The Web is an invaluable tool when it comes to travel research, so even if you don't have Web access at home, we suggest you arrange to spend some time in front of a computer, perhaps one of those available for free use at local libraries. Websites often contain the most up-to-date information (provided that the site is well maintained)—hotels, for instance, list current prices and discounts (and provide pictures of their rooms), and attraction websites provide current prices and opening and closing times. We list websites whenever possible throughout this guide.

The following websites should be able to provide you with enough info, as well as links to other websites, to keep you glued to your computer for weeks. We also recommend that you contact the tourist board websites above, as well as the websites we list throughout this guide for Visitor Information Centres in cities, towns, national parks, and elsewhere; you'll find a wealth of information specific to the places you most want to visit.

www.english-heritage.org.uk Info on hundreds of historic properties throughout England.

www.gobycoach.com Timetables and fares for the National Express coach network.

www.guardianunlimited.co.uk The Guardian and The Observer newspapers online.

www.knowhere.co.uk Oriented to skateboarders, but loaded with tips from locals on pubs, shops, and the like—some of the comments can be annoying, but in general, the insider info is useful and fun.

www.londontown.com Up-to-the-minute info on events, hotels, restaurants, sight-seeing, exhibits, and more in London.

www.nationaltrust.org.uk Lists hundreds of buildings, gardens, and preservation areas to visit.

www.ordnancesurvey.co.uk Free downloadable maps for all of Great Britain.

www.pti.org.uk Timetables and other info for all travel by rail, air, coach, bus, ferry, and tram within the United Kingdom.

www.railtrack.com Timetables and information (but not fares) for rail travel throughout Britain.

www.ramblers.org.uk All you need to know about walking in England, from trail listings to guided walks to walking holidays.

www.royal.gov.uk Info on royal palaces, castles, and museums, and other links; especially fun for royal watchers.

www.uk250.co.uk Links to hundreds of museums, galleries, and other cultural institutions throughout England.

British Consular Offices

British consulates abroad can advise you on visas for work or study in England and address many other legal and administrative questions prior to your trip.

In the United States (www.britainusa.com)

British Consulate General
Georgia Pacific Centre, Suite 3400
133 Peachtree Street NE
Atlanta, GA 30303
(404) 954-7700; fax: (404) 954-7702

British Consulate General
1 Memorial Drive, Suite 1500
Cambridge, MA 02142
(617) 245-4500; fax: (617) 621-0220

British Consulate General
The Wrigley Building, 13th Floor
400 N. Michigan Avenue
Chicago, IL 60611
(312) 970-3800; fax: (312) 970-3852

British Consulate
2911 Turtle Creek Boulevard,
Suite 940
Dallas, TX 75219
(214) 521-4090; fax: (214) 521-4807
bc1@airmail.net

British Consulate
World Trade Center
1675 Broadway, Suite 1030
Denver, CO 80202
(303) 592-5200; fax: (303) 592-5209

British Consulate General
Wells Fargo Plaza, 19th Floor
1000 Louisiana, Suite 1900
Houston, TX 77002
(713) 659-6270; fax: (713) 659-7094

British Consulate General
11766 Wilshire Boulevard,
Suite 1200
Los Angeles, CA 90025-6538
(310) 481-0031; fax: (310) 481-2960
Visa telephone: (310) 481-2900
Visa fax: (310) 481-2961

British Consulate
Brickell Bay Office Tower
1001 Brickell Bay Drive, Suite 2800
Miami, FL 33131
(305) 374-1522; fax: (305) 374-8196

British Consulate General
845 Third Avenue
New York, NY 10022
(212) 745-0200; fax: (212) 754-3062

British Consulate General
1 Sansome Street, Suite 850
San Francisco, CA 94104
(415) 617-1300; fax: (415) 434-2018

British Consulate
900 Fourth Avenue, Suite 3001
Seattle, WA 98164
(206) 622-9255; fax: (206) 622-4728

In Canada (www.britain-in-canada.org)

Honorary British Consul
British Consulate
1 Canal Street
Dartmouth, Nova Scotia B2Y 3YN
(902) 461-1381; fax: (902) 465-2578

British Consulate General
Suite 4200
1000 De La Gauchetierè West
Montreal, Quebec H3B 4W5
(514) 866-5863; fax: (514) 866-0202

British Consular Offices *(continued)*

In Canada (www.britain-in-canada.org) ***(continued)***

Honorary British Consul
British Consulate
1 Canal Street
Dartmouth, Nova Scotia B2Y 3YN
(902) 461-1381; fax: (902) 465-2578

British Consulate General
Suite 4200
1000 De La Gauchetierè West
Montreal, Quebec H3B 4W5
(514) 866-5863; fax: (514) 866-0202

Honorary British Consul
British Consulate
Le Complexe St-Amable
700-1150 Claire-Fontaine
Quebec City, Quebec G1R 5G4
(418) 521-3000; fax: (418) 521-3099

Honorary British Consul
British Consulate
PO Box 452, Station C
St. John's, Newfoundland A1C 5K4
(709) 579-2002; fax: (709) 579-0475

British Consulate General
777 Bay Street
Suite 2800, College Park
Toronto, Ontario M5G 2G2
(416) 593-1290; fax: (416) 593-1229

British Consulate General
1111 Melville Street, Suite 800
Vancouver, British Columbia V6E 4V6
(60) 683-4421; fax: (604) 681-0693

Honorary British Consul
British Consulate
229 Athlone Drive
Winnipeg, Manitoba R3J 3L6
(204) 896-1380; fax: (204) 269-3025

What to Pack

As little as possible. Be brave. Resist the urge to cram your entire closet into your luggage. Take just *one suitcase,* preferably the kind with wheels. Augment that with a backpack or some kind of useful, zippered, waterproof carry-all. Add a practical purse or bag that you can sling over your shoulder and use every day.

Keep in mind that not all English hotels have elevators or porters. In many hotels, especially smaller, less expensive establishments and bed-and-breakfasts, you're going to be lugging your own bags. Remember, too, that airlines now allow only one carry-on bag plus a purse, briefcase, or laptop. They are strict about this, and you will have to go through various security checkpoints before boarding with your personal luggage. Leave as many electric and electronic doodads as you can survive without at home; you'll have to squeeze them into your luggage, and when you're in England, you will have to get a special adapter plug to use or recharge them.

Remember, too, that in the wake of September 11, the airlines now confiscate all sharp objects, no matter how innocuous, if they are in your carry-on luggage. This includes tiny scissors, knitting and hypodermic needles (unless you have a note from your doctor explaining why you need one), corkscrews, Swiss Army or any kind of knife, and sporting equipment. And one more thing: If you forgot something, you have a good excuse to slip into a shop and indulge in a "Made in Britain" item.

Passports and Visas

If you're an American, Canadian, Australian, or New Zealand tourist visiting the United Kingdom for under three months, a valid passport is the only legal form of identification you'll need to enter England. Visas are required for any stay over three months. The U.S. State Department's Bureau of Consular Affairs' website (**www.travel.state.gov**) provides exhaustive information about passports (including a downloadable application), customs, and other government-regulated aspects of travel for U.S. citizens. Make a copy of the information page of your passport and keep it in your luggage in order to expedite replacement in case your passport gets lost or stolen.

How to Dress

Since weather in England is so unpredictable, it's wise to think in terms of layers of clothing. Bring mix-and-match coordinates that you can shed or add to as needed. Even in the summer, a sweater will be welcome. A waterproof coat or jacket with a hood will come in handy, or bring a separate rainproof hat and/or folding umbrella. A comfy and casual pair of waterproof loafers or walking shoes is a good idea. If you're traveling to England in the winter months, bring gloves, a scarf, and a warm coat.

A Word on Tourist Garb

The Brits are pretty casual about their clothes, so wearing a pair of blue jeans while sightseeing will not set you apart as a gauche tourist. But add a pair of dirty running shoes and a baseball cap and try to enter a nice restaurant, and they'll instantly peg you as an outsider and possibly suggest that you'd enjoy dining elsewhere. If you're planning to eat in good restaurants, be aware that a "smart but casual" dress code generally applies. This doesn't mean gents have to wear a tie, but they do have to wear a jacket, slacks, and something other than running shoes. Women should wear a dress or a pantsuit. There are still a few places where gentlemen are required to wear a coat and tie, but not many. You can get away with wearing just about anything to the theater, or even the opera, but you'll be in a minority if you show up in a running suit or jeans. When it comes to fashion, London is more sophisticated than the rest of England, and Londoners like to dress up for their evenings out.

Special Considerations

Traveling with Children

We have a rating system in our attraction profiles that attempts to gauge suitability for children and adults of various ages, but all children have different interests and differing levels of tolerance for museums and attractions. All in all, though, we find that kids love England—the common language provides a level of comfort, there are enough castles and suits of armor around to satisfy their romantic notions of days of yore, and a ride on a double-decker bus or in a London taxi can be sheer heaven.

You'll find kid-friendly amusements throughout England. Audio guides are available at many historic castles and palaces, making them more fun and interesting for children aged nine or ten and up. Something as low-tech and old-fashioned as the Model Village in Bourton-on-the-Water can also be enchanting to children. If your kids are resistant to visiting England, say the two magic words: "Harry Potter." That's usually all that's necessary to interest any kid in England nowadays.

If you're traveling as a family, you can usually buy money-saving "Family Tickets" at the major attractions. These tickets are available for two adults and two children (three children in some cases). Kids under five get in free almost everywhere. Finally, remember that kids get jet lag, too, so plan your first day accordingly.

Travelers with Disabilities

Many but not all English attractions are accessible to disabled visitors in wheelchairs. There are portions of some historic properties that cannot be changed to accommodate chairs. Before visiting any major attraction in England, you need to call ahead or check out an attraction's website (which we provide) to find out what, if any, arrangements have been made for wheelchairs. We try to give information relevant to travelers with disabilities throughout this guide.

Accommodations pose another problem. Bed-and-breakfasts and many hotels occupy historic buildings with steep, narrow staircases, no elevators, and doors that are too narrow for a wheelchair. Larger and newer hotels and hotel chains are where you're most likely to find special rooms designed for the disabled.

Restaurants, too, may have stairways and no ramps. The size and layout of some restaurants in old quarters make it difficult for them to accommodate wheelchairs. The following list of resources will help you plan your trip:

- *Access to the Underground,* a brochure published by London Transport, is available at tube stations or by writing the London Transport Unit for Disabled Visitors, 172 Buckingham Palace Road, London, SW1 9TN.

- *Artsline,* a charitable organization that provides access information for cultural institutions and entertainment and arts venues, distributes *Access in London,* researched by disabled people and updated regularly. Call (0207) 388-2227 or visit **www.artsline.org.uk.**
- *Can Be Done* is a tour operator specializing in British holidays and tours for travelers with disabilities; call (0208) 907-2400 or visit **www.canbedone.co.uk.**
- *Flying Wheels* is a U.S.-based organization that leads many overseas tours for travelers with disabilities, including many to England. For information, write to Flying Wheels, 143 West Bridge Street, Owatonna, MN 55060; call (507) 451-5005 or visit **www.flyingwheelstravel.com.**
- *Holiday Care Service* offers advice on disabled-friendly lodging throughout Britain, and also operates a booking service; call (0129) 377-4535 or visit **www.holidaycare.org.uk.**
- *Information for Wheelchair Users Visiting London* is a pamphlet that you can find in any tourist office in London.
- *The National Trust* provides accessibility information for its more than 300 historic buildings and gardens at **www.nationaltrust.org.uk.**
- *Tripscope* gives advice and information on transport for the elderly and disabled throughout the United Kingdom and London; call (0208) 994-9294 or visit **www.justmobility.co.uk/tripscope.**

Senior Travelers

If you're a senior who gets around easily, England won't present any particular problems for you. If you have any mobility or health issues, be aware that not all hotels have elevators, particularly less expensive bed-and-breakfasts. Before reserving a hotel room, ask whether or not you'll have access to an elevator or "lift," as they're called in England.

Being a senior may entitle you to some money-saving travel bargains, such as lower prices for BritRail passes and reduced admission at theaters, museums, and other attractions. Always ask, even if a reduction isn't posted; we give prices for seniors throughout this guide. Carrying ID with proof of age can pay off in all these situations. You may find that some discounts, such as public transportation reductions in London, are available only to U.K. residents. Most of the major U.S. domestic airlines, including American, United, and Continental, offer discount programs for senior travelers—ask before booking your flight.

The following sources can provide information on discounts and other benefits for seniors:

AARP (American Association of Retired Persons) 601 E Street NW, Washington, DC 20049; (800) 424-3410; **www.aarp.org**) Offers member discounts on car rentals and hotels; $10 yearly memberships include discounts of 12–25% on Virgin Atlantic flights to London from eight U.S. cities.

Elderhostel 75 Federal Street, Boston, MA 02110-1941; (877) 426-8056; **www.elderhostel.org**) Offers people 55 and over a variety of university-based education programs in London and throughout England. These courses are value-packed, hassle-free ways to learn while traveling. The price includes airfare, accommodations, meals, tuition, tips, and insurance. And you'll be glad to know that there are no grades. Popular London offerings have included "Inside the Parliament," "Legal London," "Classical Music and Opera in London," and "Treasures of London Galleries."

Grand Circle Travel 347 Congress Street, Boston, MA 02210; (800) 597-3644; **www.gct.com**) Another agency that escorts tours for mature travelers. Call or go online to order a copy of the publication *101 Tips for the Mature Traveler.*

SAGA International Holidays 222 Berkeley Street, Boston, MA 02116; (800) 343-0273; **www.sagaholidays.com**) Offers inclusive tours for those 50 and older. Its tours cover places outside London (such as Cornwall), but you can get a pre- or post-tour London extension.

Gay and Lesbian Travelers

The British government encourages gay tourism. Click the "Gay and Lesbian" bar on the Visit Britain website (**www.visitbritain.com**) for information on gay venues and events throughout England.

Gay theaters, gay shops, more than 100 gay pubs, famous gay discos, and gay community groups of all sorts abound in London. Old Compton Street in Soho is filled with dozens of gay pubs, restaurants, and upscale gay bars/cafés; the Earl's Court area, long a gay bastion, has gay/lesbian hotels and restaurants. Brighton, the gay-friendly resort town on the Sussex coast, is also known for its gay pub and club scene and its huge Gay Pride parade and celebrations in June, as is Manchester, in the Midlands. Elsewhere in the country, at least in the larger cities, there's usually a gay pub or two, and clubs with at least one gay-friendly night a week.

Lesbian and gay events in London include the **London Lesbian and Gay Film Festival** in March, the **Pride Parade** and celebrations in June, and the big outdoor bash known as **Summer Rites** in August. You can obtain information and dates by phone or online from the **London Lesbian and Gay Switchboard** (0207) 837-7324; **www.llgs.org.uk**).

The newest and most useful gay and lesbian travel guide, covering London, Brighton, and lots of other European destinations, is *Frommer's Gay & Lesbian Europe,* available at most bookstores or at the larger online booksellers. Several gay magazines, useful for their listings and news coverage, are available in London's gay pubs, clubs, bars, and cafes. The most popular are *Boyz, Pink Paper*, and *QX* (*Queer Xtra*; **www.qxmag.co.uk**). *Gay Times* (**www.gaytimes.co.uk**) is a monthly news-oriented mag available at most newsagents. Indispensable for its city-wide listings in London (including gay listings), *Time Out* appears at newsagents on Wednesdays. **Gay's the Word** in London (66 Marchmont Street, WC1, (0207) 278-7654; tube: Russell Square), the city's only all-round gay and lesbian bookstore, stocks a selection of new and used books and current periodicals. For a thorough online guide to gay clubs, restaurants, hotels, and events in London, visit **www.gaylondon.co.uk.**

Other Travel Concerns

Cell Phones

Having a cell phone at the ready while you're visiting England is convenient, but be prepared for some challenges. First, the cell phone you use in the United States probably won't work in England. That's because cell phones in England operate on a frequency and a network—the Global System for Mobile Communications (GSM)—that your phone probably doesn't. Plus, even if you have the right equipment, you carrier may not have global roaming arrangements that will allow you to receive calls overseas. If it does, you will probably pay at least several dollars a minute for the privilege.

So, consider some options. One is to rent a GSM phone and a calling plan geared for use in the United Kingdom, either before you leave home or in England once you arrive. You'll find several cell-phone rental outlets at Heathrow, Gatwick, Manchester, and other British airports, and many Britain-based firms will deliver a cell phone to your hotel. Many U.S.-based firms also rent cell phones and offer calling plans for use in England (some offer special plans through rental-car agencies, so ask when renting your car). They will usually ship the phone to your home. The disadvantage of these rentals is that you will be using a phone number different from your regular cell-phone number, and you will be incurring some considerable expense: a weekly rental fee for the phone, plus hefty fees for each incoming and outgoing call. A cheaper alternative is to rent or buy a GSM phone and use a SIM (Subscriber Identity Module) card, the phone's memory chip that you slip into a slot in the phone. You can buy a SIM card for use specifically in England, or one that can be used in other countries as well. The advantage of using a SIM card is that incoming calls are much cheaper than they are with carrier plans, and they are cheapest when you use a SIM card for use in England only.

To buy a GSM phone for use in England, you can check out **Ustronics.com** (580 Eighth Avenue, New York, NY 10018; (212) 840-4333; **www.ustronics.com**). To rent a GSM phone in the United States for use in England (with calling plan), try **Cellhire USA** (45 Broadway, New York, NY 10006 (and other U.S. locations); (866) CH-ONLINE; **www.cellhire.com**). To rent a mobile phone in England, contact **Rent a**

Mobile Phone (191–192 Temple Chambers, London EC4Y ODB U.K.; (0207) 353-7705; **www.rent-mobile-phone.com**). To purchase SIM cards for use in England or multiple countries, check out **Telestial** (1804 Garnet Avenue, San Diego, CA 92109; (858) 274-2686; **www.telestial.com**).

Electricity

Leave all but the most essential electric gadgets and appliances at home. The electricity supply in England is 220 volts AC, which will blow out any American 110-volt appliance you may have unless it is plugged into a transformer. British outlets are made for large three-prong plugs; you will also need to get an adapter, available at any hardware store, chemist (drugstore), supermarket, or gadget store. *Don't plug anything in until you've checked the voltage on the transformer!* It should be set to "Input AC 110 volt, output AC 220 volt." You'll know by the pop, flash, and smoke if you got it wrong. Your can equip yourself with transformers and adapters before you leave home or once you arrive in England at most major electronic stores, or order them online from website vendors such as **shopper.cnet.com, shopping.com,** and **tempestcom.com.**

Embassies and High Commissions in England

If your passport is lost or stolen, or you need some other kind of special assistance while you're traveling in England, the following embassies, all located in London, will be able to help or direct you.

United States of America The American Embassy is housed in Mayfair at 24 Grosvenor Square, London, W1A1AE; (0207) 499-9000 (Zone 8; tube: Bond Street). This is where you will go if your passport gets lost or stolen or if you have some emergency. The embassy's website is at **www.usembassy.org.uk.** The hours are 8:30 a.m.–5:30 p.m. Passports are handled from Monday to Friday, 8:30–11 a.m.; and Monday, Wednesday, and Friday, 2–4 p.m. The Passport Office is on 55 Upper Brook Street, around the corner from the main entrance (tube: Marble Arch or Bond Street).

Canada The high commission is at MacDonald House, 38 Grosvenor Square, W1; (0207) 258-6600 (tube: Bond Street). It is open Monday to Friday, 8–11 a.m.

Australia The High Commission is at Australia House, Strand, WC2; (0207) 379-4334 (tube: Charing Cross) and is open Monday to Friday, 10 a.m.–4 p.m.

New Zealand The High Commission is at New Zealand House, 80 Haymarket at Pall Mall, SW1; (0207) 930-8422 (tube: Charing Cross). It's open Monday to Friday, 9 a.m.–5 p.m.

Ireland The Irish Embassy is at 17 Grosvenor Place, SW1; (0207) 235-2171 (tube: Hyde Park Corner). Open Monday–Friday, 10 a.m.–4 p.m.

Health

You may want to take out medical insurance before you leave, since you won't be covered by the National Health Service unless you're a citizen of the European Union. Depending on the insurance you carry, you may be eligible for free emergency care, but anything else, including follow-up or specialist services, will be paid for out of your pocket. Check your existing policies to see if they cover medical services abroad. If they don't, call Travelex at (800) 228-9792 (**www.travelex.com**) or another company that offers a policy for travelers.

Pharmacies (called chemists) are open 24 hours and on Sundays on a rotating basis. Call your hotel's front desk or the local police station for a list. In London, **Bliss Chemist** is open until midnight every day; they're at 5 Marble Arch, W1; (0207) 723-6116. **Zafash Pharmacy** (233-235 Old Brompton Road, SW5, (0207) 373-2798) is open 24 hours a day.

Dentists

For dental problems, call the **Dental Emergency Care Service** 24 hours a day at (0207) 937-3951. They will give you the name of the nearest dental clinic.

Doctors

The better hotels will have their own doctor on call. If not, contact **Doctor's Call** at (0700) 037-2255. In England, the emergency room is called the Casualty Department. Call 999 or 112 for an ambulance. You'll be taken to the nearest hospital, or, if your symptoms are not life threatening, you'll be advised which is the closest hospital to you.

Prescription Medication

Be especially careful to bring with you a full supply of any prescription drugs you need, as you will find it difficult to have a prescription filled in England. British pharmacies can honor prescriptions only if they are written by physicians who are registered in the United Kingdom. This means you will have to see a doctor in England to obtain a prescription. One option is to go to a national health clinic, which will inevitably involve a wait and, unless you have travel medical insurance, an out-of-pocket expense. An alternative is to visit a private walk-in clinic, such as **Medicentre,** which has branches in Victoria Station in London and elsewhere and charges £50 for a basic consultation; call (0870) 600-0870 or visit **www.medicentre.co.uk.** If you need a medication, check first with a pharmacist (chemist); in some cases you may learn that a drug that requires a prescription in the United States is available over the counter in England.

A CALENDAR OF FESTIVALS AND EVENTS

England has a large number of special traditional events and festivals throughout the year. We list special events in the "Planning Your Visit to . . ." sections in the regional chapters. Another good resource for checking England-wide events and dates before you go is the Visit Britain site **(www.visitbritain.com).** For recorded information on weekly London events while in London, call the London Tourist Board's 24-hour London Line at (09068) 663-344; calls cost 60 pence (about $0.90) per minute; you can't call the London Line from outside the United Kingdom. As you're traveling through the rest of England, stop in at the tourist information centers to find out what's going on, or visit the regional tourist board websites, above. Other useful websites include **www.timeout.com** and the London Tourist Board's website, **www.londontown.com.**

January

Charles I Commemoration (London) Last Sunday of January. The English Civil War Society, dressed in authentic 17th-century uniforms complete with arms, follows the route King Charles I took on January 30, 1649, before he lost his head.

London Parade January 1. A big, brash spectacle with giant balloons, marching bands, clowns, vintage cars, and more. The parade starts at Parliament Square at noon and ends at Berkeley Square at 3 p.m.

February

Chinese New Year Celebrations (London) Chinese New Year changes every year, but is always in either late January or early February. The celebration is usually on the first Sunday after the first day of the Chinese New Year.

Jorvik Viking Festival (York) February 17 and 18 (dates vary). Combat (staged, of course) and a parade celebrate York's thousand-year-old Viking heritage.

March

Oxford versus Cambridge Boat Race (London/Mortlake) This takes place on a Saturday in late March or early April and has been held since 1829. Teams of eight battle the current, rowing 6.8 kilometers upriver from Putney to Mortlake.

April

Gun Salute to Mark the Queen's Birthday (London) April 21. A 41-gun Royal Salute to Queen Elizabeth II, fired at noon by the King's Troop Royal House Artillery in Hyde Park, opposite Dorchester Hotel; it's followed by a 62-gun fiesta at the Tower of London at 1 p.m.

London Harness Horse Parade Easter Monday, Battersea Park. This competition of magnificent "working" horses drawing carriages and carts makes the parade a treat unlike any other.

London Marathon Occurs on a Sunday in mid-April, starting at Greenwich Park and ending at Buckingham Palace. On average, 35,000 competitors participate, so if you want in, you'd better apply early.

The Royal Shakespeare Company (Stratford-upon-Avon) The esteemed troupe begins its performance season.

May

Brighton International Festival (Brighton) Venues all over the resort town of Brighton on the Sussex coast participate in this annual arts festival which features a wide array of drama, literature, visual art, dance, and concert programs ranging from classical to hard rock.

Chelsea Flower Show (London) Britain's largest flower show runs for two weeks at the Chelsea Royal Hospital.

Football Association FA Cup Final (London) Mid-May. Football in England is what Americans call soccer, and tickets for this major sporting event held at Wembley Stadium are difficult to come by.

Glyndebourne Opera (Lewes) The season runs into August, drawing opera lovers from around the world.

June

Beating Retreat Household Division (London) Early June, Buckingham Palace. This is a floodlit nighttime spectacle of all the queen's horses and all the queen's men.

Gay Pride Parades and other events are staged in London, Brighton, Manchester, and other British cities.

Kenwood Lakeside Concerts (London) These open-air classical concerts are held at the beautiful Kenwood House grounds in Hampstead Heath, every Saturday night until September.

Royal Academy Summer Exhibition (London) From early June to mid-August. The Royal Academy in Piccadilly shows the work of contemporary artists in its summer exhibitions. You can browse or buy.

Royal Ascot (Ascot Racecourse, Berkshire) Mid-June. Made famous to Americans by the scene in the movie *My Fair Lady,* Ascot brings out all of social London. It's almost more entertaining to dish the outfits and hats than to watch the races.

Trooping the Colour (London) Early June, Horse Guards Parade, Whitehall. Yes, the lucky queen gets two birthdays: one in April when she was actually born, and an official one in June, when the weather is better for her to inspect her troops, which parade before her. There is a procession to Buckingham Palace, where the air force flies overhead and a gun salute is fired.

Wimbledon Lawn Tennis Championships (Southwest London) This is where all true tennis fans want to be from late June to early July, and everyone else loves the strawberries and cream.

July

BBC Henry Wood Promenade Concerts Mid-July through September, Royal Albert Hall, Kensington Gore, London. Known affectionately as the "Proms," these eight weeks feature a variety of orchestral concerts, from classical to contemporary, which can be seen for a small fee (standing) or for significantly more (sitting). The last night is the big extravaganza.

A CALENDAR OF FESTIVALS AND EVENTS *(continued)*

July (continued)

Hampton Court Flower Show First week in July. Held on the palace grounds in East Molesey, Surrey (part of Greater London), this annual floral event shows off one of the loveliest gardens in England.

Henley Royal Regatta (Henley) First week in July. This championship rowing tournament, one of England's premiere sporting and social events, takes place on the Thames just downstream from Henley, an Oxfordshire town 35 miles west of London.

Winchester, Salisbury, Chichester Late July. The Southern Cathedrals Festival brings together the choirs of the cathedrals in these three cities.

August

Opening of Buckingham Palace (London) Early August to early October. While the queen's away, the tourists will play. Lines of camera-laden hoi polloi wait to take the grand tour through Queen Elizabeth's townhouse while she summers in Scotland.

Notting Hill Carnival (London) End of August, Ladbroke Grove and Portobello Road. It's the biggest street fair in all of Europe, held on a rather slim street, so be ready to stand shoulder to shoulder to enjoy the Caribbean flavor of steel bands and wild partying.

September

Great River Race (London) Mid-September, starting on the Thames at Richmond. Over 200 traditional crafts—including whalers, Viking longboats, Chinese dragon boats, and canoes—race from Ham House in Richmond at 10:30 a.m., finishing at Island Gardens, across from Greenwich Pier about three hours later.

Open House London Mid-September. Finally, a chance to look inside (for free!) more than 500 amazing houses and buildings usually off-limits to the likes of us commoners.

October

Costermongers Pearly Harvest Festival (London) First Sunday in October, St. Martin-in-the Fields, Trafalgar Square. An old cockney tradition celebrating the apple ("coster") harvest that starts with a service at the church and displays a Pearly King or Queen decked out in a costume with thousands of white buttons. Musical merrymakers everywhere. Service starts at 3 p.m.

Money

Pounds and Pence

The British are going slowly into this European Union business, taking a wait-and-see attitude toward the euro unit of currency. At this writing, they are still using pounds (£), and the pound converts to about 1.5 U.S. dollars. Check any major newspaper's business section for current exchange rates, or go to **www.travlang.com** or **www.x-rates.com.** The pound is a unit divided into 100 pence, abbreviated "p."

Harvest festivals are held in rural towns and villages all over England on weekends throughout the month.

November

Bonfire Night and Guy Fawkes Day Firework Displays November 5, all over London and in towns and villages throughout England. Guy Fawkes was the Catholic conspirator who gave his name to history to commemorate the narrowly averted Gunpowder Plot to blow up King James I and Parliament.

London Film Festival Through November. Although based at the National Film Theatre on the South Bank, the prestigious festival of new films presents screenings all over town.

Lord Mayor's Show (London) Mid-November. In this event, which goes back 700 years, the lord mayor rides through the city in a spectacular gilded carriage (which can be seen at the Museum of London during the rest of the year), followed by a retinue of floats, bands, and military marchers.

Remembrance Day November 11. At the 11th hour on the 11th day of the 11th month, all of England falls silent in remembrance of those who died in the two World Wars. Red poppies are bought and worn to show respect for the soldiers who gave their lives for England. On the nearest Sunday to the 11th, there is a service for the war dead at the Cenotaph in Whitehall, London.

State Opening of Parliament (London) First week in November. The Queen in all her finery sets out from Buckingham Palace in her royal coach and heads to Westminster, where she reads out the government's program for the coming year.

December

Christmas Lights and Tree Late November and December. Various Christmas lighting ceremonies take place throughout England, with especially big shows in London and Brighton and even tiny Mousehole in Cornwall. Trafalgar Square is the focus of England's New Year's Eve celebrations.

There are no longer any £1 notes. There are red 50s, purple 20s, brown 10s, and green 5s. Coins are divided into £2, £1, 50p, 20p, 10p, 5p, 2p, and 1p. Coins cannot be changed into foreign cash, so spend them while you're in England; better still, donate them on your way home to the UNICEF Change Collection sponsored by most airlines.

ATMs, Banks, and Bureaux de Change

There are ATMs with Cirrus, MAC, and credit-card account systems all over London and in cities and towns throughout the country. This is your best bet for getting the best rate when you withdraw money. Just slip in your ATM card or a credit card with cash-advance privileges, punch in your code, and the machine will dispense pounds, drawn against your bank account at home. Remember, you can't access funds from a bank account or credit-card account without a PIN (personal identification number). If you're unsure of how to access funds electronically, call your bank or credit-card company to find out how to access your money while in England.

You can change cash or traveler's checks for pounds at a bank or *bureaux de change.* Currency-changing services are available at major airports, at any branch of a major bank (throughout the country), at all major rail and underground stations in Central London, at post offices countrywide, at many tourist information centers, and at American Express or Thomas Cook offices.

Weekday hours for banks are generally 9:30 a.m.–4:30 p.m. All banks are closed on public holidays, but many branches have 24-hour banking lobbies with ATMs and/or ATMs on the street outside. Banks and *bureaux de change* exchange money at a competitive rate but charge a commission (typically 1–3% of the total transaction). All U.K. *bureaux de change* and other money-changing establishments are required to clearly display exchange rates and full details of any fees and rates of commission. Steer clear of *bureaux de change* that offer good exchange rates but charge a heavy commission (up to 8%). You'll find them in major tourist sections of London (some are open 24 hours). Before exchanging your money, always check to see the exchange rate, how much commission will be charged, and whether additional fees apply.

Value-Added Tax (VAT)

The VAT is a 17.5% tax slapped on everything from hotel rooms to lipstick; the only exceptions are food, children's clothing, and books. There are ways to get this tax refunded; see "VAT Refunds" on page 71. Almost everything has the VAT added into the sticker price, except for merchandise sold in some small shops, as well as various services. Check before you book a hotel as to whether the quoted price includes VAT.

Telephones, E-mail, and Postal Services

Telephones

Three types of public pay phones are available: those that take only coins (increasingly rare), those that accept only phone cards, and those that take both phone cards and credit cards. Phone cards are available in £2, £4, £10, and £20 valuations and are usable until the total value has expired. You can buy the cards from newsstands and post offices. At coin-operated phones, insert your coins before dialing. The minimum charge is 10p. The credit-call pay phones operate on credit cards (Access or MasterCard, Visa, American Express, and Diners Club).

Local and International Phone Codes The country code for the United Kingdom is 44. To call England from the United States, dial 011-44; the area or city code; and then the six, seven, or eight-digit phone number. If you're in England and dialing a number within the same area code, the local number is all you need.

To make an international call from England, dial the international access code (00), then the country code, then the area code, and finally the local number. Or call through one of the following long-distance access codes: **AT&T USA Direct** (0800-890-011), **Canada Direct** (0800-890-016), **Australia** (0800-890-061), and **New Zealand** (0800-890-064). Country codes for these nations are: United States and Canada, 1; Australia, 61; New Zealand, 64.

IMPORTANT PHONE NUMBERS

00	International dialing code if calling from England: dial 00 + 1 for U.S. and Canada, 61 for Australia, 64 for New Zealand
100	General operator
112	Emergency for police, fire, or ambulance
153	International-directory inquiries
155	International operator
192	U.K. directory inquiries

E-mail

You'll find Internet cafés all over London and in England's major cities. It's more difficult to find them in smaller towns. If you're outside of London and in dire need of a computer to check or send e-mail, go to the local library. Even the smallest libraries have at least one computer; you may have to pay for the service, or you may have to wait to use it. Using computers at an Internet café is not cheap: £1 for 15 minutes is not unusual. That wouldn't be so bad, but the connections are often slow.

The telephone jacks in England will not fit a standard American modem cord, so if you have your laptop and want to get online, you may have to ask the hotel desk for a telephone cord adapter, or buy one. You should be able to find one easily in both England and in the United States at major electronics stores, or you can order one online from such sources as **shopper.cnet.com, shopping.com,** and **tempestcom.com.**

Post Offices

Mail is called "the post" in England. Mailboxes ("postboxes") are red with "Royal Mail" lettered on them. In London, the **Main Post Office** (24

William IV Street, WC2; (08457) 223344; tube: Charing Cross), is open Monday through Friday, 8:30 a.m.–6:30 p.m., and Saturday, 9 a.m.–5:30 p.m. Other post offices and sub-offices throughout the country are open Monday through Friday, 9 a.m.–5:30 p.m., and Saturday, 9 a.m.–12:30 p.m. Many sub-offices and some main post offices close for an hour at lunchtime. In the post office, you can buy phone cards and often cash traveler's checks. You can also buy stamps at a newsagent.

Part Two

Arriving and Getting around in England

Arriving by Air

London is the main point of entry for most visitors to England. The city has five airports, but only two of them—**Heathrow Airport** and **Gatwick Airport**—are used for regularly scheduled international flights from North America, Australia, and New Zealand. Heathrow, the busiest airport in the world, offers more options for getting into London. Gatwick is much smaller, which is why some travelers prefer it. The other London airports—Stansted, Luton, and London City—are used for charter flights or flights from elsewhere in Europe. If you are spending most of your time in the west or north of England, you can bypass London entirely and fly into Manchester from a few American cities.

British airports have direct rail links to stations throughout the country, so it's possible to arrive, deplane, hop on a train, and head off to your destination. You can also pick up a rental car at the airport (see "Getting around in England" on page 53 for more details on trains and renting a car in England).

Passport Control and Customs

Regardless of which airport you fly into, procedures for entering the country are standard. On the plane, you will receive a landing card that asks for your name, address, passport number, and the address of where you'll be staying in the United Kingdom. Present this completed form and your passport at Passport Control. When your passport is stamped, proceed on to pick up your luggage. From there, you'll wend your way out through the Customs Hall.

At the Customs area there are two choices: "Nothing to Declare" and "Goods to Declare." Limits on imports for visitors 17 and older entering England include 200 cigarettes, 50 cigars, or 250 grams (8.8 ounces) of loose tobacco; 2 liters (2.1 quarts) of still table wine and 1 liter of liquor (over 22% alcohol content), or 2 liters of liquor (under 22%); and 2 fluid ounces of perfume. The total of goods brought in must not exceed £136 (about $225). You may not bring in controlled drugs (any medication you have should be in its original bottle with your name on it), firearms and/or ammunition, plants and vegetables, fresh meats, or any kind of animals. If you fall within these limits, go through the "Nothing to Declare" area at Customs. Otherwise, go through the "Goods to Declare" area, where a Customs official will assess the amount of duty that must be paid.

Heathrow Airport

Heathrow Airport (phone (0870) 0000-123; **www.baa.co.uk**), London's main international airport, is 15 miles west of Central London. Airlines that serve it include **Air Canada** (flights from Calgary, Montreal, Ottawa, Toronto, Vancouver, and St. John's); **Air New Zealand** (flights from Australia and New Zealand); **American Airlines** (flights from Boston, Chicago, Los Angeles, New York, Miami); **British Airways** (U.S. flights from Boston, Chicago, Detroit, Los Angeles, Miami, Newark, New York JFK, Philadelphia, San Francisco, Seattle, and Washington, D.C.; Australian flights from Brisbane, Melbourne, Perth, and Sydney; New Zealand flights from Auckland); **Continental** (flights from Houston, Los Angeles, New York JFK, Newark, San Francisco, and Washington, D.C.); **Icelandair** (flights from Baltimore, Boston, Minneapolis/St. Paul, and New York JFK); **Qantas** (flights from Melbourne, Perth, Sydney, Australia and Auckland, New Zealand); **United** (flights from Boston, Chicago, Los Angeles, Newark, New York JFK, San Francisco, and Washington, D.C.); **Virgin Atlantic** (flights from Chicago, Newark, New York JFK, San Francisco, and Washington, D.C.).

Heathrow has four passenger terminals. Terminal 1 is mainly for short-haul British Airways flights; Terminal 2 is for the European services of non-British airlines; Terminal 3 handles non-British long-haul flights; and Terminal 4 is used for British Airways intercontinental flights.

All sorts of services are available in the main concourses, including ATMs, hotel booking agencies, theater booking services, and several banks and bureaux de change for changing currency. There are so many shops in the departure areas that Heathrow can seem a lot more like a big shopping mall than an airport. You can pick up a free map and general tourist information at the **Tourist Information Centre** in the Terminal 3 Arrivals Concourse (open 6 a.m.–11 p.m.) and another in the Underground concourse of Terminals 1, 2, and 3 (open daily 8 a.m.–6 p.m.).

Getting into London from Heathrow

You have several options for getting into the city from Heathrow. The **London Underground,** called the **Underground** or **the tube,** is the cheapest. All terminals at Heathrow link up with the tube (subway) system. The **Piccadilly Line** gets you into Central London in about 50 to 60 minutes. The fare is £3.70 for adults, £1.50 for children ages 5–15. Underground trains run from all four Heathrow terminals every five to nine minutes Monday through Saturday, 5:08 a.m.–11:49 p.m., and arrive there 6:20 a.m.–1:07 a.m. (shorter hours on Sunday).

If the Underground has closed, the **N97** night bus connects Heathrow with central London. Buses (located in front of the terminals) run every 30 minutes, Monday through Saturday, midnight–5 a.m.; and Sunday, 11 p.m–5:30 a.m. The trip takes about an hour; a one-way fare is £1.50.

National Express' Airbus Heathrow Shuttle (phone (0207) 222-1234; **www.airbus.co.uk**) may be a better alternative to the Underground if you have lots of heavy luggage. There are two routes—the A1 and the A2—with a total of some 23 stops in central London (ask your hotel or bed-and-breakfast if there is a stop close by). The **A1** goes from Heathrow to Victoria station via Cromwell Road, Knightsbridge, and Hyde Park Corner. The **A2** goes to Kings Cross station via Bayswater, Marble Arch, Euston, and Russell Square. Travel time for both routes is about 75 minutes. The fare is £10 adults and £5 children. You can purchase your tickets on the bus. Up to three buses an hour depart between 4 a.m. and 11:23 p.m. from the front of Heathrow's terminals.

Heathrow Express (phone (0845) 600-1515; **www.heathrowexpress.co.uk**) is a fast train line that runs from all four Heathrow terminals to Paddington station in just 15 minutes. The fare is £11.70 standard class, £18.90 first class for adults; £5.40 standard class, £9 first class for children. Tickets can be purchased in the airport, on board the train (with a £2 surcharge), or online (there's a 10% discount for online purchases). Service begins at 5:07 a.m. and ends at 12:08 a.m.

Taking a **taxi** directly to your hotel is cost-effective if three or four people are sharing the cost. You can order a taxi at the **Taxi Information booths** in all four terminals. Expect to pay about £40–£45 plus tip. The trip should take about 45 minutes; cabs are available 24 hours a day.

Gatwick Airport

A smaller airport about 28 miles south of London, **Gatwick Airport** (phone (0870) 000-2468; **www.baa.co.uk**) is served by **American Airlines** (flights from Boston, Dallas/Ft. Worth, and Raleigh/Durham); **British Airways** (flights from Atlanta, Baltimore, Charlotte, Dallas/Ft. Worth, Denver, Houston, New York JFK, Miami, Orlando, Phoenix, and Tampa); **Delta** (flights from Atlanta and Cincinnati); **Continental** (flights from Boston, Cleveland, Houston, Miami, Newark, and Orlando); **Northwest** (flights from Detroit and Minneapolis/St. Paul); **Qantas** (flight from Sydney, Australia); and **Virgin Atlantic** (flights from Boston, Las Vegas, Miami, Newark, Orlando, and San Francisco).

Gatwick has two terminals: North and South. International flights come in at the South Terminal. In the main concourse, you'll find the same array of services that Heathrow offers, except there's no Visit Britain office.

Getting into London from Gatwick

Your hands-down best bet for getting into Central London is the **Gatwick Express** train (phone (08700) 002468), which is right in the terminal. It will whiz you from the airport to Victoria Station in about half an hour for £11 (express class) or £17.50 (first class). Trains run every 15 minutes at peak times and hourly throughout the night. The local **Connex South Central** train (phone (01332) 387-601) also runs to Victoria and costs £8.20. There are four trains an hour during the day; they run every half-hour between midnight and 5 a.m. Another train service, **Thameslink** (phone (0845) 748-4950), runs between Gatwick and King's Cross station. The fare is £9.50, service is every 15 minutes, 3:45 a.m.–12:15 a.m., and trip time is about 45 minutes.

Checker Cars, the official taxi company used by Gatwick, provides 24-hour **taxi service** between Gatwick and Central London. You can order a taxi when you arrive at the **Taxi Information booth.** Expect to pay about £65 (plus tip) for the 90-minute journey.

The Smaller London Airports

Stansted Airport (08700) 000303; **www.baa.co.uk.** Fifty miles northeast of London, Stansted is used for national and European flights. The **Stansted Express (www.stanstedexpress.com)** to Liverpool Street Station takes 45 minutes and costs £13 for express class, £19 for business class.

London City Airport (0207) 646-0088; **www.londoncityairport.com.** The closest airport to central London (only six miles east of downtown), London City Airport services European destinations. A bus charges £5 to take passengers on the 25-minute trip from the airport to Liverpool Street Station.

Luton Airport (01582) 405100; **www.london-luton.com.** Luton is 28 miles northwest of London and services mostly charter flights. You can travel by **Thameslink CityFlier** train from Luton Airport Parkway Station to King's Cross Station for £9.50; the trip takes about 30 minutes. The **Greenline 757 bus** (phone (08706) 087261; **www.greenline.co.uk**) departs the airport hourly for the 70-minute trip into London. The fare is £8.

Manchester Airport

Travelers who want to bypass London for western, middle, or northern England may find it more convenient to fly into **Manchester Airport** (phone (0161) 489-8000; **www.manchesterairport.com**). There are direct flights to Manchester from Chicago (**American Airlines**), New

York's JFK **(Pakistani International, Delta, British Airways),** Newark **(Continental),** Orlando **(Virgin Atlantic),** Philadelphia **(US Airways),** and Washington, D.C. **(British Midland).** The airport, located 10 miles from the center of Manchester, is linked to a major rail station, so you can connect to other cities in England. The easiest way to get into Manchester is by the **Manchester Piccadilly** light-rail service. Up to six trains an hour make the 15-minute journey; the fare is £2.15.

Arriving by Train and Ferry

If you're traveling to England from another destination in Europe, flying isn't the only option. Train and car ferries and high-speed hovercraft cross the English Channel throughout the year from ports in France, Holland, and Belgium. The high-speed **Eurostar (www.eurostar.co.uk)** zips from Paris to London through the Chunnel, a tunnel beneath the English Channel, in three hours.

Eurostar service connecting Paris and Brussels to London via the Chunnel arrives at **Waterloo International Station.** Trains from Amsterdam arrive at **Liverpool Street Station.**

Crossing time for the car, train, and passenger ferries that regularly crisscross the English Channel can be anywhere from 90 minutes to 5 hours, depending on the point of departure. Various hovercraft skim over the water in as little as half an hour. Frequent train service to London is available from all the Channel ports.

Getting around in England

Traveling by Train

From London, you can easily reach cities and towns throughout England by train. The trains in England and the rest of the United Kingdom are separate from those in continental Europe, so a Eurail pass isn't valid. If you're going to travel by train, check out the various BritRail passes available by calling (877) 257-2887 (in the United States) or (800) 361-RAIL (in Canada) or by checking out **www.raileurope.com.** A wide variety of money-saving passes is available. For current train schedules and fares within England, call **National Rail Enquiries** (phone (08457) 484950; **www.railtrack.co.uk**).

The British train system was deregulated in the 1980s with, many would say, deplorable results. Several private train companies now use the track system. Breakdowns and delays are commonplace. Don't let that deter you, however, from taking the train in England. Just be prepared not to arrive on time.

You can buy tickets at any station window, and pay with cash or credit card. A one-way trip is called a "single" and a round trip is called a "return."

If you're making day trips from London or another major city, you can get what's called a "cheap day return"; this fare is available only at certain non-peak hours.

Trains are divided into first-class and second-class (now sometimes called standard-class) compartments. First class costs about one-third more than second class. What are the advantages? First class offers seats that are larger and more comfortable and, in some cases, more personalized service with small perks like free newspapers or free tea and coffee. Both first- and second-class passengers use the same café cars or, on longer hauls, restaurant cars. Vendors come through on many trains selling beverages and snacks.

The most dependable and comfortable trains are the high-speed Intercity trains that run between London and heavily traveled main-line routes. You can get one of these fast trains to York, Stratford-upon-Avon, Bath, Oxenholme (closest station to the Lake District), Exeter, and Penzance. For shorter trips, such as to Brighton and Cambridge, commuter trains are used. Local trains connect small towns between larger towns. The local stations are small, and sometimes (particularly on Sundays) there's no one to help with information or ticket sales. Train schedules are always posted in the local stations, and if there is no window service, you can buy your ticket on the train. Local trains are smoke-free. Smoking is confined to designated areas in the other trains.

Train Stations in London

If you're going to travel around England or the rest of the United Kingdom from London, you'll be departing from one of the following train stations; all are served by Underground (subway):

Charing Cross Station For trains going southeast to Canterbury, Hastings, Dover, and Channel ports that connect with ferry service to the Continent.

Euston Station For trains going north to the Lake District and up to Scotland.

King's Cross Station For trains to destinations in the east of England, including Cambridge and York.

Liverpool Street Station For trains to Channel ports with continuing service to the Netherlands, northern Germany, and Scandinavia.

Paddington Station For trains going southwest to Bath, Plymouth, and Penzance in Cornwall, stopping at cities along the way.

St. Pancras Station Currently being renovated, it will eventually provide expanded Eurostar service to Paris and Brussels from the Midlands.

Victoria Station For trains heading to the south and southeast of England, including Canterbury, Brighton, and Gatwick Airport.

Waterloo Station Primarily for trains going to the south of England; Waterloo International is the station for Eurostar trains to and from Paris and Brussels.

Traveling by Car

If your trip is going to be confined to London, with maybe some easy day trips to places like Windsor or Oxford, don't rent a car. Driving in London is a nightmare, and you don't need the hassle or the added expense, particularly since the public transportation options in London are so good. But having a car does open up scenic regions of the English countryside, like the Cotswolds and the Lake District, where villages are not served by trains and local bus service is erratic.

Before you consider renting a car, however, ask yourself if you'd be comfortable driving with a steering wheel on the right-hand side of the vehicle while shifting with your left hand (you can get an automatic shift, but it'll cost considerably more).

DRIVING ON THE LEFT

The good news is, with a little time and practice, you should become used to driving on the left side of the road. After all, millions of British drivers manage to do it every day. Some tips to make the adjustment easier and safer:

- If you're not comfortable driving a manual transmission (with which most cars in Britain are equipped), pay the extra for an automatic. You'll have enough to adjust to when driving on the left without trying to teach yourself how to drive a manual.
- Make sure you are well rested when you first hit the road, as you'll need to keep your wits about you. Consider taking it easy on your arrival day and getting a good night's sleep rather than driving right after you step off the plane.
- Once you pick up your car, take some time to adjust–even practice getting into the car on the correct side—because chances are, you'll probably be tempted to throw open the the front-left-side door and climb right into the passenger seat. Without turning on the car, fiddle with the gearshift for awhile, as it might take a while to adjust to shifting with your left hand, not your right. When you are ready to switch on the ignition, drive around the car park for as long as it takes to feel comfortable.
- Always keep these two concepts in mind. First, look to the right, because that is the direction from which traffic will be approaching. Second, make sure the center line of the roadway is next to the driver's side of the car—this way, you'll know you're on the right (as in "correct") side of the road.

For more information and to bone up on the rules of the road in Britain before you leave home, check out the British Department of Transport's Highway Code at **www.highwaycode.gov.uk.**

Car Rentals

Renting a car in England generally costs more than it does in the United States, unless you can find a special promotional offer from an airline or a car-rental agency. Americans, Canadians, Australians, and New Zealanders renting a car in England need a valid driver's license that they've had for at least one year. In most cases, you must be 23 years old (21 in some instances, 25 in others), and no older than 70 (some companies have raised this to 75).

You can often get a lower car-rental rate if you reserve seven days in advance through the toll-free reservations offices. On a per-day basis, weekly rentals are almost always less expensive than daily rates. And the rate, of course, depends on the size of the vehicle. In general, you'll save money by renting your car before you arrive in England.

When you make your reservation, ask if the quoted price includes the 17.5% VAT (value-added tax) and unlimited mileage. Then find out whether personal accident insurance (PAI), collision-damage waiver (CDW), and any other insurance options are included. For your own peace of mind, arrange for as much coverage as possible; many credit cards cover collision-damage waiver automatically, but check to make sure.

One car-rental option to consider is **AutoEurope** (phone (888) 223-5555 U.S., (0800) 899-893 U.K.; **www.autoeurope.com**). Depending on your travel plans, AutoEurope can arrange for rentals from a variety of vendors and locations, sometimes with a substantial discount. They also offer advantages like transfers, prepaying, and vouchers that help insure a car will really be waiting when you arrive.

You can rent a car before you go at any of the following car-rental agencies. Some airlines offer package deals that include car rental. Remember, it will probably be cheaper if you rent the car at least seven days in advance. Also, many of the Web-based services offering inexpensive flights also provide rental cars at substantial discounts; see "Surf the Web" on page **28**.

Alamo	(800) 462-5266 U.S. (0800) 272200 U.K.	www.alamo.com
Avis	(800) 331-1084 U.S. (0990) 900-500 U.K.	www.avis.com
Budget	(800) 527-0700 U.S. (0541) 565656 U.K.	www.budget.com
Hertz	(800) 654-3131 U.S. (0990) 6699 U.K.	www.hertz.com
National	(800) 227-7368 U.S. (0990) 565-656 U.K.	www.nationalcar.com

Picking Up Your Rental Car Large international car-rental companies have outlets at airports in London and Manchester. It is also possible to arrange to pick up cars from main railway stations, or from an office in a city. You might want to consider taking a train to a hub city or town

(Bath, Exeter, or York, for example) and renting a car there to explore the surrounding countryside.

Roads and Roundabouts

What drivers in the United States would call a freeway, the Brits call a "motorway" (indicated on maps by "M" plus a number). You must not stop on a motorway unless there is an emergency. A two-way road is called a "single carriageway," and a four-lane divided highway (two lanes in each direction) is a "dual carriageway." Roads in the countryside are often barely wide enough for two cars to pass, and full of twists and turns. "Roundabouts" are traffic junctions where several roads meet at one traffic circle. On a roundabout, the cars to your right (i.e., already on the roundabout) always have the right-of-way.

RULES OF THE ROAD

Here are some general rules of the road you'll need to know if you're going to be driving in England:

- In England, all distances and speed limits are shown in miles and miles per hour. If you need to translate from the metric system, a kilometer is 0.62 of a mile, and a mile is 1.62 kilometers.
- Speed limits are usually 30 miles per hour (48 kph) in towns; 40 mph (65 kph) on some town roads where posted; 60 mph (97 kph) on most single carriageway (two-way) roads; and 70 mph (113 kph) on dual carriageways and motorways.
- Road signs are usually the standard international signs.
- Using seat belts is required by law. If you have children, make sure that the correct seat belts or car seats are available before you rent.
- At roundabouts, traffic coming from the right has the right-of-way.
- You can pass other vehicles only on the right.
- Parking in the center of most big towns is difficult and expensive. Make sure you read all posted restrictions, or park in a lot.
- You must stop for pedestrians in striped (zebra) crossings. They always have the right-of-way.

Road Emergencies

All motorways have emergency telephones every kilometer. There are markers every tenth of a kilometer which also point to the nearest phone. The phone operator will obtain breakdown or emergency services if you require them. Park as near to the edge of the shoulder as possible. Motorway service stations are usually about 25 miles apart, and occasionally as far as 50 miles apart.

Buying Gasoline

Gasoline is called "petrol." Petrol stations are self-service. The green filler pipe is for unleaded petrol, the red filler pipe is for leaded petrol, and the black filler pipe is for diesel.

Petrol is often cheapest at supermarkets (yes, they may have pumps outside) but more convenient to find at motorway service stations. Petrol is purchased by the liter (3.78 liters equals one U.S. gallon). Expect to pay about 85p per liter (approximately $5 per gallon) for unleaded petrol.

Traveling by Bus and Coach

A long-distance touring bus in England is called a "coach." "Buses" are what you take for local (including regional) transportation. And what's true is that more and more people are taking coaches and buses because they are more reliable than trains.

The main long-distance coach company is **National Express,** with routes covering the entire country. The coaches are equipped with reclining seats, a toilet, and often a food and beverage service. Tickets are usually half of what the train costs, and even cheaper if you buy a return ticket.

If you're going to travel around England by coach from London, you'll be departing from **Victoria Coach Station** at Buckingham Palace Road (phone (0207) 730-3466; tube: Victoria), located just two blocks from Victoria Station. Coach stations in cities outside of London are always close to the city center, often next to the train station. For information on travel by coach, and on the money-saving **Tourist Trail Pass,** contact National Express (phone (08705) 808080); you can access schedules and fares online at **www.gobycoach.com.** Any Tourist Information Centre will also have information on local and regional bus routes.

Tours and Exploring

Area attractions are profiled the "Exploring" section of each regional chapter of this guidebook. In these sections, we often give you a brief walking tour and some idea of how to get to know a place, and we also mention secondary sights that may be worth a visit or just a glance. If an attraction is not profiled, it's not a major sight. In the "Tours" section of each regional chapter, we provide details of our favorite tours of the cities, towns, and areas covered.

Walking Tours

Walking tours are one of the most enjoyable ways to see a city and learn more about its history. The historic hearts of most English cities outside of London are compact and full of architectural and historical treasures that add to their charm, character, and fascination. Part of the fun is simply listening to the tour guide. The English love to show off their history and usually do so with intelligence and enthusiasm.

Walking tours (including those provided by Visitor Information Centres) are often led by **Blue Badge** guides, who are registered with official British tourist boards, have usually undergone fairly rigorous training, and tend to be fonts of knowledge about a particular place. In using a Blue Badge guide, you will be assured of putting yourself in the hands of a expert and not a smooth-talking huckster. For information on Blue Badge guides in the places you plan on visiting, contact the **Guild of Registered Tourist Guides** (The Guild House, 52D Borough High Street, London SE1 1XN; (0207) 378-1705; guild@blue-badge.org.uk). Or simply check with the Visitor Information Centre when you arrive in a city or town. Fees for local walking tours are usually about £5.

Bus Tours

Another good way to introduce yourself to a place is by taking a guided bus tour. All major tourist towns and cities offer bus tours, often by a company called **City Sightseeing** (home office: Juliette Way, Purfleet Industrial Park, Purfleet, Essex RM15 4YA; (1708) 866-000; **www.city-sightseeing.com**). This company recently acquired Guide Friday, which you may have used on previous trips to England. These tours usually last 45 minutes to an hour and make a circuit of all the major sights. Frequently they are on open-top buses and offer "hop on, hop off" service, so you can get off, visit an attraction, and reboard the next bus. The kind and quality of commentary varies from company to company, and is sometimes canned—opt for live commentary, if you have a choice. Expect to pay about £8 for adults and £6 for children; family rates are often available.

Touring on Your Own or on an Escorted Tour

This is purely a matter of individual preference. If you choose not to rent a car, you'll find that it's easy to travel to most of England's scenic and historic cities and towns on the train, and then easily walk everywhere or use public transportation. The exceptions are villages in the Cotswolds and in the Lake District, where public transportation from place to place is erratic or time-consuming, and getting around by car is almost a necessity. Some major attractions are in the countryside, miles from the nearest town or train station. For these—Castle Howard in Yorkshire is an example—you can take a train to the nearest station and a taxi from the station. If a taxi isn't waiting at the rank outside the station, ask in the station for the number of the local company.

Escorted tours do all the logistical work for you. A coach or minivan takes you to the attraction and someone explains it all to you. Under

"Tours of London" on page 118, we provide the names of some well-regarded companies that offer escorted tours around London; they also lead tours to points outside the capital, so call or check out their websites to get a list of tours, specific itineraries, and other details.

Using London as a Base for Touring

You might want to consider using London as your base of operation and taking day trips from there. With fast trains, it's possible to reach destinations such as Stratford-upon-Avon, Salisbury, Winchester, Oxford, Cambridge, Bath, Rye, Brighton, and even York within a couple of hours. You can spend the day, see the sights, have tea, and be back in London in time for a play or concert (or to have a quick bite and fall into bed). Dozens of fascinating day trips to specific attractions are also possible this way; see "Day Trips from London," page 158, for more ideas.

Using Regional Bases for Touring

Another strategy is to take a train to a city or town in a specific region you want to tour. You can spend one or two nights in the town and rent a car to explore the outlying areas. If, for instance, you are interested in visiting the Cotswolds villages, you could base yourself in Bath or Oxford; if the west of England is calling you, you could base yourself in Exeter, Penzance, or St. Ives. York is the most logical base for exploring Yorkshire. You'll enjoy the historic atmosphere and amenities in these ancient English cities; then you can easily get out into the countryside that England is famous for. Consult the various regional chapters to get an idea of what each region has to offer.

Part Three

Lodging, Dining, and Shopping in England

Hotels in England

The type of accommodations you'll find in England fall into two general categories: hotels and bed-and-breakfast inns. Both hotels and bed-and-breakfasts vary greatly in price, style, and degree of luxury.

There's no getting around the fact that hotels in London are very pricey, but if you check out the various sources listed below and do some serious hotel-shopping on the Web, you may be able to snap up a bargain. A bargain in London is anything under $150 a night for a double. Prices are a bit lower in some other parts of England—provided, that is, you are not looking to stay in an elegant country-house hotel or upscale chain—but you will probably find that hotel prices are pretty high everywhere. Throughout England, bed-and-breakfasts are the best bet for budget-minded travelers.

The Brits are not as committed to smoke-free environments as Americans are, though this is changing. More and more hotels and bed-and-breakfasts in England reserve special rooms or an entire floor for nonsmokers. If the smell of stale cigarette smoke bothers you, always ask if nonsmoking rooms are available.

What to Expect in a Hotel or Bed-and-Breakfast

Hotel Choices

When possible, in this guide we usually steer you away from the more anonymous chain hotels to accommodations that offer similar amenities in more character-filled settings. However, in places where chain hotels are the best lodging options available, we recommend those properties.

Boutique Hotels Small to mid-range in size and large on character, boutique hotels are often sumptuously furnished and offer state-of-the-art amenities and full service. A new boutique hotel seems to be popping up in London every day, and a chain of boutique hotels, **Hotel du Vin**

(**www.hotelduvin.com**), is opening hotels in cities around Britain. These are some of our favorite places to stay in England, and you'll find our evaluations in the hotel sections of Brighton, Winchester, and Birmingham.

Deluxe Hotels These properties offer a distinctly English kind of style, full of charm and character. Usually housed in historic properties, these are the most atmospheric hotels in England, full of twisting stairways and oak-beamed bedrooms (the bathrooms will always be modern, though) and often fireplaces in the reception areas.

Chain Hotels England has plenty of chains familiar to Americans: **Hyatt, Sheraton, Marriott,** and **Days Inn,** to name just a few. Chain hotels are generally newer places that rely on their brand-name, no-surprises approach to win customers. Most chain hotels cater to large groups, and you may feel rather anonymous in them. On the other hand, these hotels are usually well equipped for people with disabilities and families with children. London is chock-full of chains; outside of the capital, you will find chain hotels in most medium-size towns and in tourist areas such as the Lake District, but the names may be unfamiliar to you. **Thistle** is a well-known British chain; some of their hotels are in historic properties and are well maintained, while we've found others to be rather disappointing in terms of quality and amenities. Hotels in the **Best Western** chain are often historic properties that have been brought up to date with modern amenities.

Landmark and Country-House Hotels At the top of the hotel spectrum, in both price and prestige, are the landmark and country-house hotels, where you can expect glamorous public salons, a generously proportioned and well-decorated room with a large private bath, an on-site health club or access to one nearby, and top-of-the-line service. Country-house hotels are a world unto themselves. Former private estates set within landscaped gardens, they typify a world of privilege and tradition and work hard to make their guests feel pampered and comfortable. You can always expect fine gourmet cooking at a country-house hotel.

Self-Catering Hotels In a self-catering hotel (basically, a hotel that has rooms equipped with kitchenettes), you do the cooking in your own hotel room. For short stays and for one or two people, self-catering hotels don't always beat the competition's price. But for families, groups, and those who can't afford or don't desire to eat every meal out, self-catering hotels can be a budget saver. Outside of London you will find few self-catering hotels; instead, you'll find self-catering flats (apartments) or holiday homes that can be rented for a week or more.

Many hotels provide breakfast with a room rental; others charge an additional fee for it (we indicate which hotels include breakfast in the room rate or how much breakfast will cost).

Tipping Hotel Staff

In the good hotels, just tip in pounds the same way you would at home in dollars: £1 or £2 a bag for bellhops, a fiver for the maid for stays of two or more nights, or a pound for one night.

Bed-and-Breakfasts

Bed-and-breakfast inns are rooms in private homes. They are inspected by local or regional tourist boards, but the degree of style, comfort, and service in them varies widely. Plumbing may be unpredictable, hot water scarce, and space cramped. Room amenities also vary widely. Nearly all bed-and-breakfast rooms contain wash basins, but you may have to share a bathroom down the hall, though "en-suite" (in the room) bathrooms are becoming more common. Décor is often less standardized than it is in a hotel. This can be good, and you often find yourself in character-filled surroundings; on the other hand, you may also find yourself surrounded by chintz, mismatched wallpaper, and a collection of stuffed dolls. Overall, the quality of bed-and-breakfasts has improved greatly in the past few years. The most successful bed-and-breakfasts continually upgrade their services or offer enticing amenities, such as cable TVs and direct-dial phones in the rooms. The more popular and well-appointed bed-and-breakfasts are, of course, more expensive.

What about the breakfast part of the bed-and-breakfast? In most bed-and-breakfasts, you can expect a "full English breakfast" (also known as a "fry-up") of eggs, sausages, bacon, grilled tomatoes, and beans, but a lighter Continental breakfast—roll, juice, and coffee or tea—is also usually available.

One caveat: If you're physically disabled or in any way infirm, bed-and-breakfasts may not be the best choice for you. They usually don't have elevators, so you have to carry your luggage up steep, narrow stairs.

Reserving Your Room in Advance

Take our advice and do not arrive in London without a hotel reservation. This is especially important if you're planning your trip from mid-April through August (high season). Booking ahead isn't quite as important in the rest of England, but it's still a wise idea for a Friday or Saturday night in a tourist spot like Stratford-upon-Avon or a town like Rye, where many Londoners like to get away for a weekend. Hotels in popular tourist areas such as the Cotswolds, Cornwall, and the Lake District also fill up fast on weekends and during high season in July and August. Off-season, and especially in the middle of week, you usually won't have a problem booking a room on the spot. In a small village, it may be as simple as finding a house that says "Room to Let" in the front window.

Tourist information centers in all large towns and in the national parks can always help you find a room. In most cases, they charge 10% of the first night's hotel rate, but you get that back at the hotel, so the service ends up costing nothing. If you decide to show up without a room reservation and find there's no room at the inn, check out our recommendations for booking services throughout this guide; they are often provided by Tourist Information Centres.

Hotels do not consider a room reservation confirmed until they receive partial or full payment. You can almost always confirm your reservations immediately with a credit card; otherwise, you must mail in your payment using an international money order, available at most banks. Before reserving your room, ask about the cancellation policy. At some hotels, you can get your money back if you cancel a room with 24 hours' notice; in others, you must notify the hotel five or more days in advance. After you've reserved the room, request a written confirmation by fax, e-mail, or post.

Smaller bed-and-breakfasts outside of London, especially those in country villages, do not always accept credit cards. If you're going to be rambling through the Cotswolds and choosing small hotels or bed-and-breakfasts as they strike your fancy, make sure you have enough cash on hand (but then again, you'll find ATMs in many of villages, no matter how quaint they seem).

Room Rates

Room rates change with the season and as occupancy rates rise and fall. If a hotel is close to full, don't expect to find any kind of rate reduction. If it's close to empty, you may be able to negotiate a discount. Expensive hotels catering to business travelers are most crowded on weekdays and usually offer substantial discounts for weekend stays. Likewise, hotels in the Cotswolds, the Lake District, and Cornwall are often fully booked on weekends but are happy to lure guests on weekdays, especially in the off-season, with reduced rates. Throughout this guide, we alert you to ways to secure a reduced rate at hotels; many offer lower rates for stays of multiple nights, or provide good-value dinner, bed, and breakfast packages (check out hotel websites for packages available at the time of your stay). Especially in resort areas, you may be able to save 20% or more by traveling off-season (mid-October to mid-December and January to March); even London hotels tend to be less expensive from January through March. Budget hotels and small bed-and-breakfasts rarely offer discounts, but you never know—if you're willing to share a bathroom, you often can save money. Our rule of thumb is: Never be afraid to ask for the lowest rate.

The best hotel rates of all, especially where London is concerned, are found with air/hotel packages. A good travel agent may be able to come up with an air/hotel package that saves you hundreds of dollars off the hotel's published rates.

VAT Included?

In general, the quoted room rate includes the 17.5% VAT (value-added tax). The exceptions to this are luxury hotels at the upper end of the price scale; their quoted prices—already astronomically high—sometimes add insult to injury by tacking on yet another 17.5%. Wherever you're staying, be sure to ask if the VAT is included so you won't get an unpleasant surprise when you're checking out.

Finding Hotel Deals on the Web

Although the major travel-booking websites listed in Part One, Planning Your Visit to England, offer hotel-booking services, there are other websites devoted entirely to lodging.

Bed & Breakfast (www.bedbreak.com) Can set you up in an inexpensive bed-and-breakfast anywhere in England.

British Hotel Reservation Centre (www.bhrc.co.uk) Lists current and seasonal specials at selected London and U.K.-wide hotels.

Hotel Discount!com (www.180096hotel.com) Lists bargain rates at hotels in London.

Hotel-U.K. Reservations Service (www.demon.co.uk/hotel-uk) Features best-value hotels of the month and other money-saving promotions.

InnSite (www.innsite.com) Provides bed-and-breakfast listings for inns around the globe, including the United Kingdom.

London Tourist Board (www.londontown.com) Has a long list of London properties to choose from, some with special low rates.

TravelWeb (www.travelweb.com) Focuses on chains such as Hyatt and Hilton and offers weekend deals at many leading chains.

Hotel Ratings

Prices in our listings include the 17.5% VAT (value-added tax) and refer to the starting price for standard single and standard double room. Prices for deluxe, executive, triple-occupancy, family rooms, and suites and rooms with special features (such as four-poster bed, fireplace, balcony, etc.) will be significantly higher.

Overall Ratings We have distinguished properties according to relative quality, tastefulness, state of repair, cleanliness, and size of standard rooms, grouping them into classifications denoted by stars. Overall star ratings in this guide do not correspond to ratings awarded by the British Tourism Board, automobile clubs, or other travel critics. Overall ratings are presented to show the difference we perceive between one property and another. They are assigned without regard to location or to whether a property has restaurants, recreational facilities, entertainment, or other extras.

★★★★★	Superior	Tasteful and luxurious by any standard
★★★★	Extremely Nice	Above average in appointments and design; very comfortable
★★★	Nice	Average but quite comfortable
★★	Adequate	Plain but meets all essential needs
★	Budget	Spartan, not aesthetically pleasing, but clean

Quality Ratings In addition to overall ratings (which delineate broad categories), we also employ quality ratings. They apply to room quality only and describe the property's standard accommodations. In addition to standard accommodations, many hotels offer luxury rooms and special suites that are not rated in this guide. Our rating scale is ★–★★★★★, with ★★★★★ as the best possible rating and ★ as the worst.

Value Ratings We also provide a value rating to give you some sense of the quality of a room in relation to its cost. As before, the ratings are based on the quality of room for the money and do not take into account location, services, or amenities.

Our scale is as follows:

★★★★★	An exceptional bargain
★★★★	A good deal
★★★	Fairly priced (you get exactly what you pay for)
★★	Somewhat overpriced
★	Significantly overpriced

A ★★½ room at £100 may have the same value rating as a ★★★★ room at £180, but that does not mean that the rooms will be of comparable quality. Regardless of whether it's a good deal or not, a ★★½ room is still a ★★½ room.

Dining in England

British food, of the boiled meat accompanied by boiled potatoes and boiled brussels sprouts variety, has been the brunt of jokes for centuries. Well, let's put the joke to rest: You're in for a pleasant surprise, because British cooking is more varied and interesting by the day, with an emphasis on fresh ingredients in exciting combinations. Asian and South Asian cuisines, French and Italian cooking, even old-fashioned British dishes (reinvented these days in modern British cuisine) are taken with greater seriousness these days, especially in London but just about everywhere in the country as well.

One thing that hasn't changed is the cost of a meal: British restaurants are expensive. Wherever you travel in England, it's hard to find a good three-course meal with a bottle of wine for under £25 a head. There are ways to cut costs. Pub meals are usually reasonably priced, though in many pubs you'll have to time your meal so you're not enveloped in smoke and surrounded by bellowing quaffers; many have separate dining rooms and nonsmoking areas, as well as outdoor tables. At other restaurants, lunch is likely to be considerably cheaper than dinner, and some places have prix fixe lunches as well as pre- or post-theater offers with limited choice and lower prices. With drinks making up a large part of many bills, look for house wines or order by the glass if that's all you want. And don't feel obliged to order a bottle of water (almost always marked up heavily) if tap water will please you just as well. If you're traveling with children but don't see a children's menu, ask if a child-size portion can be prepared. Finally, look for some of the better chains that have popped up in British cities in recent years—no, not McDonald's (though they are disappointingly present, too), but Pizza Express and other places serving unremarkable but palatable and modestly priced fare in pleasant surroundings.

Tipping Restaurant Staff

In many restaurants, a service charge of 12–15% is included in the bill; make sure you examine your menu and your bill to see if it has already been added. If service is not included, it will be mentioned in some obvious manner on the bill. Twelve to twenty percent is considered the normal range for tipping in restaurants.

Rating Our Favorite Restaurants

We have developed detailed profiles for the best and most interesting (in our opinion) restaurants all over England. Each profile features an easily scanned heading that allows you to quickly check out the restaurant's name, cuisine, star rating, quality rating, value rating, and cost, as well as a description of the dining experience you can expect to have there.

Cuisine This is actually less straightforward than it sounds. In some cases, we have used the broader terms (i.e., "French" or "Italian") but added descriptions to give a clearer idea of the fare (i.e., "Provençal" or "Southern Italian"). Don't hold us, or the chefs, to too strict a style, but we do try to give you some idea of what type of cuisine to expect.

Overall Rating The overall rating encompasses the entire dining experience, including style, service, and ambience, in addition to the taste, presentation, and quality of the food. Five stars is the highest rating possible and connotes the best of everything. Four-star restaurants are exceptional, and three-star restaurants are well above average. Two-star restaurants are good. One star is used to indicate an average restaurant that demonstrates an unusual capability in some area of specialization—for example, an otherwise unmemorable place that has great barbecued chicken.

Cost Our expense description provides a comparative sense of how much a complete meal will cost. A complete meal for our purposes consists of an appetizer, entree, and dessert. Drinks and tips are excluded. We use different scales for London and places other than London, since London restaurants are just that much more expensive.

In London

Inexpensive	Less than £25 per person
Moderate	£25–£50 per person
Expensive	More than £50 per person

Elsewhere in England

Inexpensive	Less than £15 per person
Moderate	£15–£30 per person
Expensive	More than £30 per person

Quality Rating Food quality is rated on a scale of one to five stars, five being the best rating attainable. The quality rating is based expressly on the taste, freshness of ingredients, preparation, presentation, and creativity of food served. There is no consideration of price. If you are a person who wants the best food available and cost is not an issue, you need look no further than the quality ratings.

Value Rating If, on the other hand, you are looking for both quality and value, then you should check the value rating. The value ratings are defined as follows:

★★★★★	An exceptional value; a real bargain
★★★★	Good value
★★★	Fairly priced (you get exactly what you pay for)
★★	Somewhat overpriced
★	Significantly overpriced

Payment We've listed the type of payment accepted at each restaurant using the following codes: AMEX equals American Express (Optima), CB equals Carte Blanche, D equals Discover, DC equals Diners Club, JCB equals Japan Credit Bureau, MC equals MasterCard, and V equals VISA.

Who's Included Our lists are highly selective. Our failure to include a particular place does not necessarily indicate that the restaurant is not good, only that we did not feel it ranked among the best we wanted to offer our readers in a particular place.

Shopping in England

It's safe to say that almost everything is cheaper in the United States than in England. That said, it's also true that London is one of the world's great shopping cities. If you come during the big sales, the best of which are found during the month of January (there's also one in August), you just might be able to pay North American prices for stuff you can't readily get at home. Outside of London, the shopping can still be fun, and you never know what you might find in a store window or small shop. Old books, engravings, and silver are things to look for. So are locally produced crafts: pottery, ceramics, and glass.

Wise Buys in England

The following items are worth buying in England because of their high quality or their unavailability in the United States.

Antiques

You find antiques shops in the old districts of every major city and town, which also usually have a market where vendors sell antiques. See our shopping sections in each regional chapter for tips on the shops and markets where you are most likely to pick up a bargain.

Aromatic Bath Goods and Toiletries

Bath oils, salts, soaps, and scents in some cases cost less than in the United States. **Culpepper the Herbalist, Neal's Yard Remedies, Floris, Lush, Crabtree & Evelyn,** and **Penhaligon** are slightly cheaper in England than they are in the few places they are sold in the States, and **Boots the Chemist** has its own line of goods of reasonable quality.

Bone China

Look in the stalls on Portobello Road in London's **Notting Hill** and other markets around the country. Even department stores and stores specializing in china offer patterns you can't find in America, often at reasonable prices. Crystal goods are often cheaper than they are in the States.

Books

England is a nation of readers, and there are thousands of bookstores that cater to readers with all possible interests. Almost every town of any size has one or two excellent shops that sell books published only in England, antiquarian volumes in gorgeous sets, and crates full of secondhand books. The old books are really worth your while.

Children's Clothing

Some children's clothing may be, if not cheaper, of better quality and value than in the States. English smock dresses and French baby clothes are beautiful, and you don't have to pay VAT on children's clothing.

Designer Clothing

Secondhand, that is. There are tons of resale shops that sell "pre-owned" **Chanel, Voyage, Gucci, Westwood,** or whatever for reasonable prices. A lot of ladies seem to have worn these clothes twice and then moved on to the next big thing. Many savvy clotheshorses turn up amazing finds at Oxfam charity shops.

Fabrics

England has long been known for its gorgeous fabrics; try **John Lewis** or **Peter Jones** in London for the best deals on locally made material and things like trim and curtain swags.

Stationery

Filofax, the personal organizer so well loved by type-A professionals in the States, is an indigenous English product and much cheaper here than anywhere else, especially at sale time.

Time to Shop

Stores in England tend to open late and close early. The usual hours are 10 a.m.–6 p.m., with a few opening at 9 a.m. (but closing at 5 p.m.), and a very few, like **Waterstone's Bookstores,** staying open until 9:30 p.m.

Stores all over England stay open one night a week. In London, stores stay open until 7 or 8 p.m. on Thursdays on Oxford Street, Regent Street, and the West End. Just to keep you on your toes, for stores in Knightsbridge and Chelsea, late night is Wednesday. Sunday is still relatively sacrosanct as a day of rest for shopkeepers, although more stores on the major shopping streets are starting to open for a half day, from noon to 5 or 6 p.m. Street markets follow their own muse as far as opening hours and days go.

Paying Up

Most shops take all major credit cards (though some small shops in small towns and villages outside of London may not). Some stores will take traveler's checks in British sterling, but they don't even want to hear about U.S. dollar traveler's checks. If they are kind enough to cash them, it may not be at a rate favorable to you. (Bring a passport to cash traveler's checks.) The credit card is a good way to go, as you'll have a record of your purchases and the exchange rate will be fair. The rate used will be that on the day the credit purchase clears the credit card company or bank.

The VAT

The VAT (value-added tax) is the mind-boggling 17.5% the British government adds on to the cost of all goods and services except for books, food, and children's clothing. Most goods will have the VAT already figured into the price on the tags, but other items, especially those sold at fancy knickknack stores and other high-priced shops, try to prevent total sticker shock by placing a discreet "+VAT" after all those zeros. If you have your goods shipped directly overseas from the store, the VAT will be deducted from the price, but you'd have to be paying a lot of money to have the cost of shipping balance out. There's also the important subject of paying duty on your imported goods when you arrive in the United States.

You are allowed $800 per person of goods duty free, and families may combine this allowance, so that a family of five is allowed $4,000 worth of goods. The next $1,000 worth of goods gets charged a flat 10%—after that it will vary according to what type of import you're bringing.

Yes, you may be able to get a refund of some of the VAT you've paid (see "VAT Refunds" below), but it requires a little footwork—and it may not be worth the time and bother if all you've purchased is £50 or £100 worth of goods.

VAT Refunds

Only those who are not British subjects or citizens of other European Union countries qualify for VAT refund, and they have to leave the country with their goods within six months.

Refund companies handle the VAT refund for different shops, and they have set the refund at different rates. Many stores are starting to use **Tax-Free Europe** to expedite the VAT returns; they give you a cash refund at the airport, but a lot of your money stays in their hands. There's also **VATBack,** which will do a credit-card refund by mail; this takes about three months, but you'll get a bigger percentage back. They also give immediate cash back, £8.60 for over £100 of goods or £18.50 for over £500 of goods.The clerk can tell you which company the shop uses and help you decide whether it's worth your while or not. In any case, you will not get the entire 17.5% back—it's more like 10–15% (plus an additional fee that you pay for the processing of the papers), and it can actually be as little as 4% with some refund companies.

Ask what is the minimum you must spend in a given shop to qualify for the papers being filled out—it can vary, although the law puts the minimum at £50. Some shops will refuse outright; some will charge at least £5 for issuing the papers. You must have the refund form filled out at the place of purchase! You cannot get it done anywhere else by anyone else. Bring your passport to the store to help make your case.

You must show your VAT-refund purchases at the airport Customs area; this is easiest if you keep your purchases in your carry-on luggage. Factor the size of the item against the amount of the refund times the degree of hassle you're willing to go through.

Go to the Customs official to get the VAT papers before you check in your luggage. Allow time for all the forms to be filled out—about five minutes for each one. After you go through passport control, line up at the VAT desk to show them what you've bought and the papers that go with them. You then get the papers back; you can mail the completed paperwork back to the shop, or take the papers to one of the desks that some refund companies, such as Tax-Free Europe, have at the airports.

If your VAT-refund items are too big to carry on, budget an extra hour at the airport, as you will need to have a security guard watch you go through passport control and then return the items to your airline for checking.

You can also sometimes get a VAT refund from a hotel or holiday apartment, or from a car-rental agency; ask the concierge or the person with whom you book your travel arrangements for the forms and the information.

Salespeople's Attitudes and Behavior

Except in a few upscale stores, where the staff is rigorously trained to look like they give a damn, the salespeople in England will surprise and perhaps bewilder you with their laissez-faire attitudes. It's not that they don't want to make a sale; it's just that they don't want to be perceived as pushing anyone to buy something. If you are in need of assistance, just approach them—you'll probably find that they will help you eagerly and with great courtesy.

Part Four

London

Be prepared: You may not hear this name too often as you wander through this ancient and fascinating conglomeration on the Thames. London, you see, is still a collection of villages that sprawl across the Thames basin. Oh, London has a center all right, many of them—Knightsbridge (the center of shopping), the West End (the center of nightlife and entertainment), the City (center of finance and old London), Westminster (center of British government), and on and on it goes.

While the lack of an epicenter may confuse a visitor and mandate the purchase of a good map, the sheer number of thriving, bustling neighborhoods in London accounts for much of the city's appeal. You will not, to invoke good old Dr. Johnson, ever tire of London. Should you exhaust the sights of Westminster, you can simply stroll into another London stage set, like Covent Garden or Belgravia or the trendy new South Bank across the river. Within this maze of neighborhoods are the London attractions and institutions that seem to improve all the time—the museums, historic monuments, restaurants, shops, and parks—reminders of the past and emblems of the future. Wherever you wander in London, you can't help but notice how this city embraces the new, welcomes folks from all over the world, and, despite some frustrating inconveniences like tube stoppages and high prices, is one of the most exhilarating places on earth to spend time.

The Zones

The post codes that appear at the end of a London address represents a geographic area of the city. SW1, for instance, is the royal borough of Westminster and includes the neighborhoods of Victoria, Pimlico, and parts of Knightsbridge and Belgravia. Chelsea and Kensington are in the SW3 and SW7 codes.

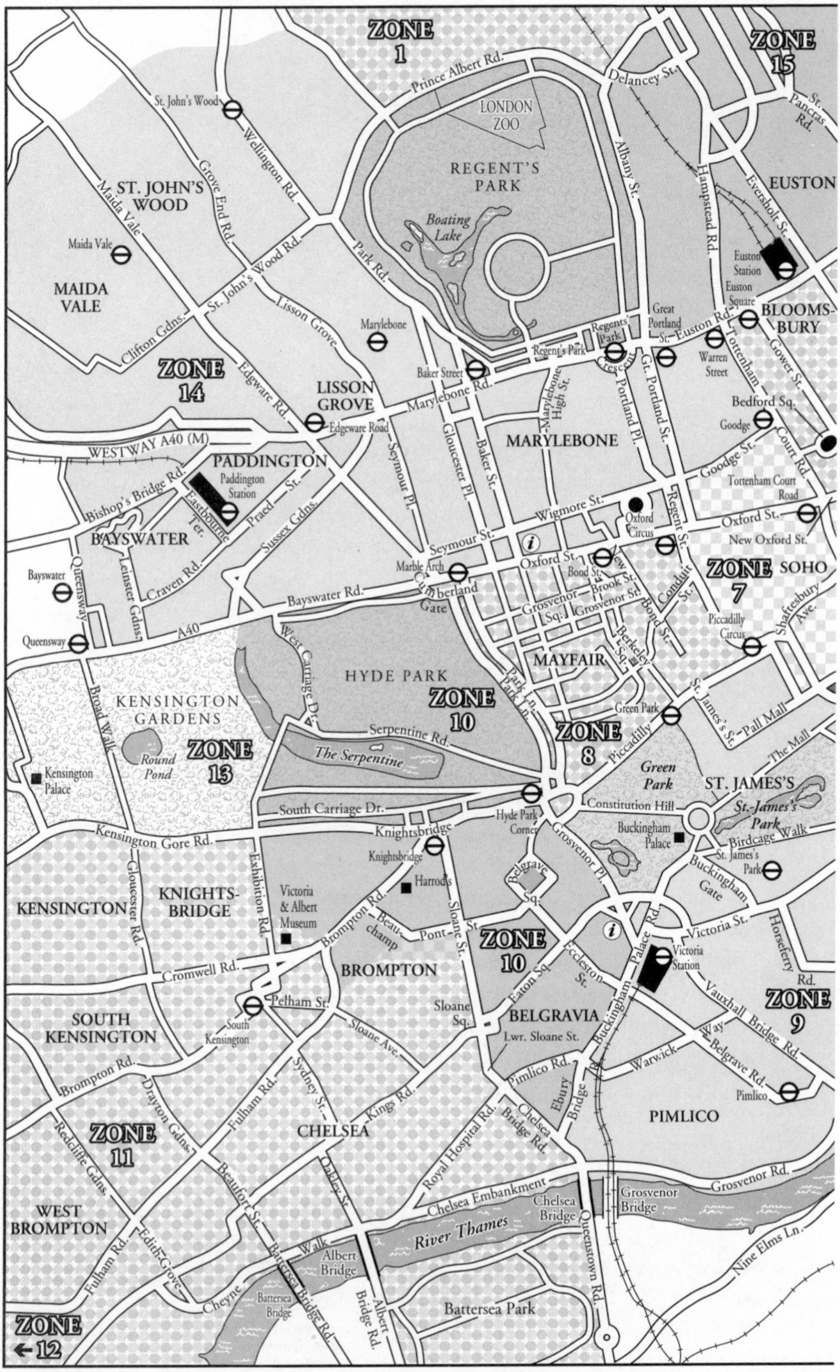

ZONE 1
ZONE 15
Prince Albert Rd.
Delancey St.
St. Pancras Rd.
LONDON ZOO
REGENT'S PARK
Boating Lake
EUSTON
Albany St.
Hampstead Rd.
Eversholt St.
Euston Station
Euston Square
BLOOMSBURY
St. John's Wood
Wellington Rd.
Grove End Rd.
ST. JOHN'S WOOD
Maida Vale
MAIDA VALE
St. John's Wood Rd.
Park Rd.
Lisson Grove
Clifton Gdns.
Marylebone
ZONE 14
Edgware Rd.
LISSON GROVE
Baker Street
Regent's Park
Great Portland St.
Euston Rd.
Warren Street
Tottenham
Gower St.
Marylebone Rd.
Crescent
Gt. Portland St.
Portland Pl.
Marylebone High St.
Bedford Sq.
Goodge
Edgeware Road
WESTWAY A40 (M)
PADDINGTON
Paddington Station
Seymour Pl.
Gloucester Pl.
Baker St.
MARYLEBONE
Goodge St.
Court Rd.
Tottenham Court Road
Bishop's Bridge Rd.
Eastbourne Ter.
Praed St.
Sussex Gdns.
Wigmore St.
Oxford Circus
Regent St.
Oxford St.
New Oxford St.
BAYSWATER
Seymour St.
Marble Arch
Oxford St.
New Bond St.
Brook St.
Conduit St.
ZONE 7
SOHO
Bayswater
Queensway
Leinster Gdns.
Craven Rd.
Bayswater Rd.
Cumberland Gate
Grosvenor Sq.
Grosvenor St.
Bond St.
Shaftesbury Ave.
Piccadilly Circus
Queensway
A40
West Carriage Dr.
Berkeley Sq.
MAYFAIR
HYDE PARK
KENSINGTON GARDENS
Broad Walk
ZONE 10
Park Ln.
Green Park
St. James's St.
Pall Mall
Serpentine Rd.
ZONE 8
Piccadilly
The Mall
ZONE 13
Round Pond
The Serpentine
Green Park
ST. JAMES'S
Kensington Palace
Constitution Hill
St. James's Park
South Carriage Dr.
Hyde Park Corner
Buckingham Palace
Birdcage Walk
Kensington Gore Rd.
Knightsbridge
Knightsbridge
St. James's Park
Grosvenor Pl.
Belgrave Sq.
Buckingham Gate
Harrods
Gloucester Rd.
Exhibition Rd.
KENSINGTON
KNIGHTSBRIDGE
Victoria & Albert Museum
Brompton Rd.
Beauchamp
Pont St.
Sloane St.
ZONE 10
Palace Rd.
Victoria St.
Horseferry Rd.
Victoria Station
Eccleston St.
Cromwell Rd.
BROMPTON
Eaton Sq.
ZONE 9
Pelham St.
Sloane Sq.
BELGRAVIA
Vauxhall Bridge Rd.
SOUTH KENSINGTON
South Kensington
Sloane Ave.
Lwr. Sloane St.
Buckingham
Way
Belgrave Rd.
Warwick
Brompton Rd.
Pimlico Rd.
Sydney St.
Pimlico
Drayton Gdns.
Fulham Rd.
Kings Rd.
Ebury Bridge
PIMLICO
ZONE 11
CHELSEA
Royal Hospital Rd.
Chelsea Bridge Rd.
Redcliffe Gdns.
Oakley St.
Grosvenor Rd.
Beaufort St.
Chelsea Embankment
Chelsea Bridge
Grosvenor Bridge
WEST BROMPTON
River Thames
Nine Elms Ln.
Walk
Albert Bridge
Edith Grove
Fulham Rd.
Cheyne
Battersea Bridge
Battersea Bridge Rd.
Albert Bridge Rd.
Queenstown Rd.
Battersea Park
ZONE ← 12

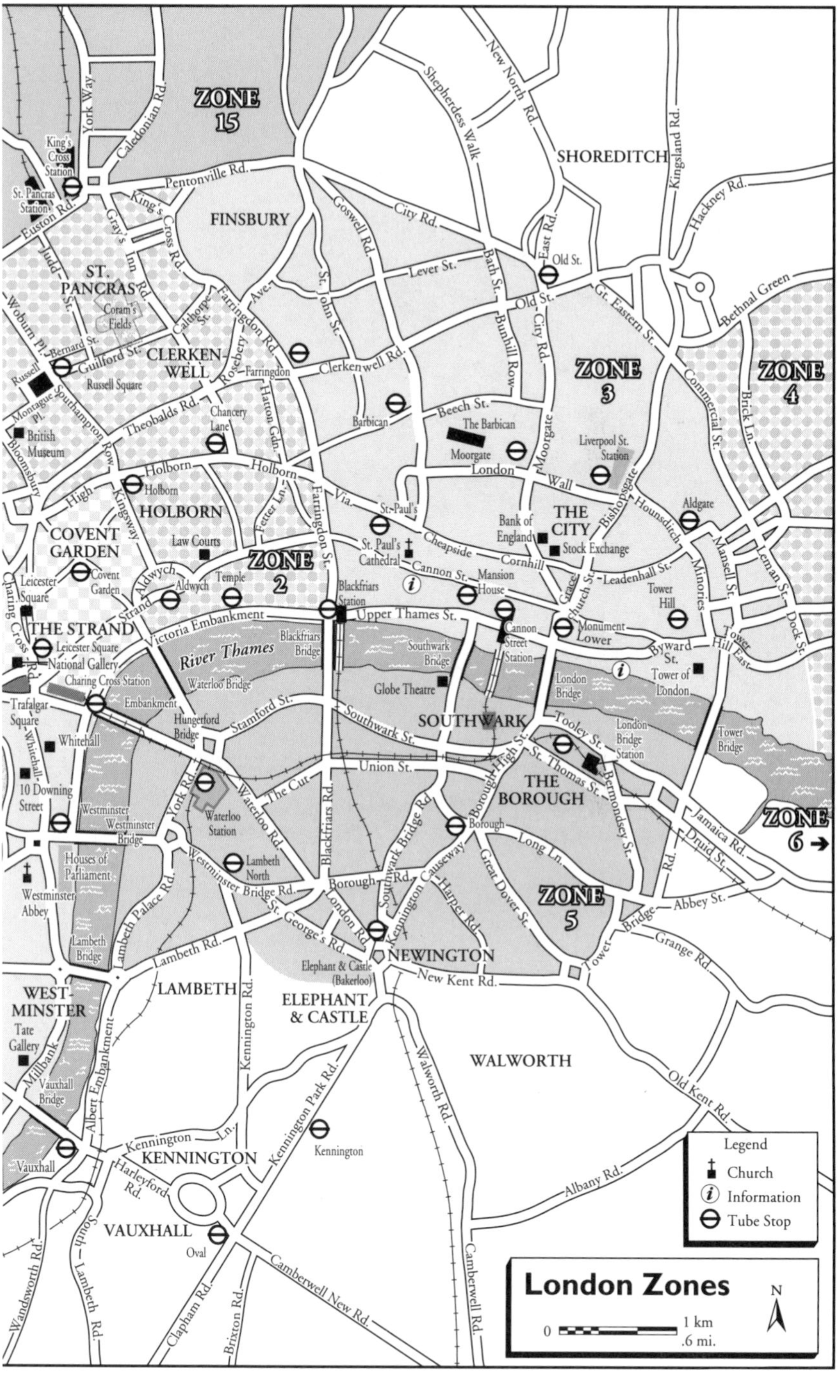
London Zones
ZONE 15
ZONE 2
ZONE 3
ZONE 4
ZONE 5
ZONE 6 →
SHOREDITCH
FINSBURY
ST. PANCRAS
CLERKENWELL
HOLBORN
COVENT GARDEN
THE STRAND
THE CITY
SOUTHWARK
THE BOROUGH
NEWINGTON
ELEPHANT & CASTLE
LAMBETH
WESTMINSTER
WALWORTH
KENNINGTON
VAUXHALL
River Thames
York Way
Caledonian Rd.
King's Cross Station
St. Pancras Station
Euston Rd.
Pentonville Rd.
King's Cross Rd.
Gray's Inn Rd.
Judd St.
Woburn Pl.
Coram's Fields
Calthorpe St.
Farringdon Rd.
Rosebery Ave.
Goswell Rd.
St. John St.
City Rd.
Shepherdess Walk
New North Rd.
Kingsland Rd.
Hackney Rd.
East Rd.
Old St.
Lever St.
Bath St.
Bunhill Row
Gt. Eastern St.
Bethnal Green
Commercial St.
Brick Ln.
Bernard St.
Guilford St.
Russell Square
Russell
Montague Pl.
Southampton Row
British Museum
Bloomsbury
Theobalds Rd.
Farringdon
Clerkenwell Rd.
Hatton Gdn.
Chancery Lane
Barbican
Beech St.
The Barbican
Moorgate
London Wall
Liverpool St. Station
High Holborn
Holborn
Kingsway
Fetter Ln.
Holborn Via.
Farringdon St.
St. Paul's
St. Paul's Cathedral
Cheapside
Bank of England
Stock Exchange
Cornhill
Bishopsgate
Houndsditch
Aldgate
Leadenhall St.
Minories
Mansell St.
Leman St.
Dock St.
Law Courts
Aldwych
Temple
Blackfriars Station
Cannon St.
Mansion House
Gracechurch St.
Tower Hill
Leicester Square
Covent Garden
Charing Cross Rd.
Strand
Victoria Embankment
Upper Thames St.
Cannon Street Station
Monument
Lower Thames St.
Byward St.
Tower Hill East
Tower of London
Leicester Square
National Gallery
Charing Cross Station
Blackfriars Bridge
Southwark Bridge
Waterloo Bridge
Globe Theatre
London Bridge
Trafalgar Square
Embankment
Hungerford Bridge
Stamford St.
Southwark St.
Tooley St.
London Bridge Station
Tower Bridge
Whitehall
10 Downing Street
Union St.
High St.
St. Thomas St.
Bermondsey St.
York Rd.
The Cut
Waterloo Rd.
Waterloo Station
Blackfriars Rd.
Southwark Bridge Rd.
Borough High St.
Borough
Long Ln.
Jamaica Rd.
Druid St.
Westminster
Westminster Bridge
Houses of Parliament
Lambeth North
Westminster Bridge Rd.
Borough Rd.
Southwark Causeway
Harper Rd.
Great Dover St.
Abbey St.
Westminster Abbey
Lambeth Palace Rd.
St. George's Rd.
London Rd.
Kennington Rd.
Tower Bridge Rd.
Grange Rd.
Lambeth Bridge
Lambeth Rd.
Elephant & Castle (Bakerloo)
New Kent Rd.
Tate Gallery
Millbank
Vauxhall Bridge
Albert Embankment
Kennington Rd.
Kennington Park Rd.
Walworth Rd.
Old Kent Rd.
Vauxhall
Kennington Ln.
Kennington
Harleyford Rd.
Oval
Albany Rd.
Wandsworth Rd.
South Lambeth Rd.
Clapham Rd.
Brixton Rd.
Camberwell New Rd.
Camberwell Rd.
Legend
Church
Information
Tube Stop
0
1 km
.6 mi.
N

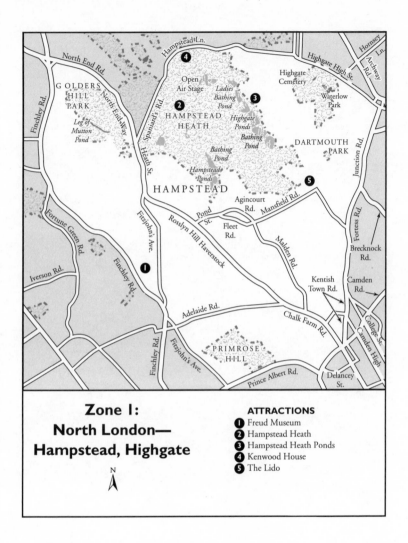

Zone 1: North London—Hampstead, Highgate

ATTRACTIONS

1 Freud Museum
2 Hampstead Heath
3 Hampstead Heath Ponds
4 Kenwood House
5 The Lido

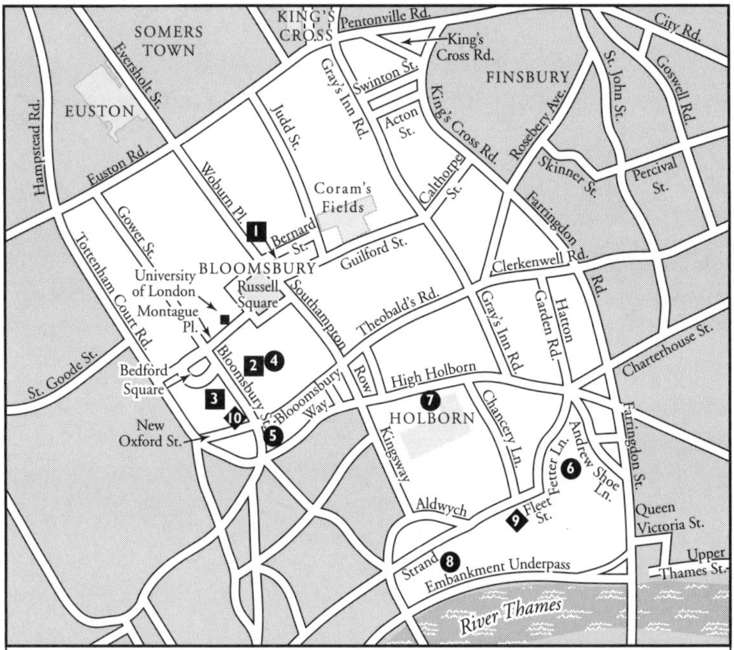

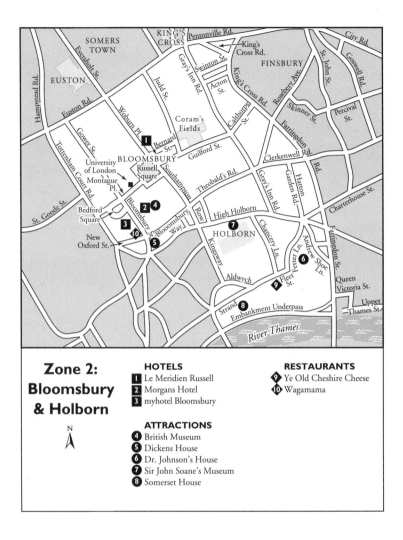

Zone 2: Bloomsbury & Holborn

N

HOTELS

1 Le Meridien Russell
2 Morgans Hotel
3 myhotel Bloomsbury

ATTRACTIONS

4 British Museum
5 Dickens House
6 Dr. Johnson's House
7 Sir John Soane's Museum
8 Somerset House

RESTAURANTS

9 Ye Old Cheshire Cheese
10 Wagamama

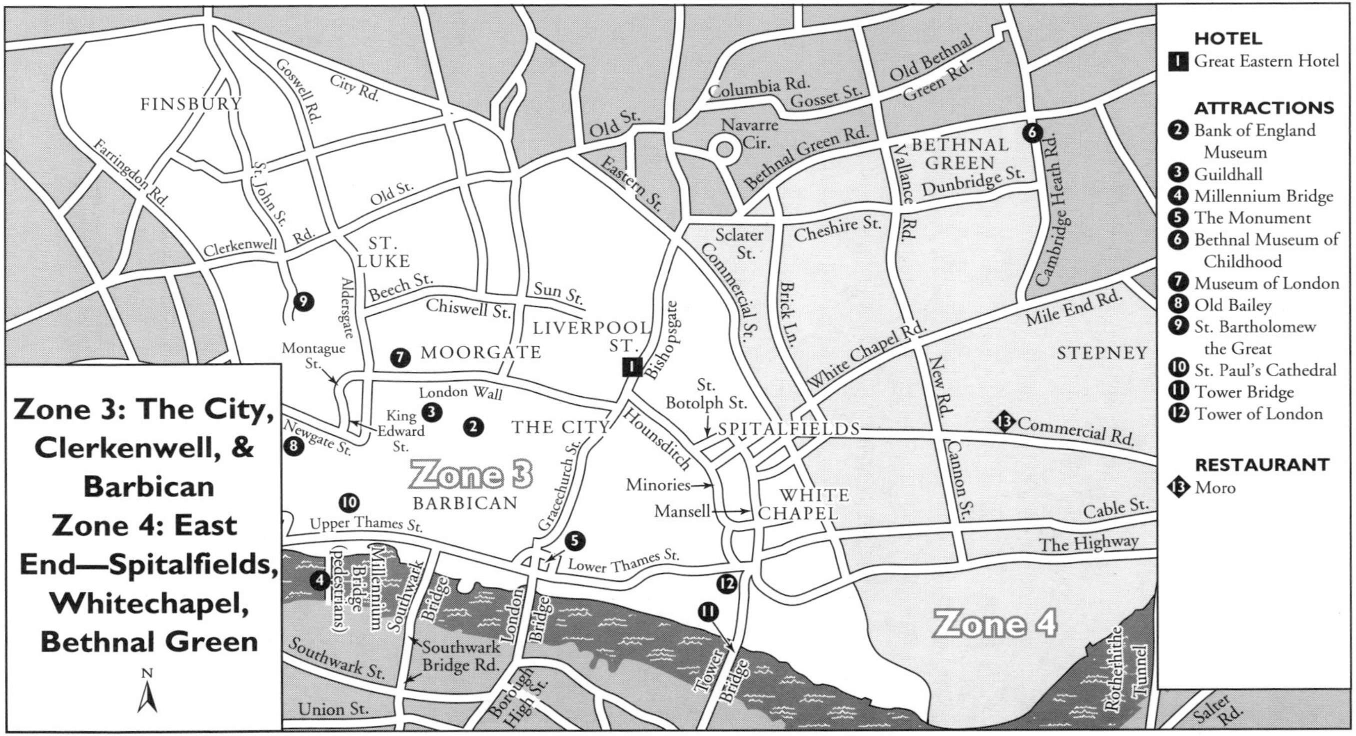
Zone 3: The City, Clerkenwell, & Barbican
Zone 4: East End—Spitalfields, Whitechapel, Bethnal Green
N
HOTEL
1 Great Eastern Hotel
ATTRACTIONS
2 Bank of England Museum
3 Guildhall
4 Millennium Bridge
5 The Monument
6 Bethnal Museum of Childhood
7 Museum of London
8 Old Bailey
9 St. Bartholomew the Great
10 St. Paul's Cathedral
11 Tower Bridge
12 Tower of London
RESTAURANT
13 Moro
Zone 3
Zone 4
FINSBURY
ST. LUKE
MOORGATE
LIVERPOOL ST.
THE CITY
BARBICAN
SPITALFIELDS
WHITE CHAPEL
BETHNAL GREEN
STEPNEY
Goswell Rd.
City Rd.
Farringdon Rd.
St. John St.
Old St.
Clerkenwell Rd.
Beech St.
Sun St.
Chiswell St.
Aldersgate
Montague St.
London Wall
King Edward St.
Newgate St.
Upper Thames St.
Millennium Bridge (pedestrians)
Southwark Bridge
Southwark Bridge Rd.
Southwark St.
Union St.
London Bridge
Borough High St.
Gracechurch St.
Lower Thames St.
Tower Bridge
Minories
Mansell
Houndsditch
St. Botolph St.
Bishopsgate
Eastern St.
Old St.
Columbia Rd.
Gosset St.
Navarre Cir.
Bethnal Green Rd.
Old Bethnal Green Rd.
Vallance Rd.
Dunbridge St.
Cambridge Heath Rd.
Sclater St.
Commercial St.
Cheshire St.
Brick Ln.
White Chapel Rd.
Mile End Rd.
New Rd.
Commercial Rd.
Cannon St.
Cable St.
The Highway
Rotherhithe Tunnel
Salter Rd.

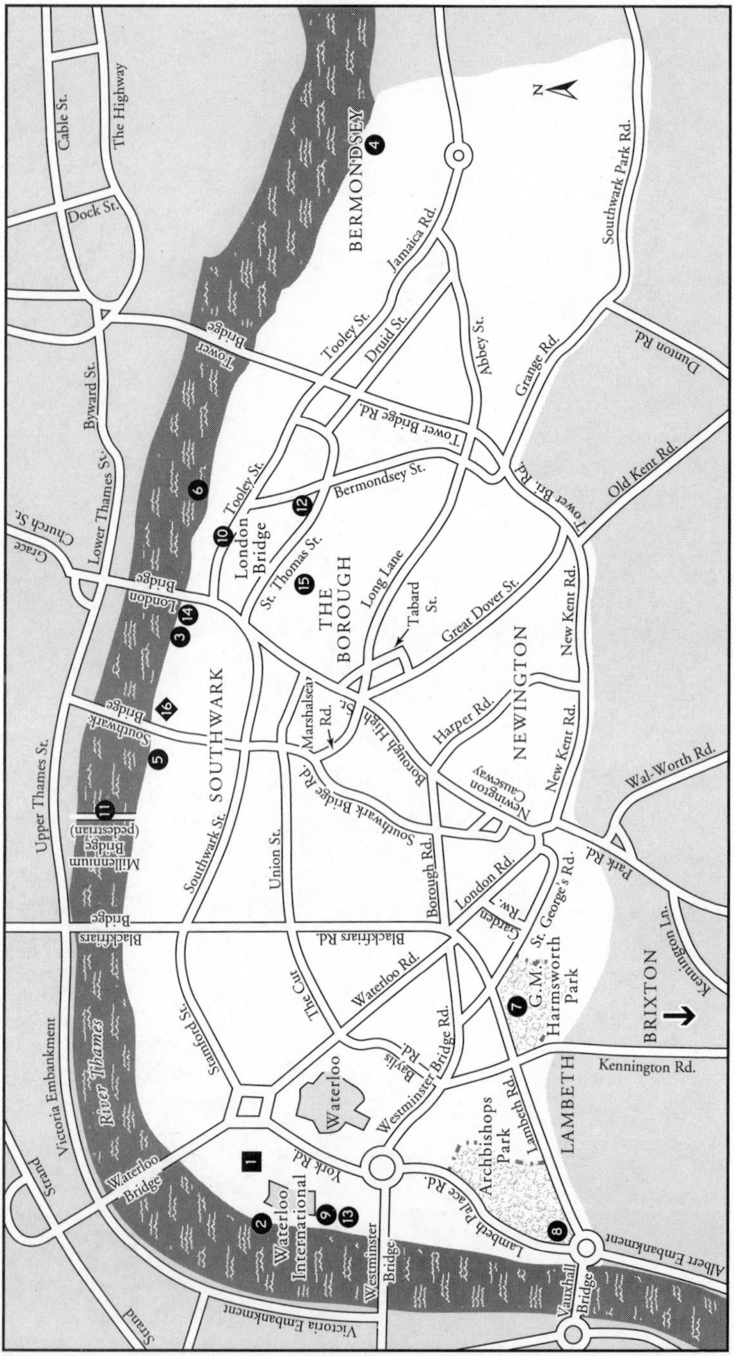
Cable St.
The Highway
Dock St.
BERMONDSEY
Jamaica Rd.
Southwark Park Rd.
Tooley St.
Druid St.
Tower Bridge
Abbey St.
Grange Rd.
Dunton Rd.
Byward St.
Tower Bridge Rd.
Tower Bri. Rd.
Old Kent Rd.
Lower Thames St.
Bermondsey St.
Grace Church St.
London Bridge
St. Thomas St.
THE BOROUGH
Long Lane
Tabard St.
Great Dover St.
New Kent Rd.
SOUTHWARK
Marshalsea Rd.
Borough High St.
Harper Rd.
NEWINGTON
Upper Thames St.
Southwark Bridge
Millennium Bridge (pedestrian)
Southwark Bridge Rd.
Newington Causeway
Wal-Worth Rd.
Park Rd.
Southwark St.
Union St.
Borough Rd.
London Rd.
Garden Rw.
St. George's Rd.
Kennington Ln.
Blackfriars Bridge
Blackfriars Rd.
The Cut
Waterloo Rd.
G.M. Harmsworth Park
BRIXTON
Stamford St.
River Thames
Victoria Embankment
Baylis Rd.
Westminster Bridge Rd.
Kennington Rd.
LAMBETH
Waterloo
Archbishops Park
Lambeth Rd.
Strand
Waterloo Bridge
York Rd.
Waterloo International
Lambeth Palace Rd.
Westminster Bridge
Vauxhall Bridge
Albert Embankment
N
1
2
3
4
5
6
7
8
9
10
11
12
13
14
15
16

Zone 5:
South London—South Bank, Lambeth, Brixton

HOTEL

1 Travel Inn

ATTRACTIONS

2 The British Airways London Eye
3 Clink Exhibition
4 Design Museum
5 The Globe Theatre
6 *HMS Belfast*
7 Imperial War Museum
8 Lambeth Palace
9 London Aquarium
10 London Dungeon
11 Millennium Bridge
12 Old Operating Theatre, Museum, and Herb Garrett
13 Saatchi Gallery
14 Southwark Cathedral
15 Tate Gallery of Modern Art

RESTAURANT

16 Cantina Vinopolis

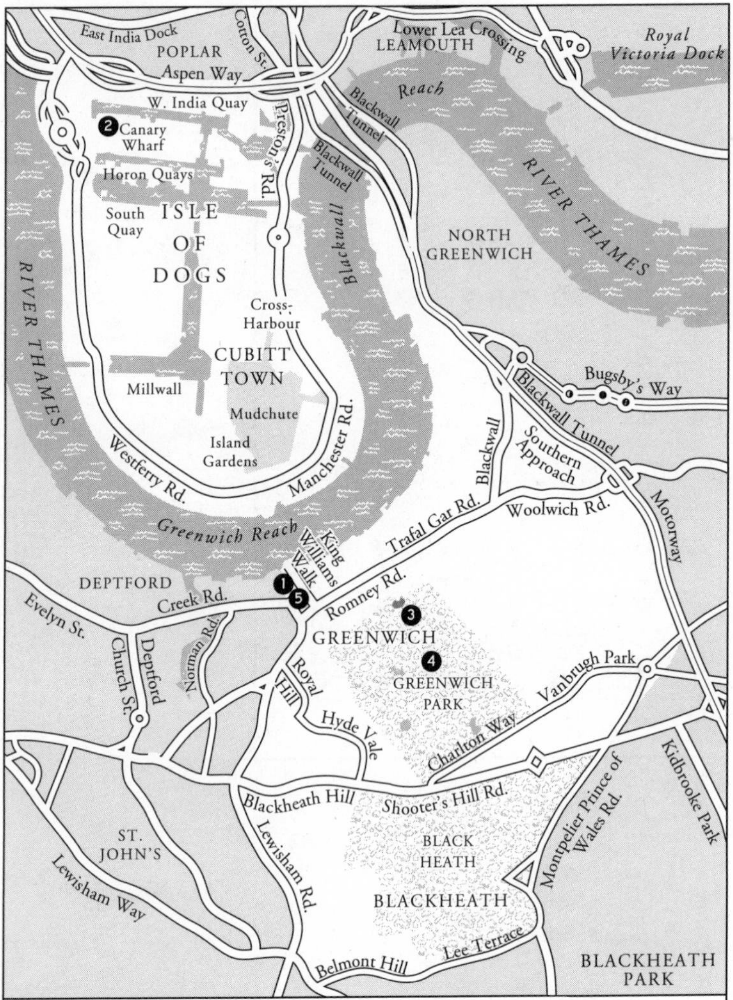

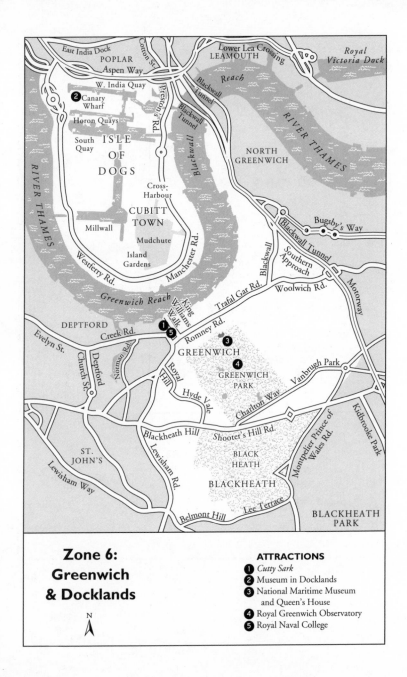

Zone 6: Greenwich & Docklands

N

ATTRACTIONS

1. *Cutty Sark*
2. Museum in Docklands
3. National Maritime Museum and Queen's House
4. Royal Greenwich Observatory
5. Royal Naval College

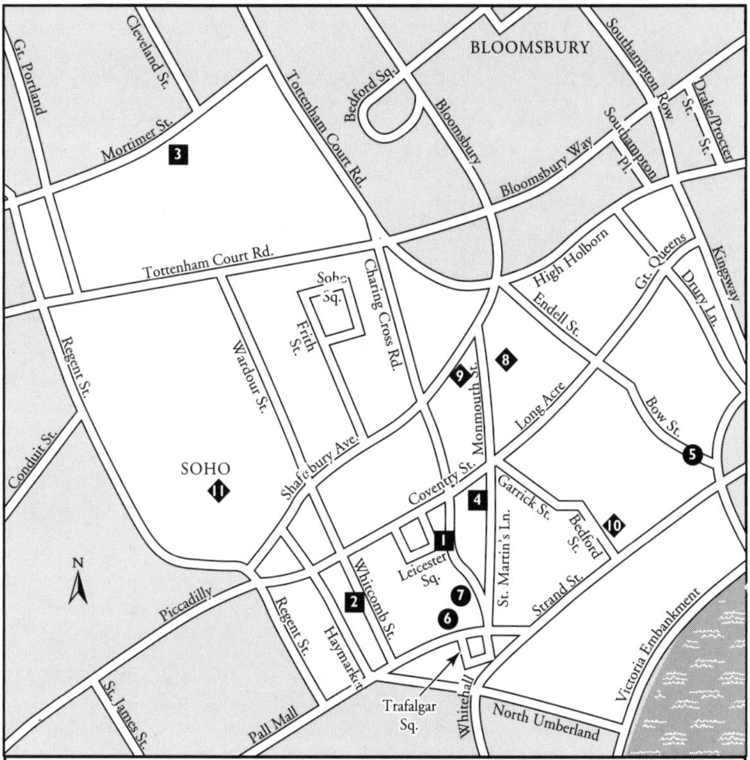

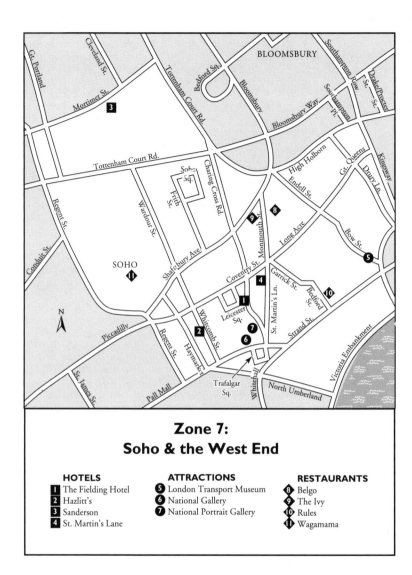

Zone 7:
Soho & the West End

HOTELS
- 1 The Fielding Hotel
- 2 Hazlitt's
- 3 Sanderson
- 4 St. Martin's Lane

ATTRACTIONS
- 5 London Transport Museum
- 6 National Gallery
- 7 National Portrait Gallery

RESTAURANTS
- 8 Belgo
- 9 The Ivy
- 10 Rules
- 11 Wagamama

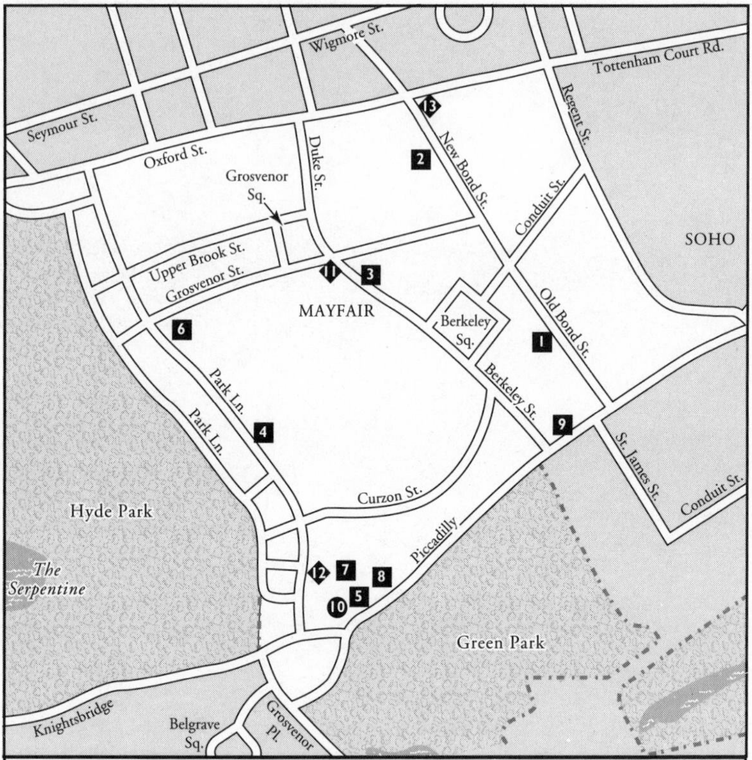

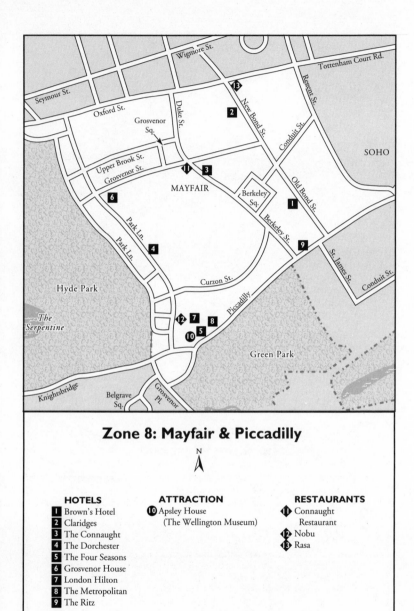

Zone 8: Mayfair & Piccadilly

N

HOTELS
1 Brown's Hotel
2 Claridges
3 The Connaught
4 The Dorchester
5 The Four Seasons
6 Grosvenor House
7 London Hilton
8 The Metropolitan
9 The Ritz

ATTRACTION
10 Apsley House (The Wellington Museum)

RESTAURANTS
11 Connaught Restaurant
12 Nobu
13 Rasa

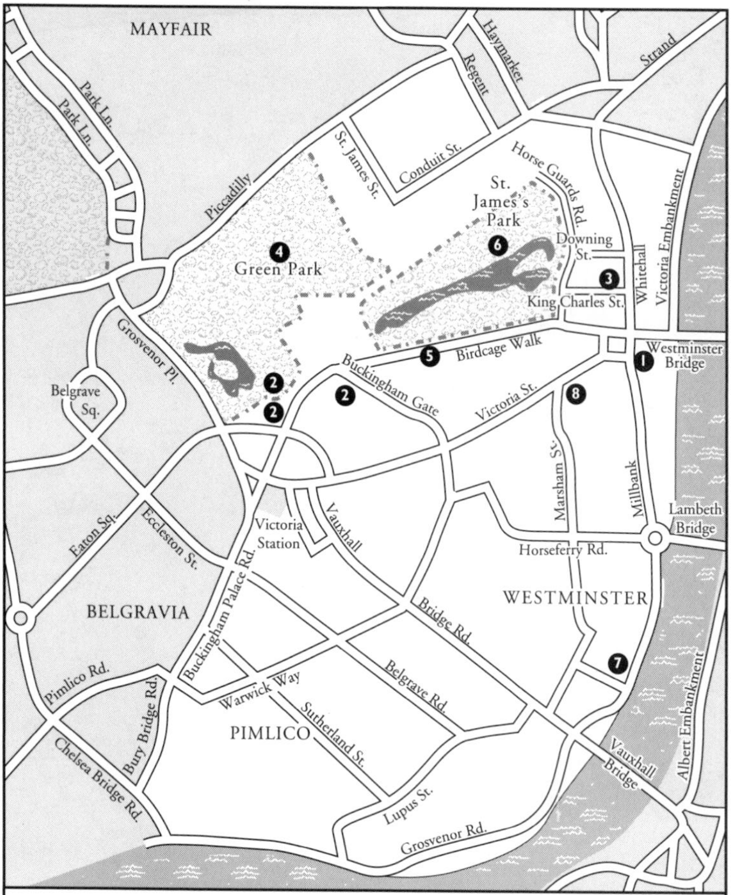

Zone 9: Victoria & Westminster

N

ATTRACTIONS

1. Houses of Parliament and Big Ben Clock Tower
2. Buckingham Palace, the Queen's Gallery, and Royal Mews
3. The Cabinet War Rooms
4. Green Park
5. Guards Museum
6. St. James's Park
7. Tate Britain
8. Westminster Abbey

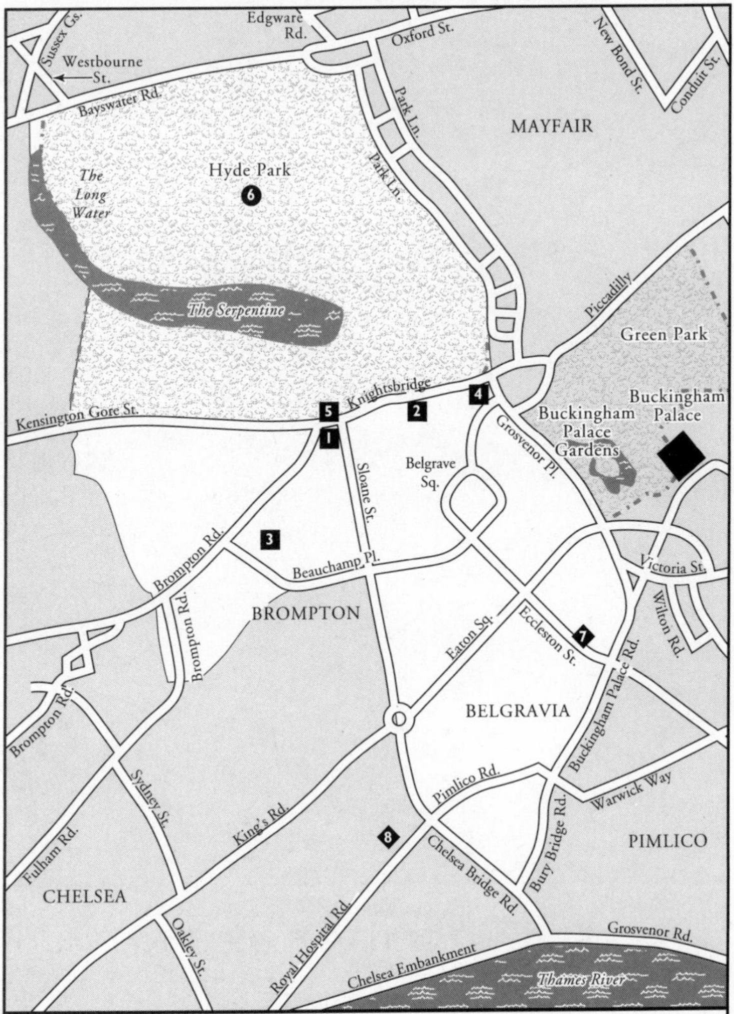

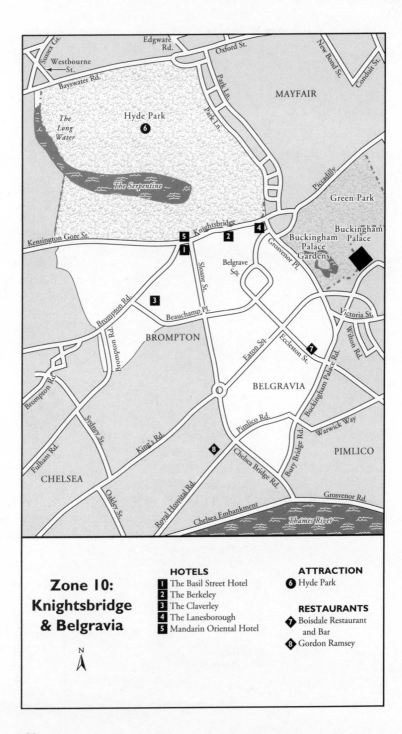

Zone 10: Knightsbridge & Belgravia

N

HOTELS

1 The Basil Street Hotel
2 The Berkeley
3 The Claverley
4 The Lanesborough
5 Mandarin Oriental Hotel

ATTRACTION

6 Hyde Park

RESTAURANTS

7 Boisdale Restaurant and Bar
8 Gordon Ramsey

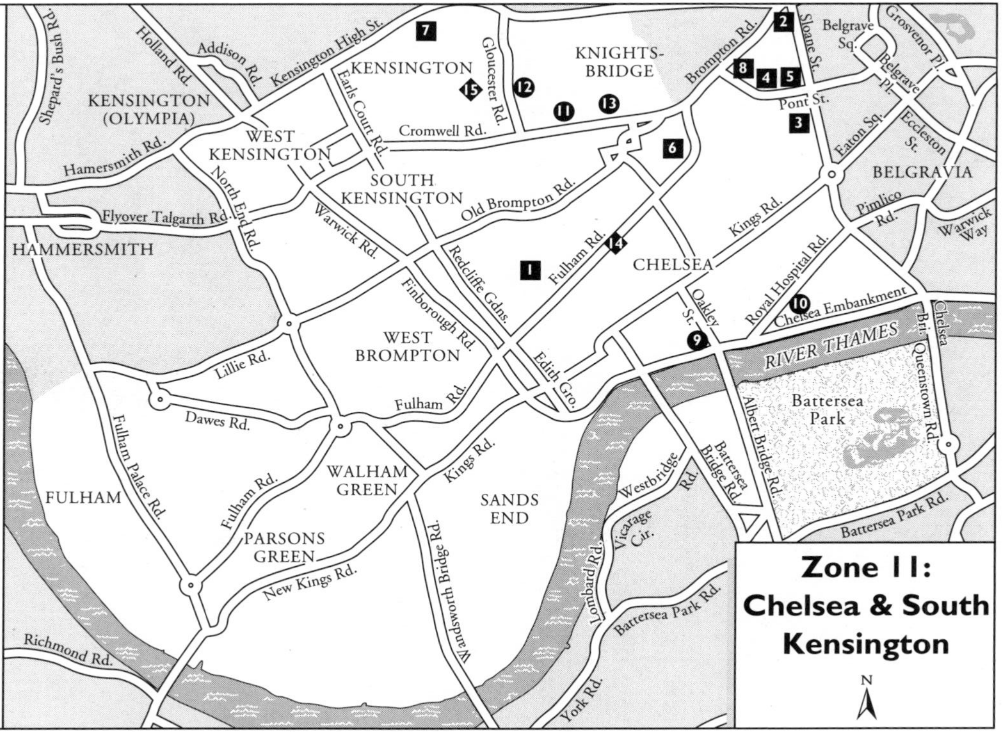

HOTELS

1 Blakes
2 Draycott Hotel
3 Five Sumner Place Hotel
4 The Gainsborough
5 The Gallery
6 The Gore
7 The Milestone Hotel
8 Number Sixteen

ATTRACTIONS

9 Carlyle's Museum
10 Chelsea Physic Garden
11 Natural History Museum
12 Science Museum
13 Victoria and Albert Museum

RESTAURANTS

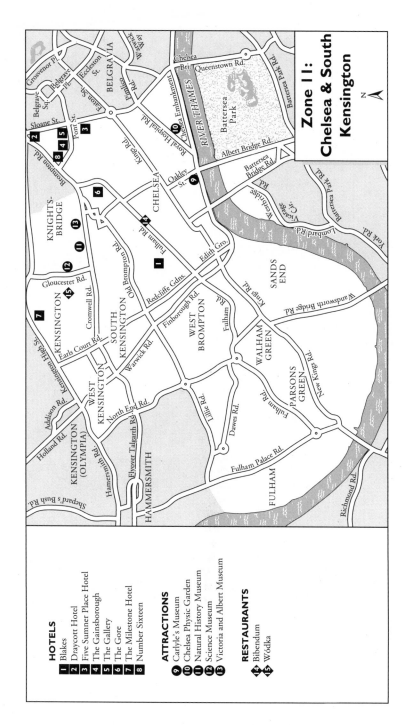

14 Bibendum
15 Wódka

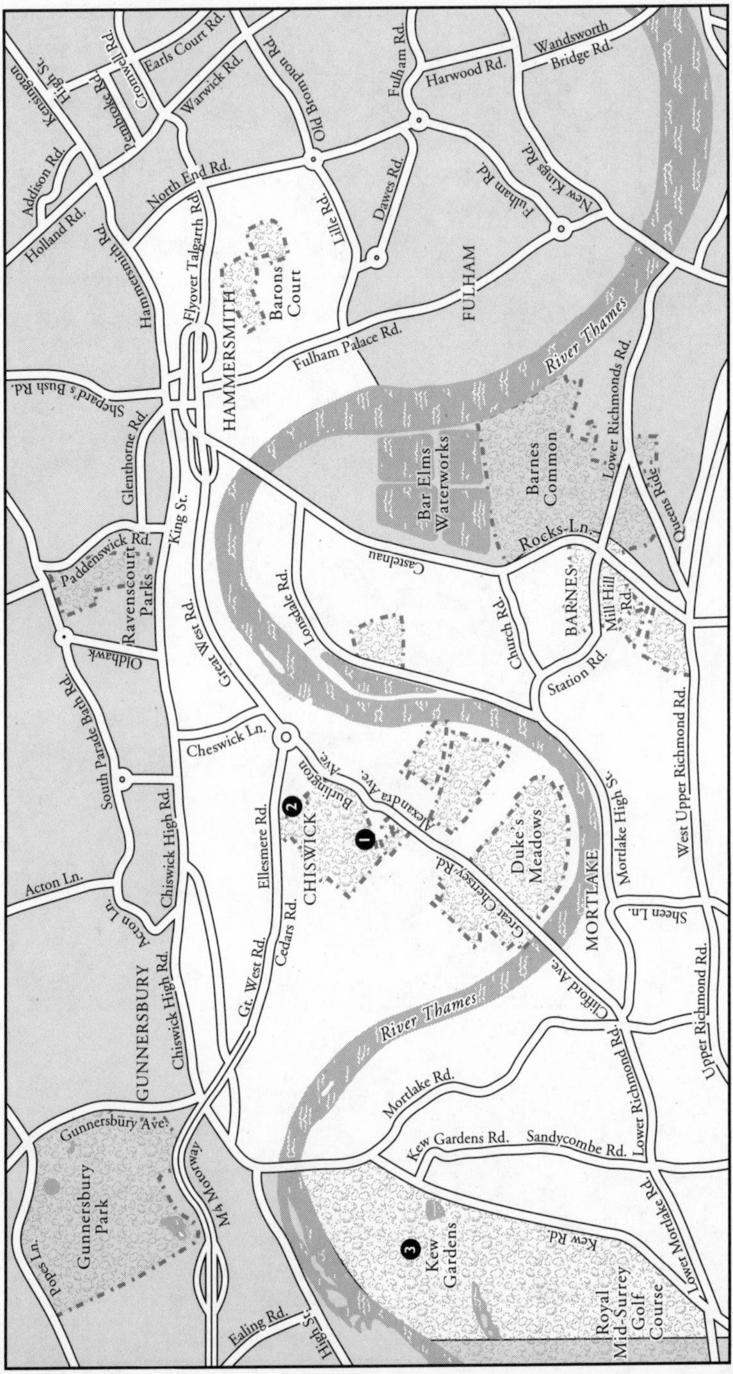
Kensington High St.
Pembroke Rd.
Cromwell Rd.
Earls Court Rd.
Warwick Rd.
Old Brompton Rd.
Fulham Rd.
Harwood Rd.
Wandsworth Bridge Rd.
Addison Rd.
Holland Rd.
North End Rd.
Hammersmith Rd.
Flyover Talgarth Rd.
Lille Rd.
Dawes Rd.
Fulham Rd.
New Kings Rd.
Barons Court
HAMMERSMITH
FULHAM
Fulham Palace Rd.
River Thames
Shepard's Bush Rd.
Glenthorne Rd.
King St.
Bar Elms Waterworks
Barnes Common
Lower Richmonds Rd.
Paddenswick Rd.
Ravenscourt Parks
Great West Rd.
Lonsdale Rd.
Castelnau
Rocks Ln.
Queens Ride
Church Rd.
BARNES
Mill Hill Rd.
Oldhawk
Station Rd.
South Parade Bath Rd.
Cheswick Ln.
Burlington Ave.
Alexandra Ave.
West Upper Richmond Rd.
Mortlake High St.
Ellesmere Rd.
CHISWICK
1
2
Chiswick High Rd.
Acton Ln.
Duke's Meadows
Great Chertsey Rd.
Sheen Ln.
MORTLAKE
Cedars Rd.
Gt. West Rd.
Clifford Ave.
Upper Richmond Rd.
GUNNERSBURY
Chiswick High Rd.
River Thames
Mortlake Rd.
Lower Richmond Rd.
Gunnersbury Ave.
Kew Gardens Rd.
Sandycombe Rd.
M4 Motorway
Gunnersbury Park
Popes Ln.
Kew Rd.
3
Kew Gardens
Lower Mortlake Rd.
Royal Mid-Surrey Golf Course
Ealing Rd.
High St.

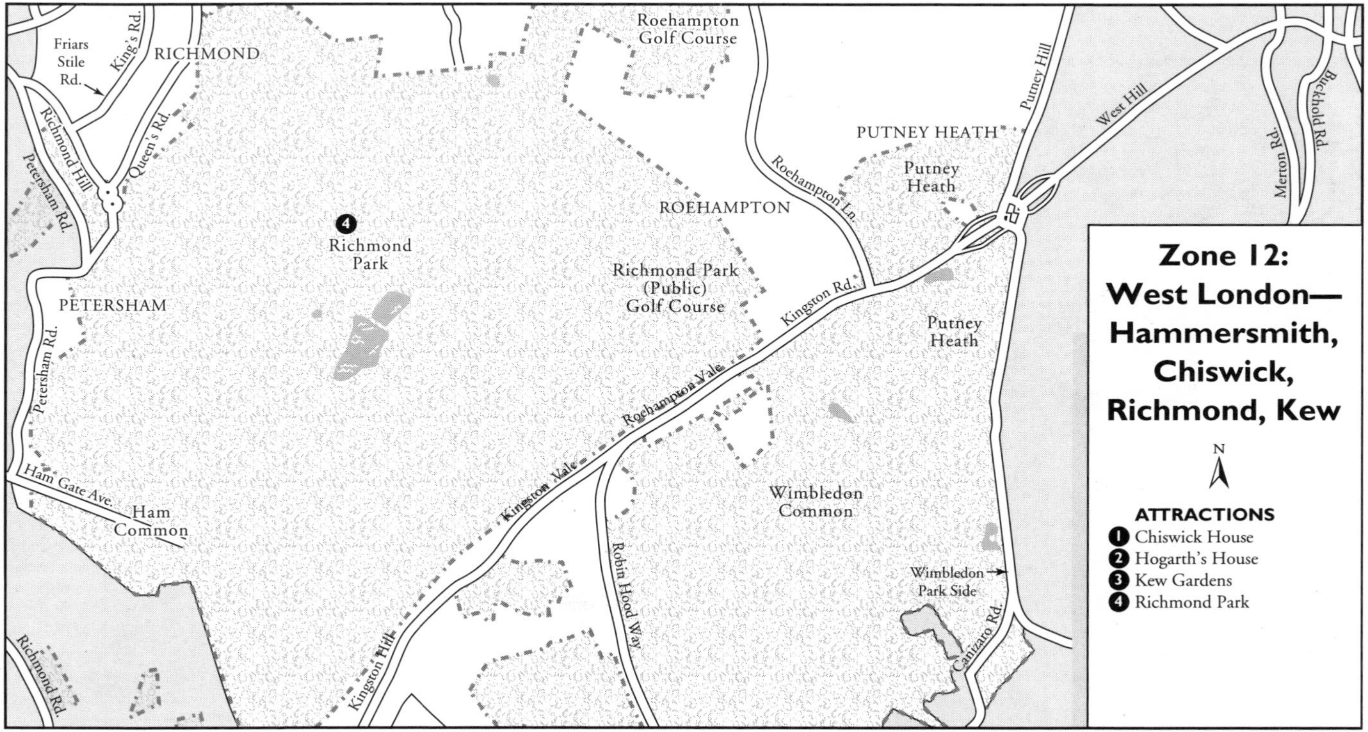

Zone 12:
West London—
Hammersmith,
Chiswick,
Richmond, Kew
N
ATTRACTIONS
1 Chiswick House
2 Hogarth's House
3 Kew Gardens
4 Richmond Park
Friars Stile Rd.
King's Rd.
RICHMOND
Richmond Hill
Queen's Rd.
Petersham Rd.
PETERSHAM
Ham Gate Ave.
Ham Common
Richmond Rd.
4 Richmond Park
Roehampton Golf Course
ROEHAMPTON
Richmond Park (Public) Golf Course
Roehampton Ln.
PUTNEY HEATH
Putney Heath
Putney Hill
West Hill
Merton Rd.
Buckhold Rd.
Kingston Rd.
Roehampton Vale
Kingston Vale
Kingston Hill
Robin Hood Way
Wimbledon Common
Wimbledon Park Side
Canizaro Rd.

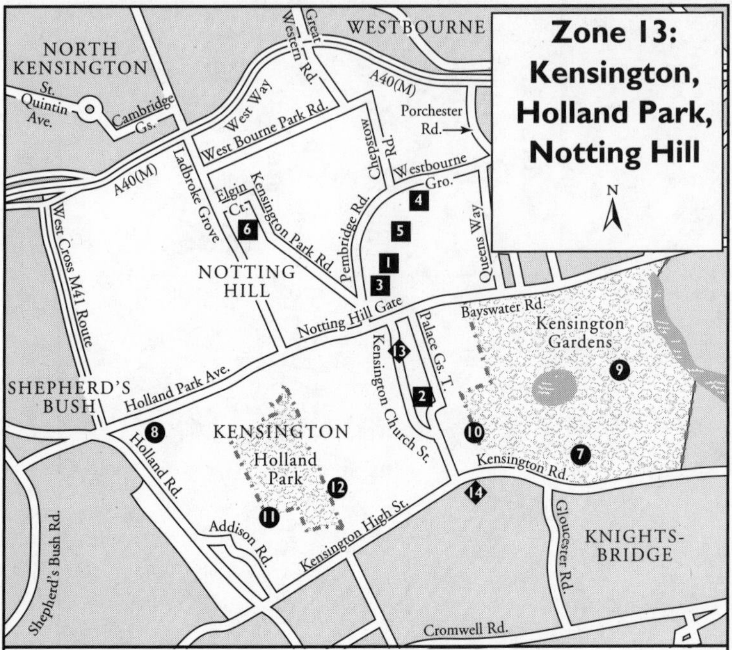

HOTELS

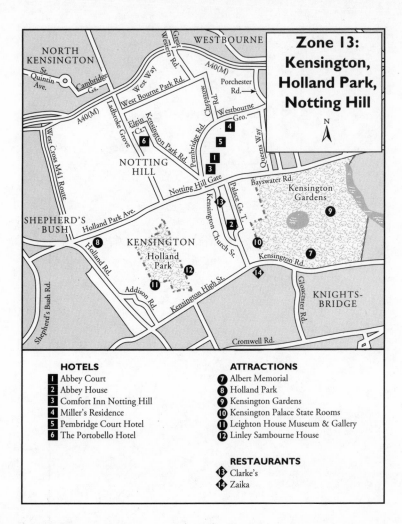

1 Abbey Court
2 Abbey House
3 Comfort Inn Notting Hill
4 Miller's Residence
5 Pembridge Court Hotel
6 The Portobello Hotel

ATTRACTIONS

7 Albert Memorial
8 Holland Park
9 Kensington Gardens
10 Kensington Palace State Rooms
11 Leighton House Museum & Gallery
12 Linley Sambourne House

RESTAURANTS

13 Clarke's
14 Zaika

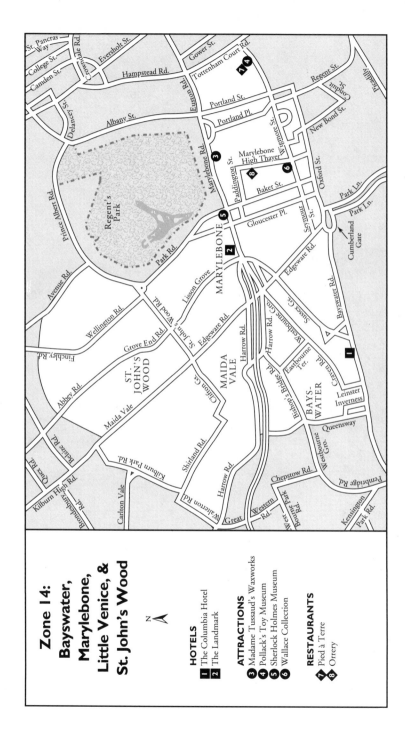

Zone 14: Bayswater, Marylebone, Little Venice, & St. John's Wood

N

HOTELS

1. The Columbia Hotel
2. The Landmark

ATTRACTIONS

3. Madame Tussaud's Waxworks
4. Pollack's Toy Museum
5. Sherlock Holmes Museum
6. Wallace Collection

RESTAURANTS

7. Pied à Terre
8. Orrery

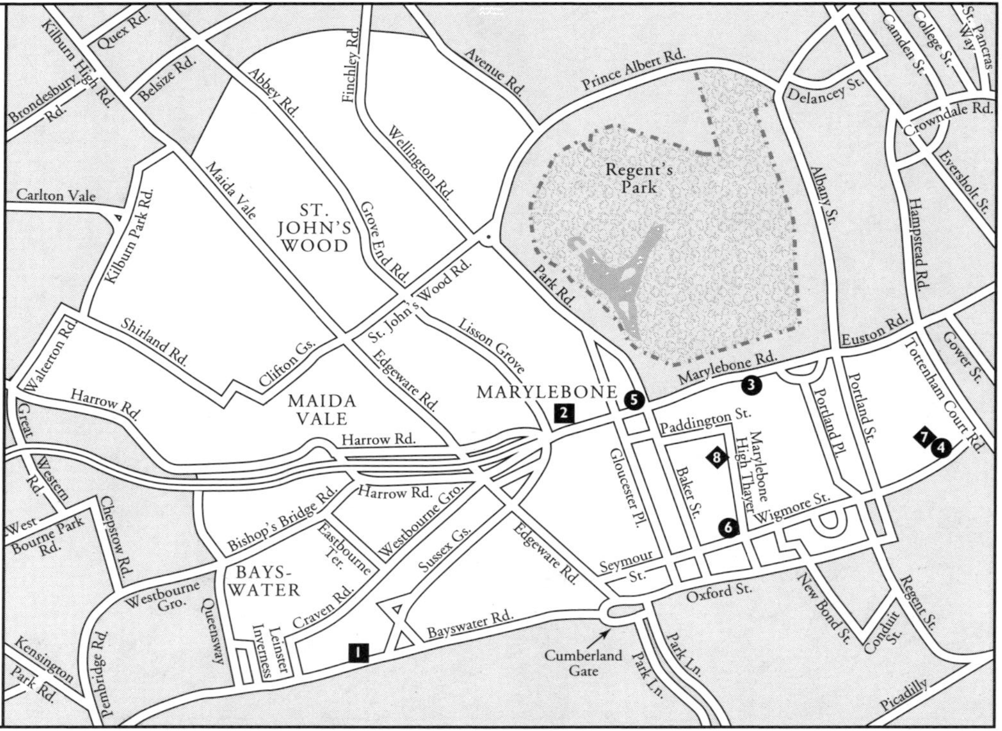

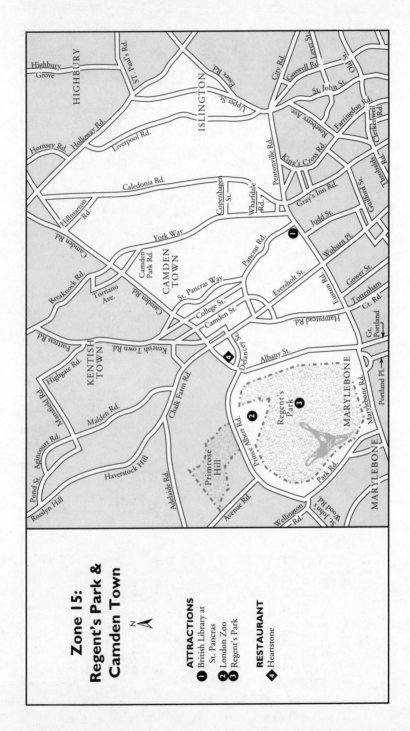

Zone 15: Regent's Park & Camden Town

N

ATTRACTIONS

1 British Library at St. Pancras
2 London Zoo
3 Regent's Park

RESTAURANT

4 Heartstone

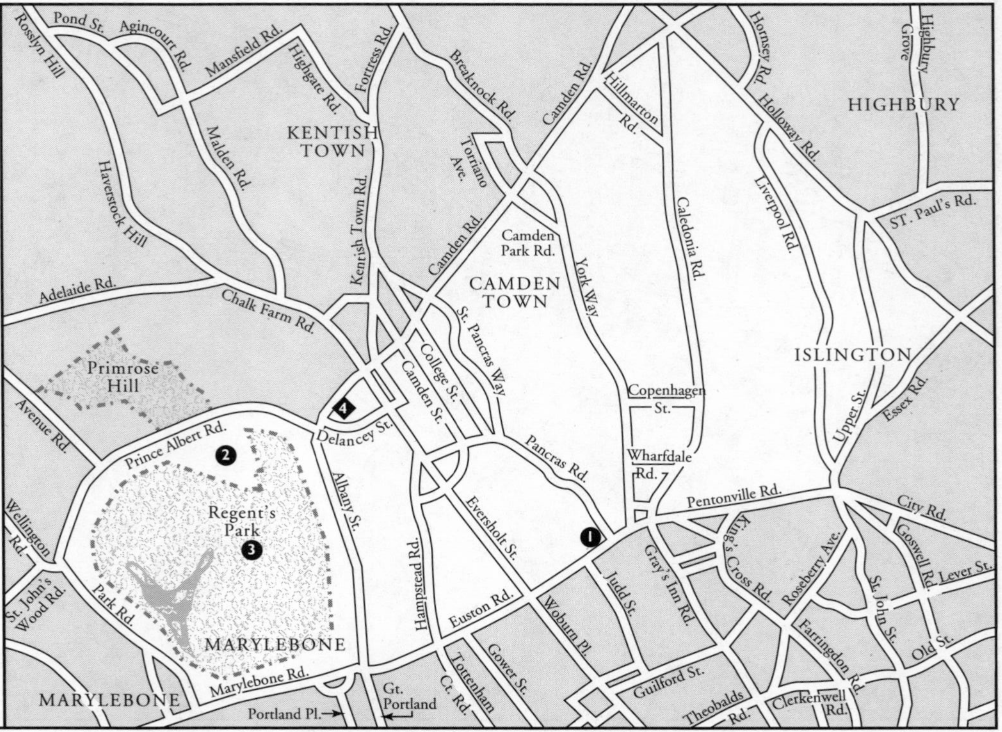

In this book, we have divided London into geographic zones (independent of the postal codes) that provide a handy way to identify neighborhoods. If you are staying in Knightsbridge, for example, and are interested in a place to eat within walking distance, look at the profiles for restaurants in Zone 10.

Zone 1: North London—Hampstead, Highgate

If you make the trip out to North London to escape the city crush amid the bucolic beauty of Hampstead Heath, you'll be following a long-standing tradition. Londoners once fled to Hampstead to escape the Black Death and, later, to soak up the fresh air and healthy springwater. The 19th century saw an influx of artists, writers, and intellectuals, a community still found here. Views from Highgate and Hampstead extend across the whole of London.

Zone 2: Bloomsbury and Holborn

Bloomsbury is dominated by the **British Museum** and the **University of London;** the area has a number of reasonably priced lodgings, and it will forever be associated with the Bloomsbury Group. This early-20th-century group of writers and artists included Virginia Woolf, Lytton Strachey, and Duncan Grant; blue plaques mark the houses where they lived.

Zone 3: The City, Clerkenwell, and Barbican

This is the oldest part of London, where you will find **St. Paul's Cathedral,** the occasional whispers of a medieval past, and some remnants of the town the ancient Romans called Londinium. The City is also where most of the financial business of London is conducted.

Zone 4: East End—Spitalfields, Whitechapel, Bethnal Green

The **Tower** of London is at the edge of the East End, where new luxury apartments, artsy nightspots, galleries, and even the **Prince of Wales's School of Architecture** now share the streets where Jack the Ripper stalked his prey and Sweeney Todd made mincemeat of his customers. Here, too, you can get boats to Greenwich, see some of the old Roman wall around London, and visit **Tower Bridge.**

Zone 5: South London—South Bank, Lambeth, Brixton

Here you'll experience the South Bank renaissance—the **London Aquarium,** the **National Theatre,** the **Hayward Gallery, British Airways London Eye,** the **Saatchi Gallery,** the **Tate Modern,** and the reconstructed **Globe Theatre** are here, as are the ancient palace of **Lambeth,** where the archbishop of Canterbury lives; **Waterloo Station,** terminus of the Eurostar; and the **Old Vic Theatre.** The South Bank promenade affords the best views of **Westminster** and **Big Ben,** and for a different take on London, step into the reggae clubs in Brixton.

Zone 6: Greenwich and Docklands

The attractions of Greenwich are within walking distance of each other, and there are many of them: the **Old Royal Observatory,** the **National Maritime Museum,** the **Royal Naval College,** Inigo Jones's **Queen's House,** and two old tea clippers. You could easily spend a full day seeing Greenwich, which is why we cover it in "Day Trips from London" on page 158. The drab Docklands are enlivened a bit by the new **Museum in Docklands.**

Zone 7: Soho and the West End

Trafalgar Square, rowdy Leicester Square, Chinatown, the **National Gallery,** and theaters, theaters, theaters and pubs, pubs, pubs—this is London's center for nightlife, and Carnaby Street and Covent Garden keep the area lively by day as well.

Zone 8: Mayfair and Piccadilly

This is the district for expensive shops—from the designers on New and Old Bond streets to the bespoke trade in St. James—and luxury hotels, of the **Atheneum, Park Lane, Ritz, Brown's, Dorchester,** and **Claridges** ilk . . . the list is impressive. **Hatchard's,** the oldest bookstore in London, is on Piccadilly, as are Fortnum and Mason's, the **Burlington Arcade,** and the **Royal Academy.**

Zone 9: Victoria and Westminster

This zone encompasses the halls of government and power in London: **Whitehall, Westminster Abbey, Parliament,** and **Buckingham Palace,** as well as the surrounding greenery of **St. James's Park** and **Green Park** and the bustle of **Victoria Station.** There are plenty of hotels, but beware—much of Westminster closes down at night and on weekends.

Zone 10: Knightsbridge and Belgravia

Welcome to the stronghold of the rich and sometimes even famous—expatriate entrepreneurs, British aristocrats, movie stars, rock-and-roll gods, and sultans, who live in splendid Georgian townhouses and deceptively simple mews houses within walking distance of **Hyde Park, Harrods,** and **Harvey Nichols.** Sloane Street, Walton Street, and Beauchamp Place are the prime Knightsbridge shopping streets; Belgravia is quieter, as enclaves of ambassadors and billionaires tend to be.

Zone 11: Chelsea and South Kensington

South Kensington, a.k.a. "Albertopolis" or "Museumland," is where Prince Albert chose to locate the cultural institutions he founded: the **Victoria & Albert** and the **Natural History Museums, Royal Albert Hall,** the **Royal Art College, Imperial College,** and numerous other learned societies. In Chelsea, to the south, once-swinging King's Road is surrounded by the neighborhoods where many of Britain's most illustrious writers and artists have lived, among them Oscar Wilde, George Eliot, Thomas Carlyle, Dante Gabriel Rossetti, and James Whistler.

Zone 12: West London—Hammersmith, Chiswick, Richmond, Kew

You may find your way to these primarily residential areas outside of central London to visit such places as **Hogarth's House, Chiswick House,** and **Richmond Park.** Two of our favorite places for day trips are in this zone: Kew Gardens and Hampton Court.

Zone 13: Kensington, Holland Park, Notting Hill

Kensington, once a country village, became fashionable when King William and Queen Mary moved their royal residence here in 1689, and along with nearby Holland Park it's still a posh place to live. Kensington High Street is a bustling shopping street, and Kensington Church Street is lined with interesting, although expensive, antiques shops. Notting Hill, once a Jamaican enclave, is a very happening place these days, and its famous **Portobello Market** draws huge Saturday crowds.

Zone 14: Bayswater, Marylebone, Little Venice, St. John's Wood

In Bayswater and Marylebone, at the north border of Hyde Park, is an assortment of attractions that include the **Wallace Collection, Sherlock Holmes Museum,** and **Madame Tussaud's.** Some of London's least expensive hotels (and not all of them are dismal) are near **Paddington Station,** the terminus for the train from Heathrow. Farther north is Little Venice, so called for the canals running through it. The main attraction in St. John's Wood, a tony residential neighborhood, is the Abbey Road crosswalk, where tourists annoy the locals by taking pictures of themselves re-creating the Beatles' famous album cover.

Zone 15: Regent's Park and Camden Town

Regent's Park houses the **London Zoo** and affords some of the most beautiful 18th-century vistas in London. Designed in concert with King George IV, who was regent at the time, this residential district is the crowning achievement of architect John Nash. The market in Camden

Town, to the northwest, rivals Portobello Road for good buys. Primrose Hill is another sylvan glade in this zone.

Not To Be Missed in London

The British Museum (page 126)
The Globe Theatre (page 131)
Hampton Court Palace (page 162)
Hyde Park (page 158)
Knightsbridge shopping (page 189)
Millennium Bridge (page 156)
The National Gallery (page 140)
Play at a West End theater (page 177)
St. James's Park (page 158)
St. Paul's Cathedral (page 145)
Walthamstow market (page 191)
Tate Modern and Tate Britain (page 149)
The Tower of London (page 150)
Victoria & Albert Museum (page 151)
Westminster Abbey (page 152)

Planning Your Visit to London

The **London Tourist Board** operates tourist centers throughout London, where you can pick up maps, pamphlets, listings, and a wealth of other information. The centers also book hotels, sell theater tickets, arrange sight-seeing tours, and offer many other services that will make your stay in London more enjoyable. Before you arrive, visit the organization's extensive website at **www.londontown.com.** Center locations include:

British Visitor Center Zone 8; 1 Regent Street, Piccadilly Circus, W1. Open June–September: Monday, 9:30 a.m.–6:30 p.m.; Tuesday–Friday, 9 a.m.–6:30 p.m.; Saturday, 9 a.m.–5 p.m.; Sunday, 10 a.m.–4 p.m. October–May: Monday, 9:30 a.m.–6:30 p.m.; Tuesday–Friday, 9 a.m.–6:30 p.m.; Saturday–Sunday, 10 a.m.–4 p.m.

Heathrow Airport Terminals Terminals 1, 2, and 3. Open daily, 8:30 a.m.–6 p.m.

Liverpool Street Underground Station Zone 3. Open Monday–Friday, 8 a.m.–6 p.m.; Saturday, 8:30 a.m.–5:30 p.m.; Sunday, 9 a.m.–5:30 p.m.

Victoria Station Zone 9, in forecourt. Open Monday–Saturday, 7:45 a.m.–7 p.m.; Sunday, 8:45 a.m.–7 p.m.

See also the resources we recommend in "Websites for Further Research," pages 32.

Hotels in London

One of the great pleasures of visiting London is staying in one of the city's hotels. Whether you want to surround yourself with country house–style opulence, high-tech minimalism, or perhaps something in between, it's actually quite easy to find grand accommodations and indulgent amenities in London. Of course, you might have to hand over the family fortune to foot the bill. But not necessarily. Following are our selections for what we consider to be the best choices in a wide range of prices.

Remember that, with many, many exceptions, especially in the grander establishments, hotel rooms in London are often rather small, especially when compared to typical American accommodations. Air-conditioning is not to be taken for granted, except at the grand hotels. On the other hand, even the more modest hotels often include such useful amenities as tea and coffeemakers, irons and hair dryers, and TVs. Be forewarned that rates usually do not include VAT (17.5%) and, in some cases, service charges. Finally, do some shopping on the Web before booking (we supply hotel websites): Not only can you view photos of the premises, but you'll be pleasantly surprised to see special promotions, weekend rates, and other offers for discounts that can substantially lower the price of a stay.

Choosing Your Hotel Zone

Where you decide to stay in London will probably depend on what you want to spend your time doing. Our top choices to meet your needs would be: **Zone 2** (Bloomsbury) for its convenience to the British Museum, the West End theaters, and the City and the Tower of London; **Zone 7** (Soho and the West End), which is great for theaters, clubs, Soho restaurants, Charing Cross bookstores, and the National Gallery; **Zone 11** (Chelsea and South Kensington), excellent for all those South Ken Museums, with plenty of shops and restaurants and streets lined with lovely houses; and **Zone 13** (Kensignton and Noting Hill), for antique shopping, the Portobello Road market, access to Kensignton Gardens and Holland Park, and a real "London neighborhood" feel.

Of course, there are down sides to some of these neighborhoods, too. Parts of Zone 2 can be desolate at night, while many streets in Zone 7 are fiendishly busy and noisy day and night both. Remember, too, that London is a large and diverse city, and you may well find the corner of the city that suits you best, even if it's not our cup of tea. Many visitors prefer **Zone 8** (Mayfair and Picadilly) for upscale shopping and convenience to the West End, and this is indeed where many of the city's poshest hotels are located (but we find this part of London to be a bit stuffy and dull, not to mention expensive). **Zone 5** (especially trendy South Bank) is becoming a popular place to stay, and the Globe Theatre, the Tate Modern, and the Saatchi Gallery are among the local amusements. (For us, this is a very long way from the places we most enjoy in London.) A good selection of less-expensive hotels in can be found in Victoria, Paddington/Bayswater, and Earl's Court, but *caveat emptor*—these kinds of neighborhoods can be dreary even in the light of a sunny day.

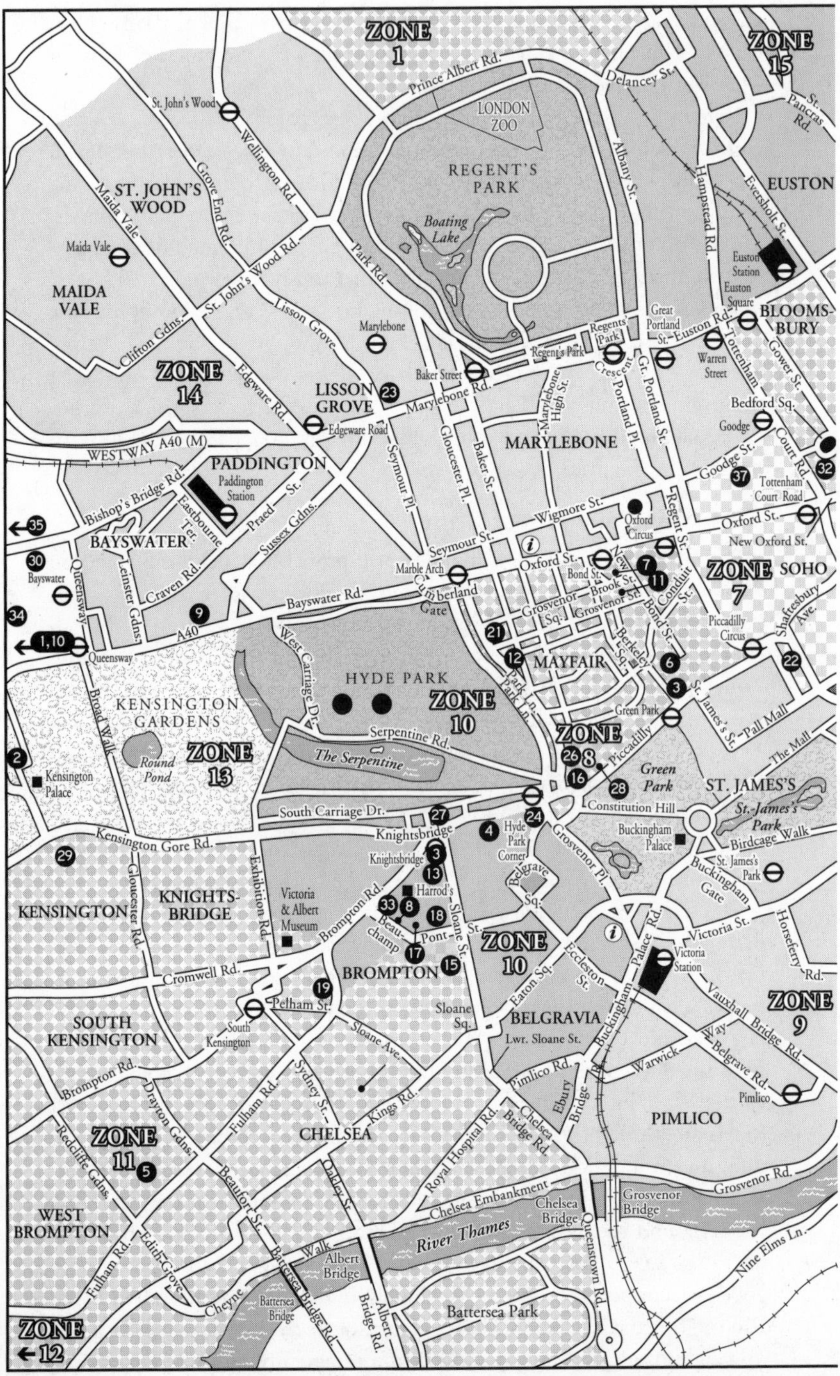
ZONE 1
ZONE 15
Prince Albert Rd.
Delancey St.
St. Pancras Rd.
LONDON ZOO
REGENT'S PARK
Boating Lake
St. John's Wood
Wellington Rd.
Grove End Rd.
ST. JOHN'S WOOD
Maida Vale
Albany St.
Hampstead Rd.
Eversholt St.
EUSTON
Euston Station
Euston Square
BLOOMSBURY
Park Rd.
St. John's Wood Rd.
Lisson Grove
MAIDA VALE
Clifton Gdns.
Marylebone
Great Portland St.
Euston Rd.
Regents' Park
Warren Street
Tottenham
Gower St.
Regent's Park
Crescent
ZONE 14
Edgware Rd.
Baker Street
LISSON GROVE
Marylebone Rd.
Marylebone High St.
Portland Pl.
Gt. Portland St.
Bedford Sq.
Goodge
Court Rd.
Edgeware Road
WESTWAY A40 (M)
Seymour Pl.
Gloucester Pl.
Baker St.
MARYLEBONE
PADDINGTON
Paddington Station
Goodge St.
Tottenham Court Road
Bishop's Bridge Rd.
Eastbourne Ter.
Praed St.
Sussex Gdns.
Wigmore St.
Oxford Circus
Regent St.
Oxford St.
New Oxford St.
BAYSWATER
Seymour St.
Bayswater
Queensway
Leinster Gdns.
Craven Rd.
Marble Arch
Cumberland Gate
Bayswater Rd.
Oxford St.
Bond St.
New Bond St.
Brook St.
Grosvenor Sq.
Grosvenor St.
Conduit St.
ZONE 7
SOHO
Shaftesbury Ave.
Piccadilly Circus
A40
West Carriage Dr.
Berkeley Sq.
MAYFAIR
Park Ln.
HYDE PARK
KENSINGTON GARDENS
Broad Walk
ZONE 10
Green Park
St. James's St.
Pall Mall
Serpentine Rd.
The Serpentine
ZONE 8
Piccadilly
The Mall
Kensington Palace
Round Pond
ZONE 13
Green Park
ST. JAMES'S
St. James's Park
South Carriage Dr.
Constitution Hill
Knightsbridge
Hyde Park Corner
Grosvenor Pl.
Buckingham Palace
Birdcage Walk
Kensington Gore Rd.
Knightsbridge
Belgrave Sq.
St. James's Park
Buckingham Gate
Exhibition Rd.
Harrod's
KENSINGTON
Gloucester Rd.
KNIGHTSBRIDGE
Victoria & Albert Museum
Brompton Rd.
Beauchamp
Pont St.
Sloane St.
ZONE 10
Victoria St.
Horseferry Rd.
Palace Rd.
Victoria Station
Eccleston St.
Cromwell Rd.
BROMPTON
Eaton Sq.
Vauxhall Bridge Rd.
ZONE 9
Pelham St.
South Kensington
Sloane Sq.
BELGRAVIA
Lwr. Sloane St.
Buckingham
Warwick Way
Belgrave Rd.
SOUTH KENSINGTON
Sloane Ave.
Brompton Rd.
Drayton Gdns.
Sydney St.
Pimlico Rd.
Ebury Bridge
Pimlico
Fulham Rd.
Kings Rd.
Royal Hospital Rd.
Chelsea Bridge Rd.
PIMLICO
ZONE 11
CHELSEA
Redcliffe Gdns.
Beaufort St.
Oakley St.
Grosvenor Rd.
Chelsea Embankment
Chelsea Bridge
Grosvenor Bridge
WEST BROMPTON
Queenstown Rd.
River Thames
Nine Elms Ln.
Fulham Rd.
Edith Grove
Cheyne Walk
Albert Bridge
Battersea Bridge
Battersea Bridge Rd.
Albert Bridge Rd.
Battersea Park
ZONE 12

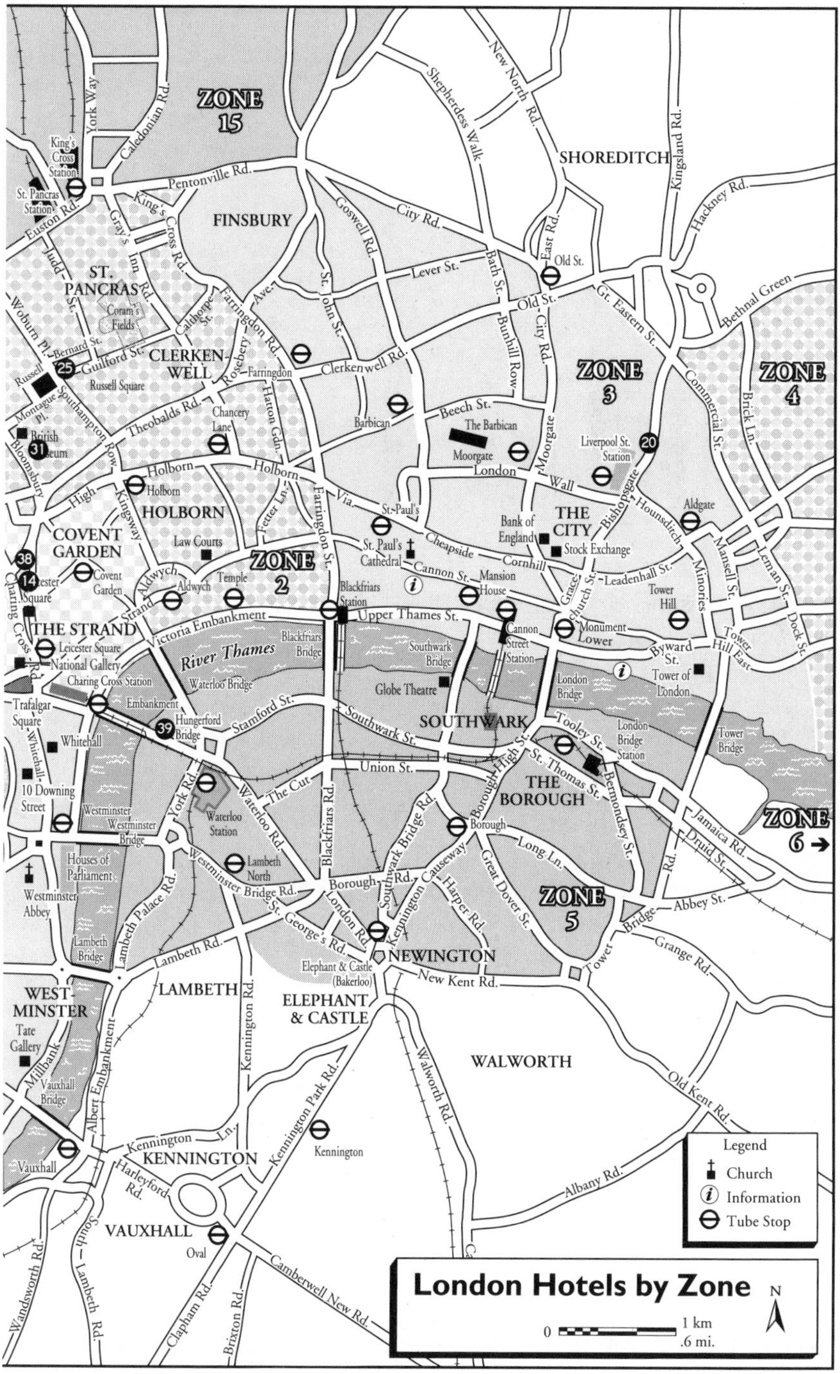
London Hotels by Zone
Legend
Church
Information
Tube Stop
N
0
1 km
.6 mi.
ZONE 15
ZONE 2
ZONE 3
ZONE 4
ZONE 5
ZONE 6
FINSBURY
SHOREDITCH
ST. PANCRAS
CLERKENWELL
HOLBORN
COVENT GARDEN
THE STRAND
THE CITY
SOUTHWARK
THE BOROUGH
NEWINGTON
LAMBETH
ELEPHANT & CASTLE
WALWORTH
WESTMINSTER
KENNINGTON
VAUXHALL
River Thames
York Way
Caledonian Rd.
Pentonville Rd.
King's Cross Station
St. Pancras Station
Euston Rd.
King's Cross Rd.
Gray's Inn Rd.
Judd St.
Coram's Fields
Calthorpe St.
Farringdon Rd.
Rosebery Ave.
Goswell Rd.
St. John St.
City Rd.
Lever St.
Bath St.
Bunhill Row
Old St.
City Rd.
East Rd.
New North Rd.
Shepherdess Walk
Kingsland Rd.
Hackney Rd.
Gt. Eastern St.
Bethnal Green
Commercial St.
Brick Ln.
Woburn Pl.
Bernard St.
Guilford St.
Russell Square
Russell
Montague Pl.
Southampton Row
Theobalds Rd.
Farringdon
Hatton Gdn.
Clerkenwell Rd.
Barbican
Beech St.
The Barbican
Moorgate
Chancery Lane
British Museum
Bloomsbury
Holborn
High
Kingsway
Fetter Ln.
Farringdon St.
Holborn Via.
St. Paul's
London Wall
Liverpool St. Station
Bishopsgate
Houndsditch
Aldgate
Bank of England
Stock Exchange
Cheapside
Cornhill
Leadenhall St.
St. Paul's Cathedral
Cannon St.
Mansion House
Law Courts
Temple
Aldwych
Covent Garden
Leicester Square
Charing Cross Rd.
Strand
Victoria Embankment
Blackfriars Station
Upper Thames St.
Gracechurch St.
Tower Hill
Minories
Mansell St.
Leman St.
Dock St.
Blackfriars Bridge
Southwark Bridge
Cannon Street Station
Monument
Lower Byward St.
Tower Hill East
Tower of London
Leicester Square
National Gallery
Charing Cross Station
Waterloo Bridge
Globe Theatre
London Bridge
Trafalgar Square
Embankment
Stamford St.
Southwark St.
Tooley St.
London Bridge Station
Tower Bridge
Whitehall
Hungerford Bridge
10 Downing Street
Union St.
St. Thomas St.
Bermondsey St.
York Rd.
Waterloo Station
The Cut
Blackfriars Rd.
Borough High St.
Jamaica Rd.
Druid St.
Westminster Bridge
Waterloo Rd.
Southwark Bridge Rd.
Borough
Long Ln.
Houses of Parliament
Lambeth North
Westminster Bridge Rd.
Borough Rd.
Kennington Causeway
Harper Rd.
Great Dover St.
Westminster Abbey
Lambeth Palace Rd.
St. George's Rd.
London Rd.
Tower Bridge Rd.
Abbey St.
Grange Rd.
Lambeth Bridge
Lambeth Rd.
Elephant & Castle (Bakerloo)
New Kent Rd.
Kennington Rd.
Tate Gallery
Millbank
Albert Embankment
Walworth Rd.
Old Kent Rd.
Vauxhall Bridge
Kennington Park Rd.
Kennington
Kennington Ln.
Vauxhall
Harleyford Rd.
Albany Rd.
Oval
South Lambeth Rd.
Wandsworth Rd.
Clapham Rd.
Brixton Rd.
Camberwell New Rd.
25
31
38
14
39
20

LONDON HOTELS BY ZONE

1. Abbey Court
2. Abbey House
3. The Basil Street Hotel
4. The Berkeley
5. Blakes
6. Brown's Hotel
7. Claridges
8. The Claverley
9. The Columbia Hotel
10. Comfort Inn Notting Hill
11. The Connaught
12. The Dorchester
13. The Draycott Hotel
14. The Fielding Hotel
15. Five Summer Place Hotel
16. The Four Seasons
17. The Gainsborough
18. The Gallery
19. The Gore
20. Great Eastern Hotel
21. Grosuenor House
22. Hazlitt's
23. The Landmark
24. The Lanesborough
25. Le Meridien Russell
26. The Metropolitan
27. The Milestone Hotel
28. London Hilton
29. Mandarian Oriental Hotel
30. Miller's Residence
31. Morgans Hotel
32. myhotel Bloomsberry
33. Number Sixteen
34. Pembridge Court Hotel
35. The Portobello Hotel
36. The Ritz
37. Sanderson
38. St. Martin's Lane
39. Travel Inn

Arriving in London without a Hotel Reservation

If you arrive without a hotel reservation—*not* a good idea—you can book rooms through the London Tourist Board; visit one of the visitor centers (see "Planning Your Visit to London," page 96, for locations) or call the London Tourist Board Hotline at (0207) 604-2890, (0208) 8759, or (0207) 802-5480, or, your best option, visit **www.londontown.com.**

Bed-and-Breakfasts and Flats in London

One of the best sources for rooms in private homes in London is **Uptown Reservations** (phone (0207) 351-3445; fax (0207) 351-9383; **www.uptownres.co.uk**), with appealing accommodations in houses in such central neighborhoods as Kensington, Chelsea, Knightsbridge, Belgravia, the West End, and along the top of Kensington Gardens from Holland Park to Marble Arch; singles are £72 a night, doubles £95, family rooms £135. Another such firm is **The Bulldog Club** (phone (0207) 371-3202; fax (0207) 371-2015; (877) 727-3004 U.S.; (612) 9960-5812 Australia; **www.bulldogclub.com**). Prices range from £85 for a single to £105 for a double, plus a fee of £25 for a three-year club membership. **London Homestead Services** (phone (0208) 949-4455; fax (0208) 549-5492; **www.lhslondon.com**) lists about 200 private homes that rent rooms in the London area, many of which are pretty far out of central London; doubles go for as little as £16, but they cost more the closer you are to the city center.

Home From Home (phone (0207) 233-8111; fax (0207) 233-9101; **www.homefromhome.co.uk**) offers some very nice apartments in central

London, with studios from £500 a week and one-bedrooms from £650 a week. **London First Choice Apartments** (phone (0208) 990-9033; fax (0208) 754-1200; **www.lfca.co.uk**) offers flats by the day; prices vary according to neighborhood and type of accommodation, from £89 for a studio in Earl's Court to £650 for a three-bedroom apartment in Mayfair.

HOW THE HOTELS COMPARE IN LONDON

Hotel	Overall Rating	Quality Rating	Value Rating	Price
The Milestone Hotel	★★★★★	★★★★★	★★★★	£250–£270
The Draycott Hotel	★★★★★	★★★★½	★★★★	£100–£220
The Basil Street Hotel	★★★★½	★★★★½	★★★	£145–£205
The Gore	★★★★	★★★★½	★★★★	£130–£170
Number Sixteen	★★★★	★★★★	★★★★	£95–£165
St. Martin's Lane	★★★★	★★★★	★★★★	£190–£210
Brown's Hotel	★★★★	★★★★	★★★	£320–£360
Hazlitt's Hotel	★★★½	★★★★	★★★★	£175–£195
myhotel Bloomsbury	★★★★	★★★	★★★	£150–£185
Abbey Court	★★★½	★★★★	★★★★	£105–£155
Pembridge Court Hotel	★★★½	★★★★	★★★★	£125–£185
The Claverley	★★★½	★★★½	★★★★	£85–£120
Le Meridien Russell	★★★½	★★★	★★★★	£79–£89
The Portobello Hotel	★★★½	★★★	★★★	£120–£160
Five Sumner Place	★★★	★★★★	★★★★	£85–£130
Miller's Residence	★★★	★★★★	★★★	£150-£185
The Gallery Hotel	★★★	★★★½	★★★★	£120–£145
The Gainsborough	★★★	★★★	★★★★	£75–£120
Travel Inn	★★★	★★★	★★★★	£80–£83
Morgans Hotel	★★	★★★½	★★★★★	£59–£85
The Columbia Hotel	★★	★★★½	★★★★★	£65–£83
Comfort Inn Notting Hill	★★	★★½	★★★★★	£52–£60
Abbey House	★★	★★	★★★★★	£45–£74
The Fielding Hotel	★★	★★	★★★	£76–£100

Cream of the Crop

In addition to the more typical hotels in the chart above and the profiles below, you can count on the following London hotels for luxurious accommodation, impeccable service, and amenities you probably didn't even know you needed. They are, after all, some of the finest hotels in the world. We list them only briefly because we assume that travelers who desire this sort of lodging and are equipped to pay the price for it have a good idea of where they want to stay. You can count on prices to begin at about £300 per night and go up from there. For more about these hotels, check out the websites—and while there, be sure to look at special offers and promotions, because you can often nab a room at one these hotels at a relative bargain.

The Berkeley Contemporary chic near Hyde Park Corner, rooftop pool. 157 rooms. Zone 10; Wilton Place, SW1; (0207) 235-6000; fax (0207) 235-4330; **www.savoy-group.com;** tube: Knightsbridge.

Blakes Hip, stylish, gorgeous, popular with a clientele of whom the same could be said. 51 rooms. Zone 11; 33 Roland Gardens, SW7; (0207) 370-6701; fax (0207) 373-0442; **www.blakeshotel.com;** tube: South Kensington.

Brown's This old landmark is so popular with even first-time visitors to London that we give it a full profile below.

Claridges Art Deco glamour, low-key luxury. 203 rooms. Zone 8; Brook Street, W1; (0207) 629-8860; fax (0207) 499-2210; **www.savoy-group.com;** tube: Bond Street.

The Connaught Country-house style, impeccable service. 90 rooms. Zone 8; 16 Carlos Place, W1; (0207) 499-7070; fax (0207) 495-3262; **www.savoy-group.com;** tube: Bond Street.

The Dorchester Legendary lodgings overlooking Hyde Park. 244 rooms. Zone 8; 53 Park Lane, W1; (0207) 629-8888; fax (0207) 409-0114; **www.dorchesterhotel.com;** tube: Marble Arch.

The Four Seasons Part of the international chain, but distinctive nonetheless. 220 rooms. Zone 8; Hamilton Place in Park Lane, W1; (0207) 499-0888; fax (0207) 493-6629; **www.fourseasons.com;** tube: Hyde Park Corner.

Great Eastern Hotel Lots of hype, flash, and chic comfort, convenient to the City. 267 rooms. Zone 3; Liverpool Street, EC2; (0207) 618-5000; fax (0207) 618-5001; **www.great-eastern-hotel.co.uk;** tube: Liverpool Street.

Grosvenor House Distinguished address, luxurious accommodations. 586 rooms. Zone 8; Park Lane, W1; (0207) 499-6363; fax (0207) 493-3341; **www.lemeridien-grosvenorhouse.com;** tube: Hyde Park Corner.

The Landmark A great Victorian railway hotel, beautifully restored. 298 rooms. Zone 14; 222 Marylebone Road, NW1; (0207) 631-8000; fax (0207) 631-8033; **www.landmarklondon.co.uk;** tube: Marylebone.

The Lanesborough Former hospital, now a formal hotel. 95 rooms. Zone 10; Hyde Park Corner, SW1; (0207) 259-5599; fax (0207) 259-5606; **www.lanesborough.com;** tube: Hyde Park Corner.

London Hilton Good-sized rooms, good views of Hyde Park. 449 rooms. Zone 8; 22 Park Lane, W1; (0207) 493-8000; fax (0207) 208-4140; **www.hilton.com;** tube: Green Park.

Mandarin Oriental Hotel Elegant Edwardian architecture, great location. 200 rooms. Zone 10; 66 Knightsbridge, SW1; (0207) 235-2000; fax (0207) 235-2001; **www.mandarinoriental.com;** tube: Knightsbridge.

The Metropolitan Beige fabrics, beechwood furnishings, blank walls, high-tech lighting, hip clientele. 155 rooms. Zone 8; Old Park Lane, W1; (0207) 447-1000; fax (0207) 447-1147; **www.metropolitan.co.uk;** tube: Hyde Park Corner.

The Ritz Versailles on Piccadilly; the very name is synonymous with luxury and extravagance. 131 rooms. Zone 8; 150 Piccadilly, W1; (0207) 493-8181; fax (0207) 493-2687; **www.theritzlondon.com;** tube: Green Park.

Sanderson The latest, hippest addition to the Ian Schrager chain, a dreamlike mirage of white and chrome, accented with the occasional celeb. 150 rooms. Zone 7; 50 Berners Street, W1; (0207) 300-9500; fax (0207) 300-1401; **www.ianschragerhotels.com;** tube: Oxford Circus or Tottenham Court Road.

The Savoy London landmark, with the Thames on one side and West End theaters on the other. 161 rooms. Zone 7; 1 Savoy Hill, Strand, WC2; (0207) 836-4343; fax (0207) 240-6040; **www.savoy-group.co.uk;** tube: Charing Cross.

Hotel Profiles

Abbey Court *£105–£155*

OVERALL ★★★½ | QUALITY ★★★★ | VALUE ★★★★ | ZONE 13

20 Pembridge Gardens, W4; phone (0207) 221-7518; fax (0207) 792-0858; info@abbeycourthotel.co.uk; www.abbeycourthotel.co.uk

Location Notting Hill; tube: Notting Hill Gate.

Amenities & Services 22 rooms. Free newspapers, bathrobes, biscuits, and bottled water; associated with nearby health club; 24-hour room service, bellhop, laundry; Jacuzzi baths.

Elevator No.

Parking Metered spaces on street; nearby car parks (about £22 for 24 hours).

Pricing Includes Continental breakfast; reduced rates for stays of a week or more.

Credit Cards All major.

This comfortable old Victorian house in a lovely neighborhood of white stucco–front row houses is beautifully appointed throughout with fine old furnishings. Downstairs, there's a small conservatory where breakfast is served and an honor bar is set out all day. Newspapers are free, and the comfortable, tasteful guest rooms are well stocked with magazines. In fact, the quarters are so appealing that you may choose to curl up with reading material and not venture out, but when you do, Portobello Road and the other Notting Hill attractions are a short walk away.

Abbey House *£45–£74*

OVERALL ★★ | QUALITY ★★ | VALUE ★★★★★ | ZONE 13

11 Vicarage Gate, W8; (0207) 727-2594; fax (0207) 727-1873; abbeyhousedesk@btconnect.com; www.abbeyhousekensington.com

Location Kensington; tube: High Street Kensington, Notting Hill Gate.

Amenities & Services 22 rooms. Shared baths; large, pleasant breakfast room; free coffee and tea.

Elevator No.

Parking In nearby car parks (about £20 for 24 hours).

Pricing Includes full English breakfast.

Credit Cards Not accepted.

Our favorite budget digs in London occupy a fine old house on a beautiful street just behind Kensington Palace. The pluses include friendly management; an elegant entrance hall and staircases; pristine rooms that are basic but large and furnished with good beds; and an excellent breakfast, included in the price. Baths are shared, though they are sparkling clean, and the hotel is so popular with return guests that it can be difficult to book a room here—reserve as far in advance as you can.

The Basil Street Hotel *£145–£205*

OVERALL ★★★★½ | QUALITY ★★★★½ | VALUE ★★★ | ZONE 10

Basil Street, Knightsbridge, SW3; (0207) 581-3311, in U.S. (800) 448-8355; fax (0207) 581-3693; thebasil@aol.com; www.thebasil.com

Location Knightsbridge; tube: Knightsbridge.

Amenities & Services 93 rooms. Dining room, lounge; air-conditioning in some rooms. Women's club (The Parrot Club) into which men can only go if accompanied by a woman; concierge, bellhop, laundry; smoking and nonsmoking rooms.

Elevator Yes.

Parking In nearby car park (about £41 for 24 hours).

Pricing Continental breakfast, £11.75; English breakfast, £15.50.

Credit Cards All major.

Homey, comfortable, and not in the least bit ostentatious, the Basil Street has been the preferred choice of discerning travelers for close to a century. A lovely dining room, gracious sitting room where afternoon tea is served, and large, non-frilly guest rooms with sitting alcoves and convenient amenities (like well-stocked writing desks) lend the air of a stately and tasteful home. Though the Basil seems like a country-house hotel, Harrods, Hyde Park, the South Ken museums, and Sloane Street boutiques are an easy walk away.

Brown's Hotel *£320–£360*

OVERALL ★★★★ | QUALITY ★★★★ | VALUE ★★★ | ZONE 8

30–34 Albemarle Street, W1; (0207) 493-6020; fax (0207) 493-9381; brownshotel@brownshotel.com; www.brownshotel.com

Location Mayfair; tube: Green Park.

Amenities & Services 118 rooms. Afternoon teas, fitness center, business center; concierge, 24-hour room service and valet, laundry; multiline phones, voice mail, sitting areas and writing desks in all rooms, air-conditioning, working fireplaces in some rooms.

Elevator Yes.

Parking In nearby car parks.

Pricing Includes English breakfast.

Credit Cards All major.

Lord Byron's valet, James Brown, opened this hotel in 1837, and Brown's has acquired a storied past ever since. Alexander Graham Bell made the first telephone call in Britain from Brown's, Rudyard Kipling wrote from here, and Theodore Roosevelt got married while a guest. Brown's was the first hotel in London to have an elevator, telephone, and electricity, and the hotel continues to go out of its way to make a stay here memorable. The service is excellent (there are 180 staff members) and good-natured in that arch English way, and the food, though sky-high in price, is simple and good (especially the afternoon cream teas). Since the hotel grew from 1 town house to 11, the configurations of the rooms are unpredictable, but all are charming and comfortable.

The Claverley *£85–£120*

OVERALL ★★★½ | QUALITY ★★★½ | VALUE ★★★★ | ZONE 10

13–14 Beaufort Gardens, SW3; (0207) 589-8541, in U.S. (800) 747-0398; fax (0207) 823-3410; reservations@claverleyhotel.co.uk; www.claverleyhotel.co.uk

Location Knightsbridge; tube: Knightsbridge.

Amenities & Services 29 rooms. Sitting room with carved fireplace and complimentary papers and magazines; concierge, bellhop, laundry, faxing; airport transfer and taxis; no wheelchair access.

Elevator Yes.

Parking In nearby car parks (about £30 for 24 hours).

Pricing Includes full English breakfast.

Credit Cards V, MC, AMEX, D, DC, CB, JCB.

This award winner for Best Bed-and-Breakfast Hotel in Central and Greater London is well located, friendly, clean, well decorated, and has a selection of rooms that range from serviceable to lovely. The single rooms all have large three-quarter beds, and some of the doubles have four-poster beds, balconies, pull-out sofas, writing desks, sitting areas, and walk-in closets. Number 12 is our favorite, with a balcony, French windows, and four-poster.

The Columbia Hotel — *£65–£83*

OVERALL ★★ | QUALITY ★★★½ | VALUE ★★★★★ | ZONE 14

95–99 Lancaster Gate, W2; (0207) 402-0021; fax (0207) 706-4691; columbiahotel@btconnect.com; www.columbiahotel.co.uk

Location Lancaster Gate; tube: Lancaster Gate.

Amenities & Services 100 rooms. Dining room, bar, 24-hour reception desk, laundry, showers in most baths; family rooms; one room for guests with disabilities and one for hearing impaired.

Elevator Yes.

Parking Eight spaces available on a first-come, first-served basis (free).

Pricing Includes full English breakfast.

Credit Cards All major.

This is probably one of the best deals in the area—there may be cheaper rooms to be had, but not with the amenities and friendliness of the Columbia. Rooms are plain hotel style, but they're clean and some are fairly large and overlook Hyde Park. The hotel is comprised of five Victorian houses strung together, so as with all such buildings, there is great disparity among the size and shapes of the rooms. Queensway, a few minutes' walk away, has lots of great restaurants.

Comfort Inn Notting Hill — *£52–£60*

OVERALL ★★ | QUALITY ★★½ | VALUE ★★★★★ | ZONE 13

6–14 Pembridge Gardens, W2; (0207) 221-3433; fax (0207) 229-4808; hillgate@lth-hotels.com; www.londonhotels.net

Location Notting Hill Gate; tube: Notting Hill Gate.

Amenities & Services 66 rooms. Satellite TV in bar, video games; reception acts as concierge; laundry.

Elevator Two elevators.

Parking In nearby car park (about £25 for 24 hours).

Pricing Includes Continental breakfast.

Credit Cards All major.

Clean and serviceable, one of London's best budget choices is within a short walk of Portobello Road and Kensington Church Street—so it's perfect for antique hunters who want to spend all their money on treasures instead of accommodation. Though the hotel comprises three old houses on a lovely street, don't expect much in the way of luxury or architectural distinction. Furnishings are plain and beds are firm—but take a twin if you're with a mate, since the double beds are small.

The Draycott Hotel — *£100–£220*

OVERALL ★★★★★ | QUALITY ★★★★½ | VALUE ★★★★ | ZONE 11

26 Cadogan Gardens, SW3; (0207) 730-6466; fax (0207) 730-0236; reservations@draycotthotel.com; www.draycotthotel.com

Location Knightsbridge/Chelsea; tube: Knightsbridge, Sloane Square.

Amenities & Services 35 rooms. Private dining room, drawing room, smoking room, afternoon tea, honor bar, breakfast room, garden; concierge, complimentary chauffeur service into city each weekday, 24-hour room service, laundry, baby-sitting; fax and modem lines, air-conditioning, VCRs, CDs, gas fires in all but the single rooms.

Elevator Yes.

Parking In nearby car park (about £20 for 24 hours).

Pricing Includes full English breakfast.

Credit Cards All major.

This town-house hotel, formerly the Cliveden Town House, really does feel like a beautiful home. Urns on either side of the front door are filled with apples, the first of many appealing touches; the lovely drawing room has a welcoming, comfortable atmosphere and opens onto a garden square that makes for a wonderful place to sit in good weather. All the rooms are beautifully appointed, but the best are junior suites overlooking the garden—settle into one and you'll soon forget that Sloane Square and Knightsbridge are only a short walk away.

The Fielding Hotel *£76–£100*

OVERALL ★★ | QUALITY ★★ | VALUE ★★★ | ZONE 7

4 Broad Court at Bow Street, WC2; (0207) 836-8305; fax (0207) 497-0064; info@the-fielding-hotel.co.uk; www.the-fielding-hotel.co.uk

Location Covent Garden; tube: Covent Garden.

Amenities & Services 24 rooms.

Elevator No.

Parking In nearby car park (about £30 for 24 hours).

Pricing Breakfast, about £4.

Credit Cards All major.

Location, location, location—these three words sum up the appeal of this bare-bones hotel on an attractive pedestrian street across from the Royal Opera House. Indeed, some might say that location is the only thing going for the Fielding, but we would add that the premises are clean, serviceable, and a great bargain for central London. The orange hallways are a tipoff to the prevailing design sense, the cheap pine furnishings are more spartan than comfortable, and bathrooms are small (but serviceable). But at this price and location, what do you expect? One quibble comes by way of guests who report run-ins with surly members of the management, and that's not acceptable at any price.

Five Sumner Place *£85–£130*

OVERALL ★★★ | QUALITY ★★★★ | VALUE ★★★★ | ZONE 12

5 Sumner Place; (0207) 584-7586; fax (0207) 823-9962; no.5@dial.pipex.com; www.sumnerplace.com

Location South Kensington; tube: South Kensington.

Amenities & Services 13 rooms. Concierge, bellhop, laundry, room service 8 a.m.–8 p.m.; refrigerators in some rooms.

Elevator Yes.

Parking In nearby car park (about £28 for 24 hours).

Pricing Includes breakfast.

Credit Cards All major.

Our only real complaint about Number Five is that it's not Number Sixteen, a hotel that we prefer just down the street. Even so, this Victorian town house on a lovely street of white terrace houses is elegant and appealing, with a small garden and a conservatory where breakfast is served. Décor throughout is of the uninspired but eye-pleasing, traditional British variety, and rooms are commodious and comfortable. Given the comfort provided and the superb location near the South Kensington museums, the hotel is very fairly priced.

The Gainsborough *£75–£120*

OVERALL ★★★ | QUALITY ★★★ | VALUE ★★★★ | ZONE 11

7–11 Queensberry Place, SW7; (0207) 838-1700, in U.S. (800) 270-9206; fax (0207) 957-0001; gainsborough@eeh.co.uk; www.eeh.co.uk

Location South Kensington; tube: South Kensington.

Amenities & Services 49 rooms. Fax in lobby, discount at two fitness clubs nearby; concierge, room service, laundry, bellhop, room service for snacks and sandwiches.

Elevator Yes.

Parking In nearby car park (about £34 for 24 hours).

Pricing Includes English or Continental breakfast.

Credit Cards All major.

A pleasant sitting room and bright breakfast room that doubles as a tearoom occupy the ground floor of what was once a private home on a sunny corner of Queen's Gate Gardens. Upstairs, the traditionally furnished guest rooms are unusually comfortable and tasteful for the cost; the first-floor rooms facing the front of the house are the most spacious and have high ceilings, and number 112 has a balcony and French windows.

The Gallery Hotel *£120–£145*

OVERALL ★★★ | QUALITY ★★★½ | VALUE ★★★★ | ZONE 11

8–10 Queensberry Place, SW7; (0207) 915-0000, in U.S. (800) 270-9206; fax (0207) 915-4400; gallery@eeh.co.uk; www.eeh.co.uk

Location South Kensington; tube: South Kensington.

Amenities & Services 36 rooms. Concierge, 24-hour room service; breakfast room; room service for sandwiches and snacks, access to nearby fitness club, fax in lobby; minibars.

Elevator Yes.

Parking In nearby car park (about £34 for 24 hours).

Pricing Includes English or Continental breakfast.

Credit Cards V, MC, AMEX, D, DC, CB, JCB.

Like its slightly less stylish companion hotel across the street, the Gainsborough, the Gallery is a good choice if you want to be near the South Kensington museums (the Natural History Museum is at the end of the street, and Kensington Gardens are just five minutes away). There's a clubby, paneled lounge and an Arts and Crafts–style drawing room, and while the guest rooms are not large (except for the suite with the private terrace), they are newly refurbished and handsomely appointed; indeed, everything here seems to shine and sparkle, especially the mahogany-and-marble bathrooms.

The Gore *£130–£170*

OVERALL ★★★★ | QUALITY ★★★★½ | VALUE ★★★★ | ZONE 11

189 Queen's Gate, SW7; (0207) 584-6601; fax (0207) 589-8127; reservations@gorehotel.co.uk; www.gorehotel.com

Location South Kensington/Kensington border; tube: Gloucester Road.

Amenities & Services 54 rooms. Concierge, room service, bellhop, laundry; use of two nearby fitness centers.

Elevator Yes.

Parking In nearby car park (about £25 for 24 hours).

Pricing Excellent special promotions available; Contiental breakfast, £9.95; English breakfast, £15.95.

Credit Cards All major.

The antiques dealers turned hoteliers who created the Gore (they also operate Hazlitt's in Soho) claim that 4,500 prints and paintings hang on the walls of these two fine old connected houses just off Kensington Gardens. Victorian antiques fill the guest rooms, each a throwback to ornate, 19th-century splendor. Provided you don't favor minimalist surroundings, all are delightful, though a few are small and dark, and some of the beds are better to look at than to occupy. For a truly over-the-top experience, check into the Tudor suite, a Victorian re-creation of an Elizabethan gallery, with a huge stone fireplace; in the feminine Venus Room, you can dream of love in an antique rococo bed once owned by Judy Garland. The bistro and restaurant downstairs are both excellent, and the bar and sitting room are appropriately homey.

Hazlitt's Hotel *£175–£195*

OVERALL ★★★½ | QUALITY ★★★★ | VALUE ★★★★ | ZONE 7

6 Frith Street, Soho Square, W16; (0207) 434-1771; fax (0207) 439-1524; reservations@hazlitts.co.uk; www.hazlittshotel.com

Location Soho; tube: Tottenham Court.

Amenities & Services 23 rooms. Receptionist, bellhop, laundry, 24-hour room service, data ports.

Elevator No.

Parking In nearby car parks (about £15 for 24 hours).

Pricing Continental breakfast, £8.95.

Credit Cards All major.

Hazlitt's Hotel, by the creators of the Gore, evokes a bygone era—the Georgian era, to be exact, when the 18th-century house was home to writer William Hazlitt. The house is filled with handsome antiques and prints, creating a décor that manages to be atmospheric without overdoing it. The guest rooms are attractive and luxuriously comfortable, with fine cotton sheets on the antique beds; many of the bathrooms are outfitted with deep, claw-footed tubs. Hazlitt's is especially popular with writers, whose books fill bookshelves in the sitting room; should your hunger extend beyond words, Soho's eateries are just outside the door.

Le Meridien Russell *£79–£89*

OVERALL ★★★½ | QUALITY ★★★ | VALUE ★★★★ | ZONE 2

Russell Square, WC1; (0207) 837-6470; fax (0207) 837-2857; russell@lemeridien.com; www.lemeridien.com

Location Bloomsbury; tube: Russell Square.

Amenities & Services 329 rooms. Concierge, 24-hour room service, bellhop, laundry, conference rooms; full business support, including e-mail; executive floor with lounge and Continental breakfast.

Elevator Three.

Parking In nearby car parks (about £25 for 24 hours).

Pricing Includes Continental breakfast.

Credit Cards V, MC, AMEX.

One of London's great Victorian hotel palaces, and overlooking Russell Square to boot, this place was for a long time one of London's best-valued hostelries. That's changed a bit since a recent purchase by Le Meridien Hotel group, but for the most part the changes have been for the good. The tired old décor is getting a redo, service (which had been abysmal) is improving, and many of the guest rooms are being brought up to snuff. For the moment, at least, the hotel offers a choice of décor and price. Rooms with basic décor are still quite a bargain, some more expensive rooms have been redone in traditional style, and the pricey, so-called Art + Tech rooms are filled with snappy modern pieces and high-tech gizmos like plasma-screen TVs. Whatever you pay for a room here, the Bloomsbury location is great, especially if you can't get your fill of the British Museum. There's a fairly uninspired restaurant, Virginia Woolf's, and the clubby King's Lounge off the Victorian lobby.

The Milestone Hotel *£250–£270*

OVERALL ★★★★★ | QUALITY ★★★★★ | VALUE ★★★★ | ZONE 11

1 Kensington Court, W81; (0207) 917-1000; fax (0207) 917-1010; www.themilestone.com

Location Kensington; tube: High Street Kensington.

Amenities & Services 57 rooms. Dining room, elegant lounge, concierge, butler, 24-hour room service, business support, health club; opulent marble baths, electronic blinds, in-room exercise equipment on request, white noise machines on request, choice of pillows and duvets.

Elevator Yes.

Parking In nearby car parks (about £25 for 24 hours).

Pricing Includes full breakfast; excellent special promotions and Web offers available.

Credit Cards All major.

The Milestone wins our prize for the best small hotel in London. We base our kudos on a wonderful location (near the end of Kensington High Street across the street from Kensington Gardens), service (which is exemplary and, with such flourishes as the presence of an attentive butler, manages to make guests feel cared for without a trace of ostentation), and style (the surroundings are both comfortable and sumptuous). Each guest room is different and lavishly decorated: some are duplex or split level, several have fireplaces, a few have terraces. One room is tented to resemble safari accommodations; another is lined with flannel to suggest a tailoring motif; a large suite is Elizabethan in feel, with beams, leaded windows, and a massive hearth. If the hotel is not full, guests are welcome to choose the décor that best suits their tastes. Our favorite accommodations face Kensington Gardens (through double-paned windows). Six stylish and commodious apartments in an adjoining building are available by the week.

Miller's Residence *£150-£185*

OVERALL ★★★ | QUALITY ★★★★ | VALUE ★★★ | ZONE 13

111A Westbourne Grove, W2 (entrance on southeast side of Hereford Road; (0207) 243-1024; fax (0207) 243-1064; enquiries@millersuk.com; www.millersuk.com

Location Notting Hill Gate; tube: Bayswater.

Amenities & Services Six rooms, two apartments. Reception acts as concierge, limited room service (from local restaurants), laundry.

Elevator No.

Parking In nearby car parks (about £25 for 24 hours).

Pricing Includes Continental breakfast.

Credit Cards All major.

Miller's Residence is not for those who object to clutter. But, if you like to surround yourself with antiques and quirky décor, this small, self-proclaimed "rooming house" is just the place. The drawing room (candlelit at night) and guest rooms are filled with the trophies that Martin Miller, of *Miller's Antique Guide,* and Kay Raveden have scavenged over the years; the bedsteads may be antique, but the mattresses are modern and firm, and the modern bathrooms are well equipped. Book well in advance, because Miller's is quite popular these days.

Morgans Hotel *£59–£85*

OVERALL ★★ | QUALITY ★★★½ | VALUE ★★★★★ | ZONE 2

24 Bloomsbury Street, WC1; (0207) 636-3735; fax (0207) 636-3045

Location Bloomsbury; tube: Tottenham Court Road.

Amenities & Services 21 rooms and 4 flats. Air-conditioning, bellhop.

Elevator No.

Parking In nearby car parks (about £30 for 24 hours).

Pricing Includes breakfast; flats: £90–£120.

Credit Cards MC, V.

Cheapskates in the know flock to this tidy, family-run hotel that's practically on the doorstep of the British Museum. We only wish that the breakfast room, set up with booths and filled with English ceramics, set the tone for the rest of the décor; alas, the rooms are not much more than serviceable. The flats are nicer, and are quite a good deal given their size and amenities, which include well-stocked kitchenettes.

myhotel Bloomsbury *£150–£185*

OVERALL ★★★★ | QUALITY ★★★ | VALUE ★★★ | ZONE 2

11–13 Bayley Street, WC1; (0207) 667-6000; fax (0207) 667-6001;
guestservicesbloomsbury@myhotels.co.uk; www.myhotels.co.uk

Location Bloomsbury; tube: Tottenham Court Road.

Amenities & Services 73 rooms. Restaurant, bar, therapy room with spa treatments, fitness room, business center, library, room service, personal stereos, VCRs, laptop-sized safes.

Elevator Yes.

Parking In nearby car parks (about £30 for 24 hours).

Pricing Special weekend rates from £115.

Credit Cards V, MC, AMEX, DC.

Tired of chintz and clutter? These sparse, tranquil surroundings may be just the answer. Guest rooms incorporate feng shui principles, which may explain why they seem so relaxing—that, along with the neutral color schemes and simple modern furnishings. The handsome library is especially soothing, a massage or facial Jinga therapy room even more so. Naysayers may scoff at this New Age approach to lodging, but for some travelers it's just the ticket—provided they're prepared to mellow out. There are also myhotels in Chelsea and Paddington.

Number Sixteen *£95–£165*

OVERALL ★★★★ | QUALITY ★★★★ | VALUE ★★★★ | ZONE 11

16 Sumner Place, South Kensington, SW7; (0207) 589-5232, in U.S. (800) 592-5387; fax (0207) 584-8615; sixteen@firmdale.com; www.numbersixteenhotel.co.uk

Location South Kensington; tube: South Kensington.

Amenities & Services 40 rooms. Concierge, laundry, 24-hour room service.

Elevator Yes.

Parking In nearby car parks (about £28 for 24 hours).

Pricing Includes breakfast.

Credit Cards All major.

These four interconnected Victorian town houses, with a lovely garden and conservatory, set the gold standard for small town-house hotels in London. Public rooms include a stylish library and a sitting room, both equipped with honor bars. Bedrooms vary in size, but many are quite large, and all provide a pleasing level of sophisticated comfort that rises far above your typical British hotel traditional look, with comfy chairs or sofas, attractive fabrics, fine linens and draperies. Sumner Place is a relatively quiet street, so we opt for the front rooms to enjoy the outlook onto the white facades of the terrace houses; others prefer rooms in back, which overlook the garden. Service here is attentive and gracious.

Pembridge Court Hotel *£125–£185*

OVERALL ★★★½ | QUALITY ★★★★ | VALUE ★★★★ | ZONE 13

34 Pembridge Gardens; (0207) 229-9977, in U.S. (800) 709-9882; fax (0207) 727-4982; reservations@pemct.co.uk; www.pemct.co.uk

Location Notting Hill Gate; tube: Notting Hill Gate.

Amenities & Services 20 rooms. 24-hour room service, limited menu, bellhop, laundry, arrangements with nearby health club, fax on request, air-conditioning.

Elevator Yes.

Parking Two spaces available on first-come, first-served basis (free); or in nearby car parks (about£22 for 24 hours).

Pricing Includes full English breakfast.

Credit Cards All major.

This excellent town-house hotel manages to be quirky (antique gloves, dresses, belts, fans, and other accessories provide the décor) without being over the top, and it's quite stylish and completely comfortable at the same time. The sitting room with a fireplace is delightful, and many of the attractive guest rooms are of a good size (singles tend to be small, though); most baths have deep tubs. Best of all for antiques hounds, Portobello Road is just outside the back door.

The Portobello Hotel *£120–£160*

OVERALL ★★★½ | QUALITY ★★★ | VALUE ★★★ | ZONE 13

22 Stanley Gardens, W11; (0207) 727-2777; fax (0207) 792-9641; info@portobello-hotel.co.uk; www.portobello-hotel.co.uk

Location Notting Hill Gate; tube: Notting Hill Gate.

Amenities & Services 24 rooms. Bar, concierge, 8 a.m.–4 p.m. room service, breakfast sent to room, laundry.

Elevator Yes, but only to the third floor.

Parking In nearby car parks (about £22 for 24 hours).

Pricing Includes Continental breakfast.

Credit Cards All major.

Many travelers (including a lot of folks in the music biz) swear they wouldn't think of staying anywhere else in London. We're not among them, though the Portobello has a lot of funky charm, nice outlooks onto a communal garden, and some great rooms (like number 16, with a round bed and a tub right in the room). Some of the rooms, though, are a shade shabby, and the tiny singles are too cell-like for comfort; likewise, some of the baths are generously sized and equipped with big tubs, while others are uncomfortably cramped. But . . . you may well find that the place oozes bohemian charm.

St. Martin's Lane *£190–£210*

OVERALL ★★★★ | QUALITY ★★★★ | VALUE ★★★★ | ZONE 7

45 St. Martin's Lane; (0207) 300-5500; fax (0207) 300-5501; sml@ianschragerhotels.com; www.ianschragerhotels.com

Location Covent Garden; tube: Covent Garden, Leicester Square.

Amenities & Services 204 rooms. Two restaurants, including trendy Asia de Cuba and 24-hour Tuscan; business center, gym, garden concierge, room service, data ports, CD and DVD players, walk-in showers.

Elevator Yes.

Parking In nearby car parks (about £25 for 24 hours); free parking available with special Internet offers.

Pricing Breakfast included with special Internet offers.

Credit Cards All major.

A bit too much hype, attitude, and enforced hipness puts us off of this Ian Schrager hotel at the edge of Covent Garden. But if it's smartness you're after, you won't be disappointed, and it must be said that the St. Martin's Lane pays attention to comfort, too, with nice details like state-of-the-art baths, fine cotton sheets, and, of course, plenty of soothing minimalist touches from designer Philippe Starck. If you want to mingle with a fashionable set, hang out in the public spaces that include Asia de Cuba restaurant and the Light Bar. You may want to spend most of the time in your room, though, fiddling with the gadget next to your bed that changes the white décor to pink, blue, yellow, or whatever color suits your mood.

Travel Inn *£80–£83*

OVERALL ★★★ | QUALITY ★★★ | VALUE ★★★★ | ZONE 5

County Hall, Belvedere Road SE1; (0870) 238-3300; fax (0207) 902-1619; www.travelinn.co.uk

Location South Bank; tube: Waterloo.

Amenities & Services 350 rooms. Restaurant, bar; king-size beds, nonsmoking rooms, rooms for travelers with disabilities.

Elevator Yes.

Parking In nearby car parks (about £25 for 24 hours).

Pricing Continental breakfast, £4.50; full breakfast, £6.50.

Credit Cards All major.

If you don't need to surround yourself with character, you can't beat these generic hotels popping up all over London for price, cleanliness, and solid comfort. All the rooms are the same, and the only concession they make to style are colorful duvets and handsome wood headboards and desks. But if you stay at this branch, with the London Eye rotating outside the window and all the other South Bank attractions at the doorstep, you're not going to spend much time in the room anyway. You'll find other Travel Inns at Tower Bridge, in Chelsea (Puney Bridge), Kensington, the Docklands, and Euston, and at Heathrow Airport.

Getting around London

For information on arriving in London by plane or train, and how to get into London from the airports, see Part Two, Arriving and Getting around in England.

Public Transportation

The most important thing to take out with you in London is a good map and/or the *London A to Z* (called *"A to Zed"* here), a pocket-sized book available in any bookshop and at many newsstands; this handy reference contains detailed maps, with tube stops, and a detailed street index. For any questions you might have regarding London travel information, call **London Transport** at (0207) 222-1234. You can get information on any facet of travel, including how everything is running.

Travel Zones

London Transport has divided London into six travel zones (which have nothing to do with the zones outlined in this book); zone 1 is central London, and the other zones radiate outward from there. Most of your travel in London will fall within zones 1 and 2. Bus and tube fares vary with the number of zones through which you travel; the fare for travel in zone 1 is £1.60, and for travel in zones 1 and 2 is £2; you can buy a carnet of ten tickets for travel within zone 1 for £11.50, lowering the fare to £1.15 a ride.

Travel Cards

The best deal for traveling on public transportation is the Travel Card, which gives you unlimited travel on the tube, buses, and most overland rail services in Greater London, including the Docklands Light Rail. A one-day travel card for zones 1 and 2 costs £5.10, £2.50 for children. Travel Cards can be bought at tube stations and also at certain newsagents; they are not valid on designated night buses or Airbuses.

Buses

There are 17,000 bus stops all over London, so you should be able to get pretty close to whatever your destination may be. Be careful that you're standing at the correct bus stop—on Oxford Street or Hyde Park Corner, for example, there are many buses and many stops. In most bus-stop shelters you'll find a map of London displaying the bus routes, along with a list of the stops of each number bus on the route. Many stops also have electronic signs that inform you of how long the wait should be for the next bus on your route. You pay the fare on the bus, and the driver or fare collector will make change. Fares are determined by how far you travel, so you should know the name of your destination.

The Tube

The tube runs between roughly 5:30 a.m. and midnight. You can buy tickets from a window or at machines in the underground stations. To enter a turnstile, you must put the ticket in a designated slot and retrieve it on the other side of the turnstile; you will then need to put the ticket into another turnstile as you exit your destination. If you lose your ticket, you will have to pay £10 to retrieve it, so hold on to it.

Taxis

Taxis in London cruise the streets or line up in queues at designated taxi stands. If a taxi is available, the yellow light atop the car will be lit. Zigzag lines running along the curb indicate that the taxi cannot legally stop; move to where those lines end to get picked up. In London (unlike New York), it's good form to tell the driver where you are going before you get into the taxi. Cabbies are a talkative and opinionated lot, and they can be a font of information about London. Tip about 10% of the fare. You can call a black taxi, though some companies charge extra for booking over the phone or using a credit card—ask when you call. Established cab companies include **Computer Cabs** (phone (0207) 286-0286), **Data Cab** (phone (0208) 964-212), **Dial a Cab** (phone (0207) 253-5000), and **Radio Taxis** (phone (0207) 272-0272).

Minicabs

Minicabs are a less reliable option than the black cabs, but they are cheaper and are often available when taxis are not. You must call to book a car; make sure you agree on a price when booking the cab, and confirm the price with the driver when you get in. Tipping is normally 10–15%. Companies include **Addison Lee** (phone (0207) 387-8888) and **Lady Cabs** (phone (0207) 254-3501), which, for the reassurance of women traveling alone, employs only female drivers.

Docklands Light Rail

The **Docklands Light Rail** (phone (0207) 363-9700) services the East End, Canary Wharf, Greenwich, the *Cutty Sark,* and Lewisham. These special trains leave from Tower Gateway and Bank, roughly between 5:30 a.m. and 12:30 a.m., with slightly reduced hours on the weekends. Fares begin at £1.60 each way and vary with distance traveled; one-day rail and riverboat tickets are also available.

Lost and Found

If you have left something in one of the above public conveyances, you might be able to retrieve it by calling one of these numbers: buses, (0207) 486-2496; taxis, (0207) 833-0996; trains, (0207) 928-5151; tube, (0207) 486-2496.

Getting around London on Your Own

Driving

If you can possibly avoid it, don't. Traffic is hellish, parking is expensive and scarce, and driving is now costly—the city imposes a congestion charge of $5 a day for driving in central London between 7 a.m. and 6:30 p.m., Monday–Friday. If you happen to be approaching London from elsewhere in Europe by car, leave your car at one of the airports or use one of the costlier **National Car Parks** (signs say NCP) around central London; call (0207) 499-7050, or go **to www.ncp.co.uk** for locations. Parking regulations on the street are strictly enforced—look at lampposts to find signs outlining where you may and may not park. If you park illegally and are clamped, a sticker telling you where to pay to have the clamp removed and the additional fine will be affixed to the windshield; if you're towed, call (0207) 747-7474 to find out where your car was taken.

Bicycling

Limit your riding to the many paths in the London parks. Call the **London Cycling Campaign** at (0207) 928-7220 for information about renting bikes, cycling routes, safety, and security.

Walking

London is bliss for walkers, and we strongly recommend that you spend as much time as you can trodding the streets through the various neighborhoods of this fascinating city. Since driving is on the left in England, please be sure to look to your right when crossing a street; at many crossings, the city has posted notices alerting pedestrians as to which way to look. At zebra crossings, pedestrians have the right-of-way. Around big intersections such as Piccadilly Circus, Marble Arch, and Hyde Park Corner, "subways" provide subterranean crossings. They are well indicated with signposts.

Exploring London

This is where we should roll out the old Samuel Johnson quote about London offering all that life can afford. Visit even a fraction of our selection of attractions and you'll no doubt agree. It's a good idea to call an attraction or check out the website before visiting, because hours and prices change all the time in fast-moving London.

Tours of London

Bus Tours

A hop-on, hop-off bus tour provides a good introduction to the city. They make stops at most of the major attractions and intersections, such as the Tower of London, Madame Tussaud's, Green Park, Hyde Park Corner, Harrods, in front of the Victoria & Albert Museum, and so on. You can choose to disembark, look around, and get back onto the next bus, or you can simply sit back and enjoy the ride (all the better if the sun is out and you can bask on an open-air upper deck, found on most buses). Tour-bus options include:

Big Bus Company (0207) 233-9533; **www.bigbus.co.uk.** Offers a Green Route (90 minutes) and a Blue Route (60 minutes), with live commentary. Buses run every 15 minutes or so. Tickets, which cost £17 for adults and £8 for children ages 5–15, are good for 24 hours.

Original London Sightseeing Tour (0208) 877-1722; **www.theoriginaltour.com.** Provides a variety of tour routes. Buses run approximately every 15–20 minutes and include 90 stops. Tickets cost £15 for adults and £7.50 for children ages 5–15. The Blue Tour offers eight language options and 100 hop-on, hop-off stops good for 24 hours.

You can do some cheap touring on your own on the number 11 bus. Pick it up at the King's Road at World's End or the Chelsea Town Hall stops, for a ride through Victoria and past Westminster Abbey, Whitehall, Trafalgar Square up the Strand to St. Paul's Cathedral. The number 15 will take you from Paddington to Marble Arch, up Oxford Street, down Regent to Piccadilly Circus, down Haymarket to Trafalgar Square, up the Strand (which turns into Fleet Street), and past St. Paul's Cathedral and the Tower of London to Petticoat Lane (Middlesex Street), where there's a market on Sunday mornings.

Tour Companies

There are a lot of tour companies in London doing very similar tours for roughly the same amount of money. You can find their brochures in any hotel lobby. These companies usually offer half-day, morning, night, full-day, or two-day tours of London, plus tours to such places as Windsor and Leeds Castles, even Paris and Amsterdam. The price of the tour almost always includes entrance fees for the attractions and the cost of meals, and in the case of the overnight trips, the cost of accommodations. Here are some of the major London tour companies; take a look at their websites for tour descriptions:

Astral Travels (0700) 078-1016; **www.astraltravels.co.uk.**

Evan Evans (0208) 332-2222; **www.evanevans.co.uk.**

Frames Rickards (0207) 233-7030; **www.framesrickards.co.uk.**

Thames River Services (0207) 930-4097; **www.westminsterpier.co.uk.** For tours along the river.

London Waterbus Company (0207) 482-2660; **www.camdenlockmarket.com.** For boat rides along the canals of Little Venice and Camden Lock.

Walking in and around London

Walking is by far the best way to experience London. Grab a map and simply wander. When you've had enough, you can just get on the Underground and head back to your hotel. If you want to walk in the company of knowledgeable Londoners, try **Original London Walks** (phone (0207) 624-3978; **www.walks.com**). London's oldest walking tour company leads scores of themed walks along the lines of Jack the Ripper, ghosts, the Beatles . . . you get the idea. If you prefer to walk at your own pace, here a few suggestions:

Chelsea (Zone 11) Cheyne Walk runs parallel to the Thames and is lined with handsome houses that have been occupied by some of Britain's greatest creative talents: George Eliot lived at number 4, Gabriel Rossetti lived at number 16, J. M. W. Turner at 119. Near the end of Cheyne Walk is the Chelsea Physic Garden. You'll find plaques commemorating the famous on surrounding streets, too: Oscar Wilde lived on Tite Street, and Thomas Carlyle at 24 Cheyne Row.

South Bank of the Thames (Zone 5) Begin at the east end of Lambeth Bridge and follow the river north (we know it's called the "South" Bank, but the Thames twists and turns, so compass directions get a bit muddled). You'll pass Lambeth Palace and, depending on how far you walk, a succession of sights, new and old: the Saatchi Galleries, the London Eye, Jubilee Gardens and Royal Festival Hall, the Tate Modern, Shakespeare's Globe, and Southwark Cathedral among them.

Royal and Official London (Zone 9) On Lower Grosvenor Place you'll come to the Royal Mews, the Buckingham Palace stables, and just beyond it, the Queen's Gallery, where Her Majesty shows off her art collection.

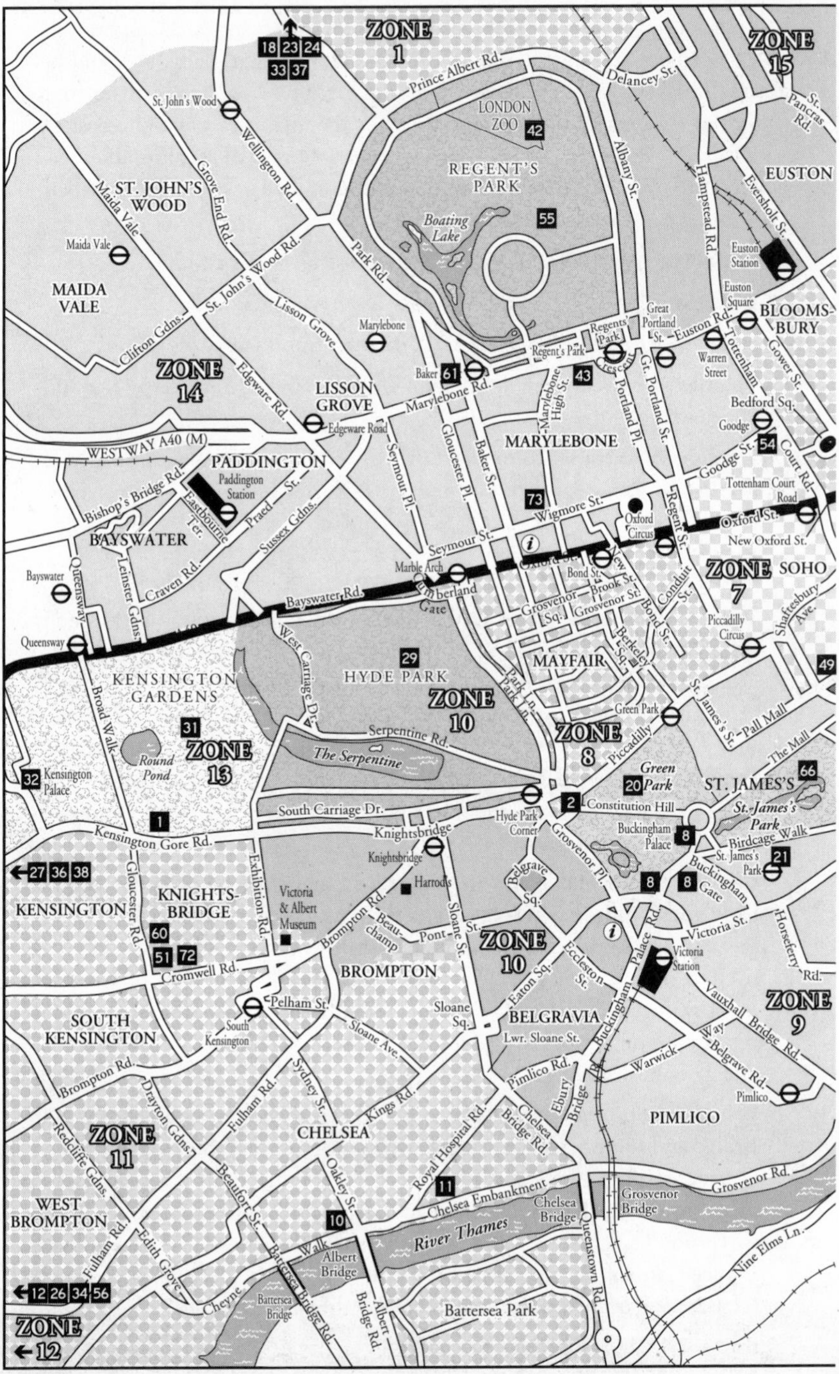
ZONE 1
ZONE 15
ZONE 14
ZONE 7
ZONE 10
ZONE 8
ZONE 13
ZONE 9
ZONE 11
ZONE 12
18 23 24
33 37
Prince Albert Rd.
Delancey St.
St. Pancras Rd.
EUSTON
LONDON ZOO
42
REGENT'S PARK
Boating Lake
55
St. John's Wood
Wellington Rd.
Grove End Rd.
ST. JOHN'S WOOD
Maida Vale
Albany St.
Hampstead Rd.
Eversholt St.
Euston Station
Euston Square
BLOOMS-BURY
Park Rd.
St. John's Wood Rd.
MAIDA VALE
Lisson Grove
Marylebone
Clifton Gdns.
Great Portland St.
Regents Park
Regent's Park
Euston Rd.
Warren Street
Tottenham
Gower St.
Baker
61
43
Crescent
Portland Pl.
Gt. Portland St.
Marylebone High St.
Edgware Rd.
LISSON GROVE
Marylebone Rd.
Bedford Sq.
Goodge
54
Edgeware Road
Seymour Pl.
Gloucester Pl.
Baker St.
MARYLEBONE
WESTWAY A40 (M)
PADDINGTON
Paddington Station
Bishop's Bridge Rd.
Eastbourne Ter.
Praed St.
Sussex Gdns.
73
Goodge St.
Court Rd.
Tottenham Court Road
Wigmore St.
Oxford Circus
Regent St.
Oxford St.
New Oxford St.
BAYSWATER
Leinster Gdns.
Queensway
Bayswater
Craven Rd.
Seymour St.
Marble Arch
Cumberland Gate
Bond St.
New Bond St.
Brook St.
Grosvenor Sq.
Grosvenor St.
Conduit St.
SOHO
Shaftesbury Ave.
Bayswater Rd.
Piccadilly Circus
West Carriage Dr.
29
HYDE PARK
MAYFAIR
Berkeley Sq.
49
KENSINGTON GARDENS
Broad Walk
Park Ln.
St. James's St.
Pall Mall
Green Park
31
Serpentine Rd.
The Serpentine
Piccadilly
The Mall
Round Pond
32
Kensington Palace
Green Park
20
ST. JAMES'S
66
St. James's Park
South Carriage Dr.
2
Constitution Hill
1
Hyde Park Corner
Buckingham Palace
8
Birdcage Walk
Kensington Gore Rd.
Knightsbridge
Grosvenor Pl.
St. James's Park
21
27 36 38
Harrods
Belgrave Sq.
Buckingham Gate
KENSINGTON
Gloucester Rd.
KNIGHTS-BRIDGE
Exhibition Rd.
Victoria & Albert Museum
Brompton Rd.
Beauchamp
Pont St.
Sloane St.
Victoria St.
Horseferry Rd.
60
51
72
Palace Rd.
Cromwell Rd.
BROMPTON
Eaton Sq.
Eccleston St.
Victoria Station
Pelham St.
Vauxhall Bridge Rd.
SOUTH KENSINGTON
South Kensington
Sloane Sq.
BELGRAVIA
Buckingham
Lwr. Sloane St.
Sloane Ave.
Warwick Way
Belgrave Rd.
Brompton Rd.
Sydney St.
Pimlico Rd.
Pimlico
Drayton Gdns.
Fulham Rd.
Kings Rd.
Ebury Bridge
PIMLICO
Royal Hospital Rd.
Chelsea Bridge Rd.
Redcliffe Gdns.
CHELSEA
Beaufort St.
Oakley St.
11
Grosvenor Rd.
Chelsea Embankment
Grosvenor Bridge
WEST BROMPTON
10
Chelsea Bridge
River Thames
Queenstown Rd.
Nine Elms Ln.
Fulham Rd.
Edith Grove
Walk
Albert Bridge
12 26 34 56
Battersea Bridge
Battersea Bridge Rd.
Cheyne
Albert Bridge Rd.
Battersea Park

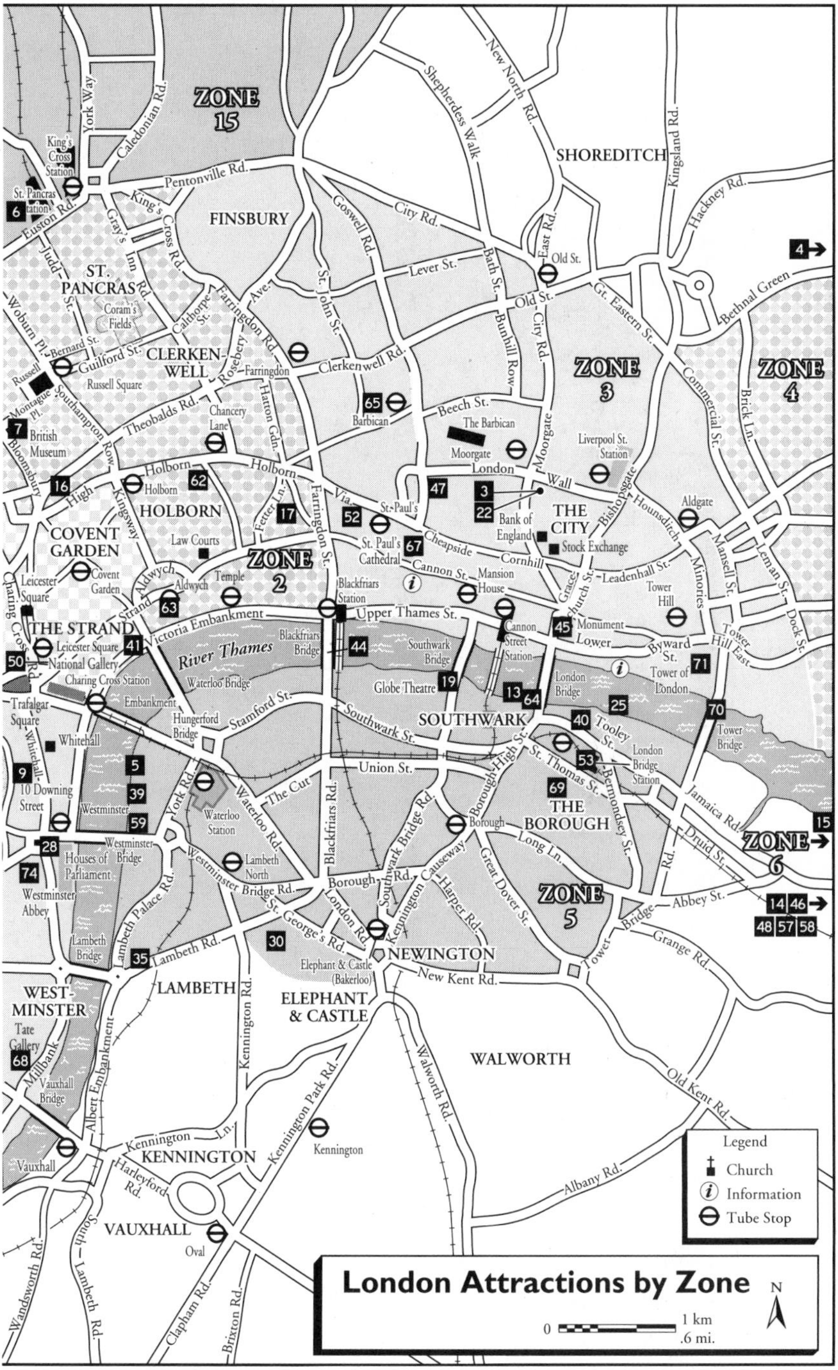
London Attractions by Zone
ZONE 15
ZONE 2
ZONE 3
ZONE 4
ZONE 5
ZONE 6
SHOREDITCH
FINSBURY
ST. PANCRAS
CLERKENWELL
HOLBORN
COVENT GARDEN
THE STRAND
THE CITY
SOUTHWARK
THE BOROUGH
NEWINGTON
ELEPHANT & CASTLE
LAMBETH
WESTMINSTER
WALWORTH
KENNINGTON
VAUXHALL
River Thames
King's Cross Station
St. Pancras Station
Euston Rd.
York Way
Caledonian Rd.
Pentonville Rd.
King's Cross Rd.
Gray's Inn Rd.
Judd St.
Woburn Pl.
Coram's Fields
Calthorpe St.
Farringdon Rd.
Rosebery Ave.
Goswell Rd.
St. John St.
City Rd.
Shepherdess Walk
New North Rd.
Kingsland Rd.
Hackney Rd.
East Rd.
Old St.
Lever St.
Bath St.
Bunhill Row
City Rd.
Gt. Eastern St.
Bethnal Green
Commercial St.
Brick Ln.
Bernard St.
Guilford St.
Russell Square
Russell
Montague Pl.
Southampton Row
British Museum
Bloomsbury
Theobalds Rd.
Chancery Lane
Farringdon
Clerkenwell Rd.
Hatton Gdn.
Barbican
Beech St.
The Barbican
Moorgate
Liverpool St. Station
London Wall
Holborn
High
Kingsway
Fetter Ln.
Farringdon St.
Via
St. Paul's
Bank of England
Bishopsgate
Houndsditch
Aldgate
Law Courts
St. Paul's Cathedral
Cheapside
Cornhill
Stock Exchange
Leadenhall St.
Minories
Mansell St.
Leman St.
Dock St.
Leicester Square
Covent Garden
Aldwych
Temple
Strand
Blackfriars Station
Cannon St.
Mansion House
Gracechurch St.
Tower Hill
Charing Cross Rd.
Victoria Embankment
Upper Thames St.
Cannon Street Station
Monument
Lower
Byward St.
Tower Hill East
Leicester Square
National Gallery
Blackfriars Bridge
Southwark Bridge
Tower of London
Charing Cross Station
Waterloo Bridge
Globe Theatre
London Bridge
Trafalgar Square
Embankment
Whitehall
Hungerford Bridge
Stamford St.
Southwark St.
Tooley St.
Tower Bridge
Union St.
High St.
St. Thomas St.
London Bridge Station
10 Downing Street
York Rd.
Waterloo Rd.
The Cut
Blackfriars Rd.
Southwark Bridge Rd.
Borough
Bermondsey St.
Jamaica Rd.
Westminster
Waterloo Station
Druid St.
Westminster Bridge
Houses of Parliament
Lambeth North
Long Ln.
Westminster Bridge Rd.
Borough Rd.
Kennington Causeway
Great Dover St.
Westminster Abbey
Lambeth Palace Rd.
St. George's Rd.
London Rd.
Harper Rd.
Abbey St.
Tower Bridge
Grange Rd.
Lambeth Bridge
Lambeth Rd.
Elephant & Castle (Bakerloo)
New Kent Rd.
Kennington Rd.
Tate Gallery
Millbank
Albert Embankment
Vauxhall Bridge
Walworth Rd.
Kennington Park Rd.
Old Kent Rd.
Kennington Ln.
Kennington
Vauxhall
Harleyford Rd.
Albany Rd.
Oval
Wandsworth Rd.
South Lambeth Rd.
Clapham Rd.
Brixton Rd.
Legend
Church
Information
Tube Stop
N
0
1 km
.6 mi.

LONDON ATTRACTIONS BY ZONE

1 Albert Memorial
2 Apsley House (The Wellington Museum)
3 Bank of England Museum
4 Bethnal Museum of Childhood
5 The British Airways London Eye
6 British Library at St. Pancras
7 British Museum
8 Buckingham Palace, the Queen's Gallery, and Royal Mews
9 The Cabinet War Rooms
10 Carlyle's Museum
11 Chelsea Physic Garden
12 Chiswick House
13 Clink Exhibition
14 *Cutty Sark*
15 Design Museum
16 Dickens House
17 Dr. Johnson's House
18 Freud Museum
19 The Globe Theater
20 Green Park
21 Guards Museum
22 Guildhall
23 Hampstead Heath
24 Hampstead Heath Pond
25 *HMS Belfast*
26 Hogarth's House
27 Holland Park
28 House of Parliament and Big Ben Clock Tower
29 Hyde Park
30 Imperial War Museum
31 Kensington Gardens
32 Kensington Palace State Rooms
33 Kenwood House
34 Kew Gardens
35 Lambeth Palace
36 Leighton House Museum & Gallery
37 The Lido
38 Linley Saunbourne House
39 London Aquarium
40 London Dungeon
41 London Transport Museum
42 London Zoo
43 Madame Tussaud's Waxworks
44 Millennium Bridge
45 The Monument
46 Museum of Docklands
47 Museum of London
48 Natinal Maritime Museums and Queen's House
49 National Gallery
50 National Portrait Gallery
51 Natural History Museum
52 Old Bailey
53 Old Operating Theatre, Museum, and Herb Garrett
54 Pollack's Toy Museum
55 Regent's Park
56 Richmond Park
57 Royal Greenwich Observatory
58 Royal Naval College
59 Saatchi Gallery
60 Science Museum
61 Sherlock Holmes Museum
62 Sir John Soane's Museum
63 Somerset House
64 Southwark Cathedral
65 St. Bartholomew the Great
66 St. James's Park
67 St. Paul's Cathedral
68 Tate Britan
69 Tate Gallery of Modern Art
70 Tower Bridge
71 Tower of London
72 Victoria and Albert Museum
73 Wallace Collection
74 Westminster Abbey

Walk past Buckingham Palace and head east through St. James's Park on Birdcage Walk, enjoying the views back across the pond to the palace. At the east end of the park you'll come to the Cabinet War Rooms, and just south, Westminster Abbey, Big Ben, and the Houses of Parliament.

Saving Money on Museum Admissions

London Pass, a program launched by the London Tourist Board in 1999, affords entry into more than 60 fee-charging attractions, free travel on tubes, trains, and buses, and a color guide to London. A one-day pass costs

£23 for adults and £15 for children; a two-day pass costs £36 for adults and £25 for children; a three-day pass costs £44 for adults and £29 for children; and a six-day pass costs £62 for adults and £41 for children. Now that so many London museums are free, we question how much the pass is really going to save you; you might want to buy a one- or two-day pass and concentrate on visiting fee-charging attractions on those days. Passes are available from offices of the London Tourist Board (see "Planning Your Visit to London, page 96) and from **www.londontown.com.**

HOW LONDON-AREA ATTRACTIONS COMPARE

Attraction	Comments	Author's Rating
London		
The British Museum	Colossal museum housing treasures of British empire	★★★★★
National Gallery	700 years of European painting	★★★★★
The National Portrait Gallery	The most famous faces in British history	★★★★★
Sir John Soane's Museum	Eccentric sculpture, art, and antiquities	★★★★★
Somerset House	Magnificent edifice and art galleries	★★★★★
The Tower of London	Ancient fortress on banks of the Thames	★★★★★
Victoria & Albert Museum	Decorative arts and design	★★★★★
British Library at St. Pancras	Collections formerly housed in British Museum	★★★★
The Globe Theatre	Magnificently reconstructed Shakespearean theater	★★★★
Kensington Palace State Rooms	Stately home in middle of Kensington Gardens	★★★★
Kenwood House (The Iveagh Bequest)	Georgian villa filled with art masterpieces	★★★★
London Transport Museum	Trams, buses, and trains of old and new London	★★★★
Museum of London	Thousands of years of London history	★★★★
Pollock's Toy Museum	Castle-like adventure into toys of the past	★★★★
Royal Academy of Arts	Summer Exhibition of contemporary artists	★★★★
Saatchi Gallery	Contemporary art	★★★★
The Science Museum	Scientific/technological odds and ends	★★★★
Tate Britain	English painters	★★★★
Tate Modern	International modern art	★★★★
The Wallace Collection	19th-century Anglo-French art	★★★★

HOW LONDON-AREA ATTRACTIONS COMPARE *(continued)*

Attraction	Comments	Author's Rating
***London** (continued)*		
Westminster Abbey	England's most historically important church	★★★★
The Cabinet War Rooms	World War II shelter for Winston Churchill and his cabinet	★★★½
Carlyle's House	Victorian home of Thomas Carlyle	★★★½
Linley Sambourne House	Perfectly preserved home of Victorians	★★★½
Natural History Museum	History of natural world	★★★½
St. Paul's Cathedral	London's most prominent cathedral	★★★½
The British Airways London Eye	World's biggest observation wheel	★★★
Freud Museum	English home of famous psychoanalyst	★★★
Leighton House Museum and Art Gallery	House of pre-Raphaelite painter	★★★
London Zoo	Modernized old zoo	★★★
Museum of Childhood at Bethnal Green	World's largest museum of toys	★★★
Old Operating Theatre, Museum, and Herb Garret	Old medical equipment and early Victorian operating theater	★★★
Buckingham Palace	Stately home of the Queen	★★½
Changing of the Guard	A London tradition	★★
Design Museum	Four floors featuring design of everyday items	★★
Dr. Johnson's House	Literary attraction in historic house	★★
Guildhall	Corporate headquarters for City of London	★★
Imperial War Museum	Highlights 20th-century British military actions	★★
London Aquarium	Wonderland of fish on bank of the Thames	★★
Madame Tussaud's	World-famous display of wax dummies	★★
Greenwich		
National Maritime Museum and Queen's House	World's largest maritime museum	★★★★
Cutty Sark	Restored clipper ship	★★★
Royal Greenwich Observatory	Location of the Prime Meridian	★★★
Royal Naval College	Renaissance architecture and interiors	★★★

HOW LONDON-AREA ATTRACTIONS COMPARE *(continued)*		Author's
Hampton Court		
Hampton Court Palace	London's most impressive royal palace	★★★★★
Royal Botanic Gardens at Kew		
Kew Gardens	Botanical extravaganza with 30,000 species of plants	★★★½
Windsor		
Windsor Castle	A royal residence	★★★★

Attraction Profiles

The British Airways London Eye — *Zone 5*

Type of Attraction The world's biggest observation wheel

Location In Jubilee Gardens, next to County Hall by Westminster and Hungerford Bridges, on the south bank of the Thames; tube: Westminster or Waterloo

Admission £11 adults; £10 seniors and the disabled; £5.50 children ages 5–16; free for children under age 5

Hours January–April: daily, 9:30 a.m.–8 p.m.; May and September: Monday–Thursday, 9:30 a.m.–8 p.m., Friday–Sunday, 9:30 a.m.–9 p.m.; June: Monday–Thursday, 9:30 a.m.–9 p.m., Friday–Sunday, 9:30 a.m.–10 p.m.; July–August: daily, 9:30 a.m.–10 p.m.; October–December, 9:30 a.m.–8 p.m.

Phone (0820) 500-0600

Website www.ba-londoneye.com

When to Go A sunny day or clear night

Special Comments This is not a trip for those suffering from vertigo; the Eye is handicapped-friendly.

Overall Appeal by Age Group

Preschool ★★★	Teens ★★★★	Over 30 ★★★
Grade school ★★★★★	Young Adults ★★★★	Seniors ★★★

Author's Rating ★★★

How Much Time to Allow If you haven't ordered tickets ahead of time, you may have to wait in line for as long as an hour, depending on the season and the weather. If you have reserved tickets by phone or on the Web, show up with your credit card and retrieve them from one of the handy machines; you must still wait about a half hour for boarding. The rotation takes 30 minutes.

Description & Comments Let's face it: When it comes to height, London isn't New York. Unlike an ascent to the top of the Empire State Building, which affords stunning views into the concrete canyons of Manhattan, a ride on the London Eye seems fairly mellow. Oh, it's perfectly pleasant looking over Westminster and the rest of London from 450 feet atop the Eye. There was never a view like this before the Eye went up as part of London's somewhat cursed Millennium celebrations, and the design—32 glass cabins carrying 25 people on a half-hour rotation—is ingenious. It's just that (and call us cranky) after about ten minutes, we begin to get a bit bored with the view and are eager to hit the streets again.

Touring Tips Combine your visit with a trip to the aquarium, the Globe, or any of the other South Bank attractions.

British Library at St. Pancras *Zone 15*

Type of Attraction New location of collections formerly housed in the British Museum

Location 96 Euston Road, NW1; tube: King's Cross

Admission Free

Hours Public areas open Monday and Wednesday–Friday, 9:30 a.m.–6 p.m.; Tuesday, 9:30 a.m.–8 p.m.; Saturday, 9:30 a.m.–5 p.m.; Sunday, 11 a.m.–5 p.m.

Phone (0207) 412-7000

Website www.bl.uk

When to Go Anytime

Special Comments Full wheelchair/disabled access

Overall Appeal by Age Group

Preschool —	Teens ★★	Over 30 ★★★
Grade school ★★	Young Adults ★★★	Seniors ★★★★

Author's Rating ★★★★

How Much Time to Allow 1 hour

Description & Comments Prince Charles scorned the exterior as "a collection of brick sheds groping for significance," but even he was impressed with the interior of this new home for the collections once housed in cramped quarters in the British Museum. The library shows off its treasures in three exhibition halls. The real trove is the John Riblat Gallery, where you can see the Lindisfarne Gospels from the tenth century, James Joyce's first draft of *Finnegan's Wake,* a copy of the Magna Carta from 1215, the Gutenberg Bible, documents related to Shakespeare, and the Magna Carta; here, too, you can listen to James Joyce and other writers read from their works.

Touring Tips Sign up for a guided tour to see the parts of the library not open to the public.

The British Museum *Zone 2*

Type of Attraction Colossal museum housing treasures of the British empire

Location Great Russell Street, WC1; tube: Tottenham Court Road

Admission Free

Hours Saturday–Wednesday, 10 a.m.–5:30 p.m.; Thursday and Friday, 10 a.m.–8:30 p.m.

Phone (0207) 323-8299 (information desk)

Website www.british-museum.ac.uk

When to Go Early mornings

Special Comments Obtain a leaflet from the information desk for details about wheelchair accessibility; wheelchairs are also available to borrow.

Overall Appeal by Age Group

Preschool ★★★★	Teens ★★★★★	Over 30 ★★★★★
Grade school ★★★★	Young Adults ★★★★★	Seniors ★★★★★

Author's Rating ★★★★★

How Much Time to Allow 2–4 hours

Description & Comments London's number-one tourist attraction houses more than 50,000 items in 100 galleries. The Rosetta Stone, the Lindow Man, the Egyptian mummies, and the Sutton Hoo treasures are the big stars, but you're bound to come across dozens of other curiosities among the clocks (high on our list of favorites), prehistoric tools, precious stones, and other displays that will stop you in your tracks. One of the most remarkable recent additions is the Queen Elizabeth II Great Court, the largest covered square in Europe, topped with more than 3,000 panes of glass surrounding what was once the domed Reading Room of the British Library (until it was removed to St. Pancras in 1997). The newest attraction, as of Fall 2003, are the Ethnography galleries.

Touring Tips The museum is far too big to try to cover in one visit, so consult the free handout map and pinpoint the galleries that might interest you. There's a good guidebook sold in the excellent bookstore. The museum has numerous gift shops and a restaurant at the top of the courtyard that lends wonderful views.

Buckingham Palace — *Zone 9*

Type of Attraction Stately home of the Queen

Location Buckingham Palace Road, SW1; tube: Green Park

Admission Palace: £12 adults; £6 children ages 5–16; free for children under age 5; £30 families. Royal Mews: £5 adults; £4 seniors and students; £2.50 children; £12.50 families. Queen's Gallery: £5 adults; £3 children

Hours Palace: August–September, daily, 9:30 a.m.–4:30 p.m. Royal Mews: October–July, daily, 11 a.m.–4 p.m.; August–September, daily, 10 a.m.–5 p.m. Queen's Gallery: daily, 10 a.m.–5:30 p.m. Closed between exhibitions, so call ahead.

Phone (0207) 799-2331 for recorded information; (0207) 321-2233 for credit-card ticket purchases; and (0207) 839-1377 for general inquiries/group booking

Website www.royal.gov.uk

When to Go If you purchase tickets for the palace visit from the ticket office in Green Park, go at 9 a.m. The lines are murder otherwise.

Special Comments Wheelchair users are required to arrange a visit to the palace in advance; the Royal Mews and Queen's Gallery are accessible to travelers with disabilities.

Overall Appeal by Age Group

Preschool ★	Teens ★★	Over 30 ★★★
Grade school ★★	Young Adults ★★★	Seniors ★★★

Author's Rating ★★½

Description & Comments Time was, the likes of us could never hope to set foot in Buckingham Palace. This is, after all, the private residence of the monarch, purchased by King George III in 1761 from the duke of Buckingham and, at the request of George IV, remodeled by John Nash in the grandiose style you see today. In 1996, Queen Elizabeth II decided to open some of the palace to the public to pay for the restoration of Windsor Castle, which was severely damaged by a fire in 1992. So, in August and September, more than 7,000 visitors a day troop past the Queen's paintings, sculpture, furniture, and decorative objects. It's quite a thrill to look into the surrounding gardens and parkland and enjoy the feeling of being in the country (as well as, of course, enjoying the voyeuristic pleasure of actually being in the Queen's house). Even when the palace is closed, you can still take a look at the stables in the Royal Mews—which, actually, are pretty palatial themselves, and the royal coaches, cars, and horses are magnificent. Another "outbuilding" is the Queen's Gallery, where selections from the massive royal holdings of Old Master and English paintings and drawings are on display.

The Cabinet War Rooms — *Zone 9*

Type of Attraction World War II shelter for Winston Churchill and his cabinet

Location Clive Steps, King Charles Street, SW1; tube: Westminster or St. James's Park

Admission £7 adults; £5.30 seniors and students; free for children under age 16; admission includes audio guide

Hours April–September: daily, 9:30 a.m.–5:15 p.m.; October–March: daily, 10 a.m.–5:15 p.m.

Phone (0207) 766-0120

Website www.iwm.org.uk, click on Cabinet War Rooms

When to Go Anytime

Special Comments Good disabled access, including wheelchairs on loan and accessible toilets

Overall Appeal by Age Group

Preschool ★	Teens ★★★	Over 30 ★★★
Grade school ★★	Young Adults ★★★	Seniors ★★★★

Author's Rating ★★★½

How Much Time to Allow 1 hour

Description & Comments During the six years of World War II, when Hitler's bombs rained with grim regularity on London, Winston Churchill met with his staff, heads of state, and military personnel in this subterranean bunker. Churchill made his historic broadcasts to buck up the public from these rooms, and many of the crucial decisions that won the war were made here. When the war ended, the lights were turned off and the door shut, and the rooms remained exactly as they were left until the 1980s, when they were opened to the public. As a result, from the sandbags that line the front of the shelter to the old telephones and notepaper on Churchill's desk, a visit provides a realistic experience of wartime Britain.

Touring Tips Combine a stop here with a visit to St. James's Park; the free self-guided audio tour is excellent.

Carlyle's House *Zone 11*

Type of Attraction Victorian home of Thomas Carlyle

Location 24 Cheyne Row, SW3; tube: Sloane Square

Admission £3.70 adults; £1.80 children under age 16

Hours April–October 31: Wednesday–Friday, 2–5 p.m.; Saturday–Sunday, 11 a.m.–5 p.m.

Phone (0207) 352-7087

Website www.nationaltrust.org.uk

When to Go Anytime it's open

Special Comments It's an old house with steep stairs; no wheelchair access.

Overall Appeal by Age Group

Preschool ★	Teens ★★	Over 30 ★★★
Grade school ★★	Young Adults ★★★	Seniors ★★★

Author's Rating ★★★½

How Much Time to Allow 60–90 minutes

Description & Comments Not only was Thomas Carlyle (1795–1881) a great essayist and historian, but his salon brought together luminaries such as Charles Dickens, George Eliot, Alfred Lord Tennyson, and Frederic Chopin, drawn as much by the sage of Chelsea's wisdom as by the famous wit of his wife, Jane. Since the house was made a museum only 15 years after Carlyle's death, there's an abundance of authentic minutiae—a hat hung on a hook, clothing in a drawer. All the furnishings are authentic, and the atmosphere is beyond the wildest dreams of a Victoriana-phile.

Touring Tips Be sure to walk around the neighborhood, where many other literary lions once lived.

Changing of the Guard *Zone 9*

Type of Attraction A London tradition

Location In the forecourt of Buckingham Palace, at the end of Pall Mall, SW1; tube: Green Park, then walk directly through the park to the palace

Admission Free

Hours April–July: daily at 11:30 a.m.; August–March: every other day at 11:30 a.m.

Phone (0207) 799-2331

Website www.royal.gov.uk

When to Go Arrive by 10:30 to get a good place by the railings or on the statue of Victoria, especially in the summer on a nice day

Special Comments The pageant is canceled in very wet weather.

Overall Appeal by Age Group

Preschool ★	Teens ★★	Over 30 ★★
Grade school ★★	Young Adults ★★	Seniors ★★

Author's Rating ★★

How Much Time to Allow The actual ceremony lasts 40 minutes, but if you want to get a good vantage point, you may want to show up an hour earlier.

Description & Comments The Queen's Guard, often accompanied by a band, leaves Wellington Barracks at 11:27 and marches along Birdcage Walk to the palace, where they . . . well, change. That's about all there is to the ceremony, though hordes of people stand around to watch.

Touring Tips If it's too crowded for you around the palace, go to the Horse Guards Parade on Horse Guards Parade Road, which is on the far eastern perimeter of St. James's Park (tube: Embankment or Charing Cross).

Design Museum — *Zone 5*

Type of Attraction Four floors featuring the design of everyday items

Location 28 Shad Thames, Butler's Wharf, SE1; tube: Tower Hill or London Bridge

Admission £6 adults; £4 seniors, students, and children ages 5–16; £16 families of up to two adults and two children

Hours Daily, 10 a.m.–5:45 p.m.

Phone (0207) 940-8790

Website www.designmuseum.org

When to Go Anytime

Special Comments Wheelchair/disabled accessible

Overall Appeal by Age Group

Preschool ★	Teens ★	Over 30 ★★
Grade school ★	Young Adults ★★	Seniors ★★

Author's Rating ★★

How Much Time to Allow 60–90 minutes

Description & Comments Homage is paid here to cars, office furniture, radios, TVs, household utensils, and other mass-produced, everyday items of the 20th century. They are part of a permanent collection that shares the modern, bright space with rotating exhibits.

Touring Tips Plan on coffee or a meal in the café or restaurant, which have splendid views of the Thames.

Freud Museum — *Zone 1*

Type of Attraction English home of famous psychoanalyst Sigmund Freud

Location 20 Maresfield Gardens, South Hampstead, NW3; tube: Finchley Road

Admission £5 adults; £2 seniors and students; free for children under age 12

Hours Wednesday–Sunday, noon–5 p.m.

Phone (0207) 435-2002

Website www.freud.org.uk

When to Go Anytime

Special Comments Limited access for disabled; no lift to upper floor

Overall Appeal by Age Group

Preschool ★	Teens ★	Over 30 ★★
Grade school ★	Young Adults ★★	Seniors ★★

Author's Rating ★★★

How Much Time to Allow 2 hours

Description & Comments The "father of psychoanalysis" lived in this house for the last year of his life, after he fled Vienna and the Nazis in 1938. His daughter, Anna Freud, lived here until her death in 1982, and on her request, the house is now a museum celebrating Freud's life and work. Rooms are decorated as they were in 1938, and possessions from the house in Vienna where Freud lived for half a century are here, too. The exhibition's centerpiece is Freud's library and study, including his famous analytic couch and numerous antiquities.

Touring Tips A 45-minute film, partially narrated by Anna Freud, contains silent black-and-white footage of Freud at home in Vienna as well as a description of the family's harrowing escape in 1938.

The Globe Theatre — *Zone 5*

Type of Attraction Magnificently reconstructed Shakespearean theater

Location New Globe Walk, Bankside, SE1; tube: Mansion House or London Bridge

Admission Globe Exhibition and guided tour: £8 adults, £6.50 seniors and students, £5.50 children ages 6–16; £24 families of up to two adults and three children. Prices for performances run from £5 (standing room) to £29 (tiered seating).

Hours October–April: daily, 10 a.m.–5 p.m.; May–September: daily, 9 a.m.–noon and 12:30–4 p.m. (no theater tours after noon in summer); check with the box office for performance times and dates

Phone (0207) 902-1500

Website www.shakespeares-globe.org

When to Go Anytime

Special Comments The exhibition is easily accessible for individuals in wheelchairs. The complex contains a café, as well as a more upscale restaurant with a view of the river and the City.

Overall Appeal by Age Group

Preschool ★	Teens ★★	Over 30 ★★★★
Grade school ★★	Young Adults ★★★	Seniors ★★★★

Author's Rating ★★★★

How Much Time to Allow 1–2 hours for museum and tour

Description & Comments Shakespeare made his literary name at this open-air theater, now faithfully restored. Actors who lead the tours are fountains of knowledge when it comes to Elizabethan theater, Shakespeare's life, and the London of his time. For more immersion in Shakespeareana, step into the Globe Exhibition beneath the theater, a fact-filled museum devoted to the life and times of the bard, as well as to the actors and the audiences who have made Shakespeare's plays so enduring. Performances run in the summer months, and are held outdoors, under natural light, as they used to be.

Touring Tips The best "seats" in the house are the standing area in front of the stage.

Guildhall — *Zone 3*

Type of Attraction Corporate headquarters for the City of London

Location Gresham Street; tube: St. Paul's, Mansion House, or Bank

Admission Free

Hours Guildhall: May–September, daily, 9:30 a.m.–5 p.m.; October–April, Monday–Saturday, 9:30 a.m.–5 p.m.; Art Gallery: Monday–Saturday, 10 a.m.–5 p.m., Sunday, noon–4 p.m.

Phone (0207) 606-3030

Website www.corpoflondon.gov.uk

When to Go Anytime

Special Comments Partial access for disabled

Overall Appeal by Age Group

Preschool ★	Teens ★★	Over 30 ★★
Grade school ★★	Young Adults ★★	Seniors ★★

Author's Rating ★★

How Much Time to Allow 60–90 minutes

Description & Comments Largely reconstructed after a World War II bombing, the Guildhall—seat of London's municipal government for more than 800 years—is the venue for official ceremonies, state banquets, and the annual installation of the lord mayor of London. Monuments honor national figures from the past three centuries, and banners of the 12 Great Livery Companies hang in the Hall. The small Clock Museum shows off more than 700 historic timepieces; choice selections from the Corporation of London's impressive collection of British art rotate in the Art Gallery; and the premises also include a small Roman amphitheater unearthed beneath the Guildhall yard in 1987.

Touring Tips The 15th-century crypt and 19th-century Old Library are generally off-limits to the public, but it is well worth asking if it might be possible to see them. Guided tours include these spots.

Imperial War Museum — *Zone 5*

Type of Attraction Highlights 20th-century British military actions

Location Lambeth Road, SE1; tube: Elephant and Castle or Lambeth North

Admission Free

Hours Daily, 10 a.m.–6 p.m.

Phone (0207) 416-5320

Website www.iwm.org.uk

When to Go Anytime

Special Comments Limited access for disabled; wheelchairs can be booked by calling (0207) 416-5397.

Overall Appeal by Age Group

Preschool ★	Teens ★★	Over 30 ★★★
Grade school ★★★	Young Adults ★★	Seniors ★★★

Author's Rating ★★

How Much Time to Allow 1 hour

Description & Comments Appropriately housed in the former lunatic asylum known as Bedlam, this museum is dedicated to 20th-century war. This is a sobering place, full of guns, tanks, zeppelins, V2 rockets, and bombers. There are vivid re-creations of the sights, sounds, and smells of the Blitz and the nightmare of life in a World War I trench, a clock counts down the numbers of war deaths in this century, and a new wing is dedicated to the Holocaust. On the grounds is a beautiful Peace Garden, which was dedicated by the Dalai Lama.

Dr. Johnson's House — *Zone 2*

Type of Attraction Literary attraction in historic house

Location 17 Gough Square, EC4; tube: Blackfriars

Admission £4 adults; £3 children ages 10–16; free for children under age 10; £9 families

Hours May–September: Monday–Saturday, 11 a.m.–5:30 p.m.; October—April: Monday–Saturday, 11 a.m.–5 p.m.

Phone (0207) 353-3745

Website www.drjh.dircon.co.uk

When to Go Anytime

Special Comments No wheelchair access; steep stairs

Overall Appeal by Age Group

Preschool ★★	Teens ★★	Over 30 ★★
Grade school ★★	Young Adults ★★	Seniors ★★

Author's Rating ★★

How Much Time to Allow 27 minutes for video, 20 minutes for house

Description & Comments Samuel Johnson, who claimed that to tire of London is to tire of life, spent 11 years in this house, the only one of his 17 London homes to survive. He worked on his famous dictionary in a garret here, and on the floors below are the doctor's furnishings and artifacts, as well as a collection of mezzotints and books on Johnson.

Touring Tips A video makes the remarkable Johnson and his biographer, Boswell, come to life.

Kensington Palace State Rooms — *Zone 13*

Type of Attraction Stately home in the middle of Kensington Gardens

Location Kensington Gardens, Broad Walk; tube: Kensington High Street

Admission £10.20 adults; £7.70 seniors and students; £6.60 children ages 5–16, free for children under age 5; £31 families of up to two adults and three children

Hours March–October 31: daily, 10 a.m.–5 p.m.; November–February: daily, 10 a.m.–4 p.m.

Phone (0870) 751-5170

Website www.hrp.org.uk

When to Go Mornings in summer; anytime in winter

Special Comments There are wheelchair-accessible toilets and a ramp to Orangery, but many steps inside the palace. Upstairs is inaccessible.

Overall Appeal by Age Group

Preschool ★★	Teens ★★★★	Over 30 ★★★★
Grade school ★★★	Young Adults ★★★★	Seniors ★★★★

Author's Rating ★★★★

How Much Time to Allow 60–90 minutes

Description & Comments Kensington Palace was the home of Diana, Princess of Wales, and Princess Victoria was born, baptized, and told that she had become queen here. Kensington is not a grandiose palace like Buckingham or Windsor, and it entered the roster of residences in 1689, when King William and Queen Mary began to use the estate as a country escape, hiring Christopher Wren and Nicholas Hawksmoor to make the necessary improvements. George I added most of the palatial elements; notice the difference between the simple oak-paneled dining room of William and Mary and the over-the-top decor of the innovations that architect William Kent provided for George. His son, George II, graced the gardens with Broad Walk, the Round Pond, the Serpentine, and other improvements we still enjoy today. In 1841, the gardens were opened to the public, and the palace became a source of "grace and favour," apartments for offshoots of the royal family, as it remains. Among the memories of Diana you'll encounter here are some of her dresses, which are a much-admired part of the Royal Ceremonial Dress Collection.

Touring Tips Take advantage of the informative audio tour, and follow up a visit with tea in the Orangery.

Kenwood House (The Iveagh Bequest) *Zone 1*

Type of Attraction Georgian villa filled with art masterpieces

Location Hampstead Lane, Hampstead Heath, NW3; tube: Archway or Golders Green

Admission Free

Hours April–September: daily, 10 a.m.–5:30 p.m.; October: daily, 10 a.m.–5 p.m.; November–March: daily, 10 a.m.–4 p.m.

Phone (0208) 348-1286

Website www.english-heritage.org.uk

When to Go Anytime, but preferably on weekdays and in good weather so you can enjoy the Heath

Special Comments Call (0207) 973-3372 to arrange limited wheelchair access.

Overall Appeal by Age Group

Preschool ★	Teens ★★★	Over 30 ★★★
Grade school ★★★	Young Adults ★★★	Seniors ★★★

Author's Rating ★★★★

How Much Time to Allow 2 hours in the house

Description & Comments Kenwood is the most elegant exponent of architects Robert and James Adams's early Georgian design. Built in 1700, the house changed hands several times, until brewery magnate Edward Guinness, earl of Iveagh, purchased it to display his extensive collection of 17th-century Dutch and Flemish and late-18th-century British paintings, including works by Sir Joshua Reynolds, George Romney, J. M. W. Turner, and Thomas Gainsborough. Among the old masterpieces here are Rembrandt's *Self Portrait* and Vermeer's *The Guitar Player.*

Touring Tips Combine this visit with a trip to Hampstead Village and the Heath.

Leighton House Museum and Art Gallery *Zone 13*

Type of Attraction House of pre-Raphaelite painter Lord Frederick Leighton

Location 12 Holland Park Road; tube: High Street Kensington, then bus 9, 10, 27, 33, or 49 to Odeon Cinema, then walk through Holland Park

Admission Free; £3 for audio tour

Hours Monday–Saturday, 11 a.m.–5:30 p.m.; Tuesday, closed

Phone (0207) 602-3316

Website www.rbkc.gov.uk/leightonhousemuseum

When to Go Anytime

Special Comments Not wheelchair accessible; many steps to top floor

Overall Appeal by Age Group

Preschool ★	Teens ★★	Over 30 ★★
Grade school ★	Young Adults ★★	Seniors ★★

Author's Rating ★★★

How Much Time to Allow 30 minutes

Description & Comments The pre-Raphaelite painter Frederick Leighton, whose magnificent painted hallway can be seen in the Victoria & Albert Museum, dedicated his home as "a private palace devoted to art." The main attraction is the Arab Hall, a Victorian fantasy of the Middle East straight out of the pages of *The Arabian Nights,* with Isniuk tiles, elaborately carved and gilded woodwork, mosaics, and a sunken fountain. The top floor is Leighton's old studio, and the huge windows, skylights, and dome are clearly the heart's desire of any 19th-century painter. There's a good collection of Victorian paintings on the lower floor, including Leighton's *Roman Mother.*

Touring Tips Combine this with a trip to Holland Park and the Linley Sambourne House.

Linley Sambourne House — *Zone 14*

Type of Attraction Perfectly preserved home of Victorians

Location 18 Stafford Terrace, Kensington, W8; tube: High Street Kensington

Admission £6 adults; £4 seniors and students, free for children under age 18

Hours Saturday and Sunday, guided tours at 10 a.m., 11:15 p.m., 1 p.m., 2:15 p.m., 3:30 p.m.

Phone (0207) 602-3316

Website www.rbkc.gov.uk/linleysambournehouse

When to Go Anytime it's open

Special Comments Lots of stairs and no wheelchair access

Overall Appeal by Age Group

Preschool ★	Teens ★★	Over 30 ★★★
Grade school ★★	Young Adults ★★★	Seniors ★★★

Author's Rating ★★★½

How Much Time to Allow 1 hour

Description & Comments *Punch* cartoonist Linley Sambourne and his family moved into this commodious house in 1874, and the place is a shrine to the late Victorian/early Edwardian era. All the fittings and furnishings are intact, and the sumptuous clutter includes ornate furnishings, clocks, vases, and knickknacks. William Morris designs adorn both walls and floors, and there are some sumptuous stained-glass windows. The house reopened in April 2003 after being closed for conservation for two years, so this homage to a domestic lifestyle long since vanished is once again a popular Kensington attraction.

Touring Tips Combine with a trip to Holland Park and/or to the Leighton House Museum.

London Aquarium — *Zone 5*

Type of Attraction Wonderland of fish on the bank of the Thames

Location County Hall, Riverside Building, Westminster Bridge Road, SE1; tube: Westminster or Waterloo

Admission £8.75 adults; £6.50 seniors and students; £5.25 children; free for children under age 3; £25 families

Hours Daily, 10 a.m.–6 p.m. (last entry at 5 p.m.)

Phone (0207) 967-8000

Website www.londonaquarium.co.uk

When to Go Avoid weekends and school holidays if possible; go early

Special Comments Fully accessible for disabled persons. To avoid steps, go around building to Belvedere Road to reach entrance. Picnic area available.

Overall Appeal by Age Group

Preschool ★★★★	Teens ★★★	Over 30 ★★
Grade school ★★★★	Young Adults ★★★	Seniors ★★

Author's Rating ★★

How Much Time to Allow 2 hours

Description & Comments If you live in North America, you've probably visited more elaborate and exciting aquariums. Even so, kids love wandering through these three dimly lit floors where enormous tanks are brimming with sea life and freshwater fish of every kind. Young visitors especially enjoy the petting pool, where they can stroke manta rays, and the piranha tank is a big hit at feeding time.

Touring Tips There's a McDonald's next door, with its own entrance to the aquarium. There's also a wonderful gift shop.

London Transport Museum — *Zone 7*

Type of Attraction A fun, interactive museum of trams, buses, and trains of old and new London

Location 39 Wellington Street, off Covent Garden Piazza, WC2; tube: Covent Garden, Leicester Square

Admission £5.95 adults; free for children

Hours Saturday–Thursday, 10 a.m.–6 p.m.; Friday, 11 a.m.–6 p.m.

Phone (0207) 379-6344

Website www.ltmuseum.co.uk

When to Go Anytime

Special Comments Wheelchair and stroller access; café and gift shop where you can find just about anything, even slippers, emblazoned with Underground maps

Overall Appeal by Age Group

Preschool ★★★★	Teens ★★★	Over 30 ★★★
Grade school ★★★★	Young Adults ★★★	Seniors ★★★

Author's Rating ★★★★

How Much Time to Allow 1 hour

Description & Comments This is one of the best venues for kids in London, and adults love it, too. And why not, when there are horse-drawn stagecoaches and omnibuses that you can climb on, buses on which you can sit behind the wheel, and switches you can pretend to throw to direct the Underground? Among the exhibits are excellent videos of old-time trams and buses and a wonderful short film on the touching last trip of the last tram in London, with everyone singing "Auld Lang Syne."

Touring Tips Buy the museum guide if you have children under age 12—there's a fun pull-out section with games and educational pursuits. Combine a trip here with a visit to Covent Garden, also fun for the kids. Call or visit the museum website to check for lectures, tours, films, and family activities.

London Zoo — *Zone 15*

Type of Attraction Modernized old zoo set at the edge of Regent's Park

Location Regent's Park; tube: Camden Town

Admission £12 adults; £10.20 seniors and students; £9 children ages 3–15; £38 families of one adult and three children or two adult and two children

Hours Mid-March–late October: Monday–Saturday, 10 a.m.–5:30 p.m.; late October–mid-February: Monday–Saturday, 10 a.m.–4 p.m.; mid-February–mid-March, Monday–Saturday, 10 a.m.–4:30 p.m.

Phone (0207) 722-3333

Website www.zsl.org

When to Go When it's warm and not raining

Special Comments Wheelchair access

Overall Appeal by Age Group

Preschool ★★★★	Teens ★★★	Over 30 ★★★
Grade school ★★★★	Young Adults ★★★	Seniors ★★★

Author's Rating ★★★

How Much Time to Allow 2 hours

Description & Comments The London Zoo puts great emphasis on educating the public about endangered species, houses 150 threatened species, has a world-renowned breeding program, and celebrates biodiversity in the wonderful Millennium Conservation Centre. Opened in 1828, the zoo has also done an admirable job of being a fun spot for an outing, and these days it counts among its most popular attractions a magnificent reptile house, a penguin pool, and extensive petting zoo.

Touring Tips The shop is fantastic and will fulfill all your animal-paraphernalia needs, with books, stuffed animals, and knickknacks.

Madame Tussaud's — *Zone 14*

Type of Attraction World-famous display of wax dummies

Location Marylebone Road, NW1; tube: Baker Street

Admission £18.95 adults; £14.80 seniors; £14 children under age 16; free for children age 4 and under. Includes admission to London Planetarium show.

Hours May–September: daily, 9 a.m.–5:30 p.m.; October–April: Monday–Friday, 10 a.m.–5:30 p.m., Saturday–Sunday, 9:30 a.m.–5:30 p.m.

Phone (0870) 400-3000 to book tickets in advance and avoid the queue (for £1 extra on each ticket) or (0207) 935-6861

Website www.madame-tussauds.com

When to Go They advise that you go in the afternoon, but there always seems to be a line there, no matter what the time, even a half hour before it opens. Go a day before or book over the phone and get a ticket so you can get in the prepaid line. Forget the weekends.

Special Comments Limited wheelchair access: call in advance, (0207) 935-6861

Overall Appeal by Age Group

Preschool ★★	Teens ★★★	Over 30 ★★
Grade school ★★★	Young Adults ★★★	Seniors ★★

Author's Rating ★★

How Much Time to Allow 1 hour

Description & Comments The young Marie Grosholtz Tussaud got her start making death masks of aristocrats during the French Revolution, and the training has paid off—just look at the lines outside this perennially popular attraction. Why folks are so eager to get inside is a mystery to us, because nothing here is particularly appealing—not the ride through London history in a miniature black taxi traveling at breakneck speed, not the waxy celebs we are tired of looking at anyway, and certainly not the truly tasteless Chamber of Horrors; in a weird juxtaposition that somehow captures the character of this creepy place, you are moved from this stomach-turning exhibit straight into the café. The admission fee includes a 20-minute film (and another wait to see it) projected onto the dome of the London Planetarium; you won't be missing much if you decide to leave without seeing this rather shallow introduction to the heavens.

Touring Tips Book a ticket in advance by phone or in person, so that you can avoid the lines, or at least minimize waiting time.

Museum of Childhood at Bethnal Green *Zone 4*

Type of Attraction Largest museum of toys in the world

Location Cambridge Heath Road, E2; tube: Bethnal Green

Admission Free; play area, £1.80

Hours Saturday–Thursday, 10 a.m.–5:50 p.m.

Phone (0208) 980-2415 (recording); (0208) 983-5200 (duty officer)

Website www.museumofchildhood.org.uk

When to Go Anytime

Special Comments Call ahead to arrange wheelchair access (phone (0208) 983-5205). Art workshops for children over age 3 and a soft play area for children ages 5 and under are available only on weekends.

Overall Appeal by Age Group

Preschool ★★★	Teens ★★★	Over 30 ★★★
Grade school ★★★	Young Adults ★★★	Seniors ★★★

Author's Rating ★★★

How Much Time to Allow 90 minutes

Description & Comments The Museum of Childhood is a branch of the Victoria & Albert Museum and houses an unparalleled collection of children's toys and accessories: dollhouses from as far back as the 17th century, model trains, hobby horses, old mechanical games and toys, dolls of every possible kind, teddy bears, and old-fashioned prams and nursery furniture. Not surprisingly, these curiosities often seem to be of more interest to adults than to the kids they have in tow—you might want to think of setting yours free in the play area, open weekends and school holidays.

Museum of London — *Zone 3*

Type of Attraction Museum covering thousands of years of London history

Location London Wall and Aldersgate; tube: St. Paul's or Barbican

Admission Free

Hours Monday–Saturday, 10 a.m.–5:50 p.m., Sunday, noon–5:50 p.m.

Phone (0207) 600-3699 or (0207) 600-0870

Website www.museumoflondon.org.uk

When to Go Anytime, although you may be navigating around large groups of schoolchildren if you go too early on weekdays while school is in session; after 2:30 p.m., they're gone.

Special Comments Good handicapped accessibility, with a number of ramps and lifts for all floors.

Overall Appeal by Age Group

Preschool ★★	Teens ★★★★	Over 30 ★★★★
Grade school ★★★★	Young Adults ★★★★	Seniors ★★★★

Author's Rating ★★★

How Much Time to Allow 2–3 hours

Description & Comments If you are even slightly interested in London's history, this museum is a must-see; if you're not, you will be after you view the new London Before London exhibit, take a good look at the large section of London's fourth-century town wall, see the gilded Lord Mayor's coach, and walk through Victorian shops. Even the hokey re-creation of the Great Fire is riveting, and the real cell from Newgate Prison is downright chilling. The gift shop has a huge assortment of books on London and English history for all ages. There's a good café, too.

Touring Tips Call ahead to find out how many schools are booked to visit the day of your visit—if the place is going to be inundated, come after 2:30 p.m.

National Gallery — *Zone 7*

Type of Attraction Splendid art gallery of 700 years of European painting

Location Trafalgar Square, WC2; tube: Leicester Square or Charing Cross

Admission Free, though there is a charge for special exhibits

Hours Monday, Tuesday, Thursday–Sunday, 10 a.m.–6 p.m.; late view, Wednesday, 10 a.m.–9 p.m.

Phone (0207) 747-2885

Website www.nationalgallery.org.uk

When to Go Anytime, but avoid major exhibits on weekends

Special Comments Wheelchair accessible

Overall Appeal by Age Group

Preschool ★	Teens ★★★	Over 30 ★★★★★
Grade school ★★★	Young Adults ★★★★★	Seniors ★★★★★

Author's Rating ★★★★★

How Much Time to Allow As much as you can manage

Description & Comments This is our favorite place to spend a rainy day in London. The museum contains many of the great art treasures of Britain, and it shows them in pleasant surroundings that are conducive to serious art appreciation. Founded in 1824 under King George IV, when the government purchased 38 paintings by such artists as Raphael, Van Dyck, and Rembrandt from the estate of John Julius Angerstein, the museum now houses 2,300 works from 700 years of European art. Holbein's *The Ambassadors,* Van Gogh's *Sunflowers,* and Monet's *Water Lily Pond* are among the museum's big crowd pleasers, but a walk through any gallery is rewarding (we suggest you grab a floor plan from the information desk and head to the galleries most likely to interest you, then amble through the rest of the museum at your leisure). The new Sainsbury Wing houses the oldest paintings, dating from 1260 to 1510, among them Jan Van Eyck's *Arnolfini Marriage.* The West Wing has paintings dating from 1510 to 1600, including Tintoretto's *St. George and the Dragon.* The North Wing has paintings from 1600 to 1700, including works by Rembrandt and Vermeer; and the East Wing takes us up to 1920, with works by Canaletto, Turner, Gainsborough, and the ever popular Impressionists, who are represented here by Rousseau's *Tropical Storm with Tiger,* Renoir's *Umbrellas,* and Van Gogh's *Chair.* The museum has just begun major renovations that will include one of those glassed-in courtyards that are all the rage in museums these days, but most galleries will remain open during the work.

Touring Tips Take advantage of the guides and recorded tours and lectures; they are excellent. The Pret a Manger in the basement serves (relatively) inexpensive sandwiches and salads, and a restaurant in the Sainsbury Wing serves full meals. The gift shops sell an enticing selection of books, postcards, and calendars.

The National Portrait Gallery — *Zone 7*

Type of Attraction Collection of the most famous faces in British history

Location 2 St. Martin's Place, W2; adjacent to the National Gallery; tube: Leicester Square or Charing Cross

Admission Free (except for special exhibitions)

Hours Monday–Wednesday, Saturday, and Sunday, 10 a.m.–6 p.m.; Thursday and Friday, 10 a.m.–9 p.m.

Phone (0207) 306-0055

Website www.npg.org.uk

When to Go Anytime

Special Comments Very accessible to disabled individuals

Overall Appeal by Age Group

Preschool ★	Teens ★★★★	Over 30 ★★★★
Grade school ★★	Young Adults ★★★★	Seniors ★★★★

Author's Rating ★★★★★

How Much Time to Allow 2–3 hours

Description & Comments If you have any stamina left after a visit to the National Gallery, pop around the corner for a look at this Who's Who of British history. Take the escalator to the top floor, where you'll encounter the lean faces of the early medieval kings and Henry VIII (and his many wives). As you walk down through the newly refurbished galleries, you'll come to Dickens and other Victorians, and, finally, on the ground floor, to portraits and photos of the current royal family. With the help of the audio guides, the amount of history you absorb will change how you perceive London's most famous sights.

Touring Tips The top-floor restaurant offers glorious views over Trafalgar Square, and there is a café in the basement.

Natural History Museum — *Zone 11*

Type of Attraction Exhibits on the history of the natural world

Location Cromwell Road, South Kensington, SW7; tube: South Kensington

Admission Free

Hours Monday–Saturday, 10 a.m.–5:50 p.m.; Sunday, 11 a.m.–5:50 p.m.

Phone (0207) 942-5000 weekdays, (0207) 942-5011 weekends

Website www.nhm.ac.uk

When to Go Anytime during the weekdays, although watch out for lines of buses along Cromwell Road, which indicate hordes of schoolkids; weekends can be quite crowded, so go early

Special Comments Complete disabled access

Overall Appeal by Age Group

Preschool ★★★	Teens ★★★	Over 30 ★★★
Grade school ★★★★	Young Adults ★★★	Seniors ★★★

Author's Rating ★★★½

How Much Time to Allow 2 hours or more

Description & Comments There's plenty of flash in this grand old institution, founded around the collections of Sir Hans Sloane in the 1860s. You can walk through a rain forest in the Ecology Gallery, ride an escalator through a model of the earth to enter the Earth Galleries, and cower beneath life-size models of blue whales and dinosaurs. At its core, though, the museum is a repository of scientific specimens, many of them brought back from the far-flung reaches of the empire, and the museum is currently renovating galleries to show off these invaluable items. The new Darwin Centre displays some 20 million zoological specimens, from the now-extinct dodo bird to butterflies, displayed in cabinets, glass jars, and huge tanks. Next on tap, scheduled to open in 2007, are halls housing equally sizable collections of plants and insects.

Touring Tips Be sure to look at the entire front of the building on Cromwell Road, where the facade is graced with statues of animals. If the line at the Cromwell Road entrance is long, enter at the Earth Galleries on Exhibition Road. Once inside, try to join one of the hourly tours.

Old Operating Theatre, Museum, and Herb Garret — *Zone 5*

Type of Attraction Haunting museum of old medical equipment and an early Victorian operating theater

Location Zone 5; 9A St. Thomas's Street, SE1; tube: London Bridge

Admission £4 adults; £3 seniors and students; £2.50 children under age 16; £10 families

Hours Daily, 10:30 a.m.–5 p.m.

Phone (0207) 955-4791

Website www.thegarret.org.uk

When to Go Anytime

Special Comments The stairs in this old house are very, very steep. There is no wheelchair access.

Overall Appeal by Age Group

Preschool †	Teens ★★	Over 30 ★★★
Grade school ★	Young Adults ★★★	Seniors ★★★

† *Not appropriate for preschoolers.*

Author's Rating ★★★

How Much Time to Allow 1 hour

Description & Comments Climb the spiral staircase and you'll be confronted with a reason to be glad you didn't live in the early 19th century—the old operating theater of St. Thomas Hospital. A wooden table, a box of sawdust to mop up the blood, and displays of massive forceps and amputation knives provide a look at early surgery, while a fragrant herb garret filled with comfrey, penny royal, willow bark, and elderflowers represents the medical arsenal of the day.

Touring Tips Include this museum with a trip to Southwark.

Pollock's Toy Museum — *Zone 14*

Type of Attraction Castle-like adventure into toys of the past

Location 1 Scala Street, W1P; tube: Goodge Street

Admission £3 adults; £1.50 children

Hours Monday–Saturday, 10 a.m.–5 p.m.

Phone (0207) 636-3452

Website www.pollocks.cwc.net

When to Go Anytime, but call and check to see if a school group is planned.

Special Comments This museum consists of six rooms on three floors connected by very steep stairs; it is not disabled or wheelchair accessible. Sometimes the museum presents puppet shows—call ahead to see if you can time your visit to coincide with one.

Overall Appeal by Age Group

Preschool ★★	Teens ★★★	Over 30 ★★★★
Grade school ★★★★	Young Adults ★★★	Seniors ★★★★

Author's Rating ★★★★

How Much Time to Allow 1 hour

Description & Comments Benjamin Pollock's famous toy theaters of the 19th century are the centerpiece of this museum, but just as enticing are the rocking horses, American automatic money boxes, magic lanterns, jack-in-the-boxes, toy soldiers, folk dolls from around the world, dollhouse rooms, puppets, and teddy bears. Refreshingly, there's not an interactive display in sight, just old-fashioned toys charmingly displayed. There's a shop on the ground floor with books, toy reproductions, and other fun stuff.

Touring Tips Kids will appreciate a stop here after a romp through the nearby British Museum.

Royal Academy of Arts — *Zone 8*

Type of Attraction Venue for the world-famous Summer Exhibition of contemporary artists and a small collection of past academicians

Location Burlington House, Piccadilly, W1; tube: Piccadilly Circus, Green Park

Admission £6–£8, depending on exhibition

Hours Saturday–Thursday, 10 a.m.–6 p.m.; Friday, 10 a.m.–10 p.m.

Phone (0207) 300-8000 (recording); (0207) 300-5760 or (0207) 300-5761

Website www.royalacademy.org.uk

When to Go The biggest crowds will be when there's a very popular exhibition; weekends are normally crowded. Go in the morning if possible.

Special Comments Wheelchair access

Overall Appeal by Age Group

Preschool ★	Teens ★★★	Over 30 ★★★★
Grade school ★	Young Adults ★★★★	Seniors ★★★★

Author's Rating ★★★★

How Much Time to Allow About 2 hours

Description & Comments Founded by Thomas Gainsborough and Joshua Reynolds, among others, in 1768, England's first art school is still sacred ground in much of the British art world. A permanent collection includes works from past academicians, as well as a Michelangelo marble frieze of the Madonna and child. But what really brings the crowds here to beautiful old Burlington House are stunning temporary exhibitions and the 200-year-old Summer Exhibition, in which painters and sculptors from throughout Britain compete for the honor of displaying their work in these hallowed halls.

Touring Tips Call or check the website for the dates of the Summer Exhibition and special exhibitions.

Saatchi Gallery — *Zone 5*

Type of Attraction Gallery of contemporary art

Location County Hall, Westminster Bridge Road SE1; tube: Westminster or Waterloo

Admission £8.50 adults; £6.50 seniors and students

Hours Sunday–Thursday, 10 a.m.–6 p.m.; Friday and Saturday, 10 a.m.–10 p.m.

Phone (0207) 823-2363

Website www.saatchi-gallery.co.uk

When to Go A visit on Friday or Saturday evening is a nice way to begin a night on the town.

Special Comments Some of the material is gruesome and sexually provocative.

Overall Appeal by Age Group

Preschool †	Teens †	Over 30 ★★★★
Grade school †	Young Adults ★★★★	Seniors ★★★:

† *Many of the exhibits may be upsetting to young children, and you might want to exercise caution in exposing younger teens to some of the works.*

Author's Rating ★★★★

How Much Time to Allow About 3 hours

Description & Comments The newest attraction on the trendy South Bank is this collection of contemporary British art, collected by advertising czar Charles Saatchi and hanging in grandiose Edwardian surroundings that once housed the London government. We'll let the art critics debate the relative merits of some of the works here, especially the dead critters, blood, and sexually provocative images by such artists as the omnipresent Damien Hirst; we'll simply say that it's wonderful to see so much contemporary art made so readily accessible. Visitors from the United States might remember that some of the pieces here, including Chris Ofili's *Holy Virgin Mary,* were not well received on American soil—they were condemned by Rudolph Giuliani, then-mayor of New York, when they were included in a show at the Brooklyn Museum of Art.

Touring Tips For another look at contemporary art, walk down the Thames and take a look at the Tate Modern, too.

St. Paul's Cathedral — *Zone 3*

Type of Attraction London's most prominent cathedral

Location Ludgate Hill, EC4; tube: St. Paul's or Mansion House

Admission Cathedral, galleries, and crypt entry: £6 adults; £5 seniors and students; £3 children. Self-guided tours (with cassette) and guided tours are also available.

Hours Visitors to cathedral: Monday–Saturday, 8:30 a.m.–4 p.m.; choral evensong occurs weekdays at 5 p.m. and Sunday at 3:15 p.m.

Phone (0207) 236-4128

Website www.stpauls.co.uk

When to Go Early in the day on weekdays to avoid the crowds and catch the best chances for clear-sky views from the dome

Special Comments Good disabled access to cathedral's nave and crypt, but there is no lift access to the galleries.

Overall Appeal by Age Group

Preschool ★	Teens ★★	Over 30 ★★★
Grade school ★★	Young Adults ★★★	Seniors ★★★★

Author's Rating ★★★½

How Much Time to Allow 30 minutes to 1 hour, depending on whether you plan to climb to the top of the dome

Description & Comments A Roman temple to the goddess Diana once stood here, and Viking raids, lightning strikes, and fires laid waste to the churches that followed it. Most notable of these catastrophes was the Great Fire of 1666: Christopher Wren was put in charge of rebuilding the cathedral, which became his masterpiece (as well as his final resting place; Lord Admiral Horatio Nelson and the Duke of Wellington are buried here, too). The stone English baroque–style edifice is now dwarfed by skyscrapers but is still a majestic presence. The dome is one of the highest in the world, at 360 feet, and second in size only to St. Peter's Basilica in Rome. After taking a look at the mosaics, frescoes, and choir-stall carvings designed by master craftsman Grinling Gibbons, climb the 530 steps to the open-air Golden Gallery for stunning views of London (take a breather on the way up in the Whispering Gallery, where a whisper uttered into one side of the dome will be heard on the other side).

Touring Tips Other nearby Wren churches include St. Mary-le-Bow (Cheapside), St. Bride's (Fleet Street), and the tower of Christ Church (Newgate Street).

The Science Museum — *Zone 11*

Type of Attraction Abundant collection of scientific/technological odds and ends that add up to a fascinating experience

Location Exhibition Road, SW7; tube: South Kensington

Admission Free

Hours Daily, 10 a.m.–6 p.m.

Phone (0870) 870-4771

Website www.sciencemuseum.org.uk

When to Go Avoid school holidays and weekends, unless you're there at 10 a.m. It's one of London's most popular museums, so go early or on weekdays.

Special Comments Good wheelchair and disabled access

Overall Appeal by Age Group

Preschool ★★★★	Teens ★★★★	Over 30 ★★★
Grade school ★★★★	Young Adults ★★★★	Seniors ★★★

Author's Rating ★★★★

How Much Time to Allow As much as you can spare—you could easily spend all day here, there's so much to see. If you're there with children who want to play in the interactive areas, plan to spend at least three hours.

Description & Comments The Science Museum seems to keep getting bigger and bigger (a recent expansion added a whole new wing), but after all, you need a lot of space to show off rockets, missiles, and spacecraft. Despite flashy shows of technology and re-creations of space and the lunar surface, the museum also takes you back to simpler times—there's a great display of early hourglasses, and the huge mill engine in the middle of the East Hall is practically a London landmark. If you have little ones with you, head downstairs to the hands-on gallery, where kids can build things with giant Legos and play with trucks and trolleys.

Touring Tips If you arrive and find a line, go across the street to the Victoria & Albert Museum or the Natural History Museum, and come back late in the afternoon when the families have left.

Sir John Soane's Museum — *Zone 2*

Type of Attraction Fascinating, eccentric collection of sculpture, art, and antiquities belonging to neoclassical architect Sir John Soane

Location 13 Lincoln's Inn Fields, WC2; tube: Holborn, Central line

Admission Free; tours, £3

Hours Tuesday–Saturday, 10 a.m.–5 p.m.; first Tuesday of each month, also 6 p.m.–9 p.m.

Phone (0207) 405-2107

Website www.soane.org

When to Go Anytime, although there is an excellent tour of the museum on Saturday at 2:30 p.m., which is limited to 20 people; arrive early to secure a spot.

Special Comments The museum is not handicapped accessible and is not recommended for very young children with the tendency to touch everything.

Overall Appeal by Age Group

Preschool †	Teens ★★★	Over 30 ★★★★
Grade school ★	Young Adults ★★★★★	Seniors ★★★★★

† *Not appropriate for young children*

Author's Rating ★★★★★

How Much Time to Allow 1½–2½ hours

Description & Comments Sir John Soane, one of London's great late-18th, early-19th-century architects, did some major remodeling when he bought the Georgian homes at 12, 13, and 14 Lincoln's Inn Fields. He added a glass-domed roof and central atrium; a mock medieval monk's parlor containing gloomy casts and gargoyles; a sarcophagus of Seti I surrounded by rows of antique statuary; and an impressive picture gallery of false and hidden walls. Saturday's hour-long tour takes you through all of this and into number 12 as well, where you can see Soane's enormous research library, complete with architectural plans for the Bank of England and Whitehall, and numerous models of Pompeiian temples.

Touring Tips If you can't manage the Saturday tour, definitely strike up a conversation with any of the museum curators.

Somerset House — *Zone 2*

Type of Attraction Magnificent edifice with river views, a classical courtyard, a river terrace, and three separate art galleries

Location Strand, WC; tube: Covent Garden; Temple (except on Sunday)

Admission Free for Somerset house and grounds. Courtauld Institute Gallery: £5 adults; £4 seniors and students; free for children under age 18; free on Monday, 10 a.m.–2 p.m. Gilbert Collection: £5 adults; £4 seniors and students; free for children under age 18 (an audio guide and magnifying glass are included in the price). Combined admission adult tickets for the Courtauld Gallery and Gilbert collection are £7. Hermitage Rooms: £6 adults; £4 seniors and students; free for children under age 18.

Hours Somerset House and all galleries are open daily, 10 a.m.–6 p.m.; during the summer, the house itself and its terrace and courtyard stay open on Friday till 10 p.m.

Phone Somerset: (0207) 845 4600; Courtauld: (0207) 848-2526; Gilbert: 020 7420 9400; Hermitage: (0207) 845 4630

Website www.somerset-house.org.uk; www.courtauld.ac.uk; www.gilbert-collection.org.uk; www.hermitagerooms.com

When to Go On a sunny day to enjoy courtyard, with a spectacular fountain, and the riverside terrace

Special Comments The house and the galleries are all wheelchair accessible. Because the Hermitage Rooms are small, the tickets are sold for timed slots, on the hour and on the half hour; about 60 at a time can go in. Check the Hermitage website to be sure they are not in the middle of staging a new exhibit.

Overall Appeal by Age Group

Preschool ★★★	Teens ★★★	Over 30 ★★★★★
Grade school ★★★	Young Adults ★★★★★	Seniors ★★★★★

Author's Rating ★★★★★

How Much Time to Allow Depends on whether you go to any or all of the art galleries and on how long you stroll around or linger in the cafés or on the terrace. You could spend the day here.

Description & Comments The recent makeover of Somerset House, a masterpiece from 1547 and one-time royal residence, is one of the great successes of London's otherwise ill-fated millennium projects. In 2000, the Gilbert Collection and the Hermitage Rooms joined the Courtauld Gallery Institute as tenants, so on a visit you can see three of London's top collections of art. The Courtauld Gallery grew from textile magnate Samuel Courtauld's private collection to include one of the world's most impressive assemblage of Impressionist works, among them Van Gogh's *Self Portrait with Bandaged Ear,* Degas's *Two Dancers,* Renoir's *La Loge,* and Manet's *Déjeuner sur l'herbe.* The medieval and early Renaissance works are nothing to sniff at either. The Gilbert Collection shows off the horde of decorative arts collected by Sir Arthur Gilbert, a Londoner who made his fortune in evening gowns and emigrated to California in the 1940s. The Hermitage Rooms rotate selections from the Hermitage Museum of St. Petersburg, Russia, every ten months, bringing the treasures of the czars to the banks of the Thames.

Touring Tips The Courtauld offers a fantastic educational booklet called "Courtauld Gallery Trail," available at the admissions desk, that instructs children (ages 5–12) in the study of the gallery's fine-art collection. Plan on having lunch or tea during your visit.

Tate Britain — *Zone 9*

Type of Attraction Museum of English painters

Location Millbank, on Thames, SW1; tube: Pimlico

Admission Free, except for special exhibits

Hours Daily, 10 a.m.–5:50 p.m.; tours, Monday–Friday, 11 a.m., noon, 2 p.m., 3 p.m.; Saturday–Sunday, 3 p.m.

Phone (0207) 887-8000 (recorded information)

Website www.tate.org.uk

When to Go Anytime, but avoid midday if there's a big exhibition on

Special Comments Access-for-disabled leaflet is available at information desks. Parking spaces and wheelchairs are available, but must be booked in advance.

Overall Appeal by Age Group

Preschool ★	Teens ★★	Over 30 ★★★★
Grade school ★★	Young Adults ★★★★	Seniors ★★★★

Author's Rating ★★★★

How Much Time to Allow 2 hours or more

Description & Comments The much talked-about Tate Modern didn't exactly leave the original Tate behind in the dust when it opened across the river (see below). The Tate Britain galleries, including those in a new wing, show off a stunning collection of English paintings and sculptures from the 16th to the early 20th century. Hogarth, Stubbs, Reynolds, Blake, Burne-Jones, Constable, even an honorary Englishman, the American expat James Whistler, are here. J. M. W. Turner, whose paintings fill the Clore Gallery, takes pride of place.

Touring Tips Leave time to check out the gift shop, with a great selection of books, gifts, and postcards, and enjoy a meal or snack in the excellent café; a boat service connects the two Tates.

Tate Modern — *Zone 5*

Type of Attraction Museum of international modern art

Location 25 Sumner Street, Bankside, SE1; tube: Southwark or Blackfriars

Admission Free, except for special exhibitions, lectures, and films

Hours Sunday–Thursday, 10 a.m.–6 p.m.; Friday and Saturday, 10 a.m.–10 p.m.

Phone (0207) 887-8000 (recorded information)

Website www.tate.org.uk

When to Go Anytime

Special Comments Individuals with wheelchairs or strollers should use the north entrance from river walkway or the west entrance on Holland Street. To reserve a parking space or wheelchair, call (0207) 887-8888.

Overall Appeal by Age Group

Preschool —	Teens ★★	Over 30 ★★★★
Grade school ★★	Young Adults ★★★	Seniors ★★★

Author's Rating ★★★★

How Much Time to Allow 1–2 hours

Description & Comments The old Bankside Power Station is the striking setting for the Tate Modern, where the works of Dali, Picasso, Matisse, Duchamp, Warhol, and Rothko fill a series of rooms surrounding the turbine hall, now the setting for changing exhibitions. The museum elicits strong opinions from all who visit—some say the place was more interesting when it was a power station, some hate the fact that the art is arranged thematically rather than chronologically. But the crowds keep pouring in, and we are among those who love this museum and are pleased to see such a fine collection of modern art on display in one place. The shop and two restaurants are excellent.

Touring Tips The best way to approach the museum is on the Millennium Bridge—follow it across the river from St. Paul's; check out the boat service between the Tate Britain and the Tate Modern.

The Tower of London — *Zone 3*

Type of Attraction Ancient, history-rich fortress on the banks of the Thames

Location Tower Hill, EC3; tube: Tower Hill

Admission £11.50 adults; £8.75 seniors and students; £7.50 children ages 5–15; free for children under age 5; £31 families

Hours March–October: Monday–Saturday, 9 a.m.–5 p.m.; Sunday, 10 a.m.–5 p.m.; November–February: Sunday and Monday, 10 a.m.–4 p.m.; Tuesday–Saturday, 9 a.m.–4 p.m.

Phone (0870) 756-6060

Website www.hrp.org.uk

When to Go The lines are LONG in the summer; plan on visiting very early or very late

Special Comments The tower is a warren of steep stairs and passageways. A limited number of wheelchairs is available; ask at the group ticket office.

Overall Appeal by Age Group

Preschool ★	Teens ★★★★	Over 30 ★★★★★
Grade school ★★★★	Young Adults ★★★★	Seniors ★★★★★

Author's Rating ★★★★★

How Much Time to Allow 3 hours or more

Description & Comments One of the most important sites in all of England is soaked in the blood of Thomas More, Anne Boleyn, Lady Jane Grey, King Henry VI, Sir Walter Raleigh, and countless others who ran afoul of the powers that be. Even so, the Tower is a surprisingly appealing and friendly place. What began as a simple fortification on the Thames in 1066 is now an airy assemblage of 13 towers and numerous other buildings of mellow old stone, surrounded by soothing greenery. The Yeoman Warders, also known as Beefeaters, have been at the tower since the 1300s and now give fascinating free tours. They're joined by the famous ravens, whose presence is most welcome—legend has it that if they ever fly away, the Tower will fall and England is doomed. The Crown Jewels are kept here, but these glittering prizes somehow pale next to the armor, the graffiti you can still see in some of the cells, and other evidence of this place's long and storied past.

Touring Tips The audio tours are great and can be done at your own pace, and the guidebook is an excellent investment. There is a security check that slows down the entrance; if possible, leave your knapsack or bag at home when you visit.

Victoria & Albert Museum — *Zone 11*

Type of Attraction Breathtaking collection of decorative arts and design

Location Cromwell Road (second entrance on Exhibition Road), South Kensington, SW7; tube: South Kensington

Admission Free

Hours Thursday–Tuesday, 10 a.m.–5:45 p.m.; Wednesday, 10 a.m.–10 p.m.

Phone (0207) 942-2000

Website www.vam.ac.uk

When to Go Anytime

Special Comments Wheelchair access is from the Exhibition Road entrance; there are ramps over most of the many small sets of steps.

Overall Appeal by Age Group

Preschool ★★★	Teens ★★★	Over 30 ★★★★★
Grade school ★★★	Young Adults ★★★★★	Seniors ★★★★★

Author's Rating ★★★★★

How Much Time to Allow As much as possible

Description & Comments When you visit this marvelous museum, founded by Prince Albert in 1852, be prepared to be overwhelmed. Armor, religious artifacts, stained glass, sculptures, wood carvings, jewelry, musical instruments, ironwork, furniture, glass, clothing, paintings, and photographs are among the holdings. Though this booty is divided into some semblance of order in the World Galleries, British Galleries, and Design Galleries, the place still seems like an eclectic hodgepodge. Just wander from room to room and admire what's here, or join one of the excellent tours led throughout the day. The red-brick Victorian buildings, with their domes, skylights, and courtyards, are themselves a treasure; the Pirelli courtyard and Morris room are especially appealing.

Touring Tips On Wednesday evenings, there's usually a lecture and a gallery talk. The restaurant downstairs is excellent, and there's a small café in the front lobby; the gift shop is huge and full of affordable treasures.

The Wallace Collection — *Zone 14*

Type of Attraction Collection of 19th-century Anglo-French art

Location Hertford House, Manchester Square, W1; tube: Bond Street

Admission Free

Hours Monday–Saturday, 10 a.m.–5 p.m.; Sunday, noon–5 p.m.

Phone (0207) 563-9500

Website www.the-wallace-collection.org.uk

When to Go Anytime

Special Comments Good disabled access including an outdoor ramp, lifts to the upper floors, and mostly uncluttered rooms in which it is easy to maneuver

Overall Appeal by Age Group

Preschool ★	Teens ★★	Over 30 ★★★★
Grade school ★	Young Adults ★★★	Seniors ★★★★

Author's Rating ★★★★

How Much Time to Allow 1–3 hours

Description & Comments Between 1750 and 1880, five generations of marquesses of Hertford amassed one of the world's most outstanding collections of paintings, furniture, and *ojets,* and it's all here, in the original rooms of the family's 18th-century mansion and in attractive new galleries. Standouts are the European and Asian armor and the works by Titian, Poussin, Rembrandt, Rubens, Van Dyck, and Velázquez. Even the café is stunning.

Touring Tips Try to catch one of the free lectures and tours; call or check the website for schedules.

Westminster Abbey — *Zone 9*

Type of Attraction England's most historically important church

Location Broad Sanctuary, just off of Parliament Square; tube: St. James's Park or Westminster

Admission Free admission for services or to visit the nave and cloisters. Royal chapels and tombs: £6 adults; £4 students and seniors; £2 children ages 11–15; free for children under age 11; £12 families of two adults and two children. Chapter House, Pyx Chamber, and museum: £1 with royal chapels admission; or £2.50 adults; £1.90 students and seniors; and £1.30 children

Hours Royal chapels: Monday–Friday, 9 a.m.–3:45 p.m.; Saturday, 9 a.m.–1:45 p.m. (closing times given are for last admission). Chapter House, Pyx Chamber: daily, 10 a.m.–3:30 p.m. The abbey is closed before special services, on Sundays (except for services), December 24–28, Good Friday, and Commonwealth Observance Day.

Phone (0207) 654-4840

Website www.westminster-abbey.org

When to Go Early mornings on weekdays, especially during the busy summer months, and at 5 p.m. evensong; those who are first in line, which starts forming at about 4:15, are seated in the stately choir stalls, where the atmosphere and view of the Westminster Boys Choir is the best.

Special Comments Audio guides are available in seven languages for £2.50, Monday–Friday, 9:30 a.m.–3 p.m., and Saturday, 9:30 a.m.–1 p.m.

Overall Appeal by Age Group

Preschool ★	Teens ★★★★	Over 30 ★★★★
Grade school ★★★	Young Adults ★★★★	Seniors ★★★★

Author's Rating ★★★★

How Much Time to Allow 60–90 minutes for audio guides; evensong is about 45 minutes

Description & Comments The beauty of the interiors (displaying at least four different eras of architecture), the sheer numbers of people buried here (more than 3,000), and the incredible amount of history that this building has seen (900 years' worth) are what make a visit to the Abbey so rewarding. Some of the Abbey's most fantastic architecture is in the Henry VII Chapel; buried here are Henry VII and his wife; King George II and Queen Caroline; Henry VIII's only son, Edward VI; and James I and his lover, George Villiers, the first nonroyal to be buried in this part of the Abbey. The South Transept, or Poet's Corner, however, is the crowd pleaser, containing the grave slabs of, to name but a few, Geoffrey Chaucer, Robert Browning, Alfred Lord Tennyson, Charles Dickens, Rudyard Kipling, and Thomas Hardy, as well as impressive memorials to William Shakespeare and George Frideric Handel. After exploring the Abbey's interior, be sure you find your way out to the cloisters, which these days contain a small shop and café.

Touring Tips Before you enter Westminster Abbey, take the time to enjoy its lesser-known neighbor, tiny St. Margaret's Church, built in 1523. Photography is permitted only on Wednesday between 6 and 7 p.m.

The Other Sights

Albert Memorial Zone 13; Kensington Gardens, west of Exhibition Road, SW7; tube: High Street Kensington. When Prince Albert succumbed to typhoid at age 42, a grieving Queen Victoria put up this extravaganza of gilded gold in his honor. Restored to its former glory, the spectacle puts a new shine on this edge of Kensington Gardens.

Apsley House (The Wellington Museum) Zone 8; 149 Piccadilly, W1; tube: Hyde Park Corner; (0207) 499-5676; £4.50 adults; £3 seniors and students; free for children under age 12; open Tuesday–Sunday, 11 a.m.–5 p.m.; last entry at 4:30 p.m.; **www.vam.ac.uk.** This grand house was the Duke of Wellington's reward for a job well done in the Napoleonic Wars. Political cartoons and other displays in the basement provide a lesson in the duke and his times, and upstairs are paintings by Velázquez, Goya, Rubens, and other masters.

Bank of England Museum Zone 3; Threadneedle Street, EC2; tube: Bank; (0207) 601-5545; free; open Monday–Friday, 10 a.m.–5 p.m.; **www.bankofengland.co.uk.** Obviously, the Bank of England, known as "The Old Lady of Threadneedle Street," knows a thing or two about money, and with exhibits ranging from replicas of early banks to interactive computer displays, does a fine job of instructing us on the evolution of the banknote from 1694, how our precious pounds are printed, and other fiscal matters.

Big Ben Clock Tower Zone 9; Parliament Square, SW1; tube: Westminster. You can set your watch by London's favorite landmark—the big bell has been ringing out since 1862.

Chelsea Physic Garden Zone 11; 66 Royal Hospital Road, SW3; tube: Sloane Square; (0207) 352-5646; £5 adults; £3 seniors, students, and children ages 5–16; open April–late-October, Wednesday, noon–5 p.m., Sunday, 2–6 p.m.; **www.chelseaphysicgarden.co.uk.** Tucked away behind high walls, this little garden contains some 5,000 species of flora, many of them from the Mediterranean and the Canary Islands and used over the years for healing; they flourish in greenhouses, lovely rock gardens, and lovingly tended planting beds.

Chiswick House Zone 12; Burlington Lane, W4; tube: Turnham Green, or Chiswick by rail; (0208) 995-0508; £3.30 adults; £2.50 seniors and students; £1.70 children ages 5–16; free for children under age 5; open April–September, daily, 10 a.m.–6 p.m.; October, 10 a.m.–5 p.m. Lord Burlington's art treasures have long since disappeared from the 1725 house he built to contain them, but the famous domed octagonal room remains, as do carvings, statuary, sumptuous William Kent ceilings, and a lovely garden.

Clink Exhibition Zone 5; 1 Clink Street, SE1; tube: London Bridge; (0207) 403-6515; £4 adults; £3 seniors, students, and children under age 16; £9 families; open September–June, daily, 10 a.m.–6 p.m.; July–September, 10 a.m.–9 p.m.; **www.clink.co.uk.** Another stop on the ghoulish London tour, this medieval prison manages to be quite boring, with dismal cell re-creations, diagrams of medieval torture devices, and dull text panels on former inhabitants.

Dickens House Zone 3; 48 Doughty Street, WC1; tube: Russell Square; (0207) 405-2127; £4 adults; £2 children ages 5–15; free for children under age 5; £9 families; open Monday–Saturday, 10 a.m.–5 p.m.; **www.dickensmuseum.com.** London should honor the master with a shrine that's a bit more riveting than this house where he lived for two years; the most evocative of the relics on view are the manuscript pages.

Dulwich Picture Gallery West of Zone 6; Gallery Road, SE21; North Dulwich or West Dulwich railway stops, ten minutes from Victoria; (0208) 693-5254; free on Friday; £4 adults; £3 seniors and students; free for children under age 16; open Tuesday–Friday, 10 a.m.–5 p.m.; Saturday–Sunday, 11 a.m.–5 p.m.; **www.dulwichpicturegallery.org.uk.** This gem of a small gallery, tucked away in a wealthy residential enclave, is one of our favorite London "finds." Assembled in a magnificent neoclassical building by Sir John Soane is a remarkable collection of paintings by Rembrandt, Poussin, Watteau, Rubens, Canaletto, Gainsborough, and others. The café is a great spot for lunch.

Guards Museum Zone 9; Wellington Barracks, Birdcage Walk, SW1; tube: St. James's Park; (0207) 414-3271; £2 adults; £1 seniors and students; free for children; open daily, 10 a.m.–4 p.m. This museum honors the 300-year-old history of those fellows you see performing the Changing of the Guard; the shop is an excellent source for toy soldiers.

HMS Belfast Zone 5; Morgans Lane, Tooley Street, SE1; tube: London Bridge; (0207) 940-6328; £5.80 adults; £4.40 seniors and students; free for children under age 16; open March–October, daily, 10 a.m.–6 p.m., November–February, daily, 10 a.m.–5 p.m.; **www.iwm.org.uk.** Climb aboard this World War II–era vessel and check it out from stem to stern, from officers cabins to the boiler rooms.

Hogarth's House Zone 12; Hogarth Lane, Great West Road, W4; tube: Turnham Green or BritRail to Chiswick; (0208) 994-6757; free; open April–October, Tuesday–Friday, 1–6 p.m., Saturday and Sunday, 1–6 p.m., November–March, Tuesday–Friday, 1–4 p.m., Saturday and Sunday, 1–5 p.m.; closed January. More than 200 of Hogarth's most famous prints, including *Marriage a la Mode, A Rake's Progress,* and *A Harlot's Progress,* hang in what was once the country retreat of the 18th-century painter and satirist.

Hungerford Bridge Zone 5; Embankment on north side of River, Royal Festival Hall on south side; tube: Embankment. This old railway bridge was an eyesore for years, but now it's straddled by flashy new pedestrian walkways that are wonderful to look at and practical, too, making it much easier to get to Royal Festival Hall, the London Eye, the Aquarium, and other South Bank attractions.

Lambeth Palace Zone 5; Lambeth Palace Road; (0207) 898-1200; bus number 3 or number 159, both via Whitehall and Westminster; tube: Lambeth North; £6.50 per person; usually open mid-afternoon on Wednesday and Thursday only. You can visit the Thames-side 13th-century palace of the Archbishop of Canterbury, with its ancient chapel and library full of illuminated manuscripts, only by appointment, but it's worth the trouble of getting one; write well in advance of your visit.

London Dungeon Zone 5; 28–34 Tooley Street, SE1; tube: London Bridge; (0207) 403-7221; £10.95 adults; £6.95 seniors, students, and children ages 5–14, free for children under age 5; open mid-March–July, daily, 10 a.m.–5:30 p.m.; mid-July–mid-September, daily, 9:30

a.m.–7:30 p.m.; mid-September–October, 10:30 a.m.–5:30 p.m.; November–mid-March, 10:30 a.m.–6 p.m.; **www.thedungeons.com.** Lots of blood, heads rolling around, piercing screams—London's most gruesome attraction is a downright gross-out fest.

Millennium Bridge Zones 3–5; Upper Thames Street on north bank of river; Bankside on south side of river; tube: Mansion on north, London Bridge on south. No sooner had this pedestrian span, designed by Lord Norman Foster, opened to great fanfare in 2000 than it began to sway and had to be closed for some serious re-engineering. Now the first bridge to be built over the Thames since 1894 is open again, providing a convenient link between St. Paul's and the South Bank.

The Monument Zone 3; Monument Street, EC3; tube: Monument; (0207) 626-2717; £1.50 adults; 50p children ages 5–15; free for children under 5; open daily, 9:30 a.m.–5 p.m. If laid down on its side, this tower designed by Sir Christopher Wren would reach directly to the spot on Pudding Lane where the Great Fire of 1666 started—which is, not by coincidence, what the 202-foot-high Monument topped by a viewing platform commemorates.

Museum in Docklands Zone 6; West India Quay; Docklands Light Railway, Canary Wharf stop; (0207) 001-9800; **www.museumindocklands.org.uk.** Opened in mid-2003, this long-awaited museum plots the history of the Thames docks and their importance in London's larger story.

Old Bailey Zone 3; Old Bailey Street, EC4; tube: St. Paul's; (0207) 248-3277; ask for List Office; free; children under age 14 not admitted; open Monday–Friday, 10:30 a.m.–4:30 p.m.; closed for lunch 1–2 p.m.; **www.courtservice.gov.uk.** You don't have to be a law freak to be intrigued by wigged and traditionally robed barristers addressing each other as "friend" and the judge as "milord" in London's ornate and formal criminal court.

St. Bartholomew-the-Great Zone 3; Little Britain Street, off West Smithfield, EC1; tube: St. Paul's or Barbican; (0207) 606-5171; free; open Monday–Friday, 8:30 a.m.–4 p.m.; Saturday, 10:30 a.m.–1:30 p.m., Sunday, 2–6 p.m.; **www.greatbarts.com.** London's oldest monastic church dates from 1123 and is a masterpiece of Romanesque architecture and medieval stonework. Regular Sunday services are at 9 a.m. and 11 a.m. (choral); evensong is at 6:30 p.m.

Sherlock Holmes Museum Zone 14; 221B Baker Street, NW1; tube: Baker Street; (0207) 935-8866; £6 adults; £4 children under age 16; free for children under age 5; open daily, 9:30 a.m.–6 p.m.; **www.sherlock-holmes.co.uk.** See the rooms full of Victorian furniture, the sleuth's violin, typewriter, and a chess set in which the pieces are characters from the

Arthur Conan Doyle books, and you'll begin to believe there really was a Sherlock Holmes.

Southwark Cathedral Zone 5; Montague Close, Southwark, SE1; tube: London Bridge; (0207) 367-6700; free; exhibitions, £3 adults, £2.50 seniors and students; £1.50 children ages 5–15; free for children under age 5; £12 families of up to two adults and three children; open daily, 8 a.m.–6 p.m.; **www.dswark.org.** Will Shakespeare attended services here, and John Harvard, founder of the noted university in the New World, was baptized in what began in the 12th century as the church of an Augustinian priory. But Southwark doesn't rest on its laurels: A new visitors' center treats visitors to time-lapse photography views of London and other high-tech exhibits.

Tower Bridge Zone 3; Tower Bridge, SE1; tube: Tower Hill or London Bridge; (0207) 357-7935; £4.50 adults; £3.50 seniors and students; £3 children ages 5–15; open daily, 9:30 a.m.–6 p.m., last admission is 75 minutes before closing; **www.towerbridge.org.uk.** This is the bridge that everyone thinks is London Bridge (the one that's now in the middle of the Arizona desert), but it's much more interesting, a marvel of Victorian engineering. You can easily appreciate this wonder from afar, but if you decide to hand over the admission fee, plan on taking a quick look at the exhibits on the bridge's history and spending most of your time looking out on London from the tower windows and the walkway high above the Thames.

The Wellington Arch Zone 10; middle of Hyde Park Corner roundabout, SW1; tube: Hyde Park Corner; (0207) 973 3494; £2.50 adults; £1.90 seniors and students; £1.30 children ages 5–16; free for children under age 5; open April–September, daily, 10 a.m.–6 p.m.; October, Wednesday–Sunday, 10 a.m.–5 p.m.; November–March, Wednesday–Sunday, 10 a.m.–4 p.m.; **www.english-heritage.org.uk.** Views to be had from the observation platforms include a peek at the tennis courts in the "backyard" of Buckingham Palace. A photo display of Londoners' snapshots of their city is quite riveting, too.

City of Parks

No small part of the appeal of London are the sweeping swaths of greenery that provide a bit of the countryside amid the concrete jungle; a retreat to one of them can be most refreshing after a session of slogging through the sights. For more information about London city parks, contact the **Royal Parks Agency** at (0207) 298-2000 or go to **www.royalparks.gov.uk.**

Green Park Zone 9; between Piccadilly and Constitution Hill (between Hyde Park and St. James's Park); enter at Hyde Park Corner; tube: Green Park. This expanse of green lawn and old trees is a backyard to Buckingham Palace.

Hampstead Heath Zone 1; Hampstead; tube: Highgate, then take 210 bus to West Gate. These 1,600 acres of hills, lakes, wild woods, and landscaped gardens offer stunning views over London.

Holland Park Zone 13; Holland Park, between Kensington and Shepherd's Bush; tube: Holland Park Avenue (then a ten-minute walk to park) or Kensington High Street and take westbound bus 9, 10, 27, 28, 31, or 49. A 54-acre landscaped marvel with a Japanese garden.

Hyde Park Zone 10; bordered by Park Lane, Knightsbridge, and Bayswater Road; tube: Hyde Park Corner. A 350-acre escape from the noise of Park Lane, Knightsbridge, and Bayswater, with fountains (soon to include the Diana, Princess of Wales Memorial Fountain), plazas, a lake (the Serpentine), and Speaker's Corner, where anyone can get on a soapbox and have his or her say.

Kensington Gardens Zone 13; Kensington Gore; tube: Kensington High Street. The backyard of Kensington Palace, complete with sunken gardens, an orangery, tree-lined avenues, and the Albert Memorial.

Regent's Park Zone 15; at end of Baker Street; for south entrance, take the tube to Regent's Park or Baker Street. The London Zoo is just one of many attractions on these 490 acres—a boating lake, waterfall, open-air theater, and 6,000 trees are also part of the landscape.

Richmond Park Zone 12; southwest London; tube: Richmond Station, then take bus 72, 265, 371, or 415. Some 400 fallow deer and 250 red deer live and graze in this 2,470-acre preserve, only a stone's throw (well, seven miles) from the center of the city.

St. James's Park Zone 9; east of Buckingham Palace gates; tube: St. James's Park. Green acres between Buckingham and St. James's Palaces, with great views of turrets, steeples, and even a pelican or two.

Day Trips from London

In addition to our suggestions below, you should also consider Canterbury and Rye (see Part Five, The Southeast of England); Brighton, Salisbury, and Winchester (see Part Six, The South of England); Bath and Oxford (see Part Eight, Bath, Oxford, and the Cotswolds); Stratford-upon-Avon (see Part Nine, The Heartland and Welsh Border); Cambridge (see Part Ten, Cambridge and East Anglia); or even York (see Part Eleven, York and Yorkshire). To get the full flavor of these places, though, we prefer spending at least a night.

Greenwich

Not only does Greenwich defy its urban setting with a cozy, villagelike atmosphere and acres of parkland, but the onetime royal retreat is also graced with a remarkable assemblage of architecture. Not that Greenwich is a stuffy relic of the past: The riverside promenades and Georgian and Regency buildings, some of them the work of Sir Christopher Wren and Inigo Jones, are a perfect backdrop for a huge weekend market. We recommend, though, that you visit this atmospheric old place on a weekday, when a quiet charm pervades the streets.

Just downriver from London, Greenwich is a 20-minute ride away from Bank Street and Tower Hill on the Docklands Light Railway (DLR), with a stop at **Greenwich Pier**. The most picturesque way to reach Greenwich is via riverboat, affording stunning views of **St. Paul's Cathedral, Tower Bridge,** and the **Docklands.** Boats leave from Westminster, Charing Cross, and Tower Pier for Greenwich approximately every 45 minutes, and the trip takes 40 minutes to an hour, depending on where you embark; call (0207) 930-4097 or (0207) 987-1185 for more information. Fares run about £8 adults, £6 seniors, and £4 children. The **Greenwich Tourist Information Center** (Greenwich Church Street, London SE10 9BL; (0208) 858-637646) provides information on sights, guided tours, and other Greenwich particulars.

Greenwich Attractions

Cutty Sark

Type of Attraction Last of the great sailing clipper ships, now restored

Location Zone 6; Greenwich Pier

Admission £3.90 adults; £2.90 children, students, and seniors; £9.70 families

Hours Daily, 10 a.m.–5 p.m.; last admission at 4:30 p.m.

Phone (0208) 858-3445

Website www.cuttysark.org.uk

When to Go Early

Special Comments Access for the disabled is limited to the entrance level of the ship, as the ship contains stairways that may prove difficult for some to maneuver.

Overall Appeal by Age Group

Preschool ★★	Teens ★★★★	Over 30 ★★★
Grade school ★★★★	Young Adults ★★★	Seniors ★★★

Author's Rating ★★★

How Much Time to Allow 45–90 minutes

Description & Comments First launched in 1869, the *Cutty Sark* earned its famous-clipper status as one of the fastest merchant vessels on the seas, transporting tea and wool around the globe in its enormous hold. You can now climb below decks to enjoy the exhibits celebrating the *Cutty Sark's* history and to view merchant-ship figureheads collected by Long John Silver.

Touring Tips Tours of the ship can be arranged at no additional charge; from the *Cutty Sark's* bow you can also see the much smaller *Gipsy Moth IV,* in which Francis Chichester sailed solo around the world.

National Maritime Museum and Queen's House

Type of Attraction Largest maritime museum in the world

Location Zone 6; Romney Road, Greenwich

Admission Free

Hours Daily, 10 a.m.–5 p.m.

Phone (0208) 312-6565

Website www.nmm.ac.uk

When to Go Anytime on weekdays; early in the day on weekends

Special Comments Fully accessible with lifts for disabled, touch talks for visually impaired, and sign-interpreted talks. Call for details.

Overall Appeal by Age Group

Preschool ★★★	Teens ★★★	Over 30 ★★★★
Grade school ★★★★	Young Adults ★★★★	Seniors ★★★★

Author's Rating ★★★★

How Much Time to Allow 2–3 hours for the museum and 1–2 hours for Queen's House Millennium Exhibition

Description & Comments The National Maritime Museum pays homage to the sea and seafaring in handsome galleries filled with exhibits on exploration, ocean-liner travel, marine ecology, maritime London, and great sea battles. All are clever, and the collections range from re-creations of passenger-ship cabins to nautical instruments to old maps and uniforms. In a hall geared to young visitors, kids get to raise and lower signal flags, load a cargo ship, and engage in other fun activities that will keep them happily occupied for hours. The adjacent Queen's House, a beautiful architectural triumph of 17th-century architect Inigo Jones, displays a fine collection of maritime art. See also the profile for the Royal Greenwich Observatory, below.

Touring Tips The museum offers a wide range of children's educational workshops and activities, many free of charge. For details and a full schedule of planned events, call (0208) 312-6608, or write the National Maritime Museum, Greenwich, London SE10 9NF.

Royal Greenwich Observatory

Type of Attraction Location of the world's Prime Meridian (0° longitude)

Location Zone 6; Blackheath Avenue, hilltop of Greenwich Park

Admission Free

Hours Daily, 10 a.m.–5 p.m.

Phone (0208) 312-6565

Website www.nmm.ac.uk

When to Go Anytime

Special Comments Not all observatory buildings are fully accessible. Special-access days are arranged with BSL signed tours and touch sessions. For details call (0208) 312-6522.

Overall Appeal by Age Group

Preschool ★	Teens ★★★	Over 30 ★★★
Grade school ★	Young Adults ★★★	Seniors ★★★

Author's Rating ★★★

How Much Time to Allow 1–2 hours

Description & Comments Sir Christopher Wren designed and built this observatory in the 1670s to further the cause of celestial navigation. While the crowd pleaser is the chance to straddle the Prime Meridian that marks 0° longitude (so you have one foot in the Orient and one foot in the Occident), other exhibits chronicle early astronomy, timekeeping, and navigation. The Telescope Dome houses Britain's largest telescope.

Touring Tips Planetarium shows are given at 2:30 p.m. on weekdays.

Royal Naval College

Type of Attraction Extraordinary example of Renaissance architecture and interiors

Location Zone 6; King William Walk

Admission Free

Hours Daily, 10 a.m.–5 p.m.

Phone (0208) 269-4741

Website www.greenwichfoundation.org.uk

When to Go Anytime

Special Comments Be prepared to have your bags searched on entry as part of security procedures.

Overall Appeal by Age Group

Preschool ★	Teens ★★	Over 30 ★★★
Grade school ★	Young Adults ★★★	Seniors ★★

Author's Rating ★★★

How Much Time to Allow Approximately 30 minutes

Description & Comments When Charles II decided not to use the palace that Christopher Wren built on the banks of the Thames, a naval hospital moved in. The next tenant was the Royal Naval College, and the premises now house the University of Greenwich. The fine old buildings are a pleasure to look at, and the views from the grounds over the river are memorable; step inside to see the Painted Hall, with its 3-D ceiling and wall murals.

Touring Tips It's worth the expense to join one of the frequent guided tours (£5).

Hampton Court

This 16th-century castle rises like a Tudor fantasy from the banks of the Thames just 13 miles west of London. You can easily get to Hampton Court by train from Waterloo or Wimbledon Stations (the trip takes less than half an hour), but if you have time, the best way to approach the palace is by water from Westminster Pier; boats depart at 11 a.m. and noon, with returns at 3 p.m. and 5 p.m.; fares are £18 adults, £12 seniors, £9 children, and £45 families. If time is short, consider taking the boat one way and the train the other; one-way fares on the boat are £12 adults, £8 seniors, £6 children, and £30 families. For more information, call **Westminster Passenger Services Administration** at (0207) 930-2062, or visit **www.wpsa.co.uk.**

Hampton Court Palace

Type of Attraction London's most impressive royal palace

Location Zone 12; East Molesey, Surrey

Admission £11.30 adults; £8.50 seniors and students; £7.40 children ages 5–15; £34 families of up to two adults and three children; prices include admission to the gardens and maze

Hours Late March–late October: Monday, 10:15 a.m.–6 p.m., Tuesday–Sunday, 9:30 a.m.–6 p.m. Late October–late March: Monday, 10:15 a.m.–4:30 p.m.; Tuesday–Sunday, 9:30 a.m.–4:30 p.m.

Phone (0870) 752-7777

Website www.hrp.org.uk

When to Go Anytime

Special Comments Disabled access, including ramps to the Tudor kitchens, access to some areas of the gardens, lifts to the first floor, and equipped toilets

Overall Appeal by Age Group

Preschool ★★	Teens ★★★★★	Over 30 ★★★★★
Grade school ★★★	Young Adults ★★★★★	Seniors ★★★★★

Author's Rating ★★★★★

How Much Time to Allow Head out early to give yourself the full day to enjoy Hampton Court.

Description & Comments Cardinal Wolsey, Henry VIII's lord chancellor, built Hampton Court Palace on the banks of the Thames in 1516, and the palace has been inhabited continuously ever since—by kings, queens, Oliver Cromwell, and these days, pensioners of the crown. Henry VIII is the sovereign most connected with the palace, and his kitchens and Great Hall are splendid examples of Tudor architecture. Christopher Wren left his mark on the palace, in the state apartments he designed for King William and Queen Mary. Though a fire raged through the palace in 1986, most of the masterpieces, including the palace's collection of 500 Renaissance paintings, were saved.

Touring Tips You can tour the palace on six short walking tours and amble at your leisure through the gardens, where visitors have been known to get lost in the famous half-mile-long maze for hours. A sunny day makes Hampton Court's ornate gardens a fantastic picnic spot for families. Alternately, you might head to the Tiltyard Tearoom for an enjoyable light meal, or wander beyond the Lion Gates and find a pub.

Royal Botanic Gardens at Kew

While Kew is at the western edge of London proper—and directly beneath the flight paths of Heathrow Airport—a trip to these beautiful gardens provides an easy getaway into a landscape far removed from the city bustle.

The easiest way to get to Kew is on the Underground to the Kew Gardens stop. The walk from the station to the garden entrance takes about ten minutes. In summer, you can take a boat from Westminster Pier; the trip takes about 90 minutes, and boats leave at 10:30 a.m. and 2 p.m., returning at noon and 4:30 p.m.; the round-trip fare is £15 adults, £10 seniors, £7 children ages 5–15; and £37.50 families. For more information, call **Westminster Passenger Services Administration** at (0207) 930-2062 or visit **www.wpsa.co.uk.**

Kew Gardens

Type of Park Botanical extravaganza with 30,000 species of plants and flowers planted over 300 acres; follies, water features, and conservatories

Location Zone 12; southwest London on the Thames; tube: Kew Gardens

Admission £7.50 adults; £5.50 seniors and students; free for children under age 16

Hours March 31–October 31: Monday–Friday, 9:30 a.m.–6:30 p.m., Saturday and Sunday, 9:30 a.m.–7:30 p.m.; late October–mid-February: daily, 9:30 a.m.–4:15 p.m., mid-February–late March: daily, 9:30 a.m.–5:30 p.m.

Phone (0208) 332-5197

Website www.kew.org

When to Go Any time of year, since so many of the displays are in glass houses

Special Comments We recommend climbing aboard the garden train for the 40-minute introductory tour of the gardens; you can hop on and off at eight stops along the route; price £3 adults, £1.50 children ages 5–16.

Overall Appeal by Age Group

Preschool ★★	Teens ★★★	Over 30 ★★★
Grade school ★★★	Young Adults ★★★	Seniors ★★★

Author's Rating ★★★½

Description & Comments These 300 acres of trees and shrubs date from the 18th century, when explorers began bringing specimens back from every corner of the world. Today Kew is one of the world's leading centers for botanical research. While there are many quiet corners in which to relax and pleasant walks along the Thames to be enjoyed, Kew's busiest and most popular attractions are the enormous glass houses—the Palm House, Water Lily House, and Temperate House shelter exotic flora beneath elaborate, Victorian glass structures that seem more whimsical than scientific. Two art galleries, a palace, a Japanese pagoda, and numerous follies and conservatories are scattered among the luxuriant grounds.

Touring Tips: The stately home you can see on the other side of the Thames from Kew is Syon House, home to the Duke of Northumberland; the gardens are the work of Capability Brown, and the Robert Adams neoclassical manor house is filled with paintings by Gainsborough, Van Dyck, and other masters. Gardens open daily, 10 a.m.–5:30 p.m.; house open late March–early November, Wednesday, Thursday, and Sunday, 11 a.m.–5 p.m. House and garden admission: £6.95 adults; £6.50 seniors and students; £5.95 for children ages 5–15; free for children under age 5; garden alone: £3.50 adults; £2.50 seniors, students, and children ages 5–15; free for children under age 5. Call (0208) 560-0883 for more information. From the Gunnersbury tube stop, one stop north of the Kew Gardens stop, take buses 237 or 267.

Windsor

The towers and crenellated walls of this 900-year-castle rise above the town of Windsor, just 20 miles west of London. While the castle is what brings most visitors to town, Windsor's winding, narrow streets are a pleasure to explore, and the adjoining village of Eton is home to the famous school, founded in 1440 to educate new generations of British leaders. You can wander through parts of the Eton grounds between 10:30 a.m. and 4:30 p.m. (shorter hours at certain times during term) for £3.70 adults, £2.50 children under age 15; or in summer, join a guided tour, given daily at 2:15 p.m. and 3:15 p.m., for £4.70 adults, £3.50 children under age 15. For more information, call (01753) 671177.

Trains leave for Windsor from London's Waterloo Station about every hour; the trip takes about 45 minutes and costs about £8.

Windsor Castle

Type of Attraction A royal residence

Location Windsor, Hertsfordshire

Admission £11.50 adults; £9.50 seniors and students; £6 children ages 5–16; £29 families of up to two adults and three children

Hours March–October: daily, 9 a.m.–5:15 p.m., last admission at 4 p.m.; November–February: daily, 9:45 a.m.–4:15 p.m., last admission at 3 p.m. St. George's Chapel closed Sunday.

Phone (0207) 321-2233

Website www.royal.gov.uk

When to Go Windsor Castle is subject to regular, annual, and sudden closures due to various royal ceremonies and events.

Special Comments Limited wheelchair access, lots of walking

Overall Appeal by Age Group

Preschool ★	Teens ★★★	Over 30 ★★★★
Grade school ★★	Young Adults ★★★★	Seniors ★★★★

Author's Rating ★★★★

How Much Time to Allow 2–3 hours

Description & Comments The world's oldest and largest occupied castle (its beginnings date back to William the Conqueror) consists of 13 acres of staterooms, chapels, galleries, courtyards, and, of course, the private royal quarters. The staterooms look especially well polished these days, having just been restored after a fire in 1992. Amidst the pomp and splendor are two particularly charming attractions. Queen Mary's Dolls' House, designed by Sir Edward Luytens in the 1920s and assembled by a thousand craftsmen and artists over the course of three years, is complete with running water, electric lights, a working elevator, fine art, gorgeous furniture, and even two tiny thrones. St. George's Chapel, started in 1475, is a medieval masterpiece and the resting place of ten monarchs.

Touring Tips Leave time for the walk through Windsor and Eton.

Dining in London

London has always embraced food from around the world, and it continues to do so in stylish new ways. Meanwhile, old British standards are popping up on menus in new preparations loosely referred to as "Modern British." Then, too, prices are now incredibly reasonable . . . er, just kidding about this last point. London restaurants are indeed expensive, but you're not going to be thrown out on your ear if you settle for soup and an appetizer. Plus, you can often sample even the capital's finest cuisine at reasonably priced set lunch menus.

For our profiles, we've chosen a broad selection that represents the spectrum of dining experiences London offers. Food trends move at an alarming pace in London, and new restaurants open all the time, so we suggest you check some of the Web resources and magazines and newspapers we recommend under "Gathering Information," page 30, to catch the very latest happenings on the London restaurant scene.

Tea Time

For seasoned Londoners and foreigners alike, a nice way to spend time in the late afternoon is to sit in pleasant surroundings at a table piled high with plates of sandwiches, cakes, and scones, along with an assortment of clotted creams and jams. Quite a few London spots are eager to indulge our pleasure; plan on showing up between 4 and 5 p.m. and lay out from £15 to £25 for the experience.

Fortnum and Mason (Zone 8, 181 Piccadilly, W1; (0207) 734-8040; tube: Picadilly Circus), the venerable department store, serves tea Monday–Saturday in the St. James room and the Fountain. **Harrods** (Zone 10; 87–135 Brompton Road, SW1; (0207) 225-6800; tube: Knightsbridge) does the honors in the Georgian Restaurant. Among the many hotels that serve tea, we recommend the **Lanesborough** (Zone 10;

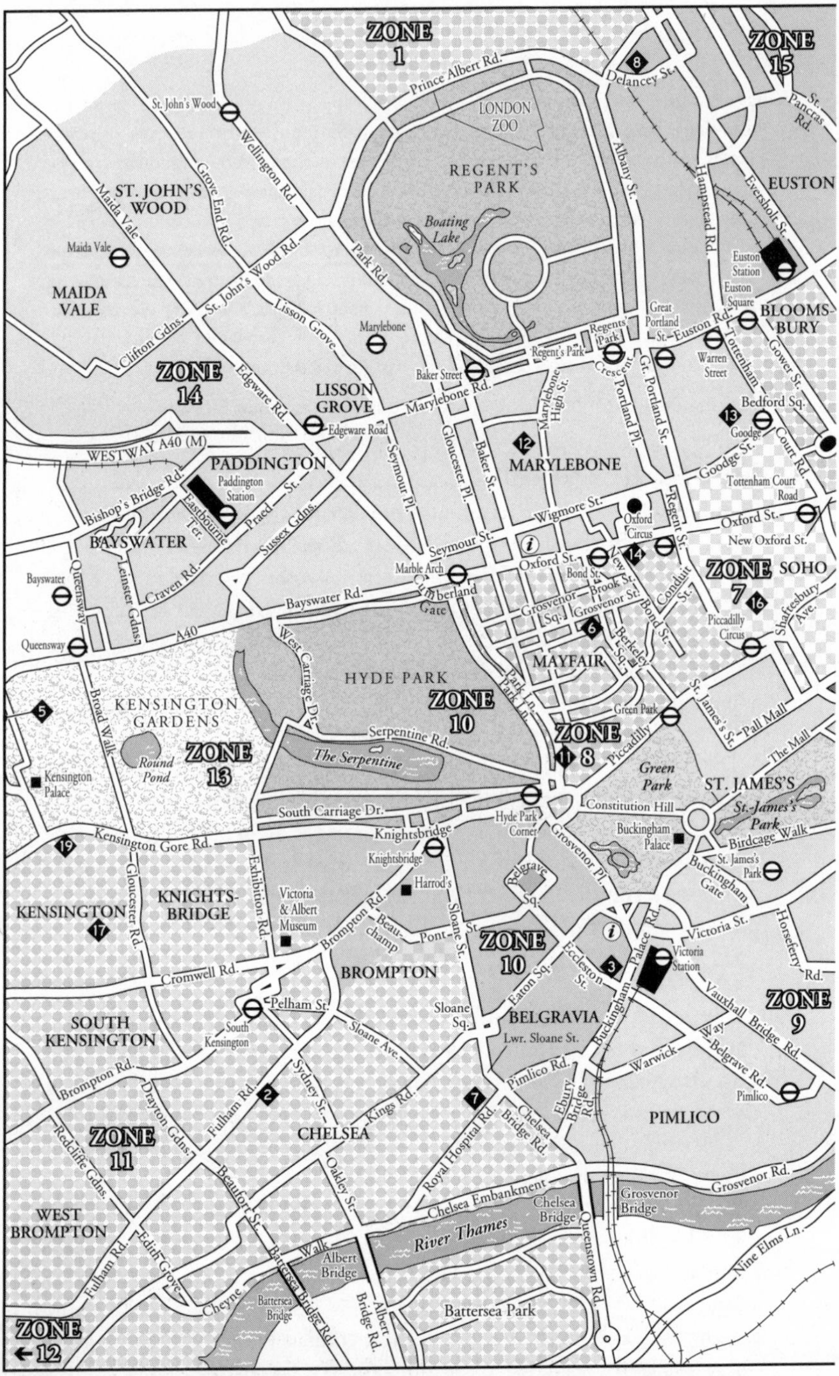
ZONE 1
ZONE 15
Prince Albert Rd.
Delancey St.
LONDON ZOO
St. Pancras Rd.
St. John's Wood
Wellington Rd.
REGENT'S PARK
Albany St.
Hampstead Rd.
Eversholt St.
EUSTON
ST. JOHN'S WOOD
Maida Vale
Grove End Rd.
Boating Lake
Maida Vale
St. John's Wood Rd.
Park Rd.
Euston Station
Euston Square
MAIDA VALE
Lisson Grove
Marylebone
Great Portland St.
Euston Rd.
BLOOMSBURY
Regents Park
Clifton Gdns.
Regent's Park
Crescent
Warren Street
Tottenham
Gower St.
ZONE 14
Baker Street
LISSON GROVE
Marylebone High St.
Marylebone Rd.
Gt. Portland St.
Portland Pl.
Edgware Rd.
Bedford Sq.
Edgeware Road
Goodge
Court Rd.
WESTWAY A40 (M)
PADDINGTON
Seymour Pl.
Gloucester Pl.
Baker St.
MARYLEBONE
Goodge St.
Paddington Station
Tottenham Court Road
Bishop's Bridge Rd.
Eastbourne Ter.
Praed St.
Sussex Gdns.
Wigmore St.
Regent St.
Oxford Circus
Oxford St.
BAYSWATER
Seymour St.
New Oxford St.
Bayswater
Queensway
Leinster Gdns.
Craven Rd.
Marble Arch
Oxford St.
Bond St.
New Bond St.
Brook St.
ZONE 7
SOHO
Cumberland Gate
Conduit St.
Bayswater Rd.
Grosvenor Sq.
Grosvenor St.
Shaftesbury Ave.
Piccadilly Circus
Queensway
A40
West Carriage Dr.
MAYFAIR
Berkeley Sq.
HYDE PARK
St. James's St.
Pall Mall
KENSINGTON GARDENS
Broad Walk
ZONE 10
Park Ln.
Green Park
ZONE 8
Piccadilly
Serpentine Rd.
The Mall
The Serpentine
Green Park
ST. JAMES'S
Round Pond
ZONE 13
Kensington Palace
South Carriage Dr.
Constitution Hill
St. James's Park
Hyde Park Corner
Buckingham Palace
Birdcage Walk
Kensington Gore Rd.
Knightsbridge
Grosvenor Pl.
St. James's Park
Knightsbridge
Belgrave Sq.
Buckingham Gate
Harrod's
KNIGHTSBRIDGE
Victoria & Albert Museum
Exhibition Rd.
Gloucester Rd.
KENSINGTON
Brompton Rd.
Beauchamp
Pont St.
ZONE 10
Victoria St.
Horseferry Rd.
Sloane St.
Eccleston St.
Victoria Station
Palace Rd.
Cromwell Rd.
BROMPTON
Eaton Sq.
Pelham St.
ZONE 9
Sloane Sq.
BELGRAVIA
Buckingham
Vauxhall Bridge Rd.
SOUTH KENSINGTON
South Kensington
Lwr. Sloane St.
Sloane Ave.
Way
Belgrave Rd.
Warwick
Brompton Rd.
Sydney St.
Pimlico Rd.
Pimlico
Fulham Rd.
Kings Rd.
Royal Hospital Rd.
Chelsea Bridge Rd.
Ebury Bridge Rd.
Drayton Gdns.
PIMLICO
ZONE 11
CHELSEA
Redcliffe Gdns.
Oakley St.
Beaufort St.
Grosvenor Rd.
Chelsea Embankment
Chelsea Bridge
Grosvenor Bridge
WEST BROMPTON
River Thames
Queenstown Rd.
Nine Elms Ln.
Walk
Albert Bridge
Fulham Rd.
Edith Grove
Cheyne
Battersea Bridge
Battersea Bridge Rd.
Albert Bridge Rd.
Battersea Park
ZONE ← 12

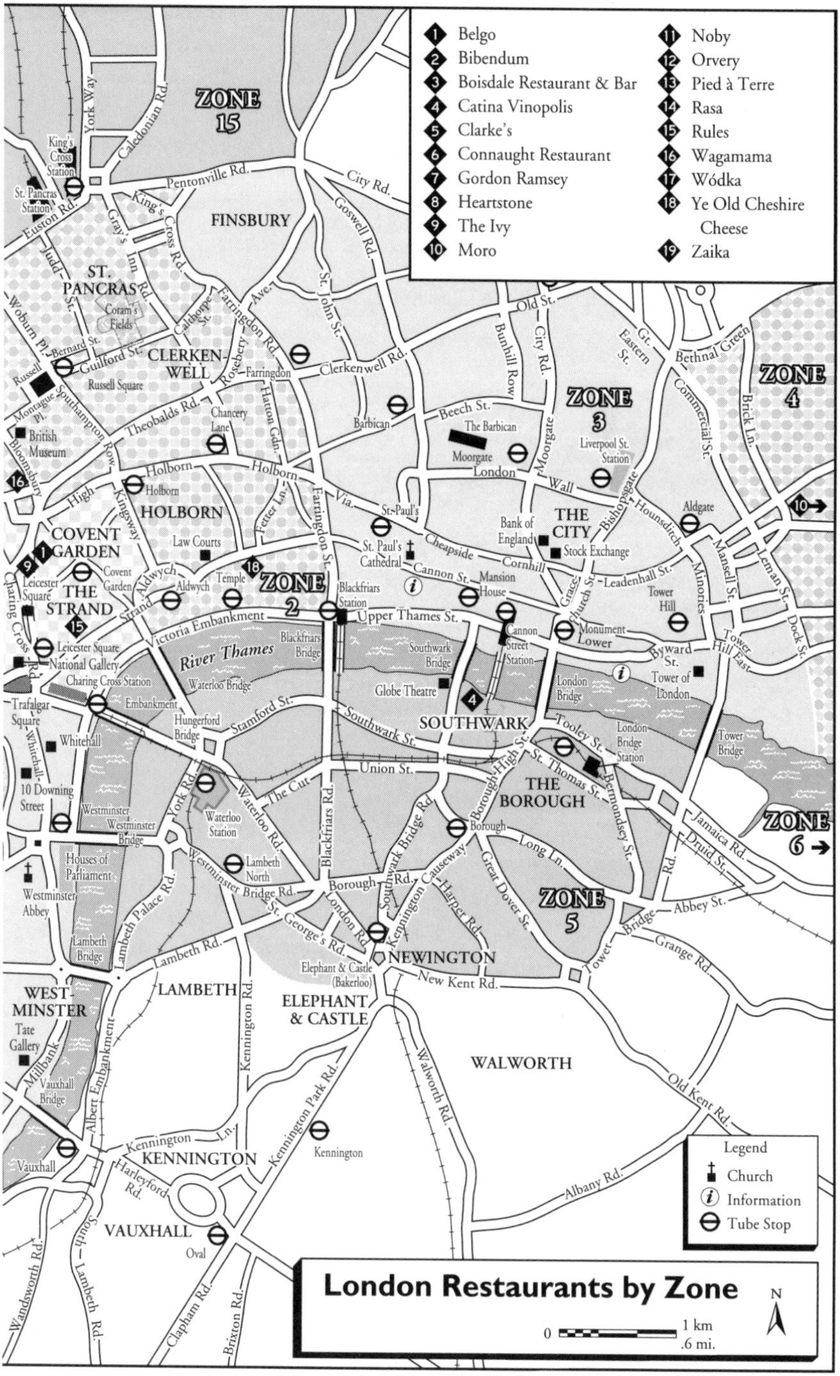
London Restaurants by Zone
1 Belgo
2 Bibendum
3 Boisdale Restaurant & Bar
4 Catina Vinopolis
5 Clarke's
6 Connaught Restaurant
7 Gordon Ramsey
8 Heartstone
9 The Ivy
10 Moro
11 Noby
12 Orvery
13 Pied à Terre
14 Rasa
15 Rules
16 Wagamama
17 Wódka
18 Ye Old Cheshire Cheese
19 Zaika
Legend
Church
Information
Tube Stop
0
1 km
.6 mi.
N
ZONE 15
ZONE 2
ZONE 3
ZONE 4
ZONE 5
ZONE 6
FINSBURY
ST. PANCRAS
CLERKEN-WELL
HOLBORN
COVENT GARDEN
THE STRAND
THE CITY
SOUTHWARK
THE BOROUGH
NEWINGTON
LAMBETH
ELEPHANT & CASTLE
WEST-MINSTER
WALWORTH
KENNINGTON
VAUXHALL
River Thames
Pentonville Rd.
City Rd.
Goswell Rd.
Clerkenwell Rd.
Old St.
Euston Rd.
Holborn
High Holborn
Cheapside
Cannon St.
Upper Thames St.
Victoria Embankment
Southwark St.
Stamford St.
Union St.
The Cut
Tooley St.
Long Ln.
Borough Rd.
New Kent Rd.
Old Kent Rd.
Albany Rd.
Walworth Rd.
Kennington Park Rd.
Kennington Rd.
Lambeth Rd.
Albert Embankment
Kennington Ln.
Harleyford Rd.
South Lambeth Rd.
Wandsworth Rd.
Clapham Rd.
Brixton Rd.
Jamaica Rd.
Druid St.
Abbey St.
Grange Rd.
Tower Bridge Rd.
Great Dover St.
Commercial St.
Brick Ln.
Leman St.
Minories
Leadenhall St.
Houndsditch
Bishopsgate
Moorgate
London Wall
Farringdon Rd.
Farringdon St.
Blackfriars Rd.
Waterloo Rd.
York Rd.
Westminster Bridge Rd.
Lambeth Palace Rd.
Whitehall
Kingsway
Aldwych
Strand
Charing Cross Rd.
Theobalds Rd.
Southampton Row
Woburn Pl.
Gray's Inn Rd.
King's Cross Rd.
Caledonian Rd.
York Way
King's Cross Station
St. Pancras Station
Russell Square
British Museum
Law Courts
St. Paul's Cathedral
The Barbican
Bank of England
Stock Exchange
Liverpool St. Station
Aldgate
Tower Hill
Tower of London
Tower Bridge
London Bridge
London Bridge Station
Globe Theatre
Waterloo Station
Waterloo Bridge
Blackfriars Bridge
Southwark Bridge
Hungerford Bridge
Westminster Bridge
Lambeth Bridge
Vauxhall Bridge
Houses of Parliament
Westminster Abbey
10 Downing Street
Trafalgar Square
National Gallery
Leicester Square
Charing Cross Station
Embankment
Tate Gallery
Millbank
Vauxhall
Oval
Kennington
Elephant & Castle (Bakerloo)
Lambeth North
Borough
Monument
Cannon Street Station
Mansion House
Blackfriars Station
Temple
Covent Garden
Holborn
Chancery Lane
Farringdon
Barbican
Moorgate

Hyde Park Corner, SW1; (0207) 259-5599; tube: Hyde Park Corner); the **Milestone** (Zone 11, 1 Kensington Court, W81; (0207) 917-1000; tube: High Street Kensington); the **Ritz** (Zone 8; 150 Piccadilly, W1; (0207) 493-8181; tube: Green Park); and the **Savoy** (Zone 7; 1 Savoy Hill, Strand, WC2; (0207) 836-4343; tube: Charing Cross).

HOW RESTAURANTS COMPARE IN LONDON

Name	Cuisine	Overall	Quality	Value	Price	Zone
Gordon Ramsay	European	★★★★★	★★★★★	★★★★	Very Exp	10
River Café	Italian	★★★★★	★★★★★	★★★	Very Exp	12
Orrery	European	★★★★½	★★★★½	★★★	Exp	14
Pied à Terre	British/ French	★★★★½	★★★★½	★★★	Exp	14
Zaika	Indian	★★★★½	★★★★½	★★★	Exp	13
Connaught Restaurant	French	★★★★	★★★★½	★★★	Exp	8
Moro	Spanish/Middle Eastern	★★★★	★★★★	★★★★	Mod	3
Clarke's	European	★★★★	★★★★	★★★	Mod–Exp	13
The Ivy	European	★★★★	★★★★	★★★	Mod	7
Bibendum	European	★★★★	★★★★	★★	Exp	11
Nobu	Japanese	★★★★	★★★★	★★	Exp	8
Heartstone	European	★★★½	★★★½	★★★★★	Inexp–Mod	15
Rasa	Indian	★★★½	★★★½	★★★★	Mod	8
Fifteen	British	★★★	★★★★	★★	Very Exp	3
Cambio de Tercio	Spanish	★★★	★★★½	★★★★	Mod	11
Rules	British	★★★	★★★½	★★★	Mod–Exp	7
Fish!	Seafood	★★½	★★★	★★★★	Inexp–Mod	7
Boisdale Restaurant and Bar	British	★★½	★★★	★★★	Mod	10
Cantina Vinopolis	European	★★½	★★★	★★★★	Mod	5
Wódka	Polish	★★½	★★★	★★★	Mod	11
Wagamama	Asian	★	★★	★★★★	Inexp	2, 7
Belgo	Belgian	★	★★	★★★★	Inexp–Mod	7

Restaurant Profiles

Belgo ★

BELGIAN | INEXPENSIVE–MODERATE | QUALITY ★★ | VALUE ★★★★ | ZONE 7

50 Earlham Street, WC2; (0207) 813-2233; tube: Covent Garden

72 Chalk Farm Road, NW1; (0207) 267-0718; tube: Chalk Farm, Camden Town

Reservations Recommended

Entrée Range £5–£16.95 **Payment** VISA, MC, AMEX, D, DC, CB **Bar** Outstanding beers **Disabled Access** Yes

Hours Monday–Friday, 12:30–3 p.m., 6–11 p.m.; Saturday, noon–11:30 p.m.; Sunday, noon–10:30 p.m.

House Specialties Croquettes de fromage; salade Liègoise; tomato crevettes; Belgian braised meats; mussels in all guises; Belgian crêpes and waffles; the beer list.

The formula here is simple: Sell Belgian food and drink at low prices, dress the waiters in monks' robes, and provide monastic surroundings. Not everyone's a fan, and the food (especially more complicated dishes) can be of variable quality. But settle in with a platter of mussels and a beer, and you should be quite content.

Bibendum ★★★★

MODERN EUROPEAN | EXPENSIVE | QUALITY ★★★★ | VALUE ★★ | ZONE 11

Michelin House, 81 Fulham Road, SW3; (0207) 581-5817; tube: South Kensington

Reservations Recommended

Entrée Range Lunch, £15.50–£26.50; dinner, £17.50–£31 **Payment** VISA, MC, AMEX, D, DC **Bar** Excellent but expensive wine selection **Disabled Access** Yes

Hours Monday–Friday, noon–2:30 p.m., 7–11:30 p.m.; Saturday, 12:30–3 p.m., 7–11:30 p.m.; Sunday, 12:30–3 p.m., 7–10:30 p.m.

House Specialties Escargots de Bourgogne; soupe de poisson; fish and chips; roast poulet de Bresse à l'estragon.

Bibendum was the first restaurant in Sir Terence Conran's soon-to-be empire, and it remains one of the best exponents of modern cooking in London. The sublime fare is served in airy Art Deco surroundings beneath exquisite stained-glass windows.

Boisdale Restaurant and Bar ★★½

BRITISH | MODERATE | QUALITY ★★★ | VALUE ★★★ | ZONE 10

15 Eccleston Street, SW1; (0207) 730-6922; tube: Victoria

Reservations Recommended

Entrée Range £16–£26.50; 2-course menu, £17.45 **Payment** VISA, MC, AMEX, D, DC, CB **Bar** Yes, with a good wine selection **Disabled Access** No

Hours Monday–Saturday, noon–2:30 p.m., 7–10:30 p.m.; Saturday, 7–10:30 p.m.

House Specialties Anything with a Scottish element, such as smoked salmon, smoked grouse, venison, Highland lamb, and Aberdeen Angus beef.

London's most serious champion of the food and drink of Scotland uses the freshest ingredients, prepares them well, and presents them in an attractive, welcoming setting that includes a bar where jazz is played. Boisdale's Back Bar, open throughout the day, has London's largest selection of single-malt scotch (whisky).

Cambio de Tercio ★★★

SPANISH | MODERATE | QUALITY ★★★½ | VALUE ★★★★ | ZONE 11

163 Old Brompton Road, SW5; (0207) 244-8970; tube: Gloucester Road

Reservations Recommended

Entrée Range £13.50–£15.50 **Payment** VISA, MC, AMEX **Bar** Yes; excellent selection of Spanish wines **Disabled Access** Restaurant only

Hours Daily, noon–2:30 p.m.; Monday–Saturday, 7–11:30 p.m.; Sunday, 7–11 p.m.

House Specialties Suckling pig; tapas.

One of London's best Spanish restaurants occupies a colorful basement room and is especially adept at reinterpreting classics with a modern slant. You can fashion a satisfying and varied meal from the tapas menu.

Cantina Vinopolis ★★½

MODERN EUROPEAN | MODERATE | QUALITY ★★★ | VALUE ★★★★ | ZONE 5

1 Bank End, SE1; (0207) 940-8333; tube: London Bridge

Entrée Range £11.50–£13.50 **Payment** VISA, MC, AMEX, DC **Bar** An enormous selection of wines available **Disabled Access** Yes

Hours Tuesday–Thursday, Sunday, noon–6 p.m.; Monday, Friday, Saturday, noon–9 p.m.

House Specialties An excellent selection of salads, including a cheese, pear, and beetroot concoction that can serve as an entrée, as can the house caesar; the simple chicken and fish dishes are nice accompaniments to the well-chosen wines.

Beneath a vaulted brick ceiling, London's "wine museum" serves a huge selection of vintages by the glass, and you can accompany your choices with pastas and other selections from a brasserie menu.

Clarke's ★★★★

MODERN EUROPEAN | MODERATE–EXPENSIVE | QUALITY ★★★★ | VALUE ★★★ | ZONE 13

124 Kensington Church Street, W8; (0207) 221-9225; tube: Notting Hill Gate

Reservations Essential

Entrée Range Lunch, £14; dinner, prix fixe, £48 for 4 courses **Payment** VISA, MC, AMEX, D, DC **Bar** Outstanding wine selection **Disabled Access** Restaurant yes, toilets no

Hours Monday–Friday, 12:30–2 p.m., 7–10 p.m.

House Specialties Menu changes daily.

No one in London understands Californian cooking better than Sally Clarke, who worked there years ago (at Chez Panisse, among other restaurants). Back home in London, she bases her deceptively simple preparations on the seasons and on what's available in the market on a given day. Accordingly, menus change daily, with a short carte at lunchtime and fixed menus at dinner. Even if you don't dine here, make a stop at Clarke's, an exquisite bakery known throughout all of London for its breads and tartes.

Connaught Restaurant ★★★★

FRENCH HAUTE CUISINE | EXPENSIVE | QUALITY ★★★★½ | VALUE ★★★ | ZONE 8

Carlos Place, W1; (0207) 499-7070; tube: Green Park

Reservations Essential

Entrée Range 3-course dinner menu, £45; 3-course lunch menu, £25 **Payment** VISA, MC, AMEX, D, DC, CB **Bar** Full service; excellent but expensive wine selection **Disabled Access** Limited

Hours Monday–Friday, noon–3 p.m.; Saturday and Sunday, noon–3:30 p.m.; Monday–Saturday, 5:45–11 p.m.; Sunday, 6–10:30 p.m.

House Specialties Classic French and British cooking; roasts from the trolley; game (in season).

Take a seat on a banquette in this elegant restaurant and give in to the experience: The cooking is never less than assured and can sometimes reach dazzling heights, and the service is as good as service ever gets.

Fifteen ★★★

MODERN BRITISH | VERY EXPENSIVE | QUALITY ★★★★ | VALUE ★★ | ZONE 3

Westland Place, N1; (0207) 251-1515, tube: Old Street

Reservations Required—months in advance

Entrée Range £25–£30 **Payment** VISA, MC, AMEX, D **Bar** Full service **Disabled Access** Limited

Hours Monday–Saturday, noon–3 p.m., 7–11 p.m.

House Specialties Slow-roasted pork with polenta and braised fennel; roasted sea bass.

If you don't know who Jamie Oliver is, you will by the time you leave London: You're sure to encounter the so-called "Naked Chef" on his TV show, in ads for Sainsbury's grocery stores, and on the covers of his books. Now he's opened what must be London's most popular restaurant, where he's devised an admirable twist—15 previously unemployed young people cook and run the premises under his stewardship, and the profits (which are surely hefty) go to charity. You must book several months in advance and then endure being squeezed into the rather unappealing pink and plastic surroundings. But take these shortcomings in stride if you can—the food lives up to its reputation. If you can't book a table, stop by the adjoining café for breakfast, which starts at 8 a.m.

Fish! ★★½

SEAFOOD | INEXPENSIVE–MODERATE | QUALITY ★★★ | VALUE ★★★★ | ZONE 7

3B Belvedere Road, SE1; (0207) 401-6734; tube: Waterloo

Cathedral Street, London Bridge, SE1; (0207) 407-3803; tube: Westminster

Reservations Call (0207) 234-3333 for all

Entrée Range £8.50–£16.95 **Payment** VISA, MC, AMEX, D, DC, JCB **Bar** Full service, good wine list **Disabled Access** Yes

Hours Borough Market, 10:30 a.m.–11 p.m.; County Hall, 11:30 a.m. –3 p.m., 5–11 p.m.

House Specialties Fresh fish, plainly cooked.

The Fish! empire is a swimming success throughout Britain, and that's because the simple formula is just right: offer the freshest fish and seafood, steam it or grill it, and serve it with a choice of sauces in attractive, spartan surroundings and they will come—especially families, for whom the reasonable prices and fun, informal surroundings seem to be tailor-made.

Gordon Ramsay ★★★★★

MODERN EUROPEAN | VERY EXPENSIVE | QUALITY ★★★★★ | VALUE ★★★★ | ZONE 10

68–9 Royal Hospital Road; (0207) 352-4441; tube: Sloane Square

Reservations Required, months in advance

Entrée Range Lunch, £35 for 3 courses; dinner, £65 for 3 courses, £80 for 7 courses **Payment** VISA, MC, AMEX, DC **Bar** Full service **Disabled Access** Yes

Hours Monday–Friday, noon–2 p.m. , 6:45–11 p.m.

House Specialties Panache of roasted sea scallops; salad of caramelized sweetbreads; oven-roasted duck.

It wouldn't be entirely cavalier to conjecture that Gordon Ramsay, London's favorite chef of the moment, provides the city's best dining experience. Quite simply, the food is sublime (and has earned three Michelin stars), and it is served in a small, elegant room in which the lighting is painstakingly designed so that spotlights over each table bring out the color of each dish. Service is so finely honed that diners are actually made to feel welcome and comfortable—quite an accomplishment in a veritable temple of gastronomy like this.

Heartstone ★★★½

MODERN EUROPEAN | INEXPENSIVE–MODERATE | QUALITY ★★★½ | VALUE ★★★★★ | ZONE 15

106 Parkway, NW1; (0207) 485-7744; tube: Camden Town

Reservations Advisable for dinner

Entrée Range £8.50–£15 **Payment** VISA **Bar** No **Disabled Access** Yes

Hours Tuesday–Saturday, 9 a.m.–9 p.m.; Sunday, 10 a.m.–4 p.m.

House Specialties Grilled fish; risotto.

Good ingredients (often organic) expertly prepared (often grilled)—a meal in these mellow, skylit surroundings shows you just how enjoyable healthy eating can be. A lot of the choices are vegetarian, but the menu includes some choices for fish eaters and carnivores, too.

The Ivy ★★★★

MODERN EUROPEAN | MODERATE | QUALITY ★★★★ | VALUE ★★★ | ZONE 7

1 West Street, WC2; (0207) 836-4751; tube: Leicester Square

Reservations Essential

Entrée Range Lunch £9–£23.50 **Payment** VISA, MC, AMEX, D, DC **Bar** Full service **Disabled Access** Restaurant only

Hours Monday–Saturday, noon–3:30 p.m., 5:30 p.m.–midnight; Sunday, 5:30 p.m.–midnight

House Specialties Simple classics such as steak tartare; calf's liver; smoked salmon with scrambled eggs; shepherd's pie; eggs Benedict; grilled or fried fish.

It's actually worth going to the trouble to book months in advance at this fashionable celeb hangout. But once in, don't spend too much time looking to see who's at the next table—just enjoy the simple but expert renditions of French and British classics.

Moro ★★★★

SPANISH/MIDDLE EASTERN | MODERATE | QUALITY ★★★★ | VALUE ★★★★ | ZONE 3

34–36 Exmouth Market, EC1; (0207) 833-8336; tube: Farringdon, Angel

Reservations Essential

Entrée Range £10.50–£15.50 **Payment** VISA, MC, AMEX, D **Bar** Excellent wine selection **Disabled Access** Yes

Hours Monday–Saturday, 12:30–2:30 p.m., 7–10:30 p.m.

House Specialties Any dish cooked in the wood-fired oven, such as cod with saffron rice, caramelized onions, and tahini; charcoal-grilled dishes like lamb kebab with egg and mint salad and bulgur; homemade breads and yogurt.

Moro is one of the most popular restaurants in London, and it's an emblem of the city's gastronomic renaissance. The area is off the beaten track as far as sightseeing is concerned (apart from Sadler's Wells Theatre, that is) but the neighborhood is becoming trendy, partly because of Moro's presence. If you can't nab a table, take a seat at the long bar and feast on tapas.

Nobu ★★★★

NEW JAPANESE | EXPENSIVE | QUALITY ★★★★ | VALUE ★★ | ZONE 8

19 Old Park Lane, W1; (0207) 447-4747; tube: Hyde Park Corner

Reservations Essential

Entrée Range £11.75–£27.50 **Payment** VISA, MC, AMEX, DC, CB **Bar** Full service **Disabled Access** Yes

Hours Monday–Friday, noon–2:15 p.m., 6–10:15 p.m.; Saturday, 6–11:15 p.m.; Sunday, 6–9:30 p.m.

House Specialties "Special appetizers" such as yellowtail sashimi with jalapeño and tomato rock shrimp ceviche; all traditional sushi and sashimi.

Nobu is a one-of-a-kind restaurant (even though there are branches in New York City and Beverly Hills). In a minimalist and chic setting with views of Hyde Park, Japanese staples take on Latin American influences, and the results are memorable.

Orrery ★★★★½

MODERN EUROPEAN | EXPENSIVE | QUALITY ★★★★½ | VALUE ★★★ | ZONE 14

55 Marylebone High Street, W1; (0207) 616-8000; tube: Baker Street

Reservations Essential

Entrée Range £17–£30 **Payment** VISA, MC, AMEX, D, DC, JCB **Bar** Full service, outstanding wine selection **Disabled Access** Yes

Hours Monday–Saturday, noon–3 p.m., 7–11 p.m.; Sunday, noon–3 p.m., 7–10:30 p.m.

House Specialties Menu changes all the time; duck and seafood preparations are excellent in any guise.

This small, skylit restaurant, one of several excellent dining experiences that Sir Terence Conran and his group own around London, offers chic, intimate surroundings and some of the best cooking in the city. The wine list is one of the finest in London, too, the presentation is brilliant, and the views over the gardens of St. Marylebone Church are sublime.

Pied à Terre ★★★★½

MODERN BRITISH/FRENCH | EXPENSIVE | QUALITY ★★★★½ | VALUE ★★★ | ZONE 14

34 Charlotte Street, W1; (0207) 636-1178; tube: Goodge Street

Entrée Range Lunch, £19.50 for 2 courses, £23 for 3 courses; dinner, £35 for 2 courses, £43.50 for 3 courses, £59.50 for 8 courses **Payment** VISA, MC, AMEX, D, DC, JCB **Bar** Exceptional wine selection **Disabled Access** Yes

Hours Monday–Friday, 12:15–2:30 p.m., 7–11 p.m.; Saturday, 7–11 p.m.

House Specialties Ceviche; other innovative fish preparations; eight-course tasting menu.

Diners take the sophisticated offerings here seriously and don't mind at all that the quiet, simply decorated room has little of the splash of some other well-known London eateries. The set meals are invariably a success, and the staff is expert at matching wine with food.

Rasa ★★★½

INDIAN | MODERATE | QUALITY ★★★½ | VALUE ★★★★ | ZONE 8

6 Dering Street, W1; (0207) 629-1346; tube: Oxford Circus

55 Stoke Newington Church Street, N16; (0207) 249-0344; tube: Manor House

5 Charlotte Street, W1; (0207) 637-0222; tube: Goodge Street

Reservations Recommended

Entrée Range £8–£14 **Payment** VISA, MC, AMEX, D, DC, CB **Bar** Full service **Disabled Access** Restaurant only

Hours Monday–Saturday, noon–3 p.m., 6–11 p.m.; Sunday, 6–11 p.m.

House Specialties Southern Indian vegetarian dishes.

The Rasa chain has introduced Londoners to Keralan (southern Indian) vegetarian cuisine, and it is served in stylish, pleasant surroundings. Multicourse Keralan feasts are available on request, and they are a treat that you'll long remember.

River Café ★★★★★

MODERN ITALIAN | VERY EXPENSIVE | QUALITY ★★★★★ | VALUE ★★★ | ZONE 12

Thames Wharf, Rainville Road W6; (0207) 386-4200, tube: Hammersmith

Reservations Required

Entrée Range £20–£35 **Payment** VISA, MC **Bar** Full service **Disabled Access** Yes

Hours Monday–Saturday, 12:30–3 p.m., 7–9:15 p.m.; Sunday, 12:30–3 p.m.

House Specialties Grilled squid; taglianni with red mullet.

The River Café has been receiving accolades ever since the 1990s, when Ruth Rogers, wife of architect Lord Richard Rogers (who designed the loftlike space), and Rose Gray began serving their beautiful fare based on fresh seasonal ingredients. The River Café upholds its standards, and a meal in this relaxed and minimalist space overlooking the Thames through huge windows is still a memorable event.

Rules ★★★

BRITISH | MODERATE–EXPENSIVE | QUALITY ★★★½ | VALUE ★★★ | ZONE 7

35 Maiden Lane, WC2; (0207) 836-5314; tube: Covent Garden, Charing Cross

Reservations Recommended

Entrée Range £16.95–£22.50 **Payment** VISA, MC, AMEX, D, DC, JCB **Bar** Good wine selection **Disabled Access** Yes

Hours Monday–Saturday, noon–11:30 p.m.; Sunday, noon–10:30 p.m.

House Specialties Game dishes; Aberdeen Angus beef.

Rules has been serving since 1798, and it seems to be improving with age. The old-fashioned interior is as charmingly stodgy as ever, and Rules is still one of the best places in London for an old-fashioned rib of beef, or steak and kidney pie.

Wagamama ★

ASIAN | INEXPENSIVE | QUALITY ★★ | VALUE ★★★★ | ZONES 2, 7

4A Streatham Street, WC1; (0207) 323-9223; tube: Tottenham Court Road

10A Lexington Street, W1; (0207) 292-0990; tube: Oxford Circus, Piccadilly Circus

Reservations Not accepted

Entrée Range £5.50–£8.50 **Payment** VISA, MC, AMEX, D, DC, JCB **Bar** Limited wine selection **Disabled Access** Yes, in most branches

Hours Monday–Saturday, noon–11 p.m.; Sunday, 12:30–10:30 p.m.

House Specialties Soup noodles, fried noodles, dumplings.

At this chain with outposts throughout the city, it's difficult to get too enthused about anything other than the bill. But that's saying a lot in high-priced London, and the noodles and other Asian dishes, served at long communal tables in minimalist settings, provide a filling and no-fuss meal.

Wódka ★★½

POLISH | MODERATE | QUALITY ★★★ | VALUE ★★★ | ZONE 11

12 St. Albans Grove, W8; (0207) 937-6513; tube: High Street Kensington

Reservations Recommended

Entrée Range £10.90–£13.90; set lunch menu, £10.90 for 2 courses, £13.50 for 3 courses **Payment** VISA, MC, AMEX, DC **Bar** Full service, specialty vodkas **Disabled Access** Yes

Hours Monday–Friday, 12:30–2:30 p.m., 7–11:15 p.m.; Saturday and Sunday, 7–11:15 p.m.

House Specialties Traditional Polish dishes such as blinis, dumplings, and herring.

Innovative interpretations of old classics prove that traditional Polish fare needn't be heavy and can be much more elegant than you might imagine. Meals are served in two plain, unpretentious rooms and are nicely accompanied by choices from the extensive vodka list.

Zaika ★★★★½

INDIAN | EXPENSIVE | QUALITY ★★★★½ | VALUE ★★★ | ZONE 13

1 Kensington High Street, W8; (0207) 795-6533; tube: South Kensington

Reservations Recommended

Entrée Range £12–£31 **Payment** VISA, MC, AMEX, D, DC, JCB **Bar** Wine and beer only **Disabled Access** Yes, but not to toilets

Hours Monday–Friday, noon–2:30 p.m., 6:30–10:45 p.m.; Saturday, 6–10:45 p.m.; Sunday, 6:30–9:45 p.m.

House Specialties "Jugalbandi" menu, tasting menu at £33.50 or £40 with selected wines; roast lamb; curry dishes.

Chef Vineet Bhatia's innovative take on Indian classics has earned him a Michelin star, and he serves his creations in swanky surroundings filled with antiques from the subcontinent.

Entertainment and Nightlife in London

To keep up with what's happening in London, pick up copies of *Time Out, What's On, Hot Tickets,* the Thursday supplement of *The Evening Standard,* or the Friday *Times.* If you are planning to enjoy some theater when you're in London, check out **www.officiallondontheatre.co.uk** for a listing of current plays, plus reviews, phone numbers, and tips.

You can obtain advance tickets for many performing arts in London with your credit card via Ticketmaster (phone (0207) 344-4444; **www.ticketmaster.co.uk**) and Firstcall (phone (0207) 420-0000; **www.firstcalltickets.com**). Just be advised that you'll add 10–20% to the price of a ticket in booking and service fees. Another option is **TKTS** booth in Leicester Square (see below) or turn up at the box office—you'll pay less and will get some assistance in choosing the best seat available.

Theater

London theater comes in three categories: the West End, off–West End, and fringe. Whichever category the play you want to see might fall into, here are some tips on obtaining tickets. Visit the **TKTS** discount ticket booth in Leicester Square (tube: Leicester Square), where you'll pay about half price for a ticket plus a £2.50 per-ticket service fee. The downside is that you'll have to spend precious vacation time (an hour or more) waiting in line. The booth accepts cash or credit cards (no traveler's checks) and is open Monday–Saturday, 10 a.m.–7 p.m., and Sunday, noon–3:30 p.m. (for matinees only). Do not go to one of the many shop fronts around Leicester Square that call themselves discounters but actually offer no deals at all; and do not buy from a tout, who will charge an astronomical sum. Many theaters offer half-price tickets on Mondays and for dress rehearsals. Some also grant discounts to students and seniors, and some sell discount tickets immediately before a performance. Lastly, it never hurts to check with your hotel concierge to see if there might be any special ticket allotments for hotel guests, or if the concierge can acquire tickets for you outright.

The West End

This term refers to an area of central London where many theaters are located, but some theaters are well outside this geographic area. The term is equivalent to "on Broadway" in terms of describing upper-echelon productions. West End theater includes big musicals and mainstream plays. Some of Britain's most esteemed theater companies, with permanent locations, are "West End," and on their stages you are going to see some of the most reliably good theater in London.

Royal National Theatre Zone 5; South Bank, SE1; (0207) 452-3400; **www.nationaltheatre.org.uk;** tube: Embankment or Southwark. Presents new works and classical drama, as well as musical works for children and other entertainment. Tickets run £10–£30; the box office is open Monday–Saturday, 10 a.m.–8 p.m.

Royal Court Zone 11; Sloane Square, SW1; (0207) 565-5000; **www.royalcourttheatre.com;** tube: Sloane Square. Considered the most important venue for new writers in Britain, as it has been for almost 40 years. There are two theaters: the "Downstairs" main theater and the "Upstairs" studio. Performances are held Monday–Saturday at 7:30 p.m., and the Saturday matinee is held at 3:30 p.m. Tickets are £10–£26 (£7.50 on Monday); the box office is open Monday–Saturday, 10 a.m.–6 p.m.

The Royal Shakespeare Company After a major shakeup, the company recently left its London base at the Barbican Centre. These days, the world's most esteemed performers of Shakespeare tour for six months a year, do a season at their home in Stratford-upon-Avon, and perform in different London theaters. For information, call (01789) 296-655 or visit **www.rsc.org.**

Shakespeare's Globe Theatre Zone 5; New Globe Walk, SE1; (0207) 401-9919; **www.shakespeares-globe.org;** tube: Blackfriars. A faithful reconstruction close to the original site of the theater where Shakespeare staged his plays. The Globe is a major London tourist attraction and a museum honoring the Bard, and from April to October it stages excellent renditions of the work in the open air. The box office is open Monday–Friday, 10 a.m.–6 p.m. during the off-season; it's open daily, 10 a.m.–8 p.m. during the season. Tickets are £5–£29 (the best "seats" in the house are the £5 standing-room spots in front of the stage).

Off–West End

You'll usually find the most creativity in Off–West End theaters, where writers, directors, and actors enjoy artistic freedom that can sometimes be lacking in the more commercially motivated West End. Expect to pay anywhere from £5 to £20 for tickets.

The Almeida Near Zone 3; Almeida Street, N1; (0207) 359-4404; **www.almeida.co.uk;** tube: Angel. With emphasis firmly on the modern and avant-garde, the Almeida features cerebral drama from top writers and actors.

Bush Theatre West of Zone 13; Shepherd's Bush Green, W12; (0207) 610-4224; **www.bushtheatre.co.uk;** tube: Shepherd's Bush or Goldhawk Road. The intimate, 105-seat Bush Theatre is considered the next-most important spot (after the Royal Court Theatre) for productions by new writers, many of whom have gone on to greater successes.

The Gate Zone 13; at the Prince Albert, 11 Pembridge Road, W11; (0207) 229-0706; tube: Notting Hill Gate. The Gate has a fine reputation for its low-budget yet high-quality drama from all over the world. Performances run Monday–Saturday; tickets are £6–£12.

The King's Head Zone 15; 115 Upper Street, N1; (0207) 226-8561; **www.kingsheadtheatre.org;** tube: Angel. London's most venerable pub theater, frequently putting on top-quality, small-scale revues and musicals.

Regent's Park Open Air Theatre Zone 14; Regent's Park, NW1; (0207) 486-2431 or (0207) 486-1933; **www.open-air-theatre.org.uk;** tube: Baker Street. Set in the eponymous park, this venue presents high-quality productions from June to September.

Riverside Studios Zone 12; Crisp Road, W6; (0208) 237-1111; **www.riversidestudios.co.uk;** tube: Hammersmith. Overlooks the river Thames near Hammersmith bridge and presents theatrical and dance productions in three studio spaces.

Young Vic Zone 5; 66 The Cut, SE1; (0207) 928-6363; **www.youngvic.org;** tube: Southwark. Standing in the shadows of the Old Vic theater, the Young Vic attracts big-name actors and touring companies such as the Royal Shakespeare Company.

Fringe

Fringe theater can be bold, but not necessarily so—just because a theater company struggles doesn't mean it puts on good productions. A reliably worthy fringe theater is **The Finborough** (at Finborough Arms, Finborough Road, SW10; (0207) 373-3842; **finboroughtheatre.itgo.com**), a small pub venue that hosts new writers, some of whom end up in the West End or on Broadway.

Classical Music, Opera, and Dance

London is arguably the music capital of the world. While Ticketmaster and other booking agencies provide tickets to some music, opera, and dance events, your best bet is to contact the box offices directly.

The Barbican Centre Zone 3; Silk Street; (0207) 638-8891 or (0207) 638-4141; **www.barbican.org.uk.** This ugly, modernist complex is fortunately blessed with superb acoustics and is home to the London Symphony Orchestra; it also hosts the "Great Orchestras of the World" series. Other great orchestras that perform a wide range of classical music at the Barbican are the BBC Symphony Orchestra, the City of London Sinfonia, and the English Chamber Orchestra.

The London Coliseum Zone 7; St. Martin's Lane, WC2; (0207) 632-8300, **www.eno.org;** tube: Charing Cross. A grand venue that is home to the English National Opera, which takes a populist approach with affordable tickets and a selection of accessible works sung in English, from Mozart's *The Marriage of Figaro* to Gilbert and Sullivan's *The Mikado.*

The Place Theatre Zone 15; 17 Duke's Road WC1; (0207) 387-0031; **www.theplace.org.uk;** tube: Euston, Euston Square, or British Rail: Euston. Hosts more than 32 dance events annually, featuring British and international contemporary dance companies, with a platform for new and emerging choreographers. The theater also features a special children's season.

Royal Albert Hall Zone 13; Kensington Gore, SW; (0207) 589-3203 or (0207) 589-8212; **www.royalalberthall.com;** tube: Gloucester Road or South Kensington. A prodigious Victorian building that sometimes plays host to pop gigs, Cirque du Soleil, and even wrestling bouts. Yet it recalls the glories of its heyday during the Henry Wood Promenade Concerts (more affectionately known as "The Proms"), held each year from July to September.

Royal Opera House Zone 7; Covent Garden, WC2; recording (0207) 304-4000 or box office (0207) 240-1200; **www.royalopera.org;** tube: Covent Garden. Mounts lavish classical productions of operas and ballets, and the price of the tickets is as breathtaking as the venue: up to £175! Within the Royal Opera House, there are two more intimate venues for opera and dance: the Linbury Studio Theater, with 420 seats, and the Clore Studios, a 200-seat space which is ideal for workshops and performances.

Sadler's Wells Zone 2; Rosebury Avenue, EC1; (0207) 863-8000; tube: Chancery Lane; more intimate and central branch: Peacock Theatre; Zone 2; Portugal Street, off Kingsway, WC2; (0207) 314-8800; **www.sadlers-wells.com;** tube: Holborn. Both houses feature contemporary ballet performances.

South Bank Centre Zone 5; Belvedere Road, South Bank, SE1; box office (0207) 960-4242; recording (0207) 633-0932; **www.sbc.org.uk;** tube: Waterloo. Perched just above the Thames next to Waterloo Bridge, this is home to the London Philharmonic and the Philharmonia. Its Royal Festival Hall is the main auditorium for symphony concerts; the smaller Queen Elizabeth Hall puts on semi-stage operas and chamber groups; and recitals as well as ensembles are performed in the intimate setting of the adjacent Purcell Room.

Wigmore Hall Zone 8 at 36 Wigmore Street, W1; (0207) 935-2141; **www.wigmore-hall.org.uk;** tube: Bond Street. The best place in town to hear piano recitals and chamber groups.

Festivals

London stages several open-air festivals over the summer, such as the **Hampton Court Palace Festival** (west of Zone 12; Hampton Court, East Molsey, Surrey; (0207) 344-4444; **www.hamptoncourtfestival.com**), when the palace grounds are the setting for classical music. **The Holland Park Theatre** (Zone 13; Holland Park, Kensington High

Street, W8; box office (0207) 602-7856; information (0207) 603-1123; **www.operalondon.com;** tube: High Street Kensington or Holland Park) stages an array of music, theater, and dance performances in one of London's loveliest parks from June to August. Tickets are £10–£30.

Free Concerts

Many churches in central London offer free lunchtime classical concerts and recitals; among them are **St. John's** (Zone 7; Waterloo Road; tube: Waterloo), **St. Martin-in-the-Fields** (Zone 7; St. Martin's Place; tube: Leicester Square or Charing Cross), and **St. Pancras Church** (Zone 15; Euston Road; tube: Euston). The **Royal College of Music** (Zone 13; Prince Consort Road, SW7; (0207) 591-4314; **www.rcm.ac.uk;** tube: Gloucester Road, High Street Kensington) has free performances Monday–Thursday at 1:05 p.m., and during term at 7 p.m. The **Royal Academy of Music** (Zone 14; Marylebone Road; (0207) 873-7300; **www.ram.ac.uk;** tube: Marylebone or Baker Street) offers performances every day at 1:05 and 5:05 p.m.

Live Jazz, Pop, and Rock

London is a mecca for live music. In addition to clubs around town (see nightclub profiles, below), the Barbican and South Bank Centre often present top international stars, and two big jazz festivals are held in the autumn: the **Soho Jazz Festival** and the **Oris London Jazz Festival.** The **Notting Hill Carnival,** Europe's largest street fest, pumps jazz into the London sky in late August.

Gargantuan rock structures include the 11,000-seat **Wembley Arena** (west of Zone 14; Empire Way, Wembley, Middlesex; (0208) 902-0902; **www.wembleyticket.com;** tube: Wembley Park); the 20,000-seat **Earl's Court Exhibition Centre** (Zone 11; Warwick Road, SW5; (0207) 385-1200, **www.eco.co.uk;** tube: Earl's Court); and the 12,000-capacity **London Arena** (Zone 6; Limeharbour, Isle of Dogs, E14; (0207) 538-1212; **www.londonarena.co.uk;** rail: Docklands Light Rail, Crossharbour and London Arena).

Among the smaller-scale venues are the **Shepherd's Bush Empire** (near Zone 12; Shepherd's Bush Green, W12; (0208) 354-3300; **www.shepherds-bush-empire.co.uk;** tube: Shepherd's Bush), a top popular music spot with an excellent sound system. The **Carling Academy Brixton** (Zone 5; 211 Stockwell Road, SW9; (0207) 771-3000; **www.brixton-academy.co.uk;** tube: Brixton) has a 4,300-person capacity and attracts many popular bands.

Laughs in London

You might not catch all the references or innuendo, but these London clubs will keep you laughing.

Chuckle Club Zone 2; Houghton Street, WC2; (0207) 476-1672; tube: Holborn. An itinerant club with some brilliant comedy that resides at the London School of Economics. Performances are held on Saturday only, starting at 8:30 p.m.

Comedy Café Zone 3; 66 Rivington Street, EC2; (0207) 739-5706; tube: Old Street. Grants free admission on Wednesday, when new acts make their debuts. Comedy Café is open Wednesday–Sunday.

Comedy Store Zone 7; at Haymarket House, Oxedon Street, SW1; (0207) 344-0234; **www.thecomedystore.co.uk;** tube: Piccadilly Circus. The venue from which alternative comedy exploded onto British television screens. Many stars began their careers here, and the comedy remains fresh and top-notch.

Jongleurs Zone 11; The Cornet, 49 Lavender Gardens, SW11; (0207) 564-2500; **www.jongleurs.com;** tube: Clapham Junction. Hosts an impressive lineup of performances at the address above and at its chain of clubs around the capital.

Bars and Pubs

If you want to enjoy a pint in olde-worlde surroundings, you could not do better than the **Prospect of Whitby** (Zone 4; 57 Wapping Wall, E1; (0207) 481-1095; tube: Wapping), with trappings that include an Elizabethan pewter bar, flagstone floors, cast-iron hearths, and small round windows. The atmospheric old place dates back to 1520. A haven for journalists and scribblers of all types since before 1666, **Ye Old Cheshire Cheese** (Zone 2; 145 Fleet Street, EC4; (0207) 353-6170; tube: Blackfriars) has served such regulars as Thackeray, Johnson, Voltaire, Pope, Dickens, and Tennyson in its nooks and crannies warmed by blazing fires.

On a more modern note, you can enjoy cocktails in opulent settings and often to the accompaniment of a piano at the city's noted hotel bars, among them the Windows Bar on the 28th floor of the **Hilton** (Zone 8; Park Lane, W1; (0207) 493-8000; tube: Hyde Park Corner or Green Park), with a dazzling view thrown in. The Art Deco ambience of the **Savoy** (Zone 7; 1 Savoy Hill, Strand, WC2; (0207) 836-4343; tube: Charing Cross) competes with the sheer opulence of the **Dorchester** (Zone 8; 53 Park Lane, W1; (0207) 629-8888; **www.dorchesterhotel.com;** tube: Marble Arch). For more on the London drinking scene, see our nightclub profiles, below.

Casinos

The gaming industry in Great Britain is one of the most carefully regulated in the world. All casinos are licensed under the Gaming Act of 1968, which stipulates that players who are not members of a gaming club or the guest of a member must register at the casino 24 hours before entering to play; a passport, driver's license, or other suitable identification is required. Casinos are generally open 2 p.m.–4 a.m. and require either jacket and tie or, at least, some form of dressy attire. Clubs include the posh **50 St. James** (Zone 7; 50 St. James Street, SW1; (0207) 491-4678; tube: Piccadilly), which opened in 1828 as London's first club built for the purpose of gaming, and is, along with the legendary **Les Ambassadeurs Club** (Zone 8; 5 Hamilton Place, W1; (0207) 495-5555; tube: Hyde Park), at the top end of the market. More proletarian venues include the **Rendezvous Casino** (Zone 8; 14 Old Park Lane, W1; (0207) 491-8586; tube: Hyde Park); the **Sportsman Casino** (Zone 8; 40 Bryanston Street, W1; (0207) 414-0061; tube: Hyde Park), and the mass-market **Golden Nugget Casino** (Zone 7; 22 Shaftesbury Avenue, W1; (0207) 439-0099; tube: Piccadilly). For more on all these casinos, visit **www.clublci.com.**

HOW LONDON NIGHTCLUBS COMPARE

Name	Comments	Cover
Bagley's	Gigantic disco and bar	None–£20
Bull's Head	Jazz club	£4–£10
Café de Paris	London's most renowned club	£15
The Fridge	Brixton's most celebrated disco	£5–£12
Heaven	Gay paradise	£12
Jazz Café	Modern club geared toward rap, soul, funk, and jazz	£8–£20
Ministry of Sound	The U.K.'s most famous disco	None–£15
Pizza Express	Intimate jazz club and restaurant	£15–£20
Pizza on the Park	Upmarket jazz/cabaret/restaurant	£10–£20
Ronnie Scott's	London's premier jazz club	£15–£25
606	Highly regarded jazz club and restaurant open for over 25 years	£6–£8
Turnmills	Disco where all-night clubbers end up	None–£10
The Vortex Jazz Bar	Popular jazz club-cum-café, bar, and restaurant	£4–£10

Nightclub Profiles

London has a huge range of nightclubs offering everything from hardcore techno to smooth jazz to tabletop dancers. London's clubs generally provide excellent quality. Many clubs offer reduced admission rates before 10:30 p.m., and it is easier to gain admittance at that hour. A club that is quiet at 11 p.m. can often be packed to the rafters by midnight. Some clubs in London start late and carry on until 6 a.m., with their busiest period being between 11:30 p.m. and 2 a.m. If you intend to dine at the club, we recommend you book a table for 10 p.m., after which you will be permitted to stay on for the dancing. Not all clubs serve dinner; call the club and ask for information.

Bagley's

GIGANTIC DISCO AND BAR

Who Goes There Youthful dancers and soaks

King's Cross Depot, York Way, N1; tube: King's Cross/St, Pancras; (0207) 278-2777 | Zone 15

Cover Friday, £14–£20; Saturday, £14 **Prices** Cheap by club standards **Dress** Smart, casual **Food Available** Snacks

Hours Friday–Saturday, 10:30 p.m.–6:30 a.m.

What Goes On Sweat rises like smoke off the dance floor.

Setting & Atmosphere Bagley's is colossal, with five dance floors, six bars, and something different going on in every room.

If You Go You will be part of a heaving, throbbing mob of young movers in one of the many rooms.

Bull's Head

JAZZ CLUB

Who Goes There The 25–55 age group; actors, musos, film and telly people

373 Lonsdale Road, SW13; tube: East Putney; (0208) 876-5241 | Zone 12

Cover £4–£10, depending on the celebrity of the band **Prices** Modest **Dress** Anything goes **Food Available** Excellent Thai cuisine

Hours Monday–Saturday, 11 a.m.–11 p.m.; Sunday, noon–10:30 p.m.

What Goes On Most of the modern greats have played here.

Setting & Atmosphere The Bull's Head, built in 1684, is a beautiful pub facing the Thames. The mood is convivial.

If You Go Offer to buy the musicians a pint.

Café de Paris

LONDON'S MOST RENOWNED CLUB

Who Goes There Everyone who is anyone in London

3–4 Coventry Street, W1; tube: Piccadilly Circus; (0207) 734-7700 | Zone 7

Cover £15 **Prices** Somewhat pricey **Dress** Elegant **Food Available** French cuisine presided over by an ex–Anton Mosimann chef

Hours Closes at 3 a.m.

What Goes On Live jazz music accompanies dinner, after which a DJ spins records for the more athletically inclined. The café is furnished with numerous bars.

Setting & Atmosphere Since its launch in the 1920s, Café de Paris has been synonymous with high society—even the queen has given a party here. Such luminous performers as Marlene Dietrich, Maurice Chevalier, Fred Astaire, Noël Coward, Frank Sinatra, and Edith Piaf have graced its stage. The Café's Art Deco design was influenced by the operas *Don Giovanni* and *La Bohème*. A 50-foot bar encompasses the oval ballroom, and the restaurant is highly regarded.

If You Go Circumvent any nonsense at the door by booking a table for dinner. Please do not turn up in your baseball cap and sneakers.

The Fridge

BRIXTON'S MOST CELEBRATED DISCO

Who Goes There Clientele varies according to what's on any given night, but it's played host to the gay and lesbian scene for some time now

Town Hall Parade, Brixton Hill, SW2; tube: Vauxhall; (0207) 326-5100 | Zone 5

Cover £5–£12 **Prices** Average **Dress** Casual **Food Available** Fast

Hours Daily, 10 p.m.–6 a.m.

What Goes On Dancing and trancing out to techno.

Setting & Atmosphere A vast dance floor, a huge bar, capacious balconies, and a place to really let it all hang out. Highly recommended for the open-minded. Renowned DJs spinning every night. Call for special-event information.

If You Go Call a respectable minicab company to get home.

Heaven

GAY PARADISE

Who Goes There Straights and gays

The Arches, Villiers Street, WC2; tube: Charing Cross; (0207) 930-2020 | Zone 7

Cover £12 **Prices** Average **Dress** Flamboyant **Food Available** Coffee bar–type sandwiches and munchies

Hours Monday and Wednesday, 10:30 p.m.–3 a.m.; Friday and Saturday, 10 p.m.–5 a.m.

What Goes On Saturday night is gay night, but all are welcomed.

Setting & Atmosphere The crowded rooms don't make any claim to be stylish, the place pulsates to techno music, it can be impossible to get near any of the three bars, and the dancers are far from angelic-looking. Unless you're into this kind of scene, you're likely to think you've wound up in Hell.

If You Go Arrive before 10:30 p.m. Heaven is notorious for its hellish queues.

Jazz Café

MODERN CLUB GEARED TOWARD RAP, SOUL, FUNK, AND JAZZ

Who Goes There 20–55-year-olds, depending on whether jazz or rap is featured

5 Parkway, N1; tube: Euston; (0207) 916-6060 | Zone 15

Cover £8–£20 according to the popularity of the act **Prices** Average **Dress** Anything goes **Food Available** Dinner from modern European menu

Hours Monday–Thursday, 7 p.m.–1 a.m.; Friday and Saturday, 7 p.m.–2 a.m.; Sunday, 7–11 p.m.

What Goes On This club's name is something of a misnomer, since the Jazz Café may have rap, soul, or funk bands performing rather than jazz groups; consult the listings pages of *Time Out* or call before going.

Setting & Atmosphere The bar leads onto the dance floor, where there are some seats available. The restaurant is situated on the balcony overlooking the stage and projectors transmit arty neon images onto the awnings.

If You Go Get into the mood of whatever music happens to be featured

Ministry of Sound

THE U.K.'S MOST FAMOUS DISCO

Who Goes There Regulars who've been coming for years, newcomers

103 Gaunt Street, SE; tube: Vauxhall; (0207) 378-6528 | Zone 5

Cover Friday, £12; Saturday, £15 **Prices** Slightly expensive **Dress** Glamorous **Food Available** None

Hours Friday, 10:30 p.m.–5 a.m.; Saturday, 11 p.m.–8 a.m.

What Goes On Young to youngish clubbers bopping to monotonously loud and repetitious drum 'n' bass grooves.

Setting & Atmosphere Ministry of Sound is a vast converted warehouse located in the not exactly salubrious boondocks of Elephant and Castle. You will find yourself dancing to everything from U.K. garage to R&B hits; check listings or call for the nights on which American DJs are imported to show the locals how it is done.

If You Go Wear your dancing shoes.

Pizza Express

INTIMATE JAZZ CLUB AND RESTAURANT

Who Goes There Pizza and jazz lovers of both tourist and local variety

10 Dean Street, W1; tube: Tottenham Court Road; (0207) 439-8722 | Zone 7

Cover £15–£20, depending on status of band **Prices** Average **Dress** Smart, casual **Food Available** Pizza, pasta, lasagna, salad Niçoise, etc.

Hours Daily, 7:45 p.m.–midnight; shows begin at 9 p.m.

What Goes On Eighty percent of the bands booked are celebrated Americans of the status of Tal Farlow, Art Farmer, Kenny Garret, and Roy Haynes. Pizza Express also books top British talent such as Martin Taylor and Guy Barker.

Setting & Atmosphere An intimate basement equipped with modern stage lighting and sound. The environment is friendly, sophisticated, and relaxed. The food and wine are excellent, and the music is superb. A memorable night out. The place has been dubbed London's best live music venue by *Time Out* magazine.

If You Go You will enjoy yourself.

Pizza on the Park

UPMARKET JAZZ/CABARET/RESTAURANT

Who Goes There Generally older crowd of 45+ category

11–13 Knightsbridge, SW1; tube: Knightsbridge; (0207) 235-5273 | Zone 10

Cover £10–£20 **Prices** Fairly average, which is somewhat surprising considering the posh location **Dress** Smart, casual **Food Available** Yes

Hours Monday–Friday, 8:30 a.m.–midnight; Saturday, 9:30 a.m.–midnight

What Goes On Jazz and cabaret shows begin at 9:15 p.m. and end at 11:15 p.m.

Setting & Atmosphere The club is located on the site of a Victorian tea shop, which was saved from demolition in 1986 by Peter Boizot, who then commissioned Enzu Apicella to transform the place into a modern jazz/cabaret club. POTP is clubby, intimate, dimly lit, and freshly flowered.

If You Go Try the wild Scottish smoked salmon, reputed to be the best in town.

Ronnie Scott's

LONDON'S PREMIER JAZZ CLUB

Who Goes There Yuppies, buppies, musicians, arty types

47 Frith Street, WI; tube: Tottenham Court Road; (0207) 439-0747 | Zone 7

Cover £15–£25 **Prices** A little lower than average **Dress** Smart **Food Available** Full menu of modern European cuisine and à la carte as well

Hours Monday–Saturday, 8 p.m.–3 a.m.; gigs at 9:30 p.m.

What Goes On Affluent diners and drinkers are serenaded by famous musicians downstairs, while others choose to attend the upstairs disco.

Setting & Atmosphere Ronnie's is pushing 40 now and is as close as London will ever get to the classic sort of jazz club you have seen in countless films. The large, dark room is comfortable, with enough space between tables that you won't feel like you've been crammed onto a bus. The walls are lined with photos of jazz greats.

If You Go Prepare for an enjoyable evening.

606

HIGHLY REGARDED JAZZ CLUB AND RESTAURANT OPEN FOR OVER 25 YEARS

Who Goes There Yuppies, buppies, and bohemians, young and old

90 Lots Road, SW10; tube: South Kensington; (0207) 352-5953; www.606.co.uk | Zone 11

Cover No cover per se, but there is a per-person "music charge": £6 Sunday–Thursday, £8 Friday and Saturday, £7 Sunday **Prices** Modest to reasonable **Dress** Casual **Food Available** Extensive European-based menu, featuring a wide selection of meat, fresh fish, vegetarian

Hours Friday and Saturday, 8 p.m.–2 a.m.; Sunday, 8 p.m.–midnight; Monday–Wednesday, 8 p.m.–1 a.m.; Thursday, 9:30 p.m.–2 a.m.

What Goes On There are two jazz groups on each night from Monday through Wednesday playing from 7:30 p.m. until midnight. One band is featured, playing from around 8 p.m. until 11 p.m. The groups are selected from a variety of up-and-coming players and more established musicians. The music ranges from traditional to contemporary, with an emphasis on the modern.

Setting & Atmosphere A basement club with a brick-walled entrance, frescoes of jazz legends, and a relaxed, comfortable vibe. The 606 is a great place to take a date.

If You Go Have a late supper. The cuisine at the 606 has been praised by the *Sunday Times* and TV's *The Restaurant Show,* among others.

Turnmills

DISCO WHERE ALL-NIGHT CLUBBERS END UP

Who Goes There Hard-core club hoppers

63B Clerkenwell Road, EC1; tube: Moorgate; (0207) 250-3409 | Zone 3

Cover £10 Saturday only **Prices** Lowish **Dress** Casual **Food Available** Bar food

Hours Tuesday, 6:30 p.m.–midnight; Friday, 10:30 p.m.–7:30 a.m.; Saturday, 10 p.m.–5 a.m.

What Goes On In addition to the mandatory drinking and dancing, this club provides a few pinball machines.

Setting & Atmosphere Candlelit tables and an electronica bar area provide a refreshing contrast to the throbbing chaos of the dance floor.

If You Go Check out Anexo, a sister club next door. Turnmills also hosts Trade, Britain's top gay night.

The Vortex Jazz Bar

HIGHLY REGARDED JAZZ CLUB-CUM-CAFÉ, BAR, AND RESTAURANT

Who Goes There Arty types

139–141 Stoke Newington Church Street, N16; tube: Moorgate; (0207) 254-6516 | Zone 3

Cover £4–£10 **Prices** Reasonable **Dress** Informal **Food Available** The café serves coffee, cappuccino, teas, cakes, and mainly vegetarian hot meals, soups, and salads

Hours Daily, 10 a.m.–5 p.m., 8 p.m.–midnight

What Goes On Mainstream and avant-garde jazz music is presented here. The Vortex also plays host to special-guest club nights devoted to international music, cabaret, women musicians, and young contemporary artists. The club welcomes visiting musicians from America and mainland Europe.

Setting & Atmosphere The Vortex is a first-floor venue in the heart of Stoke Newington. It's intimate, shadowy, and seedy.

If You Go Seek out the nonsmoking areas.

Shopping in London

The bad news first: Goods are expensive in London. Now, the good news: There is a bounty of wonderful merchandise to be had in London, and many of the stores, even large department stores, are extremely pleasant places to browse and buy.

The Big Shopping Neighborhoods

Knightsbridge Zone 10; tube: Knightsbridge. **Harrods** is here, as are the boutiques of Beauchamp (pronounced "Beecham") Place and Walton Street.

Fulham Road Zone 11; tube: South Kensington. Before you get to the trendy **Joseph Boutique** at Brompton Cross, where Fulham Road actually starts, you'll pass some very haut monde stores of fashion: **Tokio, The Library**, and **NK Space** (two designer boutiques and a designer and cosmetics place). From Brompton Cross to Edith Grove, Fulham Road is lined with a stretch of shops whose goods cover the gamut, from the height of fashion and the latest housewares, to the best used treasures.

New and Old Bond Streets Zone 8; tube: Bond Street. **Chanel, Tiffany, Cartier**—they're all here in this swath of expensive real estate.

Kensington Church Street Zone 11; tube: High Street Kensington. This street of antiques, with shops stretching from Kensington High Street all the way to Notting Hill Gate, is great for window-shopping, and though prices are high, you may just find the objet you can't live without.

King's Road Zone 11; tube: Sloane Square. This stretch is no longer as quite as hip as it was in the 1960s and 1970s, when Mary Quant set up shop to sell her revolutionary miniskirts, but boutiques and trendy stores continue to come and go.

Sloane Street Zone 10; tube: Knightsbridge. The two blocks between Brompton Road and Sloane Square house every hot designer you can think of; and if you don't find the designer store you're looking for, check out **Harvey Nichols,** famed for its fashionable merchandise, at the end of the street.

Oxford and Regent Streets Zone 7; tube: Oxford Circus. Department stores line these streets, along with outlets of such ubiquitous retailers as **Gap** and **Virgin Megastores;** the crème de la crème includes **Liberty,** the Tudor-style department store, as well as such traditional British emporia as **Burberry's, Jaeger,** and **Aquascutum.**

Markets

The Apple Market Zone 7; tube: Covent Garden. A must-see, especially on the weekends when the buskers (street entertainers) and throngs are milling. Just about anything—crafts, woolens, fruits, vegetables, flowers, upscale clothing—is available at this lively market, open daily from 10 a.m. to 7 p.m. A Mondays-only antiques market sells jewelry, silver, and knickknacks at relatively reasonable prices.

Bermonsey Market Zone 5; Bermonsey Square; tube: London Bridge, Borough. Since this market , also known as the New Caledonian, is open Friday only, from 5 a.m. to 2 p.m., it pays to be the early bird to pick over the selection of antiques of every description, including clothing and jewelry.

Brick Lane Market Zone 3; Brick Lane; tube: Aldgate East, Shoreditch, Liverpool Street. This East End market is open only on Sundays from 8 a.m. to 1 p.m. It is still kind of basic, without much of the sexy stuff, but it does have its fans. As the East End becomes more fashionable, this market is becoming a bit more fashionable, with hip, young designer gear vying with chipped crockery for your attention.

Camden Market Zone 15; Camden Town; tube: Camden Town. Huge crowds converge to pore over the hip clothing, jewelry, and records. The Victorian Market Hall, open daily, sells everything from London souvenirs to antiques to books on three floors. Camden Market is open Thursday and Friday from 9 a.m. to 5 p.m. and weekends from 10 a.m. to 6 p.m. Follow Chalk Farm Road to the Stables, a weekend market of antiques and secondhand goods.

Camden Passage Market Zone 3; Camden Passage; tube: Angel. The outdoor stalls at this market offer an interesting array of antiques and collectibles, open Wednesday, 10 a.m.–2 p.m., and Saturday, 10 a.m.–5 p.m. The Passage also houses many antiques stores. For a preview, visit **www.antiquescamdenpassage.co.uk.**

Columbia Flower Market Zone 3; Columbia Road east of Ravenswood Street; tube: Old Street. Beautiful flowers, as well as gift items and jewelry, are sold here on Sundays only, from 8 a.m. to 1 p.m.

Greenwich Markets Zone 5; take Greenwich Docklands Light Rail (DCR) or Cutty Sark DCR from Tower Tube. The charming streets of Greenwich host several markets on Saturday and Sunday, from 9 a.m.–6 p.m.: a crafts market in the center of town; the Bosun's Yard market, also specializing in crafts and such; the Canopy Antiques Market, a flea market with plenty of interesting junk; and the Greenwich Antiques Market, with many stalls of vintage clothes, as well as a variety of collectibles and antiques.

Leather Lane Market Zone 2; tube: Chancery Lane. A market has been doing business on this site at Leather Lane for more than 300 years. Leather goods are indeed available, and they're not too expensive either, nor are electrical and household items, CDs, and the like. The market is open Monday–Friday, 10:30 a.m.–2 p.m.

Petticoat Lane Market Zone 3; Middlesex Street and environs; tube: Liverpool Street. There was indeed a street of this name, until the Victorian sensibilities found the reference to ladies' unmentionables to be unsuitable for municipal nomenclature. These days hundreds of stalls—selling clothing, shoes, household goods, crafts, you name it—line a number of streets in the area. The market is open on Sunday only, 9 a.m.–2 p.m.

Portobello Market Zone 3; tube: Notting Hill Gate. Located on Portobello Road, from the Notting Hill end to the Ladbroke Grove end, this market is really several markets in one. Come on Saturday, the liveliest day at Portobello. The antiques stores are at the Notting Hill end; as you head toward Ladbroke Grove, clothing takes over, and at the end of the street, as you turn left on Westbourne Grove Road, you'll walk through densely packed stalls of secondhand clothes, head shop–type paraphernalia, vintage shoes, food, and loud music. The antiques market is held on Saturday, 7 a.m.–6 p.m.; the more general market is open Monday–Wednesday, 9 a.m.–5 p.m.; and the organic market takes place Thursday, 11 a.m.–6 p.m. Clothing and knickknacks are for sale Friday, 7 a.m.–4 p.m.; Saturday, 8 a.m.–5 p.m.; and Sunday, 9 a.m.–4 p.m.

Spitalfields Market Zone 3; Commercial Street between Lam and Brushfield; tube: Liverpool Street. Stalls sell a bounty of organic foods, as well as lots of ethnic fast food. Combine your trip to Spitalfields with a stop at the Petticoat Lane and/or Brick Lane Markets. Visit on Sunday, because both the general market and the organic market are open, starting at 9 a.m. (The general market is also open Monday–Friday, 11 a.m.–3 p.m., and the organic market is open Friday, 11 a.m.–3 p.m.)

Walthamstow Walthamstow High Street; tube: Walthamstow Central. Europe's longest daily street market, open Monday–Saturday, 8 a.m.–6 p.m., has 450 stalls and 300 shops. The goods are pretty ordinary—food, clothes, electrical equipment—but the market is fun to see, there's plenty of good eats, and in the summer, there's live entertainment.

Department Stores

Fortnum & Mason Zone 9; 181 Piccadilly, W1; (0207) 734-8040; **www.fortnumandmason.co.uk;** tube: Green Park. You might not think of this as anything other than a food emporium, but in fact F&M has floors that carry clothing, clocks, and gifts above its ground floor stocked with jellies and jams. The interior is beautiful, and the cream tea is classic.

Harrods Zone 10; 87 Brompton Road, SW1; (0207) 730-1234; **www.harrods.com;** tube: Knightsbridge. Harrods made its 100-plus-year-old reputation by satisfying every possible whim: The store once famously delivered a camel to a customer. The array of merchandise is still impressive, and the food halls live up to their international reputation.

Harvey Nichols Zone 10; 109–125 Knightsbridge, SW1; (0207) 235-5000; **www.harveynichols.com;** tube: Knightsbridge. Beloved by rich fashionistas, Harvey Nichols offers floors of designer clothes, plus a good restaurant on the fifth-floor food hall.

John Lewis/Peter Jones John Lewis: Zone 14; 278–306 Oxford Street, W1; (0207) 629-7711; **www.johnlewis.co.uk;** tube: Oxford Circus. Peter Jones: Zone 11; Sloane Square, SW1; (0207) 730-3434; tube: Sloane Square. No one is going to accuse either of these stores of being trendy, but they really do carry everything, from picture hooks to computers, at good prices.

Liberty Zone 7; 210–220 Regent Street, W1; (0207) 734-1234; **www.liberty-of-london.co.uk;** tube: Oxford Circus. This Tudor-style emporium is famous for its fabrics, and it also sells many antiques, prints, and other goods from the Far East.

Marks and Spencer Main branch: Zone 14; 458 Oxford Street, W1; (0207) 935-7954; **www.marks-and-spencer.co.uk;** tube: Bond Street. M&S, or Marks and Sparks as it's known, provides food and fashion, as well as some of London's most popular brands of underwear.

Selfridges Zone 14; 400 Oxford Street, W1; (0207) 629-1234; **www.selfridges.co.uk;** tube: Marble Arch. Ongoing improvements are bringing this huge old emporium up to date and giving it a natty image to match its extravagant facade. Designer wear, silver, beauty products, furniture, as well as restaurants and a very comprehensive food hall, make a stop here a satisfying shopping experience.

Where to Find . . .

Antiques

In addition to the large markets that sell antiques—Bermonsey, Camden Passage, and Portobello—antiques arcades include **Alfie's Antique Market** (Zone 14; 13–15 Church Street, NW8; (0207) 723-6066; tube: Edgeware Road), open Tuesday–Saturday, 10 a.m.–6 p.m., and **Gray's Antiques Market** and **Gray's Mews Market** (Zone 8; off Oxford Street at 58 Davies Street, W1; (0207) 629-7034; **www.graysantiques.com;** tube: Bond Street), open Monday–Friday, 10 a.m.–6 p.m.

Beauty and Bath

Culpepper the Herbalist (Zone 7; 8 The Market, Covent Garden Piazza, WC2; (0207) 379-6698; tube: Covent Garden) sells bath salts, oils, teas, spices, essential oils—they've got it all here. A branch is located at 21 Bruton Street, W1; (0207) 629-4559. **MAC Cosmetics** (Zone 11; 109 King's Road, SW3; (0207) 349-0022; tube: Sloane Square) offers new, trendy makeup that doesn't cost the world. **Neal's Yard Remedies** (Zone 7; 15

Neal's Yard, WC2; (0207) 379-7222; tube: Covent Garden) is a great place for homeopathic remedies, fresh herbs, essential oils, soaps, and hair-care products, all in beautiful blue glass bottles; call for branches. **SPace.NK Apothecary** (Zone 7; 37 Earlham Street, WC2; (0207) 379-7030; tube: Covent Garden) offers the latest and greatest in cosmetics and beauty products at its popular store; call for branch locations.

Books

In addition to the ubiquitous branches of **Borders, Waterstone's,** and the other chains, London is blessed with such long-standing institutions as **Hatchard's** (Zone 8; 187 Piccadilly, W1; (0207) 439-9921; **www.hatchards.co.uk;** tube: Piccadilly Circus), the city's oldest bookstore, with a very fine selection. The city also has any number of specialist bookshops, such as **Books for Cooks** (Zone 13; 4 Blenheim Crescent, Notting Hill, W11; (0207) 221-1992; tube: Ladbroke Grove), with a vast selection of cookbooks and books about food, plus a café. **Edward Stanford** (Zone 7; 12–14 Long Acre, WC2; (0207) 836-1321; tube: Leicester Square) stocks a huge collection of maps, globes, and travel books. **Forbidden Planet** (Zone 2; 71–75 New Oxford Street, WC1; (0207) 836-4179; tube: Tottenham Court Road) is billed as "The Science Fiction Entertainment Store" and has indeed got it all, from toys to videos to all kinds of printed matter. **Gay's the Word** (Zone 2; 66 Marchmont Street, Bloomsbury, WC1; (0207) 278-7654; tube: Russell Square) carries an extensive selection of books on gay and lesbian subjects. **Grant & Cutler** (Zone 8; 55–57 Great Marlborough Street, W1; (0207) 734-2012; **www.grant-c.demon.co.uk;** tube: Oxford Street), Great Britain's largest foreign language bookshop, has books, videos, cassettes, and more in about 200 languages. **Helter Skelter** (Zone 2; 4 Denmark Street, St. Giles, WC2; (0207) 836-1151; tube: Tottenham Court Road) is a music bookshop with sheet music, mags, music-related art, and all possible fiction and nonfiction about the subject.

If you're interested in secondhand books, take a walk down Charing Cross Road. You should also seek out **Any Amount of Books** (Zone 7; 56 Charing Cross Road, WC2; (0207) 836-3697; tube: Leicester Square) and **Unsworths Booksellers** (Zone 2; 12 Bloomsbury Street, WC1; (0207) 436-9836; **www.unsworths.com;** tube: Tottenham Court Road). **Henry Southeran** (Zone 8; ground floor at 2 Sackville Street, W1; (0207) 429-6151; tube: Green Park) deals in rare antiquarian books, as well as reproductions of antiquarian volumes.

Clothing

Harvey Nichols, Harrods, Selfridges, and **Liberty** carry good selections of designer clothes (see "Department Stores," page 191). **Browns** (Zone

7; 23–27 South Moulton Street, W1; (0207) 514-0000; tube: Bond Street) has a huge selection of all the big names, while **Koh Samui** (Zone 7; 65 Monmouth Street, WC2; (0207) 240-4280; tube: Covent Garden) carries a mix of fashion from both the established big names and the avant-garde.

For traditional British fashions, the major houses are **Aquascutum** (Zone 8; 100 Regent Street, W1; (0207) 675-9050; tube: Piccadilly Circus), **Burberry's** (161-165 Regent Street, W1; (0207) 734-4060; tube: Piccadilly Circus), and, for the ultimate in men's shirts, **Turnbull & Asser** (Zone 8; 70 Jermyn Street, W1; (0207) 808-3000; tube: Piccadilly Circus).

Gifts

Asprey and Garrard (Zone 7; 167 New Bond, W1; (0207) 493-6767; tube: Bond Street) is the perfect place to pick up a cut-glass paperweight or other frivolous yet classy mementos. For a supply of the national beverage, check out **R. Twining and Company** (Zone 7; 216 Strand, WC2; (0207) 353-3511; tube: Temple), where tea has been sold since 1706. If the pampered pet you left behind is expecting a rhinestone collar or other souvenir from London, make a trip to **Woof Woof** (Zone 11; 178A King's Road, SW3; (0207) 352-6244; tube: South Kensington).

Home Accessories

The Conran Shop (Zone 11; Michelin House, 81 Fulham Road, SW3; (0207) 589-7401; tube: South Kensington) sets the standard for stylish, clean-lined modern items for bed, bath, kitchen, and nursery. Very traditionally English in style are the wares at **General Trading Company** (Zone 11; 2 Symons Street, SW3; (0207) 730-0411; tube: Sloane Square), which offers everything you can imagine wanting for the home or tabletop. **Thomas Goode** (Zone 8; 19 South Audley Street, W1; (0207) 499-2823; tube: Green Park) provides a genuine English shopping experience, with major china, silver, and crystal, as well as knickknacks. Have a spot of tea here, too.

Kids' Things

Hanley's (Zone 7; 188-196 Regent Street, W1; (0208) 752-2278; tube: Piccadilly Circus) is the first place to stop for toys, which are displayed on seven fun-filled floors. For old-fashioned toys, check out the amazing collection at **Benjamin Pollock's Toyshop** (Zone 7; 44 The Market, WC2; (0207) 636-3452; tube: Covent Garden). You can dress the little ones in Italian style at **Iana** (186 King's Cross Road, SW3; (0207) 352-0060; tube: South Kensington), or go for a Dutch designer look at Oilily (Zone 10; 9 Sloane Street, SW1; (0207) 823-2505; tube: Sloane Square). **Peter Rabbit and Friends** (Zone 7; 42 The Market; (0207) 497-1777; tube: Covent Garden) is heaven for a Beatrix Potter buffs, and the popular critters appear as stuffed toys, emblazoned on T-shirts, and in many other forms as well.

Perfume

Floris (Zone 8; 89 Jermyn Street, SW1; (0845) 702-3239; tube: Piccadilly Circus) is the classic English fragrance and soap maker, in business since 1730. Also offered are potpourri and candles. **Penhaligons** (Zone 7; 41 Wellington Street, WC2; (0207) 629-1416; tube: Covent Garden), making scents since 1870, is great for gifts and has numerous branches.

Woolens and Linens

Irish Linen Company (Zone 8; 35–36 Burlington Arcade, W1; (0207) 493-8949; tube: Piccadilly Circus) sells Irish linen and Egyptian cotton sheets and tablecloths. **Scotch House** (Zone 7; 191 Regent Street, W1; (0207) 581-2151; tube: Oxford Circus) has scarves, kilts, jackets, capes, gloves, and everything else that can be made from wool and cashmere. Call for information on branches. **Shirin Cashmere** (Zone 11; 12 Beauchamp Place, SW3; (0207) 581-1936; tube: Knightsbridge) purveys an extremely elegant (and expensive) selection of sweaters, scarves, and other garments. The **White House** (Zone 8; 40–41 Conduit Street, W1; (0207) 629-3521; tube: Bond Street) sells unbelievably lovely bedclothes at unthinkably extravagant prices.

Exercise and Recreation in London

Spectator Sports

Cricket

You can see this game played throughout England from mid-April to early September, and there are two main venues in London:

Lord's Zone 14; St. John's Wood Road, NW8; (0207) 432-1000; **www.lords.org.uk;** tube: St. John's Wood. Home of the Marylebone Cricket Club and often considered the home of cricket. Tickets begin at £18.

Oval Cricket Ground South of Zone 5; Kennington Oval, SE11; (0207) 582-6660; tube: Oval. International cricket is often played here. Tickets are £30–£50.

Football

The football (soccer to Americans) season runs from August to May. Leading London teams include:

Arsenal Zone 15; Arsenal Stadium; Avenell Road, N5; (0207) 704-4000; **www.arsenal.co.uk;** tube: Arsenal. Tickets £23.50–£43.50.

Chelsea Zone 11; Stamford Bridge; Fulham Road, SW6; (0207) 385-5545); **www.chelseafc.co.uk;** tube: Fulham Broadway. Tickets £28–£40.

Charlton Athletic East of Zone 6; The Valley; Floyd Road, SE7; (0208) 333-4010; **www.cafc.co.uk;** BritRail: Charlton. Tickets £15–£30.

Tottenham Hotspur West of Zone 1; White Hart Lane; High Road, N17; 0208) 365-5000; **www.spurs.co.uk;** BritRail to White Hart Lane. Tickets £25–£55.

West Ham United East of Zone 4; Boleyn Ground; Green Street, E13; (0208) 548-2748; **www.westhamunited.co.uk;** tube: Upton Park. Tickets £26–£46.

Greyhound Racing

Greyhound-racing venues include:

Catford Stadium South of Zone 6; Adenmore Road, SE6; (0208) 690-8000; BritRail: Catford, Catford Bridge. Tickets £4.50.

Romford Stadium North of Zone 4; London Road, Romford, Essex; (0170) 876-2345; **www.coraleurorbet.co.uk;** BritRail: Romford. Tickets £1.50–£5.

Walthamstow Stadium East of Zone 15; Chingford Road, E4; (0208) 531-4255; **www.wsgreyhound.co.uk;** tube: Walthamstow Central and then a minicab. Tickets £2.50–£5.

Wimbledon Stadium Zone 12; Plough Lane, SW17; (0208) 946-8000; **www.wimbledonstadium.co.uk;** tube: Wimbledon. Tickets £3–£5.

Horse Racing

The flat season runs from April to September, and the jumps or steeplechase runs from October to April. Racing venues include:

Ascot Race Course High Street, Ascot, Berkshire; (0134) 462-2211; **www.ascot.co.uk;** BritRail: Ascot. Tickets £10–£48, depending on whether you sit in the grandstand or the silver ring.

Epsom Downs Epsom, Surrey; (0137) 272-6311; **www.epsomderby.co.uk;** British Rail: Epsom Downs. Tickets £11–£20.

Kempton Park Staines Road East; (0193) 278-2292; **www.kempton.co.uk;** BritRail: Sunbury on Thames, Kempton Park. Tickets £6–£18.

Sandown Park The Racecourse, Portsmouth Road, Esher, Surrey; (0137) 246-3072; **www.sandown.co.uk;** BritRail: Esher. Tickets £11–£18.

Windsor Maidenhead Road, Windsor, Berks; (0175) 386-5234; **www.windsor-racecourse.co.uk.** BritRail: Windsor, Eton Riverside. Tickets £5–£16. The castle overlooks the course.

Rugby

Rugby League is the professional form of rugby; Rugby Union is traditionally the amateur form of rugby football. The season runs from August to May. Teams to watch out for are the Harlequins, London Irish, Saracens, and the Wasps. A major venue is **Twickenham Rugby House** (Zone 12; 21 Rugby Road; Twickenham Middlesex; (0208) 892-2000; **www.rfu.com**). Ticket prices vary.

Tennis

In the build-up to the world-famous Wimbledon championships, the smaller but equally popular **Stella Artois** tournament takes place in mid-June at Queens Club (Palliser Road, W14; (0207) 385-3421; tube: Barons Court). Tickets are £24–£57; book early.

Wimbledon fortnight starts the last week in June, and demand for tickets always far exceeds the supply. To obtain tickets for Centre Court or Number One Court, you must write for an application form, enclosing a self-addressed envelope, between September 1 and December 31: The All England Lawn Tennis Club, P.O. Box 98, Church Road, London, SW19; call (0208) 778-0131 or visit **www.wimbledon.org.** Late in the day, you can often purchase returned show court tickets at a reduced price. Take the tube to Wimbledon (District line).

Recreation

Bicycling

The London Bicycle Tour Company runs guided tours and also rents out bikes; call (0207) 928-6838 or visit **www.londonbicycle.com.**

Golf

The **English Golf Union** (National Golf Centre, Woodhall Spa, Lincolnshire LN10 6PM; (01526) 354-500; **www.englishgolfunion.org**) is an excellent source of information on courses that can be reached with relative ease from London. These include:

Brent Valley Zone 13; Church Road Cuckoo Lane, W7; (0208) 567-1287; BritRail: Hanwell.

Chingford Golf Course East of Zone 4; Bury Road, E4; (0208) 529-5708; BritRail: Chingford.

Richmond Park Zone 12; Roehampton Gate, Richmond Park, SW15; (0208) 876-3205; BritRail: Barnes.

Royal Mid-Surrey Golf Club Zone 12, Old Deer Park, Twickenham Road, Richmond, Surrey; (0208) 940-1894; BritRail, tube to Richmond.

Gyms and Leisure Centers

Many hotels in London have their own facilities or have arrangements under which guests can use the facilities at a nearby club. Some sport and leisure clubs in central London are:

Chelsea Sports Center Zone 11, Chelsea Manor Street, SW3; (0207) 352-6985; tube: Sloane Square, South Kensington. Offers a 25-meter pool and the usual weights, aerobics classes, and so on.

Jubilee Hall Leisure Center Zone 7, 30 The Piazza, Covent Garden, WC2; (0207) 836-4835; **www.jubileehallclubs.co.uk;** tube: Covent Garden. Has a new cardio theater, free weights, and resistance machines; yoga and various exercise classes.

Queen Mother Sports Center Zone 9, 223 Vauxhall Bridge Road, SW1; (0207) 630-5522; tube: Victoria. Very central, this complex has a complete range of facilities, equipment, and classes.

Seymour Leisure Center Zone 14, Seymour Place, W1; (0207) 723-8019; tube: Marble Arch. This center has an Olympic-size pool, steam rooms, cardiovascular machines, and a snooker room.

Horseback Riding

Hyde Park is popular with riders, who enjoy paths that include Rotten Row. You can rent horses for group riding at **Hyde Park and Kensington Stables** (Zone 14; 63 Bathurst Mews, W2; (0207) 723-2813; **www.hydeparkstables.com;** tube: Lancaster Gate, Paddington; closed Mondays). The cost for group riding is £39 an hour.

Ice Skating

A popular and central rink is **Leisurebox** (Zone 14; 17 Queensway, W2, (0207) 229-0172; tube: Bayswater or Queensway). Admission is £6–6.50, including skate hire; Friday and Saturday nights are disco nights.

Inline Skating

There are good skating tracks around Hyde Park and Battersea Park. You can rent skates at several outlets near Hyde Park/Kensington Gardens, including **Snow and Rock** (Zone 13; 19 Kensington High Street, W8; (0207) 937-0872; **www.snowlandrock.com;** tube: Kensington High Street).

Swimming

Almost every borough of London has at least one public pool. Here are some popular swimming spots in London:

Hampstead Heath Ponds Zone 1, Millfield Lane, NW3; (0207) 485-3873; tube: Hampstead, Hampstead Heath; BritRail: Cospel Oak. Three ponds in picturesque surroundings; free.

The Lido Zone 1, Gordon House Road, NW3; (0207) 485-3873; BritRail: Gospel Oak. London's biggest outdoor pool; open daily, April–September; £3.50, £1.50 for concessions.

The Oasis Zone 7, 32 Endell Street, WC2; (0207) 831-1804; tube: Covent Garden, Holborn. Indoor and outdoor pool; £3 adults, £1.10 children over age 5, and free for children under age 5.

Serpentine Lido Zone 14, Hyde Park; (0207) 298-2100; tube: Hyde Park Corner, Lancaster Gate, Marble Arch. July–September only, daily, 10 a.m.–6 p.m.; £2.70 adults and 60p children.

Tennis

Almost all London parks have tennis courts, which are available at very little cost; call the **Lawn Tennis Association** at the Queens Club in West Kensington (phone (0207) 381-7000) for a booklet called "Where to Play Tennis in London."

Part Five

The Southeast of England

The rolling fields, orchards, pastoral villages, and chalky downs of southeastern England have nurtured any number of great figures, from Charles Dickens to Henry James to Winston Churchill, to name just a few. Once you begin exploring the back roads of this small corner of England—the most remote bit of which is only two hours from London—it's easy to see why so many writers, kings, queens, statesmen, and, especially in recent times, untold numbers of vacationers seeking a rural retreat have taken refuge in these landscapes. In these southern counties of Kent and Sussex, you'll find beautiful countryside, miles of English Channel beaches, and the palaces, gardens, cathedrals, and historic homes that past residents have left behind. As you maneuver the twisting lanes, you may want to remember a line from another great English writer, C. K. Chesterton: "Before the Roman came to Rye or out to Severn strode, the rolling English drunkard made the rolling English road."

Not To Be Missed in the South of England

- Canterbury, cathedral and town (page 201)
- Dover Castle (page 217) and the White Cliffs (page 218)
- The town of Rye (page 221)
- Ightham Mote, a medieval manor house (page 234)
- Gardens at Sissinghurst (page 237)

Canterbury

Bell Harry, the famous bell tower of **Canterbury Cathedral,** is visible for miles across the orchards and fields of the Kentish countryside. As you enter the beautiful city beneath the towers, you're in good company. Pilgrims have made their way here for centuries, and in their footsteps you'll find one of England's great cathedrals, the seat of the Anglican church since 597, and a small, friendly medieval city that is a pleasure to explore.

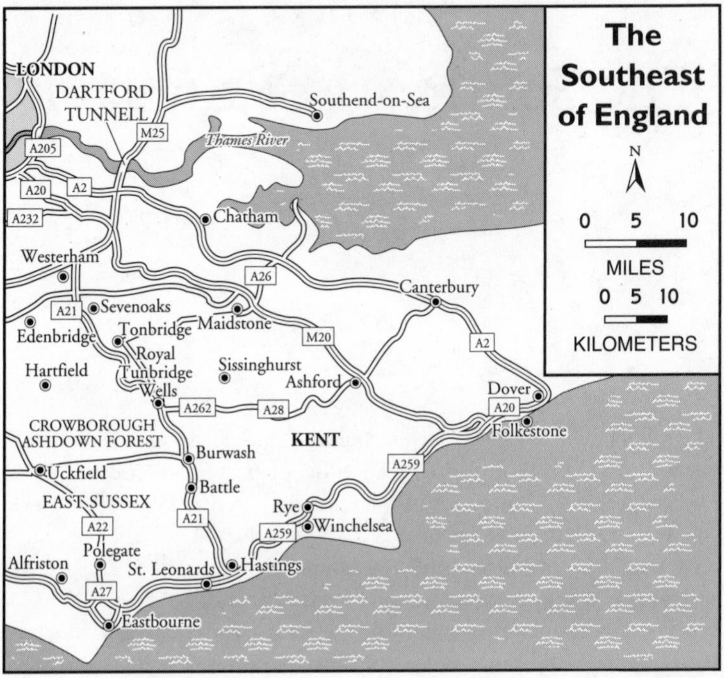

Canterbury, of course, was the goal of the pilgrims in Geoffrey Chaucer's *The Canterbury Tales,* and the medieval lanes and squares still seem as lively as Chaucer depicted them. In fact, it's all the easier to step back in time a bit in Canterbury because that intrusive beast of modern times, the automobile, has been banned from most of the city center.

Planning Your Visit to Canterbury

The Canterbury **Visitor Information Centre** (2/3 Sun Street, Canterbury CT1 2HX; **www.canterbury.co.uk**) provides maps, listings of major attractions, and notices of special events and can help you find a room—a blessing in the busy summer months when the city fills to bursting. For information, call (01227) 378100; for accommodations, call (01227) 378108. Open January–March: Monday–Saturday, 9:30 a.m.–5 p.m.; April–October: Monday–Saturday, 9:30 a.m.–5:30 p.m., Sunday, 10 a.m.–4 p.m.; November–December: Monday–Saturday, 9:30 a.m.–5 p.m., Sunday, 10 a.m.–6 p.m.

Special Events in Canterbury

Canterbury hosts many performing-arts events throughout the year. Some are held in the cathedral and, given this setting, provide a memorable experience. Check with the Visitor Information Centre when you arrive for a list of goings-on; the center also sells tickets to many events.

For two weeks in October, the **Canterbury Festival** presents a superb program of concerts, dance performances, plays, and readings at the cathedral and other venues around the city; the festival also stages a carnival procession that brings a great deal of color to Canterbury's medieval streets. For information and tickets, call (01227) 378188.

December music programs in the cathedral include traditional English carols and a performance of *The Messiah*—not to be missed if you are anywhere near Canterbury at this time; for information and tickets, call (01227) 378188.

Arriving and Getting Oriented in Canterbury

Canterbury is 62 miles southeast of London. Trains run about every half hour from London's Victoria Station to Canterbury East Station, and about every hour from London's Charing Cross Station to Canterbury West Station. The trip takes about an hour and a half and costs about £18. For information, call (08457) 484950 or go to **www.railtrack.co.uk.** Both train stations are at the edge of the city center and within easy walking distance of the cathedral and other sights.

By car, the quickest route from London is the M25/M20 toward Folkstone; exit at Ashford onto the A28 for the short drive north to Canterbury. The trip takes just over an hour, but traffic in and around London can add considerable time. Several car parks are located on the outskirts of Canterbury and are well marked along the routes into the city. Free shuttle buses connect these car parks with the city center and operate Monday–Saturday, 7 a.m.–7 p.m.; at other times, parking attendants provide a token for a free ride on city buses. The fee is £1.50 per car per day. You can also use the car parks at the fringes of the city center; in these, obtain a ticket from a machine by punching in numbers from your license plate and place it on the dashboard in easy view; the fee is about £1 an hour, 7 a.m.–7 p.m., and about £2 flat rate, 7 p.m.–7 a.m.

National Express buses leave London's Victoria Coach Station for Canterbury about every hour. The trip takes about one hour and 50 minutes and costs £14.50. For more information, call (08705) 808080 or go to **www.gobycoach.com.** The bus station is on St. George's Lane at the edge of the pedestrian zone of the city center and within easy walking distance of the cathedral and other sights.

Canterbury is small and compact, and strolling along its medieval lanes is a pleasure. You can easily walk to all of the major sights in town. The main thoroughfare changes its name from St. George's Street to Parade Street to High Street to St. Peter's Street as it bisects the center of the old city; signposts along the street point the way to all the major attractions.

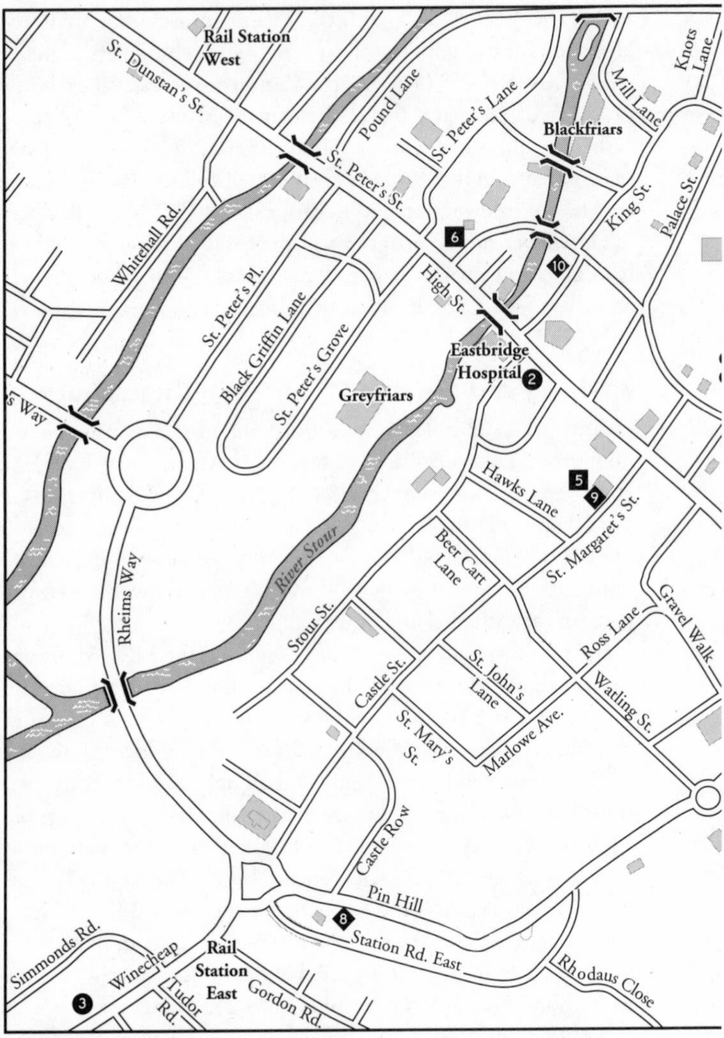

Hotels in Canterbury

Canterbury Gate — *£47–£84*

OVERALL ★★★★ | QUALITY ★★★½ | VALUE ★★★★

Canterbury Gate Hotel, 36 Burgate, Canterbury, Kent CT1 2HA; (10227) 464381; fax (10227) 462800; cgate@cgate.demon.co.uk; www.cathgate.co.uk

Location 30 paces away from the cathedral.

Amenities & Services 26 rooms. The public areas are unusually pleasant, and include a comfy lounge, a rooftop patio with view of the cathedral towers, and a bow-windowed breakfast room overlooking medieval Burgate.

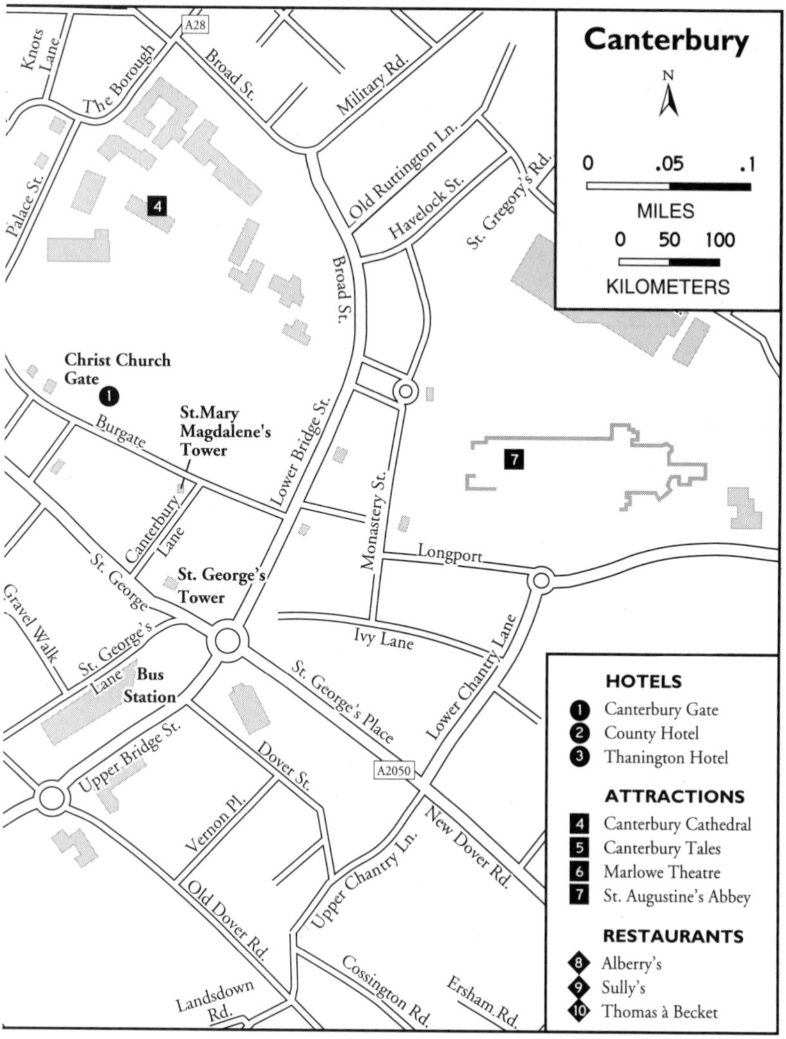

Elevator No.

Parking For £3 a day, the hotel provides a voucher for city-run car parks.

Pricing Includes Continental breakfast; full English breakfast available for £6.

Credit Cards V, MC, AMEX, D

The character-filled and atmospheric Canterbury Gate is wonderfully located in a 1438 building that abuts Cathedral Gate and overlooks the cathedral and precincts. In the spacious and comfortable rooms, you'll find all the sloping floors, heavy beams, leaded windows, and low doorways you need to take you back several centuries. Furnishings are comfortably old-style without being coyly antique, and they include a few modern amenities, such as TVs and telephones.

HOW HOTELS COMPARE

Hotel	Overall Rating	Quality Rating	Value Rating	Price
Canterbury				
Canterbury Gate	★★★★	★★★½	★★★★	£47–£84
Thanington Hotel	★★★	★★★	★★★★	£55–£78
County Hotel	★★★	★★★	★★★	£120–£160

Bathrooms were carved out of the ancient warren of rooms late in the hotel's life, so they tend to be a bit small but nonetheless are well-maintained, and many have shower-tub combinations. Rooms on the top floor are bathless and are at the bottom of the price range; while they are quite spartan, some have views of the cathedral and are an exceptional bargain. Ask for a room at the rear of the hotel (and preferably one with a cathedral view); those in front can be noisy at night when Canterbury's young people congregate in the square below. Steep stairs render the Canterbury Gate a poor choice for travelers with mobility problems.

County Hotel — *£120–£160*

OVERALL ★★★ | QUALITY ★★★ | VALUE ★★★

High Street, Canterbury, Kent CT1 2RX; (01227) 766266; fax (01227) 451512; county@macdonaldhotels.co.uk; www.macdonaldhotels.co.uk

Location In the center of town.

Amenities & Services 73 rooms. With its paneling, fireplace, and leaded windows overlooking High Street, the Tudor Bar off the lobby is one of the most pleasant places in town for tea, a drink, or a light lunch or snack. Service throughout the hotel is friendly and attentive.

Elevator Yes.

Parking The hotel has a garage (£2 a day) and free outdoor parking.

Pricing Includes a lavish buffet breakfast.

Credit Cards V, MC, AMEX, D

The County is the best hotel in town, and the handsome brick building has an air of solid comfort. Part of the hotel dates from the 17th century, while a new wing has been seamlessly added, and all rooms have been fitted with spacious, well-appointed modern baths. Unfortunately, the standard rooms have been brought up to date in fairly bland hotel style. If you're looking for atmosphere, ask for one of the "specialty" rooms in the old wing. These are larger and nicely furnished with wing chairs, four-poster beds, and other distinctive touches. The hotel dining room, Sully's, is the finest restaurant in town (see profile under "Restaurants in Canterbury," below).

IN THE SOUTHEAST OF ENGLAND

Hotel	Overall Rating	Quality Rating	Value Rating	Price
Rye				
Jeake's House	★★★★★	★★★★	★★★★★	£34–£84
King Charles II Guest House	★★★★	★★★★	★★★★★	£80–£95
The Mermaid Inn	★★★	★★★★	★★	£75–£150
White Vine House	★★★	★★★	★★★	£50–£100

Thanington Hotel *£55–£78*

OVERALL ★★★ | QUALITY ★★★ | VALUE ★★★★

140 Wincheap, Canterbury, Kent CT1 3RY; (01227) 453227; fax (01227) 453225; www.thanington-hotel.co.uk

Location Just outside the old city walls, about ten minutes' walk from the center.

Amenities & Services 15 rooms. Drawing room, bar/lounge, indoor heated swimming pool, walled garden.

Elevator No.

Parking Free, on premises.

Pricing Includes English breakfast.

Credit Cards V, AMEX, D

This bed-and-breakfast in a Georgian house is really more like a small hotel and offers a great deal of comfort for the price. Ten rooms are in a modern wing linked to the main HOUSE by a conservatory; two are especially large and suitable for families; and four rooms are on the ground floor, making this a good choice if hauling bags up a flight of stairs is a problem. All of the rooms are furnished with traditional pieces (and with a few too many frilly pillows and accessories for our tastes); some have antique bedsteads or four-posters, and all have well-equipped adjoining bathrooms.

Exploring Canterbury

To the west, the main street of Canterbury is known as St. Peter's Street as it passes **West Gate Tower,** a perfectly intact, fortified medieval gate house on the banks of the River Stour. The street then crosses town to the eastern section of the old walls near St. George's Tower, which rose above a medieval church bombed in World War II. A walk down this busy, pedestrian-only street takes about 15 minutes. Many of the major shops and restaurants are on and off High Street, as are some of Canterbury's finest medieval buildings, including Greyfriar's hospital and the Weaver's House. To reach the cathedral precincts from High Street, walk north on Mercery Lane through Christ Church Gate, built in 1517.

HOW ATTRACTIONS COMPARE

Attraction	Comments	Author's Rating
Canterbury		
Canterbury Cathedral	Seat of Archbishop of Canterbury and mother church of Anglicanism	★★★★
St. Augustine's Abbey	Ruins of monastic sites and Tudor palace	★★★
The Canterbury Tales	Multimedia exhibition recreating Chaucer's story	★★
Broadstairs		
Bleak House	House where Charles Dickens wrote	★★
Dover		
Dover Castle	One of England's most famous castles	★★★
Gateway to the White Cliffs	Famous cliffs facing the English Channel	★★★
Maidstone and Leeds Castle		
Leeds Castle	Romantic castle in lake	★★

Tours in Canterbury

While you are not going to have a difficult time finding your own way around Canterbury, guided walking tours of the cathedral precincts and other sights provide an excellent introduction to the city. From April through October, the 90-minute walks leave daily at 2 p.m. from the front of the **Canterbury Visitor Information Centre** (2⁄3 Sun Street); in July and August, walks also leave at 11:30 a.m. Monday through Saturday. For information, call (01227) 459-779 or visit **www.canterburyguidedwalks.uk.com.** The fee is £3.75 adults; £3.25 students, seniors, and children ages 14–17; and £2.75 children under age 14 .

Half-hour **Canterbury Historic River Tours** on the River Stour allow you to relax while a rower provides lively commentary on bridges, mills, riverside chapels, and other Canterbury sights you might otherwise overlook. Tours depart from the ducking-stool dock (where miscreants were once submerged for their infractions) behind the 15th-century Weaver's House (1 St. Peter's Street). Tours operate April–September, Monday–Saturday, 10 a.m.–5 p.m., and Sunday, 11 a.m.–5 p.m. (weather and river conditions permitting). The fee is £5 adults, £3.80 children under age 16, and £15.50 families of two adults and two children.

The **Ghostly Tour of Old Canterbury** will amuse young travelers. The one-hour guided walk departs from the corner of St. Margaret's Street and Alberry Street every Friday and Saturday evening at 8 p.m.

IN THE SOUTHEAST OF ENGLAND

Attraction	Comments	Author's Rating
Rye		
Lamb House	Historic home of famous writers	★★★
Rye Castle Museum	History of Rye area	★★
Battle		
Battle of Hastings 1066, Battlefield and Abbey	Scene of England's most important battle	★★★★
The Historic Houses of Kent		
Ightham Mote	Medieval manor house	★★★★
Sissinghurst Castle Garden	Elizabethan manor house and world-famous gardens	★★★★
Chartwell	Historic home of Winston Churchill	★★★
Hever Castle	Medieval castle	★★★
Knole	Historic home	★★★
Penshurst Place	Historic home	★★★

and explores nooks and crannies of the town that are allegedly haunted by ghosts from the city's 2,000-year past. The fee is £5 adults, £4 children, and £17.50 families of two adults and two children.

Attractions in Canterbury

Canterbury Cathedral

Type of Attraction Seat of the Archbishop of Canterbury and mother church of Anglicanism

Location The Precincts

Admission £3.50 adults; £2.50 seniors and students; free for children under age 5

Hours Easter–September 30: Monday–Saturday, 9 a.m–6:30 p.m.; Sunday, 12:30–2:30 p.m., 4:30–5:30 p.m. (and for services). October 1–Easter: Monday–Saturday, 9 a.m–5 p.m.; Sunday, 12:30–2:30 p.m. (and for services)

Phone (01227) 762-862

Website www.canterbury-cathedral.org

When to Go Very crowded in summer, so go late in the day, when many visitors have left Canterbury; the cathedral is especially atmospheric and quiet on a winter weekday.

Special Comments For a memorable experience, try to attend one of the recitals, classical musical concerts, and other performing-arts events the cathedral hosts. These are listed on the cathedral's recorded phone message and website and with the Canterbury Visitor Information Centre.

Overall Appeal by Age Group

Preschool ★★	Teens ★★★	Over 30 ★★★
Grade school ★★★	Young Adults ★★★★	Seniors ★★★

Author's Rating ★★★★

How Much Time to Allow At least 1 hour

Description & Comments You are bound to feel a bit humbled upon entering this soaring, vaulted edifice, destination of Chaucer's pilgrims, scene of the murder of Thomas à Becket, and arguably the most famous cathedral in England. Despite the cathedral's ecclesiastic importance and its august history, which begins in 1070, the structure is surprisingly inviting. Soft gray stone, much of it shipped to England from French quarries, lends a great deal of warmth to the long interior, and a holiday atmosphere prevails as thousands of modern pilgrims troop through daily.

The cathedral is most famously associated with Thomas à Becket, the archbishop of Canterbury whom knights of Henry III murdered in 1170 (a slab in the northwest transept marks the spot). The zealously loyal knights had heard the King cry out, "Who will rid me of this turbulent priest?"—this was not an execution order, the penitent king later claimed, but simply frustration at Thomas's relentless defense of the church against encroachment by the state. Thomas was canonized three years later, and pilgrims began coming to Canterbury from all over Europe to worship the fallen martyr. In the Trinity Chapter, at the end of the longest choir in Europe, stood an elaborate shrine to Becket, who, even in death, ran afoul of another king—Henry VIII had the shrine destroyed as part of his campaign to diminish the power of the church. But he did not remove the chapel's magnificent stained-glass windows that depict the miracles of Christ, nor could he erase the grooves that thousands of pilgrims made in the tiles as they made their way past the shrine on their knees. Henry did manage, however, to have most of the wall paintings that once covered the interior removed. A vivid remaining fragment depicts St. Paul and the Viper; you can see it high in the northeastern corner of the chapel.

One of the of the most enticing regions of the cathedral is the 12th-century crypt, where Henry II did his penance for Becket's murder; a fantastic bestiary is carved into the capitals of the support pillars. Just off the northwest transept, next to the crypt staircase, is the vast and beautiful Great Cloister. Before leaving the walled Cathedral Precinct, walk past the buildings of King's College, founded as a monastery in the seventh century and converted to a boy's school by Henry VIII. Alumni include 16th-century dramatist Christopher Marlowe and 20th-century novelist and short-story writer W. Somerset Maugham.

Touring Tips The admission fee is often waived late in the day; the church is less crowded then, too.

The Canterbury Tales

Type of Attraction Multimedia exhibition that re-creates Chaucer's story

Location St. Margaret's Street

Admission £6.50 adults; £5 children under age 16; £2.50 seniors and students; £20 families of two adults and two children

Hours January 1–February 10: daily, 10 a.m.–4:30 p.m.; February 11–June 30: daily, 10 a.m.–5 p.m.; July 1–September 1: daily, 9:30 a.m.–5 p.m.; September 2–October 27: daily, 10 a.m.–5 p.m.; October 28–December 31: daily, 10 a.m.–4:30 p.m.

Phone (01227) 479-227

Website www.canterburytales.org.uk

When to Go Early or late, when the exhibition is less crowded and you will find it easier to get into the spirit of medieval misadventures

Special Comments Stairs and dark passageways make a visit treacherous for anyone with limited mobility or vision. A kids' version of the audio tape edits out Chaucer's ribald language and sexual innuendo.

Overall Appeal by Age Group

Preschool ★★	Teens ★★★	Over 30 ★★★
Grade school ★★★	Young Adults ★★★	Seniors ★★

Author's Rating ★★

How Much Time to Allow About 1 hour

Description & Comments Visitors who prefer to absorb history through serious reading and the touch of old stone will probably not be amused by the theatrics that have taken over the medieval church of St. Margaret. Walk-through sets depicting scenes from *The Canterbury Tales*—from Tabard Inn in London, where Chaucer's pilgrims begin their journey, to Becket's shrine in Canterbury—accompanied by a lively audio-tape commentary, all meant to provide a taste of what it was like to be a 13th-century pilgrim. Along the way, animated puppets re-create the lusty wife of Bath, the chivalrous knight, the uncouth miller, and other pilgrims, who recite their particular tales. For young visitors especially, the colorful animations may bring history alive. Others may well ask why they're spending their time in a Hollywood spectacle when so much real history lies just beyond the exit—which, not surprisingly, can only be reached through a large souvenir shop.

Touring Tips If you plan on including this exhibition in your visit to Canterbury, stop here before walking through town or visiting the cathedral so you can get the most out of the historical perspective the commentary provides.

St. Augustine's Abbey

Type of Attraction Ruins of one of Britain's oldest monastic sites and a Tudor palace

Location Long Port

Admission £2 adults; £1.50 children under age 16

Hours March 22–October 31: daily, 10 a.m–6 p.m..; November 1–March 31: daily, 10 a.m.–4 p.m.

Phone (01227) 767-345

HOW RESTAURANTS COMPARE

Name	Cuisine	Overall	Quality	Value	Price
Canterbury					
Alberry's	Continental	★★★★	★★★	★★★	Mod
Sully's	British/Continental	★★★½	★★★★	★★★	Exp
Thomas à Becket	British/Pub	★★★	★★	★★★	Inexp
Maidstone					
Ringlestone Inn	British	★★★	★★★	★★★	Mod
Rye					
Landgate Bistro	French/ British	★★★★	★★★★	★★★★	Mod
The Flushing Inn	British	★★★★	★★★★	★★	Exp

Website www.thycotic.com/guide/sights/staugabb.html

When to Go In good weather, since you'll be spending most of the time here outdoors

Special Comments The sight is accessible to visitors in wheelchairs

Overall Appeal by Age Group

Preschool ★	Teens ★★	Over 30 ★★★½
Grade school ★★	Young Adults ★★	Seniors ★★★½

Author's Rating ★★★

How Much Time to Allow At least 1 hour

Description & Comments These highly evocative ruins encompass a huge sweep of British history and are set in a grassy field just outside Canterbury's medieval walls. St. Augustine founded an abbey here in 598, when Kentish King Ethelbert granted him permission to preach Christianity in Britain. By 1500, the complex was one of the world's leading centers of learning, with a scriptorium and 2,000-volume library. Henry VIII gave orders to destroy the abbey in the middle of the 16th century and constructed a palace on the grounds to welcome Anne of Cleves when she arrived from France to marry him. The ruins are now a UNESCO World Heritage Site, and an intelligent and informative self-guided audio tour shows off the Saxon and Norman churches, tombs, the palace and its gardens, and other ruins. Some fascinating finds, including carved stonework and the remains of a young woman buried on the grounds in the Middle Ages, are housed in a small museum.

Touring Tips After touring the abbey ruins, continue east up Long Port to North Holmes Road and an even older remnant of early Canterbury, St. Martin's Church. Parts of the small church date to the Roman period. It is known that King Ethelbert presented the church to his Christian bride, Queen Bertha, making it the oldest parish church in Britain that has been in continuous use. The church is open from 9 a.m. to 5 p.m., and admission is free.

IN THE SOUTHEAST OF ENGLAND

Name	Cuisine	Overall	Quality	Value	Price
Rye *(continued)*					
The Union Inn	Pub	★★★	★★★	★★★	Inexp
Mermaid Bar	Pub	★★★	★★	★★	Inexp
Battle					
Orangery	British/French	★★★★	★★★★	★★★	Mod
The Historic Houses of Kent					
The Spotted Dog	Pub/British	★★★	★★★	★★★	Mod

Restaurants in Canterbury

Alberry's ★★★★

CONTINENTAL | MODERATE | QUALITY ★★★ | VALUE ★★★

38 St. Margaret Street; (01227) 452-378

Reservations Not necessary **Entrée Range** £8.25–£9.25 **Payment** V, MC, AMEX, D **Bar** Full service **Disabled Access** Yes

Hours Monday–Saturday, noon–11 p.m. for food, later for bar service

House Specialties Mussels in white wine sauce; Kentish chicken and leek pie; fish and chips.

This friendly bistro in the center of town is a little of everything—snack bar, restaurant, and late-night retreat. While this variety of purpose might suggest a lack of focus on cuisine, the kitchen is serious about what it sends out and changes the menu daily to ensure that all the selections are made with the freshest local ingredients. Offerings include pastas and salads as well as full meals.

Sully's ★★★½

BRITISH/CONTINENTAL | EXPENSIVE | QUALITY ★★★★ | VALUE ★★★

County Hotel, High Street; (01227) 766-266

Reservations Recommended **Entrée Range** £14.95–£18.50 **Payment** V, MC, AMEX, D **Bar** Full service **Disabled Access** Yes

Hours Daily, noon–2:30 p.m., 7–9:30 p.m.

House Specialties Rack of Kentish lamb; filet of salmon with fennel; pan-roasted breast of duck with red onions; start with the vodka and lemon-scented risotto.

Ask anyone in Canterbury for a restaurant suggestion, and you will be whisked here to undeniably the best place in town. The food is memorable and raises the restaurant to the status of one of southern England's most noted gourmet stops. Service is impeccable, too, yet Sully's retains a comfortable, welcoming air. Our only complaint is the rather bland and uninspired décor, which doesn't do justice to the fare that comes out of the kitchen.

Thomas à Becket ★★★

BRITISH/PUB | INEXPENSIVE | QUALITY ★★ | VALUE ★★★

21 Best Lane; (01227) 464-384

Reservations Recommended on weekends **Entrée Range** £5–£8 **Payment** V, MC, AMEX, D **Bar** Full service **Disabled Access** Yes

Hours Daily, noon–11:30 p.m.

House Specialties Stick to the basic pub fare: liver and bacon casserole; lamb and apple pie; lamb shank. A selection of vegetarian dishes (including a delicious stir-fry) are available, and daily specials often include fresh fish.

The Becket is the favorite of the many locals who crowd into the cozy, beamed rooms every evening. This is not just a place for drinking—the food is good, filling, quite inventive for pub fare, and very fairly priced. Service is remarkably attentive given the number of customers that pack in here.

Entertainment and Nightlife in Canterbury

The **Gulbenkian Theatre** is part of the University of Kent, which spreads across a hill above the town named for Wat Tyler, who led the Peasant's Revolt of 1381. The theater, on Giles Lane, hosts a year-round program of theater, dance, and many visiting entertainers, and also includes a British Film Institute cinema that shows classic and contemporary films. The Visitor Information Centre has listings of Gulbenkian events; call (01227) 769-075 or visit **www.ukc.ac.uk/gulbenkian.** The **Marlowe Theatre,** in the center of the medieval city on the Friars, is named for the 16th-century dramatist who was born in Canterbury. It is the major regional theater for southeastern England and, in addition to dramatic productions, hosts many visiting theater, dance, and music groups. For information, check with the Visitor Information Centre, call (01227) 787-787, or go to **www.marlowetheatre.com.**

Recreation in and around Canterbury

Some of the most enjoyable hiking in England is along the **North Downs National Trail.** This much-trod path follows the route of Chaucer's pilgrims across the beautiful Kent countryside for 150 miles, passing through orchards, forests, and villages and ending at the **White Cliffs of Dover** (see profile, page 218). **Leeds Castle** (see profile, page 220) is on the route, and a northern spur passes through Canterbury. The Visitor

Information Centre in Canterbury provides maps of the North Downs Way and related literature. In addition, the National Trails website (**www.nationaltrails.gov.uk**) is a great source of info on the route.

Around Canterbury

Sooner or later the green downs and fertile farmland surrounding Canterbury may entice you to venture out, and there's much to see within a short distance.

Broadstairs

Any devoted reader of Charles Dickens will want to make the short pilgrimage from Canterbury to this attractive seashore town, where brick houses climb steep streets above a snug little harbor and pebbly beach. Dickens began coming here in 1837 when he was just 25 and already famous for *The Pickwick Papers.* To him, Broadstairs "beat all other watering places" and the author began returning every summer to watch his growing brood become "brown as berries," "to walk upon the sands at low-water," and to commit to paper the words that flowed out of him at a prodigious volume.

Arriving and Getting Oriented in Broadstairs

Broadstairs is about 15 miles northeast of Canterbury along A28. Trains from Canterbury West make the trip in half an hour or 45 minutes, depending on whether or not it's necessary to change; the trip costs about £9. For information, call (08457) 484-950 or go to **www.railtrack.co.uk.** The **Broadstairs Visitor Information Centre** is at 6B High Street (phone (10843) 583-333).

Exploring Broadstairs

Like Dickens, you can walk on the sands and follow the author's footsteps through narrow streets where signs inscribed with "The Old Curiosity Shop" and other Dickensian monikers swing in front of many businesses. For a bracing adventure, walk along the seaside promenade facing Viking Bay just north of the harbor, where winds whip the North Sea high into the air and send it crashing over the walkway.

You'll be in for a bit of a shock if you pull into town in mid-June, during the annual **Broadstairs Dickens Festival.** Dickens enthusiasts dress like their favorite characters from the master's novels and promenade on the seafront, play croquet, and swim in Victorian bathing costumes. In mid-August, the town hosts the **Broadstairs Folk Week,** one of England's larger folk festivals, with a program of dance, music, and a crafts fair.

Bleak House

Type of Attraction The cliff-top house where Charles Dickens spent his summers and wrote some of his most famous works

Location On cliff top above Viking Bay

Admission £3 adults; £2.50 seniors and children under age 16

Hours End of February–mid-December: daily, 10 a.m.–6 p.m. (to 9 p.m. in July and August)

Phone (01843) 862-224

Website www.bleakhouse.ndo.co.uk

When to Go Any time a school group is not tromping through the house

Special Comments If you're a Dickens fan, you'll want to linger over the writer's ephemera at leisure; others in your party may be bored, so leave them on the beach.

Overall Appeal by Age Group

Preschool ★	Teens ★★	Over 30 ★★★
Grade school ★★	Young Adults ★★	Seniors ★★★

Author's Rating ★★

How Much Time to Allow About half an hour

Description & Comments The souvenir shop and garish signs that surround the entrance to this handsome brick house overlooking the English Channel can dissuade a serious Dickens fan from entering. Don't let the clutter deter you, though, because inside several rooms poignantly capture the daily life of the writer, who wrote the eponymous *Bleak House* and most of *David Copperfield* in a bright upstairs study overlooking the sea. Dickens's pen, pocketknife, corrected proofs, the lectern he used at public readings, and other personal effects look as if the author has just stepped out for one of his daily 12-mile walks on the beach; upon his return, he would enjoy a hearty lunch in the dining room. Cellars beneath the house are filled with exhibits that trace Broadstairss' infamy as a smuggling port, and a downstairs parlor pays tribute to the ships that floundered on the treacherous Goodwin Sands, visible just beyond the windows.

Touring Tips Visitors are welcome to picnic in the house's extensive gardens, and it's hard to find a more appealing spot in Broadstairs.

Dover

While nearby Folkstone is the terminus of the Chunnel link between France and England, this busy Channel port, for centuries Britain's portal to the Continent, still bustles with nonstop activity as ferries continually move in and out of its extensive docks. Dover was an important Roman settlement, and became the chief city of the Cinque Ports (Five Ports), which also included Sandwich, Hythe, Romney, and Hastings. These seaside towns were afforded special privileges in return for defending the land and fitting out the Royal Fleet for skirmishes with the

French and Spanish. Dover came under continual bombardment and shelling during World War II, when the townspeople frequently took shelter in the castle. Postwar builders launched their own assault on Dover with acres of ugly concrete, but the magnificent castle and famous **White Cliffs** are among the great sights of England.

Arriving and Getting Oriented in Dover

Dover is about 12 miles southeast of Canterbury along A2. Trains from Canterbury East make the trip in about half an hour; the trip costs about £9. Call (08457) 484-950 or go to **www.railtrack.co.uk.** The **Dover Visitor Information Centre** is in the Old Town Gaol, on Biggin Street (phone (01304) 205-108; **www.whitecliffscountry.org.com**).

Exploring Dover

Aside from the castle, one of the other major remnants of old Dover is the **Masion Dieu Hall** in the town hall on Biggin Street. The cavernous room, built in 1221 as a hostel for Canterbury-bound pilgrims, is open to the public for free Tuesday–Saturday, 10 a.m.–4:30 p.m., and Sunday, 2–4:30 p.m. Even older is the **Roman Painted House,** which, ironically, is on New Street. Vivid paintings and an elaborate, under-floor heating system are preserved within a modern shelter. The house is open April–June, Tuesday–Sunday, 10 a.m.–5 p.m.; July and August, daily, 10 a.m.–5 p.m.; and September, Tuesday–Sunday, 10 a.m.–5 p.m.; for information, call (01304) 203-279. You can enjoy stunning views of the White Cliffs and see the hubbub of busy Dover Harbour—without boarding a boat to France or beyond—on **White Cliff Boat Tours;** daily trips leave hourly from DeBradelei Wharf and cost £5 for adults and £3 for children ages 3–15.

Dover Castle

Type of Attraction One of England's most famous castles

Location On cliffs above the east side of town

Admission £7 adults; £3.50 seniors and children ages 5–15; free for children under 5; £17.50 families of two adults and two children

Hours April–September: daily, 10 a.m.–6 p.m. October: daily, 10 a.m.–5 p.m.; November–March: daily, 10 a.m.–4 p.m.; closed December 24–25, January 1

Phone (01304) 201-628

Website www.theheritagetrail.co.uk/castles/dover-castle.htm

When to Go Try to avoid weekends, when the castle fills up with day-trippers from London and France.

Special Comments The compound covers 70 acres, so pick up a free map at the entrance gate and plan your visit before setting off. A Land Train (free) makes a circuit of the grounds, and you can hop on and off at the attractions you want to see.

If you are accompanied by restless children, you may want to head right to the kid-pleasing highlights: the 1216 Siege Experience, the Secret Wartime Tunnels, and a view over the Channel from one of the lookouts.

Overall Appeal by Age Group

Preschool ★★	Teens ★★★	Over 30 ★★★
Grade school ★★★	Young Adults ★★★	Seniors ★★★

Author's Rating ★★★

How Much Time to Allow About 2 hours

Description & Comments A fortification has stood on the site of Dover Castle since Roman times, and the Roman pharos (lighthouse) still stands, making it the oldest building in Britain. Much of the castle's mighty fortifications date from the 12th century, when the castle came to be known as the "key of England" because to take it would have meant to take the rest of the country.

There's a lot to see in the castle, and even the most ardent history buff may tire before touring the many rooms, towers, and dungeons. To maintain a historical perspective, look at the pharos and the Saxon church next to it, then enter the Keep Yard, where a short introductory film is shown. Before exploring the rest of the castle, climb up to Battlement Walk or Admiralty Look-out—here you'll get a sense of its strategic location high above the Channel. Make your next stop the 1216 Siege Experience, an audio tour that uses sound and light effects to dramatize a French attempt to seize the castle. It's possible to walk through a portion of the medieval tunnels that were cut into the chalky cliffs on which the castle is built, but the Secret Wartime Tunnels are far more interesting. During World War II, these housed a hospital, living quarters, and a military command center and can be visited only on a 40-minute guided tour that is accompanied by the sound of shells, airplanes, and air-raid sirens.

Touring Tips If Dover Castle whets your appetite for more castles, travel north up the coast to two fortifications that Henry VIII built. Walmer Castle, seven miles northeast of Dover, is the official residence of the Lord Warden of the Cinque Ports. Among those holding this post have been the Duke of Wellington, who lived at Walmer from 1829 to 1852; Sir Winston Churchill; and the late Queen Mother. Deal Castle, a mile north of Walmer, is built on a plan of concentric circles. The small port of Deal looms large in history—Caesar landed here in 55 B.C. and William Penn set sail from here for the American colonies in 1682. Both castles are open April–October, daily, 10 a.m.–6 p.m.; and November–March, Wednesday–Sunday, 10 a.m.–4 p.m.

Gateway to the White Cliffs

Type of Attraction Trails across the top of the famous cliffs facing the English Channel

Location Langdon Cliffs

Admission £1.50 per car

Hours March 1–October 31: daily, 10 a.m.–5 p.m.; November 1–February 28: daily, 11 a.m.–4 p.m. Closed Christmas Day.

Phone (01304) 202-756

Website www.nationaltrust.org.uk

When to Go Not in the rain, when the trails can be treacherously slippery and views are obscured

Special Comments Parking and some of the paths to the viewpoints are wheelchair accessible; with its isolated location and spiral staircase, the lighthouse is not easily accessible to visitors with limited mobility. Children will love running around the downs and watching the shipping traffic in the Channel, but keep a close eye on them—some of the trails are close to the edge of the cliffs.

Overall Appeal by Age Group

Preschool ★★★	Teens ★★★	Over 30 ★★★
Grade school ★★★★	Young Adults ★★★	Seniors ★★★

Author's Rating ★★★

How Much Time to Allow If you're going to walk as far as the lighthouse, allow at least two hours. But even a brief 15-minute excursion from the parking areas to one of the many viewpoints along the clifftop is rewarding.

Description & Comments This National Trust recreation area comprises the rolling downs atop the famous White Cliffs of Dover and affords a chance for a memorable walk in the bracing sea air. The big draw, of course, is the exhilarating view of the Channel, Dover Castle perched high above, and the chalk cliffs. The cliffs are indeed white, though slowly browning because of air pollution; they are made up of millions of fossilized sea creatures and coral that aeons ago thrived on the bottom of a tropical sea. The Straits of Dover at the bottom of the cliffs are the narrowest part of the Channel, and just 17 miles of water separate Dover from Cape Gris Nez, in France. This proximity has proved irresistible to generations of adventurers, from Francois Blanchard, who floated across the Straits in a balloon in 1785, to Captain Webb, who became the first swimmer to complete the crossing, in 1875; he reached Calais from Dover in 21 hours and 45 minutes.

From the parking areas near Dover Castle, a two-mile-long trail crosses grazing lands and follows the cliff top to South Foreland Lighthouse, built in 1843. Guglielmo Marconi made the first shore-to-ship radio transmissions from here on December 24, 1898, and these days a climb to the top affords memorable views of the Channel and the White Cliffs. The lighthouse is open March 1–June 30, Thursday–Monday, 11 a.m.–5:30 p.m.; and July and August, daily, 11 a.m.–5:30 p.m. Admission is £2 adults, £1 children under age 16, £5 families of two adults and three children.

Touring Tips A coffee shop near the parking area offers snacks and light lunches on a terrace or in a bright, airy room overlooking the downs and Channel.

Maidstone and Leeds Castle

Maidstone (pronounced "MED-stun") is the county seat of Kent and straddles both banks of the River Medway. Its most notable attraction, **Leeds Castle,** lies just five miles east on A20.

Arriving and Getting Oriented at Maidstone and Leeds Castle

Maidstone is about 17 miles west of Canterbury, via M2 and M26. Trains from Canterbury West and East run to Maidstone about every 45 minutes. Try to take a route that requires only one change, which will shorten the travel time from about one hour and 50 minutes to about one hour and 20 minutes; the trip costs about £10. Bearsted Station is closer to Leeds Castle, and the trip from Canterbury can be as quick as 50 minutes; the cost is also about £10. For more information, call (08457) 484-950 or go to **www.railtrack.co.uk.**

Leeds Castle is a popular day trip from London, and it's just 40 miles southeast of the city. **National Express** (phone (08705) 808080; **www.gobycoach.com**) offers all-inclusive packages that include round-trip transportation to and from Leeds from Victoria Coach Station and admission to the castle and grounds. The price is £14 adults Monday–Friday, £15 Saturday and Sunday; and £11 children ages 4–15 Monday–Friday, £12 Saturday and Sunday. **Connex** (phone (0870) 030405; **www.connex.co.uk**), the rail operator, offers a similar package with train service from Victoria Station, transportation between Bearsted Station and Leeds Castle, and admission to the castle and grounds. The price is £21.50 adults and £10.80 children ages 4–15.

Exploring Leeds Castle

Leeds Castle

Type of Attraction A romantic castle in the middle of the lake

Location Outside Maidstone

Admission March 1–October 31: £11 adults; £9.50 seniors and students; £7.50 children ages 4–16; £32 families of two adults and three children. November 1–Feburary 28: £9.50 adults; £8 seniors and students; £6 children ages 4–16; £27 families of two adults and three children.

Hours March–October: daily, 10 a.m.–5 p.m.; November–February: daily, 10 a.m.–3 p.m.

Phone (0870) 600-8880

Website www.leeds-castle.com

When to Go Unlike most historic properties in Britain, Leeds Castle is open year-round. However, you probably won't want to fork over the substantial admission fees in inclement weather when you can't enjoy the grounds.

Special Comments There are several refreshment concessions on the grounds.

Overall Appeal by Age Group

Preschool ★★★	Teens ★★★	Over 30 ★★
Grade school ★★★	Young Adults ★★★	Seniors ★★

Author's Rating ★★

How Much Time to Allow 2–3 hours

Description & Comments "The Loveliest Castle in the World" is how this fairy-tale home of queens, kings, and nobility bills itself, and it's hard to argue. The castle is a mirage of light gray stone that seemingly floats on a lake. However, the mirage is soon shattered by the aura of commercialism that pervades the castle, which now hosts flower shows, fireworks displays, vintage car exhibits, Christmas pageants, and many other flashy events. Four restaurants, several shops, a Dog Collar Museum (housed in the castle's gate house), a well-stocked aviary, and a nine-hole golf course are among other recent additions.

Leeds traces its origins to ninth-century fortifications and was transformed into a royal palace for Edward I in 1278. Henry VIII was one of many kings who resided at Leeds, and the castle was later the country estate of Lord Culpepper, governor of Virginia from 1680 to 1683. While the Gloriette, the keep that rises from the lake waters at the north end of the castle, is authentically medieval, much of the castle was rebuilt in the 19th and 20th centuries. Olive, Lady Baillie, purchased the castle in 1926 and amassed many of the furnishings and paintings that are on view in a series of salons and state rooms; the medieval Queen's Rooms and Henry VIII's banqueting hall retain some of their original furnishings.

The grounds are beautiful. Black swans and other waterfowl swim in the stream that bubbles through the Wood Garden and Duckery, and the castle's own vineyard has been yielding grapes since the 11th century and is listed among the tax records of the Doomsday Book. An English cottage garden and a Mediterranean bower are delightful, and a maze of 3,000 yew trees surrounding a secret tunnel and an underground grotto festooned with seashells will keep youngsters amused for hours.

Touring Tips A nice time to enjoy the grounds is during one of the summertime outdoor concerts the castle hosts.

Dining in Maidstone

Ringlestone Inn ★★★

BRITISH | MODERATE | QUALITY ★★★ | VALUE ★★★

Near Harrietsham, Maidstone (about a mile east of Leeds Castle on A20); (01323) 870-218

Reservations Recommended **Entrée Range** £4–£9 **Payment** V, MC, AMEX **Bar** Full service, plus 36 varieties of English fruit wines and liqueurs **Disabled Access** Yes

Hours Monday–Saturday, noon–2 p.m., 7–10 p.m.; Sunday, 12:30–2:30 p.m., 7–10 p.m.

House Specialties A cold buffet lunch features salads and meat and vegetable pies made from fresh ingredients from the surrounding farms. The Sunday roast-beef lunch is excellent, and evening fish specials are fresh and simply but adeptly prepared.

Wayfarers have been snuggling into this cozy inn, with its beamed ceilings, brick walls, plank floors, and roaring fire, since the 16th century. Service is friendly, and the emphasis is on providing a comfortable and relaxed atmosphere. The Ringlestone is a pleasant alternative to the dining options on the grounds of Leeds Castle.

Rye

Rye is the English equivalent of an Italian hill town and just as charming, set on an outcropping above the plain and salt marshes, surrounded by walls, and entered through medieval gates. Once a port and now two miles inland, Rye has fought off pirates and invaders, provided hideouts

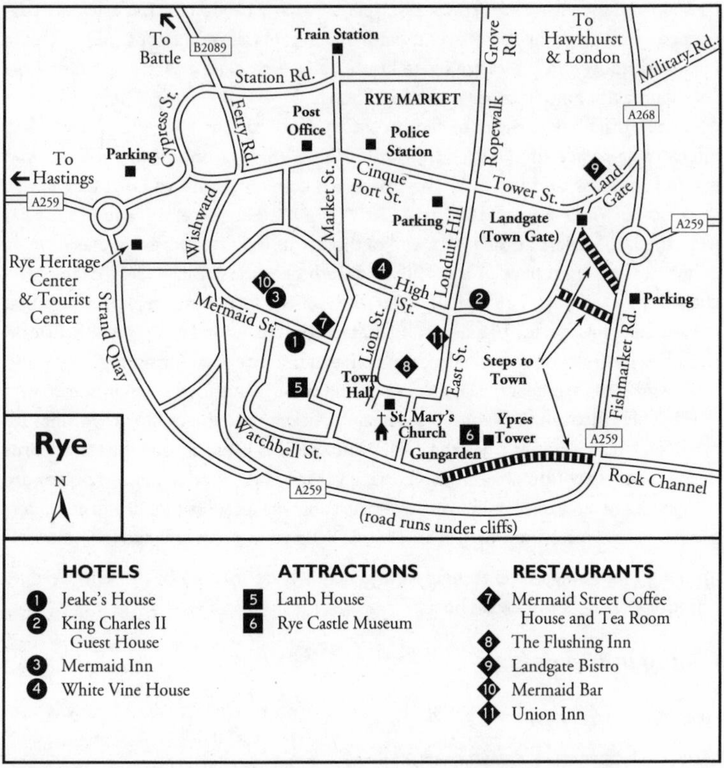

for smugglers, and harbored an unusually large number of writers, whose presence you will encounter all over town.

Rye is today a much-visited weekend retreat for Londoners, and with its cobbled lanes and half-timbered houses, one of the most beautiful towns of England. Rye is a lovely place to stay, with many historic inns where you can curl up with a pint and a copy of Henry James or E. F. Benson (among the aforementioned local writers). The town is an excellent base from which to explore the surrounding countryside of Sussex and Kent. For more of the same, all you need to do is pop over to Winchelsea, two miles southwest of Rye, a picturesque village perched on a hill above marshes and the sea, with an old church of time-mellowed stone that dates from 1300.

Planning Your Visit to Rye

The Rye Tourist Information Centre is part of the **Rye Heritage Center,** located in an old sail-making workshop on Strand Quay (phone (01797) 226-696; Rye TN31 7AY; **www.rye-tourism.co.uk**). The office provides a wealth of information on local sights, services, and events; sells bus tickets and tickets for ferry service to France; and provides an accommodation booking service, which can be especially handy on weekends when Rye's hotels often fill up with Londoners. Open daily: November–February, 10 a.m.– 4 p.m.; and March–October, 9 a.m.–5:30 p.m.

Special Events in Rye

Rye hosts the **Rye Winter Festival** in late January–early February and the **Rye Festival** in September; both bring classical music, jazz, theater works, and films to town. For information and tickets, call (01797) 22444 or visit **www.ryefestival.co.uk.** Rye gets into the spirit of Guy Fawkes Day (November 5) on November 9 with the **Rye Bonfire Night,** which includes an evening torchlight procession through town, an enormous bonfire, and fireworks.

Arriving and Getting Oriented in Rye

Rye is 60 miles southeast of London. Trains run about every hour from London's Victoria Station with a change in Ashford, and also about every hour from London's London Bridge Station with a change at Hastings. The trip from either station takes about two hours and costs about £20. For information, call (08457) 484950 or go to **www.railtrack.co.uk.** The Rye station is just north of the town center, about a ten-minute walk away along Market Street.

By car, the quickest route from London is M25/M20 toward Folkstone; exit at Ashford onto the A2070 and A259 for the drive east to Canterbury. The trip takes just over an hour, but traffic in and around London can add considerable time. Several short-stay car parks are located at the edge of the town center, just a few minutes away by foot. In these you obtain a ticket from a machine and place it on the dashboard in easy view; the fee is about £1 an hour, 7 a.m.–7 p.m., and about £2 flat rate, 7 p.m.–7 a.m. Long-term visitor parking is available in a car park off the Battle road; the fee is £1.50 per car per day. Car parks are well signed off A259 and the other routes that ring the old town.

Hotels in Rye

Jeake's House — *£34–£84*

OVERALL ★★★★★ | QUALITY ★★★★ | VALUE ★★★★★

Mermaid Street, Rye, East Sussex TN31 7ET; (01797) 222828; fax (01797) 222623; jeakeshouse@btinternet.com; www.jeakeshouse.com

Location On a cobbled street in the old town.

Amenities & Services 12 rooms. Drinks are available on the honor system in the book-lined bar, and a small, beamed parlor provides a quiet place to relax in front of the fire; breakfast is served in a two-story high, galleried room that once served as a Quaker chapel.

Elevator No.

Parking Available in a private lot a short walk away from the inn for £3 a day.

Pricing Includes traditional English or vegetarian breakfast.

Credit Cards V, MC

Managing to provide atmosphere and comfort without overdoing the "cute" quotient is an accomplishment, and this wonderful inn that comprises several historic buildings does so seamlessly. In the early 20th century, Jeake's House was home to the American poet Conrad Aiken and is now in the capable hands of Jenny Hadfield, a former opera singer, and John Burke. They have made the award-winning Jeake's House into what may well be the most inviting and comfortable bed-and-breakfast inn in England. All of the rooms are attractively furnished with a fine eye to comfort, with wonderful old beds, fine linens, and plush reading chairs. Many are quite large, encompassing sitting alcoves or loft bedrooms, and most have well-equipped baths, though a few share facilities. Reserve well in advance, especially on weekends; many repeat visitors to Rye would not think of staying anywhere else, and you may well become one of them.

King Charles II Guest House — *£80–£95*

OVERALL ★★★★ | QUALITY ★★★★ | VALUE ★★★★★

4 High Street, Rye, East Sussex TN31 7JE; (01797) 224954;
www.rye-tourism.co.uk/kingcharles

Location In the center of town.

Amenities & Services 3 rooms. Lovely lounge and breakfast room.

Elevator No.

Parking In nearby municipal lots.

Pricing Includes a full buffet breakfast; two-night minimum stay on weekends, reduced rates on weekdays.

Credit Cards No.

This medieval house dates to 1420, and it is said that Charles II stayed here on his secret trips back to England during his 17th-century exile in France. In more recent times, the novelist Radclyffe Hall lived here in the 1930s. The current owners, Nicola and Margrit, have restored every square inch of the house down to the last beam and filled it with polished antiques and rich fabrics, creating an exquisite little inn where the level of comfort and charm of the surroundings far exceed the price. The three rooms are furnished with carved-wood beds, antique writing desks, and other unique pieces and have modern baths. The Country Room is especially pleasant, with a four-poster bed and views over the countryside through leaded-glass windows.

The Mermaid Inn — *£75–£150*

OVERALL ★★★ | QUALITY ★★★★ | VALUE ★★

Mermaid Street, Rye, Sussex TN31 7EY; (0179) 223065; fax (0179) 225069;
mermaidinnrye@btclick.com; www.mermaidinn.com

Location On a cobblestone street in the old town.

Amenities & Services 31 rooms. One of England's oldest inns has two cozy lounges in which plump furniture is grouped around hearths, a heavily beamed bar with a roaring fire, and a formal dining room; steep and creaky staircases make many rooms inaccessible to guests with disabilities. Bellhop.

Elevator No.

Parking Free outdoor parking behind the hotel.

Pricing Includes early-morning tea, breakfast, and VAT; Sunday–Thursday, the inn provides room, early-morning tea, breakfast, and a four-course dinner for £100 per person per night.

Credit Cards V, MC, AMEX

The Mermaid dates from 1300 and is full of enough beams, polished wood floors, and blazing hearths to satisfy any connoisseur of the quaint old English look. The atmosphere extends to the guest rooms, all of which are furnished distinctively. Eight of the rooms have four-poster beds; Dr. Syn's Bedchamber once accommodated the late Queen Mother and has a richly carved mantel and a secret passage that leads to the bar below; the Nutcracker is a cozy family suite tucked beneath the beams. All rooms have private bathrooms, which are relatively late additions and may tend to be small. While a stay in this character-filled and well-run hotel is bound to be comfortable, you can find an equal amount of charm in slightly less precious and less expensive surroundings at many of Rye's other inns.

White Vine House — *£50–£100*

OVERALL ★★★ | QUALITY ★★★ | VALUE ★★★

24 High Street, Rye, East Sussex TN31 7JF; (01797) 224748; fax (01797) 223599; irene@whitevinehouse.freeserve.co.uk; www.rye.uk.co/whitevine

Location In the center of town.

Amenities & Services 7 rooms. Guests can relax in a handsome lounge (the Elizabeth Room), and breakfast is served in a sunny parlor in front of a blazing hearth.

Elevator No.

Parking In nearby municipal car parks or on street.

Pricing Includes breakfast. A family room sleeps four and costs £140.

Credit Cards V, MC

This gracious Georgian house in the center of town on High Street was once the home of a 19th-century mayor of Rye, and the inn still seems like a grand private home. Guest rooms have enough beams and antique furnishings to provide character without being overwhelmingly quaint. The best rooms in the house are the two large doubles with canopied four-poster beds, but all of the rooms are spacious, nicely appointed, and extremely comfortable. Bathrooms throughout are large and well equipped, and all the modern amenities are here, including color TV.

Exploring Rye

Rye claims to have more historic buildings per square foot than any other town in England. Although this claim has never been officially authenticated, walking through the small town center along cobbled lanes past medieval and Georgian houses is a satisfying experience that will keep you pleasantly occupied for several hours.

A good place to begin is the **Rye Heritage Centre,** on Strand Quay (phone (01797) 226-696; Rye TN31 7AY; **www.rye-tourism.co.uk**). The center presents a free exhibit of artifacts and historic photos and a 20-minute sound and light show, *The Story of Rye,* that uses a town model to re-create some 700 years of smugglers, highwaymen, royals, and other characters from local history. The fee is £2.50 adults, £1 children, £1.50 seniors, and £6 families. Open daily: November–February, 10 a.m.– 4 p.m.; and March–October, 9 a.m.–5:30 p.m.

From the Heritage Centre, follow Wish Street and Cinque Ports Street to **Landgate,** the main entrance to the old city and part of the medieval fortifications that for many centuries protected the town from French incursions. The climb into town up East Cliff affords views over salt marshes and the River Rothner and soon comes to High Street. From here Lion Street leads north toward the castle and St. Mary's Church, and the narrow lanes that surround them.

Commanding a hilltop above the old town, **St. Mary's Church** dates to the 11th century and has withstood raids, fires, and pirate attacks. French looters took the church bells off to France in 1377, but a rescue party from Rye retrieved them a year later. The giant bells continue to toll the hour, though the church's so-called "Quarter Boys," which strike the quarter hours, are more of an auditory presence in Rye. The enormous 1561 pendulum clock on the turret is said to be the oldest in England that still works, though the stained-glass windows are relatively recent; one, from 1891, is by Edward Burne-Jones, the pre-Raphaelite painter. A climb to the tower is rewarded with a view across the salt marshes that surround Rye to the sea. The church is open daily, 9 a.m.–6 p.m. (until 4 p.m. in the winter); admission to the tower is £1.50. Mermaid Street leads out of the historic warren of streets and lanes that surround the church down to the riverside quays, where 19th-century warehouses once bustled with seafaring trade.

Tours in Rye

The **Rye Heritage Centre** (Strand Quay; (01797) 226-696; Rye TN31 7AY; **www.rye-tourism.co.uk**) equips visitors with headsets for self-guided **Historic Audio Walking Tours;** an Audio Ghost Walks version is available for nighttime explorations and is an excellent way to entertain young travelers. Both take one to three hours, depending upon how long you choose to spend at each stop.

Anyone who's read the Mapp and Lucia novels by E. F. Benson will enjoy **Mapp and Lucia's Rye,** a walking tour with the Secretary of the

E. F. Benson Society. Benson lived and wrote in Rye (see profile for Lamb House, below), and turned the town into Tilling for his humorous and astute novels set in the 1920s and 1930s. The walk begins at **Hidler's Cliff Belvedere** at the east end of High Street, lasts about an hour and a half, and ends at **Lamb House,** passing many of the locales that Benson worked into his delightful novels. The walks are conducted on Wednesdays and the first and third Saturday of each month; starting time is 2 p.m., and the cost is £4.50 per person. You may want to read the novels before coming to Rye, or watch the ten-part series based on the novels produced in the 1980s and now available on video; much of the series was filmed in Rye.

Attractions in Rye

Lamb House

Type of Attraction Historic home of famous writers

Location West Street

Admission £2.60 adults; £1.30 children ages 5–15; £6.50 families of two adults and two children

Hours April–October: Wednesday and Saturday, 2–5.30 p.m.

Phone (01372) 453-401 (National Trust regional office)

Website www.nationaltrust.org.uk

When to Go The house is open so seldom you won't have a choice, but if possible, visit on Wednesday to avoid the weekend crowds.

Special Comments The house stewards are well-versed in the history of the house and its residents and are eager to share their knowledge.

Overall Appeal by Age Group

Preschool ★	Teens ★★	Over 30 ★★★
Grade school ★★	Young Adults ★★	Seniors ★★★

Author's Rating ★★★

How Much Time to Allow 30 minutes

Description & Comments Anyone who has read the novels of Henry James or E. F. Benson will enjoy seeing this house, which still seems to resound with their presence. James moved here in 1898 and remained until his death in 1916. The American man of letters wrote some of his most famous novels at Lamb House, including *The Wings of the Dove, The Ambassadors,* and *The Golden Bowl;* H. G. Wells, Rudyard Kipling, and Edith Wharton were among his visitors. Some of the handsome, paneled rooms still contain James's personal effects, and the garden is especially charming. James often worked there, in a pavilion that was leveled by a bomb in 1940. E. F. Benson lived in the house from 1918 until his death in 1940; he wrote his humorous Mapp and Lucia novels here, and they provide a good introduction to the house, which figures in many of the scenes. Even without these literary associations, Lamb House would have a worthy past: The house was only three years old when King George I was forced to come ashore during a storm and take lodgings here. The King could not have spent a restful time here, though, as Mrs. Lamb gave birth the night of this arrival.

Touring Tips You may want to linger in the garden with a copy of a book by James or Benson.

Rye Castle Museum

Type of Attraction History museum occupying the castle and another historic building

Location Ypres Tower and East Street

Admission £2.90 adults; £2 seniors and students; £1.50 children ages 7–16; £5.90 for families of two adults and two children

Hours April 1–October 31: Ypres Tower, Monday, Thursday, and Friday, 10:30 a.m.–1 p.m., 2–5 p.m.; East Street building, Saturday and Sunday, 10:30 a.m.–1 p.m., 2 p.m.–5 p.m..; November 1–March 31: Ypres Tower only, Saturday and Sunday, 10 a.m–3 p.m.

Phone (01797) 226728

Website www.rye-tourism.co.uk

When to Go Anytime; the museum is rarely crowded.

Overall Appeal by Age Group

Preschool ★★	Teens ★★	Over 30 ★★
Grade school ★★	Young Adults ★★	Seniors ★★

Author's Rating ★★

How Much Time to Allow 30 minutes for a quick run-through

Description & Comments Ypres Tower, named for 15th-century inhabitant John de Ypres and known locally as "Wipers," is what remains of Rye's castle. Built in 1249 and surviving numerous fires and attacks, the tower's past is more colorful than the collection of medieval pottery and torture items now filling its rooms would suggest. Over the years, the structure has served as a fortification, a residence, a mortuary, and a prison. One of the most interesting displays is a series of maps showing how the coastline has changed over the years, which helps illuminate how landlocked Rye could once have been a major port. Part of the collection is housed across Church Square in a former bottling factory on East Street, where Rye's 18th-century fire engine is on display among other historic items.

Touring Tips If you want to enjoy the castle precincts while sparing yourself the price of admission, take a stroll in the Gungarden, a patch of lawn beneath the tower.

Dining in Rye

Rye seems to have a teashop on every corner. One of the most charming is the **Mermaid Street Coffee House and Tea Rooms** (corner of Mermaid and West Streets at 13 West Street; (01797) 223-272), which serves light lunches (including excellent homemade soups) and cream teas; it's open daily, 10:30 a.m.–5 p.m. If you decide to take a stroll in nearby

Winchelsea, the **Tea Tree** on High Street (phone (01797) 226-102) is a good place to stop for a light meal or tea; it's open Wednesday–Monday, 10 a.m.–6 p.m. (until 5 p.m. November–March).

Restaurants in Rye

The Flushing Inn ★★★★

MODERN BRITISH | EXPENSIVE | QUALITY ★★★★ | VALUE ★★

4 Market Street ; (01797) 223-292

Reservations Recommended **Entrée Range** 3-course dinner, £26.50–£36; 3-course lunch, £16.50–£18; light meals, £7–£11 **Payment** V, MC, AMEX, D **Bar** Beer and wine only **Disabled Access** Yes

Hours Wednesday–Monday, noon–2 p.m., 7–9 p.m.

House Specialties Fresh seafood any way it appears on the menu: Dover sole caught in Rye Bay; fish soup with garlic sauce; mussels; oysters; and for a light meal, crab sandwiches; lamb from nearby farms is also memorable.

This handsome inn dates from the 13th century, though the present building has been restored and rebuilt many times over the centuries. It seems that everyone who enjoys a meal beneath the dining room's wall frescoes knows each other, and service is attentive and friendly.

Landgate Bistro ★★★★

FRENCH/MODERN BRITISH | MODERATE | QUALITY ★★★★ | VALUE ★★★★

5–6 Landgate; (01797) 222-829

Reservations Recommended on weekends **Entrée Range** £9– £15 **Payment** V, MC, AMEX **Bar** Beer and wine only, with a thoughtful selection of French wines **Disabled Access** Yes

Hours Tuesday–Saturday, 7–10 p.m.

House Specialties Fish of the day, which is always fresh and beautifully prepared, and fresh lamb. Starters often include fresh-caught squid and fresh, local asparagus with hollandaise, or tomatoes with goat cheese and other vegetable creations.

The atmosphere in this bright, pleasant, ground-floor restaurant in an old building near the center of town is that of a simple bistro, and it soon becomes clear that the emphasis is on excellent, straightforward cuisine. The service matches the surroundings—it's welcoming and unfussy, and you'll probably want to linger over coffee and dessert.

Mermaid Bar ★★★

PUB | INEXPENSIVE | QUALITY ★★ | VALUE ★★

Mermaid Street; (01797) 223-065

Reservations Not necessary **Entrée Range** £5.50–£14.50 **Payment** V, MC, AMEX, D **Bar** Full service **Disabled Access** Yes

Hours Daily, 11 a.m.–11 p.m.

House Specialties Sandwiches; seafood platter.

We recommend the beamed and paneled bar at the back of this historic inn rather than the formal and expensive hotel restaurant because the bar is a pleasant, atmospheric setting for a light meal or snack. Some excellent wines and ales are available, and service is attentive. Should you want more than bar fare, you can also order from the full restaurant menu. In good weather, there is seating on a small terrace that, unfortunately, overlooks the car park.

The Union Inn ★★★

PUB | INEXPENSIVE | QUALITY ★★★ | VALUE ★★★

East Street; (01797) 222-334

Reservations Not necessary **Entrée Range** £5.95–£12.95 **Payment** V, MC **Bar** Full service **Disabled Access** Yes

Hours Monday–Saturday, 11 a.m.–3 p.m., 6–11 p.m.; Sunday, noon–3 p.m., 7–10:30 p.m.

House Specialties Steak and ale pie; plaice and other fresh fish from local waters.

The Union is one of Rye's busiest and friendliest pubs, and it offers a nice alternative to more formal restaurants if you want a light meal in a relaxed atmosphere. Plus, in a town with very little nightlife, the Union is one of the liveliest places around after dark.

Recreation in and around Rye

Rye Harbour Nature Reserve lies between the town walls and the sea, and it's laced with footpaths that lead to pools where seabirds gather, old fortifications, and the ruins of **Camber Castle,** built by Henry VIII and abandoned in 1642. Viewpoints overlook the marshes, sea, and islands, and part of the walk is along windswept beaches. Walks are well marked and take from one to three hours; the entrance is off Harbour Road. The **Rye Tourist Information Centre** (Strand Quay; (01797) 226-696; Rye TN31 7AY; **www.rye-tourism.co.uk**) provides a walking map.

Around Rye

Rye is a convenient base from which to explore many of the attractions of the southeast. Driving is the easiest way to get around these parts.

Battle

The Battle of Hastings, that decisive event in English history, took place not in Hastings but at what is now the site of this pleasant country town, 6 miles north of Hastings and some 17 miles southwest of Rye. Here, on October 14th, 1066, Duke William of Normandy slew Harold, the Saxon king of England. The king, who would become known as William the Conqueror, was crowned in London on Christmas Day of that year and during his tumultuous reign brought some degree of unity to England. The Tower of London is among his accomplishments, as is the Doomsday Book—the king had this listing of property throughout England compiled for purposes of taxation, and it survives as one of the most illustrative records of the times.

Arriving and Getting Oriented in Battle

It's possible to reach Battle from Rye by train, though the trip requires a change in London and takes about an hour and a half. Trains run about every half hour throughout the day, and the fare runs about £20. For information, call (08457) 484-950 or go to **www.railtrack.co.uk.** Battle is less than half an hour from Rye by car, via the A259 coast road to Hastings and then a short trip inland on A2100. The **Battle Tourist Information Centre** (88 High Street; (01424) 773-721; **www.battletown.co.uk**) provides a town map and information about the battlefield and other local attractions.

Exploring Battle

A stroll down High Street and Upper Lake Street leads past handsome homes, shops, and the town's Romanesque church of **St. Mary the Virgin.** The big attraction, though, is the open field where the monumental event in English history was played out.

Battle of Hastings 1066, Battlefield and Abbey

Type of Attraction Scene of England's most important battle

Location Off High Street

Admission £4.30 adults; £3.20 seniors and students; £2.20 children ages 5–15; £10.80 families of two adults and two children

Hours April 1–September 30: daily, 10 a.m.–6 p.m.; October 1–October 31: daily, 10 a.m.–5 p.m.; November 1–March 31: daily, 10 a.m.–4 p.m. Closed December 24–26 and January 1.

Phone (01424) 773792

Website www.battletown.co.uk

When to Go Avoid the weekend crush if you can, and try to visit in good weather so you can linger comfortably on the battlefield and in the abbey ruins.

Special Comments Mock battles and other events are staged throughout the year and can be quite colorful.

Overall Appeal by Age Group

Preschool ★	Teens ★★★★	Over 30 ★★★★
Grade school ★★★	Young Adults ★★★	Seniors ★★★★

Author's Rating ★★★★

How Much Time to Allow About 2 hours for everything

Description & Comments A video, an exhibit, and a self-guided audio tour of the battleground precincts, cleverly produced by the English Heritage preservation society, bring the most famous date in England history vividly to life. The tour begins with a video presentation and a museum-like exhibition of maps, drawings, and text panels; both put the battle in historical context and thoroughly explain the events and circumstances leading up to the Norman conquest. Visitors then wander at leisure through the site, which encompasses the battleground and the ruins of the massive abbey that William the Conqueror erected to atone for the bloodshed. (A later king, Henry VIII, had the abbey destroyed when he broke with the Church of Rome.) At marked spots along the paths, visitors stop to listen to fictional firsthand accounts of the battle from the perspective of Aelfric, a Saxon soldier; Henri, a Norman knight; and Edith, mistress of King Harold.

Touring Tips Visitors have a choice of an in-depth version of the audio tour or a shorter one; opt for the longer version, as there is much to be learned here and the presentation is excellent.

Dining in Battle

Orangery ★★★★

BRITISH/FRENCH | MODERATE | QUALITY ★★★★ | VALUE ★★★

PowderMills Hotel, PowderMills Lane, behind the abbey; (01424) 772035

Reservations Recommended **Entrée Range** £8–£13 **Payment** V, MC, AMEX, D **Bar** Full service **Disabled Access** Yes

Hours Daily, 7–9 a.m., noon–2 p.m., 7–9 p.m.

House Specialties Seafood, especially fresh fish of the day and a delicious seafood ravioli.

Battle's finest restaurant, in a country-house hotel just outside of town, is a restful place to take a break during a sight-seeing visit to the battleground and abbey. The service is warm, and the surroundings are airy and casually attractive, with wicker furniture and marble floors. This is an especially nice place to dine in good weather, when meals are served on a flowery terrace overlooking the gardens; allow time to take a stroll around the 150-acre grounds after your meal. Children are not welcome in the restaurant in the evenings.

The Historic Houses of Kent

Rye is well situated for a drive north into Kent and the rolling forests and farmland known as the Weald. Some of England's finest houses are located on the Weald, and many are open to the public. A relatively easy drive through some lovely countryside will bring you to all the houses we list here.

Arriving and Getting Oriented in Sussex and Kent

A good map is essential when you set off into the twisting lanes of Sussex and Kent. All the houses can be reached from turnings off A268 and

A21, which lead north from Rye, and are well signed; the drive to any of these houses should take from half an hour to an hour. These houses are not well served by public transportation, but an alternative to driving is to travel to the town of **Royal Tunbridge Wells** by train and then to reach the houses of your choice by taxi from there. Tunbridge Wells is about 18 miles north of Rye; all of the houses we list below are within a ten-mile radius. Trains between Rye and Tunbridge Wells run about every half hour; the trip takes an hour, and fares run about £9. For information, call (08457) 484-950 or go to **www.railtrack.co.uk.**

Exploring the Historic Houses of Kent

Chartwell

Type of Attraction Historic home of Winston Churchill

Location 2 miles south of Westerham (fork left off B2026 after 1.5 miles); 12 miles northwest of Tunbridge Wells

Admission £5.80 adults; £2.90 children; £14.50 families

Hours March 22–June 29, September 3–November 9: Wednesday–Sunday, 11 a.m.–5 p.m.; July 1–August 31: Tuesday–Sunday, 11 a.m.–5 p.m.

Phone (01732) 868-381

Website www.nationaltrust.org.uk/places/chartwell

When to Go In good weather, as you'll want to enjoy the house and the grounds

Special Comments Chartwell provides an evocative glimpse into the life of Winston Churchill, and anyone with an interest in the remarkable man should go out of the way to visit this house; young people will probably find that the surroundings provide an especially rich introduction to the life of one of England's greatest 20th-century statesmen and the country's wartime prime minister.

Overall Appeal by Age Group

Preschool —	Teens ★★★	Over 30 ★★
Grade school ★★★	Young Adults ★★	Seniors ★★★★

Author's Rating ★★★

How Much Time to Allow At least 2 hours for the house and grounds

Description & Comments Sir Winston and Lady Churchill moved into this brick house overlooking hills and a wooded valley in 1924 and made it their home for the next 40 years. The house, still furnished as the Churchills left it, not only provides a glimpse into the home life of the couple but still seems to resound with activity. The couple entertained many of the great statesmen of the 20th century in the five reception rooms, Sir Winston wrote his *History of the English-Speaking Peoples* and other books here, and the couple planted gardens and transformed the 80-acre grounds with ponds and a swimming pool. The carpet of the study is worn with the path Sir Winston made while dictating through many nights, the wall he built around the kitchen garden still stands, and the rose garden Lady Churchill planted blooms throughout much of the summer. Many of Sir Winston's paintings hang in the studio where he often retreated.

Touring Tips The grounds are ideal for walking and provide stunning views over the Kentish countryside. You can easily combine a visit to Chartwell with visits to nearby Ightham Mote and Knole.

Hever Castle

Type of Attraction Medieval castle

Location 3 miles west of Penshurst on B 2026, 10 miles northwest of Tunbridge Wells

Admission Castle and gardens: £8.40 adults; £7.10 seniors; £4.60 for children ages 5–14; £21.40 families. Gardens only: £6.70 adults; £5.70 seniors; £4.40 children ages 5–14; £17.80 families.

Hours March 1–November 30: daily, noon–5 p.m. Grounds open at 11 a.m.

Phone (01732) 865-224

Website www.hevercastle.com

When to Go In good weather, because you'll want to spend time in the gardens

Special Comments The castle is well equipped for visitors with disabilities, and visitors in wheelchairs are admitted free of charge.

Overall Appeal by Age Group

Preschool —	Teens ★★★	Over 30 ★★★
Grade school ★★★	Young Adults ★★★	Seniors ★★★

Author's Rating ★★★

How Much Time to Allow At least 2 hours

Description & Comments This squat, stone fantasy of crenellation and turrets, all of it surrounded by a moat, fits just about anyone's image of what a medieval castle should look like. Hevers has a colorful history, too. Anne Boleyn, the second wife of Henry VIII, grew up here, and Henry later gave the house to his fourth wife, Anne of Cleves. William Waldorf Astor, the American millionaire, bought the castle in 1903, restored it, built a mock Tudor village alongside the moat to house his staff, and had himself named a viscount. Among Viscount Astor's many additions were the classical and natural gardens, on which some 1,800 workers toiled for more than two years. The Italian Gardens surround a 35-acre lake and contain a stunning collection of classical sculpture, including portions of the triumphal arch that the Roman Emperor Claudius erected on the nearby coast in A.D. 52. A massive topiary maze is especially popular with young visitors.

Touring Tips There are two restaurants on the castle grounds, one overlooking the moat and one near the lake and Italian Gardens.

Ightham Mote

Type of Attraction Medieval manor house

Location Ivy Hatch, 6 miles east of Sevenoaks, 10 miles north of Tunbridge Wells

Admission £5.40 adults; £2.70 children; £13.50 families

Hours March 23–November 7: Monday, Wednesday–Friday, Sunday, 10 a.m.–5:30 p.m.

Phone (01732) 810-378

Website www.nationaltrust.org.uk/places/ighthammote

When to Go During the week, to avoid weekend crowds

Special Comments The garden and ground-floor rooms are wheelchair accessible. The Mote Restaurant is open year-round, Thursday–Sunday, and serves lunches and dinners. Part of the 15th-century stable blocks have been converted into two vacation cottages; call (0870) 458-4411 for information.

Overall Appeal by Age Group

Preschool ★★	Teens ★★★	Over 30 ★★★★
Grade school ★★★	Young Adults ★★★	Seniors ★★★★

Author's Rating ★★★★

How Much Time to Allow At least 1 hour

Description & Comments This moated manor house dates from 1330; it's one of the oldest residences in England and one of the best-preserved medieval houses anywhere. ("Mote," incidentally, is a reference not to the romantic water that surrounds the mellowed stone structure but to the fact that it once served as a spot where local landowners would meet.) Ightham Mote seems to have remained nestled in its hidden valley over the centuries without being touched by time, though the rooms show signs of just about every period of British architecture. As a result, a tour of the Great Hall drawing room, billiards room, and family chapels provides a wonderful look into domestic life amidst constantly shifting styles and tastes of centuries gone by. While much of the house is remarkably intact, some parts are under restoration, and the work is of great interest: Instructive panels explain what's being done and how various preservation methods are applied. The gardens have recently been beautifully restored.

Touring Tips The docents are a font of knowledge about architecture and domestic life; try to join one of the tours or talks they sometimes offer. The grounds surrounding the house are open year-round and are laced with woodland trails.

Knole

Type of Attraction Historic home

Location Outskirts of Sevenoaks, 11 miles north of Tunbridge Wells

Admission £5 adults; £2.50 children; £12.50 families

Hours March 23–November 3: Wednesday–Sunday, 10:30 a.m.–5 p.m.

Phone (01732) 810-378

Website www.nationaltrust.org.uk/places/knole

When to Go On a weekday if possible, because the house is popular with Londoners on weekend day trips

Special Comments The gardens are lovingly tended by the Sackville family but are open only on Wednesdays, May–September.

Overall Appeal by Age Group

Preschool —	Teens ★★	Over 30 ★★★
Grade school ★★	Young Adults ★★	Seniors ★★★

Author's Rating ★★★

How Much Time to Allow An hour and a half

Description & Comments Knole was built on grand scale for the Archbishop of Canterbury in the 15th century and remains perfectly intact, one of the great treasure houses of England. Queen Elizabeth I presented the house to Thomas Sackville in 1603, and the Sackville-West family has lived here ever since. Vita Sackville-West, the 20th-century poet, writer, and friend of novelist Virginia Woolf, grew up here. Woolf, who set her novel *Orlando* here, described Knole as "a town rather than a house," and Sackville-West once wrote of footmen being stationed at the edges of carpets during dinner to keep them from floating up in the drafts that rush through the 365-room house. Aside from having a room for every day of the year, Knole also has a courtyard for every day of the week and a staircase for every week of the year. The labyrinth of galleries and rooms houses an unmatched collection of 17th- and 18th-century furniture, rare textiles, and a collection of portraits by such masters as Sir Anthony Van Dyck, Sir Joshua Reynolds, and Thomas Gainsborough. Most rooms are the private quarters of the Sackville family; public visits are confined to 13 staterooms and the grounds.

Touring Tips A tearoom on the grounds is a good spot for a light lunch and can be followed by a walk in the park, where deer roam freely.

Penshurst Place

Type of Attraction Historic home

Location Village of Penshurst, 7 miles northwest of Tunbridge Wells

Admission House and grounds: £6.50 adults; £6 seniors and students; £4.50 children; £18 families. Grounds only: £5 adults; £4.50 seniors and students; £4 children, £15 families

Hours March 1–March 28: grounds only, Saturday and Sunday, 10:30 a.m.–6 p.m.; March 29–November 2: grounds, daily, 10:30 a.m.–6 p.m.; house, noon–5:30 p.m.

Phone (01892) 870-307

Website www.penshurstplace.com

When to Go With many stands of trees, the grounds are quite colorful in the autumn.

Special Comments Parts of the house and much of the grounds are wheelchair accessible. The house is especially child-friendly; printed guides for young visitors are available, and there are child-oriented nature paths and a large playground.

Overall Appeal by Age Group

Preschool ★	Teens ★★	Over 30 ★★★
Grade school ★★★	Young Adults ★★	Seniors ★★★

Author's Rating ★★★

How Much Time to Allow 2 hours for house and grounds

Description & Comments This lovely manor house dates from the 13th century, though it has been embellished upon many times since then. The stone-floored Baron's Hall, with a ceiling of chestnut wood, a huge, octagonal-shaped central hearth, and a minstrel's gallery, is considered to be among the finest interiors to come down to us from the Middle Ages. Indeed, it's easy to imagine the servants and estate workers huddled around the fire and sleeping on mats on the stone floor; the family of the house resided in paneled rooms upstairs. Many of the grander staterooms and the Long Gallery date from the Elizabethan period, by which time the house had passed into the Sidney family, a gift of King Edward VI; the Sidneys have lived at Penshurst ever since. Sir Philip Sidney, the soldier, courtier, poet, and personification of an Elizabethan gentleman, was born here. Ben Jonson, the Elizabethan poet and playwright, wrote a long, admiring poem about the house, "To Penshurst," in which he rhapsodizes, "Thou art not, Penshurst, built to obvious show." With its solid stone exterior and battlements, Penshurst is indeed not showy, though the current resident, Viscount de L'Isle, does an admirable job of maintaining the old place in all its grandeur.

Touring Tips Take a break in the tearoom; seating on a pleasant terrace is available in good weather.

Sissinghurst Castle Garden

Type of Attraction A partially ruined Elizabethan manor house surrounded by some of the world's most renowned gardens

Location 1 mile east of Sissinghurst village, off A262; 12 miles east of Tunbridge Wells

Admission £6.50

Hours March 22–November 2: Monday, Tuesday, Friday, 11 a.m.–6:30 p.m.; Saturday and Sunday, 10 a.m.–6:30 p.m.

Phone (01580) 710-700

Website www.nationaltrust.org.uk/places/sissinghurst

When to Go The gardens are a delight at any time but are especially colorful in May and June when many of the flowers are blooming. Because Sissinghurst is so popular, it's best to try to visit on a weekday.

Special Comments Sissinghurst attracts hundreds of thousands of visitors a year, and at busy times the number of visitors allowed into the garden may be controlled. Don't be surprised if you are told you must wait for entry.

Overall Appeal by Age Group

Preschool ★★★★★	Teens ★★★	Over 30 ★★★★
Grade school ★★★	Young Adults ★★★	Seniors ★★★★

Author's Rating ★★★★

How Much Time to Allow 2 hours

Description & Comments The poet and writer Vita Sackville-West and her husband, the diplomat Harold Nicolson, bought this property, then derelict, in the 1930s. They restored part of the house, furnishing it richly, and converted the first floor of the Tudor Gatehouse into Vita's study. Their greatest accomplishment, though, was the creation of the gardens, now some of the most famous in the world. They are laid out as ten outdoor rooms, each with a distinct look and feel; one is planted almost entirely in whites and grays, another in bright reds and oranges.

Touring Tips Don't miss the exhibition in the Oast House, one of the buildings on the estate, that traces the history of Sissinghurst and the transformation of the gardens.

Dining near the Historic Houses of Kent

The Spotted Dog ★★★

PUB/BRITISH | MODERATE | QUALITY ★★★ | VALUE ★★★

About a half mile south of Penshurst village center on Smarts Hill, off B2188; (01892) 870-253

Reservations Recommended for Sunday lunch and evening meals **Entrée Range** £7–£12 **Payment** V, MC **Bar** Full service **Disabled Access** Yes

Hours Daily, 11 a.m.–3 p.m., 6–10:30 p.m.

House Specialties The local sausages and kidney pie top the list of the pub fare; for more elaborate meals, the kitchen prepares locally caught fish and an excellent Sunday roast.

With its heavy beams, paneled alcoves, inglenook fireplace, and views over Penshurst Place and the lush Kentish Weald, this 16th-century pub provides plenty of atmosphere. In good weather, you may want to forego the cozy atmosphere and enjoy drinks and meals on the stone terrace. Locals crowd into this place day and night, but outsiders are made to feel most welcome.

Part Six

The South of England

Three of England's most intriguing cities are in the south. Depending on your tastes, **Brighton** may impress or appall you with its garish seaside atmosphere and exotic palace, the **Royal Pavilion.** The cathedral cities of **Winchester** and **Salisbury** are a bit less exciting but certainly more soothing; in fact, many travelers find these quintessentially English cities to be two of the most appealing places in the land.

Around these cities are meadow-covered downs and plains that invite easygoing exploration. Every bend in the lane hides pleasant inns and pubs where you'll feel comfortable plunking down in front of a fire and taking in a slice of British provincial life. You'll also come upon stately country houses, including the majestic **Wilton House** near Salisbury; the homes of such luminaries as Jane Austen, at Chawton outside of Winchester, and the country retreats of Virginia Woolf and the Bloomsbury group near Brighton; and one of the world's greatest prehistoric treasures, **Stonehenge,** just north of Salisbury.

Not To Be Missed in the South of England

- Brighton Pavilion (page 239)
- The town of Lewes (page 256)
- Salisbury, town, cathedral, and Cathedral Close (page 274)
- Stonehenge (page 284)
- Winchester, town and cathedral (page 262)

Brighton

Brighton has been London's seaside getaway for two centuries now, ever since King George IV discovered the little town named Brighthelmston when he was Prince of Wales. "Prinny," as the high-living prince was called, installed his morganatic wife, the Catholic Mrs. Maria Fitzherbert, here and eventually built Brighton's most famous structure, the exotic palace known as **Brighton Pavilion.** In Prinny's wake came the

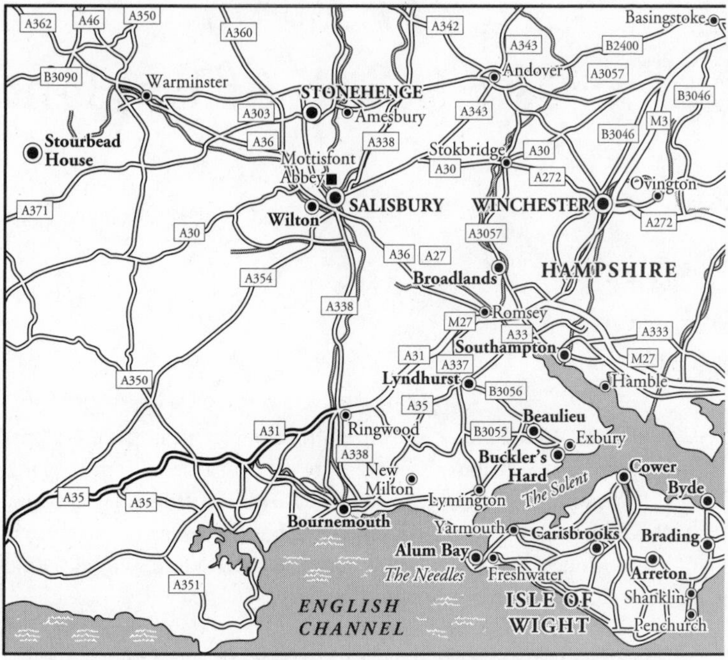

world-weary looking for sea air, a little fun, and perhaps a weekend with a mistress or some other form of illicit pleasure. For years, Brighton was the place where a gentleman would come with a paid companion and a photographer, with the purpose of being caught en flagrante and thereby expediting a divorce. Others came simply to enjoy the easygoing, seaside atmosphere. After the pavilion, Brighton's most notable structures are the amusement piers that stretch from shore far into the English Channel and the handsome Regency-style terraces (blocks of houses built around gardens) that stretch for miles from the town center.

The years have taken their toll on Brighton. One of the main amusements of the past, the **West Pier,** is now a rusting hulk that seems like it might at any minute succumb to the waves that batter its pilings. Shops are boarded up, streets are often unkempt, and a general air of decay pervades the place. Even so, Brighton has its ardent supporters, and efforts to retrieve some of the former glory days are ongoing—including restoration of the West Pier. The town is a bedroom community for London, and Brighton's recent popularity with gays and lesbians has reinvigorated the town center. Seeing the rows of terrace houses facing gardens that thrive in the mild climate, it's easy to understand why many Brighton fans are able to find a great deal of charm in an atmosphere that others find melan-

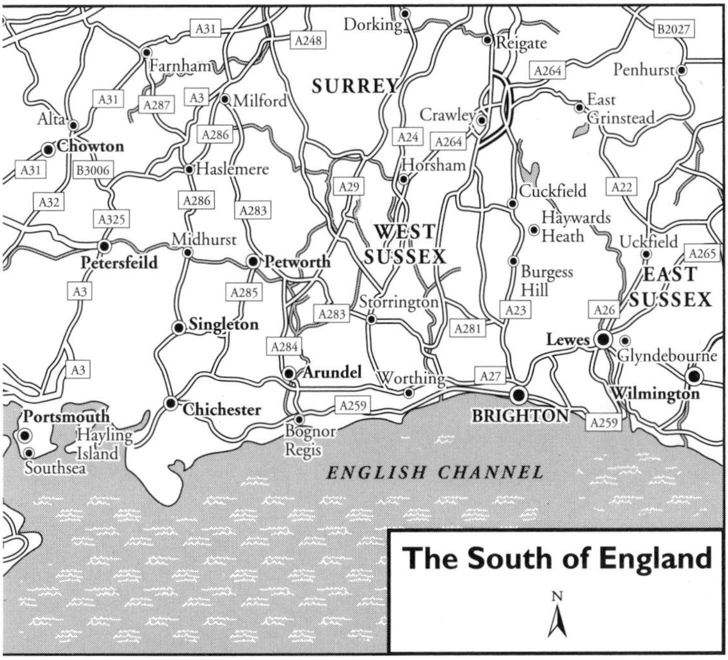

cholic. Whatever you think of Brighton, the town and its surroundings have plenty of appealing attractions to keep you busy for several days.

Planning Your Visit to Brighton

The **Brighton Visitor Information Centre** is at 10 Bartholomew Square, in the center of town just off the seafront between West Street and Old Steine (**www.brighton-hove.gov.uk** or **www.tourism.brighton.co.uk**). The center provides information on places to stay, what to see and do, where to dine and shop, and how to get around, as well as information on guest houses, clubs, shops and other Brighton businesses that cater to gay and lesbian visitors. The office also offers a same-day accommodation booking service. For information, call (0906) 711-2255; the center is open Monday–Friday, 9 a.m.–5 p.m., and Saturday, 10 a.m.–5 p.m.; in summer, it's also open Sunday, 10 a.m.–4 p.m.

Special Events in Brighton

Brighton hosts many events throughout the year. The **Brighton Festival** is the largest performing-arts festival in Britain and runs throughout May, bringing theater, opera, film, classical music, and dance to the concert halls, theaters, and streets of the city; for tickets and information, call

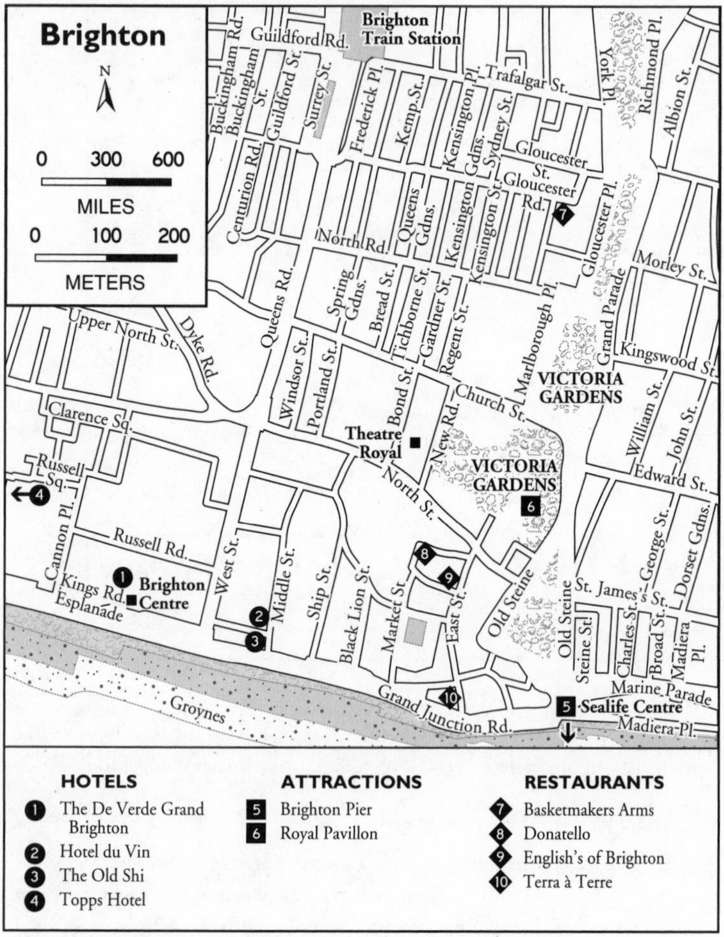

(01273) 709-709. Brighton's **Gay Pride parade,** held the second weekend in August, draws more than 50,000 participants; for information, call (01273) 775-939 or visit **www.prideinbrightonandhove.com.** On the first weekend in November, antique cars crowd the seafront when Brighton becomes the terminus of a 50-mile drive from London during the **Vintage Car Rally.** The seafront is aglow on December 22, when thousands of townspeople turn out to celebrate the shortest day of the year with a candlelight procession accompanied by fireworks; for information, call (01273) 57110628.

Arriving and Getting Oriented in Brighton

Brighton is 50 miles due south of London. Trains run about every half hour from London's Victoria Station to Brighton, and with a little less frequency from London Bridge and London King's Cross stations. The trip takes about an hour and 20 minutes and the round trip costs about £22. For information, call (08457) 484-950 or go to **www.railtrack.co.uk.** The Brighton train station is at the end of Queens Road, about a ten-minute walk north of the city center and seafront; city buses (see "Getting around Brighton," page 247) run from the station to the seafront and other locations around town.

By car, the quickest route from London is the M23. The trip often takes just over an hour, but traffic in and around London can add considerable time. Several car parks are located throughout Brighton and are well marked along the routes into the city. When using car parks and when parking on the street, you must obtain a ticket from a machine and place it on the dashboard in easy view through the windshield. Fees vary from place to place, but in the city center, expect to pay £1.40 for the first hour and up to £12 for eight hours. In many car parks, you can park overnight for fees that range from £2 to £4. Much of the street parking in Brighton is reserved for residents, so pay close attention to signs.

National Express buses leave London's Victoria Coach Station for Brighton every hour. The trip takes about an hour and 45 minutes and costs £8.50. For more information, call (08705) 808-080 or go to **www.gobycoach.com.**

Hotels in Brighton

The De Vere Grand Brighton — *£155–£220*

OVERALL ★★★★★ | QUALITY ★★★★ | VALUE ★★★

Kings Road, Brighton BN1 2FW; (01273) 224-300; fax (01273) 224-321; reservations@grandbrighton.co.uk; www.grandbrighton.co.uk

Location On the seafront.

Amenities & Services 200 rooms. Indoor pool and spa, fitness center, restaurant, bar/lounge, nightclub (see profile for Midnight Blues under "Nightclubs in Brighton," below), concierge, 24-hour room service, bellhop, laundry, satellite TV.

Elevator Yes.

Parking Yes, £20.

Pricing Includes lavish buffet breakfast in an atrium-like room overlooking the sea.

Credit Cards V, MC, AMEX, D

With its gleaming white façade, bow windows, and elegant balconies facing the waves, the Grand may outshine the Royal Pavilion as Brighton's most magnificent palace. The Italian Renaissance interior is both intriguing and welcoming, and as you soon as you enter the column-filled lobby and see the soaring grand staircase, it becomes clear that a stay at the Grand will be a memorable experience. Service manages to be super-efficient, comfortably obliging, and gracious at the same time. The seafront rooms are enormous and are filled with cushy couches and armchairs—you may well want to consider paying the additional charge for one of these extraordinary accommodations, especially if they are available as part of the

HOW HOTELS COMPARE

Hotel	Overall Rating	Quality Rating	Value Rating	Price
Brighton				
The De Vere Grand Brighton	★★★★★	★★★★	★★★	£155–£220
Topps Hotel	★★★★	★★★★	★★★★★	£45–£84
Hotel du Vin	★★★★	★★★★	★★★	£140–£180
The Old Ship	★★★	★★★	★★★	£125–£155
Lewes				
Shelleys Hotel	★★★★½	★★★★½	★★★★½	£110–£170
Salisbury				
White Hart	★★★★	★★★★	★★★	£105–£130

special offers the hotel often posts on its website. Rooms in the back of the hotel are also large and well appointed with staid, colonial furnishings enlivened with shades of blue and gold, and most have commodious marble baths with deep tubs, hair dryers, and other amenities. Ongoing improvements—some occasioned by the explosion of an IRA bomb during Margaret Thatcher's stay here in the 1980s—keep the Grand in pristine condition.

Hotel du Vin — *£140–£180*

OVERALL ★★★★ | QUALITY ★★★★ | VALUE ★★★

Ship Street; (01273) 718-588; fax (01273) 718-599; info@brighton.hotelduvin.com; www.hotelduvin.com

Location Just off the seafront and near the Lanes.

Amenities & Services 37 rooms. Sumptuous bathrooms with deep tubs and "rain" showerheads; Egyptian linens; bistro, bar with billiards table and cigar gallery; courtyard; satellite TV; room service for breakfast only.

Elevator Yes.

Parking In nearby municipal car parks.

Pricing Continental breakfast, £9.50; full English breakfast, £13.50.

Credit Cards V, MC, AMEX, D

We were delighted when another link in this small, chic English chain of boutique hotels opened in Brighton in the winter of 2003, because we rate these hostelries to be among the best hotels in the other cities where they operate (see hotel profiles in Winchester and Birmingham). Like all Hotels du Vin, this one is stunningly decorated throughout, and guest rooms are done in rich hues and fine fabrics, creating an atmosphere that is both relaxed and stylish. Bathrooms are exquisite, with deep tubs and special "rain" showerheads. A pleasant courtyard provides a chance to enjoy the sea air without dealing with Brighton's summertime crowds.

IN THE SOUTH OF ENGLAND

Hotel	Overall Rating	Quality Rating	Value Rating	Price
Salisbury (continued)				
Red Lion Hotel	★★★★	★★★	★★★	£88–£109
Grasmere House Hotel	★★★	★★★	★★★	£65–£85
Winchester				
Hotel du Vin	★★★★	★★★★	★★★★	£115–£135
Lainston House Hotel	★★★★	★★★★	★★★	£110–£260
Winchester Royal Hotel	★★★	★★★	★★★	£90–£120
Portland House	★★	★★	★★★	£48–£60

The Old Ship *£125–£155*

OVERALL ★★★ | QUALITY ★★★ | VALUE ★★★

Kings Road, Brighton BN1 2FW; (01273) 329-001; fax (01273) 820-718; oldship@paramount-hotels.co.uk; www.paramount-hotels.co.uk/oldship

Location On the seafront.

Amenities & Services 152 rooms. Restaurant, bar/lounge, use of nearby health clubs; the lobby is unusually pleasant and is divided into several different seating areas.

Elevator Yes.

Parking On site, £10.

Pricing Includes buffet breakfast.

Credit Cards V, MC, AMEX, D, DC

The Old Ship is Brighton's oldest hotel—an inn has stood here since 1559—and throughout much of the 19th and early 20th centuries it was one of Brighton's grandest hostelries. Recent refurbishment is doing much to bring the interior back up to high standards, though the dreary exterior is in need of work. Inside, the lobby is broken into several stylish seating areas, some of them overlooking the sea, and many of the guest rooms have been redone in a chic, casual style, with wicker, bright colors, high-tech lighting, and gleaming white baths with tub and shower combinations. (Some of the rooms have not been touched for years, so ask for a refurbished room when booking.) The staff will gladly take you on a tour of the hotel's 16th-century cellars, which were once smugglers' lairs and are now sometimes used for special candlelit dinners—ask if you might be able to partake of one of these weird experiences.

HOW ATTRACTIONS COMPARE

Attraction	Comments	Author's Rating
Brighton		
Royal Pavilion	Historic palace with exotic design	★★★½
Preston Manor	Manor house	★★★
Brighton Pier	Historic pier lined with arcades and amusements	★★
Lewes and Surroundings		
Charleston	Home of members of Bloomsbury group	★★★★
Monk's House	Home of writer Virginia Woolf	★★★★
Sheffield Park Garden	Spectacular garden	★★★
Lewes Castle and Anne of Cleves House	Historic buildings	★★
Winchester		
Winchester Cathedral	Great cathedral	★★★
Great Hall	Medieval hall once part of Norman castle	★★

Topps Hotel *£45–£84*

OVERALL ★★★★ | QUALITY ★★★★ | VALUE ★★★★★

17 Regency Square, Brighton BN1 2FW; (01273) 729-334; fax (01273) 203-679; toppshotel@aol.com; www.brighton.co.uk/hotels/topps

Location In a Regency square just off the seafront.

Amenities & Services 15 rooms. Two nonsmoking rooms; meals prepared on request.

Elevator Yes.

Parking Street parking and municipal car parks nearby.

Pricing Includes breakfast.

Credit Cards V, MC, AMEX, DC

Brighton is liberally graced with beautiful 19th-century squares, and this excellent small hotel occupies two converted town houses on one of the most beautiful of them, facing the sea just down Kings Road from the Grand Hotel. While Topps doesn't provide the full service of a hotel like the Grand, it is one of the nicest places to stay in Brighton—and justifiably popular with return guests, so reserve as far in advance as you can. Owners Paul and Pauline Collins have kept the original layout of the houses intact, so all rooms but one single are large, and the high-ceilinged rooms occupying former parlors at the front of the hotel are especially gracious. All of the rooms are pleasantly and individually decorated with antique beds (including some four-posters), couches, and reading chairs, and many have large, windowed bathrooms equipped with deep tubs and, in some, rocking chairs next to the tubs.

IN THE SOUTH OF ENGLAND

Attraction	Comments	Author's Rating
Winchester (continued)		
The Military Museums	Collections of regimental history	★★
Around Winchester		
Chawton	Home of writer Jane Austen	★★★
Mottisfont Abbey	Norman abbey	★★★
Salisbury		
Mompesson House	Historic house	★★★★
Salisbury Cathedral	Great cathedral	★★★
Around Salisbury		
Stonehenge	World-renowned prehistoric site	★★★★★
Longleat House	Historic house and safari park	★★★★
Wilton House	Historic estate and lavish gardens	★★★★
Stourhead	Country house and garden	★★★

Getting around Brighton

Brighton is compact, and most of the places where you'll want to spend time are an easy walk from the center of town, the Steine (pronounced "steen"). This large, open area is planted with gardens that grow on land reclaimed when George IV drained a river that once flowed into the sea here; the name refers to a stone on which fishermen used to dry their nets. The **Brighton Pavilion** is on the Steine, and the southern end of the gardens opens onto the seafront. The medieval enclave of twisting alleyways and hidden squares known as the Lanes (and the one section of Brighton that can be considered quaint) is just to the west of the Steine.

Brighton's efficient bus system is operated by **Brighton and Hove Bus and Coach Company.** The fare for travel anywhere in Brighton is £1. For information on routes and times, call (01273) 886-200 or visit **www.buses.co.uk.** The company also operates the 1 Stop Travel Store at 16 Old Steine, which sells bus tickets as well as tickets for long-distance coach, train, and ferry travel.

Exploring Brighton

You can't come to Brighton without taking a stroll along the seafront, known simply as "the front." Most popular is the mile or so stretch between **Brighton Pier** and the **West Pier,** reminders of the days when the amusement pier was at the height of holiday fashion. Brighton Pier

HOW RESTAURANTS COMPARE

Name	Cuisine	Overall	Quality	Value	Price
Brighton					
English's of Brighton	Seafood	★★★½	★★★½	★★★	Exp
Terra à Terre	Vegetarian	★★★	★★★★	★★★	Mod
Basketmakers Arms	Pub	★★★	★★★	★★★★	Inexp
Donatello	Italian	★★★	★★½	★★★	Inexp
Lewes and Surroundings					
Shelleys Hotel	British/ Continental	★★★★	★★★★	★★★★	Exp
The Hungry Monk	British	★★★★	★★★★	★★★	Exp

(see profile under "Attractions in Brighton," below), now more than a hundred years old, continues to dazzle visitors with its bright lights and kitschy amusements. West Pier has long since been abandoned and, now ravaged by the elements, is just a ghostly reminder of the sensation it created when it opened in 1866. A portion of the pier collapsed in 2002, but a restoration project is slated to have the full length of the pier looking just as it did in the 1920s by 2005.

The **Volk Electric Railway** runs for about a mile from Brighton Pier west to the Black Rock Station. Britain's first electric railway (and the world's oldest operational public electric railway) has been hauling passengers up and down the Brighton seafront since 1883. Magnus Volk, who built the railway, had already made an impressive show of his knowledge of electricity by illuminating the turrets and domes of Brighton Pavilion with thousands of electric lights, and the magical effect can still be witnessed nightly. A ride along the beach in one of the open-air cars costs £1.40 adults (£2.40 round trip), £1 seniors (£1.60 round trip), £0.70 children under age 14 (£1.20 round trip), and £3.20 families (£5.80 round trip). Trains operate Monday–Friday, 11 a.m.–5 p.m., and Saturday and Sunday, 11 a.m.–6 p.m. One stretch of sand along the route is the section reserved for nudists, the only such beach in England.

What remains of the original fishing village of Brighthelmston now clusters along the twisting narrow alleyways and compact squares of the quarter known as **the Lanes** (the name is a reference not to the small streets but to the lines that fishermen used to stretch out along the streets to dry). The simple houses now accommodate Brighton's famous

IN THE SOUTH OF ENGLAND

Name	Cuisine	Overall	Quality	Value	Price
Winchester					
Hotel du Vin	French Bistro	★★★★½	★★★★½	★★★★	Exp
La Bodega	Mediterranean	★★★★	★★★★	★★★★	Mod
Wykeham Arms	English	★★★★	★★★★	★★★★	Mod
Salisbury					
Squires Restaurant	British	★★★★	★★★½	★★★	Mod
Haunch of Venison	British/Pub	★★★★	★★★	★★★	Inexp–Mod
Harper's Restaurant	British	★★★½	★★★	★★★	Mod
Prezzo	Italian	★★★	★★½	★★★	Mod

antiques trade (see "Shopping in Brighton," below) as well as pubs, restaurants, coffee houses, and boutiques. Brighton's small **Fishing Museum,** on the seafront near the Lanes at 201 King's Road Arches, chronicles the days when the residents of this quarter set out to sea in search of their livelihood. The museum is open daily, 10 a.m.–5 p.m. Admission is free; for more information, call (01273) 723-064.

Attractions in Brighton

Brighton Pier

Type of Attraction A historic pier lined with arcades and amusements

Location Grand Junction Road and Marine Parade

Admission Free

Hours Summer: daily, 9 a.m.–2 a.m.; winter, 10 a.m.–midnight

Phone (01273) 609-361

Website www.brightonpier.co.uk

When to Go In daylight, because the views up and down the Channel coast are magnificent. Besides, at night the pier seems a bit tawdry.

Special Tips The pier looks a lot more romantic from the shore than it does on closer inspection, so you may want to keep your feet on terra firma and enjoy the spectacle from afar.

Overall Appeal by Age Group

Preschool ★★★	Teens ★★★	Over 30 ★★
Grade school ★★★★	Young Adults ★★★	Seniors ★★

Author's Rating ★★

How Much Time to Allow About 1 hour for a walk to the end of the pier and back; longer for games of chance, roller coaster, and other rides

HOW NIGHTCLUBS COMPARE

Name	Comments	Cover
Brighton		
Club Revenge	Brighton's top gay club	0–£7
Cricketers	Pub and drinking spot	None

Description & Comments Brighton's famous seaside attraction extends a third of a mile into the English Channel and is lined with arcades, bars, restaurants, shops selling candy and fast food, and amusement rides. The atmosphere is anything but restful, and for a whiff of sea air and a view of the coast you'll need to stand at the railing and turn your back to all the noise and lights. Brighton's civic leaders are quick to point out that the pier is a place for family fun, and kids will probably love it; but when walking past all the tacky attractions on the pier, it's hard not to think of Graham Greene's sinister novel about the local underworld, *Brighton Rock* (the title is a reference to the hard candy that is readily available on the pier).

Touring Tips If it's bracing sea breezes you're after, walk about two-thirds of the way out to the open space between the covered arcades and the amusement park. This is the quietest part of the pier, and you can sit on a bench and enjoy the view.

Preston Manor

Type of Attraction Manor house

Location Preston Park, 2 miles north of city center off the London Road (A23)

Admission £3 adults; £2.50 seniors and students; £1.80 children ages 5–15; £7.85 families of two adults and up to four children; £4.85 families of one adult and up to four children

Hours Tuesday–Saturday, 10 a.m.–5 p.m.; Sunday, 2–5 p.m.; Monday, 1–5 p.m., holidays, 10 a.m.–5 p.m.; closed December 25 and 26 and Good Friday

Phone (01273) 292-770

Website tourism.brighton.co.uk

When to Go On a rainy day, or a pleasant alternative to the beach

Special Tips Only the gardens are accessible to wheelchairs

Overall Appeal by Age Group

Preschool ★★	Teens ★★★	Over 30 ★★★
Grade school ★★★	Young Adults ★★★	Seniors ★★★

Author's Rating ★★★

How Much Time to Allow About 1 hour

Description & Comments This handsome residence was built in 1738 on medieval foundations and extensively remodeled and enlarged in 1903. The house reflects the style and taste of the early-20th-century Edwardian era and is remarkably intact, with furniture, paintings, and even table settings in the same place they were a hundred years ago. (If you've watched *Upstairs, Downstairs,* you get the idea.) Unlike many historic homes where visitors are allowed access to only a few rooms, all of Preston Manor is open for inspection, from the basement kitchens to

IN THE SOUTH OF ENGLAND

Name	Comments	Cover
Brighton (continued)		
Legends	Brighton's "second" gay club	None
Midnight Blues	Upscale dance club	£5–£7

the attic nursery, so a visit is especially satisfying and provides a rich glimpse into how upper-class Edwardian families once lived.

Touring Tips The 13th-century parish church of St. Peter is next door and usually open during daylight hours.

Royal Pavilion

Type of Attraction Historic palace with an exotic design

Location On the Steine off the Grand Parade

Admission £5.35 adults; £3.85 seniors and students; £3.30 children under age 16; £14 families of two adults and up to four children; £8.65 families of one adult and up to four children

Hours October–March: daily, 10 a.m.–5:15 p.m.; April–September: daily, 9:30 a.m.–5:45 p.m.

Phone (01273) 2909-00

Website www.royalpavilion.org.uk

When to Go Avoid school holidays, when hundreds of screeching youngsters descend upon the palace.

Special Tips Ground-floor rooms, which include the State Rooms, Drawing Rooms, the Great Kitchen, and the King's Apartments are accessible to wheelchair users.

Overall Appeal by Age Group

Preschool ★★	Teens ★★★	Over 30 ★★★
Grade school ★★★	Young Adults ★★★	Seniors ★★★

Author's Rating ★★★½

How Much Time to Allow About 1 hour

Description & Comments George IV, the womanizing, heavy-drinking, gambling prince regent and son of the insane George III, let his tastes run wild when he asked architect John Nash to build this palace in the early 19th century. With a profusion of onion domes and minarets, the pavilion looks like it belongs in a palm-filled garden in India, and the interior is just as exotic, filled with chinoiserie, carvings of dragons and other whimsical creatures, and masses of Regency furniture and fine china and crystal. The Music Room is especially rich, a fantasy of red wall paintings depicting Chinese scenes beneath a domed ceiling encrusted with gilded shells, but even the kitchen is exotic, with a high ceiling supported by iron palm trees. A walk through the King's Apartments provides an intimate look at royal life and more evidence of George's taste for ornate furnishings. Queen Victoria didn't care for the palace and in 1850 sold it for a song to the city of Brighton, which in recent years has taken great care to restore the structure to its original splendor. The Dome, built at the same time as the Pavilion as a riding school and stables, now houses the Dome Theater, home of the Brighton Philharmonic Orchestra, and the Brighton Museum and Art Gallery, a mediocre collection that you can easily forego.

Touring Tips Guided tours at 11:30 a.m. and 2:30 p.m. reveal a lot about the palace's rich past and enhance a visit considerably. The Queen Adelaide tearoom is one of the best and most atmospheric places in Brighton for lunch, a light meal, or a cream tea. The restaurant occupies the former apartments of George IV's long-suffering wife and is open daily, 10:30 a.m.–4:30 p.m. (until 5 p.m. June–September); meals and teas cost £3–£6.

Restaurants in Brighton

Basketmakers Arms ★★★

PUB | INEXPENSIVE | QUALITY ★★★ | VALUE ★★★★

East end of Gloucester Road, just off Cheltenham Place; (01273) 689006

Reservations Not necessary **Entrée Range** £2–£6 **Payment** V, MC **Bar** Full service; excellent selection of ales **Disabled Access** Yes

Hours Monday–Saturday, 11 a.m.–11 p.m.; Sunday, noon–10:30 p.m.; food served Monday–Friday, noon–3 p.m., 5:30–8:30 p.m.; Saturday, noon–3:30 p.m.; Sunday, noon–4 p.m.

House Specialties Burgers, potatoes filled with shrimp, fish and chips (Fridays only).

It's a pleasure to wander off the busy seafront and find your way to this small pub, tucked away on a quiet street between the Lanes and the train station. Walls and beams are cluttered with old photos, prints, and whatever else seems to have caught the proprietors' fancy, and the overall ambience is mellow and friendly. Basketmakers is a favorite with many locals, and it fills up on weekend evenings.

Donatello ★★★

ITALIAN | INEXPENSIVE | QUALITY ★★½ | VALUE ★★★

3 Brighton Place; (01273) 775-477

Reservations Not necessary **Entrée Range** £6–£8; 2 courses, £7.95; 3 courses, £9.25 **Payment** V, MC, AMEX, D **Bar** Full bar **Disabled Access** Yes

Hours Daily, 11:30 a.m.–11 p.m.

House Specialties Mussels; thin-crust pizzas.

It seems like much of Brighton dines regularly in this cheery, brick-walled Italian restaurant in the Lanes. Donatello is associated with Pinocchio's, a much larger Italian restaurant that is a big presence in the Lanes; Donatello is smaller, friendlier, and much more appealing. If you don't expect more than the basic Italian preparations and stick to simple pastas and the pizzas, you'll be satisfied with the food.

English's of Brighton ★★★½

SEAFOOD | EXPENSIVE | QUALITY ★★★½ | VALUE ★★★

29–31 East Street; (01273) 327-980

Reservations Recommended **Entrée Range** £10.95–£21.95 **Payment** V, MC, AMEX **Bar** Full service **Disabled Access** Yes

Hours Monday–Saturday, noon–10:15 p.m.; Sunday, noon–9:30 p.m.

House Specialties Dover sole, prepared here seven different ways—the two best ways to enjoy it are simply grilled or with the house Veronique preparation, poached and served with grapes and white wine sauce.

This 150-year-old restaurant is one of the most venerable seafood houses in England and occupies three ancient fishermen's cottages in the heart of the Lanes. The terrace in front is delightful in good weather, but a meal in the cramped dining rooms is quite an experience; seating is on banquettes lining the plush, red-velvet walls decorated with murals. Tables are so close together that diners inevitably strike up conversations with one another and often pass dishes around so everyone can try the house delicacies, which include many kinds of oysters. Service, provided by a staff that seems to have been here for decades, is extremely attentive.

Terra à Terre ★★★

VEGETARIAN | MODERATE | QUALITY ★★★★ | VALUE ★★★

77 East Street; (01273) 729051

Reservations Recommended on weekends **Entrée Range** £9–£12 **Payment** V, MC, DC **Bar** Organic beer, wine, and cider **Disabled Access** Yes

Hours Monday, 6–10:30 p.m.; Tuesday–Saturday, noon–10:30 p.m.; Sunday, 10 a.m.–10:30 p.m.

House Specialties The Terra à Tapas, a sampling of the house specialties; a chocolate mess of a dessert called Gufelhopf proves that vegetarian cuisine can be downright decadent.

Even if the notion of a meal without meat or fish seems unpalatable, step into this sunny restaurant in the Lanes at least once during your stay in Brighton. For many visitors, Terra à Terre is the reason they come to Brighton, and the place is earning a reputation as the best vegetarian restaurant in England. Don't worry if the names of many of the items on the menu seem like exotic foreign terms—the staff is patient and most willing to explain the offerings.

Entertainment and Nightlife in Brighton

Brighton's major center for the performing arts is the **Dome,** originally King George IV's stable block and converted into a theater in 1867. The Dome was modernized in 1935, and after a recent restoration, it retains its Art Deco interior; the complex also includes smaller stages at the Corn Exchange and at the Pavilion Theatre. Something always seems to be happening at the Dome: The main hall is home to the Brighton Philharmonic, and the stages welcome a range of visiting performing artists who in any given year might include the Moscow Philharmonic, Wynton Marsalis, and Tap Dogs. For tickets and information, call (01273) 709-709 or visit **www.brighton-dome.org.uk.** Big-name entertainers likely to draw crowds often appear at the **Brighton Centre,** a huge convention and exhibition complex facing the sea on Kings Road; for tickets and information, call (01273) 290-131 or visit **www.brightoncentre.com.**

The **Theatre Royal Brighton,** on New Road near the Pavilion, is a lovely old theater that opened in 1807 with a performance of *Hamlet.* Since then, just about every actor of note on the British stage has performed in this multitiered, Regency-style theater. A different traveling company appears at the Theatre Royal almost every week, bringing first-rate drama, dance, and musical comedy to Brighton. Call (01273) 328-488 or visit **www.theambassadors.com/brighton.**

Another performing arts venue in Brighton is the **Gardner Arts Centre** at the University of Sussex, about three miles outside the city center. The Gardner presents innovative drama, performance art pieces, dance, and film. For information and tickets, call (01273) 685-861 or visit **www.artsoutheast.co.uk.**

Brighton retains its centuries-old reputation for naughtiness and still serves up lively nightlife. *What's On* is a magazine distributed free all over town. It lists clubs, restaurants, pubs, and theaters in Brighton and adjoining communities. If you want to plan your nighttime forays in Brighton before you leave home, visit **whatson.brighton.co.uk.** Much of Brighton's nightlife is geared toward gays and lesbians and is concentrated on and off St. James Street, east of Old Steine.

Nightclubs in Brighton

Club Revenge

BRIGHTON'S TOP GAY CLUB

Who Goes There Londoners

32–34 Old Steine; (01273) 606064; www.revenge.co.uk

Cover 0–£7, depending on time (cover usually charged weekends and weekdays after 11 p.m.) **Prices** Moderate **Dress** Casual **Food Available** None

Hours 9 p.m.–2 or 3 a.m.

A very friendly crowd frequents this two-tier club, which appears to be a mandatory stop for every gay visitor to Brighton. In fact, on weekends it seems that about half of the regulars are Londoners catching up with their local pals. Lasers, smoke machines, and thumping music provide an edgy atmosphere, but at heart Revenge is a sociable, everyone-is-welcome sort of place—a lot of the crowd is just looking for a good place to dance.

Cricketers

PUB AND DRINKING SPOT

Who Goes There A lot of locals

Black Lion Street, in the Lanes; (01273) 329-472

Cover None **Prices** Moderate **Dress** Casual **Food Available** Pub snacks that aren't bad

Hours Monday–Saturday, 11 a.m.–11 p.m.; Sunday, noon–10:30 p.m.

This century-old pub is also one of Brighton's most popular meeting spots and serves a wide selection of beers in three bar areas spread over two floors. While the place seems to be a favorite of Brighton's young professional set, plenty of visitors find their way up to the lounge on the first floor to enjoy the resortlike atmosphere and sea views.

Legends

BRIGHTON'S "SECOND" GAY CLUB

Who Goes There Locals, Londoners

31–32 Marine Parade; (01273) 024-462; www.legendsbar.co.uk

Cover None **Prices** Moderate **Dress** Trendy **Food Available** Sandwiches, salads, and light meals

Hours Monday–Saturday, noon–11 p.m.; Sunday, noon–10:30 p.m.

This smartly decorated club/cabaret in the New Europe Hotel provides great sea views, but that's not really why anyone is here. Legends was the first gay bar to open in Brighton and is still one of the most popular stops on the Brighton club circuit, with more than 7,000 mostly male patrons passing through on a weekend evening. There's a cabaret show and, of course, a dance floor.

Midnight Blues

UPSCALE DANCE CLUB IN THE GRAND HOTEL

Who Goes There Older folks

Kings Road; (01273) 321-188; www.midnightblues.co.uk

Cover Friday, £5; Saturday, £5 before 11 p.m., £7 after 11 p.m. **Prices** Expensive **Dress** Dressy **Food Available** None

Hours Saturday and Sunday; 8 p.m.–until

Brighton's most upscale nightspot attracts a crowd of well-dressed, well-heeled twenty- and thirty-somethings, with plenty of older folks joining in. The resident DJ has a strong preference for 80s disco music, but no one seems to mind.

Exercise and Recreation in Brighton

The long, paved seafront is well-suited to cycling and roller-blading or roller-skating. Bicycles are available for rent from **Sunrise Cycle Hire** (West Pier; (01273) 748-881); the shop is open late March–late September and charges £3 an hour, £12 for the day. **Oddballs Skate Hire** at the West Pier rents roller skates, roller blades, and skateboards for about £3 an hour. If you're interested in dipping your toes in the water, you can set yourself up on the beach (which is pebbly) with a deck chair for £1.25 for the day, a beach mat for £2 a day, or a chaise longue for £3—all are available from vendors who make themselves known all along the beach.

Shopping in Brighton

Some of the best shopping in Brighton is concentrated in the Lanes, where the old cobbled streets are lined with interesting shops. **Pecksmith's**

(45–46 Meeting House Lane; (01273) 723-292) is an old family-run business that is also one of England's best-known fragrance houses. The staff ushers customers into a room lined with wooden drawers filled with bottles from which a custom-made scent is concocted. **Dermot–Jill Palmer Antiques** (7–8 Union Street; (01273) 328-669) fills three floors with a remarkable collection of English and French furniture and decorative objects. True antiques aficionados will enjoy wandering through **Brighton Architectural Salvage** (just north of the Lanes at 33–34 Gloucester Road; (01273) 681-656), where mantle pieces, garden ornaments, stained glass, and other items salvaged from old buildings fill a jumbled shop. For a souvenir that's easier to pack, try **Rin-Tin-Tin** (34 North Road; (1273) 672-424), where the specialties are labels, posters, magazines, and other memorabilia from the 20th century; or **Holleyman and Treacher** (21 Duke Street; (01273) 328-007), one of many bookshops in the Lanes and one of the most respected rare-book dealers in England. The **Royal Pavilion Shop** (next to the Royal Pavilion; (01273) 292-792) carries a huge selection of books on the Regency period and the Pavilion, as well as fascinating reproduction glassware, china, fabrics, and decorative items based on the palace collections.

Around Brighton

Lewes

Lewes is a solid-looking country town, where handsome houses line steep, narrow streets. Past residents include Anne of Cleves, who received a house here as part of her divorce settlement from Henry VIII; the 17th-century diarist John Evelyn; and Thomas Paine, who later became an American patriot and penned the incendiary pamphlet urging independence, *Common Sense.* Paine lived in a half-timbered house on High Street and presided over a debating club that met just down the road in the **White Hart Hotel,** where many of the ideas that would emerge in the American Declaration of Independence took shape. (The hotel bar still serves good British ales.)

In the early 20th century, the countryside around Lewes became popular with the writers, artists, and intellectuals who belonged to the so-called Bloomsbury group; the houses of two of them, Virginia Woolf and Vanessa Bell, are open to the public. The town is now famous for its opera house, **Glyndebourne,** and for its Guy Fawkes celebrations on November 5, and it's surrounded by rolling countryside known as the **Sussex Downs.** You can enjoy Lewes and its surroundings on an easy day trip from Brighton, but you may well be charmed enough that you'll want to stay for a while.

Arriving and Getting Oriented in Lewes

Lewes is about eight miles east of Brighton along the A27. The **Lewes Tourist Information Centre** (187 High Street; (01273) 483-448; lewestic@lewes.gov.uk). Trains from Brighton run about every 20 minutes throughout the day and make the trip in 15 minutes; the trip costs about £5. Lewes is also an easy trip from London on a direct train line, with service every half hour; the trip takes a few minutes over an hour and costs about £20. For information, call (08457) 484-950 or go to **www.railtrack.co.uk.**

Shelleys Hotel — *£110–£170*

OVERALL ★★★★½ | QUALITY ★★★★½ | VALUE ★★★★½

High Street, Lewes, East Sussex BN7 1XS; (01273) 472-361; fax (01273) 483-152; info@shelleys-hotel-lewes.com; www.shelleys-hotel.com

Location In the center of the historic towns.

Amenities & Services 19 rooms; restaurant. The hotel has a pleasant sitting room and a large garden where tea and light meals are served in good weather.

Elevator No.

Parking Free parking at side of hotel.

Pricing Includes breakfast.

Credit Cards V, MC, AMEX, D

Though this gracious house once belonged to the family of the poet Percy Bysshe Shelley, it's hard not to think of Jane Austen the moment you step into the entryway. There, you'll be greeted by a staff member sitting behind an antique desk and taken up the grand staircase to one of the guest rooms that are luxuriously appointed with traditional but not-too-fussy furnishings. Shelleys is a country-house hotel that's done superbly, providing excellent accommodation and service to match, and rates are relatively reasonable considering the surroundings. Special offers (check out the hotel's website) can make a stay here even more of a good value; such rates usually include dinner in the restaurant. Shelleys provides a pleasant and well-priced alternative to the Brighton hotels, provided you don't require sea air or the convenience of being able to crawl home after nighttime forays.

Special Events in Lewes

Every summer, the **Glyndebourne Opera festival** stages six operas from May through August. The performances, held in a stunning opera house completed in 1994, are considered to be one of the finest opera festivals in the world, bringing leading voices and their ardent fans in droves to Lewes. The box office is open Monday–Saturday, 10 a.m.–7 p.m., and Sunday, 10 a.m.–5 p.m. For information, call (01273) 813-813 or visit **www.glyndebourne.com.**

The other big annual event in Lewes is **Guy Fawkes Night,** on November 5. On this evening in 1605, Guy Fawkes and members of the

Gunpowder Plot attempted to blow up Parliament in retaliation for penal laws against Catholics; Fawkes was caught and executed. Other towns in England now commemorate the anniversary with displays of fireworks, but Lewes celebrates most grandly, with costumed processions and an enormous bonfire.

Exploring Lewes

Lewes is a good base from which to visit many of the attractions below; alternatively, the town and its surrounding sights can easily be included in a day trip from Brighton.

Charleston

Type of Attraction Home of members of the Bloomsbury group

Location 7 miles east of Lewes off A27

Admission House and grounds: £6 adults; £4 students and seniors; £4.50 children ages 6–16. Grounds only: £2.50 adults; £1 children ages 6–16

Hours March 27–October 31: Wednesday–Sunday, 2–6 p.m.

Phone (01323) 811-265

Website www.charleston.org.uk

When to Go Since the main attractions are indoors, Charleston is a pleasure even in bad weather.

Special Tips The shop sells reproductions of many of the textiles and ceramics you'll see in the house, as well as books by and about members of the Bloomsbury group. A gallery on the premises shows works by contemporary artists, and a tea-room provides teas and snacks. In late May, the Charleston Festival presents a series of talks in which authors discuss their works; the festival is part of the Brighton Festival (see "Special Events in Brighton," page 241).

Overall Appeal by Age Group

Preschool —	Teens ★★★	Over 30 ★★★
Grade school ★★★	Young Adults ★★★	Seniors ★★★

Author's Rating ★★★★

How Much Time to Allow 1–2 hours

Description & Comments Virginia Woolf discovered this rambling old farm-house in the 1920s and told her sister, the painter Vanessa Bell, "If you lived there you could make it absolutely divine." Vanessa, her husband, Clive Bell, and her friend and sometime lover, Duncan Grant, took Virginia's advice and lived at Charleston until their deaths many years later. The three painted all the surfaces and furniture in colorful swirls, creating an artistic backdrop in which they hung a collection of art that includes works by Picasso and Renoir and entertained the finest intellectual, literary, and artistic talents of the day. The walled garden is filled with statuary, mosaics, and plantings reminiscent of the great gardens of Italy.

Touring Tips Bus 125 from Lewes passes the entrance to Charleston Wednesday–Saturday; for timetable information, call (08706) 082-608.

Lewes Castle and Anne of Cleves House

Type of Attraction Historic buildings

Location High Street and Southover High Street

Admission Castle: £4.40 adults; £3.70 students and seniors; £2.10 children ages 5–15; £11.40 families of two adults and two children; £8.40 families of one adult and up to four children. House: £2.80 adults; £2.50 students and seniors; £1.40 children ages 5–15; £7 families of two adults and two children; £5.50 families of one adult and up to four children.

Hours Castle: Monday–Saturday, 10 a.m.–5:30 p.m.; Sunday and holidays, 11 a.m.–5:30 p.m. (closed Mondays in January). House: Monday–Saturday, 10 a.m.–5 p.m. (closed Mondays in January and February).

Phone (01273) 405-732

Website www.sussexpast.com/lewescastle1.htm

When to Go Since the visit to both requires a ten-minute walk, try to find a day when it's not pouring.

Special Tips The castle and house are not equipped for wheelchairs.

Overall Appeal by Age Group

Preschool —	Teens ★★	Over 30 ★★
Grade school ★★	Young Adults ★★	Seniors ★★

Author's Rating ★★

How Much Time to Allow About an hour and a half for both

Description & Comments You might know more about Lewes than you wished by the time you tour these two historic sites. Lewes Castle was constructed soon after the Norman Conquest in 1066 to secure William the Conqueror's stronghold in Sussex, and its strategic importance becomes clear when you look from the ramparts over the town and what seems to be most of the county. Tour the castle first, with the help of the audio guide, then take time to see *The Story of Lewes Town* sound-and-light show in the adjoining Barbican House Museum; having seen the castle, the show will be a lot more relevant. The Anne of Cleves House is about a ten-minute walk from the castle, and the steep climb downhill and back up is well worth the effort. The house is filled with cannonballs and other rather boring historical bric-a-brac, but the structure itself, a half-timbered house that Henry presented to Anne upon their divorce in 1541, is quaint. The kitchen and bedroom have been restored to look as they did in the days of the discarded Queen and, with their rough floors and rustic appearance, they reveal just how simply even the upper classes once lived.

Touring Tips If you've had your fill of historic houses and museums, buy a castle-only ticket so you can enjoy the view from the castle towers.

Monk's House

Type of Attraction Home of writer Virginia Woolf

Location Village of Rodmell, 4 miles southwest of Lewes

Admission £2.60 adults; £1.30 children; £6.50 families

Hours April 1–November 2: Wednesday and Saturday, 2–5:30 p.m.

Phone (01372) 453-401

Website www.nationaltrust.org.uk

When to Go Only 15 visitors are allowed into the house at a time, so try to visit on a Wednesday.

Special Tips Monk's House and nearby Charleston will be of special interest to readers of Virginia Woolf; *Virginia Woolf, A Biography,* by Virginia's nephew Quentin Bell, contains detailed accounts of life at both houses.

Overall Appeal by Age Group

Preschool —	Teens ★★★	Over 30 ★★★
Grade school ★★	Young Adults ★★★	Seniors ★★★

Author's Rating ★★★★

How Much Time to Allow About 1 hour

Description & Comments Beginning in the years immediately after World War I, Leonard and Virginia Woolf often retreated from their home in London's Bloomsbury neighborhood to this modest, clapboard house. Virginia wrote several of her novels in the study, and the couple entertained the artistic and intellectual set of the 1920s and 1930s here; the biographer Lytton Strachey, economist John Maynard Keynes, the poet T. S. Eliot, and painter Duncan Grant were frequent guests. The house is filled with paintings by members of this circle, known as the Bloomsbury group, as well as furniture painted by Virginia's sister, Vanessa Bell. In 1941, Virginia walked from Monk's House to the nearby River Ouse, put stones in her pockets, and drowned herself. Her ashes are buried in the garden. Leonard remained at Monk's House until his death in 1969, and the garden he carefully tended is much as he left it.

Touring Tips From the garden and garden house there are lovely views toward the river and hills beyond.

Sheffield Park Garden

Type of Attraction A spectacular garden

Location About 8 miles north of Lewes, off A275

Admission £4.80 adults; £2.40 children ages 5–15; £12 families of two adults and two children

Hours January 4–February 28: Saturday and Sunday, 10:30 a.m.–4 p.m. March 1–October 31: 10:30 a.m.–6 p.m. November 1–December 22: 10:30 a.m.–4 p.m.

Phone (01825) 790-231

Website www.nationaltrust.org.uk/sheffieldpark

When to Go In any season; the azaleas and rhododendrons bloom in early summer, the fall foliage is magnificent, and there are winter gardens housed in greenhouses.

Special Tips Most of the garden paths are accessible to wheelchairs.

Overall Appeal by Age Group

Preschool —	Teens ★★	Over 30 ★★★
Grade school ★★★	Young Adults ★★	Seniors ★★★

Author's Rating ★★★

How Much Time to Allow About 1 hour

Description & Comments Sheffield is one of the most spectacular gardens in England, and, given the mild climate of Sussex, flourishes for much of the year. Capability Brown, the 18th-century landscape architect who also designed the gardens at Kew and Blenheim Palace, designed Sheffield around four lakes and several streams. Many colorful plants bloom at the water's edge, and the sound of rushing water permeates the garden.

Touring Tips Picnics are not allowed in the garden, but there is a pleasant picnic area near the entrance.

Dining in and around Lewes

The Hungry Monk ★★★★

INNOVATIVE BRITISH | EXPENSIVE | QUALITY ★★★★ | VALUE ★★★

Route B2105, in the village of Jevington, near Polegate; about 10 miles east of Lewes and 16 miles east of Brighton on A27; (01323) 482-178

Reservations Required **Entrée Range** Prix fixe: £24.90 lunch, £28.95 dinner **Payment** V, MC, AMEX, D **Bar** Full service **Disabled Access** Yes

Hours Daily, 7:15–10 p.m.; Sunday lunch, noon–2:30 p.m.

House Specialties Tiger prawn and smoked salmon tart or sweet potato and red pepper soup to start, followed by lamb with feta crust or breast of duckling; the dessert of choice is banoffi pie (a banana cream concoction, which was invented here in 1972). The menu changes frequently, depending on what's fresh at the markets.

Roaring fires, cozy sitting rooms where guests enjoy cocktails and after-dinner coffee, and an intimate beamed dining room provide the perfect country-inn atmosphere at this legendary restaurant, one of South England's best, in a 14th-century stone cottage. We only wish this spot would open for lunch on days other than Sunday, because it's a perfect stop on a day of sight-seeing on the Sussex Downs.

Shelleys Hotel ★★★★

BRITISH/CONTINENTAL | EXPENSIVE | QUALITY ★★★★ | VALUE ★★★★

High Street, Lewes; (01273) 472-361

Reservations Recommended; required at time of Glynbourne Festival Entrée Range Lunch, £9.50–£14.50; dinner, £15.50–£17 Payment V, MC, AMEX, D Bar Full service Disabled Access Yes

Hours Daily, 12:15–2:15 p.m., 7–9:15 p.m.

House Specialties Fresh scallops or a vegetable tart to start, followed by roast saddle of lamb filled with asparagus or a seared fillet of turbot.

It's well worth the drive out from Brighton to enjoy a meal in the dining room of this gracious country-house hotel. Chef Tim Earley uses fresh produce and local lamb and game to prepare inventive cuisine that's served in a handsome room overlooking the garden. The setting and service are in keeping with the high standards found throughout this lovely hotel.

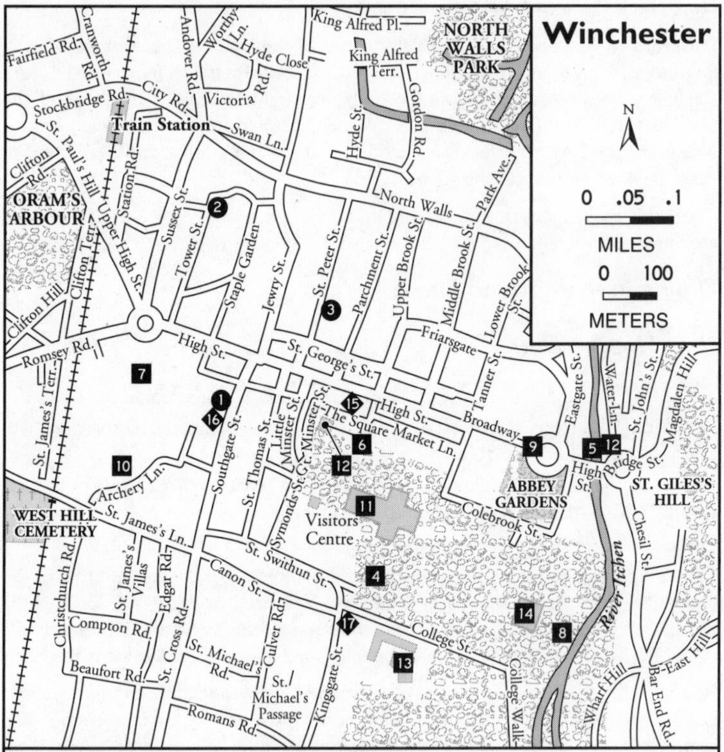

HOTELS

1. Hotel du Vin
2. Portland House
3. Winchester Royal Hotel

ATTRACTIONS

4. Cathedral Close
5. City Bridge
6. City Museum
7. Great Hall
8. Hospital of St. Cross
9. King Alfred's Statue
10. Military Museums
11. Winchester Cathedral
12. Winchester City Mill
13. Winchester College
14. Wolvesey Castle

RESTAURANTS

15. La Bodega
16. Hotel du Vin
17. Wykeham Arms

Winchester

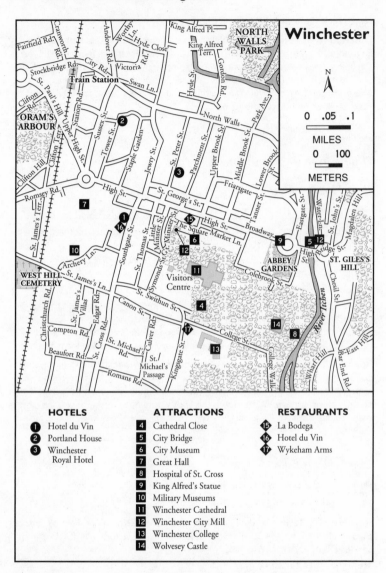

Now a small cathedral city and county seat of Hampshire, Winchester has been thriving since Roman times. Egbert and Alfred the Great, the first kings of England, ruled from Winchester, and the Normans made the city their capital when they took England in 1066. In fact, it wasn't until the 13th century that power began to shift north from Winchester to London, with its advantageous position on the Thames. Even then, Winchester continued to thrive as a medieval center of the wool trade.

Today, Winchester is hands-down one of the most beautiful small cities in England, with a mighty cathedral and what is arguably the country's oldest public school, **Winchester College.** Winchester is a pleasant, easygoing place where you can stroll through the **Water Meadows** alongside the River Icthen, browse on medieval lanes for old books and antiques, and even take a look at a colorful sham that is purported to be the famous **Round Table of King Arthur.**

If you want to venture forth from London and experience one typical, small English city, Winchester should be among your first choices. Adding to its appeal is that another city near the top of that list, **Salisbury,** is only about 20 miles away. A trip to Winchester and Salisbury will show you a slice of England at its best, and near to them are historic homes (including the house where the novelist Jane Austen lived and wrote), gardens, abbeys, and England's best-known prehistoric monument, **Stonehenge.**

Planning Your Visit to Winchester

The **Tourist Information Centre** (Winchester S023 9LJ; (01962) 840-500; **www.winchester.com**) is on the ground floor of the Guildhall, in the center of the city on Broadway. The office is unusually helpful, even by the high standards of tourist info offices throughout England. It provides maps, guides to major attractions, and notices of special events; has a gift shop where you can stock up on maps and photo books on Britain; and can help you find a room. The center is open May–September: Monday–Saturday, 9:30 a.m.–5:30 p.m., and Sunday, 11 a.m.–4 p.m.; and October–April: Monday–Saturday, 10 a.m.–5 p.m.

Special Events in Winchester

The annual **Winchester Festival** brings drama, classical music and jazz, and theater to indoor and outdoor settings around Winchester for ten days in early July. For information and tickets, call (01962) 877-977 or visit **www.winchesterfestival.co.uk.**

Right on the heels of the Winchester Festival comes, in alternating years, the **Southern Cathedrals Festival,** which for several days in late July brings together the choirs of Salisbury, Chichester, and Winchester cathedrals for performances in Winchester Cathedral and in the cathedrals of the other two cities. So, if you are in Winchester or Salisbury at a time when they are hosting the festival, you have the chance to hear three of the world's finest choirs in some of Europe's greatest architectural masterpieces. For information and tickets, call (01962) 857-2000 or visit **www.southerncathedralsfestival.org.uk.**

Arriving and Getting Oriented in Winchester

Winchester is 70 miles southwest of London. Trains run frequently, as often as every 15 minutes for much of the day, from London's Waterloo Station. The trip takes anywhere from just over an hour to just under two hours, depending on the number of stops, and the round trip costs about £20. Call (08457) 484-950 or go to **www.railtrack.co.uk.** The train station is at the edge of the city center, off Upper High Street, and within easy walking distance of the cathedral and other sights.

By car, the quickest route from London is the M3. The trip takes about an hour and a half, depending on traffic in and around London. Several car parks are located on the outskirts of the city center, and more are well marked along the routes into the city. One of the closest to the city center is the **Chesil,** about a five-minute walk from the cathedral. Fees at most car parks near the center are £2.80 per day. A **Park and Ride** facility just off the Junction 10 exit of the M3 provides all-day parking for £1.50 and free shuttle service to the city center, Monday–Friday, 7:30 a.m.–6:30 p.m.

National Express buses leave London's Victoria Coach Station for Winchester about every hour, though check the time of the trip carefully—it can take anywhere from two to four hours, depending on the number of stops and changes. The round trip costs about £11. For more information, call (08705) 808-080 or go to **www.gobycoach.com.** The bus station is near the King Alfred Statue in the center of town and within easy walking distance of the cathedral and other sights.

Hotels in Winchester

Hotel du Vin — *£115–£135*

OVERALL ★★★★ | QUALITY ★★★★ | VALUE ★★★★

Southgate Street, Winchester, Hampshire SO23 9EF; (01962) 841-414; fax (01962) 842-458; info@winchester.hotelduvin.com; www.hotelduvin.com

Location Near the top of High Street, about a five-minute walk from the center of town.

Amenities & Services 23 rooms. Sumptuous bathrooms with deep tubs and "rain" showerheads; Egyptian linens; stylish bistro and wine bar; garden; satellite TV; room service for breakfast only.

Elevator No.

Parking Yes, next to hotel; free.

Pricing Continental breakfast, £9; full English breakfast, £12.50.

Credit Cards V, MC, AMEX, D

If Winchester's many charms don't tempt you to spend a night or two, this stylish and exciting hotel will. This member of a small chain of chic hotels occupies a lovely 18th-century house where the public rooms have been strikingly redone in deep colors and handsome classic and contemporary furnishings. Each bedroom is named for a different wine house; the best open onto the garden and are reached through a gate to the side of the hotel. While most rooms are tastefully equipped with classic pieces, including wingbacked reading chairs covered in white, a few show the mark of an overzealous decorator with a gloomy disposition, as evidenced by dark gray walls and black linens and furniture.

Lainston House Hotel — *£110–£260*

OVERALL ★★★★ | QUALITY ★★★★ | VALUE ★★★

Sparsholt, Winchester, Hampshire SO21 2LT; (01962) 863-588; fax (10962) 776-672; enquiries@lainstonhouse.com; www.exclusivehotels.co.uk

Location In a small community about 2.5 miles northwest of Winchester.

Amenities & Services 40 rooms. Tennis, putting green, trout fishing, clay pigeon fishing, restaurant, room service.

Elevator No.

Parking Free, on site.

Pricing Includes breakfast; check website for room and meal packages.

Credit Cards V, MC, AMEX, D

One of southern England's most luxurious hotels occupies a 17th-century manor house set in 63 acres of parkland. While this is in every way a country-house hotel, with lovely views from the rooms over the gardens, the center of Winchester is less than ten minutes away. The drawing room and bar are graciously appointed in period furniture. Guest rooms are located throughout the main house, in an adjoining residence known as Chudleigh Court, and in a renovated stable block; all are large and sumptuous. Many have fireplaces and four-poster beds, and bathrooms are huge and well equipped, often with Jacuzzis. The hotel restaurant, Avenue, serves excellent French-inspired cuisine and achieves the same level of formal opulence as the rest of the hotel.

Portland House — *£48–£60*

OVERALL ★★ | QUALITY ★★ | VALUE ★★★

63 Tower Street, Winchester, Hampshire SO23 8TA; (01962) 865-195; tony@knightworld.com

Location On a quiet street off the top of High Street.

Amenities & Services 5 rooms. Drawing room for guests, cable TV, in-room coffee facilities.

Elevator No.

Parking In nearby municipal Tower Street car park.

Pricing Includes breakfast.

Credit Cards Not accepted.

This pleasant bed-and-breakfast in a Regency town house is well located on a quiet street just five minutes from the center of town. The surroundings are quite attractive, with an airy lounge and breakfast room on the ground floor and large guest rooms comfortably furnished with pine furniture and bright fabrics upstairs. All rooms have private baths, which have been added recently and are small with showers only.

Winchester Royal Hotel — *£90–£120*

OVERALL ★★★ | QUALITY ★★★ | VALUE ★★★

St. Peter Street, Winchester, Hampshire SO23 8BS; (01962) 840-840; fax (01962) 841-582; royal@marstonhotels.com; www.marstonhotels.com

Location Off High Street in the city center.

Amenities & Services 75 rooms. Walled garden, turndown service includes nightcap; walking tours of city available; satellite TV.

Elevator Yes.

Parking Free, on site.

Pricing Includes full English breakfast.

Credit Cards V, MC, AMEX, DC

Built in 1657, the Royal has been a private residence, a convent, and a hotel for 150 years. Though the hotel is in the center of town only a few steps from the cathedral, the premises are usually quiet and have the feel of a country-house hotel—unless the hotel is hosting a coach tour, which it sometimes does. The rooms are well maintained; traditional furnishings are a tad dull but comfortable, and the garden is a welcome retreat after a round of sight-seeing. Drinks and meals are served outdoors in good weather.

Exploring Winchester

You'll want to spend the better part of a day ambling around Winchester. Begin at **Winchester Cathedral,** then take time to explore the **Cathedral Close,** one of the oldest and most picturesque sections of Winchester. Adjacent to the church are the **Deanery and Pilgrims' Hall,** from the 13th and 14th centuries respectively, and Cheyney Court, the half-timbered porter's lodge that once served as the courthouse for the Bishop of Winchester. **Kingsgate,** one of two surviving gates to the medieval city, is now the southern entrance to the Cathedral Close; the simple church of **St. Swithun** is located at the archway of the gateway. Jane Austen spent the last six weeks of her life in a house just a few steps down College Street, and died there on July 18, 1817. The novelist, who probably suffered from Addison's disease, came to Winchester from her home in nearby Chawton (see page 273) to be near her physician. College Street takes its name from **Winchester College,** founded in 1382 by Bishop William of Wykeham; alumni are known as "Wykehamists." The school claims to be the oldest continually running school in England, though King's School in Canterbury disputes the claim.

The ruins of **Wolvesey Castle,** the 12th-century Bishop's Palace, is at the edge of the Cathedral Close, near the banks of the River Icthen. A footpath leads south from here along the river, through the tranquil and mellow **Water Meadows,** which inspired the poet John Keats to write his poem "To Autumn"; the path is part of an amble that the tourist office labels as "Keats' Walk" and leads to the **Hospital of St. Cross,** a medieval almshouse founded in 1132 by William de Blois, a grandson of William the Conqueror. The hospital is now home to 25 brothers who continue to dispense the wayfarer's dole of bread and ale, though these days in tiny portions. The hospital is open summer: daily, 9:30 a.m.–5 p.m.; winter: daily, 10:30 a.m.–3:30 p.m. Admission (£2 adults, £1.25 seniors and students, and £0.50 children) entitles you to a look at the kitchen, brethren's hall, and garden, and your dole, obtained on request from the Porter's Lodge.

If you follow the footpath along the River Icthen back to the Cathedral Close and the center of town, you will come to **City Bridge,** a 19th-century reconstruction of the river crossing the Saxons built here more than a thousand years ago. The **Winchester City Mill,** spanning the river just north of the bridge, dates to 1744; the equipment is in full working order and is put into use for demonstrations, and an island next to the mill is now a lovely garden. The mill is open March: Saturday and Sunday, 11 a.m.–5 p.m.; April–June: Wednesday–Sunday, 11 a.m.–5 p.m.; July–August: Monday–Sunday, 11 a.m.–5 p.m.; and September–October: Wednesday–Sunday, 11 a.m.–5 p.m. Admission is £2 adults, £1 children, and £5 families of two adults and two children; call (10962) 870-057 for information.

From the bridge, the medieval thoroughfare known as Broadway, then High Street, leads through the center of town. Alfred, the ninth-century king who ruled the southern lands known as Wessex from his court at Winchester, presides over the foot of the street in the form of the town's famous, bronze **King Alfred the Great statue.** The **Tourist Information Centre** is housed on the ground floor of the Victorian Guildhall, just opposite. A little way up High Street, in the old marketplace known as the Square, is the **City Museum.** Take 20 minutes or so to step into this collection of municipal history to see the mosaics, pottery, and other relics from Roman Winchester. The museum is open April–October: Monday–Saturday, 10 a.m.–5 p.m., Sunday, noon–5 p.m.; November–March: Tuesday–Saturday, 10 a.m.–4 p.m., Sunday, noon–4 p.m. Admission is free; call (01962) 848-269 for more information. High Street continues west through another medieval gateway, **Westgate,** and just beyond are the **Great Hall** and other scant remains of Winchester's once mighty castle.

Tours in Winchester

The only way to enjoy Winchester is on foot, and a good way to get your bearings is on one of the guided walking tours organized by the Tourist Information Centre. The guides, Winchester locals who seem to love their city and have encyclopedic knowledge about its nooks and crannies, lead the 90-minute walks that show off the cathedral, Great Hall, and other highlights of the town. We highly recommend that you join one of these walks, then amble back at your leisure to the places that capture your interest. Tours leave from the front of the Tourist Information

Centre, across from the Alfred statue on Broadway. Tour times are April: Monday–Friday, 2:30 p.m., Saturday, 11:30 a.m. and 2:30 p.m.; May–September: Monday–Saturday, 11 a.m. and 2:30 p.m., Sunday, 11:30 a.m.; October: Monday–Friday, 2:30 p.m., Saturday, 11 a.m. and 2:30 p.m.; November–March: Saturday, 11 a.m. For information, call (01962) 840-500 or visit **www.visitwinchester.com.** The fee is £3 adults, free for accompanying children.

If you'd rather see the city on your own, equip yourself with one of the self-guided walking tour maps the Tourist Information Centre provides. You might also want to ask for the brochure on the self-guided poet's walk, which retraces the route past the cathedral and through the Water Meadows that the poet John Keats took daily during his stay in Winchester in 1819; the walk inspired his poem "To Autumn."

Winchester College opens its beautiful grounds and historic buildings to the public for guided tours only. Included on the 45-minute walks are the chapel, scholar's dining room, cloister, and several other buildings; tours are conducted year-round on Monday, Wednesday, Friday, and Saturday at 10:45 a.m., noon, 2:15 p.m., and 3:30 p.m.; on Tuesday and Thursday, at 10:45 a.m. and noon; and on Sunday, at 2:15 p.m. and 3:30 p.m. The fee is £2.50 adults, £2 seniors and children.

Attractions in Winchester

Great Hall

Type of Attraction A medieval hall that was once part of a Norman castle

Location Castle Avenue, near the top of High Street

Admission Free

Hours March–October: daily, 10 a.m.–5 p.m.; November–February: Monday–Friday, 10 a.m.–5 p.m., Saturday and Sunday, 10 a.m.–4 p.m.

Phone (01962) 846-476

When to Go Any time

Special Tips Accessible to visitors with disabilities

Overall Appeal by Age Group

Preschool —	Teens ★★★	Over 30 ★★
Grade school ★★★	Young Adults ★★★	Seniors ★★

Author's Rating ★★

How Much Time to Allow 15 minutes

Description & Comments This medieval hall is all that remains of mighty Winchester Castle, built during the reign of William the Conqueror and destroyed when Parliamentary forces under Cromwell laid siege to Winchester in 1646. Cromwell spared this hall—which was a 13th-century addition to the fortress—to be used for assemblies. One of Winchester's main courts until the late 20th century, the hall is now best known as the repository of King Arthur's Round

Table, a massive piece of brightly colored wood that could accommodate 24 knights—and a forgery that has been dated to around 1400. The sixth-century Arthur, king of the Britons, is legendary, based perhaps on a military leader of the time. The table on display here would be the Round Table around which, according to the legend, Arthur's Order of Knights would convene. Aside from the shadowy presence of King Arthur, the hall also resounds with some of the other great figures of British history. In this hall, the English Parliament met for the first time in 1246, and Sir Walter Raleigh was tried for conspiracy in 1603.

Touring Tips Changing exhibits relating to local history and other topics are hung in the hallways leading to the Great Hall.

The Military Museums

Type of Attraction Collections of regimental history

Location Peninsula Barracks

Admission Gurkha Museum: £1.50 adults; £0.75 children and seniors. Royal Green Jackets Museum: £2 adults, £1 children and seniors. Other museums are free.

Hours Light Infantry Museum: Tuesday–Saturday, 10 a.m.–4 p.m.; Sunday, noon–4 p.m. Gurkha Museum: Monday–Saturday, 10 a.m.–5 p.m.; Sunday, noon–4 p.m. King's Royal Hussars Museum: Tuesday–Friday, 10 a.m.–12:45 p.m., 1:15–4 p.m.; Saturday and Sunday, noon–4 p.m. Royal Hampshire Regiment Museum: Monday–Friday, 11 a.m.–3:30 p.m.; Saturday and Sunday (April–October), noon–4 p.m. Royal Green Jackets Museum: Monday–Saturday, 10 a.m.–1 p.m., 2–5 p.m.; Sunday, noon–4 p.m.

Phone Light Infantry Museum, (01962) 828-550; Gurkha Museum, (01962) 842-832; King's Royal Hussar's Museum, (01962) 828-541; Royal Hampshire Regiment Museum, (01962) 863-658; Royal Green Jackets Museum, (01962) 828-528

Website Gurkha Museum: www.thegurkhamuseum.co.uk; Royal Green Jackets Museum: www.royalgreenjackets.co.uk

When to Go Anytime; these museums are almost never crowded

Special Tips All the museums are accessible to visitors with disabilities, and guided tours are available by special arrangement at all.

Overall Appeal by Age Group

Preschool —	Teens ★★	Over 30 ★★★
Grade school ★★★	Young Adults ★★	Seniors ★★★

Author's Rating ★★

How Much Time to Allow Depending on how much time you want to spend looking at medals, about 1 hour

Description & Comments You don't have to be a military hound to enjoy these small, quirky museums that pay tribute to different regiments. All but one of them occupy Winchester's historic military barracks; the Royal Hampshire Regiment Museum is just around the corner on Southgate Street. Since admission is free or reasonably priced, you may want to take a stroll through all of them. The Gurkha Museum tells the fascinating story, through dioramas and models, of the Nepalese troops who have paid service to the British Crown. The King's Royal Hussars Museum exhibits items from the Charge of the Light Brigade; in the Royal Green Jackets Museum, a huge diorama depicts the Battle of Waterloo.

Touring Tips Take a casual stroll through all the museums; in each, an exhibit or two are likely to catch your eye.

Winchester Cathedral

Type of Attraction One of England's great cathedrals

Location Cathedral Close, off High Street

Admission Suggested donations: £3.50 adults; £2.50 seniors and students; £7 families of two adults and two children; £0.50 children. Library: £1 adults; £2 families; £0.50 children.

Hours Monday–Saturday, 8:30 a.m.–6 p.m.; Sunday, 8:30 a.m.–5:30 p.m. Library: Wednesday and Saturday, 11:30 a.m.–3:30 p.m.

Phone (01962) 857-200

Website www.winchester-cathedral.org.uk

When to Go Any weekday, when the cathedral is less crowded than on weekends; in summer, on Tuesday afternoons beginning at 1:10 p.m., you can enjoy recitals of piano, organ, and vocal pieces (no fee, but donations welcome)

Special Tips The cathedral is accessible to disabled visitors.

Overall Appeal by Age Group

Preschool —	Teens ★★★	Over 30 ★★★
Grade school ★★★	Young Adults ★★★	Seniors ★★★

Author's Rating ★★★

How Much Time to Allow About 45 minutes

Description & Comments Winchester Cathedral has the longest nave (central aisle) of any cathedral in Europe, and it's also one of the world's finest examples of Norman architecture. Winchester became the capital of England after the Norman Conquest in 1066, and the cathedral began rising over an earlier church soon afterward, destined to be one of the mightiest structures in the land. Fittingly, some of the cathedral's most notable architectural details are the tombs of 12 English kings, though they have been eclipsed by the legends surrounding Saint Swithun. The saint, a ninth-century bishop of Winchester, was buried outside the city walls in honor of his request for a humble burial. On July 15, 971, when Swithun's bones were moved into the earlier church that stood on this site, legend has it that it began to rain and didn't stop for 40 days. It is still said that if it rains on July 15, it will do so for each of the next 40 days. Other tombs in the cathedral include a simple marker commemorating Jane Austen, who died in a house in the Cathedral Close, and Izaak Walton, who wrote the *Compleat Angler* and died in another house in the close in 1683; stained-glass windows in the church commemorate both of them. The church's 13th-century choir stalls are stunning, but more moving is a pair of simple wooden benches that date from the reigns of the Norman kings and are therefore some of the oldest pieces of wooden furniture in the world. In the church library, the oldest reading room in Europe, is a 12th-century illuminated Bible.

Touring Tips Monday–Saturday, you can join a free, hour-long tour of the cathedral, conducted on the hour 10 a.m.–3 p.m., or a crypt tour, lasting about 30 minutes, at 11:30 a.m., 12:30 p.m., and 2:30 p.m. Tours of the roof and tower are conducted Wednesday at 2:15 p.m., and Saturday at 11:30 a.m. and 2:15 p.m.; the fee is £2, and the tours are open only to visitors between the ages of 12 and 70. For more information, check with the visitors' center near the West Front.

Dining in Winchester

Finding a casual meal is easy to do in Winchester. The **Courtyard Café** (behind the Tourist Information Centre in the Guildhall; (01962) 622-177) serves coffee, sandwiches, and light meals daily, 9:30 a.m.–5 p.m. The **Cathedral Rectory** (in the Cathedral Close; (01962) 857-258) serves snacks, teas, and lunches in a medieval setting, Monday–Saturday, 9:30 a.m.–5 p.m., and Sunday, 10 a.m.–5 p.m. Café Renée (the Square; (10962) 870-0722) is a patisserie and tearoom that serves breakfast, sandwiches, cream teas, and delicious pastries Monday–Saturday, 8:30 a.m.–5 p.m.

Restaurants in Winchester

La Bodega ★★★★

MEDITERRANEAN | MODERATE | QUALITY ★★★★ | VALUE ★★★★

9 The Square; (01962) 864-004

Reservations Recommended on weekend evenings **Entrée Range** £9.25–£12.95; tapas from £2.50 and pastas from £6.95 **Payment** V, MC **Bar** Beer and wine only **Disabled Access** Yes

Hours Monday–Saturday, noon–2:30 p.m., 6:30–10:30 p.m.

House Specialties Any of the tapas, especially the char-grilled vegetables and the *pan con tomate* (bread with olive oil and tomatoes); pasta with artichokes and shrimp; ravioli with bass and prawn sauce.

This bright, airy, simply decorated room near the cathedral is one of the most innovative restaurants in Winchester and serves Mediterranean-inspired dishes. You can enjoy a good sampling by sticking to the tapas menu, and the delicious pasta dishes constitute a meal in themselves. If you move onto a main course, ask for the daily specials, which often include fresh fish.

Hotel du Vin ★★★★½

FRENCH BISTRO | EXPENSIVE | QUALITY ★★★★½ | VALUE ★★★★

Southgate Street; (01962) 841-414

Reservations Recommended, especially on weekends **Entrée Range** £30 prix-fixe for 3-course meal **Payment** V, MC, AMEX, D **Bar** Full service, but forego hard spirits because the wine selection is extraordinary **Disabled Access** No

Hours Daily, noon–1:45 p.m., 7–9:45 p.m.

House Specialties A delicious onion soup, when available, and sea bass or other fresh fish.

This stylish bistro—in an intimate high-ceilinged room hung with old prints and paintings on the ground floor of a 17th-century house—is as appealing as the rest of the hotel, and it serves commendably simple French fare made with local ingredients. Service is pleasant and the ambience is casual (no jackets required), and diners are welcome to spend the entire evening lingering over a meal and the superb wines from the hotel cellars.

Wykeham Arms ★★★★

ENGLISH | MODERATE | QUALITY ★★★★ | VALUE ★★★★

75 Kingsgate Street; (01962) 853-834

Reservations Not accepted, so expect to wait on weekends **Entrée Range** £13–£14.50; bar fare about £3.50–£6.50 **Payment** V, MC, AMEX **Bar** Full service, with an excellent wine list **Disabled Access** Yes

Hours Monday–Saturday, 11 a.m.–11 p.m.; Sunday, noon–10:30 p.m.

House Specialties Excellent bar food, including an open-steak sandwich; on the restaurant menu, onion tart to start, followed by roast rack of local lamb or chicken breast served on a bed of risotto.

This old inn is in the Cathedral Close near Winchester College and is named for Bishop William of Wykeham, who founded the school in 1382. The proprietors appear to have inherited pews, desks, and all sorts of other bric-a-brac from that institution, and this eclectic assortment of furnishings and prints is spread through a series of dark, beamed rooms, candlelit at night and warmed by roaring fires in the winter. You can order off the lengthy bar menu at lunch and until 8:45 p.m. all evenings but Sunday, or from the accomplished restaurant menu; even the sandwiches and soups are delicious.

Entertainment and Nightlife in Winchester

Winchester's major venue for live entertainment is the **Theatre Royal** on Jewry Street, which hosts drama, dance, and opera, often performed by top touring companies, throughout the year. For tickets and information, call (01962) 840-440. The city's many pubs are the preferred places to spend an evening out. Aside from the places we recommend in "Dining in Winchester," you may want to step into two old Winchester institutions: the **Royal Oak** (Royal Oak passage; (01962) 865-676) incorporates 12th-century beams and parts of a Saxon wall, so may well be truthful in its claims to be one of Britain's oldest drinking establishments; and the **Eclipse** (The Square; (01962) 842-701), a relative newcomer dating from the 14th century.

Shopping in Winchester

Winchester is somewhat of a gold mine for shoppers who like to browse through antiques shops and secondhand and rare bookstores. Some dozen shops specializing in everything from fine furniture to bric-a-brac line Jewry Street, which is near the top of High Street. **Gerald E. Marsh** (32A The Square; (01962) 844-443) is a venerable old Winchester institution specializing in all varieties of antique timepieces, from watches to wall clocks to barometers. **P. G. Wells** (Cathedral Close at 11 College Street; (01962) 852-016) is a charming shop selling prints and old books.

Around Winchester

Aside from the places below, from Winchester you can also easily explore Salisbury and many of the sights near that city, including Stonehenge.

Chawton

Type of Attraction Home of the novelist Jane Austen

Location 16 miles northeast of Winchester; the village of Chawton is off A31, which is well-marked from the road

Admission £4 adults; £3 seniors and students; £0.50 children ages 8–18; free for children under age 8

Hours March 1–December 31: daily, 11 a.m.–4:30 p.m.

Phone (01420) 832-62

When to Go Avoid school holidays—the house is a popular destination for school outings

Special Tips If you're traveling by public transportation, Stagecoach Hampshire Bus company operates regular service from Winchester to Chawton; for information, call (01256) 464-501 or check with Winchester Tourist Information Centre

Overall Appeal by Age Group

Preschool —	Teens ★★★★	Over 30 ★★★
Grade school ★★★★	Young Adults ★★★★	Seniors ★★★★

Author's Rating ★★★

How Much Time to Allow 30 minutes

Description & Comments Jane Austen seems to become more popular with the years (and with more and more movie and television adaptations of her works), and this sturdy red-brick house modestly pays tribute to the author who so adeptly observed British provincial life. Jane and her sister, Cassandra, moved here in their thirties, leading a genteel life in these small rooms. The sitting room where Jane worked seemed to fire her creativity: She wrote *Sense and Sensibility, Pride and Prejudice, Emma, Persuasion,* and *Mansfield Park* while living in Chawton, publishing them all anonymously as "by a lady." Jane's desk and other effects, including a quilt she made with her mother, fill the rooms. In the bakehouse is the donkey cart the family used for trips into nearby Alton to shop. Jane left the house to live near her physician in Winchester, where she died in 1817 at age 42.

Touring Tips Time permitting, you may want to stop by Selborne, about two miles south along A327. Here you can visit the Wakes, the home of Gilbert White; this clergyman and amateur naturalist wrote *Natural History and Antiquities of Selborne,* an astute 18th-century account of the plants, birds, and animals of this part of Hampshire. The grounds are lovely, shadowed by a beech-covered hill called the Hanger. Call (01420) 511-275 for more information.

Mottisfont Abbey

Type of Attraction Norman abbey

Location About 1 mile north of Romsey

Admission £6; £15 families of up to two adults and two children

Hours: Garden: March 1–March 16, Saturday and Sunday, 11 a.m.–4 p.m.; March 22–June 8, Monday–Wednesday and Saturday and Sunday, 11 a.m.–6 p.m.; June 9–June 29, Monday–Wednesday and Saturday and Sunday, 11 a.m.–8:30 p.m.; June 30–August 31, Monday–Thursday and Saturday and Sunday, 11 a.m.–6 p.m.; September1–Nov. 2, Monday–Wednesday and Saturday and Sunday, 11 a.m.–6 p.m.; House: March 22–June 8, Monday–Wednesday and Saturday and Sunday, 11 a.m.–6 p.m.; June 9–June 29, 11 a.m.–6 p.m.; June 30–August 31, Monday–Thursday and Saturday and Sunday, 11 a.m.–6 p.m.; September 1–November 2, Monday–Wednesday and Saturday and Sunday, 11 a.m.–6 p.m.

Phone (01794) 340-757

Website www.nationaltrust.org.uk/places/mottisfontabbey

When to Go In June, when the roses are in bloom

Special Tips The rose garden is accessible to wheelchairs; gravel and lawns make wheelchair travel across the rest of the grounds difficult. A restaurant on the grounds serves light meals and tea.

Overall Appeal by Age Group

Preschool —	Teens ★★	Over 30 ★★★
Grade school ★★	Young Adults ★★	Seniors ★★★

Author's Rating ★★★

How Much Time to Allow An hour or two

Description & Comments An Augustinian priory was built at Mottisfont in the 12th century. Converted to a private residence in the 17th century, the house is best known for its collection of 20th-century paintings and trompe l'oeil murals. The gardens, though, are what draw most visitors to Mottisfont, especially the walled garden containing the national collection of old-fashioned roses; in fact, the grounds are open late throughout June so visitors can take full advantage of the daylight hours to see and smell the magnificent blooms. The rest of the grounds are also delightful. They are shaded by grand old trees and border the River Test, a rushing trout stream.

Touring Tips The grounds provide beautiful riverside and woodland walks and are pleasant for picnicking.

Salisbury

Even if you've never foot set in Salisbury (pronounced "SOLS-bury"), you may well experience the feeling that you've been here before. You may have seen John Constable's paintings of **Salisbury Cathedral** in the National Gallery in London and in other museums, and his images of the tall spire against a blue sky full of scudding clouds often comes vividly to life in Salisbury. Thomas Hardy and Anthony Trollope both used Salisbury for the backdrop of novels; Hardy called his city "Mel-chester," and Trollope called his fictional blending of Winchester and Salisbury "Barchester."

Even without these associations, Salisbury has an air of familiarity about it simply because it is such a quintessentially English cathedral city. Salisbury's history is linked with that of the cathedral that rises from its center. Both took shape in the 13th century, a couple of miles from the Iron Age and Roman settlement at **Old Sarum.** Salisbury is still a city of medieval

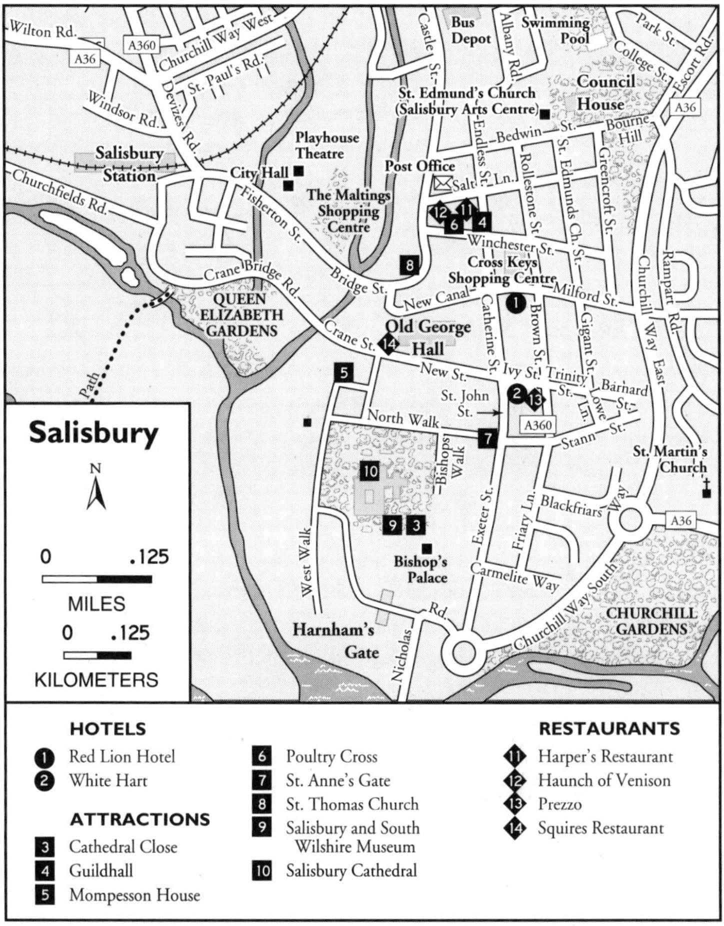

lanes, a vast marketplace where vendors have been gathering for some 800 years, and half-timbered houses and old coaching inns. The cathedral and the **Cathedral Close** create one of England's most beautiful precincts, and the **Water Meadows** that surround the banks of the Rivers Avon and Nadder, from which Constable painted his famous canvases, are unspoiled.

While it's possible to visit Salisbury on a day trip from London, the city and many nearby attractions—including **Stonehenge,** the famous prehistoric site just to the north, and nearby Winchester—can keep you agreeably occupied for much longer.

Planning Your Visit to Salisbury

The **Salisbury Information Centre** (between the Market Place and the train station on Fish Row, Salisbury, SP1 1EJ; (01722) 334-956; **www.visitsalisburyuk.com**) provides maps and information on major attractions, shops, restaurants, and local events; sells tickets to local events and attractions; and can help you find a room. The center is open:

October–April:
Monday–Saturday, 9:30 a.m.–5 p.m.

May:
Monday–Saturday, 9:30 a.m.–5 p.m.;
Sunday, 10:30 a.m.–4:30 p.m.

June–September:
Monday–Saturday, 9:30 a.m.–6 p.m.;
Sunday, 10:30 a.m.–4:30 p.m.

July–August:
Monday–Saturday, 9:30 a.m.–6 p.m.;
Sunday, 10:30 a.m.–5 p.m.

Special Events in Salisbury

The annual **Salisbury Festival** presents drama, classical music and jazz, and theater and films at the Salisbury Playhouse and at other indoor and outdoor locations around the city for ten days in late May and early June; the festival also includes architectural tours and other walks around the city. For information and tickets, call (01722) 332-241 or visit the website at **www.salisburyfestival.co.uk.**

In alternating years, Salisbury hosts the **Southern Cathedrals Festival,** which for several days in late July brings together the choirs of Salisbury, Chichester, and Winchester cathedrals for performances in Salisbury Cathedral and in the cathedrals of the other two cities. For information and tickets, contact the Salisbury Information Centre or visit **www.southerncathedralsfestival.org.uk.**

Arriving and Getting Oriented in Salisbury

Salisbury is 90 miles southwest of London. Trains run frequently, with half-hourly service at morning and evening peak travel times and hourly the rest of the day; most leave from London's Waterloo Station, though some leave from Paddington. The trip takes about an hour and a half, and the round trip costs about £22. For information, call (08457) 484-950 or go to **www.railtrack.co.uk.** The train station is at the western edge of the city center, off Fisherton Street, and within easy walking distance of the cathedral and other sights.

By car, the quickest route from London is the M3, then the A30. The trip takes about two hours, depending on traffic in and around London. Several car parks are located in and around the city center, including **Central Car Park,** west across the River Avon from the center, and **Culver Street Car Park,** a few blocks from the Cathedral Close. Fees at most car parks near the center are £3 per day. The **Beehive Park and Ride** is just north off the city off A345; it is open Monday–Friday, 6:45 a.m.–8 p.m.; and Saturday, 7:15 a.m.–7:30 p.m. The fee is £1 a day and includes free bus transportation into the city center.

National Express buses leave London's Victoria Coach Station for Salisbury every two to three hours. The train is a much better alternative, since the bus ride takes at least three hours and often longer, and sometimes requires a change at Southampton or Bristol. The round trip costs about £19.50. For more information, call (08705) 808-080 or go to **www.gobycoach.com.** The bus station is at the east end of the Market Place in the center of town and within easy walking distance of the cathedral and other sights.

Hotels in Salisbury

Grasmere House Hotel — *£65–£85*

OVERALL ★★★ | QUALITY ★★★ | VALUE ★★★

70 Harnham Road, Salisbury, Wiltshire, SP28JN; (01722) 338-388; fax (01772) 333-710; info@grasmerehotel.com

Location About a mile outside the city center.

Amenities & Services 20 rooms. Restaurant, conservatory bar and lounge, garden, satellite TV.

Elevator No.

Parking Free parking on grounds.

Pricing Includes breakfast.

Credit Cards V, MC, AMEX

This converted Victorian mansion, built for a Winchester merchant in 1896, is situated atop a hill overlooking the spires of Salisbury from a lovely garden. The spacious lawns make this an excellent choice for travelers with children, and a footpath from the bottom of the garden follows the Nadder and Avon, Salisbury's two meandering rivers, through the water meadows to the cathedral. Only four of the rooms are located in the old house, and these are larger and have a little more character than those in a new wing, though all of the rooms are tastefully done in traditional furnishings, and all have large, newly remodeled bathrooms with tub and shower combinations. Several rooms on the ground floor open onto small patios, and two are equipped for guests with disabilities.

Red Lion Hotel — *£88–£109*

OVERALL ★★★★ | QUALITY ★★★ | VALUE ★★★

Milford Street, Salisbury, Wiltshire, SP1 2AN; (01722) 323-334; fax (01722) 325-756; reception@the-redlion.co.uk; www.the-redlion.co.uk

Location In the center of the city.

Amenities & Services 54 rooms. Restaurant, bar, lounge, courtyard patio, satellite TV.

Elevator Yes.

Parking Limited free parking on the premises.

Pricing Continental breakfast, £5.50; full breakfast, £9.50.

Credit Cards V, MC, AMEX, D

The Red Lion was built more than 750 years ago as housing for laborers building the cathedral, and during the coaching era was known to any traveler as the departure point for the "Salisbury Flying Train," which dashed off nightly at 10 p.m. The hotel's public rooms, including the Vyne Restaurant, and some of the guest rooms are located in the original, half-timbered structure, while others are in more recent additions. All of the rooms are uniquely furnished, often with dramatic fabric swags over the beds and reproduction carved furniture, though the accommodations throughout the hotel are rather small and the décor is a bit fussy for the space. A few of the older rooms have fireplaces, and all have newer baths, many with large tubs. Tea and light snacks are served throughout the day in the cozy lounge, which is a popular gathering spot for shoppers from the county in town for the day and local professionals. In good weather, you can enjoy a drink in the creeper-covered courtyard.

White Hart — *£105–£130*

OVERALL ★★★★ | QUALITY ★★★★ | VALUE ★★★

St. John Street, Salisbury, Wiltshire SP1 2SD; (0870) 400-8125; fax (0172) 241-2761; general.whitehartsalisbury@macdonald-hotels.co.uk; www.macdonaldhotels.co.uk

Location In the city center.

Amenities & Services 68 rooms. Restaurant, lounge with open fire, bar.

Elevator No.

Parking Free parking behind the hotel.

Pricing Includes full breakfast.

Credit Cards V, MC, AMEX, D

Salisbury's finest hotel is a member of Macdonald Hotels, one of Britain's better chains, and dates from the 17th century. The entrance is beneath a pillared portico that is a Salisbury landmark, just as tea in the hotel foyer is something of a local institution. Most of the rooms are in a newer wing in the back, though some regulars prefer the rooms in the older part of the hotel. There's really little difference, since rooms throughout the hotel are large and luxuriously appointed with handsome wood armoires and headboards and rich, earth-toned fabrics. Four superior rooms are done in traditional style with four-poster beds, but the standard rooms are so comfortably and handsomely furnished, with large armchairs and spacious desks, that the upgrade really doesn't seem worth the added expense.

Exploring Salisbury

Salisbury rose around its cathedral in the Middle Ages, and this great monument remains the city's centerpiece. A good place to begin a tour, though, is at the city's secular heart, the vast **marketplace,** where markets have been held on Tuesday and Saturday since 1227. The market extends around the corner to Silver Street, where the **Poultry Cross,** one of four small stone shelters that once rose above the market stalls, still stands. By medieval tradition, vendors of poultry could ply their trade in the shadow of the cross with the reassurance of divine protection—or at least easy recognition of what they were selling. The **Guildhall,** at the south-eastern corner of the marketplace, is from the 18th century. This makes it a rare new incursion in the midst of **Cross Keys Chequer**, one of the city's most intact medieval neighborhoods (the precincts that grew up around the cathedral were known as "chequers," and you'll see the word often as you wander through the city).

Next to the Guildhall rises 700-year-old **St. Thomas Church,** which makes itself known with a tall spire, an enormous clock on one of the facades by which locals set their watches, and the tolling of its bells. A terrifying painting called *Doom* hangs over the chancel arch and depicts ordinary folk rising from their graves and marching toward heaven or hell. It's a great relief to flee from the painting into the mellow, friendly streets of the city. After wandering along streets whose monikers belie their medieval functions, such as Fish Row and Butcher's Row, you'll want to follow High Street south toward the **Cathedral Close,** taking time to admire the shop windows, many of which grace half-timbered houses. A particularly appealing entrance to the Close is **St. Anne's Gate,** to the east and reached via Queen Street. An imposing structure in itself, the gate houses a room where George Frederick Handel is said to have given a recital.

The Cathedral Close is a small city, contained within four gates and encompassing cobblestone lanes lined with some of the city's most gracious houses. Among them are the **College of Matrons,** founded in the 16th century for widows and the daughters of clergymen, and **Malmesbury House.** The **Salisbury and South Wiltshire Museum** (65, The Close; (01722) 332-151) is well worth a visit for its artifacts from **Stonehenge** (see page 284). The museum is open Monday–Saturday, 10 a.m.–5 p.m., and Sunday (July and August), 2–5 p.m. Admission is £3.50 adults, £2.30 seniors and students, £1 children ages 5–16, and £7.90 families of up to two adults and three children.

At some point in your explorations, you should wander along the well-maintained footpath that crosses the **Water Meadows** between Mill Road and the old **Harnham Mill.** The views toward the cathedral are unspoiled since John Constable painted them 200 years ago.

Tours in and around Salisbury

Salisbury is well endowed with historic buildings and monuments, and a good way to appreciate them is on the **Salisbury City Walk.** The hour-and-a-half-long tours start at the Tourist Information Centre in Fish Row and follow medieval streets and lanes to such sights as St. Thomas' Church and the Cathedral Close. Walks begin at 11 a.m., Saturday and

Sunday, November–March; and daily, April–October. The fee is £2.50 adults and £1 children; for information, call (01725) 518-658.

Foot Trails is a local organization that leads walking tours in the countryside around Salisbury. Walks last anywhere from two hours to a full day or weekend. Call (01747) 861-851, or inquire via e-mail to alison@footrails.co.uk.

Attractions in Salisbury

Mompesson House

Type of Attraction Historic house in Cathedral Close

Location Choristers' Green, north side of Cathedral Close

Admission £3.90 adults; £1.95 children

Hours March 24–November 3: Saturday–Wednesday, 11 a.m.–5 p.m.

Phone (01722) 335-659

Website www.nationaltrust.org.uk

When to Go Weekdays; the house is less crowded than weekends, making it easier to get into the spirit of 18th-century high life

Special Tips The ground floor and garden are accessible to visitors with disabilities.

Overall Appeal by Age Group

Preschool —	Teens ★★★★	Over 30 ★★★★
Grade school ★★★	Young Adults ★★★★	Seniors ★★★★

Author's Rating ★★★★

How Much Time to Allow About 1 hour

Description & Comments If this elegant house looks familiar, it may be because it was used as a set in the 1995 film of Jane Austen's *Sense and Sensibility*. Even without this notoriety, the house is a pleasure to visit—plasterwork, paneling, and the original layout of the rooms remain remarkably intact from 1740. The house contains a great quantity of original 18th-century furniture and decorative pieces, including a collection of drinking glasses, and there is a beautiful walled garden at the rear.

Touring Tips The tearoom overlooking the garden serves light meals and is an excellent place to stop and relax while touring the Cathedral Close.

Salisbury Cathedral

Type of Attraction One of England's great cathedrals

Location The Close

Admission Suggested donation: £3.80 adults; £3.30 seniors and students; £2 children ages 5–17; £8.50 families

Hours Cathedral: March 1–June 9, September 1–March 31, 7:15 a.m.–6:15 p.m.; June 10–August 31, 7:15 a.m.–8:15 p.m. Chapter House: Monday–Saturday, 9:30 a.m.–5:30 p.m. (until 7:45 p.m. June 10–August 31), Sunday, noon–5:30 p.m.

Phone (01722) 335-161

Website www.salisburycathedral.org.uk

When to Go Weekdays, when the cathedral is less crowded

Special Tips The cathedral's excellent choir sings evensong daily at 5:30 p.m., and the cathedral hosts noontime concerts throughout the summer.

Overall Appeal by Age Group

Preschool —	Teens ★★★	Over 30 ★★★
Grade school ★★★	Young Adults ★★★	Seniors ★★★

Author's Rating ★★★

How Much Time to Allow At least 1 hour

Description & Comments This gracious church is credited with a long list of attributes. One of the most commendable is the fact that it was built in record time, just 38 years, from 1220 to 1258. As a result, it is for the most part all of one piece, a soaring testimony to the glories of Gothic architecture. The cloisters, the largest in England, and the Chapter House were added in 1280; the spire, at 404 feet the tallest in England, was completed in 1313. The cathedral houses, in the north aisle, one of the oldest pieces of working machinery in the world, a mechanical clock that has been telling time since 1386. In the octagonal Chapter House, remarkable stone friezes from the 13th century tell Old Testament stories, and one of four copies of the Magna Carta has been housed here since 1225—with the exception of the World War II years, when the document was sheltered from German bombs in a nearby quarry.

Touring Tips Volunteers offer free guided tours of the cathedral and Chapter House throughout the day. Or, equip yourself with a leaflet, available near the entrance, for a self-guided tour. On Tower Tours, you can climb into the tower via 332 winding steps for a look at medieval scaffolding left in place after the tower's construction, a peek into the spire, and views over the city and countryside; the tours last one and a half hours and are held January–February and November–December, 2:15 p.m.; March, Monday–Saturday, 11 a.m. and 2:15 p.m.; April, Monday–Saturday, 11:15 a.m., 2:15 p.m., and 3:15 p.m.; May and September, Monday–Saturday, 11:15 a.m., 2:15 p.m., and 3:15 p.m., Sunday, 4:30 p.m.; June–August, Monday–Saturday, 11:15 a.m., 2:15 p.m., 3:15 p.m., and 6:30 p.m., Sunday, 4:30 p.m. Fees are £3 adults and £2 seniors and children.

Dining in Salisbury

Salisbury is well endowed with pleasant places to pop into for a cup of tea. The lounges of the **White Hart Hotel** on St. John Street and the **Red Lion Hotel** on Milford Street are two of the most popular spots. The **Mitre House** is an atmospheric old shop and tearoom on High Street; if you like what you drink, you can purchase a package or two.

Harper's Restaurant ★★★½

BRITISH | MODERATE | QUALITY ★★★ | VALUE ★★★

6–7 Ox Row, Market Place; (01722) 333-118

Reservations Not necessary **Entrée Range** £8.50–£12.50; 2-course prix fixe menu, £6.90 for lunch, £8 6–8 p.m., £9 after 8 p.m. **Payment** V, MC, AMEX **Bar** Full service **Disabled Access** No

Hours Monday–Saturday, noon–2 p.m., 6–9:30 p.m.; Sunday, 6–10 p.m.

House Specialties Grilled gammon (ham) steak; calf's liver; fresh fish of the day; sweet potato patties and mushroom confit; several other vegetarian dishes.

"Real food is our specialty" reads a sign in this pleasant first-floor restaurant (that's second floor to Americans), and Harper's lives up to the claim with its tasty, non-fussy meals. Soft lighting, a soothing cream-and-brown–toned décor, and friendly service provide a relaxed, casual atmosphere in a large dining room overlooking the marketplace.

Haunch of Venison ★★★★

BRITISH/PUB | INEXPENSIVE–MODERATE | QUALITY ★★★ | VALUE ★★★

1–5 Minster Street; (01722) 322-024

Reservations Recommended **Entrée Range** £9–£13; pub fare, £4–£6 **Payment** V, MC, AMEX **Bar** Full service **Disabled Access** Ground floor only

Hours Pub: daily, 11 a.m.–11 p.m. Restaurant: Monday–Sunday, noon–2:30 p.m.; Monday–Thursday, 6:30–9:30 p.m.; Friday and Saturday, 6–10 p.m.

House Specialties Roast haunch of venison, of course.

This character-filled old establishment dates from 1320, and the beams that slice through the series of small rooms are said to be much older than that and were taken from sailing vessels. Pub fare is served in the paneled rooms downstairs, and restaurant meals appear in a sloping, creaky-floored dining room upstairs, warmed by a roaring fire. The kitchen is at its best with traditional roasts and grilled chops, and the meat pies and other pub platters are delicious.

Prezzo ★★★

ITALIAN | MODERATE | QUALITY ★★½ | VALUE ★★★

52 High Street; (01722) 341-333

Reservations Recommended on weekends **Entrée Range** £8–£13; pastas and pizzas from £6.50 **Payment** V, MC, AMEX, D **Bar** Full service **Disabled Access** Yes

Hours Daily, noon–11 p.m.

House Specialties Penne with basil, tomato, and mozzarella; thin-crust pizzas.

Every English city has its share of Italian restaurants, and this one stands out not because of its cuisine, which is fairly standard, but because of a dramatic setting in a Tudor building. High-tech lighting imparts a warm glow to the otherwise stark dining room, where heavy old beams are offset by gleaming white tiles and large windows overlooking High Street. Stick to the basic pastas or excellent, individual-sized pizzas and a selection from the excellent wine list, and you'll enjoy a decent if not memorable meal here.

Squires Restaurant ★★★★

BRITISH | MODERATE | QUALITY ★★★½ | VALUE ★★★

White Hart Hotel, St. John Street; (0870) 400-8125

Reservations Recommended at dinner **Entrée Range** 2-course lunch, £6.50; 3-course lunch, £8.50; 3-course dinner, £22.95 **Payment** V, MC, AMEX, D **Bar** Full service **Disabled Access** Yes

Hours Daily, 12:30–2 p.m., 7:30–9:30 p.m.

House Specialties Char-grilled guinea fowl; any of the pan-seared or roast lamb preparations; grilled red snapper.

The combination of handsome, country-house décor and a solid menu of traditional standards provides a haven for a well-heeled, tweedy crowd of regulars. In addition to excellent cuisine, offered on a small menu that changes daily and always includes a choice of meat, fish, and vegetarian dishes, Squire's also offers a peaceful, almost hushed atmosphere that's perfect for a business meal or a good chat. The Squire's prix fixe lunch is the best-valued meal in town, making this a good choice when visiting the nearby cathedral.

Entertainment and Nightlife in Salisbury

Salisbury Playhouse (Malthouse Lane in city center; (01722) 320-33) is one of England's most respected regional theaters and stages productions of classic and contemporary dramas throughout the year, often in collaboration with other British theaters; the Playhouse is also the main stage of the Salisbury Festival in May (see "Special Events in Salisbury"). The city has any number of character-filled old pubs where residents like to while away an evening. You can join them at three of the most historic: the pub at the **Red Lion Hotel** (Milford Street; (01722) 323-334), the **Haunch of Venison** (1–5 Minster Street; (01722) 322-024), and the **New Inn** (New Street; (01722) 326-662), which isn't new at all and is a creaky old warren full of heavy beams and centuries-old hearths.

Shopping in Salisbury

Most shops in Winchester are open Monday–Saturday, 9 a.m.–5:30 p.m., with some remaining open later on Thursday evenings. Even if you're not shopping, a mandatory stop is **Watsons** (8–9 Queen Street; (01722) 320-311), where you can view a vast collection of British crystal and fine china as well as the architectural details of two of Salisbury's oldest buildings, from 1306 and 1425. A cutaway section in the flooring shows the original foundations, and old photographs show how the shop restored its historic premises. The **National Trust Shop** (41 High Street; (01722) 331-884) is another good stop for upscale souvenirs, along the lines of needlepoint kits and tea towels with designs based on those found in the Trust's many holdings. **Mitre House** (37 High Street, Salisbury; (01722) 333-705) sells many varieties of tea, which it also serves on the premises; the name comes from the generations of Salisbury bishops who were once robed on the historic premises before their enthronement.

Around Salisbury

Salisbury lies at the edge of the **Salisbury Plain,** where grass-covered downs support the sheep that have long made the region a center of the wool trade. Gardens and historic homes dot the plain, along with what may be the world's most famous prehistoric site, **Stonehenge.**

Longleat House

Type of Attraction Historic house and safari park

Location Near Warminster, 27 miles northwest of Salisbury, 6 miles north of Stourhead on B3092

Admission House and grounds: £9 adults; £6 seniors and children ages 3–14. Grounds only: £3 adults; £2 seniors and children ages 3–14. Safari Park: £9 adults; £6 seniors and children ages 3–14. Railway: £3. Safari boats: £3. Longleat Passport (provides admission to house, grounds, Safari Park, and other attractions): £16 adults; £13 seniors and children ages 3–14.

Hours House: Easter–September, daily, 10 a.m.–5:30 p.m.; October–Easter, daily, guided tours only, every hour on the hour, 11 a.m.–3 p.m. Safari Park: April 5–November 2, Monday–Friday, 10 a.m.–4 p.m., Saturday–Sunday, 10 a.m.–5 p.m.

Phone (01985) 844-400

Website www.longleat.co.uk

When to Go Try to avoid weekends and school holidays, when Longleat is packed.

Special Tips The Longleat Passport (see prices above) provides the most economical way to enjoy Longleat.

Overall Appeal by Age Group

Preschool ★★★★	Teens ★★★★	Over 30 ★★
Grade school ★★★★	Young Adults ★★★★	Seniors ★★

Author's Rating ★★★★

How Much Time to Allow At least half a day

Description & Comments Longleat is a magnificent estate, with a 16th-cenutry Italian Renaissance house filled with fine furnishings and surrounded by grounds that Capability Brown, the great master of 18th-century landscape gardening, designed according the principles of 18th-century "romantic" naturalism. The family home of the marquesses of Bath was the first country house in Britain to open to the public, in 1949; in 1966, it became one of Britain's most famous family attractions when a Safari Park opened on the grounds. Hippos now slumber on the shores of the estate lakes, gorillas inhabit islands, and lions and giraffes roam. A railway chugs through the grounds, safari boats ply the waters, and a half-mile hedge maze that contains 16,000 yews, an adventure castle, butterfly garden, petting zoo and other attractions will keep young visitors amused for hours. If you want to enjoy the atmosphere of a typical British country estate, you're better off visiting Wilton or Stourhead, both nearby. But for a day of family fun, Longleat fills the bill.

Touring Tips Longleat has fast-food kiosks, a restaurant, and a café.

Stonehenge

Type of Attraction Perhaps the world's most renowned prehistoric site

Location 8 miles north of Salisbury via A338, A303, and A360

Admission £4.40 adults; £3.40 seniors and students; £2.40 children ages 5–15; £10.80 families of up to two adults and three children

Hours March 16–May 31: daily, 9:30 a.m.–6 p.m.; June 1–August 31: daily, 9 a.m.–7 p.m.; September 1–October 15: daily, 9:30 a.m.–6 p.m.; October 16–October 23: daily, 9:30 a.m.–5 p.m.; October 24–March 15: daily, 9:30 a.m.–4 p.m.

Phone (01980) 624-715

Website www.stonehenge.org.uk

When to Go Early morning or as late in the day as possible, when crowds are likely to be thinnest. Misty, foggy, and rainy days are ideal for a visit, because the site is especially atmospheric and many would-be visitors are elsewhere.

Special Tips Stonehenge is easy to reach by public transportation. From the Salisbury train station, Wilt and Dorset buses depart for Stonehenge every hour on the hour between 10 a.m. and 5 p.m. and depart from Stonehenge for Salisbury at 20 minutes after the hour, with the last return at 6:20 p.m. The trip takes 40 minutes; the round-trip fare is about £5. For information, go to **www.wdbus.co.uk.**

Overall Appeal by Age Group

Preschool ★★★★★	Teens ★★★★★	Over 30 ★★★★★
Grade school ★★★★★	Young Adults ★★★★★	Seniors ★★★★★

Author's Rating ★★★★★

How Much Time to Allow About 30 minutes

Description & Comments This stone circle of pillars and lintels has been fascinating humankind for the better part of 5,000 years. Despite centuries of scholarly study and rumination, it is still not known why these stones are here or what they signify. It even seems difficult to arrive at the number of stones at Stonehenge; legend has it that no mortal can count them and arrive at the same number twice, proved to be true when Jonathan Swift, 18th-century century author of *Gulliver's Travels,* arrived at "93 or 94." What is known is that most of the stones, many weighing several tons, were transported from as far as hundreds of miles away, probably by raft and across the land on primitive rollers. Begun a thousand years before the Egyptian pyramids in 1800 B.C., Stonehenge may have been built by early Greek wanderers or by neolithic Britons, and, given its alignment with the summer equinox, may have been intended as an astronomical observatory. Over the years, Stonehenge has served as a burial ground and a ceremonial center. Stonehenge continues to attract modern-day druids who, to the chagrin of local authorities, converge upon the site at the summer solstice. Indeed, hordes descend upon one of Britain's most popular attractions year-round, and sadly, these are kept behind barriers placed 50 feet from the stones to the side of one section of the site. Even so, the sight of Stonehenge rising above the Salisbury plain is haunting.

Touring Tips Bring binoculars to observe lintels and other architectural details.

Stourhead

Type of Attraction Country house and garden

Location Stourton; 30 miles northwest of Salisbury via A36 and A303 to Mere, then B3092 to Stourhead

Admission April–October: Garden or house, £4.90 adults, £2.70 children ages 5–15, £12.30 families of up to two adults and three children; garden and house, £8.70 adults, £4.10 children ages 5–15, £20.50 families of up to two adults and three children. November–February: garden only, £3.80 adults, £1.85 children ages 5–15, £9.20 families of up to two adults and three children

Hours Garden: daily, 9 a.m.–7 p.m. or until sunset, whichever is earlier. House: March 23–November 3, Saturday–Wednesday, noon–5:30 p.m. or until dusk, whichever is earlier.

Phone (01747) 841-152

Website www.nationaltrust.org.uk

When to Go Any day when the weather is good, since you'll want to walk a couple of miles through the gardens

Special Tips The grounds are wheelchair accessible, but paths are steep in places. Stourhead hosts a full schedule of outdoor concerts, nature walks, and many events, such as storytelling sessions and theatrical productions, geared to youngsters.

Overall Appeal by Age Group

Preschool ★★	Teens ★★★	Over 30 ★★★
Grade school ★★★	Young Adults ★★★	Seniors ★★★

Author's Rating ★★★

How Much Time to Allow Several hours

Description & Comments The gardens at Stourhead are the first in England to reflect a change in 18th-century landscape design from the formality of French gardens to a romantic notion of "natural" settings. The gardens at Stourhead do indeed succeed in reflecting an idealized and altogether delightful version of a natural setting, with hidden grottoes, small temples, fanciful bridges, and a tranquil lake surrounded by towering trees and rare plantings. The mile-and-a-half walk around the lake with pauses to enjoy the setting is a delightful way to spend a summer afternoon. The largest monument in the garden is a freakish-looking, 150-feet-tall red brick edifice known as King Alfred's Tower; a climb to the top affords excellent views (and costs £1.65 adults and £0.85 children), but the gardens are better appreciated from terra firma. The house, built in 1722 for merchant banker Henry Hoare, is memorable, too, and it's filled with French and Chinese porcelains and early Chippendale furniture.

Touring Tips The gardens are where you will want to spend the most time, so you might want to consider buying a "garden only" ticket.

Wilton House

Type of Attraction Historic estate surrounded by lavish gardens

Location 3 miles northwest of Salisbury on A30, in village of Wilton

Admission £9.25 adults; £7.50 seniors and students; £5 children over age 5, £22 or families

Hours March 27–October 27: daily, 10:30 a.m.–5:30 p.m.

Phone (01722) 746-720

Website www.wiltonhouse.co.uk

When to Go In June, when the rose gardens are in full bloom

Special Tips The house and gardens are accessible for wheelchairs; there is a tearoom on the grounds.

Overall Appeal by Age Group

Preschool ★★	Teens ★★★	Over 30 ★★★★
Grade school ★★★	Young Adults ★★★	Seniors ★★★★

Author's Rating ★★★★

How Much Time to Allow About 2 hours for the house and grounds

Description & Comments Wilton is one of the great homes of Britain and is among the finest achievements of 17th-century architect Inigo Jones, the founder of English classical architecture whose works also include Covent Garden and the Banqueting Hall at Whitehall in London. Wilton is now the home of the 17th Earl of Pembroke, and only some of the rooms are open to the public. You see enough, though, to appreciate the architectural mastery at work here, as well as the richness of the family collections. Tours begin in the Tudor kitchen and Victorian laundry, but the crowd pleasers are a little farther on—the so-called staterooms. Most stately among them is the Double Cube Room, famous for its harmonious proportions, 60 feet long by 30 feet wide and 30 feet high. Despite its opulence, the room has served a practical function, too—it was the top-secret Operations Room for Southern Command, and it was here that General Dwight D. Eisenhower planned the logistical support for the D-Day Landings in 1944. All of the paintings in the room are by Anthony Van Dyck, and paintings by Peter Paul Rubens, Peter Brueghel, Sir Joshua Reynolds, and other masters hang throughout the other staterooms as well. With their sweeping lawns and a Palladian-style bridge crossing the River Avon, the gardens look like a painting themselves.

Touring Tips You can entertain restless children here with a look at the house's collection of 200 miniature Wareham Bears and a session in the playground at the edge of the garden; young visitors will also enjoy the water gardens, with their lily pads and carp.

Part Seven

The Southwest of England

While many regions of England greet visitors with a gentle embrace, the southwest is more likely to clap you heartily on the back. That sensation might be caused by a bracing wind racing across the desolate **Devon Moors,** or a spray of Atlantic surf crashing against the rocky coasts of **Cornwall.**

You will never be far from the sea wherever you wander in England's two southwesternmost counties; these areas occupy a long peninsula that juts into the English Channel to the south and the Atlantic Ocean on the north and comes to a breathtakingly dramatic finale at **Land's End,** the western edge of England. Altogether, some 650 miles of coastline skirt **Devon** and Cornwall. You'll soon come to associate Devon with wild moors, including those in **Dartmoor National Park** that inspired Sir Arthur Conan Doyle's *The Hound of the Baskervilles,* but desolate as the landscape can be, Devon offers plenty of civilized attractions, such as **Exeter Cathedral.** Cornwall is a place for walks along jagged coastlines (including the stretch at **Tintagel** of Arthurian legend), swims from golden sands, and a pint or two in a cozy pub alongside a snug harbor.

Not To Be Missed in the Southwest of England

- St. Peter's Cathedral (page 298)
- Dartmoor National Park (page 301)
- Buckland Abbey (page 302)
- The Lost Gardens of Heligan (page 308)
- Tintagel Castle (page 311)
- St. Michael's Mount (page 322)
- Land's End (page 322)
- The village of St. Ives (page 312)

Exeter

The street plan of the Devon county seat has not changed much since the Romans laid out what is today's High Street in the first century A.D. Even then, Exeter was already a well-established center for the Dumnonii

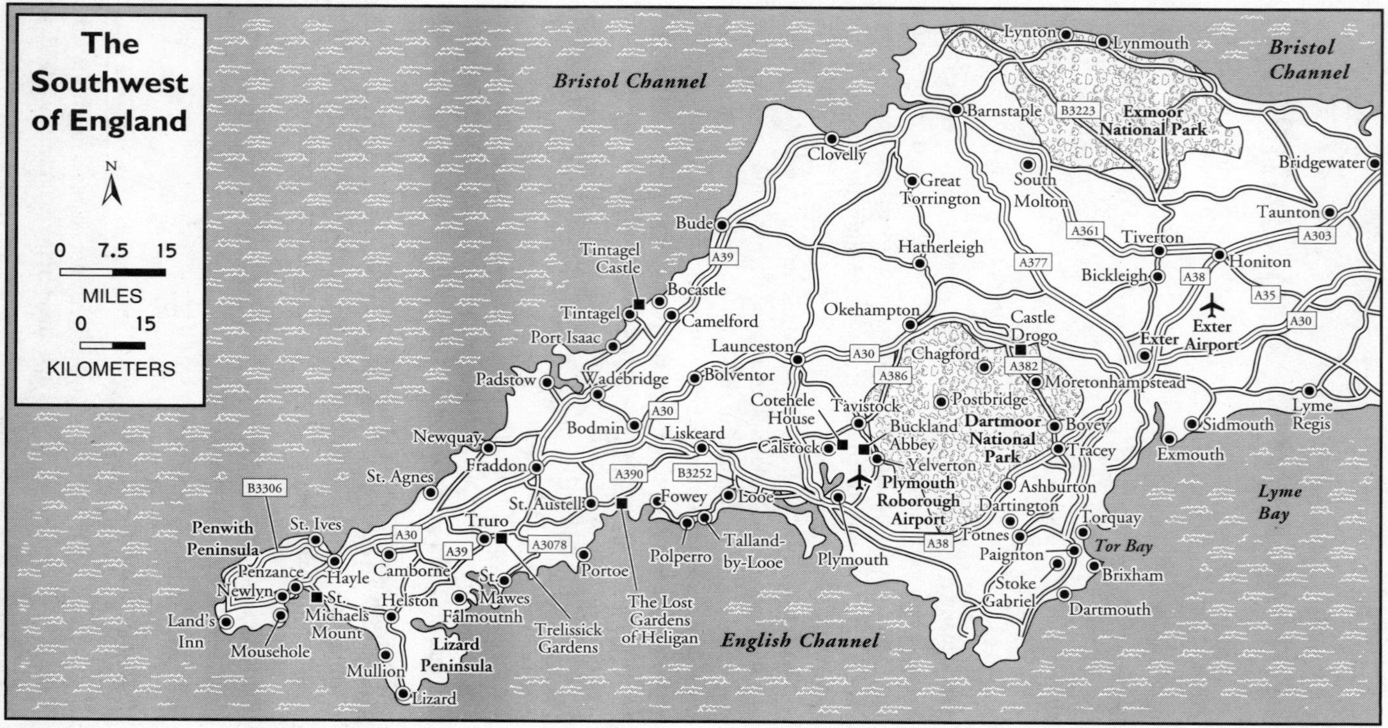

The Southwest of England
N
0 7.5 15
MILES
0 15
KILOMETERS
Bristol Channel
Bristol Channel
Lynton
Lynmouth
Barnstaple
B3223
Exmoor National Park
Bridgewater
Clovelly
Great Torrington
South Molton
Taunton
A361
Tiverton
A303
Bude
A39
Hatherleigh
A377
Honiton
Tintagel Castle
Bickleigh
A38
Bocastle
A35
Tintagel
Camelford
Okehampton
Castle Drogo
Exter Airport
A30
Port Isaac
Exter
Launceston
A30
Chagford
A382
Padstow
Wadebridge
Bolventor
A386
Moretonhampstead
Cotehele House
Tavistock
Postbridge
Lyme Regis
A30
Bodmin
Buckland Abbey
Dartmoor National Park
Bovey Tracey
Sidmouth
Newquay
Liskeard
Calstock
Exmouth
Yelverton
Fraddon
A390
B3252
Plymouth Roborough Airport
Ashburton
St. Agnes
St. Austell
Fowey
Looe
Dartington
Lyme Bay
B3306
Torquay
Penwith Peninsula
St. Ives
A30
Truro
Totnes
Tor Bay
A39
A3078
A38
Paignton
Polperro
Talland-by-Looe
Plymouth
Penzance
Hayle
Camborne
Portoe
Brixham
Newlyn
St. Mawes
Stoke Gabriel
St. Michaels Mount
Helston
Falmoutnh
The Lost Gardens of Heligan
Dartmouth
Land's Inn
Mousehole
Trelissick Gardens
English Channel
Lizard Peninsula
Mullion
Lizard

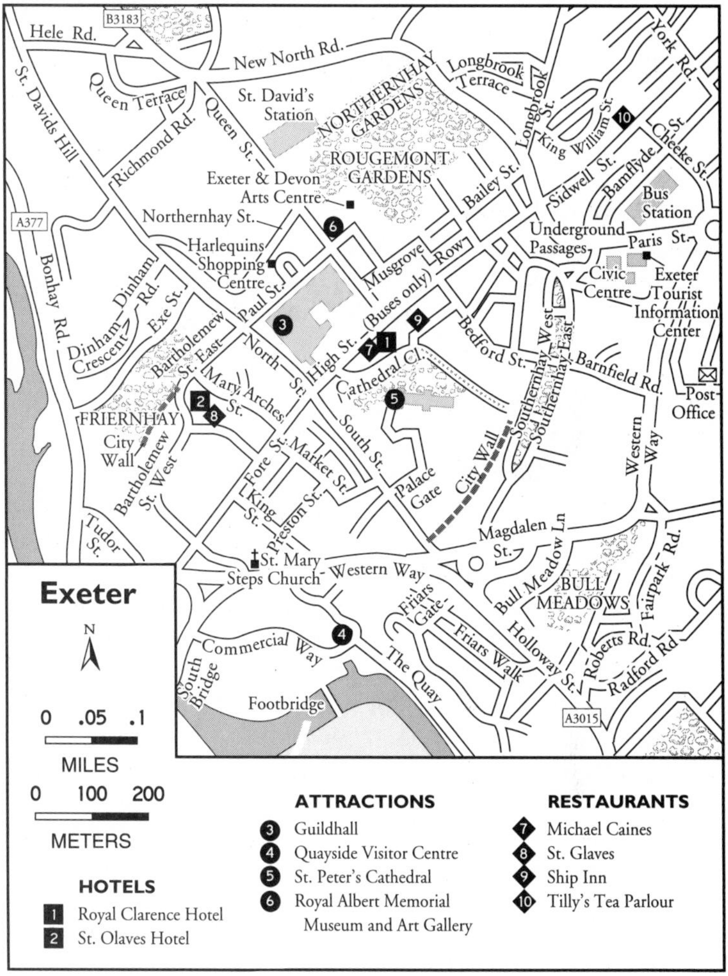

Celts. Built on a plateau above the River Exe, the old city center is still surrounded by sections of Roman and medieval walls, but rebuilding made necessary by a German bombing raid in World War II has turned Exeter into what is essentially a modern-looking town.

While Exeter warrants a leisurely look, we recommend it also as a base from which to explore the heather-covered moorlands, gardens, and historic properties that surround the city.

Planning Your Visit to Exeter

The **Exeter Tourist Information Centre** (in the Civic Centre, Paris Street; (01392) 265-2031; **www.exeter.gov.uk**) provides information on places to stay, what to see and do, and where to dine in Exeter, as well as on attractions throughout Devon. The center is open daily in the summer, Monday–Saturday, 9 a.m.–5 p.m., and Sunday, 10 a.m.–4 p.m.; and six days a week in the winter, Monday–Friday, 9 a.m.–5 p.m., and Saturday, 9 a.m.–1 p.m. and 2–5 p.m.

Special Events in Exeter

The **Exeter Festival** brings classical music, opera, ballet, and jazz to Exeter for two weeks every July. For information and tickets, call (01392) 265-200 or visit **www.exeter.gov.uk/festival.** From mid-July through mid-August, Exeter's **Northcott Theatre Company** presents Shakespearean drama outdoors in the Rougemont Gardens; for information, call (01392) 493-493 or visit **www.northcott-theatre.co.uk.**

Arriving and Getting Oriented in Exeter

Trains run every half hour to hour throughout the day from London's Paddington Station to St. Davids Station in Exeter. The trip takes about two to two and a half hours, and the fare is about £60 round trip. For information, call (08457) 484-950 or go to **www.railtrack.co.uk.** St. Davids Station is about a mile west of the city center. You can take local trains from there to Central Station, just off Queen Street, or buses to the city center; there is a taxi rank outside the station.

By car, the quickest route from London is the M4 to Bristol, then the M5 to Exeter. The trip takes about three hours (often longer at peak travel times in the summer and on weekends, when traffic can become quite heavy). Driving and parking is severely restricted in Exeter, and the entrance to the city center, through a series of one-way streets, is confusing even to residents. The city has built an extensive series of municipal car parks around the center, including a large one near the cathedral on Mary Arches Street. Fees are £0.60 per hour, £7.40 for the day.

National Express buses run from London's Victoria Coach Station to Exeter, leaving about every two hours or so. The journey takes about four and a half hours, so the train is a much faster option. The round trip costs £33.50; for more information, call (08705) 808-080 or visit **www.gobycoach.com.**

Hotels in and around Exeter

We recommend hotels in Exeter as well as in the surrounding countryside. You may want to divide your time to enjoy either of the two excellent hotels we suggest in Exeter and partake of the activity of the county seat, then move on to enjoy the pleasures of rural Devon from one of our country hotel choices.

Gidleigh Park *£275–£420*

OVERALL ★★★★★ | QUALITY ★★★★★ | VALUE ★★★

Gidleigh Road, Chagford, Devon TQ13 8HH; (01647) 432-367; fax (01647) 432-574; gidleighpark@gidleigh.co.uk; www.gidleigh.com

Location In Dartmoor National Park, 3 miles outside the village of Chagford and 25 miles from Exeter.

Amenities & Services 16 rooms. Award-winning restaurant (one of England's finest); antiques-filled drawing room and lounges, gardens, croquet, lawn bowling, tennis, walking, other outdoor activities by arrangement.

Elevator No.

Parking Yes.

Pricing Includes early-morning tea or coffee in the room, full breakfast, and dinner.

Credit Cards V, MC

Should you want to feel like Lord and Lady of the Manor for a night or two, bank balance permitting, Gidleigh Park is the place to do it. This member of the Relaix and Chateaux group is, quite simply, one of the finest country hotels in England, and while the tariffs are steep, the proprietors and staff deliver a memorable experience. The 1920s manor house and 45 acres of gardens are lovely, service is impeccable without being fussy, and the welcoming public rooms and commodious guest rooms are swathed in fine fabrics, rich paneling, and exquisite old pieces. (We stop short of saying Gidleigh Park is quintessentially British, because the proprietors who created this wonderful place in 1977, Paul and Kay Henderson, are American.) Gourmands around the world know Gidleigh Park as the home base of chef Michael Caines, whose preparations have earned two Michelin rosettes and a bounty of other commendations.

Holne Chase Hotel *£95–£130*

OVERALL ★★★★ | QUALITY ★★★★ | VALUE ★★★★

Near Ashburton, Devon TQ13 7NS; (01364) 631-471; fax (01364) 631-453; info@holne-chase.co.uk; www.holne-chase.co.uk

Location On the River Dart in Dartmoor National Park.

Amenities & Services 16 rooms. Restaurant, comfortable lounges, beautiful gardens and grounds; fishing, hunting, horseback riding, walking, and other outdoor activities; fireplaces in some rooms.

Elevator No.

Parking Yes.

Pricing Includes full English breakfast; special off-season rates and dinner, bed, and breakfast packages for longer stays available.

Credit Cards V, MC, AMEX

At Holne Chase, walking sticks and Wellingtons are lined up on the porch, bassets snore in front of the fire, ponies graze on the lawn, and a river rushes through 70 acres of gardens and woodland. It's no surprise, then, that this rambling Victorian house, a former hunting lodge, serves up the perfect setting for a country-house retreat. In addition to beautiful surroundings, hosts Sebastian and Philippa Hughes

HOW HOTELS COMPARE

Hotel	Overall Rating	Quality Rating	Value Rating	Price
Exeter				
Gidleigh Park	★★★★★	★★★★★	★★★	£275–£420
Holne Chase Hotel	★★★★	★★★★	★★★★	£95–£130
Royal Clarence Hotel	★★★★	★★★	★★★★	£105–£130
Parford Well	★★★	★★★★	★★★★	£50–£60
St. Olaves Hotel	★★★	★★★½	★★★	£95–£115
Fowey				
Fowey Hall	★★★★½	★★★	★★★★	£135–£150
Marina Hotel	★★★★	★★★	★★★★	£60–£120

provide comfortable accommodations in the main house and in the former stables, where two-level units have been fitted out with sitting rooms on the ground floor and bedrooms upstairs. The hotel is an excellent base for long walks in Dartmoor National Park, and fly-fishing is available outside the front door in the renowned waters of the River Dart, which runs through the grounds. The dining room serves fish from local waters, meat reared on nearby farms, and produce from the hotel gardens, which also keep the guest rooms supplied with fresh flowers in season.

Parford Well — *£50–£60*

OVERALL ★★★ | QUALITY ★★★★ | VALUE ★★★★

Sandy Park, Devon TQ13 8JW; (01647) 433-353

Location Near the village of Chagford, about 20 miles from Exeter.

Amenities & Services Three rooms, two with adjoining baths and one with a private bath across the hall. Pleasant lounge and garden.

Elevator No.

Parking Yes.

Pricing Includes full breakfast.

Credit Cards Not accepted.

Number Sixteen is one of our favorite hotels in London, so it's not too surprising that this small bed-and-breakfast is the creation of former owner and manager Tim Daniel. Here in his native Devon, Tim has created a stylish and secluded retreat in a well-tended garden that is within easy reach of the outdoor pleasures of Dartmoor National Park. The bedrooms, dining room (where an enormous breakfast is served), and guest rooms are delightfully and comfortably furnished, and Tim is a font of knowledge about the region.

Royal Clarence Hotel — *£105–£130*

OVERALL ★★★★ | QUALITY ★★★ | VALUE ★★★★

Cathedral Yard, Exeter, Devon EX1 1HD; (01392) 319-955; fax (01392) 439-423; marina.hotel@dial.pipex.com; www.regalhotels.co.uk/royalclarence

IN THE SOUTHWEST OF ENGLAND

Hotel	Overall Rating	Quality Rating	Value Rating	Price
St. Ives				
The Abbey Hotel	★★★★½	★★★★	★★★★	£85–£100
The Pedn-olva Hotel	★★★★	★★★½	★★★	£65–£110
The Garrack Hotel	★★★	★★★	★★★	£53–£106
Primrose Valley Hotel	★★½	★★½	★★★★	£35–£59

Location Across from St. Peter's Cathedral.

Amenities & Services 56 rooms. Michael Caines Restaurant, St Martins Cafe Bar, Well House Pub.

Elevator Yes.

Parking No; it's necessary to use nearby car parks.

Pricing Includes full breakfast; special dinner, bed, and breakfast rates including a meal in the excellent Michael Caines Restaurant are available, as are other discount packages.

Credit Cards V, MC, D, AMEX

The Clarence has been the preferred hotel in town since the 18th century and has hosted any number of royals and other dignitaries. This well-run hotel carries on its pedigree with some degree of modesty: The atmosphere is relaxed and comfortable, the high-ceilinged guest rooms are nicely but not grandly furnished in handsome old pieces, and the main asset—stunning views over the cathedral, which is quite a spectacle when it's floodlit at night—is the same now as it has been for centuries. Insist on a front room facing the cathedral (and book at the St. Olaves Hotel, below, if one isn't available), because enjoying this view is what staying at the Clarence is all about. Another tip: When booking, ask if the hotel is hosting a function the night of your stay—the function room is uncomfortably close to the guest rooms, and the merrymaking will probably keep you awake until the party breaks up.

St. Olaves Hotel *£95–£115*

OVERALL ★★★ | QUALITY ★★★½ | VALUE ★★★

Mary Arches Street, Exeter, Devon EX4 3AZ; (01392) 217-736; fax (01392) 413-054; info@olaves.co.uk; www.olaves.co.uk

Location Near the historic center of Exeter.

Amenities & Services 17 rooms. Restaurant, bar, walled garden, comfortable lounge.

Elevator No.

Parking Yes.

HOW ATTRACTIONS COMPARE

Attraction	Comments	Author's Rating
Exeter		
St. Peter's Cathedral	Historic cathedral	★★★★
Chagford		
Buckland Abbey	Former abbey buildings and home of Sir Francis Drake	★★★
Cotehele	Medieval house and gardens	★★★
Castle Drogo	20th-century castle designed by Edward Lutyens	★★
Fowey		
Eden Project	Educational garden and biospheres	★★★★
The Lost Gardens of Heligan	Magnificently restored Cornish garden	★★★★
Trelissick	Woodland garden	★★★

Pricing Includes Continental breakfast.
Credit Cards V, MC, AMEX

St. Olaves is a bona-fide find—a Georgian manor house tucked away in a walled garden in the center of busy Exeter. Guest rooms, reached via a stunning spiral staircase, are individually and a tad sedately decorated with reproduction antiques and traditional pieces and sporting prints, while the baths are contemporary and equipped with tub and shower combinations. Service, like the surroundings, is first-rate without being overbearing. The hotel sometimes offers dinner, bed, and breakfast packages on its website, and you should consider them. The dining room is excellent (see profile in "Restaurants in Exeter," below) and the St. Olaves is such a pleasant oasis that you may want to settle in and never leave the grounds.

Exploring Exeter

Exeter's ancient **St. Peter's Cathedral** lies at the heart of the old city, its massive 12th-century towers rising from a diamond-shaped green surrounded by picturesque houses and bow-fronted shops. In one of them, **Mol's Coffee House,** Sir Francis Drake met with his admirals in 1588 to plan his attack on the Spanish Armada; the half-timbered, 16th-century building, now a shop, acquired its "coffee house" appellation in the 18th century when it became a club serving the newly introduced beverage.

Sir Francis was also reportedly a regular at the **Ship Inn** (see profile in "Restaurants in Exeter," below) on Martins Lane, a narrow medieval street that leads to High Street. A remnant of old Exeter remains on this otherwise modern shopping boulevard, the 14th-century **Guildhall,** the oldest municipal building in England and for centuries the mayor's office, town prison, and center of ceremonial life. When the Guildhall is not being

IN THE SOUTHWEST OF ENGLAND

Attraction	Comments	Author's Rating
Bocastle and Tintagel		
Tintagel Castle	Cliffside ruins associated with King Arthur	★★★
St. Ives		
Barbara Hepworth Museum and Sculpture Garden	Home of sculptor Dame Barbara Hepworth	★★★★
Tate St. Ives	Contemporary British art museum	★★
The Penwith Peninsula		
St. Michael's Mount	Island castle in Mount's Bay	★★★★
Land's End	Point of land at end of England	★★★

used for city council meetings and other civic functions, it is often open to free visits by the public (Monday–Saturday, usually 10:30 a.m.–4 p.m.). You can also see a slice of medieval Exeter by descending beneath the street into the **Underground Passages,** dug in the 14th century to bring fresh water into the city. The passages can be visited on 45-minute guided tours, providing a rare look at the workings of a medieval city; tours are led June–September: Monday–Saturday, 10 a.m.–5 p.m.; October–May: Tuesday–Friday, noon–5 p.m., and Saturday, 10 a.m.–5 p.m.. Admission July and August, £3.75 adults, £2.75 seniors and children, £11 families; September–June, £3 adults, £2 seniors and children, £8 families.

The **Royal Albert Memorial Museum and Art Gallery,** an elaborate Victorian edifice north of High Street on Queen Street, houses artifacts from Exeter's Roman past, as well as a couple of other collections—one of historic timepieces, another of totem poles and other artifacts that Thomas Cook brought back from his voyages—that make it well worth your time to step in for an hour or so. Admission is free, and the museum is open Monday–Saturday, 10 a.m.–5 p.m.

In the Middle Ages, Exeter's quays on the River Exe bustled with the wool trade, and the waterfront remained active well into the 20th century. In recent years, a cluster of 18th- and 19th-century warehouses and some earlier buildings have been converted into shops, restaurants, and pubs, though **Quayside** is still not the lively quarter it once was. The **Quayside Visitor Centre** (46 The Quay; (01392) 265-213) houses exhibits showing life on the quays in days gone by, as well as "A Celebration of Exeter," a fine video presentation on the history of the city.

Admission to the center and the video showings are free, and the center is open April–October: daily, 10 a.m.–5 p.m.; and November–March: Saturday and Sunday, 11 a.m.–4 p.m.

Tours of Exeter

You'll better appreciate the city's ancient history and architecture by taking one of the free guided walking tours that start at 10:30 a.m., 11 a.m., 2 p.m., and 2:30 p.m. from April to October; and at 11 a.m. and 2 p.m., with a 7 p.m. walk on Tuesday, from November to March. Most tours begin outside the Royal Clarence Hotel in Cathedral Yard, last about 90 minutes, and focus on a different aspect of the city, such as Roman and medieval remains, the cathedral, and the quay. No advance booking is necessary; just show up at the appointed place and meet the **Red Coat Guide.** For more information, check with the **Exeter Tourist Information Centre** (in the Civic Centre; (01392) 265-203; **www.exeter.gov.uk**).

Attractions in Exeter

St. Peter's Cathedral

Type of Attraction Historic cathedral

Location 1 The Cloisters

Admission £2 (suggested donation)

Hours Monday–Friday, 7:30 a.m.–6:15 p.m.; Saturday, 7:30 a.m.–5 p.m.; Sunday, 8 a.m.–7:30 p.m.

Phone (01392) 255-573

Website www.exeter-cathedral.org.uk

When to Go Anytime

Special Comments For a memorable experience, attend a service with choir accompaniment or one of the concerts the cathedral hosts throughout the year, when the grand edifice is filled with music; the website lists daily sung services and the year-round concert schedule, as does the notice board outside the cathedral. Evensong is at 3 or 5:30 p.m.

Overall Appeal by Age Group

Preschool ★	Teens ★★★	Over 30 ★★★★
Grade school ★★★	Young Adults ★★★	Seniors ★★★★

Author's Rating ★★★★

How Much Time to Allow About 30 minutes

Description & Comments The transept towers of this mighty edifice are Norman, constructed in the 12th century, but most of the cathedral church as it exists today was erected in the 13th and 14th centuries. Constructed of gray-white Beer stone, the cathedral rises from the green amidst a showy splendor of buttresses, flying buttresses, and massive windows with tracery. Before entering, take some time to view the remarkable West Front, decorated with three rows of sculpted saints and kings—the largest array of 14th-century sculpture in England. In the nave, rows of elegant columns support the longest fan-vaulted ceiling in the world. Stretching some 300 feet, it is punctuated by brightly colored and gilded bosses.

Some original 14th-century glass still glows in the great east window (the giant rose window on the west contains 20th-century glass), and the cathedral is decorated throughout with remarkable carvings. The minstrels' gallery is carved with angels playing ancient instruments, and the cathedral claims the country's oldest complete set of misericords, carved in 1260–1280, and a 14th-century bishop's throne carved from oak. A famous 15th-century astronomical clock showing the sun and moon revolving around the earth graces the north transept.

Touring Tips Bring a pair of field glass for a close look at the carvings inside and outside the church.

Dining in Exeter

To enjoy a full Devon cream tea, with great quantities of clotted cream and homemade jams to spread on fresh-baked scones, step into **Tilly's Tea Parlour** (48 Sidwell Street, (01392) 213-633); open daily, 9 a.m.–5:30 p.m.

Restaurants in Exeter

Michael Caines at the Royal Clarence ★★★★

MODERN BRITISH | EXPENSIVE | QUALITY ★★★★ | VALUE ★★★★

Cathedral Yard, Exeter; (01392) 310-031

Reservations Essential **Entrée Range** £16.25–£22.50; 2-course prix fixe lunch, £16.5; £19.50 for 3 courses **Payment** V, MC, AMEX **Bar** Full service **Disabled Access** Yes

Hours Daily, noon–2:30 p.m., 7–10 p.m.

House Specialties Fresh fish; lamb and game dishes.

Michael Caines is one of Britain's leading chefs, and after training with such internationally known culinary stars as Raymond Blanc and Joel Robuchon, he took over the restaurant at Gidleigh Park Hotel. He has now opened this popular ground-floor restaurant across from the cathedral in the Royal Clarence Hotel, where the fairly priced meals, like the wood-floored room where they are served, are chic and elegant. The menu changes daily to reflect what's available locally, but it always includes fresh fish and shellfish and West Country cheeses. Children are welcome in the restaurant, and diners ages 5–12 are introduced to haute cuisine with a special three-course £6 menu.

St. Olaves Hotel Dining Room ★★★

BRITISH | MODERATE | QUALITY ★★★ | VALUE ★★★

Mary Arches Street; (01392) 217-736

Reservations Recommended **Entrée Range** £10.50–£15; prix fixe, £23 **Payment** V, MC, AMEX **Bar** Full service **Disabled Access** Yes

Hours Daily, noon–2 p.m., 7–10 p.m.

House Specialties Grilled lamb chops; braised duck leg; other traditional British favorites.

The dining room of this small town-house hotel is as intimate as the rest of the surroundings. Though the food and the décor are traditionally British, with old paintings and mirrors on the walls, the atmosphere is quite relaxed—especially in

HOW RESTAURANTS COMPARE

Name	Cuisine	Overall	Quality	Value	Price
Exeter					
Michael Caines at the Royal Clarence	British	★★★★	★★★★	★★★★	Exp
St. Olaves Hotel Dining Room	British	★★★	★★★	★★★	Mod
Ship Inn	Pub	★★★	★★	★★★	Inexp
Chagford					
Ring O'Bells	Pub	★★★	★★★	★★★	Inexp

good weather, when you can dine in the walled garden. St. Olaves serves a light lunch menu, and at dinner, several of the salads and other starters are also available as entrées.

Ship Inn ★★★

PUB | INEXPENSIVE | QUALITY ★★ | VALUE ★★★

Martins Lane, Exeter; (01392) 272-040

Reservations Not necessary **Entrée Range** £5.75–£6.95 **Payment** V, MC, AMEX **Bar** Full service **Disabled Access** Downstairs only

Hours Daily, 11 a.m.–11 p.m.

House Specialties Sandwiches; meat pies; other basic pub fare.

Sir Walter Raleigh allegedly used to quaff ale in this heavily beamed and timbered pub only steps from the cathedral, and on weekend evenings a sizable portion of the citizenry of Exeter follows in his footsteps. The selections of ales and ciders is mind-boggling. A paneled upstairs room serves grilled fish, chicken curries, and other dishes that are a bit more ambitious than the typical pub fare available downstairs, and the smoke and noise levels are considerably lower.

Entertainment and Nightlife in Exeter

Exeter's main entertainment venue is the **Northcott Theatre** (city center noth, Stooker Road; (01392) 493-493; **www.northcott-theatre.co.uk**) which stages productions by its own company and hosts traveling troupes as well. You can also join what seems to be a good portion of the citizenry in a pub crawl. One of the most popular spots is the well-historied **Ship Inn,** around the corner from the cathedral on Martins Lane (see "Restaurants in Exeter," above). An unusually pleasant pub is the **Imperial** (near St. Davids Station on Tiverton Road; (01392) 434-050), occupying a 19th-century house. There's enough of a regal air about the place to keep the crowd well mannered, the selection of ale and pub fare is good, and the surrounding gardens offer plenty of outdoor seating in good weather.

IN THE SOUTHWEST OF ENGLAND

Name	Cuisine	Overall	Quality	Value	Price
Fowey					
The Old Ferry	Pub	★★★	★★★	★★★	Inexp
The Waterside	Seafood	★★★	★★★	★★★	Exp
St. Ives					
The Abbey Restaurant	British	★★★★	★★★★	★★★	Mod
Russets	British/ Seafood	★★★	★★★	★★★	Mod
Caffé Pasta	Pizza/Italian	★★½	★★	★★★	Inexp
Seafood Café	Seafood	★★	★★★	★★★	Mod

Shopping in Exeter

Exeter was once well known for its silversmiths, and examples of their work, identifiable by the three castles on the assay mark, can still be found. One place to look is the **Quay Gallery Antiques Emporium** (43 The Quay; (01392) 213-283), where you might come across some antique silver among the collectibles sold by dealers; if none is available at the time of your visit, they can tell you where to look. The market is open daily, 10 a.m.–5 p.m.

Around Exeter

Dartmoor

The eastern boundary of **Dartmoor National Park,** some 368 square miles of distinctive gorse- and heather-covered moorland, begins just 13 miles west of Exeter. This protected area, with its brooding rocky outcroppings (called tors) and rushing streams, is one of the last unspoiled landscapes in England. The park is not a vast empty wilderness: land in the park, surprisingly enough, is privately owned, though it is crisscrossed with public footpaths much loved by walkers, and working farms and villages are scattered throughout. From Exeter, the quickest route into Dartmoor is the B3212. A car will make it much easier to explore Dartmoor; if you are without one, contact Transmoor Link (phone (01392) 382-800) about bus service to Chagford or one of the other villages in the park.

Dartmoor has its own windswept beauty, but the landscape is not exactly what you would call hospitable. There's a good reason Sir Arthur Conan Doyle set his chilling tale *The Hound of the Baskervilles* in Dartmoor. The park is something of a time capsule, loaded with more prehistoric stone circles, stone rows, and stone burial monuments than anywhere else in Europe. It's believed that people began clearing the land at Dartmoor some 10,000 years ago, and most of the stone remains here date from the Bronze Age, 2,500–600 B.C. These include some 5,000 houses and huts, 1,500 burial mounds (known as cairns), 70 stone rows, and 18 stone circles. Some of the most impressive stone formations are on **Long Ash Hill,** near the village of **Merivale.**

If you want to explore the park on foot, make sure you have a detailed area map and appropriate clothing, and load up with information from one of the park's visitor centers. The main one is **High Moorland Visitor Centre** (Tavistock Road, Yelverton, open daily, 10 a.m.–5 p.m. in summer, 10 a.m.–4 p.m. in winter). An excellent way to see the park is on one of the guided walks the centers lead to areas of interest throughout the year; walks are geared to the fitness level of slow walkers, last from two to eight hours, and cost £3–£5 adults (depending on the length of the walk), £1 children under age 15. For more information on the park and the walks, call (01822) 890-414 or visit **www.dartmoor-npa.gov.uk;** the website has a full schedule of upcoming walks.

Chagford

The cozy town of Chagford makes a good base for touring Dartmoor, and it is near three fascinating historic properties: **Buckland Abbey, Castle Drogo,** and **Cotehele.**

Buckland Abbey

Type of Attraction Former abbey buildings that became the home of Sir Francis Drake

Location 3 miles west of Yelverton, off A386, just south of the High Moorland Visitor Centre in Dartmoor National Park

Admission £4.70 adults; £2.35 children ages 5–15; £11.70 families of up to two adults and two children; £2.50 for grounds only

Hours March 23–November 4: Friday–Wednesday, 10:30 a.m.–5:30 p.m.; November 5–December 23, February 16–March 22: Saturday and Sunday, 2–5 p.m. (last admission 45 minutes before closing)

Phone (01822) 853-607

Website www.nationaltrust.org.uk

When to Go The house and grounds are pleasantly uncrowded on weekdays.

Special Comments Some of the grounds and the ground floor of the house are accessible to visitors in wheelchairs. Crafts shops and a tearoom have been set up in some of the old farm buildings.

Overall Appeal by Age Group

Preschool ★	Teens ★★	Over 30 ★★★
Grade school ★★	Young Adults ★★	Seniors ★★★

Author's Rating ★★★

How Much Time to Allow 1–2 hours

Description & Comments Beautifully situated in a secluded river valley, Buckland Abbey began life in the 13th century as a Cistercian monastery. The enormous stone-built tithe barn, which you pass through on your way to the house, is a remnant from the days when local farmers were expected to donate a portion of their crops to the Church. The navigator Sir Richard Grenville purchased the property in the 16th century, after the abbey was dissolved by Henry VIII, and turned it into a residence. Sir Francis Drake, the great Elizabethan mariner who circumnavigated the globe, bought Buckland Abbey in 1581. The manor house, which still retains some architectural features from its days as an abbey, is filled with memorabilia pertaining to its two seafaring owners. Old crops have been replanted in some of the abbey gardens; there is also an herb garden and an Elizabethan garden.

Touring Tips If you have the time, stroll along one of the many paths winding through the lovely, secluded grounds and woodlands that surround the manor.

Castle Drogo

Type of Attraction 20th-century castle designed by Edward Lutyens

Location 4 miles northeast of Chagford, or 5 miles south of A30 (Exeter–Okehampton Road) via Crockenwell

Admission Castle and grounds: £5.90 adults; £2.90 children; £14.70 families of two adults and two children; grounds only: £3 adults; £1.50 children

Hours March 23–November 3: Wednesday–Monday, 11 a.m.–5:30 p.m. Garden and grounds: year-round, daily, 10:30 a.m.–dusk.

Phone (01647) 433-306

Website www.nationaltrust.org.uk

When to Go On weekdays, when the house and grounds are rarely crowded

Special Comments Much of the house is accessible to visitors in wheelchairs. There is a restaurant in the castle and a tearoom and gift shop at the entrance to the grounds.

Overall Appeal by Age Group

Preschool ★	Teens ★★	Over 30 ★★★
Grade school ★★	Young Adults ★★	Seniors ★★★

Author's Rating ★★

How Much Time to Allow About 1 hour

Description & Comments This massive, medieval-looking granite structure is actually less than a century old. The last private castle to be built in England, it was constructed between 1910 and 1930 for Julius Drewe, who obviously wanted to show off his self-made grocery fortune. His choice of Sir Edwin Lutyens, one of Britain's leading 20th-century architects, to design the castle lends a certain cachet and probably saves the ostentatious property from becoming more ridiculous than it already is. Lutyens basically gave his client what he wanted: a medieval fantasy with all the comforts of 20th-century living, including elaborate bathrooms, a "modern" kitchen, and elegant living rooms. As long as you think of Castle Drogo for what it is, a white elephant from the days of early-20th-century high life, you'll enjoy the place enormously.

Touring Tips Take some time to stroll in the gardens. The castle squats on a cliff above the Teign River and commands dramatic views of Dartmoor.

Cotehele

Type of Attraction Medieval house surrounded by gardens

Location Calstock, 8 miles southwest of Tavistock, a village at the western edge of Dartmoor National Park

Admission £6.40 adults; £16 families of up to two adults and two children. Garden and mill only: £3.60 adults; £9 families of up to two adults and two children.

Hours March 23–September 30: Saturday–Thursday, 11 a.m.–5 p.m.; October–November 3: Saturday–Thursday, 11 a.m.–4:30 p.m.; gardens: year-round, daily, 10:30 a.m.–dusk

Phone (01579) 351-346

Website www.nationaltrust.org.uk

When to Go There is no electric lighting in the house, so visitors should avoid dark days early and late in the season.

Special Comments The number of visitors in the fragile house is limited to a maximum of 80 at a time and not more than 600 in one day; only the ground floor of the house is accessible to visitors in wheelchairs.

Overall Appeal by Age Group

Preschool ★	Teens ★★★	Over 30 ★★★
Grade school ★★	Young Adults ★★	Seniors ★★★★

Author's Rating ★★★

How Much Time to Allow At least half a day if you want to visit the house, mill, and quay and walk on the property

Description & Comments This granite manor house, built between 1485 and 1627 and home of the Edgcumbe family for centuries, evokes the comfortable life that a privileged few led in the late medieval period. You get a wonderful sense of what life in this remote spot might once have been like: Many of the rooms are decorated with the original, centuries-old furniture and tapestries, and the restored formal gardens overlooking the valley below are intimate and romantic, with a medieval dovecote. The property also includes a working water mill tucked away in dense woodland, as well as a quay on the River Tamar where a sailing barge, the *Shamrock*, is moored.

Touring Tips A network of footpaths laced throughout the estate provides a variety of riverside and woodland walks. There is a restaurant and an art gallery at the quay.

Restaurants in Chagford

Ring O'Bells ★★★

PUB | INEXPENSIVE | QUALITY ★★★ | VALUE ★★★

Just outside of village off A382, Chagford ; (01647) 432-466

Reservations Not necessary **Entrée Range** £5.95–£13 **Payment** V, MC **Bar** Full service **Disabled Access** Yes

Hours Monday–Saturday, 11 a.m.–3 p.m., 5–11 p.m.; Sunday, noon–3 p.m., 6–10:30 p.m.

House Specialties Soups; meat pies; roasts.

This cozy, paneled pub is the perfect place for a Sunday country-pub lunch, a pint or two, or a sandwich after a walk on the surrounding moors. The homemade soups, salads, and other fare are excellent and served in generous proportions, and some of the specials, such as the roast Dartmoor lamb, elevate the Ring to one the region's better places to dine.

Fowey

The attractive town of Fowey (pronounced "Foy"), in the middle of the south coast of Cornwall, stretches for a mile or so along the Fowey River to its mouth in St. Austell Bay. Fowey is well known to yachters, who berth thousands of boats in the town's harbor during the summer, and to fans of the 20th-century novelist Dame Daphne du Maurier, who spent much of her life here and wrote her famous novels from several houses in and around the town. Fowey also holds a special place in the hearts of gardeners and garden lovers: The mild maritime climate favors gardens and greenery, and Fowey is surrounded by some of England's most magnificent plantings and manmade landscapes.

Planning Your Visit to Fowey

The **Fowey Tourist Information Centre** (4 Custom House Hill; (01726) 833-616; **www.fowey.co.uk**) provides information on all of central Cornwall, including places to stay, what to see and do, where to dine and shop, and how to get around. The center is open May and September: Monday–Friday, 9 a.m.–5:30 p.m., and Saturday, 9 a.m.–1 p.m.

Special Events in Fowey

Fowey celebrates one of its most famous citizens with the annual **Daphne du Maurier Festival of Arts and Literature,** which includes a roster of guided walks, boat trips, theatrical performances, readings, and other events that celebrate the author's works as well as the history and charm of Fowey. For information, call (01726) 223-535 or visit **www.fowey.co.uk.**

Arriving and Getting Oriented in Fowey

Trains run about every hour throughout the day to St. Austell, the closest station to Fowey, from London's Paddington Station. The trip takes about four to four and a half hours, depending on whether or not it's necessary to change trains in Exeter, and the fare is about £60 round trip. Call (08457) 4849-50 or go to **www.railtrack.co.uk.** St. Austell is about three miles west of Fowey; you can reach Fowey on the number 24 bus or take a taxi from the station.

By car, the quickest route from London to Fowey is the M4 to Bristol, then the M5 to Exeter and the A30 to the A391, which drops south to St. Austell and Fowey. The trip takes at least four and a half hours, and often longer at peak travel times in the summer and on weekends, when traffic on the A30 can become quite heavy. Driving and parking are severely restricted in Fowey; when you reach town, leave your car at one of the car parks on the outskirts of town or use the facilities the hotels provide.

National Express buses run from London's Victoria Coach Station to St. Austell, leaving about every hour and a half or so. The journey takes at least six and a half hours and often ten hours, so the train is a much better option. The round trip costs £30 to £40, depending on day of travel; call (08705) 808-080 or visit **www.gobycoach.com.**

If you wish to avoid traffic and the long journey, you can get to Plymouth or Newquay by air from London Gatwick on **Brymon Airlines** and drive or take the train from there to Fowey. One-way fares begin at £28 but vary considerably with time and day of travel; for more information, call (0845) 773-3377 or visit **www.ba.com.**

Hotels in Fowey

Fowey Hall — *£135–£150*

OVERALL ★★★★½ | QUALITY ★★★ | VALUE ★★★★

Fowey, Cornwall PL23 1ET; (01726) 833-866; fax (01726) 834-100; info@foweyhall.com; www.foweyhall.com

Location On a hill above the town and harbor.

Amenities & Services 24 rooms. Two dining rooms; beautiful drawing room and lounges; extensive lawns, gardens, and terraces; indoor swimming pool, badminton, croquet, children's game room and play area, free nursery, baby monitoring devices, baby-sitting, free use of bicycles; complimentary fresh fruit, cookies, and mineral water.

Elevator No.

Parking On the premises.

Pricing Includes full breakfast and one other meal a day, lunch or dinner, on stays of two or more nights; special rates for connecting family rooms.

Credit Cards V, MC, AMEX

You'll feel like a guest at an easygoing country-house party the moment you walk into the grand entrance hall of this 19th-century mansion, now a character-filled member of the Luxury Family Hotels chain. The paneling, fireplaces, antiques, and other trappings combine with a casual atmosphere to suggest that a stay here will be a great deal of fun—all the more so if you have children in tow, for whom the hotel caters with games, a nursery, and special meals. Rooms vary in size and outlook, and many cost considerably more than the rates quoted above, which vary with season and the type of accommodation (almost half are suites, and others can be connected for families). All of the rooms are handsomely decorated with comfy old furnishings that seem like they belong in a family manor house (which Fowey Hall is, after all) and have large, well-equipped baths. Eight coach-house rooms are perfectly pleasant but don't afford the sweeping views of those at the front of the main house. While all of the accommodations are attractive and comfortable, you'll want to spend a lot of time in the appealing public rooms and on the delightful grounds.

Marina Hotel *£60–£120*

OVERALL ★★★★ | QUALITY ★★★ | VALUE ★★★★

The Esplanade, Fowey, Cornwall PL23 1HY; (01726) 833-315; fax (01726) 832-779; marina.hotel@dial.pipex.com; www.themarinahotel.co.uk

Location Near the center of town on the Fowey River.

Amenities & Services 12 rooms. Waterside Restaurant; several riverside terraces, comfortable lounge.

Elevator No.

Parking Yes, in nearby garage; £7.50 per day.

Pricing Includes full breakfast; dinner, room, and breakfast rates also available; rates vary with season.

Credit Cards V, MC, AMEX

The former summer home of the archbishop of Truro has been attractively transformed into this intimate, riverside hotel. Most of the bright, airy guest rooms overlook the harbor, and many have balconies perched above the busy waterway below. All are furnished differently and achieve a breezy, contemporary look; they are equipped with gleaming, new, white-tile baths. The hotel's Waterside restaurant (see "Restaurants in Fowey," below) is excellent, and a dinner, room, and breakfast package allows you to try chef Nick Fisher's seafood preparations at a very good price. If you need more space or want to settle into Fowey for a while, ask about the one- and two-bedroom apartments the hotel maintains in adjacent buildings.

Exploring Fowey

Most of old Fowey stretches along a riverside street, the Esplanade. Two of the oldest buildings are **St. Fimbarrus Church,** dedicated to St. Finnbar, who passed through Fowey in the sixth century, and the appropriately named **Old House of Fowey,** a medieval structure built in 1432. Across the river, and reached by municipal ferry, is the village of **Polruan,** where cottages climb the hillside from the riverbank.

Some of Fowey's greatest attractions are the gardens that flourish in the lush Cornish countryside surrounding the town. You can arrange with the **Tourist Information Centre** (4 Custom House Hill; (01726) 833-616; **www.fowey.co.uk**) to visit two of these gardens, the **Eden Project** and the **Lost Gardens of Heligan,** with a guide. The tour costs £10 per person for a half-day tour of one of the gardens, or £15 for a full-day tour of both gardens (includes transportation but not admission fees).

Tours in Fowey

A good way to appreciate this scenic town is on one of the two-hour guided walks that leave from the town quay on Tuesdays at 11 a.m. (April 1–October 31). Tickets can be purchased from the Tourist Information Centre (4 Custom House Hill; (01726) 833-616; **www.fowey.co.uk**) and cost £3 for adults and £1.50 for children.

Wind of the Willow cruises explore aspects of Fowey and its surroundings that inspired Kenneth Grahame, author of the classic *The Wind in the Willows.* The boat trips follow the river from Fowey to the village of Lerryn several times a month between Easter and the end of September; check with the Tourist Information Centre for dates and departure times, which depend on the tides. The trip takes two and a half hours and costs £8 for adults and £5 for children.

Attractions in Fowey

Eden Project

Type of Attraction Educational garden with huge biospheres

Location About 5 miles from Fowey outside St.Austell

Admission £9.80 adults; £7.50 seniors; £5 students; £4 children; £23 families of two adults and three children

Hours March 25–October 26: daily, 10 a.m.–6 p.m. (last entry 5 p.m.); October 27–March 24: daily, 10:30 a.m.–4:30 p.m. (last entry 3 p.m.)

Phone (01726) 811-911

Website www.edenproject.com

When to Go As early in the day as possible, to beat the lines

Special Comments Buying an advance ticket, available from most Tourist Information Centres in Cornwall and from many local hotels, allows you fast-track entry upon arrival. This is the best way to avoid what may otherwise be a very long wait to get in.

Overall Appeal by Age Group

Preschool ★★	Teens ★★★	Over 30 ★★★★
Grade school ★★★	Young Adults ★★★★	Seniors ★★★★

Author's Rating ★★★★

How Much Time to Allow 3–4 hours

Description & Comments Whether you call it a "Living Theater of Plants and People" or a "Global Garden of the 21st Century," the Eden Project will give you new insight into mankind's dependence on plants. This giant garden, built on the site of an exhausted Cornish clay pit, features two giant glass-roofed greenhouses (shown in the James Bond movie *Die Another Day*) called biomes. The Humid Tropics Biome is a rain forest under glass, filled with tropical plants found in products used every day. The Warm Temperate Biome is planted with species indigenous to South Africa and California, including orange and lemon trees and olive groves. Crescent-shaped terraces in the outdoor garden tell the story of plants that have changed the world. In a larger sense, given its setting, the Eden Project is an environmental experience that shows what can be done when people work with nature to heal damaged places.

Touring Tips Frequent bus service connects the Eden Project with the train station in St.Austell.

The Lost Gardens of Heligan

Type of Attraction Magnificently restored Cornish garden

Location About 10 miles from Fowey, outside St.Austell. From St.Austell take the

Mevagissey road (B3272) and follow brown tourist signs to "The Lost Gardens of Heligan."

Admission £6 adults; £5.50 seniors; £3 children ages 5–15; £17 families of up to two adults and three children

Hours April–October: daily, 10 a.m.–6 p.m. (last tickets 4:30 p.m.); November–March: daily, 10 a.m.–5 p.m. (last tickets 3:30 p.m.). Closed December 24–25.

Phone (01726) 845-100

Website www.heligan.com

When to Go Anytime, but the garden is at its most colorful April–July

Special Comments Most of the garden is accessible to visitors in wheelchairs.

Overall Appeal by Age Group

Preschool ★	Teens ★★	Over 30 ★★★★
Grade school ★★	Young Adults ★★★	Seniors ★★★★

Author's Rating ★★★★

How Much Time to Allow Half a day for dedicated gardenistas; otherwise 2–3 hours

Description & Comments This 1,000-acre garden, domain of the Tremayne family for 400 years, was rediscovered in 1991 after decades of neglect. Brambles and ivy had obliterated a superb garden that was one of the finest in Cornwall up until World War I. A decade of extensive restoration work has brought the "Lost Gardens" back to life, revealing the meticulous planting schemes of Victorian (and earlier) gardeners. The garden has four distinct sections. The Jungle, a subtropical valley planted with exotic specimens originally brought back by Victorian plant hunters, features bamboo tunnels, avenues of palms and tree ferns, and a banana plantation. Restored greenhouses in the Productive Gardens, once used to feed the Tremayne family, contain exotic fruits and old varieties of vegetables. New Zealand and Italian gardens are found in the romantic Pleasure Grounds, first laid out in the early 1800s; historic flowering shrubs bloom here for six months of the year. The Wider Estate contains lakes, wetlands, and old woodlands where the ancient arts of coppicing and charcoal burning are practiced.

Touring Tips A video presentation in the garden's visitors' center tells the fascinating story of how the lost gardens were rediscovered and restored.

Trelissick

Type of Attraction Woodland garden

Location About 20 miles southwest of Fowey in Feock, near Truro, on both sides of B3289 above King Harry Ferry

Admission £4.50 adults; £2.25 children ages 5–16; £11.25 families of up to two adults and three children

Hours February 16–November 3: Monday–Saturday, 10:30 a.m.–5:30 p.m.; Sunday, 12:30–5:30 p.m.

Phone (01872) 862-090

Website www.nationaltrust.org.uk

When to Go Anytime; the garden is at its best April–July

Special Comments The garden sponsors monthly walks as well as many events for children; call or visit the website for details and dates; the garden is accessible to visitors in wheelchairs.

Overall Appeal by Age Group

Preschool ★	Teens ★★	Over 30 ★★★★
Grade school ★★	Young Adults ★★	Seniors ★★★★

Author's Rating ★★★

How Much Time to Allow About 3–4 hours

Description & Comments This tranquil estate, set in 500 acres of park and farmland, is beautifully situated at the head of the Fal estuary with panoramic views down to Falmouth and the sea. The 25-acre garden is planted on many levels and renowned for its collection of hydrangeas, camellias, and rhododendrons that provide color throughout the year, making Trelissick especially appealing during spring blooming season. Beyond the garden, oak and beech woodlands stretch down to the river Fal, providing five miles of scenic riverside walks. The Visitor Centre, located in the Ladder Walk, contains an exhibition on Trelissick's development and history and provides access to a Georgian-era stable and tack room; there are an art and craft gallery, a shop, and two restaurants on the grounds.

Touring Tips A pleasant addition to a visit to the garden is a ride on the King Harry Ferry across the Fal River, providing extensive views of the estuary and woodlands surrounding it.

Restaurants in Fowey

The Old Ferry ★★★

PUB | INEXPENSIVE | QUALITY ★★★ | VALUE ★★★

Next to ferry slip in Boddinick; (01726) 870-237

Reservations Not necessary **Entrée Range** £2.75–£10 **Payment** V, MC, AMEX **Bar** Full service **Disabled Access** Yes

Hours Summer: Monday–Saturday, 11 a.m.–11 p.m.; Sunday, noon–2:30 p.m., 6:30–10:30 p.m. Winter: daily, noon–2:30 p.m., 6:30–10:30 p.m.

House Specialties Homemade savory pies; fish dishes.

A nautical theme prevails at this cozy pub, as well it might since it is right on the water, across the river from Fowey. Views from the terrace are especially nice, making the Old Ferry a good spot for lunch or a sunset drink in good weather; the daily specials often include fresh fish and seafood and are usually excellent.

The Waterside ★★★

SEAFOOD | EXPENSIVE | QUALITY ★★★ | VALUE ★★★

Abbey Street, Penzance; (01736) 330-680

Reservations Recommended **Entrée Range** £12.95–£39; prix fixe £32.50 **Payment** V, MC, AMEX **Bar** Full service **Disabled Access** No

Hours Daily, 7–10 p.m.

House Specialties Any of the shellfish or fish preparations.

Nick Fisher, formerly of the Lanseborough Hotel in London, has brought his considerable talents to Fowey and presents his preparations in the Marina Hotel's attractively casual dining room overlooking the river. In good weather, meals are served on a delightful waterside terrace. The prix fixe dinner menu is an excellent introduction to Mr. Fisher's cuisine.

Recreation and Sports in and around Fowey

Fowey is an excellent base for walks along the coast and in the countryside. A good way to explore Fowey and the neighboring village of Polruan is the **Hall Walk,** a circular route that follows both banks of the Fowey River estuary. The **Saint's Way** is a 30-mile path that traverses Cornwall from Fowey on the south shore to Padstow on the north shore and passes through many places associated with fifth- and sixth-century Celtic saints who walked the route on pilgrimages to Rome, Santiago de Compostela, and Jerusalem.

There are many beaches within easy reach of Fowey. **Readymoney Cove,** at the mouth of the River Fowey, is only a 20-minute walk from the town center. One of the most scenic beaches is **Polridmouth Cove** (pronounced "PRID-mouth") west of town and reached on the **Southwest Coast Path,** which follows most of the Cornish coast.

Around Fowey

Bocastle and Tintagel

About 35 miles north of Fowey off the A39 are two of the prettiest villages on the rugged north coast of Cornwall, **Bocastle** and **Tintagel.** The two are connected by a path atop the rocky seaside cliffs, providing what must be the most picturesque walk in Cornwall.

Bocastle is at the mouth of the River Valency, and the town's distinctive 13th-century stone and slate cottages are nestled around a tiny harbor beneath towering white cliffs. Tintagel (pronounced "tin-TAD-jell"), just a few miles south along the coast, is also graced with some distinctive medieval buildings. Among these is the stone-and-slate **Old Post Office,** a rare 14th-century manor house that was used as a post office in the Victorian era; many of the rooms are furnished with centuries-old oak furnishings. The building is open March 29–September 30: daily, 11 a.m.–5:30 p.m.; and October 1–November 2: daily, 11 a.m.–4 p.m. What brings most visitors to Tintagel, though, are the magnificent ruins said to be King Arthur's castle.

Tintagel Castle

Type of Attraction Cliffside ruins associated with King Arthur

Location Tintagel Head, half a mile from the village of Tintagel, off the A39 on the north coast of Cornwall

Admission £3 adults; £2.30 seniors; £1.50 children

Hours March 24–July 13: daily, 10 a.m.–6 p.m.; July 14–August 27: daily, 10 a.m.–7 p.m.; August 28–September 30: 10 a.m.–6 p.m.; October 1–31: daily, 10 a.m.–5 p.m.; November 1–March 23: daily, 10 a.m.–4 p.m.

Phone (01840) 770-328

Website www.english-heritage.org.uk

When to Go Not in inclement weather, when it seems like you might be blown off the island on which the ruins stand

Special Comments There is no parking at the site, so visitors must park in the village and walk about half a mile (there is a car service from the village to the site in summer). Due to the uneven pathway and rocky terrain, this site is not wheelchair accessible.

Overall Appeal by Age Group

Preschool ★	Teens ★★★	Over 30 ★★★
Grade school ★★★	Young Adults ★★★	Seniors ★★★

Author's Rating ★★★

How Much Time to Allow About 1 hour

Description & Comments Colorful legends about King Arthur have been fascinating romantics for the better part of a thousand years, and this seaside castle ruin on the rugged Cornish coast is one of many places in England that are identified with Arthurian legend. Many scholars believe that Arthur, if he existed at all, was of a mixed Roman and Celtic parentage, and he may have been a fifth-century chieftain who led his West Country comrades in their resistance against Saxon invaders. Such fanciful speculation aside, all that can be said with certainty is that in the Dark Ages there was a great warrior who had a fortress where the ruins of Tintagel Castle are today. The original fortress no longer exists, but archaeologists have found evidence that the site was inhabited during the sixth century. The replacement castle, built in the 13th century as a stronghold for the Earls of Cornwall, fell into ruins within 200 years. Today it is owned by the Duchy of Cornwall and managed by English Heritage. For more information about Tintagel and the castle, stop in first at the new Visitor Centre in the village center (phone (01840) 779-084). From there, you will make your way for half a mile along a beautiful coastal path to Tintagel Island, site of the ruins. The landscape, with Atlantic breakers crashing against the cliffs, is far more impressive than the meager remains of the castle, in which you can make out vague traces of the great hall and some other buildings. Bring your imagination, and you won't be disappointed.

Touring Tips The rocky cliffs around the castle provide breeding grounds for sea birds, lizards, and butterflies. To observe the surroundings and dip your toes in the icy Atlantic, climb down the path from the castle to the beach below.

St. Ives

On the Penwith Peninsula, Cornwall narrows and becomes little more than a narrow scrap of scrubby moors and rugged coastlines interspersed with snug harbors and tidy villages. The westernmost tip of the peninsula is known as **Land's End,** where, from the bottom of granite cliffs, the Atlantic stretches in an unbroken swath all the way to North America. **St. Ives,** perhaps the most appealing of all Cornish towns, is the best base from which to explore this fascinating peninsula at England's end.

Even summertime crowds can't rob St. Ives of its small-fishing-village charm, and the town remains a picturesque seaside resort of cobbled streets surrounding a pretty harbor. (According to the ages-old legends with which Cornwall is so well endowed, the town's name comes from St. Ia, an Irish Christian missionary of the fifth or sixth century who floated into these parts on a leaf.) Artists began discovering St. Ives more than a hundred years ago, and the town still maintains a foothold in the international art world with its two museums, the **Tate St. Ives** and the **Barbara Hepworth Museum.** For many visitors, however, St. Ives's main attractions are more prosaic: the long strands of golden sands that stretch to the east and west of the village.

Planning Your Visit to St. Ives

The **St. Ives Tourist Information Centre** (in center of town in the Guildhall; (01736) 796-297; **www.go-cornwall.com**) provides information on all of West Cornwall, including places to stay, what to see and do, where to dine and shop, and how to get around. Opening times are May and September: Monday–Saturday, 9 a.m.–6 p.m., and Sunday, 10 a.m.–2 p.m.; June 1–August 31: Monday–Saturday, 9 a.m.–6 p.m., and Sunday, 10 a.m.–4 p.m.; and October 1–April 30: Monday–Saturday, 9 a.m.–5 p.m.

Special Events in St. Ives

May Day festivities in St. Ives include maypole dancing at the harbor as well as a series of indoor and outdoor concerts. Throughout the summer, there is a **band concert on the West Pier** in St. Ives almost every evening. The nearby seaside village of **Mousehole** (see page 321) is ablaze with Christmas lights throughout December.

Arriving and Getting Oriented in St. Ives

By any means of transportation, it's a long haul out to the end of Cornwall. Trains run about every hour throughout the day to St. Ives and to Penzance from London's Paddington Station. The trip to St. Ives usually requires a change of train in the town of St. Erth, while the trip to Penzance does not usually require a change. The trip to St. Ives takes five to five and a half hours and the trip to Penzance takes four and a half to five hours; the fare is about £65 round trip. For information, call (08457) 484-950 or go to **www.railtrack.co.uk.** The St. Ives train station is at the edge of the village, just a short walk from the center; the Penzance train station is also centrally located on the harbor just outside the city center.

By car, the quickest route into the region from London is the M4 to Bristol, then the M5 to Exeter and the A30 to St. Ives or Penzance. The trip takes at least five hours, and often longer at peak travel times in the summer and on weekends, when the A30 can become quite jammed. Driving and parking in both St. Ives and Penzance is severely restricted. Most hotels provide car parking, or you can park in one of the many municipal car parks, which charge about 20 pence an hour.

National Express buses run from London's Victoria Coach Station to St. Ives and Penzance, leaving about every two hours or so. The journey is long, about eight to eight and a half hours, and is far slower than the train trip. The round trip costs £30 to £40, depending on day of travel; for more information, call (08705) 808-080 or visit **www.gobycoach.com.**

If you wish to avoid traffic and the long journey, you can get to Newquay or Plymouth by air from London Gatwick on Brymon Airlines and drive or take the train from there to St. Ives and the rest of the Penwith Peninsula. One-way fares begin at £28 but vary considerably with time and day of travel; for more information, call (0845) 773-3377 or visit **www.ba.com.**

Hotels in St. Ives

Rates vary considerably depending on season, and they are highest in July and August. Reservations are essential at those times, when most hotels are fully booked with vacationers. During the winter months, many hotels offer substantial discounts and bed, breakfast, and dinner packages to lure guests out to the far end of Cornwall.

The Abbey Hotel — *£85–£100*

OVERALL ★★★★½ | QUALITY ★★★★ | VALUE ★★★★

Abbey Street, Penzance, Cornwall TR18 4AR; (01736) 669-06; fax (01736) 511-63; glyn@abbeyhotel.fsnet.co.uk; www.abbey-hotel.co.uk

Location On a cobblestone street near the harbor.

Amenities & Services 7 rooms. Adjoining restaurant; beautiful drawing room and large garden, fireplaces in some rooms, laundry service.

Elevator No.

Parking On the premises.

Pricing Includes breakfast.

Credit Cards V, MC, AMEX

The one reason to stay in Penzance rather than in quieter, pretty St. Ives is this extraordinary small hotel in a 350-year-old house. Without fuss or show, the Abbey manages to provide an intimate atmosphere and a great deal of stylish comfort at a reasonable price. Public rooms and the large guest rooms are filled with well-chosen antiques, deep couches and armchairs, and fine old carpets. Guest rooms in the front of the house overlook Penzance Harbour, while those in the back face the garden of the medieval abbey built on the site in the 12th century; bathrooms have been updated but manage to maintain the old character of the rest of the house. Room 3 is especially commodious and pleasant and overlooks the harbor, and the two-bedroom suite, with a separate entrance onto the courtyard and garden, is an attractive base for families or groups exploring Cornwall. The Abbey is owned by the former model Jean Shrimpton, who, with husband Michael Cox, brings as much charm to the Cornwall hotel scene as she once did to the fashion pages.

The Garrack Hotel — *£53–£106*

OVERALL ★★★ | QUALITY ★★★ | VALUE ★★★

St. Ives, Cornwall, Burthallan Lane TR26 3AA; (01736) 796-199; fax (01736) 798-955; Garrack@accuk.co.uk; www.garrack.com

Location North of the village, on a hillside overlooking the sea.

Amenities & Services 18 rooms. Restaurant and comfortable lounges, heated indoor swimming pool, sauna, gym, sun terrace.

Elevator No.

Parking On the grounds.

Pricing Includes breakfast; discounts for stays of three or more nights, and good dinner, bed, and breakfast packages are available.

Credit Cards V, MC, AMEX

The Garrack comprises several buildings set among attractive gardens on a hillside above Porthmeor Beach, near the Tate and just west of the village. The hotel's excellent restaurant, comfortable lounges, and the most atmospheric guest rooms are in a vine-covered manor house; two rooms are in a separate cottage, and most are in a newer wing that, aside from attractive sea views, doesn't offer much more charm than a standard American motel. But ongoing renovations are sprucing up the premises, so if the hotel isn't full, ask to look around until you find a room that suits your tastes.

The Pedn-olva Hotel — *£65–£110*

OVERALL ★★★★ | QUALITY ★★★½ | VALUE ★★★

Porthminster Beach, St. Ives, Cornwall TR26 2EA; (01736) 796-222; fax (01736) 797-710; bookings@pednolva.freeserve.co.uk; www.walterhickshotels.co.uk

Location On a bluff above Porthminster Beach and St. Ives Harbour.

Amenities & Services 30 rooms. Lookout Restaurant and Bar; several terraces, heated outdoor swimming pool.

Elevator No.

Parking In car park at the nearby railway station, £3.

Pricing Includes breakfast; good dinner, bed, and breakfast packages also available.

Credit Cards V, MC

You might feel like you're in a ship at the Pedn-olva, where the snug rooms and lounges are perched over a rocky, wave-washed outcropping, and views extend out to sea and over sandy Porthminster Beach on one side and the village and harbor on the other. While most of the guest rooms (as well as their adjoining baths) carry out the shipboard motif by being small enough to be cabins, they are attractively furnished with rattan furniture and bright, handsome fabrics and face the sea through large plate-glass windows. Several have balconies, but the hotel terraces are so commodious that you won't feel at a loss without one (and may want to forgo the extra fee tacked on to the price of balcony rooms). The Lookout Bar is probably the most romantic place in St. Ives for a drink, which you can enjoy in front of a crackling fire to the sound of waves crashing on the rocks below.

Primrose Valley Hotel — *£35–£59*

OVERALL ★★½ | QUALITY ★★½ | VALUE ★★★★

Primrose Valley, St. Ives, Cornwall TR26 2ED; (01736) 794-939; fax (01736) 794-939; info@primroseonline.co.uk; www.primroseonline.co.uk

Location Across from Porthminster Beach, about a five-minute walk from town center.

Amenities & Services 9 rooms. Terrace facing the sea, homey lounge and bar area.

Elevator No.

Parking On grounds and in nearby lot, free.

Pricing Includes full breakfast.

Credit Cards V, MC, AMEX

Sue and Andrew Bliss took over the operation of this family-oriented bed-and-breakfast in 2001 and have been working hard to improve the property ever since. They've refurbished several of the rooms (equipping some for families with one double bed and bunk beds), added new baths, revamped and landscaped the terrace, and rebuilt wooden balconies off several of the front rooms. All the changes make the Primrose a comfortable base that is especially well-suited for travelers with children—the beach is just across a little-traveled street, and a landscaped pedestrian path leads into town. In bad weather, young guests are welcome to take over the comfortable lounge areas.

Exploring St. Ives

St. Ives is built around its harbor, which becomes a broad swathe of golden sand at low tide and is enclosed on the west by **West Pier** and on the east by **Smeaton's Pier.** The old fishing village that surrounds the harbor is known as **Downalong,** where narrow, cobbled streets are lined with small, distinctive, whitewashed granite cottages and houses. Rising above the town is the tower of quaintly beautiful **St. Ives Parish Church,** built in the 15th century.

Barbara Hepworth Museum and Sculpture Garden

Type of Attraction Studio, living quarters, and outdoor sculpture garden of famed sculptor Dame Barbara Hepworth

Location Barnoon Hill

Admission £3.95 adults; £2.25 seniors and children under 18; combined ticket with Tate St. Ives, £6.95

Hours March–October: daily, 10:30 a.m.–5:30 p.m.; November–February: Tuesday–Sunday, 10 a.m.–4:30 p.m.; closed December 24–26

Phone (01736) 796-226

Website www.tate.org.uk

When to Go On weekdays if possible to avoid weekend crowds

Special Comments The lower floor of the museum is not wheelchair accessible, and the upper floors are accessible only with prearranged assistance; space is limited in this small museum, and admission may be restricted during the summer season.

Overall Appeal by Age Group

Preschool ★	Teens ★★	Over 30 ★★★★
Grade school ★	Young Adults ★★	Seniors ★★★★

Author's Rating ★★★★

How Much Time to Allow About 30 minutes

Description & Comments Dame Barbara Hepworth (1903–1975), one of Britain's most important 20th-century artists, lived and worked in this intriguing stone house and studio in St. Ives from 1939 until her death in a fire. The house became the epicenter of British avant-garde abstract art, as other artists, including Ben Nicholson and Naum Gabo, settled in St. Ives. The coolly elegant and rather spartan living quarters on the first floor provide an unusually intimate view of Hepworth's life and work, and the adjacent garden is graced by a large collection of her sculptures. A small exhibit room on the ground floor is hung with text panels and photographs that nicely summarize Hepworth's life and work and the importance of St. Ives as an artists' colony.

Touring Tips After visiting the museum, you may want to walk around the corner to St. Ives Parish Church; a "Madonna and Child" that Dame Barbara carved for the church in memory of her son, Paul, killed in active service with the Royal Air Force over Thailand in 1953, is in the Lady Chapel. She also designed the stainless-steel "Christmas Rose" candlesticks that she presented to the church in 1972 and which are now in the Lady Chapel as well.

Tate St. Ives

Type of Attraction Contemporary art museum focusing on British artists

Location Porthmeor Beach

Admission £4.25 adults; £2.50 seniors and children under 18; combined ticket with Barbara Hepworth Museum and Sculpture Garden, £6.95.

Hours March–October: daily, 10 a.m.–5:30 p.m.; November–February: Tuesday–Sunday, 10 a.m.–4:30 p.m.; closed December 24–26 and for short periods throughout the year for gallery preparations

Phone (01736) 796-226

Website www.tate.org.uk

When to Go Anytime; the museum is most crowded during the summer, but is rarely jammed

Special Comments The flow of the museum galleries is not particularly well designed. Pick up a map at the ticket area to help you navigate.

Overall Appeal by Age Group

Preschool ★	Teens ★★★	Over 30 ★★★
Grade school ★★	Young Adults ★★★	Seniors ★★

Author's Rating ★★

How Much Time to Allow About 1 hour

Description & Comments Opened in 1993 to capitalize on St. Ives's century-plus reputation as an art colony, this stark-white and rather clumsily designed modernist building features artwork selected from the National Collection of British Modern Art. There are also exhibitions of works by major British artists and artists associated with St. Ives. Unfortunately, there is no permanent collection of works by the artists most identified with St. Ives (although chances are you will see a Ben Nicholson painting or two), so the St. Ives "connection" is at times tenuous. If you want to see the works of local artists, we suggest a stop at the Penlee House in Newlyn (see page 321). All of the exhibits in the museum change periodically, so it's best to come to Tate St. Ives with no preconceived notions about what you're going to see in the various galleries. On a walk-through, you are likely to encounter the latest video art and other work by top British artists.

Touring Tips The bookshop has an excellent collection of books on local artists; the airy, top-floor cafe provides sweeping views of the harbor and town.

Dining in St. Ives

In addition to these restaurants, we also suggest enjoying a meal or two at the historic pubs we recommend in "Entertainment and Nightlife in St. Ives," below.

The Abbey Restaurant ★★★★

INNOVATIVE BRITISH | MODERATE | QUALITY ★★★★ | VALUE ★★★

Abbey Street, Penzance; (01736) 330-680

Reservations Recommended **Entrée Range** £12.75–£16.50 **Payment** V, MC **Bar** Full service **Disabled Access** No

Hours Tuesday–Saturday, 7–9:30 p.m.; Friday and Saturday, noon–2 p.m.

House Specialties Seared scallops or lamb-kidney salad as starters, followed by any of the fish dishes.

Plan on enjoying at least one meal at this wonderful restaurant near Penzance Harbour and next to the Abbey Hotel (though the two are independent of one another, they stand out as two of the finest establishments for food and lodging in Cornwall). Downstairs is a sophisticated bar/lounge done in deep reds and purples. A curving staircase leads to a bright, airy dining room where wicker chairs and rattan carpets lend an air of casual sophistication to match the cuisine that chef Ben Tunnicliffe prepares from local, market-fresh fish, meat, and produce. Service is attentive and unhurried, and since there's only one sitting in an evening, guests are encouraged to linger and enjoy the lights twinkling in the harbor.

Caffé Pasta ★★½

PIZZA/ITALIAN | INEXPENSIVE | QUALITY ★★ | VALUE ★★★

The Wharf, St. Ives; (01736) 796-447

Reservations No necessary **Entrée Range** £4.95–£10.95 **Payment** V, MC **Bar** Full service **Disabled Access** Yes

Hours Daily, noon–3 p.m., 6–10 p.m. (coffee service starts at 10 a.m.)

House Specialties Pizza; fresh fish; seafood risotto.

A friendly, casual atmosphere prevails at this bright, attractive pizzeria/restaurant overlooking the sea. The pizza is delicious, and many of the other entrée choices, including fresh fish just off the boats and artfully prepared, are more elaborate than the setting suggests. Fresh-brewed Italian coffee is served from 10 a.m., making this a popular morning gathering spot.

Russets ★★★

BRITISH/SEAFOOD | MODERATE | QUALITY ★★★ | VALUE ★★★

18A Fore Street, St. Ives; (01736) 794-700

Reservations Recommended **Entrée Range** £9.95–£15.25 **Payment** V, MC, AMEX **Bar** Full service **Disabled Access** No

Hours Tuesday–Sunday, 7–10 p.m.

House Specialties Fresh seafood.

A good way to begin a meal at this popular restaurant in the center of town is to take a seat on one of the leather couches in the brick-walled lounge and enjoy a drink in front of the fire, then move into the airy dining room. This is an excellent place to try fresh local seafood, starting with grilled scallops or steamed mussels, then moving on to one of the many simple fish preparations.

Seafood Café ★★

SEAFOOD | MODERATE | QUALITY ★★★ | VALUE ★★★

45 Fore Street, St. Ives; (01736) 794-004

Reservations Recommended **Entrée Range** £7.50–£16 **Payment** V, MC, AMEX **Bar** Full service **Disabled Access** Yes

Hours Daily, noon–3 p.m., 6–10 p.m.

House Specialties Fresh fish.

This white-tile and chrome room looks like a fish market, and that's the point: Your meal will have been swimming in the cold waters off Cornwall just hours before. Choose your fish from one of the display cases, select a sauce and side dish, and take a seat at one of the blond-wood tables. Poultry, lamb, and beef from local farms are also available, and, like the seafood, they are about as fresh as you're ever going to find.

Entertainment and Nightlife in St. Ives

The region's most noted entertainment venue is the **Minack Theatre,** about 15 miles southwest of St. Ives in the village of Porthcurno, between Penzance and Land's End. The setting is as dramatic as the performances: The theater has been carved out of hillside overlooking the sea, and the backdrop is an ever-changing vista of waves crashing into the rocky coast. Touring companies from around the world perform at the Minack from May through September, presenting drama that ranges from Greek tragedy to Shakespeare to the latest comedies from the London stage. Plan on seeing at least one performance if you are in Cornwall during the Minack Theatre season, but book your tickets well in advance. For tickets and information, call (01736) 810-18 or visit **www.minack.com.**

A popular evening activity in these parts is to settle into one of the historic pubs that grace almost every town and village. In fact, ale quaffers can keep themselves quite busy making the rounds of pubs on the Penwith Peninsula. These establishments also serve light fare and full meals, and they are generally open seven days a week from 11 a.m. to 11 p.m., sometimes closing a bit earlier on Sundays. On the harbor in St. Ives, you can slip in for a slurp at the **Sloop** (phone (01736) 796-584). This darkly atmospheric and low-ceilinged pub claims to have been serving since 1312.

The **Turks Head** (phone (01736) 363093) claims to be the oldest pub in Penzance, and the building at 49 Chapel Street that now houses the busy, beamed bar dates from the 16th century; however, it's built over the remains of a 700-year-old inn destroyed during Spanish raids on the town. The rear garden is a pleasure on one of the sunny days that are common in this part of England. The **Ship,** on the harbor in Mousehole (phone (01736) 731234), is as delightful as the rest of the village and on the evening of your visit might be serving its famous "starry gazy pie," made from seven kinds of fish, whose heads and tails poke through the crust.

Exercise and Recreation in St. Ives

St. Ives is known for its excellent beaches. **Porthmeor Beach,** pounded by a raging sea that attracts surfers, lies on the western edge of town. The sea is usually a bit calmer at **Porthminster Beach,** on the eastern edge of town and popular with families. You can easily walk to either beach from the center of town.

St. Ives and many other towns and villages on the Penwith Peninsula are on the **Southwest Coast Path,** a 613-mile trail that skirts much of the Cornish coast. Coast-guard patrols once walked these footpaths looking for smugglers; today, the coastal route is an excellent place from which to observe sea life, rock formations, and unique flora and fauna. The Tourist Information Centre in St. Ives (in center of town in the Guildhall; (01736) 796-297; **www.go-cornwall.com**) provides information on the route and on other walks in the area.

Around St. Ives

The Penwith Peninsula

Generally treeless, the landscapes of the Penwith Peninsula dip and rise across open moors and pasturelands, and the narrow roads that traverse them offer frequent glimpses of the sea. Adding to the moody atmosphere of the landscape are the ancient Celtic crosses, reminders of the Irish missionaries who arrived here some 1,500 years ago, that still rise from the mossy churchyards; the sound of the sea crashing into the rocky shoreline is ever present.

You can explore the entire peninsula on a leisurely day's excursion, with fascinating stops along the way. From St. Ives, take the A3074 south to its junction with A30 and follow A30 west into **Penzance.** From there, the A30 continues west via **Mousehole** to **Land's End.** The B3306 winds back up the coast to St. Ives.

About three miles outside Penzance, signposts lead you to the Iron Age settlement of **Chysauster,** a village of eight stone courtyard houses inhabited from about 100 B.C. to A.D. 300. The members of the Dumnonii Tribe who lived here raised grain and livestock, and the remains of their lives—stone walls, ancient drains, grinding stones—are stirringly evocative. The site is open during daylight hours, and visitors are asked to donate £1.80 for upkeep.

Penzance, a little less then 10 miles south of St. Ives, is the largest town on the Penwith Peninsula and is a lively commercial hub (and in the eyes of Gilbert and Sullivan fans, forever associated with pirates). Spanish pirates, indeed, razed the town in the 16th century, and World War II bombings repeated the damage. While postwar development in Penzance has been uniformly uninspired, the town still enjoys a lovely view across Mount's Bay and the island castle of **St. Michael's Mount.** One of the few interesting lanes of the old town that remain intact is Chapel Street, which begins at the domed **Market House** and tumbles down to the harbor past lovely 17th- and 18th-century houses, including one called the **Egyptian House** because of its exotic, lavishly painted and ornamented facade. The tower of the church of **St. Mary the Virgin** marks the end of the street.

On its southern boundaries Penzance runs into **Newlyn,** a name you might recognize from restaurant menus, because the fleet bobbing in the port supplies much of the country with fresh fish. In the early 20th century, the town's stone cottages attracted artists who came to be known as the Newlyn School, and their works are on display in **Penlee House** (Penlee Park; (01736) 636-25), open May–September: Monday–Saturday, 10 a.m.– 5 p.m.; and October–April: Sunday, 10:30 a.m.–4:30 p.m. Admission is £2 adults and £1 seniors and students. More Newlyn heritage is on display at the **Pilchard Works Museum and Factory** (The Combe (near Newlyn Bridge); (01736) 332-112). Pilchards are sardines, and this still-working factory is the last to cure and tin what was once one of the region's major products. The museum is open Easter–October 31: Monday–Friday, 10 a.m.–6 p.m.; admission is free.

Mousehole (pronounced "MUZ-zle"), a few miles west of Newlyn, is one of the prettiest villages on the coast—a collection of stone cottages curving around the small harbor. The tiny village of **Porthcurno,** a few miles west of Mousehole, was once world famous, at least in some circles, as the home of the world's largest undersea cable system, and this claim to fame is celebrated in the **Museum of Submarine Telegraphy** (village center; (01736) 810-966). Contrary to what that somewhat dry-sounding name might suggest, the setting and displays are fascinating. A series of vast underground tunnels houses the equipment that, beginning in the 1860s, was used to transmit communications through 14 cables across the globe. The museum is open April–June and September–October: Sunday–Friday, 10 a.m.–5 p.m.; July–August: daily, 10 a.m.–5 p.m.; and November–March: Sunday and Monday, 10 a.m.–4 p.m. Admission is £4 adults, £3.50 seniors, £2.50 students and children, and £10 families of two adults and two children. A hillside above Porthcurno Bay is the setting for the dramatic **Minack Theatre,** an amphitheater carved out of stone that stages a full summer's season of drama (see page 319). The road and the peninsula come to an end at **Land's End,** the southwesternmost tip of England.

Land's End

Type of Attraction A point of land at the end of England

Location 12 miles west of Penzance at the end of the A30

Admission Free, unless you visit the theme park, which you should not do

Hours Open year-round, all day

Phone None

Website www.landsend-landmark.co.uk

When to Go During daylight hours

Special Comments Land's End is usually very windy and often wet, so wear appropriate clothing.

Overall Appeal by Age Group

Preschool ★	Teens ★★★	Over 30 ★★★
Grade school ★★★	Young Adults ★★★	Seniors ★★★

Author's Rating ★★★

How Much Time to Allow At least 30 minutes, but longer if you want to hike along the surrounding coast

Description & Comments The high cliffs and thundering seas at the southwesternmost tip of England form one of the country's best-loved and most historically significant landmarks. Indeed, according to a local saying, Land's End is to Cornwall what Jerusalem is to the Holy Land. For centuries, Land's End was the last glimpse explorers and emigrants had of England—and all known civilization. Unfortunately, the magnificent scenery of this hallowed headland has been shamelessly marred by the addition of a tacky theme park and "shopping village." You can't escape the commercial exploitation because you must pass through an outdoor shopping mall to reach the extraordinary sea views at Land's End. Once you are away from this disgraceful intrusion, however, the scenery is magnificent, and you can explore it on several well-maintained coastal paths. Except for the Scilly Islands, 28 miles out to sea, nothing stands between you and the "New World" but 3,000-plus miles of Atlantic Ocean.

Touring Tips Don't be tempted by the fast-food emporiums that you'll see among the commercial clutter—you can enjoy a meal or snack in far more authentic surroundings in any of the towns on the Penwith Peninsula.

St. Michael's Mount

Type of Attraction Island castle in Mount's Bay

Location Marazion, Mount's Bay, just east of Penzance on the A30

Admission £4.50 adults; £2.25 children ages 5-15; £12 families of up to two adults and two children

Hours April–October: Monday–Friday, 10:30 a.m.–5:30 p.m. (last admission at 4:45 p.m.); grounds open most weekends in summer; November–March: Monday, Wednesday, and Friday by conducted tour only at 11 a.m., noon, 2 p.m., and 3 p.m. (call to verify)

Phone (01736) 710-507

Website www.stmichaelsmount.co.uk

When to Go St. Michael's Mount is one of the most visited National Trust sites in England, so be prepared for crowds. Visiting the castle is easiest on weekdays April–October; if you are planning to visit on a weekend during that time, call to verify that the castle will be open.

Special Comments Access to the island is by foot on a causeway, or by ferry at high tide. For tide and ferry information, call (01736) 710-265. Wear sensible footwear because there are many stairs to climb. The island's two restaurants are open for lunch and afternoon tea April–October only.

Overall Appeal by Age Group

Preschool ★	Teens ★★★	Over 30 ★★★★
Grade school ★★★	Young Adults ★★★	Seniors ★★★★

Author's Rating ★★★★

How Much Time to Allow A minimum of 2 hours

Description & Comments Built on a rocky island that rises dramatically from Mount's Bay, this castle began life in the 12th century as a Benedictine priory, the daughter house of Mont St. Michel in Normandy. In the 16th and 17th centuries, the Mount was used as a fortress, then as a Royalist stronghold during the Civil War. For 300 years, it has been the home of the St. Aubyn family. It's a steep climb up to the West Door, which acts as the visitors' entrance. Today's entrance hall was used in the 16th and 17th centuries as living quarters by the Captain of the Mount. St. John's Room, a snug little chamber beside the entrance hall, is the private sitting room of the current owner. The Armoury contains a collection of weapons and war memorabilia. Though portions of the castle date from different periods, the effect is quite harmonious. In the oldest part of the castle, from the 12th century, there is a charming library and a dining hall that once served as the monks' refectory; the ornate Blue Drawing Room is from the 17th century. A church with lovely rose windows crowns the highest section of the castle, and nondenominational services are held there on some Sundays. The walled and terraced gardens are spectacular, but they can only be visited on special occasions; you may have to settle for viewing them from the castle windows or from one of the terraces. In fact, the castle's setting on its granite island remains its most alluring feature, and you will want to spend as much time outdoors admiring the views and the terrain as you do touring the interior.

Touring Tips Steep paths and many stairs may render the Mount inaccessible to elderly visitors and those with limited mobility. All visitors should wear sensible walking shoes.

Part Eight

Bath, Oxford, and the Cotswolds

West of the westernmost suburbs of London, the landscape begins to roll and rise through valleys and gentle uplands. Eventually the land rises into the **Cotswolds** hills, known simply as the Cotswolds—beautiful, unspoiled, and cradling villages of golden stone. This is a slice of rural England that you can't really say is too good to be true, because the Cotswolds are more or less the English countryside as we all expect it to be. As if the promise of these rural pleasures weren't enough to lure you to this part of England, at the edges of the Cotswolds are two of England's most beautiful and fascinating cities. To the south is **Bath,** founded by the Romans, a famous 18th- and 19th-century watering hole for high society, and now an architectural treasure trove. To the west is **Oxford,** center of one of the two greatest British universities and a lively and engaging city in its own right.

Not To Be Missed in Bath, Oxford, and the Cotswolds

The Royal Crescent (page 333)
Roman Baths Museum (page 339)
Oxford Colleges (page 352)
Bodleian Library (page 349)
Sheldonian Theatre (page 349)
Chipping Campden (page 368)
The Rollright Stones (page 368)
Blenheim Palace (page 360)

Bath

This gentle city on the River Avon has been going strong since the Romans occupied Britain. Actually, legend has it that Bath was known for its restorative waters as early as the ninth century B.C. when it was discovered that pigs wallowing in local mud were cured of their various ailments. The Romans channeled the healing waters into baths and pools, where the legions enjoy a little R & R from their hardship duties on the fractious borders. Taking the waters in Bath became wildly popular in the 18th century, and the city of terraced houses and elegant squares and circuses (curving

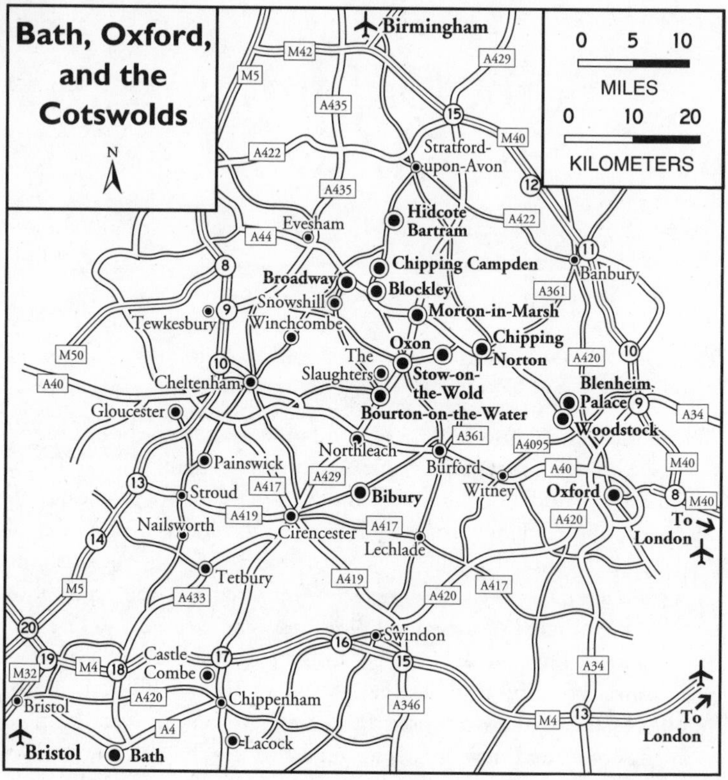

crescents) took shape to house the ladies and dandies of high society and the wannabes who came to Bath for the "season" every year. Jane Austen lived here in the early 19th century, and while she was not charmed by Bath, the city provided a wealth of social fodder for her novels.

Two hundred years after its heyday as a fashionable social resort, Bath remains an exceptionally lovely and lively city. The streets are lined with genteel Georgian houses and shops, all built in a soft, honey-colored local stone that has mellowed with time. Bath's charms are not a secret—UNESCO has designated the city as a World Heritage Site, and millions of visitors now come to Bath not necessarily to take the waters (although that can be done) but simply to enjoy its unique beauty.

Planning Your Visit to Bath

The **Bath Tourist Information Centre** (center of town, in Abbey Church Yard; (01225) 477-101; **www.visitbath.co.uk**) provides information on places to stay, what to see and do, where to dine and shop, and how to get around. Opening times are May 1–September 30: Monday–Saturday,

9:30 a.m.–6 p.m., and Sunday, 10 a.m.–4 p.m.; October 1–April 30: Monday–Saturday, 9:30 a.m.–5 p.m., and Sunday, 10 a.m.–4 p.m.

Special Events in Bath

Bath hosts a lively calendar of events year-round. The **Bath Music Festival** brings classical and popular musicians from around the world to Bath for two weeks in late May and early June. As part of the festival, galleries around Bath hang special exhibitions of contemporary art, and restaurants serve special festival menus, often accompanied by live music. Call (01225) 463-362 or visit **www.bathmusicfest.org.uk.**

Other events throughout the year include **Literature** and **Shakespeare festivals** in March; the **Puppet Festival** in April; the **Balloon** and **Flower** festivals in May; the **Guitar Festival** in July; the **Film Festival** in October; and **Mozartfest** in November. For information on these and other activities in Bath, contact the Bath Festivals office at (01225) 463-362, or visit **www.bathfestivals.org.uk.** The Bath Festivals box office is at 2 Church Street, Abbey Green, and is open Monday–Saturday, 9:30 a.m.–5:30 p.m.

Arriving and Getting Oriented in Bath

Bath is 115 miles west of London. Trains run about every half hour from London's Paddington Station to Bath. The trip takes 90 minutes and costs about £40 round trip. For information, call (08457) 484-950 or go to **www.railtrack.co.uk.** The Bath train station is at the south edge of the city center, off Dorchester Street, about a five-minute walk along Pierrepont Manvers Street from the Abbey and Grand Parade. City buses run from the station to locations around town, but most places are within walking distance; there's a taxi rank outside the station.

By car, the quickest route from London is the M4. The trip usually takes about 90 minutes. Parking can be hellish in Bath: spaces are scarce, and fines are steep. Several car parks are located throughout Bath and are well marked along the routes into the city. The most convenient places to park are the city's three **Park and Ride** facilities, at Lansdown to the north (the most convenient when entering the city from the M4 from London), Newbridge to the west, and Odd Down to the south. All are well marked from major routes into the city, and using them will spare you hours of looking for a space elsewhere. All three are open Monday–Saturday, 7:15 a.m.–7:30 p.m.; parking is free, and buses run from all three to the city center about every 10 to 15 minutes (the bus fare is £1.40 round trip). Much of the street parking in Bath is reserved for residents, so pay close attention to signs. Many hotels issue temporary parking permits to guests.

National Express buses leave London's Victoria Coach Station for Bath every hour, with some half-hourly departures. Check the schedule carefully when buying a ticket, because travel times vary from three hours

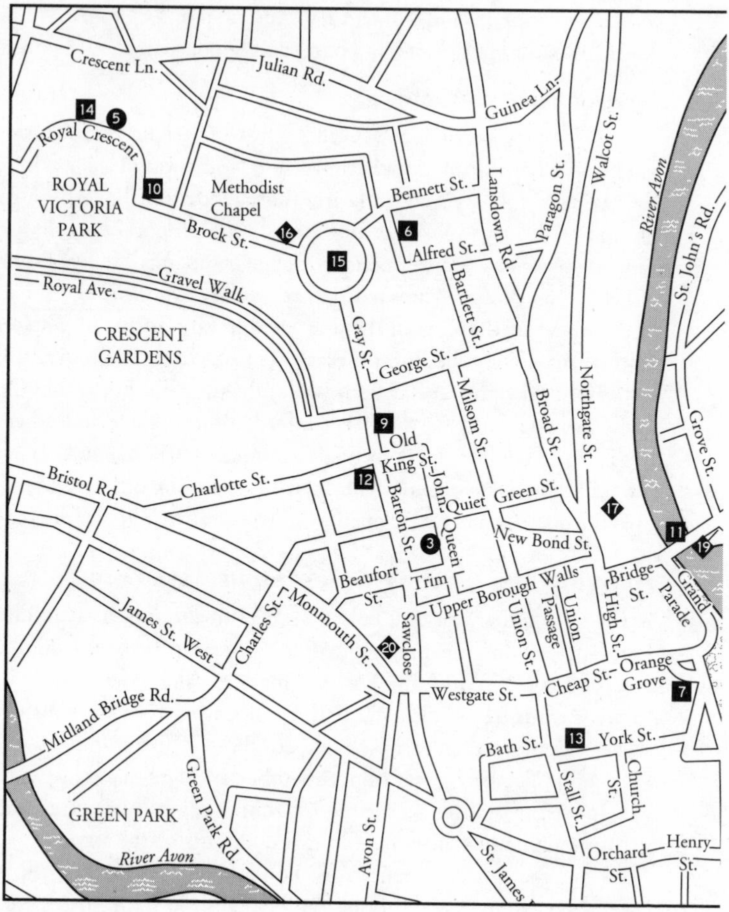

and 15 minutes for the direct trip to four or even close to five hours for trips that require a change. The round trip costs £21. The bus station is on Pierrepont Manvers Street, near the train station. For more information, call (08705) 808-080 or go to **www.gobycoach.com.**

Hotels in Bath

Carfax Hotel — £52–£75

OVERALL ★★★ | QUALITY ★★★ | VALUE ★★★

13–15 Great Pulteney Street, Bath, Somerset BA2 4BS; (01225) 462-089; fax (01225) 443-257; www.carfaxhotel.co.uk

Location Across the Pulteney Bridge from the town center.

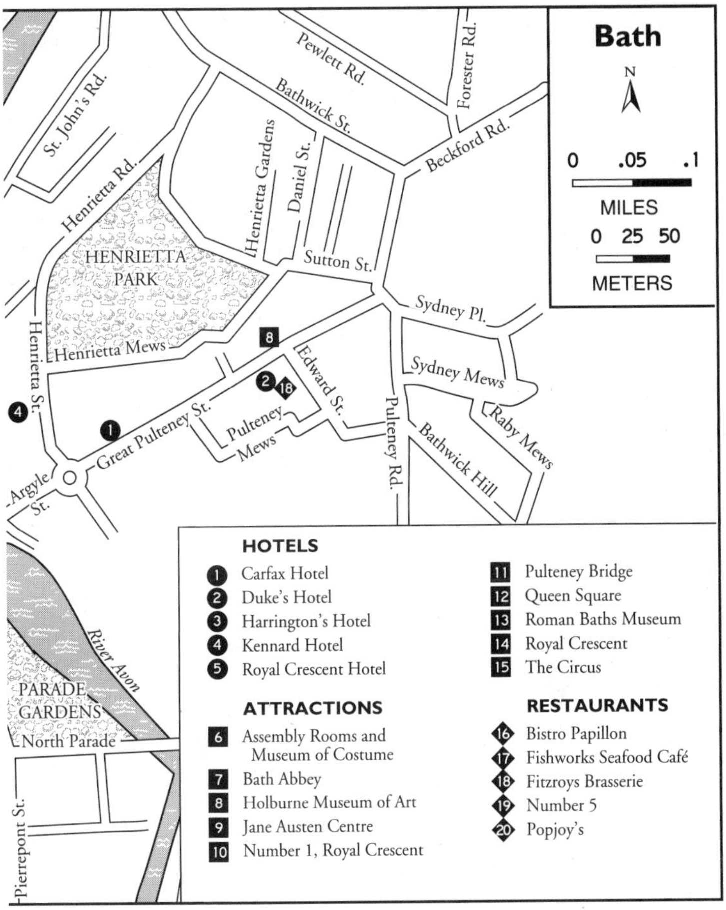

Amenities & Services 34 rooms; four share baths in the hallway. Dining room, pleasant lounge, self-service laundry.

Elevator Yes.

Parking On premises, free.

Pricing Includes English or Continental breakfast.

Credit Cards V, MC, AMEX, D

The Carfax occupies three Regency town houses on one of Bath's grandest avenues, and while the hotel is not going to win awards for style and luxury, it earns high marks for location and value. Décor throughout the public rooms and guest rooms is traditional and a bit dowdy, though the hotel is very well maintained. While the rooms are priced according to their size and location, all enjoy airy views over Great Pulteney Street or Henrietta Park. Ask to look at several

HOW HOTELS COMPARE

Hotel	Overall Rating	Quality Rating	Value Rating	Price
Bath				
Royal Crescent Hotel	★★★★★	★★★★	★★★★	£170–£240
Duke's Hotel	★★★★	★★★★½	★★★★	£115–£145
Kennard Hotel	★★★	★★★	★★★	£48–£118
Harington's Hotel	★★★	★★★	★★★★	£66–£88
Carfax Hotel	★★★	★★★	★★★	£52–£75
Oxford				
The Old Parsonage	★★★★	★★★★	★★★	£125–£135
The Old Bank	★★★★	★★★★	★★★	£140–£160
The Randolph	★★★★	★★★	★★★	£98–£160
Parklands Hotel	★★★	★★★	★★★★	£58–£86

rooms before settling on one, as they vary considerably in size; you may well want to spend the extra £15 or £20 for an upgrade to one of the "plus" or "superior" rooms. Two of the best rooms are numbers 27 and 32—large, high-ceilinged superior doubles with nice views over the city and hills.

Duke's Hotel *£115–£145*

OVERALL ★★★★ | QUALITY ★★★★½ | VALUE ★★★★

Great Pulteney Street, Bath, Somerset BA2 4DN; (01225) 787-960; fax (01225) 787-961; info@dukesbath.co.uk; www.dukesbath.co.uk

Location On one of Bath's finest avenues, a five-minute walk from the center.

Amenities & Services 18 rooms. Lounge, bar, and Fitzroy's restaurant; breakfast, other meals served in walled garden in good weather; large baths with deep tubs and power showers; porter; the hotel offers treatments at the new Thermae Bath Spa complex.

Elevator No.

Parking The hotel provides a permit for overnight street parking.

Pricing Includes breakfast; the hotel frequently offers special rates on its website.

Credit Cards V, MC, AMEX

England has no shortage of hotels claiming to provide a private town house ambience, but Duke's seamlessly achieves it. This gracious new hotel occupies an elegant and relatively unaltered Palladian-style mansion, and the original floor plans are perfectly intact, along with plasterwork, moldings, mantelpieces, and other details. All of the rooms are large and high-ceilinged, and they are tastefully (not fussily) appointed with sumptuous wallpapers, draperies, and traditional, comfort-

IN BATH, OXFORD, AND THE COTSWOLDS

Overall Hotel	Quality Rating	Value Rating	Rating	Price
The Cotswolds				
The Cotswold House	★★★★	★★★★½	★★★	£110–£120
The Royalist Hotel	★★★★	★★★★	★★★★	£50–£90
Mill House Hotel	★★★★	★★★½	★★★★	£60–£120
The Crown Inn	★★★	★★★	★★★★	£60–£90
The Swan	★★★	★★★	★★★	£180
Lygon Arms	★★★	★★★	★★	£119–£179
Bantam Tea Rooms	★★	★★★	★★★★	£30–£60

able furniture—armchairs are deep, and there's always a table and reading lamp nearby; beds are queen and king-size, and many are four-poster and canopied. The bay-windowed first-floor suite is especially pleasant. Service matches the décor, achieving just the right level of attentiveness and friendliness. There's not a bad room in the house, and since the hotel is on a corner, all are bright and command views down Great Pulteney Street or over surrounding gardens and rooftops.

Harington's Hotel — *£66–£88*

OVERALL ★★★ | QUALITY ★★★ | VALUE ★★★★

Queen Street, Bath, Somerset BA1 1HE; (01225) 461-728; fax (01225) 444-804; post@haringtonshotel.co.uk; www.haringtonshotel.co.uk

Location In the city center.

Amenities & Services 13 rooms. Café/bar open all day, serving sandwiches and other light fare until 8 p.m., drinks until midnight; cable TV.

Elevator No.

Parking In nearby garage, £6 per day.

Pricing Includes full English breakfast; the hotel often offers special rates on its website.

Credit Cards V, MC, AMEX, D, DC, CB

This tidy, small hotel may well provide the best-located lodgings in Bath. Harington's is on a quiet and atmospheric cobbled lane, just steps away from the abbey, Roman baths, Assembly Rooms, and other attractions, and shops and restaurants line the surrounding streets. What Harington's doesn't have is a great deal of character—beds are firm and the new baths are equipped with good-sized tubs or roomy shower stalls, but the décor throughout is blandly contemporary, geared more toward comfortable, informal utility than luxury. Smoking is not allowed in the guest rooms.

Kennard Hotel *£48–£118*

OVERALL ★★★ | QUALITY ★★★ | VALUE ★★★

11 Henrietta Street, Bath, Somerset BA2 6LL; (01225) 310-472; fax (01225) 460-054; reception@kennard.co.uk; www.kennard.co.uk

Location Off Great Pulteney Street, just across Pulteney Bridge from the center.

Amenities & Services 14 rooms (two singles use a bath in the hallway). Delightful breakfast room/lounge area and garden; satellite TV.

Elevator No.

Parking Upon a refundable deposit of £20, the hotel will issue a permit for free street parking.

Pricing Includes breakfast; a two-night stay is required on weekends.

Credit Cards V, MC

Built in 1794 as a lodging house during Bath's heyday, the Kennard continues to provide a welcoming place to stay at a good price for the location and the level of comfort. The public areas, including the first-floor landing that's been turned into an intimate sitting room and the gardenlike breakfast room, are ornately filled with antiques and paintings. Most of the guest rooms are more sedate and furnished in rather conventional, hotel-issue pieces. While the hotel does not welcome children under age 12, a large triple is suitable for families. Baths are new and well equipped, and the entire premises are nonsmoking.

Royal Crescent Hotel *£170–£240*

OVERALL ★★★★★ | QUALITY ★★★★ | VALUE ★★★★

16 Royal Crescent, Bath, Somerset BA1 2LS ; (01225) 823-333; fax (01225) 339-401; reservations@royalcrescent.co.uk; www.royalcrescent.co.uk

Location On the Royal Crescent, the best address in town.

Amenities & Services 45 rooms. Drawing rooms where guests can enjoy tea and drinks, bar, Pimpernel's Restaurant, gym, Bath House Spa with extensive treatment regimen and a dramatic indoor swimming pool, beautiful garden, hot-air balloon rides and river cruises available, concierge, porter, room service.

Elevator Yes.

Parking Valet parking, £20 per day.

Pricing Breakfast, £15.50–£18.50; the hotel offers special rates and packages throughout the year, so check the website or call to discuss.

Credit Cards V, MC, AMEX, DC

Excuse us if we rave about the Royal Crescent. Quite simply, we find a stay here to be a memorable experience for the following reasons: an extraordinary setting on the Royal Crescent, exemplary service, comfortable and attractive accommodations, and a gorgeous garden and swimming pool. You know you're in for a special experience as soon as you enter the handsome, tiled-floor entrance hall (warmed by a fire in the colder months) and are escorted into a drawing room for check-in. The staff manages to pull off this sort of exercise without making guests feel like country mice. Rooms are located in interconnected Regency town houses on the Crescent and in a villa in the large garden that provides the hotel with a country-house ambience. All guest rooms are large and traditionally appointed with acres of highly polished wood and rich upholstery and carpets and have sumptuous tiled baths. Actually, our one quibble is that the hotel may too successfully re-create a Georgian atmosphere, and we find the décor a bit stuffy and unimaginative. The same certainly cannot be said for the swimming pool and spa area, where stone, bamboo, and wood create an indulgently relaxing vibe that is hard to leave behind when it comes time to delve into Bath.

Exploring Bath

The best way to appreciate Bath is to walk around town and admire the architecture at your leisure. A good place to begin a walking tour is at **Bath Abbey,** established in the eighth century and site of the coronation of the first English king, Edgar, in 973. The Norman conquerors tore the church down and in 1090 began to replace it with a massive cathedral. By 1499, the church was again in ruins, and a new church was begun—only to be destroyed as part of Henry VIII's dissolution of the monasteries in 1539. The cathedral has been restored many times since, and its windows and 16th-century fan-vaulted ceiling present one of the most pleasing church interiors in England; visit during the day and you will understand why the light-filled church is known as the "lantern of the west." The abbey is open to visitors daily in summer, 9 a.m.–6 p.m., and 9 a.m.–4:30 p.m. in winter.

The **Abbey Church Yard** is the lively center of Bath, a pedestrian-only precinct that provides an outdoor foyer to the **Roman Baths Museum and Pump Room.** From here, the Grand Parade leads a few blocks north to **Pulteney Bridge,** an 18th-century span over the Avon River that, like the Ponte Vecchio in Florence, is lined with shops. Return to the west bank of the bridge and follow Upper Borough Walls Street through the city center to the **Theatre Royal** on Saw Close. The house next to this beautiful theater from 1805 was once the home of the mistress of Beau Nash, an 18th-century arbiter of taste and a high-living gambler who is credited with putting Bath on the map as a fashionable watering hole (the house is now **Popjoy's Restaurant**). Gay Street leads north past Queen Square and the **Jane Austen Centre** and comes to the **Circus,** where three semicircular terraces of Regency town houses surround a circular park. The **Assembly Rooms** and **Museum of Costume** are just northwest of the Circus, on Bennett Street. Brock Street leads west from the Circus to **Royal Victoria Park** and the amazing **Royal Crescent,** Bath's most famous architectural assemblage—a semicircle of elegant town houses facing a park.

A longer walk across Pulteney Bridge and up Great Pulteney Street brings you to the **Holburne Museum of Art.** An elegant mansion that was once Bath's finest hotel—Jane Austen watched the comings and goings from her house opposite the entrance—is now a repository of silver, glass, and other decorative objects, as well as paintings by Joseph Turner and other masters. The museum is open mid-February–mid-December, Tuesday–Saturday, 10 a.m.–5 p.m., and Sunday, 2:30–5 p.m. Admission is £3.50 adults, £1.50 children, and £7 families of up to two adults and two children; call (01225) 466-669 for information.

Another excursion from the center takes you farther afield, south of the city along the Warminster Road to **Claverton Manor,** a 19th-century mansion that houses Britain's only American museum—or what the museum describes as the "finest collection of American decorative arts outside the United States." On display are quilts, artifacts from the opening of the American West, folk art, Shaker pieces, and other Americana. The museum is open March 22–November 2, Tuesday–Sunday, 2–5 p.m.; and November 22–December 13, Tuesday and Thursday–Sunday, 1–4 p.m., and Wednesday, 1–4 p.m. and 5:30–7:30 p.m. Admission is £6 adults, £5.50 seniors and students, £3.50 children. Bus 18 runs to Claverton from the city center.

Tours of Bath

Several walking tours show off the riches of Bath. The **Mayor of Bath's Honorary Civic Walking Tour** provides a general overview of the city, taking in the Pump Room, Pulteney Bridge, Royal Crescent, and other architectural gems. Tours depart from outside the Abbey Church Yard entrance to the Pump Room, last about two hours, and are free. The schedule: May–October, daily, 10:30 a.m.; Monday–Friday and Sunday, 2:30 p.m.; Tuesday, Friday, and Saturday, 7 p.m.; November–April, daily, 10:30 a.m., Monday–Friday, 2 p.m., Sunday, 2:30 p.m. For more information, ask at the Bath Tourism and Conference Bureau office, also in the Abbey Church Yard.

Bizarre Bath is a so-called "comedy walk" and provides the most amusing evening entertainment you're going to find in the city. The 90-minute tours combine street theater, improv, pranks, and ad-libs for a humorously irreverent and refreshing look at Bath, which may not seem as stately and elegant when the fun comes to an end. Tours leave from in front of the Huntsman Inn in North Parade Passage, April 1–September 28, every evening at 8 p.m.; the cost is £5 adults, £4 students; purchase tickets, in cash, at the time of the walk. For more information, call (01225) 335-124 or visit **www.bizarrebath.co.uk.**

Ghost Walks of Bath explore supernatural appearances in the Theatre Royal, the Circus, and elsewhere, while showing off this lovely city at night. The two-hour-long walks are conducted April 1–October 31,

Monday–Saturday, at 8 p.m., and November 1–March 31, Sunday, also at 8 p.m. Walks start at the Garricks Head Pub, next to the Theatre Royal. The fee is £5 adults and £4 children and can be paid, in cash, at the time of the walk. For more information, call (01225) 463-618 or visit **www.ghostwalksofbath.co.uk.**

Bath Parade Guides, a private tour company, leads walking tours on special themes, including popular Jane Austen's Bath and Bath in Film and Literature walks, every Saturday at 2:30 p.m. Tours cost £3 and leave from the Bath Lace Shop on York Street, where you can purchase tickets. For more information, call (01225) 443-433.

The **Jane Austen Centre** sponsors walking tours that take a close look at sights around the city associated with the novelist, including some of her residences in Bath and the settings that appear in *Persuasion* and *Northanger Abbey.* Walks are conducted June–September, daily, at 1:30 p.m., and October–May, Saturday and Sunday, at 1:30 p.m. Walks begin in Abbey Church Yard and cost £3.50 adults, £2.50 seniors, students, and children. For more information, call (01225) 443-000 or visit **www.janeausten.co.uk.**

Open-top tour buses operated by **City Sightseeing,** one of Britain's largest tour operators, provide an easy way to see the city. Tours include a straightforward and rather uninspired commentary, but they provide many airy views over Bath and its rural surroundings as you are whisked past all the sights in the center and into the surrounding hills. It takes about an hour to cover the entire tour route, but you can hop off the bus at any stop and get back to a later bus as often as you like. We recommend the tours for anyone planning to spend a full day in Bath because they ensure you will see the entire city while allowing you to enjoy the sights at your leisure. Tours begin on the Grand Parade and operate daily; in summer, every 15 minutes, 9:30 a.m.–5 p.m.; and in winter, hourly, 10 a.m–3:30 p.m. The price is £8 adults, £6 seniors and students, £4 children ages 5–15; family discounts are available. For more information, call (01708) 866-000 or visit **www.city-sightseeing.com.**

From Easter through October, **Bath's Victorian Boating Station,** on the River Avon beneath the Pulteney Bridge, is the departure point for hour-long boat cruises. The fee is £4.50 adults and £2.25 children. For more information, call (01225) 466-407.

Attractions in Bath

Assembly Rooms and Museum of Costume

Type of Attraction Regency-era ballrooms with costume museum

Location Bennett Street

Admission Assembly Rooms: free. Museum of Costume: £5 adults; £4 seniors, students, and children ages 6–18; £14 families of up to two adults and four children

HOW ATTRACTIONS COMPARE

Attraction	Comments	Author's Rating
Bath		
Number 1, Royal Crescent	Regency-era town house	★★★★
Roman Baths Museum	Ancient bath complex	★★★★
Assembly Rooms and Museum of Costume	Regency-era ballrooms and costume museum	★★★
Jane Austen Centre	Jane Austen exhibit	★★
Oxford		
Oxford Colleges	Historic colleges built around inner quadrangles	★★★★

Hours Daily, 10 a.m.–5 p.m. (last admission 4:30 p.m.)

Phone (01225) 477-789

Website www.museumofcostume.co.uk

When to Go Anytime

Special Comments A visit to the Assembly Rooms is an essential part of any visit to Bath, because they still evoke the lifestyle that put the city on the map. Walk through them even if you don't plan on visiting the Museum of Costume.

Overall Appeal by Age Group

Preschool ★	Teens ★★★	Over 30 ★★★
Grade school ★★	Young Adults ★★★	Seniors ★★★

Author's Rating ★★★

How Much Time to Allow 15 minutes for Assembly Rooms, about 45 minutes for museum

Description & Comments Bath became famous as a fashionable spa in the late 18th century. Visitors came to sip the salubrious waters, check out the marriageable material, social climb, gamble, and attend glittering balls. They could enjoy all of these activities in the Assembly Rooms. There's not a great deal to see here now except the four elegant, high-ceilinged rooms—the Ballroom; the Tea or Concert Room; the Octagon Room; and the Card Room. As you stroll through them, though, it's easy to imagine the phantom hum of conversation and the sound of dancing feet. Below the Assembly Rooms, in the Museum of Costume, you can see what fashionable people wore to those social events (and are wearing today). This is one of the finest museums of fashion in the world, with a collection of some 30,000 items. The displays include 200 figures dressed in original garments that show the changing styles in fashionable clothes from the late 16th century to the present day.

Touring Tips The free audio tour available to those visiting the Museum of Costume provides rich detail about the garments on display.

IN BATH, OXFORD, AND THE COTSWOLDS

Attraction	Comments	Author's Rating
Oxford (continued)		
Ashmolean Museum	Museum of art and archaeology	★★★½
The Oxford Story	Multimedia show about Oxford	★★
Woodstock		
Blenheim Palace	Early 18th-century palace and birthplace of Sir Winston Churchill	★★★★
Chipping Campden		
Hidcote Manor Garden	Magnificent Cotswolds garden	★★★★

Jane Austen Centre

Type of Attraction Exhibition on Jane Austen and her time in Bath

Location 40 Gay Street

Admission £3.95 adults; £3.45 seniors and students; £2.45 children ages 6–15; £11.45 families of up to two adults and four children

Hours Monday–Saturday, 10 a.m.–5:30 p.m.; Sunday, 10:30 a.m.–5:30 p.m.

Phone (01225) 443-000

Website www.janeausten.co.uk

When to Go Early or late to avoid the midday crunch of visitors

Special Comments The museum shop sells more Jane Austen paraphernalia than you probably knew existed, from quill pens to mouse pads to a good selection of various editions of the author's works.

Overall Appeal by Age Group

Preschool ★	Teens ★	Over 30 ★★
Grade school ★	Young Adults ★★	Seniors ★★

Author's Rating ★★

How Much Time to Allow About 45 minutes

Description & Comments This small museum is devoted to the life and times of the novelist Jane Austen, who visited Bath twice in the late 18th century and lived here from 1801 to 1806. The witty novelist of late 18th- and early 19th-century manners took inspiration from the city and set her novels *Persuasion* and *Northanger Abbey* in Bath, and she enthuses in the latter, "Who can ever be tired of Bath." Alas, Jane did tire of Bath, and came to loathe the city's stuffy manners and garish bright-stone facades. Her feelings may well have been tainted by the fact that her family fell upon hard times in the city, and Jane, her mother, and sister Cassandra were eventually forced to lodge in a street known for its prostitutes. The museum is a bit dull but informative, with text-heavy displays (bring your reading glasses) filled with Austen letters, apparel, and other paraphernalia. The liveliest part of the tour is a brief introductory lecture in which a staff member provides an over-rehearsed but nonetheless gossipy lecture about Austen's life in Bath.

Touring Tips We found the center's walking tours of Jane Austen's Bath (see "Tours of Bath," above) to be just as informative as a visit to the center, and far more entertaining. Devoted Austen fans will want to make the pilgrimage to Chawton, about an hour from Bath near Winchester, where the novelist lived when she left Bath—the house there is quietly evocative of her life and times.

Number 1, Royal Crescent

Type of Attraction Regency-era town house furnished with period pieces

Location Royal Crescent

Admission £4 adults; £3 seniors, students, and children ages 6–18; £10 families of up to two adults and two children

Hours Mid-February–October: Tuesday–Sunday, 10:30 a.m.–5 p.m.; November: Tuesday–Sunday, 10:30 a.m.–4 p.m.

Phone (01225) 428-126

Website www.bath-preservation-trust.org.uk/museums/no1

When to Go Anytime; the house is crowded only in the peak summer months

Special Comments The house has interior stairways that are not wheelchair-accessible.

Overall Appeal by Age Group

Preschool ★	Teens ★★	Over 30 ★★★
Grade school ★★	Young Adults ★★★	Seniors ★★★

Author's Rating ★★★★

How Much Time to Allow About 30 minutes

Description & Comments Built to the designs of John Wood the Younger between 1767 and 1774, the Royal Crescent is the most famous example of Palladian architecture in Bath, and one of the most distinctive examples of residential architecture in the world. Master craftsmen created the interior decorations for this great curving row of town houses using designs taken from the many pattern books published at the time, and this beautiful museum provides an opportunity to step behind the facades and see their work. Number 1, an unusually bright and spacious "corner" house, was leased out to various seasonal visitors, among them, in 1776, the Duke of York, second son of George III. About 200 years later, the house was completely restored by the Bath Preservation Trust. Paint, wallpapers, fabrics, and other materials available in the 18th century were used in restoring the rooms on the three main floors to the way they looked when this grand abode was built; they are furnished with a superlative collection of period antiques.

Touring Tips Guides are stationed in every room to tell you about architectural details, furnishings, and the history of the house. They are very well informed and add much to a visit, so don't be afraid to ask them questions.

Roman Baths Museum

Type of Attraction Ancient bath complex

Location Pump Room, Stall Street, beside Bath Abbey

Admission £8 adults; £7 seniors and students; £5 children ages 6–16; £20 families of up to two adults and two children

Hours November–February: daily, 9:30 a.m.–4:30 p.m.; March–June, September–October: daily, 9 a.m.–5 p.m.; July–August, daily, 9 a.m.–9 p.m.

Phone (01225) 477-785

Website www.romanbaths.co.uk

When to Go Early or late, when there are fewer people and you can better soak up the atmosphere

Special Comments Take advantage of the free audio guide to learn more about this historic monument, or join one of the free hourly tours. During July and August, you can tour the museum at night by flashlight.

Overall Appeal by Age Group

Preschool ★	Teens ★★	Over 30 ★★★
Grade school ★★	Young Adults ★★★	Seniors ★★★

Author's Rating ★★★★

How Much Time to Allow About 1 hour

Description & Comments Built nearly 2,000 years ago, this bath complex reveals the engineering ingenuity of the ancient Romans. The healing hot springs on the site were allegedly discovered around 875 B.C. and used by the Celts, but it was the Romans who dubbed the sacred spot Aquae Sulis (waters of Sul, an ancient Celtic deity) and channeled the piping-hot sulfurous water into a series of baths. Much of the Roman structure remains. The springs continue to bubble forth at the rate of about 240,000 gallons a day, and the water emerges at a near-steady 116° Fahrenheit. From terraces at the top of the complex, you can look down into the large pool, and it is easy to imagine the legions and colonists coming here to relax and get a taste of the life they left behind in the far-distant Italian peninsula. (Such musings are encouraged by an excellent self-guided audio commentary that provides a wealth of information about the complex and the Roman art of bathing.) Descending into the subterranean chambers, you'll see the excavated remains of steaming pools and cleansing saunas heated by underground pipes called hypocausts, along with fragments of elaborate paving and other decorative work.

Touring Tips The self-guided tour ends in the Pump Room, where you can sample the Bath water yourself. Be warned that the stuff has, in the words of Sam Weller in Charles Dickens's *The Pickwick Papers,* "a very strong flavor o' warm flatirons." Here, too, you can enjoy coffee or tea to the accompaniment of a string trio.

Dining in Bath

Bath is the sort of place where afternoon tea figures prominently in the local lifestyle. Among the prime venues is the **Royal Crescent Hotel** (see page 332). In addition, **Hands** (next to the abbey on Abbey Street;

HOW RESTAURANTS COMPARE

Name	Cuisine	Overall	Quality	Value	Price
Bath					
Number 5	French	★★★★	★★★★	★★★	Mod
Popjoy's Restaurant	British	★★★★	★★★	★★★	Exp
Fishworks Seafood Café	Seafood	★★★	★★★½	★★★	Mod
Bistro Papillon	French	★★★	★★★	★★★	Mod
Fitzroy's Brasserie	Continental	★★★	★★★	★★★	Mod
Oxford					
Le Petit Blanc	French	★★★★	★★★★	★★★	Mod
Pierre Victoire	French Bistro	★★★½	★★★½	★★★★	Inexp–Mod

(01225) 463-928) is another popular spot, and it's well known for cream teas; you can also enjoy morning coffee and pastries and light lunches (sandwiches and salads) in this Georgian town house. Hands is open Tuesday–Saturday, 9:30 a.m.–5:30 p.m., and Sunday, 11 a.m.–4:30 p.m.

Restaurants in Bath

Bistro Papillon ★★★

FRENCH | MODERATE | QUALITY ★★★ | VALUE ★★★

2 Margarets Building, Brock Street; (01225) 310-064

Reservations Not necessary **Entrée Range** £9.95–£12.50; 2-course lunch, £7.50 **Payment** V, MC, AMEX, D **Bar** Full service **Disabled Access** Yes

Hours Tuesday–Saturday, noon–2:15 p.m., 6:30–10 p.m.

House Specialties Chicken supreme (with brie and Parma ham); lamb shank; fresh fish.

You might want to plan on having lunch here, either in the cheerful, wood-floored dining room or at a sidewalk table, after visiting the Royal Crescent. The two-course lunch special is an excellent bargain, but the straightforward bistro fare and friendly ambience provide a pleasant and well-priced dining experience at other times, too.

Fishworks Seafood Café ★★★

SEAFOOD | MODERATE | QUALITY ★★★½ | VALUE ★★★

6 Green Street; (01225) 448-707

Reservations Recommended **Entrée Range** £9–£16.90 **Payment** V, MC, AMEX, DC **Bar** Full service **Disabled Access** Yes

IN BATH, OXFORD, AND THE COTSWOLDS

Name	Cuisine	Overall	Quality	Value	Price
Oxford (continued)					
Merton's Bar and Brasserie	British	★★★	★★★	★★★	Inexp–Mod
Gee's	British	★★★	★★★	★★★	Exp
The Cotswolds					
Eagle and Child Pub	Pub	★★★★	★★★★	★★★★	Mod
Mill House Hotel	British	★★★★	★★★★	★★★★	Mod
Hicks'	Continental	★★★★	★★★★	★★★	Mod
947 AD Restaurant	British	★★★★	★★★★	★★★	Exp
Jankowski's	British/Bistro	★★★	★★★	★★★	Mod

Hours Monday–Saturday, noon–2:30 p.m., 6–10:30 p.m.

House Specialties *Zuppa de pescatore* (a hearty fish stew); fresh crab salad; skate with black butter.

This bright white-tiled room is an outlet of a growing enterprise that includes restaurants in other cities, a seafood cooking school, home delivery of fresh fish, and a line of cookbooks. The operation has a reputation to maintain for freshness, and it does so by providing fish and shellfish caught that morning in the waters off nearby Cornwall. Dishes are nicely accompanied by selections from the well-chosen wine list. To best enjoy a meal here, come early or late when the noise level may be lower.

Fitzroy's Brasserie ★★★

CONTINENTAL | MODERATE | QUALITY ★★★ | VALUE ★★★

Duke's Hotel, Great Pulteney Street; (01225) 787-960

Reservations Recommended **Entrée Range** £12.50–£14.50 **Payment** V, MC, AMEX **Bar** Full service **Disabled Access** Restaurant accessible only by stairs

Hours Daily, noon–2:30 p.m., 6:30–10 p.m.

House Specialties Onion tart or salmon blinis to start, followed by goat cheese tortellini, stir-fried mussels, or duck leg confit.

This smart little brasserie is in the cellar of Duke's Hotel and is as tasteful and pleasant as the rest of the premises. Wicker furnishings and a Mediterranean color scheme lend a casual quality to the room, which extends into a lovely walled garden in good weather. Most guests enjoy cocktails and after-dinner drinks in the cozy bar across the hall, so a dinner at Fitzroy's can become a full evening's entertainment. Pastas and salads are also served as main courses, making it easy to eat lightly if you choose to do so.

Number 5 ★★★★

FRENCH | MODERATE | QUALITY ★★★★ | VALUE ★★★

5 Argyle Street; (01225) 444-499

Reservations Recommended on weekends **Entrée Range** £12.50–£13.95 **Payment** V, MC, AMEX **Bar** Full service **Disabled Access** Yes

Hours Tuesday–Saturday, noon–2:30 p.m.; Monday–Thursday, 6:30–10 p.m., Friday–Sunday, 6:30–10:30 p.m.

House Specialties Fresh fish (served most days and on a special fish menu on Wednesday); homemade soups; veal kidneys.

One of Bath's top restaurants (just across the Pulteney Bridge from the city center) is a simple, unassuming little place with bare wood floors, cane chairs, and a friendly, casual atmosphere. Even so, there's nothing causal about chef Michel Lemoine's approach to food, and the dishes that emerge from the kitchen are consistently outstanding.

Popjoy's Restaurant ★★★★

MODERN BRITISH | EXPENSIVE | QUALITY ★★★ | VALUE ★★★

Beau Nash House, Saw Close; (01225) 460-494

Reservations Required **Entrée Range** £15–£20; lunch and pretheater menus, 2 courses for £12.50, 3 courses for £15.50; 3-course prix fixe dinner, £23 **Payment** V, MC, AMEX, D **Bar** Full service **Disabled Access** Yes

Hours Monday–Saturday, noon–2:30 p.m., 6–11 p.m.

House Specialties Fresh lobster and crab bisque; seared loin of lamb; selection of fresh seafood.

The name refers to Juliana Popjoy, for whom this handsome house next to the Theatre Royal was built in 1720. Popjoy was the lifelong mistress of Beau Nash, 18th-century dandy and arbiter of Bath taste, and her dining and drawing rooms are now an elegant and handy place to dine before or after the theater; you might want to think about dining early, because the pretheater menu is a good value.

Entertainment and Nightlife in Bath

Theater has been thriving in Bath for the past 300 years, and the **Theatre Royal** on Sawclose is one of Britain's oldest working stages. The theater now occupies a Regency building that dates from 1863 and replaces an earlier structure destroyed by fire. Even after a restoration in 1982, some sight lines remain obscured by columns, but the lavish interior is a rich setting for drama, musicals, dance performances, and other entertainment—Bath is a major stop for traveling troupes. Even if you're not able to attend a performance, you may be able to join a 45-minute theater tour, held the first Wednesday of the month at 11 a.m. and the following Saturday at noon (£3 adults, £2 children). The box office is open Monday–Saturday, 10 a.m.–8 p.m., and Sunday, noon–8 p.m. For ticket information, call (01225) 448-844 or visit **www.theatreroyal.org.uk.** Standby seats (£5) are available on the day of performances from noon on, and standing-room tickets (£3) go on sale at 6 p.m. (earlier for matinees).

Moles (14 George Street; (01225) 404-445) provides live music throughout the week and hosts bands from throughout England. The **Bell** (103 Walcot Street; (01225) 460-426) is an atmospheric old pub that presents jazz and other live music on Monday and Wednesday evenings and at Sunday lunch. The **Old Green Tree** (12 Green Street; (01225) 448-259) doesn't offer music, and the quiet, relaxing atmosphere is one of its draws; so is a wide selection of ales and light fare served in three snug rooms, making the Old Green Tree an especially nice place to settle in for an evening.

Shopping in Bath

It figures that shopping would be a popular pastime in Bath, which has always been a place for worldly diversions. Among the more interesting shops is **Hitchcocks** (just north of Queen Square at 10 Chapel Row; (01225) 330-646), which specializes in traditional wooden toys from Germany and the Czech Republic, as well as automata and other unique items that are a cross between playthings and artworks. **The Glass House** (just off the Grand Parade at 1–2 Orange Grove; (01225) 463-436) sells pieces crafted from the distinctive aqua glass and blue glass for which the region is famous. **Antique Textiles** (just east of the center off Lansdown Road at 34 Belvedere; (01225) 310-795) shows an amazing array of 18th-century textiles, from shawls to bed pulls. **The Margarets Buildings** (around the corner from the Royal Crescent on Brock Street) house many distinctive shops. One of the most unusual is **Hansel und Gretel** (9 Margarets Buildings; (10225) 464-677), which sells cuckoo clocks, tea towels, figurines, and other distinctive crafts from Germany and Switzerland.

An excellent place to browse is **Green Park Arts and Craft Market,** in the historic Green Park train station, north of the center off Charles Street; the market is open Wednesday–Saturday and hosts vendors selling everything from antiques to crafts to farm produce. Vendors at the **Bartlett Street Antique Centre,** a bit closer to the center of things near the Assembly Rooms on, naturally, Bartlett Street, and the nearly adjacent **Western Antiques Centre** specialize in jewelry, silver, prints, and other memorabilia. **Bath Antiques Market** brings together 40 or more vendors of high-quality collectibles in a hall on Guinea Lane, east of the center off Lansdown Road, on Wednesdays, 6:30 a.m.–2:30 p.m.

Exercise and Recreation in Bath

Bath is planning to replay some pages from its history with the much-delayed opening, sometime in 2004, of the **Thermae Bath Spa** (Bath Street; (1225) 780-308; **www.bathspa.co.uk**). Now that the Roman

Baths are closed to would-be soakers, the new spa provides the only way to partake of the city's healing waters. The complex encompasses five historic buildings and a futuristic-looking glass-and-stone spa structure topped with a rooftop thermal pool. Aside from the opportunity to enjoy a luxurious soak, offerings include whirlpools, steam rooms, and spa treatments. The Spa is open daily, 9 a.m.–10 p.m., and fees are £17 for two hours, £23 for four hours, and £35 for the full day.

You can also take to the waters of the River Avon in skiffs, punts, and canoes available for rental from the **Victorian Bath Boating Station,** beneath the Pulteney Bridge. The boat house is open daily, May–September, 10 a.m.–6 p.m.; call (01225) 466-407.

The paths that run alongside the River Avon, the **Kennet and Avon Canal towpath** and the **Bristol to Bath Railway Path,** are both great for hiking and cycling. The Bath Tourist Information Centre (center of town, in Abbey Church Yard; (01225) 477-101; **www.visitbath.co.uk**) offers walking and cycling guides, as well as listing places to rent bikes. **Avon Valley Cyclery** (phone (01225) 722-292) is centrally located in the railway station.

Oxford

The "sweet city with her dreaming spires," to quote the poet Matthew Arnold, is best-known as the seat of **Oxford University,** one of the world's greatest and oldest centers of learning. Oxford has been educating Britain's elite since the 13th century and continues to do so today in 39 colleges, whose chapels, quads, and lecture theaters are spread throughout the city.

While Oxford presents a visitor with a great deal of history, the city also happens to be one of Britain's most enjoyable places to spend time, proffering plenty of diversions that, depending on your tastes, can include chamber music recitals, theater, museums, riverside walks, and pub crawls. Town and gown converge on the lively commercial streets, as Oxford is also a major manufacturing center (steel and cars, in particular) and, increasingly, one of Britain's high-tech bastions. You can easily visit Oxford on a day trip from London, but once you get a taste of the city, you'll probably appreciate our recommendation that you spend at least one night here.

Planning Your Visit to Oxford

The **Oxford Tourist Information Centre** (15–16 Broad Street, Oxford, Oxfordshire OX1 3AS; (01865) 726-871; **www.oxfordcity.co.uk**) provides information on what to see and do, where to dine and shop, how to get around, and where to stay, and conducts several excellent walking tours (see "Tours of Oxford," below). Don't be surprised when you are

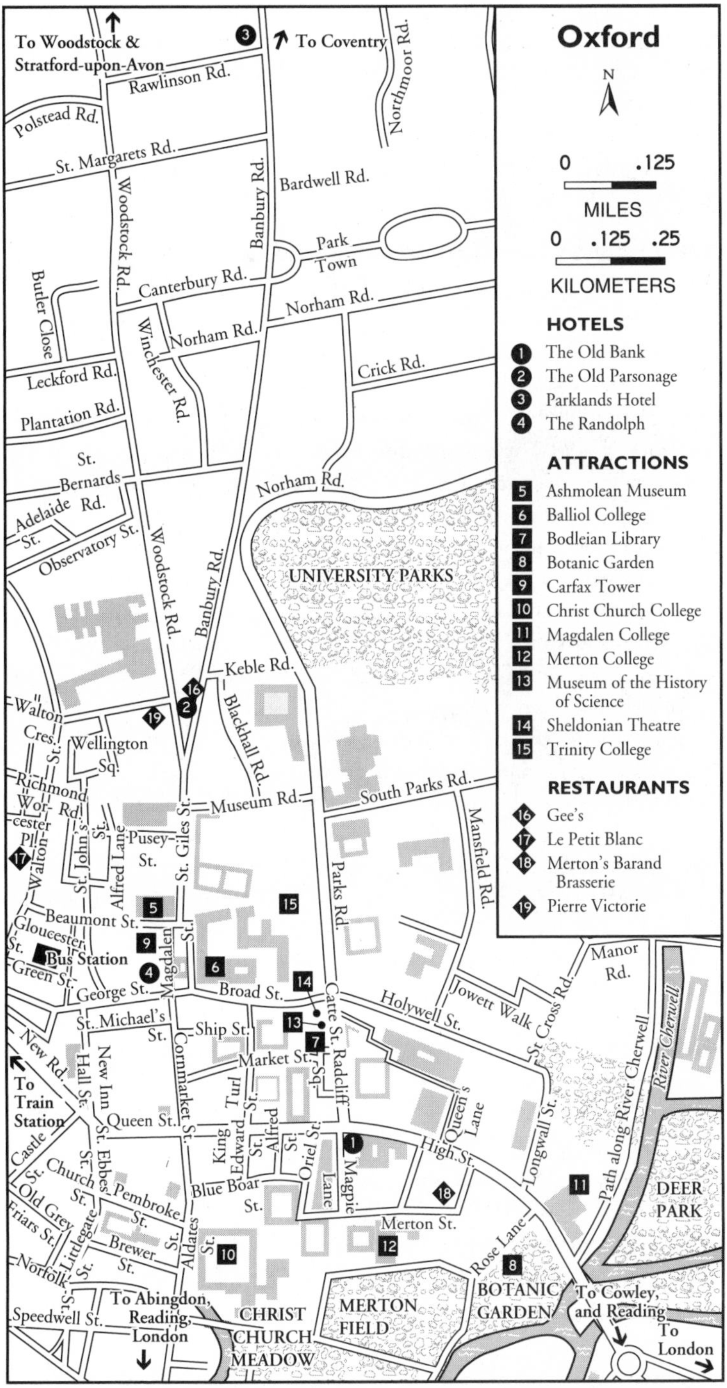
Oxford
N
0 .125
MILES
0 .125 .25
KILOMETERS
HOTELS
1 The Old Bank
2 The Old Parsonage
3 Parklands Hotel
4 The Randolph
ATTRACTIONS
5 Ashmolean Museum
6 Balliol College
7 Bodleian Library
8 Botanic Garden
9 Carfax Tower
10 Christ Church College
11 Magdalen College
12 Merton College
13 Museum of the History of Science
14 Sheldonian Theatre
15 Trinity College
RESTAURANTS
16 Gee's
17 Le Petit Blanc
18 Merton's Barand Brasserie
19 Pierre Victorie
To Woodstock & Stratford-upon-Avon
To Coventry
Rawlinson Rd.
Northmoor Rd.
Polstead Rd.
St. Margarets Rd.
Bardwell Rd.
Woodstock Rd.
Banbury Rd.
Park Town
Canterbury Rd.
Butler Close
Norham Rd.
Winchester Rd.
Crick Rd.
Leckford Rd.
Plantation Rd.
St. Bernards Rd.
Adelaide St.
Observatory St.
UNIVERSITY PARKS
Keble Rd.
Blackhall Rd.
Walton Cres.
Wellington Sq.
Richmond Rd.
Worcester Pl.
Walton St.
St. John's St.
Alfred Lane
Pusey St.
St. Giles St.
Museum Rd.
South Parks Rd.
Mansfield Rd.
Parks Rd.
Beaumont St.
Gloucester St.
Bus Station
Green St.
George St.
Magdalen St.
Broad St.
Holywell St.
Jowett Walk
St Cross Rd.
Manor Rd.
River Cherwell
St. Michael's St.
Ship St.
Catte St.
Radcliff Sq.
Market St.
New Rd.
Hall St.
New Inn Hall St.
Cornmarket St.
Turl St.
To Train Station
Queen St.
King Edward St.
Alfred St.
Oriel St.
Magpie Lane
High St.
Queen's Lane
Longwall St.
Path along River Cherwell
DEER PARK
Castle St.
St. Ebbes St.
Church St.
Pembroke St.
Blue Boar St.
Old Grey Friars St.
Littlegate St.
Brewer St.
Aldates St.
Merton St.
Rose Lane
Norfolk St.
To Abingdon, Reading, London
Speedwell St.
CHRIST CHURCH MEADOW
MERTON FIELD
BOTANIC GARDEN
To Cowley, and Reading
To London

asked to hand over a pound or two for many of the center's offerings (made necessary by budget cuts, the people behind the desk explain). The center also has a small bookshop where you can purchase photo books on Oxford and other specialized guides. The center and shop are open Monday–Saturday, 9:30 a.m.–6 p.m.; and Sunday, 10 a.m.–1 p.m. and 1:30–3:30 p.m.

Arriving and Getting Oriented in Oxford

Oxford is just 59 miles west of London. Trains run about every 15 to 20 minutes from London's Paddington Station. The trip takes about an hour and costs about £15 round trip. For information, call (08457) 484-950 or go to **www.railtrack.co.uk.** The Oxford train station is about a ten-minute walk west of the city center, off Park End Street. City buses run from the station to locations around town, but many places are within walking distance; there is a taxi rank outside the station.

By car, the quickest route from London is the M40. The trip usually takes a little over an hour. Parking is difficult in Oxford, so you are well advised to leave your car in a hotel car park or in one of the municipal car parks and get around on foot. The most convenient places to park are the city's **Park and Ride** facilities on the outskirts, at Pear Tree to the north, Seacourt to the west, Thornhill to the east, and Red Bridge to the south; all are well marked from major routes into the city. Buses run from these car parks to the city center Monday–Saturday, 5:30 a.m.–11:30 p.m., and Sunday, 8:30 a.m.–9:30 p.m. Parking at these facilities costs just £0.60 for 24 hours. There are also municipal car parks near the city center, off Beaumont Street, off Worcester Street, and off Norfolk Street; these are often full and can cost as much as £22 for a 24-hour period.

National Express buses leave London's Victoria Coach Station for Oxford every half hour. The round trip costs £12. The bus station is near the city center at Gloucester Green. For more information, call (08705) 808-080 or go to **www.gobycoach.com.**

Hotels in Oxford

The Old Bank *£140–£160*

OVERALL ★★★★ | QUALITY ★★★★ | VALUE ★★★

92–94 High Street, Oxford, Oxfordshire OX1 4BN; (01865) 799-599; fax (01865) 799-598; info@oldbank-hotel.co.uk; www.oxford-hotels-restaurants.co.uk

Location City center.

Amenities & Services 42 rooms. Restaurant and bar, the Quod; satellite TV, CD players and radios, two-line phones, modem ports. Service is understated and attentive.

Elevator Yes.

Parking In private car park, free.

Pricing Continental breakfast, £9; English breakfast, £12.

Credit Cards V, MC, AMEX, D

If you're looking for four-poster beds festooned in chintz, look elsewhere (perhaps the Old Parsonage, below, which is part of the same hotel group that owns the Old Bank). The design sense at the Old Bank, which does indeed occupy a Georgian bank, is contemporary, and the effect is calming, luxurious, and chic, but not overbearingly so. Old stonework, beveled windows, fireplaces, and other details remain, with the addition of contemporary art, handsome, unobtrusive furnishings, and subdued but rich fabrics. Rooms 10 and 15 are especially commodious, but all rooms are spacious and have large marble baths equipped with deep tubs, powerful showers, and plush towels; rooms on the higher floors in the front enjoy good views over the surrounding colleges, but all the outlooks are pleasant.

The Old Parsonage *£125–£135*

OVERALL ★★★★ | QUALITY ★★★★ | VALUE ★★★

1 Banbury Road, Oxford, Oxfordshire OX2 6NN; (01865) 310-210; fax (01865) 311-262; info@oldparsonage-hotel.co.uk; www.oxford-hotels-restaurants.co.uk

Location About a five-minute walk from the center.

Amenities & Services 30 rooms. Restaurant and bar, the Parsonage; garden and roof garden, satellite TV, 24-hour room service.

Elevator No.

Parking On premises, free.

Pricing Continental breakfast, £9; English breakfast, £12.

Credit Cards V, MC, AMEX, D

You notice that old "like a small country inn in the center of the city" quality the moment you open the creaky wooden door and step into the stone-floor lobby of this 17th-century stone inn, once home to playwright and wit Oscar Wilde. If this isn't the sort of old English charm you're in the mood for, turn around and walk out, because the country-house atmosphere doesn't let up as you settle into one of the appealing and comfy rooms, where acres of floral-print fabrics, traditional furnishings, and old paintings and prints prevail. Modern conveniences include plush marble baths. The hotel is especially pleasant in good weather, when the gardens provide a nice retreat from the busy city around you; the year-round place to relax is the cozy Parsonage Bar, open all day and long into the evening to serve drinks, snacks, and full meals.

Parklands Hotel *£58–£86*

OVERALL ★★★ | QUALITY ★★★ | VALUE ★★★★

100 Banbury Road, Oxford, Oxfordshire OX2 6JU; (01865) 554-374; fax (01865) 559-860; theparklands@freenet.co.uk; www.oxfordcity.co.uk/hotels/parklands

Location About a mile north of the city center.

Amenities & Services 15 rooms. Nice lounge and bar area, and a walled garden; Internet access.

Elevator No.

Parking On premises, free.

Pricing Includes full breakfast.

Credit Cards V, MC, AMEX

In a city where hotel rooms are quite expensive, the Parklands offers unusually pleasant accommodations at a very good price. While the traditional furnishings are of the blandly pleasant variety, the hotel occupies a Victorian house built for an Oxford don, and a great deal of original character remains. The large, high-ceilinged first-floor rooms (second floor to Americans) at the front of the house are especially nice and look out over the grounds from huge windows; newly refurbished baths, some with tubs, adjoin all of the rooms. One convenient amenity is the fact that you can park your car here and forget about it. The walk into town through Oxford's residential neighborhoods is pleasant, and there's regular bus service to and from the center along Banbury Road.

The Randolph — *£98–£160*

OVERALL ★★★★ | QUALITY ★★★ | VALUE ★★★

Beaumont Street, Oxford, Oxfordshire OX1 2UN; (0870) 400-8200; fax (01865) 791-678; enquiries@macdonald-hotels.co.uk; www.macdonaldhotels.co.uk

Location In the center of town, across the street from the Ashmolean Museum.

Amenities & Services 114 rooms. Morse Bar and Oyster Bar and Restaurant; satellite TV, room service.

Elevator Yes.

Parking Ask when you book. The Randolph's garage is currently being rebuilt; until it's done, parking is scare and inconvenient. The only nearby parking is at the Westgate Car Park, but you'll have to return to your car throughout the day to procure new park-and-display tickets.

Pricing Includes lavish buffet breakfast.

Credit Cards V, MC, AMEX, D

The Randolph inspires all the old chestnuts—grand dame, Oxford landmark, Victorian pile. It's all of these, as well as being nicely situated in the city center and the traditional place where visiting parents stay and wine and dine their young scholars. The bar and dining room remain grand and atmospheric, but the guest rooms have lost some of their creaky old character in recent renovations. Furnishings are smart and handsome, though they are a bit more corporate and anonymous than we would prefer in a hotel of this vintage. Many of the rooms are in wings that have been added to the back of the hotel over the years, and the best are the high-ceilinged old rooms in the front of the house. Baths throughout are new and luxurious, and service is efficient and gracious. The hotel offers some very good deals and will extend special offers when not fully booked, so check the website or ask when you reserve.

Exploring Oxford

The best way to get a sense of Oxford is from a perch above the domes, spires, and medieval streets. A climb up the spiral staircase of the **Carfax**

Tower, at the crossroads of the town's busiest thoroughfares (Cornmarket Street, Queen Street, St. Aldate's Street, and High Street) rewards you with the town's best bird's-eye view. The tower is all that remains after the 14th-century church of St. Martin was demolished in the late 19th century to ease traffic flow on the streets below; it's open daily, 10 a.m.–3 p.m., and admission is £1. Most of the golden-stone buildings and monuments of the **University of Oxford** stretch to the east of the tower, and a walk down High Street and then north on Cattle Street brings you to some of the university's most famous structures.

Sir Christopher Wren was a professor of astronomy at Oxford before he became famous for designing St. Paul's Cathedral in London, and his first major building was the **Sheldonian Theatre,** built between 1664 and 1668 in the style of a Roman theater. (Actually, the first building Wren designed was Pembroke Chapel at Cambridge, but work on that impressive structure began later.) The main room, richly paneled in wood beneath a painted ceiling, is used for matriculation exercises (in Latin) and other university ceremonies, and the public can step inside for a look Monday–Saturday, 10 a.m.–12:30 p.m. and 2–4:30 p.m.

The **Bodleian Library** is the oldest library in Europe (established in 1450) and one of the largest, with more than five million books stored on 80 miles of shelving. The library's main reading room, the domed and round Radcliffe Camera, was built between 1737 and 1749. High on the list of old Oxford customs is the oath "not to bring into the library or kindle therein any fire or flame" that students and academics who wish to use the collection must take. The precaution dates from the days when the library was not heated and a reading session could require no small amount of physical stamina. While most of the library is not open to the general public, exceptions are the Divinity School, a 15th-century lecture hall, and the Exhibition Room, which mounts rotating displays of the university's large collection of rare volumes, maps, and prints. These free exhibits are invariably fascinating; they're open Monday–Friday, 9:30 a.m.–4:45 p.m., and Saturday, 9:30 a.m.–12:30 p.m. You can also see Duke Humfrey's Library, with one of the world's earliest collections of books, and other parts of the library on 40-minute guided tours. The fee is £4, and it's open March–October, Monday–Friday, 10:30 a.m., 11:30 a.m., 2 p.m., and 3 p.m. Saturday, 10:30 and 11:30 a.m.; November–February, Monday–Friday, 2 and 3 p.m., Saturday, 10:30 and 11:30 a.m. For more information, call (01865) 277-224.

Near the entrance to the Bodleian, on Broad Street, is the fascinating **Museum of the History of Science.** Housed in a fine 17th-century building that was once home to Elias Ashmole's Cabinet of Curiosities—which has long since moved to grander quarters on Beaumont Street and has changed its name to the Ashmolean Museum (see below)—the collection includes early medical and scientific instruments. Among the relatively recent additions to the collection is Alfred Einstein's blackboard. The museum is open Tuesday–Sunday, 10 a.m.–4 p.m., and admission is free.

A short walk west on Broad Street takes you to Cornmarket Street, the main shopping street, and back into the city center. But we suggest you retrace your steps back past the Sheldonian Theatre and down New College Lane. **Hertford College** lies on either side of the walls that close in the street, which is crossed by a remarkable enclosed bridge, known as the **Bridge of Sighs** because of its resemblance to the Venetian landmark. New College Lane leads into Queens Lane, which soon comes to High Street. A short walk east brings you to a slice of rural Oxford, the **Botanic Garden,** on the banks of the River Cherwell. This is the oldest teaching garden in England, founded in 1621 for the study of medicinal plants—fittingly, a rose garden commemorates Oxford researchers whose work led to the discovery of penicillin. The garden is open daily, 9 a.m.–5 p.m. **Magdalen Bridge,** next to the garden, is where undergraduates follow an old Oxford tradition and gather in punts at dawn on May Day as the strains of the May Day anthem float across Oxford from the top of Magdalen bell tower.

Tours of Oxford

Oxford colleges are open to casual sightseers only for a few hours on certain days, ensuring silence and privacy for their students. To find out when colleges are open on any given day, check with the Oxford Tourist Information Centre (center of town, 15–16 Broad Street, Oxford, Oxfordshire OX1 3AS; (01865) 726-871; **www.oxfordcity.co.uk**) or go to **www.ox.ac.uk/visitors.** If you want to see at least a few of the more famous colleges, a guided walking tour is your best option. These tours also show off the rest of Oxford and its colorful associations.

Oxford's **Guild of Guides** leads two-hour walking tours of the city center and the colleges that are open to guides on that particular day. Tickets are available from the Tourist Information Centre (or from the guide if the center is closed). Numbers are limited to 19 people per tour, and tickets are sold on a first-come, first-served basis. Tours leave the Tourist Information Centre at 15/16 Broad Street daily at 11 a.m. and 2 p.m. The cost is £6 adults, £3 children under age 16. Additional tours focus on Christ Church College, which is otherwise not open to tours, and also leave from the Tourist Information Centre on Saturday at 11 a.m. and 2 p.m.; the cost is £7 adults, £3.50 children under age 16. Call (01865) 726-871 for more information.

On **Inspector Morse Tours,** fans of the popular PBS series can visit the scenes of the detective's best-known cases; tours depart from the Tourist Information Centre on Saturday at 1:30 p.m.; the fee is £6.50 adults and £3.50 children. Entertaining nighttime Ghost Tours through Oxford's medieval streets and alleys depart from the Tourist Information

Centre on Friday and Saturday evenings at 8 p.m., July 1–September 31, and on October 31 (Halloween); the fee is £5 adults and £3 children. Call (01865) 250-551 for more information on these tours and to confirm departures. Tickets are available from the Information Centre (or from the guide if the center is closed).

Blackwell's Bookshop, Oxford's largest bookstore, sponsors **Tolkien Tours** that explore the haunts of the literature professor who wrote *The Lord of the Rings* and *The Hobbit;* there's only one tour a week, on Wednesday at 11:45 a.m., March–October. The shop also leads **Civil War Tours,** which take a look at places that figured in the 17th-century struggle between King Charles I and Oliver Cromwell; the background is fascinating and will considerably enhance the rest of your travels in Britain, where you'll continually encounter evidence of Cromwell's efforts to dissolve the monarchy and divest the church of power. Tours are on Friday at 2 p.m. and cost £6 adults, £5 seniors and children. Tolkien and Civil War tours start and finish at Blackwell's (53 Broad Street; (01865) 333-606).

Attractions in Oxford

Ashmolean Museum

Type of Attraction Oxford University's museum of art and archaeology

Location Beaumont Street

Admission Free

Hours June 1–August 31: Tuesday–Wednesday, Friday, and Saturday, 10 a.m.–5 p.m.; Thursday, 10 a.m.–7:30 p.m.; Sunday, 2–5 p.m.; September 1–May 31: Tuesday–Saturday, 10 a.m.–5 p.m.; Sunday, 2–5 p.m.

Phone (01865) 278-000

Website www.ashmol.ox.ac.uk

When to Go Anytime, as the museum is rarely crowded

Special Comments The museum has a café, but you may want to pop across the street to the Randolph Hotel, an Oxford landmark, for tea after a visit.

Overall Appeal by Age Group

Preschool ★	Teens ★	Over 30 ★★★
Grade school ★★	Young Adults ★★	Seniors ★★★

Author's Rating ★★★½

How Much Time to Allow 2 hours or more, since this is a museum where you'll want to spend some time poking around

Description & Comments The Ashmolean, founded in 1683, is the oldest public museum in England and houses the vast art and antiquities collection of the University of Oxford in a grand neoclassical building dating from the 1840s. You may find that it takes a little work to appreciate this museum: The Ashmolean is a bit dusty and makes few concessions to the commercialism and showmanship that seems to be the rage in museums these days. In each of the departments you'll find some amazing works. The collections of the Department of Antiquities include a wide-ranging representation of the early cultures of Europe, Egypt, and the Near East. The Cast Gallery holds one of the largest and best-preserved collections of casts in the world—the Parthenon frieze, the Apollo from Olympia, the Nike of Samothrace, and the Prima Porta Augustus are all here, in cast form. Many of these casts were done in the 19th century and are now in better condition than the originals, which have weathered or have been lost over time. The collections in the Museum of Eastern Art, and especially the ceramics, are surpassed only by those of the British Museum and the Victoria & Albert in London; they include unique examples of early Chinese ceramics, contemporary Chinese painting, Islamic pottery, and Japanese ceramics. The Ashmolean also has one of the two largest collections of Japanese paintings in Britain, and the Indian (including Tibetan and Southeast Asian) collections are also of international importance. The works on display in the Department of Western Art include Italian, Dutch and Flemish, French Impressionist, pre-Raphaelite, and Russian paintings, drawings, prints, sculpture, applied arts, and musical instruments from the Middle Ages to the present day. Among the department's most famous holdings are Paolo Uccello's *Hunt in the Forest* and Claude Lorrain's *Ascanius Shooting the Stag of Sylvia.* The Heberden Coin Room houses a collection of some 300,000 coins and medals.

Touring Tips This is not a child-friendly museum; though the mummies will engage the little ones for a few minutes, you'll enjoy the museum a lot more if you pack them off on another excursion while you idle in the galleries. You might want to consider sending them around the corner to the Oxford Story (see below).

Oxford Colleges

Type of Attraction Historic colleges built around inner quadrangles

Location Throughout Oxford

Admission Varies from college to college; admission fees are included in price of guided walking tours; see "Tours of Oxford," above

Hours Varies from college to college and may change seasonally

Website www.ox.ac.uk/visitors; this is the official website of Oxford University and lists opening times of the colleges, as well as concerts, exhibitions, and other events

When to Go Guided walking tours are offered daily at 11 a.m. and 2 p.m.; see "Tours of Oxford," above

Special Comments It's important to check with the university website or the Tourist Information Centre for hours and admission policies if you want to visit colleges on your own, without a guided tour; they are often closed.

Overall Appeal by Age Group

Preschool ★	Teens ★★	Over 30 ★★★★
Grade school ★★	Young Adults ★★	Seniors ★★★★

Author's Rating ★★★★

How Much Time to Allow Depends entirely on how many colleges you plan to visit and how much time you plan to spend at each; guided walking tours last 2 hours

Description & Comments There are 39 colleges in Oxford, serving some 16,000 students. Most of the colleges sit behind high walls and were built around inner courtyards called "quads." The following are the most architecturally and historically significant of Oxford's colleges. These enclaves differ greatly in architectural style—from the grandiose to the restrained—but in sum, they convey the overwhelming impression that you are in one of the world's greatest centers of learning, which indeed you are.

Balliol College, on Broad Street, was founded in 1263 by John Balliol, a lord of King Henry III, and Dervorguilla, his Scottish princess wife. Noted alumni include the translator of the Bible John Wyclif, and writers Aldous Huxley, Robertson Davies, and Graham Greene; many cabinet ministers and ambassadors; two prime ministers (Harold Macmillan and Edward Heath); and even a king, Olaf of Norway. The college is also infamously associated with Oxford's martyrs, Bishops Latimer and Ridley and Archbishop Crammer, who were burned in front of the college entrance for 17th-century heresy; the entrance doors to the college still bear scorch marks. Open daily, 2 p.m.–dusk. Admission is £1.

Christ Church College, facing St. Aldate's Street, was founded by Cardinal Wolsey, King Henry VIII's powerful associate, in 1525 and has Oxford's largest quad and most majestic architecture (some of it the work of Sir Christopher Wren) of any college in Oxford. Christ Church also claims a Norman church, St. Frideswide, that is better known as Oxford Cathedral, and, over the entrance, Tom Tower, with a bell that's rung 101 times nightly at 9:05 p.m. when the college gates are closed. Among alumni who have set their watches by the tolling are Lewis Carroll, William Penn, and John Wesley. Portraits by Sir Joshua Reynolds and William Gainsborough hang in the Christ Church Picture Gallery. The college is open Monday–Saturday, 9 a.m.–6 p.m., Sunday, 1–6 p.m.; the Picture Gallery is open Monday–Saturday, 10:30 a.m.–1 p.m. and 2–5:30 p.m., Sunday, 2–5:30 p.m. (closes at 4:30 p.m. October–March). Admission to the college (includes the Picture Gallery) is £4 adults, £3 seniors and children.

Magdalen (pronounced "MAUD-lin") **College,** on High Street, dates from the mid-15th century and was laid out with extensive grounds, including a deer park, cloisters, and some lovely water meadows along the River Cherwell that can be enjoyed from Addison's Walk. The Magdalen bell tower is one of Oxford's most famous landmarks and is the center of May Day celebrations that begin at dawn, when choristers sing a hymn from the tower, signaling surrounding pubs to open and general rowdiness to begin. Sir Edward Gibbon, of *The Decline and Fall of the Roman Empire* fame, described his time here as "the most idle and unprofitable of my whole life." Oscar Wilde is another notable alumnus. Open in summer, Monday–Friday, noon–6 p.m., and Saturday and Sunday, 2–6 p.m.; and in winter, Monday–Sunday, 2 p.m.–dusk. Admission is £3 adults, £2 seniors and children.

Merton College, near Merton Street, the only medieval cobbled street left in Oxford, harks back to the 13th century. Merton vies with Balliol and University Colleges in its claim to be the first center of learning in Oxford, but it certainly wins the prize for evoking the most medieval atmosphere. Mob Quad, unquestionably the oldest in Oxford, dates from the 14th century, as does the library, which contains such treasures as Geoffrey Chaucer's astrolabe and the first Bible to be printed in Welsh. J. R. R. Tolkien taught at Merton, and T. S. Eliot is among the alumni. Open Monday–Friday, 2–4 p.m.; Saturday and Sunday, 10 a.m.–4 p.m. Admission is £1.

Trinity College, on Broad Street, is well known for its splendid gardens and 17th-century chapel, paneled exquisitely in wood. A few of the buildings date to 1280 and were once part of Durham College, dissolved under Henry VIII; Sir Thomas Pope bought the site and established Trinity in 1550. One famous alumnus, Cardinal Newman, led the so-called Oxford movement, which attempted to reintroduce Roman Catholic doctrine to the Church of England. Open Tuesday–Sunday, 10:30 a.m.–noon and 2–4 p.m. (open Mondays in summer). Admission is £1.50 adults, £0.75 seniors and children.

Touring Tips A guided tour will enhance your visit to the colleges considerably, and the fee is less than you will pay in individual admissions to the colleges.

The Oxford Story

Type of Attraction Multimedia theme show about Oxford

Location 6 Broad Street

Admission £6.50 adults; £5.50 seniors and students; £5 children ages 5–15; £20 families of up to two adults and two children

Hours January–June: Monday–Saturday, 10 a.m.–4:30 p.m.; Sunday, 11 a.m.–4:30 p.m.; July–August: daily, 9:30 a.m.–5 p.m.

Phone (01865) 728-822

Website www.oxfordstory.co.uk

When to Go Weekdays, because the place is popular with local children on weekends

Special Comments Young travelers who might otherwise find Oxford to be a big bore are the best audience for the Oxford Story.

Overall Appeal by Age Group

Preschool ★	Teens ★★★	Over 30 ★★
Grade school ★★★	Young Adults ★★	Seniors ★★

Author's Rating ★★

How Much Time to Allow About 1 hour

Description & Comments The Oxford Story is another multimedia adventure from the folks who brought us the Jorvik Viking Centre in York and Canterbury Tales in Canterbury. Here, you sit in a moving car shaped like a medieval desk and are whisked past dioramas and moving figures that depict 800 years of Oxford history and the many famous folk who have lived, worked, and studied at the university, as related by your fictional guide, Magnus Magnusson. With so much "real" history to be seen in Oxford, you may not want to spend time and money to sit through these shenanigans, which seem all the sillier given the fact you're in one of the brainiest cities on earth. This audio-visual show will, however, fill you in on pieces of Oxford history that may enhance your own explorations—but then again, a walking tour, especially in the company of a good guide, will probably be a lot more informative.

Touring Tips Don't overlook the less showy exhibits that take a serious look at the contributions of modern-day Oxford researchers in such realms as medicine and science.

Dining in Oxford

In addition to dipping into the wealth of restaurants that fit the budgets of students as well as the local business types, consider dining in the many Oxford pubs (see "Entertainment and Nightlife in Oxford," below). Most offer decent lunches and dinners, though beware that these meals are often served in smoky, noisy surroundings. If you feel like grazing for a quick meal, stroll through the covered market at the intersection of High and Cornmarket Streets. Not only will you be surrounded by all the makings of a picnic, but any number of stalls and small shops sell sandwiches and other light fare. One of them, **Aunt May's** (phone (01865) 241-613), sells authentic Cornish pasties. Be prepared to do some walking after loading up on one of these delicious meat pies, which sit a bit heavily on the stomach.

A popular place for tea, coffee, and snacks is the **Grand Café** (84 High Street; (01865) 204-463), open daily 9 a.m.–7 p.m. The ornate interior and huge selection of pastries are impressive, but somehow the Grand isn't quite as Continental and swell as it pretends. A good way to follow up a meal in Oxford is with a stroll out to Little Claredon Street, just north of the center off Woodstock Road. There at number 55 you'll find **George and Davis** (phone (01865) 516-652) for an ice cream, homemade and available in dozens of varieties; George and Davis is open Monday–Sunday, 8 a.m.–midnight.

Restaurants in Oxford

Gee's ★★★

MODERN BRITISH | EXPENSIVE | QUALITY ★★★ | VALUE ★★★

61A Banbury Road; (01865) 553-540

Reservations Required **Entrée Range** £10.95–£18.95; 2-course lunch, £12.50; 3-course lunch, £16; 3-course dinner, £24.95 **Payment** V, MC, AMEX **Bar** Full service **Disabled Access** Yes

Hours Monday–Saturday, noon–2:30 p.m., 6–11 p.m.; Sunday, noon–11 p.m.

House Specialties Seared scallops as a starter, followed by grilled duck with orange sauce.

We recommend this perennial favorite in North Oxford (a ten-minute walk from the city center) for the fun of dining in an ornate Victorian conservatory. The glass-roofed dining room and the adjoining garden are smartly done up with rattan chairs and other summery effects to create an experience likely to make even locals feel like tourists out for a night on the town. Festive as the surroundings are, the kitchen takes its job very seriously, sending out duck, salmon, and other British standards that bear the mark of French influence with results that are at times a bit fussy (we prefer our foie gras without the accompaniment of a fried egg). Kids will love the holiday atmosphere at Gee's, and the kitchen does an expensive but tasty burger.

Le Petit Blanc ★★★★

FRENCH | MODERATE | QUALITY ★★★★ | VALUE ★★★

71–72 Walton Street; (01865) 510-999

Reservations Recommended **Entrée Range** £10–£16.50; 2-course prix fixe menu, £12.50; 3-course prix-fixe menu, £15 **Payment** V, AMEX, D **Bar** Full service **Disabled Access** Yes

Hours Monday–Friday, noon–3 p.m., 6–11 p.m.; Saturday, noon–3:30 p.m., 6–11 p.m.; Sunday, noon–3:30 p.m., 6:30–10 p.m.

House Specialties Mediterranean fish soup or boudin noir as starters, followed by beef Bourguignon or grilled salmon.

Like Pierre Victoire (below), Oxford's other smart French bistro is part of a small chain, this one under the stewardship of Raymond Blanc, one of Britain's top chefs. The setting is colorful and chic, and the offerings from the kitchen are reliably good, combining hearty French cuisine with some modern innovations that include many vegetarian options. The wine list is well chosen, with many excellent, moderately priced bottles.

Merton's Bar and Brasserie ★★★

BRITISH | INEXPENSIVE–MODERATE | QUALITY ★★★ | VALUE ★★★

Eastgate Hotel, High Street; (0870) 400-8201

Reservations Recommended **Entrée Range** £5.95–£21 **Payment** V, MC, AMEX, D **Bar** Full service **Disabled Access** Yes

Hours Daily, 8–10 a.m., noon–2:30 p.m., 6–10 p.m.

House Specialties The place is meat-lover's heaven, excellent for grilled steaks and chops.

Pleasantly done up in an unobtrusive cross between clubby and chic, Merton's is a nice place to settle for drinks and a steak dinner. There's an open fire in the winter, and a great deal of grilling goes on year-round, with an emphasis on grass-fed, hormone-free Scottish beef. A few fish dishes and vegetarian choices are also available, but if you're going to have a problem with your fellow diners cutting into thick slabs of meat, you might not be able to get into the Merton's aesthetic. The restaurant also serves Continental and full English breakfasts, and is open throughout the day outside meal times for coffee, drinks, and snacks.

Pierre Victoire ★★★½

FRENCH BISTRO | INEXPENSIVE–MODERATE | QUALITY ★★★½ | VALUE ★★★★

9 Little Claredon Street; (01865) 316-616

Reservations Recommended on weekends **Entrée Range** £7.95–£11.25; 1- to 3-course lunch, £5.90–£7.90; 2-course pretheater menu, £7.90; 3-course à la carte dinner, with wine, from £15 **Payment** V, MC, D **Bar** Beer and wine only **Disabled Access** Yes

Hours Monday–Saturday, noon–3 p.m., 6–11 p.m.; Sunday, noon–3:30 p.m., 6–10 p.m.

House Specialties French onion soup or duck breast with pistachio as starters; chicken breast stuffed with spinach purée or char-grilled swordfish or tuna as entrées.

Our recommendations for this bistro (set about a ten-minute walk north from the center) might not be available, since specials change daily and are posted on blackboards. Whatever you order here will be deftly prepared from fresh local ingredients and served with style. In fact, the food is so good and the surroundings so atmospheric, with wood and tile floors, rough wood tables, and brick walls, that it's hard to believe that Pierre Victoire is part of a small chain.

Entertainment and Nightlife in Oxford

Oxford has a lot to offer by way of entertainment. While many of these diversions are appropriately highbrow, as befits this city where everyone seems to sport a high IQ, Oxford also has many cozy pubs and clubs where culture is decidedly relaxed. There's so much going on at any given time in Oxford that you should make it a point to pick up a free copy of *This Month in Oxford* or other *What's On*–type listings distributed at hotels, at the Tourist Information Centre, and elsewhere around town.

Music and Theater

Chances are your visit to Oxford will coincide with a concert of classical or contemporary music because the city stages an admirable year-round schedule of performances by musicians from around the world. The main venues include the **Apollo Theatre** (on George Street; (0870) 606-3500), which regularly hosts the Glyndebourne Opera Touring Company and the Welsh National Opera; the **Holywell Music Room** (Holywell Street; (01865) 305-305), built in 1748 as Europe's first concert hall (Franz Joseph Haydn and George Frideric Handel both performed here); and the **Jacqueline du Pré Music Room** (St. Hilda's College; (01865) 276-821), the city's newest concert hall. Concerts are also held at **Christ Church Cathedral** (Christ Church College; (01865) 276-150), at the many university chapels, and at the **Sheldonian Theatre** (Broad Street; (01865) 277-299) designed by Sir Christopher Wren (see "Exploring Oxford," above). **Music at Oxford** mounts concerts from January to July, usually on Friday and Saturday evenings, at the Sheldonian Theatre; for more information, call (01865) 242-865 or visit **www.musicatoxford.com. Oxford Coffee Concerts** is a chamber-music series performed on Sunday mornings in the Sheldonian Theatre at 11:15 a.m. Tickets cost £7 and are available from the Oxford Playhouse box office on Beaumont Street (phone (01865) 305-305); for schedules and other information, visit **www.coffeeconcerts.com.**

Oxford has a lively theater scene and is a stop for many touring theater and dance companies and big-name acts. These often perform at the **Apollo Theatre** (on George Street; (0870) 606-3500), the city's largest performance space. The **Oxford Playhouse** (phone (01865) 305-305; **www.oxfordplayhouse.com**), opposite the Ashmolean Museum on Beaumont Street, also hosts touring companies, especially theater groups. The Playhouse was for many years associated with the university, and such luminaries as Richard Burton, John Gielgud, and Dirk Bogarde have acted on its stage. The theater is now independent but continues to launch new productions, so between visiting theater and its own productions, it usually offers something worth seeing. The tiny, 50-seat **Burton-Taylor Theatre** (phone (01865) 798-600) on Gloucester Street, funded by the famous pair and associated with the Oxford Playhouse just around the corner, mounts student productions during school term and hosts touring companies outside of term. The **Pegasus Theatre** (phone (01865) 722-851; **www.pegasustheatre.org.uk**) on Magdalen Road is more inclined to the avant-garde and also hosts productions by the Oxford Youth Theatre.

Clubs and Pubs

Oxford students unwind at a fairly large selection of nightspots where they listen to live music, dance, and run up bar tabs that probably bring their hardworking parents to the point of despair. But Oxford is a working city, too, and at most places, town and gown seem to mingle effortlessly. Most clubs are open Monday–Saturday from about 9 p.m. to 2 a.m. and charge covers of £2–£3. At many, you'll feel like a Stone Age relic if you're over 25. Some popular spots of the moment include **Zodiac** (190 Cowley Road; (01865) 420-042), with well-regarded live music; **Po Na Na** (13–15 Magdalen Street; (01865) 249-171), a small, dark, cave-like space that's funky and comfortable; and the **Bridge** (6–9 Hythe Bridge Street; (01865) 242-526), which we mention because it is an exception to the comment on age we made above and caters more to professional academics than to the young scholars they teach.

Then, of course, there are the pubs, most of which are open Monday–Saturday from noon to 11 p.m. and Sunday from noon to 10:30 p.m. (We're saving some of the city's famous "summer pubs," places where you can enjoy a pint on a riverside terrace as a reward for a walk through the countryside, for our section on "Exercise and Recreation in Oxford," below.) Two historic haunts in the city center are the **Eagle and Child** (49 St. Giles, (01865) 302-925), where J. R. R. Tolkien and Lewis Carroll found inspiration at the bottom of a glass, and the **Lamb and Flag,** just down the street at 12 St. Giles (phone (01865) 515-787), where the same crowd would pop in for a change of scenery and where Thomas Hardy allegedly wrote parts of *Jude the Obscure* in front of the fire. Oxford's most popular (and most crowded) drinking spot is probably the **King's Arms** (40 Holywell Street; (01865) 242-369), which is allegedly cozy but is so noisy and smoke-filled that you really won't be able to tell (or care). Honorable mention for antiquity also goes to the Bear Inn (6 Alfred Street; (01865) 728-164), which allegedly dates from 1262 and decorates its ages-old walls with ties donated by satisfied patrons. The **Head of the River** (phone (01865) 721-600) is the only so-called summer pub near the city center; follow St. Aldate's Street south from High Street to Folly Bridge, where the pub enjoys a picturesque location beside the Thames; like the other summer pubs, it's open year-round.

Shopping in Oxford

Chances are that you will not be too tempted to part with your hard-earned vacation dollars in Oxford—unless, that is, you are a bibliophile. If you are, you should make a beeline for **Blackwell's Bookshop** (48–52 Broad Street; (01865) 792-792), which since 1879 has been selling books from an originally tiny but now-expanded shop. Despite the shop's quaint appearance, it is enormous and stocks more than 200,000 new and rare books, many of them displayed on more than three miles of shelving in a cavernous underground bunker, the Norrington Room. Oxford University Press is the world's largest university press and traces its roots to the 15th century, when movable type was invented; the Press's admirable selection of dictionaries, reference works, and other books are available from the **Oxford University Press Bookshop** (116–117 High Street; (10865) 242-913).

A walk through the covered market at the intersection of High and Cornmarket Streets is an enlivening experience, especially if you pass by the dreary stalls selling cheap clothing and housewares and concentrate on the amazing selection of foods. You'll probably see game and other animals and victuals you didn't know people ate, and the selection of British cheeses is mouthwatering. Oxfam, Britain's huge relief and charity organization, was founded in Oxford in 1947. The **Oxfam Shop** (17 Broad Street; (10865) 241-333) is the first of the now-legendary Oxfam Shops throughout England that sell donated clothing, furniture, prints, and other merchandise that often constitutes a rare find at a bargain price. Should you nurse a secret desire to pass yourself off as an Oxford alum, you can garb yourself in logo-encrusted sweats and otherwise stock up on university-related paraphernalia at the **University of Oxford Shop** (106 High Street; (01865) 247-414).

Exercise and Recreation in Oxford

Oxford is laced with the Rivers Cherwell and Thames (known here as the Isis) and the water meadows that surround their banks. You can walk alongside the rivers or enjoy them from water level in a punt, a long, romantic-looking craft propelled by a combination of pole and brute strength. You can rent them by the hour from the **Cherwell Boathouse** (Banbury Road; (01865) 515-978) and **Old Horse Ford** (off High Street under the Magdalen Bridge; (01865) 202-643). Both are open mid-March–mid-October and charge £10 an hour, plus a hefty damage and theft deposit (should you float down the Thames and end up in the middle of London).

A popular way to spend a weekend afternoon is to follow the riverside paths, or to punt for that matter, to outlying "summer pubs" (which are open year-round but are especially pleasant in warm weather when they spill outdoors). Favorites include the thatch-roofed **Perch** (phone (01865) 728-891), reached by following Walton Street toward Binsey with a generous sweep of riverside lawn; and the nearby **Trout** (phone (01865) 302-071), a favorite lunch and drinks-in-the-garden spot in Wolvercoate, which is about a two-mile walk from the center of Oxford.

You can enjoy watching punting without fear of getting your feet wet during **Oxford's Eight Week,** at the end of May, when students from the different colleges take to the waters of the River Isis to work out their rivalries.

Around Oxford

Woodstock and Blenheim Palace

Woodstock is a small, charming town eight miles north of Oxford on A44 Evesham Road. While the narrow lanes invite a stroll, the attraction is the magnificent estate of **Blenheim Palace** whose gates are at the edge of town. Buses run regularly from Oxford's bus station on Gloucester Green and other locations to Woodstock.

Blenheim Palace

Type of Attraction Early 18th-century palace and birthplace of Sir Winston Churchill

Location Woodstock

Admission £10 adults; £8 seniors and children ages 16–17; £5 children ages 5–15; £26 families of up to two adults and two children; separate admission for formal gardens: £3.80 adults; £2.50 seniors and children

Hours Palace and formal gardens: March 14–October, daily, 10:30 a.m.–5:30 p.m. Park: year-round, daily, 9 a.m.–5 p.m. (last admission 4:15 p.m.)

Phone (01993) 811-325

Website www.blenheimpalace.com

When to Go Early or late to beat the crowds

Special Comments You can tour the palace on your own, but we recommend that you join one of the free guided tours that leave from the entrance every five to ten minutes, lasting about half an hour; the commentary is quite informative. You'll probably want to return to some of the rooms on your own to take a closer look at the paintings and the Winston Churchill exhibit.

Overall Appeal by Age Group

Preschool ★	Teens ★★	Over 30 ★★★★
Grade school ★★	Young Adults ★★★	Seniors ★★★★

Author's Rating ★★★★

How Much Time to Allow About 1 hour for the palace, another 1–2 hours to explore the grounds

Description & Comments Blenheim Palace was built for John Churchill, a soldier and general who won Queen Anne's favor by defeating the armies of Louis XV at the Battle of Blenheim in 1704. In recognition of his victory, the queen made Churchill the First Duke of Marlborough and rewarded him with funds to build this extraordinary palace, now a UNESCO World Heritage Site. Sir John Vanbrugh designed the palace with the assistance of Nicholas Hawksmoor. Blenheim is generally regarded as the most beautiful Baroque palace in England and is also one of the largest private homes in the land, though there's nothing homey about the place. As Sir John commented on his commission, he approached Blenheim "more as an intended Monument of the Queen's glory than a private habitation for the Duke of Marlborough."

For today's visitors, the house is most famously associated with Sir Winston Churchill, and you can visit the modest room where Britain's wartime prime minister was born in 1874 and tour a fascinating collection of Sir Winston memorabilia. Most of the house tour comprises a walk through a series of grandiose state rooms. You will want to pay special attention to the stone carvings by Grinling Gibbons, the foremost stone and wood carver of the 18th century, in the Great Hall; the tapestry in the Green Writing Room depicting the duke accepting the French surrender; and the Marlborough family portraits by Anthony Van Dyck, Joshua Reynolds, John Singer Sargent, and others in the Green Drawing Room and the rooms beyond.

Capability Brown and Achille Duchene, two of the most famous landscape architects of their day, designed Blenheim's sweeping acres of parkland, lakes, and gardens. The 2,200 manicured acres achieve a "natural" look and comprise some of the most famous and oft-photographed vistas in England—the two lakes that meet at a point spanned by an arched bridge are especially photogenic.

Touring Tips Several attractions on the grounds are geared to young visitors: the Butterfly House, the Marlborough Maze (the world's largest), and a narrow-gauge railway.

The Cotswolds

The Cotswolds hills are gentle landscapes of green hills, rushing streams, deciduous woodlands, and high open plateaus known as "wolds." Oh, and sheep—lots of sheep. Mostly dating from the Middle Ages, when trade in Cotswolds's wool made the region prosperous and famous throughout Europe, the villages and market towns are still remarkably prosperous-looking, built with a soft local stone that glows like butterscotch in the sunlight (which itself does occasionally make an appearance in these parts, especially during the warm summers). If these attributes

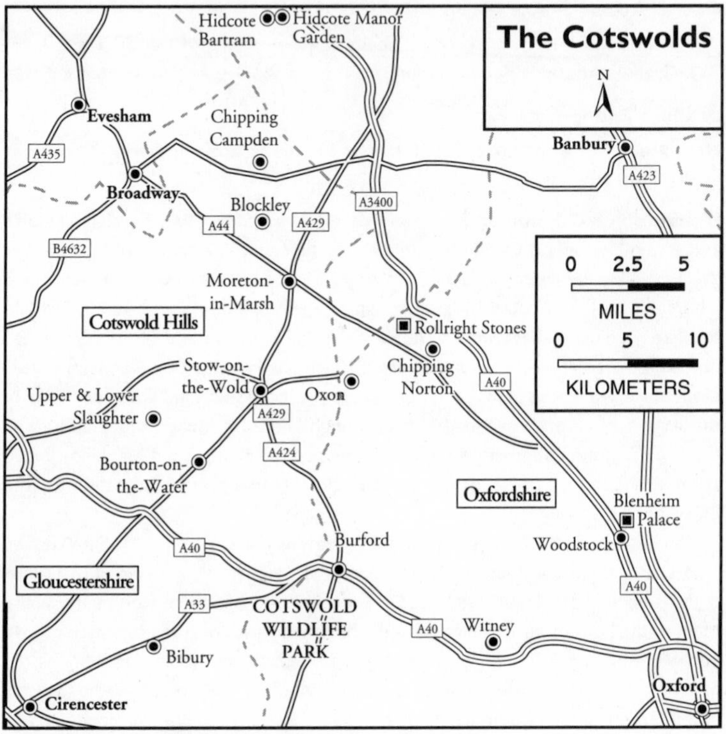

seem to comprise the English countryside as you expected it to be, you're quite right in your preconceptions. A visit here may well confirm your notion that England is full of people who live in thatch-roofed cottages, wear tweeds and sensible shoes, like long walks across sheep-studded meadows, and hang out in quaint tea shops and the paneled bars of country inns. Actually, a lot of British folks like to tour the Cotswolds to find the same sort of quintessential British charm.

In fact, so many people descend upon the Cotswolds that the region's rural pleasures can be a bit elusive at times. This is especially true in summer, when the villages are often filled to bursting. We recommend you visit in late fall, winter, or early spring, when, in a manner of speaking, you may well have the antiques shops, country inns, and lovely cobbled village marketplaces to yourself. If you visit the Cotswolds at times like this you may well come under their spell, because this is indeed a mellow and enchanting corner of the world.

Hotels in the Cotswolds

In the Cotswolds, you will find a bed, often one outfitted with the finest linen sheets, in some of the most distinctive accommodations in England. In many, room size and levels of luxury vary considerably, so some rooms may cost more than the rates we quote, which are the base prices for singles and doubles. You should reserve well in advance for stays on weekends and in summer, when hotels are often full. Out of season, and especially on weeknights, hoteliers are eager to lure guests into their empty rooms, and you'll often be able to arrange special rates that include room and dinner packages or substantial discounts for stays of two or more nights. Ask when booking or check the hotel websites.

Bantam Tea Rooms *£30–£60*

OVERALL ★★ | QUALITY ★★★ | VALUE ★★★★

High Street, Chipping Campden, Gloucestershire GL55 6HB; (01386) 840-386; thebantam@hotmail.com

Location In the center of Chipping Campden, a charming stone village.

Amenities & Services 3 rooms, all with adjoining baths and TV.

Elevator No.

Parking No.

Pricing Includes breakfast.

Credit Cards V, MC

These three rooms above a pleasant tearoom in a 17th-century stone house are several cuts above other bargain accommodations. They're large, warmly decorated with pine furniture and bright fabrics that show an eye to taste, and quite comfortable. All three have small baths with showers. The outlooks are pleasant, over a garden at the rear and Chipping Campden's marketplace to the front. Plus, if you want a cup of tea and a scone, all you need to do is walk downstairs.

The Cotswold House *£110–£120*

OVERALL ★★★★ | QUALITY ★★★★½ | VALUE ★★★

The Square, Chipping Campden, Gloucestershire GL55 6AN; (01386) 840-330; fax (01386) 840-310; reception@cotswold-house; www.cotswoldhouse.com

Location In the center of Chipping Campden, a charming stone village.

Amenities & Services 20 rooms. The Garden Restaurant and Hicks' Brasserie; Bang and Olufsen sound systems with CDs/DVDs; ISDN lines; luxurious bathrooms, most with TVs, deep tubs, and power showers; selection of pillows and bedding; working fireplaces in some rooms; beautiful gardens.

Elevator No.

Parking On grounds, free.

Pricing Includes full breakfast.

Credit Cards V, MC, AMEX, D

This lovely 17th-century house sits in the middle of Chipping Campden. Beyond the colonnaded porch and front door is a curving spiral staircase, and you soon notice an aura of drama and chic. Staying at the Cotswold House is a special and rather exciting experience. All of the rooms are distinctly decorated and manage to combine contemporary and traditional pieces effortlessly to provide comfort. The five so-called cottage rooms, in stone buildings set in the gardens, are especially nice (and cost considerably more than the rates above). In the Griggs room, centuries-old beams support the cathedral ceiling, and armchairs are grouped around a contemporary fireplace; the Hidcote cottage has a private terrace with hot tub. Service is attentive and as highly polished as the wood floors, yet a relaxed, homelike atmosphere prevails.

The Crown Inn *£60–£90*

OVERALL ★★★ | QUALITY ★★★ | VALUE ★★★★

High Street, Blockley, Gloucestershire GL56 9EX; (01386) 700-245; fax (01386) 700-247; info@crown-inn-blockley.co.uk; www.crown-inn-blockley.co.uk

Location In the center of the small village of Blockley.

Amenities & Services 24 rooms. Rafters restaurant, bar, pleasant lounge.

Elevator No.

Parking On grounds, free.

Pricing Includes breakfast; £39.95 per person for bed, breakfast, and dinner for bookings on three consecutive midweek nights.

Credit Cards V, MC, AMEX, D

A stay at the Crown provides a chance to experience a small and attractive village that's off the beaten path, yet Blockley is just a few miles from the bigger and better known towns of Chipping Campden, Stow-on-the-Wold, and Moreton-in-Marsh. The combination of hospitality and easygoing atmosphere makes the Crown popular with return guests, and if you don't know your way around the Cotswolds, the staff will gladly help you plan excursions. Actually, you may be tempted to settle in at this pleasant and well-managed inn and go nowhere at all; the hotel's dining room, Rafters, is excellent, and the friendly bar serves as the town's local pub. Rooms are unusually comfortable for the price, and many are quite distinctive: room 16 has a sitting room and terrace overlooking the garden, and room 24 is tucked under the centuries-old eaves and has an upper-level sitting room beneath the rafters.

Lygon Arms *£119–£179*

OVERALL ★★★ | QUALITY ★★★ | VALUE ★★

High Street, Broadway, Worcestershire WR12 7DU (01386) 852-255; fax (01386) 858-611; info@the-lygon-arms.co.uk; www.the-lygon-arms.co.uk

Location In the center of Broadway, one of the Cotswolds's most popular towns.

Amenities & Services 69 rooms. Great Hall dining room, Oliver's and Cotswolds bars, afternoon tea; two-line telephones, complimentary shoe shine and bathrobes, spa and indoor pool, large garden, 24-hour room service, porter, concierge, golf, horseback riding, fishing, hot-air ballooning available.

Elevator No.

Parking On grounds, free.

Pricing Includes full breakfast.

Credit Cards V, MC, AMEX, DC

This 16th-century former coaching inn and onetime headquarters for both Oliver Cromwell and King Charles I is now a member of the prestigious Savoy Group, which operates such five-star properties as the Savoy and the Berkeley in London. The Lygon Arms is also quite posh and is certainly popular, but it's a bit large, busy, businesslike (the hotel hosts many conferences), and expensive for our tastes. The rooms with the most character are in the original structure facing High Street, while others are in two newish wings. All of the rooms are comfortable, but you have to upgrade to a luxury room or a suite to surround yourself with paneling, fireplaces, beams, and the other telltale marks of a historic inn. On the plus side, the five-acre garden lends a countrylike air and is a welcome retreat from the tourist-crowded town in summer. The sitting rooms, bars, and baronial dining room are delightful, and if you don't stay here, we recommend that you stop by the Lygon Arms on your mandatory visit to Broadway to enjoy a pint or a cup of tea in front of a blazing hearth.

Mill House Hotel *£60–£120*

OVERALL ★★★★ | QUALITY ★★★½ | VALUE ★★★★

Kingham, Oxon, Oxfordshire OX7 6UH; (01608) 658-188; fax (01608) 658-492; stay@millhousehotel.co.uk; www.millhousehotel.co.uk

Location In the lovely countryside between Stow-on-the-Wold and Chipping Norton.

Amenities & Services 23 rooms. Attractive Marionette Room restaurant, bar, and lounges, beautiful grounds with trout stream.

Elevator No.

Parking On grounds, free.

Pricing Includes full breakfast.

Credit Cards V, MC, AMEX

Understated charm prevails in this converted stone mill house next to a bubbling stream in beautiful countryside. The bright, airy lounges and dining room have the feel of a family home and, like the guest rooms, are furnished comfortably and sensibly, minus the coy knickknacks that clutter up many a Cotswolds hostelry. Rooms vary considerably in size, décor, and level of luxury, though all are comfortable—since the rates are quite reasonable, we recommend making the jump from a standard room to one in the superior category. We especially like room 3, a cozy superior room under the eaves with a separate sitting area and an oversized bathroom. While the Mill House is only a short drive away from restaurants in Stow-on-the-Wold and Chipping Norton, you should plan on taking at least some of your meals in the hotel's excellent dining room (see "Dining in the Cotswolds," below).

The Royalist Hotel *£50–£90*

OVERALL ★★★★ | QUALITY ★★★★ | VALUE ★★★★

Digbeth Street, Stow-on-the-Wold, Gloucestershire GL54 1BN; (01451) 830-670; fax (01451) 870-048; info@theroyalisthotel.co.uk; www.theroyalisthotel.co.uk

Location In the center of Stow-on-the-Wold, an attractive stone village.

Amenities & Services 12 rooms. 947 AD Restaurant, Eagle and Child pub; stylish and comfortable lounge with open fire.

Elevator No.

Parking Yes.

Pricing Includes Continental breakfast; special bed breakfast and dinner packages available; rates increase on weekends.

Credit Cards V, MC, AMEX

Alan and Georgina Thompson, who received raves for their 755 Restaurant in London, took over this tenth-century inn several years ago and have created one of the Cotswolds's most distinctive hostelries. Meals in the Eagle and Child pub and 947 AD Restaurant are memorable (see "Dining in the Cotswolds," below), while the upper floors of the centuries-old inn have been refurbished to house unusually stylish and comfortable accommodations. Exposed beams, handsome wool carpets, and attractive furnishings appear throughout the hotel, and baths are new and well equipped. Even the tiny single room is appealing, and the two-floor Maugersbury Suite, with a stone-walled bedroom, upstairs sitting room, and Jacuzzi bath, is one of the best-valued hotel rooms we've seen in the Cotswolds.

The Swan *£180*

OVERALL ★★★ | QUALITY ★★★ | VALUE ★★★

Bibury, Gloucestershire, GL7 5NW; (01285) 740-695; fax (01285) 740-473; info@swanhotel.co.uk; www.swanhotel.co.uk

Location In the center of Bibury. which has been called the prettiest village in England.

Amenities & Services 20 rooms. Signet Room dining room, Jankowski's brasserie, bar, parlor and writing room, Jacuzzis in many baths.

Elevator No.

Parking On grounds, free.

Pricing Includes full breakfast.

Credit Cards V, MC, AMEX

There's no such thing as a standard room at this distinctive inn, so if the hotel isn't fully booked, ask to look around to select the room that is best suited to your taste. (Since photographs of each room and its adjoining bathroom appear on the hotel's website, you can request the room you want when you book.) All of the rooms are large, and all have luxurious bathrooms. Rooms at the front of the hotel have the advantage of facing the River Coln and the meadows that surround it;

room 14, a spacious twin-bed room, is an especially comfortable front room, while room 12 faces the rear and has a four-poster bed and other baronial furnishings. Public rooms are pleasant, especially when fires are blazing, and the hotel's pretty riverside garden is just across the road.

Exploring the Cotswolds

The Cotswolds villages are within easy driving distance from Bath and Oxford. You can easily explore them as day trips from those places, as well as from Stratford-upon-Avon (see pages 402), but part of the pleasure of touring the region is to stay in one of the inns that are thick on the ground in these parts.

On a two-day tour, you can visit several of the most beautiful Cotswolds villages. In each, you can usually see what you want within an hour or so, though you may want to linger a bit longer to shop and have tea. Though the villages are not far from each other, they are deep in the countryside on winding and sometimes confusing rural roads. A detailed road map is essential, and you will probably want to rent a car to go along with it; except for **Moreton-in-Marsh,** the villages are not served by trains, and bus service between the villages is infrequent. If you don't wish to drive, we recommend that you take one of the many tours that operate out of Bath and Oxford. One to consider is **Cotswold Roaming,** which operates day tours of the Cotswolds villages from Oxford; call (10865) 308-300 or visit **www.oxfordcity.co.uk/cotswold-roaming** for information.

In our coverage we approach the Cotswolds from Oxford, but the region is small enough—about 40 miles east to west and 25 miles north to south—that whichever route you take to reach the region and wherever you base yourself, you won't be too far from the other places you want to see.

Chipping Norton

This pleasant country town 19 miles north of Oxford via the A4144 and the A44 is a good place to begin a Cotswolds tour. Known as "the town on the hill," Chipping Norton—chipping means "market town"—is the highest town in the county of Oxfordshire and was once an important center for the Cotswolds wool trade. What you'll come to appreciate most about Chipping Norton is that it's relatively unspoiled and more concerned with going about its business than catering to tourists. The town crowds around its handsome marketplace, which is in turn surrounded by the medieval **Guildhall,** 15th-century St. Mary's Church and almshouses, Georgian houses, and a town hall dating from 1835. The **Visitor Information Centre** (in the Guildhall; (01608) 644-379; **www.oxfordshirecotswolds.org**) is a good place to stock up on information about Chipping Norton as well as other Cotswolds villages; the center is open March–October, Monday–

Saturday, 9:30 a.m.–5:30 p.m., and November–February, Monday–Saturday, 10 a.m.–3 p.m.

About four miles north of Chipping Norton, off the A3400, are the impressive remains of a Neolithic stone circle known as the **Rollright Stones** (open daily). Some 77 stones form a circle about 100 feet in diameter atop a secluded and atmospheric hilltop. The site was probably used as an ancient meeting place or sacred center during the Bronze Age.

Moreton-in-Marsh

This small, pretty village sits on a flat plain (a rarity in these parts) where the **Fosse Way,** a Roman road extending from Norfolk to Cornwall that is now the A429, crosses the old London-Worcester highway (A44); the town is about eight miles north of Chipping Norton on A44. Moreton-in-Marsh came to early prominence as a coaching stop, and it's now one of the few Cotswolds villages you can reach by train. Moreton is not huddled around a central square, like so many Cotswolds towns are; instead, elegant 17th- and 18th-century buildings are strung out for a mile or so along the broad High Street. Among them is **White Hart Royal,** a manor house in which King Charles I sheltered during the Civil War. **Curfew Tower** still sports its original clock and bell, dating from 1633, rung to tell the inhabitants to lock themselves in and cover their fires so they couldn't be seen by invaders. The village's street market, held on Tuesdays, is the largest in the Cotswolds and attracts some 200 vendors selling everything from antiques to fresh produce. You'll find information on the town and area at the **Moreton-in-Marsh Tourist Information Centre** (Cotswolds District Council Offices, High Street; (01608) 650-881; **www.moreton-in-marsh.co.uk**).

Chipping Campden

Many of the region's enthusiasts consider Chipping Campden, about ten miles northwest of Moreton-in-Marsh via A44 and B4081, to be the most beautiful of the Cotswolds villages, and the place certainly has enough charm and a lovely setting among hills and copses to win anyone over. While "Chippy" is pretty and quaint, it is by no means a sleepy little backwater. Tourists parade up and down High Street, where honey-colored stone buildings dating from the 14th to the 17th centuries house small shops, restaurants, and tea rooms. The 17th-century gabled market hall and 14th-century **Woolstaplers Hall** are surely among the most photographed buildings in England. For more information about the village and local attractions, stop in at the **Chipping Camden Tourist Information Centre** (Old Police Station, High Street; (01386) 841-206; **www.chippingcampden.co.uk**).

Hidcote Manor Garden

Type of Attraction Magnificent Cotswolds garden

Location Hidcote Bartram, just outside Chipping Camden

Admission £5.80 adults; £2.90 children; £14.50 families of up to two adults and two children

Hours March 23–May 31, August 1–September 30: Monday–Wednesday, Saturday and Sunday, 10:30 a.m.–6 p.m.; June 1–July 31: Monday–Thursday, Saturday and Sunday, 10:30 a.m.–6 p.m.; October 1–November 2: Monday–Wednesday, Saturday and Sunday, 10:30 a.m.–5 p.m.

Phone (01386) 438-333

Website www.nationaltrust.org.uk/hidcote

When to Go Early in the morning or late in the afternoon to avoid crowds

Special Comments Much of the garden is easily accessible to wheelchairs.

Overall Appeal by Age Group

Preschool ★	Teens ★★	Over 30 ★★★
Grade school ★	Young Adults ★★★	Seniors ★★★

Author's Rating ★★★★

How Much Time to Allow 1–2 hours

Description & Comments One of the most influential and inventive gardens of the 20th century, Hidcote was created by Major Lawrence Johnstone. Starting in 1907, over some 30 years Johnstone relandscaped ten acres of inhospitable terrain and designed a series of "outdoor rooms" separated by walls and terraces. Each "room" is a small, unique garden with its own special plantings and atmosphere, and Hidcote is laced with many enticing walkways and spots to sit (though weekend crowds can make contemplation difficult). Part of the garden's magic is the variety of borders and plants, and some of them always seem to be in bloom.

Touring Tips A restaurant on the site serves lunch, noon–2:30 p.m., and tea, 3–5:30 p.m.

Broadway

What must be the most popular Cotswolds village (think tour buses) is about four miles east of Chipping Campden on the B463. Artist and craftsman William Morris supposedly "discovered" Broadway in the 19th century, and artists since that time have drawn inspiration from the textures and composition of what, with a little imagination to see beyond the summertime hordes, might still be regarded as a quintessential English village. If you want to avoid the commercialism that threatens to overtake Broadway, come in winter—then you'll better be able to appreciate this village of mellow honey-colored stone that grew up as a stagecoach stop along High Street, the width of which gave the place its name and is today lined with pretty chestnut trees. The **Lygon Arms,** the town's best-known inn (see "Hotels in the Cotswolds," above) and other local establishments once supplied fresh horses for coaches making the steep haul up the escarpment that rises above Broadway. The hill is now topped by the **Broadway Tower,** an 18th-century whimsy built by the earl of Coventry. Unless you're keen on paying to see views similar to those you can glimpse for free from many a Cotswolds hilltop, there's no need to climb the tower. But should you wish to do so, the tower is open April–October, daily, 10:30 a.m.–5 p.m.; November–March, Saturday and Sunday, 11 a.m.–3 p.m. Admission is £4 adults, £2.30 children, and £11.50 families of up to two adults and three children; for more information, call (01386) 523-90. You can stock up on information about the Cotswolds at **Cotswolds Info** (Windrush House, Station Road; (01386) 853-577).

Stow-on-the-Wold

It's easy to see where the old saying, "Stow-on-the-Wold where the wind blows cold" originates if you pay a visit to this high-lying, handsome stone town in winter. Stow, 12 miles south of Broadway on A44 and A424 and surrounded by rolling grazing lands, manages to maintain a sense of a proud market town. English provincial life transpires quietly and politely on the central marketplace, surrounded by a nice blend of shops selling antiques as well as everyday essentials. There's also a well-stocked **Stow-on-the-Wold Tourist Information Centre** (in Hollis House, on the Square; (01451) 831-082; **www.glos-cotswolds.com**).

Bourton-on-the-Water

Sorry to say, one of the loveliest of the Cotswolds villages has become a victim of its charm. This still-attractive but no-longer-tranquil village, about five miles south of Stow-on-the-Wold on A429, now has the atmosphere of a theme park. Even so, it's a pleasure to walk along the River Windrush, which despite its name courses through town at a leisurely pace and is crisscrossed by a string of beautiful, low stone bridges. Bourton is usually a hit with young travelers, who enjoy the attractions that make the rest of us yearn for days gone by when we might have stumbled upon this place before it was *so* discovered. The **Model Village** (High Street behind the Old New Inn; (01451) 820-467) is a 1/9-scale miniature replica of the village built of Cotswolds stone in 1937 (you have to wonder why people are willing to pay to walk through a model of the village they're in). The model is open daily in summer, 9 a.m.–6 p.m., and in winter, 10 a.m.–4 p.m.; admission is £2.75 adults, £2.25 seniors, and £2 children. At **Birdland Park** (Rissington Road; (01451) 820-480), pelicans, penguins, cranes, and colorful toucans and parrots squawk, flutter, and wade in some 50 different aviaries; the park is open daily, April–October, 10 a.m.–6 p.m., and November–March, 10 a.m.–4 p.m.; admission is £4.60 adults, £3.60 seniors, £2.60 children, £13 families of up to two adults and two children. **Cotswold Motor Museum** (in the Old Mill, (01451) 821-255) houses a collection of cars, motorcycles, and children's pedal cars as well as a small collection of historic toys; it's open daily, February–November, 10 a.m.–6 p.m.; admission is £2.50 adults, £1.75 children. Information about the village is available at the **Bourton-on-the-Water Tourist Information Centre** (Victoria Street; (01451) 820-211; **www.bourton-on-the-water.co.uk**).

Bibury

Bibury became famous when William Morris, that arbiter of Victorian taste, described the hamlet as "the most beautiful village in England." Actually, we're not sure we would entirely agree with this bit of Victorian hyperbole, but we will go so far as to say that we think this small village, about ten miles south of Bourton-on-the-Water off A429, is certainly one of the most beautiful and unspoiled villages in the Cotswolds. The one tourist attraction, aside from the local trout farm, is **Arlington Row,** a photogenic row of stone cottages with steeply pitched stone roofs that began as a monastic sheep house or wool store some time around 1380. In the 17th century, the buildings were converted into cottages for weavers, who supplied cloth for Arlington mill. **Rack Isle,** a water meadow next to the River Coln in the center of town, was once used to hang out the cloth on racks to dry. Bounded on three sides by water and seasonally flooded, this meadow provides a good habitat for water-loving plants and birds. **St. Mary's,** near the end of town, is a small, remarkably unspoiled church that dates from Saxon times. Information about Bibury and surrounding attractions is available at the **Bourton-on-the-Water Tourist Information Centre** (Victoria Street; (01451) 820-211; **www.bourton-on-the-water.co.uk**).

Dining in the Cotswolds

You'll never go hungry in the Cotswolds, as every village and country crossroads in between has a restaurant, and many are excellent. Many of the region's best restaurants are located in hotels and inns; most of these offer attractive bed and dinner packages to overnight guests and also welcome non-guests in their dining rooms.

Eagle and Child Pub ★★★★

INNOVATIVE PUB | MODERATE | QUALITY ★★★★ | VALUE ★★★★

Royalist Hotel, Digbeth Street, Stow-on-the-Wold; (01451) 830-670

Reservations Recommended on weekend evenings **Entrée Range** £7.75–£14.25 **Payment** V, MC, AMEX **Bar** Full service **Disabled Access** Yes

Hours Monday–Saturday, noon–2:30 p.m., 6–10 p.m., Sunday, noon–3 p.m., 6–9 p.m.

House Specialties Smoked haddock chowder, smoked chicken spring rolls, or Mediterranean charcuterie to start, followed by wild mushroom and asparagus tart or local sausages.

The Eagle and Child shares the kitchen with 947 AD Restaurant in the Royalist Hotel (see below). While the setting is more informal and the menu more varied and casual, the cuisine is serious (after all, rib steak and venison is not your typical pub fare). But the Eagle and Child still has the soul of a pub—it's a popular local gathering spot, fish and chips are on the menu, and you'll be encouraged to linger over a pint or two in the beamed interior or pleasant garden as long as you wish.

Hicks' ★★★★

CONTINENTAL | MODERATE | QUALITY ★★★★ | VALUE ★★★

In the Cotswold House, The Square, Chipping Campden; (01386) 840-330

Reservations Recommended on weekends **Entrée Range** £9.50–£13.25; prix fixe at Monday–Saturday lunch and 6–7 p.m.: £12.50 for 2 courses, £15.50 for 3 courses **Payment** V, MC, AMEX **Bar** Full service **Disabled Access** Yes

Hours Daily, 9 a.m.–9:30 p.m.

House Specialties Chorizo or tiger prawn salad to start, followed by Cornish mackerel or beef Bourguignon.

This airy, bright brasserie in the Cotswold House is as stylish as the rest of the hotel, and it serves an innovative menu in a relaxed setting. Hicks' is especially welcome if you've been making the rounds of more traditional inns and dining on heavier fare. Here you can order some of the appetizer salads as main dishes, and many of the offerings are vegetarian, including a risotto of pumpkin and wild mushroom and a fennel and chicory tartlet.

Jankowski's ★★★

MODERN BRITISH/BISTRO | MODERATE | QUALITY ★★★ | VALUE ★★★

Swam Hotel, Bibury, Gloucestershire; (01285) 740-695

Reservations Not necessary **Entrée Range** £8.95–£15.95 **Payment** V, MC, AMEX **Bar** Full service **Disabled Access** Yes

Hours Daily, noon–2:30 p.m., 6–9:30 p.m.; open 10 a.m. for tea and coffee, 3–5:30 p.m. for cream tea

House Specialties Grilled Bibury trout (from the trout farm across the road); Scottish beef burger.

Jankowski's is the brasserie of the Swan inn (see "Hotels in the Cotswolds," above), and much more casual than the hotel dining room at the other end of the building. This is an especially nice warm-weather spot, when seating moves from the attractive, Mediterranean-looking main room onto a stone terrace, where a meal is accompanied by the sound of the rushing waters of the River Coln. Sandwiches, ploughman's, and other light lunches are available, and daily dinner specials usually include roast turkey and other traditional standards as well as lamb kebabs and other slightly exotic flourishes.

Mill House Hotel ★★★★

BRITISH | MODERATE | QUALITY ★★★★ | VALUE ★★★★

Kingham, Oxon, Oxfordshire OX7 6UH; (01608) 658-188

Reservations Recommended **Entrée Range** £15.95–£17.50; prix fixe: 3-course lunch, £15.75; 3-course dinner, £23.75 **Payment** V, MC, AMEX, D **Bar** Full service **Disabled Access** Yes

Hours Daily, noon–2 p.m., 7–9 p.m.

House Specialties Boudin of smoked salmon to start, followed by pot-roasted guinea fowl or roast rump of lamb.

A meal in the hotel's Marionette Room is a pleasant and easygoing event that begins with cocktails in the bar or hotel lounge. You place your order from the comfort of an easy chair, are escorted to your table when the first course is about to be served, then retire to the bar or lounge for coffee and after-dinner drinks. The staff carries these arrangements off with aplomb and gracious hospitality, and the offerings from the kitchen are creatively prepared from fresh local ingredients; the wine list is extensive and well-chosen. Lunch at the Mill House is a nice way to break up a day of sight-seeing in the surrounding hills and dales.

947 AD Restaurant ★★★★

MODERN BRITISH | EXPENSIVE | QUALITY ★★★★ | VALUE ★★★

Royalist Hotel, Digbeth Street, Stow-on-the-Wold; (01451) 830-670

Reservations Required on weekends, recommended at other times **Entrée Range** 2 courses, £27; 3 courses, £32 **Payment** V, MC, AMEX **Bar** Full service **Disabled Access** Yes

Hours Monday–Saturday, 7–9 p.m., Sunday, noon–3 p.m.

House Specialties Roast quail or seared scallops to start, followed by roast fillet of local beef or braised rack of local lamb.

Alan and Georgina Thompson, who made a great success of London's 755 Restaurant, now bring their considerable talents for hospitality and fine cuisine to one of England's oldest inns. Heavy beams and a massive old hearth lend character to the room, yet both the surroundings and the cuisine have an innovative, fresh feel. We suggest you begin a meal with cocktails in the hotel's attractive lounge, where you can also enjoy coffee and an after-dinner drink in front of the fire.

Exercise and Recreation in the Cotswolds

The Cotswolds are excellent walking country. The main walking route through the region is the 100-mile-long **Cotswolds Way,** a national trail that runs from Bath to Chipping Campden and traverses gentle hills and valleys and passes through many lovely stone villages. For the most part, a walk on the trail requires only moderate exertion, and villages, with their welcome tea shops and pubs, seem to lie around every bend in the path. You can spend a very nice week walking the entire route, covering

15 miles or so a day and stopping for the night at hotels and bed-and-breakfasts along the way. Tourist information centers in any of the Cotswolds villages, as well as in Bath and Oxford, can provide information on the walk. **Cotswold-Way** provides guidebooks to the route (which are also available in any bookshop for miles around) and will arrange accommodations and luggage transfer from point to point along the route; e-mail them at enquiries@cotswold-way.co.uk or check out **www.cotswold-way.co.uk.**

Local tourist offices can also provide information on the other footpaths in the region. Two especially scenic walks are the **Windrush Way** and **Wardens Way,** both between the villages of Bourton-on-the-Water and Winchcombe. Cotswolds lanes are especially good for cycling, and you can rent bicycles in many of the villages. Expect to pay about £10 a day and £40 a week at shops like **Hartwells** (High Street; Bourton-on-the-Water, (01451) 820-405) and **Cotswolds Country Cycles** (Longlands Farm Cottage, Chipping Campden; (01386) 438-706).

Part Nine

The Heartland and Welsh Border

This moniker is apt for a region that encompasses not only the middle part of England but also incorporates cities and towns where much of that quality we associate with "Englishness" took root. Shakespeare was born here, in **Stratford-upon-Avon;** the industrial revolution exploded in and around **Manchester** and other cities in this region; and it seems only fair to mention, the Beatles burst onto the international scene from their humble roots in **Liverpool.** What's more, here in this swath of England, you'll see the great variety of past and present that constitute British life—dark Victorian remnants, modern business complexes, popular tourist haunts, and sleepy villages.

Not To Be Missed in the Heartland and Welsh Border

- Albert Dock in Liverpool (page 390)
- Barber Institute of Fine Arts in Birmingham (page 396)
- Beatles' homes in Liverpool (page 391)
- Ludlow (page 400)
- Mappa Mundi in Hereford Cathedral (page 400)
- Shakespeare sights in Stratford-upon-Avon (page 405)
- Victorian and Edwardian architecture in Manchester (page 382)
- Walker Art Gallery in Liverpool (page 392)
- Whitworth Art Gallery in Manchester (page 385)

Manchester

Manchester, in the heart of the industrial northwest, has seen worse days. Time was, the city was the soot-choked industrial nightmare Charles Dickens wrote about in *Hard Times.* Along with atrocious working conditions and social ills, those 19th-century decades of the Industrial Revolution brought enormous wealth to Manchester, and the city became even more important with the opening of the Manchester Ship Canal, creating an inland port around the turn of the 20th century.

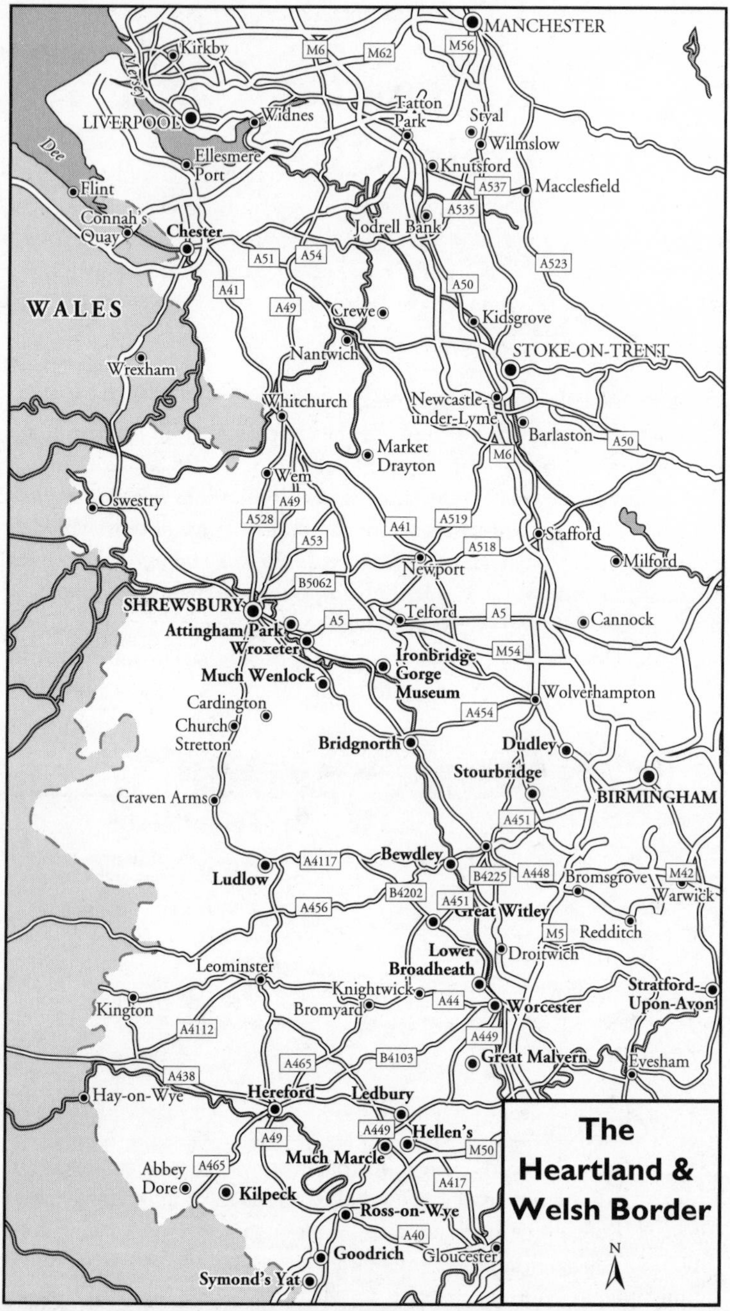

MANCHESTER
Kirkby
M6
M62
M56
Mersey
LIVERPOOL
Widnes
Tatton Park
Styal
Wilmslow
Dee
Ellesmere Port
Knutsford
Flint
A537
Macclesfield
A535
Connah's Quay
Chester
Jodrell Bank
A51
A54
A523
A41
A50
WALES
A49
Crewe
Kidsgrove
Nantwich
STOKE-ON-TRENT
Wrexham
Whitchurch
Newcastle-under-Lyme
Barlaston
A50
Market Drayton
M6
Wem
Oswestry
A49
A528
A41
A519
Stafford
A53
A518
Newport
Milford
B5062
SHREWSBURY
Telford
A5
A5
Cannock
Attingham Park
Wroxeter
Ironbridge Gorge Museum
M54
Much Wenlock
Wolverhampton
Cardington
A454
Church Stretton
Bridgnorth
Dudley
Stourbridge
BIRMINGHAM
Craven Arms
A451
Bewdley
Ludlow
A4117
B4225
A448
Bromsgrove
M42
Warwick
B4202
A451
A456
Great Witley
Redditch
M5
Lower Broadheath
Droitwich
Leominster
Knightwick
Stratford-Upon-Avon
Kington
Bromyard
A44
Worcester
A4112
A449
Great Malvern
Evesham
A465
B4103
A438
Hay-on-Wye
Hereford
Ledbury
A449
Hellen's
A49
M50
Much Marcle
Abbey Dore
A465
Kilpeck
A417
Ross-on-Wye
A40
Goodrich
Gloucester
Symond's Yat
The Heartland & Welsh Border
N

These days, following almost a hundred years of decline, the city is enjoying something of a renaissance. We don't recommend that you go too far out of your way to see Manchester, but if you are in the region anyway or come to Manchester on business, the city is well worth a look. Much of the heart of the city remains pompously Victorian and Edwardian, and the old behemoths are rather interesting to look at; huge swaths of 19th-century brick warehouses and mills are being converted to shops and housing complexes. While Manchester is hardly as cosmopolitan as London, the ongoing revitalization and an ever-burgeoning gay scene suggest that this is a city on the move.

Planning Your Visit to Manchester

The **Manchester Visitor Information Centre** (Town Hall Extension, Lloyd Street; (0161) 234-3157; **www.manchester.gov.uk**) is open Monday–Saturday, 10 a.m.–5:30 p.m., and Sunday, 11 a.m.–4 p.m. It's well-stocked with brochures on local sights and has an accommodation booking service.

Special Events in Manchester

In late winter and early spring, Manchester stages an enormous three-day gay **Mardi Gras** with a big parade and lively street performances. Manchester celebrates the **Festival Europa** in late May, when street theater, markets, live music, and dance and sports events take over the city.

Arriving and Getting Oriented in Manchester

Manchester is 207 miles north of London. Trains run about every half hour from London's Euston Station to Manchester's Piccadilly Station, about a ten-minute walk from Albert Square in the city center. The trip takes from two hours and 45 minutes to three hours, and the round-trip is about £60. For more information, call (08457) 484-950 or go to **www.railtrack.co.uk.**

By car, Manchester is about three or four hours, depending on traffic, from London on the M1 and M6 motorways to junction 21A, where you head east on the M62. The M62 becomes the M602 as you enter Manchester.

Manchester Airport, 15 miles south of the city, handles direct flights from the United States and the Continent. **Airport Link,** an aboveground train, runs from the airport terminal to Piccadilly Railway Station in downtown Manchester every 15 minutes, 5:15 a.m.–10:10 p.m., less often through the night; the trip takes about 20 minutes. Bus numbers 44 and 105 travel between the airport and Piccadilly Gardens Bus Station every 15 minutes during the day, and hourly during evenings and on Sunday; the ride takes about 55 minutes.

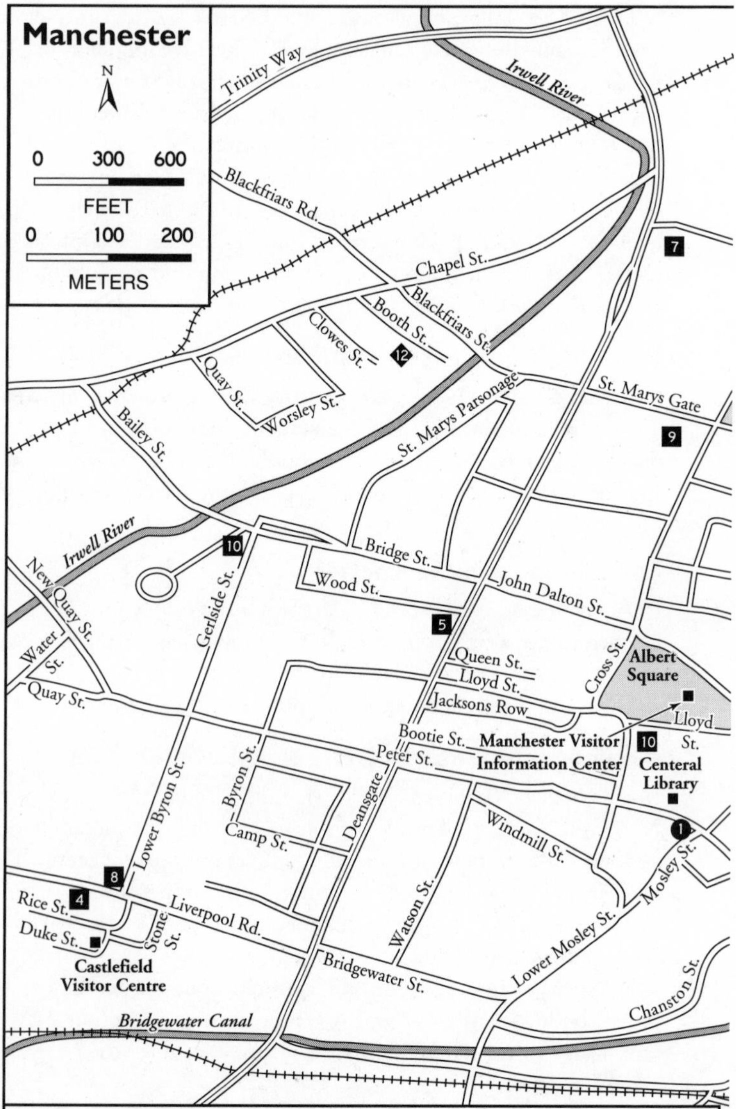

HOTELS

1. Holiday Inn Crowne Plaze Midland Hotel
2. Le Meridien Palace
3. The Place Apartment Hotel

ATTRACTIONS

4. Castlefield
5. John Rylands Library
6. Manchester Art Gallery
7. Manchester Cathedral
8. Museum of Science and Industry
9. Royal Exchange
10. Town Hall
11. Whitworth Art Gallery

RESTAURANTS

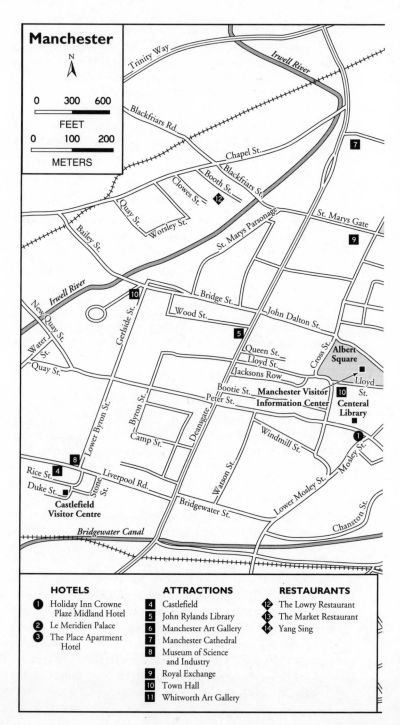

12. The Lowry Restaurant
13. The Market Restaurant
14. Yang Sing

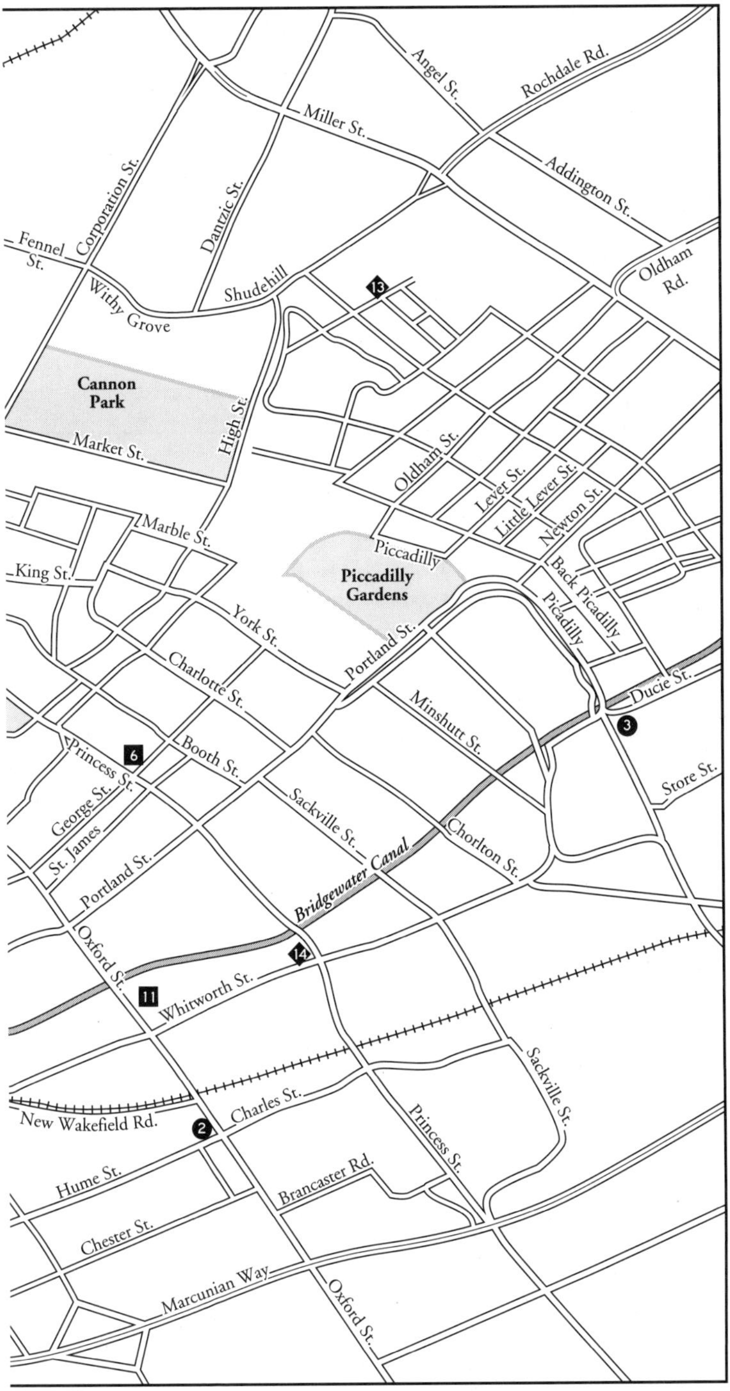
Angel St.
Rochdale Rd.
Miller St.
Addington St.
Corporation St.
Dantzic St.
Fennel St.
Oldham Rd.
Withy Grove
Shudehill
13
Cannon Park
High St.
Market St.
Oldham St.
Lever St.
Little Lever St.
Newton St.
Marble St.
Piccadilly
Piccadilly Gardens
King St.
Back Piccadilly
Piccadilly
York St.
Portland St.
Ducie St.
3
Charlotte St.
Minshull St.
6
Princess St.
Booth St.
Store St.
George St.
St. James
Sackville St.
Chorlton St.
Portland St.
Bridgewater Canal
Oxford St.
14
11
Whitworth St.
Sackville St.
Charles St.
New Wakefield Rd.
2
Princess St.
Hume St.
Brancaster Rd.
Chester St.
Marcunian Way
Oxford St.

HOW HOTELS COMPARE

Hotel	Overall Rating	Quality Rating	Value Rating	Price
Manchester				
Le Méridien Palace	★★★★	★★★½	★★★★	£75–£89
Holiday Inn Crowne Plaza Midland Hotel	★★★★	★★★	★★★	£129–£135
The Place Apartment Hotel	★★★	★★★★	★★★	£99
Birmingham				
Hotel du Vin	★★★★	★★★★	★★★½	£110
New Hall Thistle	★★★★	★★★	★★★★	£103–£110

National Express buses leave London's Victoria Coach Station for Manchester every hour to every hour and a half. The trip takes five to six hours and costs about £35 round trip. For more information, call (08705) 808-080 or go to **www.gobycoach.com.**

Getting around Manchester

Trains from London stop at Piccadilly Station on the eastern end of Manchester. Nearby Piccadilly Gardens, where the bus station is located, is a busy inner-city transportation hub. From there, Mosley Street, a major north-south artery, leads south to the city center.

Central Manchester, where you'll want to be, is compact and easily walkable. **Metrolink Trams** connect the Piccadilly bus and train stations to central Manchester. Self-service ticket machines dispense zone-based fares. Buses operate 6 a.m.–11 p.m., with limited route service until 3 a.m.; tickets are available from the driver.

Hotels in Manchester

Holiday Inn Crowne Plaza Midland Hotel — *£129–£135*

OVERALL ★★★★ | QUALITY ★★★ | VALUE ★★★

Peter Street, St. Peter's Square, Manchester, Lancashire M60 2DS; (800) 897-121, (0161) 236-3333; fax (0161) 932-4100; sales.cpmanchester@6c.com; www.ichotelsgroup.com

Location In city center off St. Peter's Square.

Amenities & Services 303 rooms. Three restaurants, two bars, fitness center with swimming pool, concierge, 24-hour room service, laundry, shoe shine.

Elevator Yes.

Parking Yes, £8 a day.

IN THE HEART OF ENGLAND AND WELSH BORDER

Hotel	Overall Rating	Quality Rating	Value Rating	Price
Birmingham (continued)				
Hyatt Regency Birmingham	★★★	★★★	★★★	£110
Stratford-upon-Avon				
Shakespeare Hotel	★★★★	★★★	★★½	£140–£165
Dukes Hotel	★★★	★★★	★★★★	£69
Thistle Stratford-upon-Avon	★★★	★★★	★★	£101–£115

Pricing Includes full breakfast.

Credit Cards V, MC, AMEX, DC

This Edwardian railroad hotel, built in 1903 is a city-center landmark easily identified by its terra cotta façade, and it's one of the city's best hostelries. Public rooms are especially grand, while guest rooms are large and high-ceilinged but, while perfectly comfortable and well appointed, are a bit bland for the atmospheric surroundings. Services, however, are plentiful, and the service is excellent.

Le Méridien Palace *£75–£89*

OVERALL ★★★★ | QUALITY ★★★½ | VALUE ★★★★

Oxford Street, Manchester, Lancashire M60 7HA; (0161) 288-1111; fax (0161) 288-2222; www.lemeridien.com

Location In the city center, opposite Palace Theatre and Oxford Road railway station.

Amenities & Services Two restaurants, bar; concierge; 24-hour room service, laundry, dry cleaning; business services; Jacuzzis.

Elevator Yes.

Parking Yes, about £8 per day.

Pricing Sometimes includes full breakfast, depending on room rate.

Credit Cards V, MC, AMEX, D

The Méridien group has done a fine job with this Edwardian hotel, nicely refurbishing the public spaces and guest rooms while leaving the original flourishes intact. There are three categories of guest rooms: Standard and Executive, both decorated in Edwardian style (Executive rooms are quite a bit larger), and Ambassador, which are cavernous and sumptuous, with canopied beds and added amenities, including refrigerators. The quietest rooms in any category face the courtyard, though the exterior rooms on the third and fourth floors have pleasant views of the city.

The Place Apartment Hotel — *£99*

OVERALL ★★★ | QUALITY ★★★★ | VALUE ★★★

Ducie Street, Manchester, Lancashire M1 2TP; (0161) 778-7500; info@theplaceforliving.com; www.theplaceforliving.com

Location In city center, near Piccadilly railway station.

Amenities & Services 100 rooms. 24-hour room service, daily maid service, CD and DVD players.

Elevator Yes.

Parking Yes.

Pricing Discounted rates on weekends.

Credit Cards V, MC, AMEX, D

One of many conversion projects in central Manchester has transformed a former industrial space into this exciting new accommodation. The one- and two-bedroom apartment units surround a dramatic atrium and are large and loftlike, with interesting architectural touches like brick walls. State-of-the-art kitchens are fully equipped, with crockery as well as washer/dryers, and there are large sitting and dining areas and separate bedrooms in all units. While the hotel is geared to professionals on long-term assignment in Manchester, a stay of even a night here provides a pleasant break from the hotel circuit.

Exploring Manchester

Though Manchester doesn't offer too much in the way of "sights," just wandering through the predominantly Victorian core can make for an interesting outing. Most of what you will want to see in Manchester is located within an easy walk of Albert Square, dominated by the massive, spooky Victorian **Town Hall.** Just to the south of this edifice, on St. Peter's Square, is another enormous civic structure, the **Central Library**, dating from the 1930s and once the largest municipal library in the world. A more interesting stop for bibliophiles would be **John Rylands Library,** a walk of a few blocks east down Brazennose Street to Deansgate. The gloomy, late Gothic–style building, erected in the 1890s, houses an impressive collection of rare manuscripts. Admission is free, and the library is open Monday–Friday, 10 a.m.–5 p.m. and Saturday, 10 a.m.–1 p.m. Manchester is also home to the oldest public library in the English-speaking world, **Chetham's Library,** near the banks of the River Irwell, on Long Millgate; the library was founded in 1653 in a medieval complex dating from 1421. Many of the works are from the 16th and 17th centuries. Admission is free; open Monday–Friday, 9:30 a.m.–12:30 p.m. and 1:30–4:30pm.; call (0161) 834-7961 for more information.

The **People's History Museum,** in the old Pump House of Manchester's municipal water supply on Bridge Street, displays a wonderful collection of artifacts, from tools to photographs, that commemorate the working people of Britain over the past two centuries. The museum is open Tuesday–Sunday, 11 a.m.–4 p.m., and admission is £1; for more information, call (0161) 839-6061. If you follow the River Irwell north to Market Street and turn inland, you will soon pass the **Royal Exchange,** an elaborate structure built to accommodate the city's cotton traders, from the days when mills still fueled the local economy. Within the shell of its brick exterior is the steel and glass Royal Exchange Theatre, where the stage productions are as innovative as the surroundings. **Manchester Cathedral** is just north, on Victoria Street; the massive structure dates from the 15th century and has the widest nave in Britain.

Back in the vicinity of St. Peter's Square, Manchester's former central railway station has been converted to the **G-Mex Centre,** which now hosts trade shows and major events. Just south is **Castlefield,** one of the city's oldest industrial districts laced with canals and now preserved as a seven-acre heritage park.

Attractions in Manchester

Manchester Art Gallery

Type of Attraction World-class art collection

Location Mosley Street

Admission Free

Hours Tuesday–Sunday, 10 a.m.–5 p.m.

Phone (0161) 235-8888

Website www.manchestergalleries.org

When to Go Anytime, weekdays if possible

Special Comments The museum has an excellent restaurant and a shop.

Overall Appeal by Age Group

Preschool —	Teens ★★★	Over 30 ★★★★
Grade school ★★	Young Adults ★★★	Seniors ★★★

Author's Rating ★★★

How Much Time to Allow About 1 hour

Description & Comments Manchester's excellent art gallery is housed in a neoclassical building in the shadows of Town Hall and has just undergone a £35 million revamp. Among the improvements is a dramatic new Gallery of Craft and Design, where the museum's collection of decorative art, craft, and design is housed, ranging from ancient Greek pottery to contemporary furniture. The museum's crowd pleasers (also surprisingly popular with youngsters and young adults) are works by pre-Raphaelite painters Dante Gabriel Rossetti, John Everett Millais, William Holman Hunt, and Ford Madox Brown. In fact, the museum is said to have the finest pre-Raphaelite collection in Britain.

Touring Tips If you have young ones with you, seek out the Clore Interactive Gallery, where exhibits are geared to introducing art to children ages 5–12.

HOW ATTRACTIONS COMPARE

Attraction	Comments	Author's Rating
Manchester		
Whitworth Art Gallery	Fine art, textiles, and wallpapers	★★★★
Manchester Art Gallery	World-class art collection	★★★
Museum of Science and Industry	Relics of Manchester's industrial past	★★★
Liverpool		
Beatles' Homes	Childhood homes of John Lennon and Paul McCartney	★★★★★
Walker Art Gallery	Magnificent art gallery	★★★★
Birmingham		
Barber Institute of Fine Arts	One of Britain's finest collections of European art	★★★★
Birmingham Museum and Art Gallery	Notable pre-Raphaelite collection	★★★

Museum of Science and Industry

Type of Attraction Old buildings housing relics of Manchester's industrial past

Location Castlefield

Admission Free

Hours Daily, 10 a.m.–5 p.m.

Phone (0161) 832-2244

Website www.msim.org.uk

When to Go Try to avoid weekends (when the museum can be quite crowded) and wet days, as it's necessary to walk outdoors to reach the different buildings.

Special Comments The museum sponsors some excellent tours on topics such as Manchester mills and the steam age; the general museum tour, the first Saturday of every month at 11:30 a.m. and 2 p.m., provides a good introduction to England's industrial past.

Overall Appeal by Age Group

Preschool ★★	Teens ★★	Over 30 ★★★
Grade school ★★★	Young Adults ★★★	Seniors ★★★

Author's Rating ★★★

How Much Time to Allow At least 2 hours

Description & Comments The world's oldest railway station (from 1830) and other buildings from Manchester's industrial past house a collection of artifacts

IN THE HEART OF ENGLAND AND WELSH BORDER

Attraction	Comments	Author's Rating
Hereford		
Hereford Cathedral	Norman cathedral with rare medieval documents	★★★★
Stratford-upon-Avon		
Anne Hathaway's Cottage	Childhood home of Shakespeare's wife	★★★
Mary Arden's House and Shakespeare Country Museum	Tudor farm where Shakespeare's mother was born	★★★
Shakespeare's Birthplace	Half-timbered house where the Bard was born	★★★
Hall's Croft	Elegant Tudor home	★★½
New Place/Nash's House	Site of Shakespeare's last home	★★
Warwick		
Warwick Castle	Medieval fortress above the River Avon	★★

that seem all the more evocative since many are in a place where they were once part of day-to-day life. Giant locomotives, huge mill engines, even a 19th-century sewer pay tribute to Manchester's past, while jet-age aircraft and helicopters incongruously fill the restored 19th-century market hall.

Touring Tips The museum has many exhibits oriented to children, as well as plenty of gadgetry that will interest them; get a map at the entrance.

Whitworth Art Gallery

Type of Attraction Museum of fine art, textiles, and wallpapers

Location Oxford Road, south of the city center on the campus of the University of Manchester

Admission Free

Hours Monday–Saturday, 10 a.m.–5 p.m.; Sunday, 2–5 p.m.

Phone (0161) 275-7451

Website www.whitworth.man.ac.uk

When to Go Anytime

Special Comments The collection is so rich that you might want to join the so-called "eye-opener" tours on Saturdays at 2:30 p.m.

Overall Appeal by Age Group

Preschool —	Teens ★★	Over 30 ★★★
Grade school ★★	Young Adults ★★★★★	Seniors ★★★

HOW RESTAURANTS COMPARE

Name	Cuisine	Overall	Quality	Value	Price
Manchester					
The Lowry Restaurant	British	★★★★	★★★★	★★★★	Mod
The Market Restaurant	British	★★★★	★★★★	★★★	Mod–Exp
Yang Sing	Chinese	★★★	★★★	★★★	Mod
Birmingham					
Bistro du Vin	French	★★★½	★★★	★★★	Exp
Titash	Balti/Tandoori	★★★	★★★½	★★★★	Inexp
Michelle's La Bastille	French	★★★	★★★	★★★★	Mod

Author's Rating ★★★★

How Much Time to Allow At least 2 hours

Description & Comments This excellent gallery is administered by the University of Manchester and is renowned for its collections of watercolors and rare textiles. A walk through the galleries is full of surprises, as you might encounter an etching by Piranesi, a Turner watercolor, a fragment of 18th-century wallpaper, or a tapestry by 20th-century artist Eduardo Paolozzi. Exhibitions change frequently, as the museum has room to show only a small portion of its holdings at any one time.

Touring Tips You might want to stroll into Whitworth Park, which adjoins the museum, and take a look at some of the buildings of the University of Manchester.

Restaurants in Manchester

The Lowry Restaurant ★★★★

MODERN BRITISH | MODERATE | QUALITY ★★★★ | VALUE ★★★★

The Lowry, Pier 8, Salford Quays; (0161) 876-2121

Reservations Recommended **Entrée Range** £7.95–£13.95; prix fixe 2-course lunch, £10.95–£14; prix-fixe 2-course pretheater dinner, £13.95–£17.90 **Payment** V, MC, AMEX, D **Bar** Full service **Disabled Access** Yes

Hours Daily, noon–3 p.m., 5:15–10 p.m.

House Specialties Any of the seafood preparations.

The Lowry is a futuristic shopping and entertainment complex on Manchester's historic quays, and the eponymous restaurant is in the hands of well-known chef Steven Saunders. The preparations are exquisite, and the multilevel, waterside, glass-enclosed dining room is dramatic—indeed, given the quality of the food, service, and setting, a meal here is an exceptional bargain.

The Market Restaurant ★★★★

BRITISH | MODERATE–EXPENSIVE | QUALITY ★★★★ | VALUE ★★★

104 High Street; (0161) 834-3743

IN THE HEART OF ENGLAND AND WELSH BORDER

Name	Cuisine	Overall	Quality	Value	Price
Stratford-upon-Avon					
Boathouse	Asian/ International	★★★★	★★★★	★★★	Mod–Exp
Quatro	British	★★★★	★★★★	★★★	Exp
Garrick	Pub	★★★★	★★★	★★★★	Inexp
1564	Café	★★★	★★★	★★★	Inexp

Reservations Recommended **Entrée Range** £12.95–£15.95 **Payment** V, MC, AMEX, DC **Bar** Full service **Disabled Access** Yes

Hours Friday, 6–10 p.m.; Saturday, 7–10 p.m.

House Specialties Traditional yet innovatively prepared British lamb and beef dishes, as well as seafood and vegetarian choices.

Our only complaint about this unpretentious, simply decorated restaurant north of the center is that its hours are so limited. Then again, serving only two meals a week seems to allow the kitchen to concentrate on its preparations, which are outstanding. The menu changes every six weeks to accommodate seasonal variations, and it always includes an appetizing mix of choices with a little exotic flair, such as risotto cakes or wild mushroom pancakes. The wine list is excellent, and there is a long list of specialty beers.

Yang Sing ★★★

CHINESE | MODERATE | QUALITY ★★★ | VALUE ★★★

34 Princess Street; (0161) 236-2200

Reservations Recommended **Entrée Range** £8.50–£15 **Payment** V, MC, AMEX **Bar** Full service **Disabled Access** Ground floor only

Hours Monday–Friday, noon.–11:30 p.m.; Saturday and Sunday, noon–12:30 a.m.

House Specialties Dim sum, daily specials.

Manchester has a large Chinese population, and it's probably second only to London when it comes to its number of good Chinese restaurants. Yang Sing has been a favorite with local Chinese and British diners for years, and the place serves excellent Cantonese dishes in two crowded rooms.

Entertainment and Nightlife in Manchester

Performing Arts

Manchester is the home of the acclaimed **Halle Orchestra,** the **BBC Philharmonic,** and the **Manchester Camerata** chamber music group.

They perform at **Bridgewater Hall,** a marvelous new concert hall with outstanding acoustics, situated just off St. Peter's Square; call (0161) 907-9000 for information. The **Royal Exchange Theatre Company** is one of England's most venerable companies and occupies a spectacular space—a new theater enclosed within the hall of the Royal Exchange, Manchester's former trading center; call (0161) 833-9833 for tickets and information. The **Library Theatre,** in the Central Library on St. Peter's Square, presents new and classic stage works; call (0161) 236-7110. The **G-Mex Centre,** on Lower Mosley Street, is a major venue for traveling shows, musicals, and dance programs; for events schedules and tickets, call (0161) 834-2700. To attend a free concert, contact BBC's **New Broadcasting House** on Oxford Road, where audiences can attend tapings of musical performances; call (0161) 244-4001.

Bars and Clubs

Over the past ten years or so, Manchester has become one of Europe's major gay centers, and, accordingly, has one of England's liveliest gay and lesbian nightlife scenes. Most of the city's gay shops, restaurants, hotels, and clubs are located in a small area just east of Town Hall, on and around Princess Street, known as Gay Village. Here, and elsewhere in Manchester, bars and pubs are open standard pub hours (to 11 p.m. Monday–Saturday and 10:30 p.m. Sunday), and clubs stay open to 2 a.m. or so.

Clubs and bars come and go as quickly in Manchester as they do anywhere else, but some that seem to be withstanding the test of time include **Churchill's** (37 Chorlton Street; (0161) 236-5529), a friendly and old-fashioned pub for Gay Village locals. **Napoleons** (35 Bloom Street; (0161) 366-8800) is one of Manchester's oldest discos, and **New Union** (111 Princess Street; (0161) 228-1492) offers a high-spirited stage show, karaoke, and disco. **New York, New York** (98 Main Street; (0161) 236-6556) boasts a neon sign of a limp-wristed Statue of Liberty out front and a wild party scene within. **Paradise Factory** (112–116 Princess Street; (0161) 273-5422) is Manchester's largest and most popular disco, with many floors packed with serious clubsters. The **Rembrandt** (33 Sackville Street; (0161) 236-1311) is Manchester's oldest and friendliest gay pub.

Some other bars to check out, regardless of sexual orientation, include **Cybercafe** (12 Oxford Street; (0161) 236-6300) a fully licensed café/bar with computer workstations, so you can drink and click. **Britons Protection** (Castle Street; (0161) 236-5895) and **Perevil of the Peak** (Great Bridgewater Street; (0161) 236-6365) are wonderfully atmospheric Victorian pubs in the historic Castlefield District.

Shopping in Manchester

For the trendiest Manchester boutiques, check out **St. Ann Square** and especially the **Royal Exchange Shopping Centre,** with many fashionable clothing stores, and the **Royal Exchange Crafts Centre,** where many shops sell glassware, dinnerware, jewelry, and crafts made in Britain. Other large shopping venues include the **Triangle,** on Exchange Square. This Victorian landmark was known as the Corn Exchange before much of the building was destroyed in a 1996 IRA bombing; after a thorough restoration, the sleek shopping center houses a not-terribly-exciting collection of housewares, clothing, and cosmetics shops in surroundings that are more appealing than the goods on sale. The **Arndale Centre,** in the city center on Market Street, is one of Europe's largest covered shopping centers and houses some 200 shops. **Chinatown**, behind Piccadilly Plaza and the City Art Gallery, is one of the most colorful quarters of the city and has many gift shops and markets.

Some shops to go out of your way to find are the **Gallery Manchester's Art House** (131 Portland Street; (0161) 237-3551), which sells work by artists from Manchester and elsewhere in northern England, and the **Manchester Craft Centre,** set in a restored Victorian glass-and-iron structure (17 Oak Street; (0161) 832-4274) and specializing in ceramics, glass, and textiles by local craft artists.

Around Manchester

Liverpool

Liverpool is just 34 miles southwest of Manchester and shares with that city the distinction of having been, as recently as a hundred years ago, one of the wealthiest cities in Europe. In the 18th century, the city made its fortune in the slave trade, shuttling human cargo from Africa across the Atlantic to the colonies. In the 19th century, Liverpool's sprawling docks took in cotton from the Americas and other raw materials from all over the world and shipped out the products of Britain's enormous mills. And yes, in the 1960s, Liverpool became famous for another export—the Beatles, who were reared in Liverpool and who are much commemorated here. These days, Liverpool seems to be waiting for better times to return, though the only place you're going to get much of an inkling that might happen is on **Albert Dock,** a vast historical conversion project on the backs of the River Mersey.

Planning Your Visit to Liverpool

The main **Liverpool Tourist Information Centre** (Atlantic Pavilion, Albert Dock; (01517) 088-854) is open daily, 10 a.m.–5:30 p.m. Another center, near Lime Street Station in the Queen's Square Centre on Roe Street (phone (01517) 093-285), is open daily, 9 a.m.–5:30 p.m.

Arriving and Getting Oriented in Liverpool

Trains run from Manchester's Piccadilly Station to Liverpool's Lime Street station about every half hour, and the trip takes about 45 minutes;

call (08457) 484-950 or go to **www.railtrack.co.uk.** Even if you have a car with you in Manchester, take the train to avoid the traffic you'll encounter getting into and out of both cities. When you arrive at Lime Street Station, take a look around—the magnificent 19th-century terminal was the largest in the world when it was built.

Exploring Liverpool

Most sights of interest in Liverpool are clustered on or around the historic preservation project known as Albert Dock. A free shuttle bus runs to this riverside quarter from Lime Street Station, but before you board or set out on foot, take time to visit some of the attractions in the immediate vicinity of the station. A ten-minute walk up Mount Pleasant Hill brings you to the Roman Catholic **Metropolitan Cathedral of Christ the King,** stirring controversy ever since the concrete, funnel-shaped structure was completed in 1967; whatever you think of the futuristic exterior, step inside, because the diffusely lit, round interior is serene and contemplative. The church is open daily, 8 a.m.–6 p.m.; call (0151) 709-9222 for information. Down Hope Street, toward the River Mersey, is the Anglican **Cathedral Church of Christ,** a neo-Gothic structure so different from the Catholic cathedral that you can't help but wonder if the architectural contrast wasn't deliberate. The massive sandstone structure—the largest church in Britain and fifth-largest in the world—wasn't completed until 1978, so for the moment at least it holds claim to be the last Gothic cathedral built anywhere in the world. The cathedral is open daily, 8 a.m.–6 p.m.; call (01517) 096-271 for information.

St. George's Hall, a massive and handsome Greek Revival building immediately across Lime Street from the station, still serves in part as a courthouse. W. S. Gilbert, of Gilbert and Sullivan fame, once practiced law here, but, fortunately, his shortcomings as a solicitor led him to his career in music. Just up the street is the **Walker Art Gallery,** one of the finest art collections in Britain (see profile below).

Albert Dock, on the River Mersey, is the center of much of the activity in Liverpool these days. You can walk to the dock in about ten minutes from the station, following Ranleigh and Hanover Streets toward the river, or take the Albert Dock shuttle, which circulates through the city center about every half hour. Albert Dock once bustled with the trade that for much of the 19th and early 20th centuries made Liverpool a wealthy trading city. The magnificent brick warehouses, resting on iron pillars along the Merseyside quays, had sat empty for years when they were converted to an appealing complex of shops, restaurants, offices, and museums.

You can learn about Liverpool's past in the **Merseyside Maritime Museum** and the **Museum of Liverpool Life,** where the fascinating exhibits trace the city's history as a major shipbuilding center and as a port. Cotton from America came through Liverpool, and finished goods were exported; it was also through Liverpool that hundreds of thousands of Irish immigrants passed on their way to a new life in America. This history is richly recounted in displays, while several historic vessels are docked outside. The museums are open daily, 10 a.m.–5 p.m., and admission is free; call (0151) 478-4499. The **Tate Liverpool,** a branch of the London museums, mounts changing exhibits of modern art in attractive galleries fashioned from a converted warehouse; it's open Tuesday–Sunday, 10 a.m.–5:50 p.m.; admission is free; call (0151) 702-7400.

The most popular attraction in Albert Dock is the **Beatles Story,** a gimcrack tourist trap that re-creates 18 scenes from the career of the Fab Four; open April–October, 10 a.m.–6 p.m., and November–March, 10 a.m.–5 p.m.; £7.95 adults, £5.45 seniors and students, £4.95 children, £23 families; for more information, call (0151) 709-1963 or visit **www.beatlesstory.com.** If you want to continue in the tracks of the famous local lads, try to book a place on one of the tours of the childhood homes of John Lennon and Paul McCartney (see below). Meanwhile, you can pay homage to another famous musical group, Gerry and the Pacemakers, and take a "Ferry cross the Mersey"; boats leave from Pier Head, just north of Albert Dock. If you don't know this famous 1960 group, who added another notch in Liverpool's fame with this hit song, you'll probably enjoy seeing the busy Liverpool docks from the water anyway.

Beatles' Homes

Type of Attraction Childhood homes of John Lennon and Paul McCartney

Location Outlying neighborhoods; buses leave from Albert Dock and Speke Hall

Admission £10

Hours Late March–late October: Wednesday–Saturday, 10:30 and 11:20 a.m. (tours leave from Albert Dock), 1:50 and 3:55 p.m. (tours leave from Speke Hall; call for directions)

Phone (0151) 427-7231

Website www.nationaltrust.org.uk

When to Go Whenever you can—spaces on the tours are limited and hard to get

Special Comments Photography is not allowed in the houses, and visitors are asked to leave all bags at the door.

Overall Appeal by Age Group

Preschool —	Teens ★★★★	Over 30 ★★★★★
Grade school ★★★	Young Adults ★★★★	Seniors ★★★★

Author's Rating ★★★★★

How Much Time to Allow At least 3 hours, for bus trip to houses and tours; you may also want to take the time to tour the house and gardens at Speke Hall, a Tudor estate included in the tours.

Description & Comments The childhood homes of John Lennon and Paul McCartney, all but national shrines, are now in the hands of the National Trust and open to the public. The McCartney House, restored to the way it looked in the 1950s when Paul grew up here, is a modest row house where the Beatles often met to rehearse and where they wrote some of their first songs. Mendnips is the middle-class, semi-detached house where John Lennon lived with an aunt from 1945 to 1963; it's furnished with period originals, right down to the checkered linoleum and 1940s kitchen appliances. Anyone who came of age during the "Beatles Revolution" will be deeply moved by seeing these unpretentious houses, and in their modesty they brilliantly pay tribute to the legendary Fab Four.

Touring Tips The houses can only be visited on guided tours that leave from Albert Dock for morning visits, and Speke Hall, a half-timbered Tudor house set in magnificent gardens near the Liverpool airport, for afternoon visits (admission price on the Beatles houses tours also includes entrance to Speke Hall). Spaces are extremely limited, so call well in advance of your visit to Liverpool to reserve.

Walker Art Gallery

Type of Attraction A magnificent art gallery

Location William Brown Street

Admission Free

Hours Monday–Saturday, 10 a.m.–5 p.m.; Sunday, noon–5 p.m.

Phone (01514) 784-199

Website www.nmgm.org.uk/walker

When to Go Monday–Saturday, 10 a.m.–5 p.m.; Sunday, noon–5 p.m.

Special Comments There's a pleasant café in the museum, and the store is one of the most interesting places to shop in Liverpool, with glassware, jewelry, and other work by local artisans.

Overall Appeal by Age Group

Preschool —	Teens ★★	Over 30 ★★★★
Grade school ★★	Young Adults ★★★	Seniors ★★★★

Author's Rating ★★★★

How Much Time to Allow At least 1 hour

Description & Comments One of the finest museums outside of London, and reason enough to come to Liverpool for an afternoon, it was founded in the 1870s by former mayor Sir Andrew Barclay Walker. Since then, the collection has grown to encompass a remarkable range of works, from those by medieval Europeans to works by Lucian Freud and other modern British artists. The museum's two strongest collections are the Netherlandish and Italian works from 1350 to 1550 and the pre-Raphaelite paintings by William Holman Hunt, John Everett Millais, and Dante Rossetti and others. Also in the wide-ranging mix are works by Thomas Gainsborough, David Hockney, and Lucas Cranach.

Touring Tips The museum often mounts special exhibits that are well worth seeing; check the website to see what is on view at the time of your visit.

Birmingham

Britain's second-largest city is not particularly appealing. Harsh, concrete buildings rise from the soulless city center, and highways rip through the center of town. Clearly, this city is about business, not easygoing lifestyle and tourism, and business—whether in one of the many factories or office complexes or exhibition halls—is what brings most visitors to Birmingham. If you do find yourself here, check out the museums we profile below and buy a ticket for one of the many excellent concerts, plays, and other performances on offer.

Planning Your Visit to Birmingham

The **Birmingham Tourism Centre** (near International Convention Centre, 2 City Arcade; (0121) 202-5000; **www.birmingham.org.uk**) is open Monday–Saturday, 9:30 a.m.–5:30 p.m., and Sunday, 10:30 a.m.–4:30 p.m. The center is well-stocked with brochures on local sights and sells tickets for the city's hefty schedule of performing-arts events.

Arriving and Getting Oriented in Birmingham

Birmingham is 120 miles northwest of London. Trains run about every 15 minutes from London's Euston Station to Birmingham's New Street Station, on Navigation Street in the city center. The trip takes from an hour and 45 minutes to two hours, and the round-trip fare begins at £26. For information, call (08457) 484-950 or go to **www.railtrack.co.uk.** By car, Birmingham is about two hours from London on the busy M40.

National Express buses leave London's Victoria Coach Station for Birmingham's Digbeth Coach Station, adjacent to the train station, every half hour to every hour throughout the day. The trip takes two hours and 40 minutes and costs about £18 round trip. For more information, call (08705) 808-080 or go to **www.gobycoach.com.**

Hotels in Birmingham

Hotel du Vin *£110*

OVERALL ★★★★ | QUALITY ★★★★ | VALUE ★★★½

Church Street, Birmingham B3 2NR; (0121) 200-0600; fax (0121) 236-0889; info@hotelduvin.com; www.hotelduvin.com

Location In the city center, near the cathedral.

Amenities & Services 66 rooms. Three bars, excellent bistro, health club with spa treatments, weekend wine courses.

Elevator Yes.

Parking In nearby car parks.

Pricing Continental breakfast, £9.50; English breakfast, £13.50; package rates available.

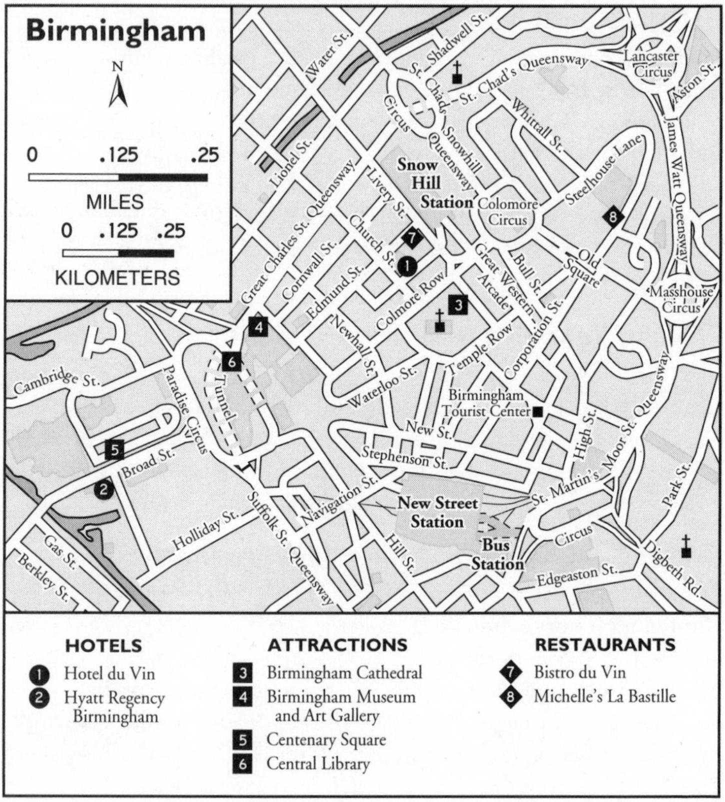

Credit Cards V, MC, AMEX, D

We'd almost go out of our way to be in Birmingham just to spend the night in this stylish and comfortable hotel, one of a small boutique chain that is enlivening the accommodation scene in cities around Britain. The hotel occupies the former Birmingham Eye Hospital, a formidable early-19th-century structure that has been stunningly converted to retain such features as an elegant grand staircase and marble foyer as well as bay windows, high ceilings, and woodwork. New touches in the comfortable guest rooms include sleek modern furniture, fine linens, large showers, and luxuriously deep tubs.

Hyatt Regency Birmingham £110

OVERALL ★★★ | QUALITY ★★★ | VALUE ★★★

2 Bridge Street, Birmingham B1 2JZ; (0121) 643-1234; fax (0121) 616-2323; birmingham@hyattintl.com; www.hyatt.com

Location In the city center, next to the convention center.

Amenities & Services 319 rooms. Restaurant, bar, café, 24-hour room service; business center, fitness center with swimming pool, Internet access.

Elevator Yes.

Parking On premises; ask for price when booking.

Pricing Continental breakfast sometimes included, depending on room rate.

Credit Cards V, MC, AMEX, D, DC

From the glossy atrium to the bland and comfortable guest rooms, you won't encounter many surprises in this generic chain hotel, an attractive, glass high-rise linked to Birmingham's International Convention Centre and geared to professionals attending events there. The location is ideal, too, if you plan on attending a concert or play at one of the city's excellent performing-arts venues. In addition to the restaurant, a cocktail-lounge area in the atrium serves tea and light meals; both eateries are most welcome in this commuter city where an evening meal can be hard to find.

New Hall Thistle — *£103–£110*

OVERALL ★★★★ | QUALITY ★★★ | VALUE ★★★★

Walmeley Road, Sutton Coldfield, Birmingham B76 1QX; (0870) 333-9147; fax (0870) 333-9247; newhall@thistle.co.uk; www.thistlehotels.com/newhall

Location About 9 miles outside city center.

Amenities & Services 62 rooms. Formal restaurant, lounge. Nine-hole golf course, tennis courts, croquet.

Elevator No.

Parking On premises, free.

Pricing Includes full breakfast.

Credit Cards V, MC, AMEX, D

A good way to enliven a visit to Birmingham is with a stay in this unique and pleasant hotel occupying the oldest inhabited manor house in England. The moated, 12th-century stone house is set in 26 acres of gardens and has been tastefully outfitted with gracious guest rooms decorated in fairly sumptuous country-house style. The oak-paneled public rooms, including the award-winning restaurant, are particularly grand and, with their open hearths, are especially inviting in a grim Birmingham drizzle. The location outside the city makes a car a necessity, but a stroll on the lush grounds more than justifies any inconvenience.

Exploring Birmingham

A look around won't take too much time, because there's really not a whole lot to see in Birmingham. What's here is concentrated around the huge **International Conventional Centre,** where the city hosts majors conventions and trade shows. The center sits on Centenary Square, around which are clustered the **Symphony Hall** and **Birmingham Repertory Theatre,** both of which put the city on the performing-arts map (see "Entertainment and Nightlife in Birmingham," below). The octagonal **Hall of Memory,** also on the square, commemorates the city's World War I dead.

Walking west from Centenary Square you will soon come to Chamberlain Square, above which rises the concrete hulk of the **Central Library.** Prince Charles, a harsh critic of many of the trends in modern British architecture, once said this building looks like a place where books should be incinerated. The **Birmingham Museum and Art Gallery** is across the square (see the profile below), and just north on Waterloo Street is a building that might meet with the approval of His Royal Highness, the 18th-century **Birmingham Cathedral.** Take the time to step inside this pleasantly small-scale stone structure that's built in the English Baroque style and surrounded by plane trees. The stained-glass windows behind the altar were designed by the pre-Raphaelite painter Edward Burne-Jones and manufactured by his close friend and fellow artist, William Morris. The cathedral is open Monday–Friday, 8 a.m.–6 p.m., and Saturday and Sunday, 9 a.m.–4 p.m.; call (0121) 262-1840 for information.

It's well worth your time to leave the center for an excursion out to the **University of Birmingham** to visit the exquisite collection of the Barber Institute of Fine Arts (see profile below).

Attractions in Birmingham

Barber Institute of Fine Arts

Type of Attraction One of Britain's finest collections of European art

Location Campus of University of Birmingham, 3 miles southwest of city center

Admission Free

Hours Monday–Saturday, 10 a.m.–5 p.m.; Sunday, noon–5 p.m.

Phone (0121) 414-7333

Website www.barber.org.uk

When to Go Anytime; the museum is seldom crowded. You may also want to visit the museum to attend one of the excellent concerts it hosts; call or the check the website for schedules.

Special Comments To reach the museum from the city center, take a train from New Station to University Station (the trip takes ten minutes and the station is a five-minute walk from the Institute) or buses 61, 62, or 63 from the city center to Navigation Street (tell the driver where you want to get off and get directions to the museum).

Overall Appeal by Age Group

Preschool —	Teens ★★★	Over 30 ★★★★
Grade school ★★	Young Adults ★★★	Seniors ★★★★

Author's Rating ★★★★

How Much Time to Allow At least 2 hours

Description & Comments Dame Barber, wife of a wealthy Birmingham real-estate developer, founded this collection in 1932. Since then, the Institute has acquired a remarkable collection of European art that includes works by such Renaissance masters as Jacopo Bellini and Sandro Botticelli as well as René Magritte, Egon Schiele, and other modern icons. The collection is housed in a fine Art Deco building by British architect Robert Atkinson that shows off the works to their best advantage. Newly renovated galleries house an extensive collection of coins, including many from the Byzantine Empire.

Touring Tips The museum hosts a series of excellent concerts; call or the check the website for schedules.

Birmingham Museum and Art Gallery

Type of Attraction An art museum with a notable pre-Raphaelite collection

Location Chamberlain Square

Admission Free

Hours Monday–Thursday and Saturday, 10 a.m.–5 p.m.; Friday, 10:30 a.m.–5 p.m.; Sunday, 12:30–5 p.m.

Phone (0121) 303-2834

Website www.bmag.org.uk

When to Go Anytime; the museum is rarely crowded

Special Comments The pre-Raphaelite works, as well as some of the crafts pieces (including a six-foot-tall statue of the Buddha) are surprisingly popular with young visitors.

Overall Appeal by Age Group

Preschool —	Teens ★★★	Over 30 ★★★
Grade school ★★	Young Adults ★★★	Seniors ★★★

Author's Rating ★★★

How Much Time to Allow 1 hour, more if you are a fiend for the pre-Raphaelites

Description & Comments Founded in 1883, the Birmingham Museum has the world's largest collection of works by Edward Burne-Jones, who was born in Birmingham in 1833 and became one of the leading figures in the pre-Raphaelite and 19th-century Arts and Crafts movements. Works by many other Victorian artists are here, too, as befits an institution built from riches garnered during Birmingham's 19th-century industrial heyday, and many hang beneath a vast glass dome in the so-called Round Room. Throughout the museum, the ornate Victorian architecture provides an evocative setting for works by William Holman Hunt *(The Two Gentlemen of Verona)*, Ford Madox Brown *(The Last of England)*, and John Everett Millais *(The Blind Girl)*. The museum also houses a collection of tiles, ceramics, and metalwork, with many pieces fashioned in Birmingham.

Touring Tips If possible, try to take one of the free guided tours on Tuesdays at 1 p.m., and Saturday and Sunday at 2:30 p.m.; they show off the museum's treasures and provide a fascinating look at fine and applied arts in Birmingham.

Dining in Birmingham

Bistro du Vin ★★★½

FRENCH | EXPENSIVE | QUALITY ★★★ | VALUE ★★★

Church Street; (0121) 200-0600

Reservations Recommended **Entrée Range** Three-course menus about £40 **Payment** V, MC, AMEX, D **Bar** Full service **Disabled Access** Yes

Hours Daily, noon–2 p.m., 7–10 p.m.

House Specialties Any of the daily specials.

It's a pleasure to discover that the proprietors of this stylish bistro in Birmingham's chic Hotel du Vin pay as much attention to cuisine as they do to the surroundings. Fresh ingredients make their way into preparations that often include hearty soups and classic chicken and seafood dishes. The wine list is extensive, and the sommelier will help you select the perfect bottle to accompany a meal.

Michelle's La Bastille ★★★

FRENCH | MODERATE | QUALITY ★★★ | VALUE ★★★★

200 Corporation Street; (0121) 236-1171

Reservations Not necessary **Entrée Range** £8.50–£13.50 **Payment** V, MC, AMEX **Bar** Full service **Disabled Access** Yes

Hours Monday–Friday, noon–2 p.m., 6–10 p.m.; Saturday, 6–10 p.m.

House Specialties The evening prix fixe menu (£15.95) is an excellent value.

This attractive bistro is a find in the center of town, where welcoming restaurants are few and far between. The mirrored walls and hardwood floors provide an authentic bistro flair that reflect the offerings on hand—flavorful shrimp bisque, excellent fish and meat dishes (including a hearty cassoulet), and some inventive vegetarian choices. An adjoining café is open 11 a.m.–10 p.m. and serves sandwiches and other light fare.

Titash ★★★

BALTI/TANDOORI | INEXPENSIVE | QUALITY ★★★½ | VALUE ★★★★

2278 Coventry Road; (0121) 722-2080

Reservations Not necessary **Entrée Range** £4.90–£8.50; set meals for two, £21 **Payment** V, MC **Bar** Beer and wine only **Disabled Access** Yes

Hours Daily, 5:30 p.m.–12:30 a.m.

House Specialties Any of the Balti dishes.

Birmingham has a large population of Kashmiris, and they have brought with them a style of cooking known as Balti. In these preparations, marinated meat or seafood is cooked with spices over high heat in a wok-like pan that is brought to the table and from which diners scoop the contents with bread. Titash is one of many such

Balti places in the city; the premises are colorful and pleasantly informal, and the friendly staff is eager to introduce newcomers to this delicious cuisine.

Entertainment and Nightlife in Birmingham

While Birmingham is not particularly oriented to tourism, the city treats its residents to a first-rate performing-arts lineup. If you're in town for business, it's well worth your while to check out the performance schedule of any of the following companies that call Birmingham home. The **City of Birmingham Symphony Orchestra,** now under the musical direction of Sakari Oramo, performs in Symphony Hall, a glass-enclosed structure on Centenary Square; call (0121) 200-2700 or visit their website at **www.cbso.co.uk.** The **Birmingham Royal Ballet,** once the London-based touring company of the Royal Ballet, now calls Hippodrome Theatre on Hearst Street home; call (0121) 245-3500 or visit their website at **www.brb.org.uk.** In addition to the renowned dance company, which tours the world outside of its Birmingham season, the ballet incorporates the Royal Ballet Sinfonia, which performs with many other leading ballet companies as well and performs concerts at Symphony Hall in Birmingham and elsewhere. The Birmingham Repertory Company is one of Britain's leading drama companies and performs classical as well as modern works in its theater next to the International Convention Centre on Centenary Square; for tickets and information, call (0121) 245-2025 or visit **www.birmingham-rep.co.uk.**

Around Birmingham

Hereford

In this pretty, unspoiled agricultural town, 56 miles southwest of Birmingham, you'll usually find a cart or shop selling cider and fruit from the prosperous farms and orchards in the green hills of surrounding Herefordshire; the town's bustling main market is held Wednesday and Saturday mornings, 8:30 a.m.–3:30 p.m. What will bring you to this pleasant place, though, is the massive Norman cathedral built of red sandstone.

The tourist information center is open in summer, Monday–Saturday, 9 a.m.–5 p.m., and Sunday, 10 a.m.–4 p.m.; and in winter, Monday–Saturday, 9 a.m.–5 p.m. Trains run from Birmingham's New Street Station to Hereford about every hour; the trip takes about an hour and a half, and the round-trip fare is £12. By car, the quickest route is to follow the M5 south to A4103, which leads west to Hereford. From Hereford, a drive farther west along A438 follows the Wye River and, after about 12 miles, crosses the Welsh border at the town of **Hay-on-Wye.** If you're a bibliophile, you'll think you've died and gone to heaven: This tiny town of fewer than 1,500 inhabitants supports some 25 secondhand bookshops, where you can pick up a cheap thriller or a rare, centuries-old manuscript.

Hereford Cathedral

Type of Attraction A Norman cathedral with rare medieval documents

Location Center of town

Admission Free; Mappa Mundi and Chained Library: £4.50 adults, £3.50 seniors and children, £11 families of up to two adults and three children

Hours Monday–Saturday, 10 a.m.–4:15 p.m.

Phone (01432) 374-202

When to Go Anytime; the cathedral is almost never crowded

Special Comments The Mappa Mundi alone merits a special trip to Hereford.

Overall Appeal by Age Group

Preschool ★★★★★	Teens ★★★	Over 30 ★★★★
Grade school ★★★	Young Adults ★★★	Seniors ★★★★

Author's Rating ★★★★

How Much Time to Allow At least 1 hour

Description & Comments Though this proud cathedral was overzealously restored in the 19th century, the massive pillars and semicircular arches in the nave are telltale signs of the church's Norman origins. The attractions here, though, are not architectural. In the cathedral library is a collection of more than 1,700 "chained" books, so called because they are mounted on rods and attached to cases; among them is an eighth-century Anglo-Saxon gospel. The cathedral's most famous treasure occupies a new, specially built annex, funded by John Paul Getty Jr. The extraordinary, five-foot-wide Mappa Mundi is a medieval map of the world, depicting the earth as flat with Jerusalem at its center. As many times as you might have seen reproductions of such maps, seeing an original stirringly evokes the medieval view of the world.

Touring Tips As you leave the cathedral, step into the 15th-century College of Vicars' Choral, a group of cottages where priests who chanted the services once lived.

Ludlow

Many are those who consider Ludlow, about 15 miles west of Birmingham, to be the prettiest town in England, and we can't really disagree. There's not a whole lot in particular to see, which can be a blessing if you're sight-soaked. Instead, the pleasure of being in Ludlow is to walk along streets lined with handsome black-and-white half-timbered houses; the **Feathers Hotel,** on the street called the Bull Ring, is especially elaborate. The **Church of St. Lawrence** is one of the largest medieval churches in England, and the ashes of A. E. Housman, who extolled the beauty of the surrounding Shropshire hills in "A Shropshire Lad" and other poems, were scattered in the churchyard.

Ludlow's other formidable structure is the Norman **Ludlow Castle,** built in the 11th century as a border defense again possible incursions from Wales. Much of the castle is in ruin, though the chapel of **St. Mary Magdalene,** with a rare circular nave, still stands. The castle and chapel are open January, Saturday and Sunday, 10 a.m.–4 p.m.; February–March, daily, 10 a.m.–4 p.m.; April–July, daily, 10 a.m.–5 p.m.; August, daily, 10 a.m.–7 p.m.; September, daily, 10 a.m.–5 p.m.; October–December, daily, 10 a.m.–4 p.m. Admission is £3.50 adults, £3 seniors, £1.50 children, £9.50 families; for more information, call (01584) 873-355 or visit **www.ludlowcastle.com.**

In the last week of June and first two weeks of July, the castle serves as a creative backdrop for Shakespeare plays performed during the **Ludlow Festival;** the festival also brings classical music, dance, and opera, along with many world-renowned performing artists, to Ludlow. For more information, call (01584) 872-150 (phone lines are open May–July).

Local buses make the short trip from Birmingham to Ludlow regularly; check with the Birmingham tourist office for schedules (phone (0121) 202-5000). While it is possible to reach Ludlow by train from Birmingham, the trip takes at least two hours. In a car, you can zip to Ludlow from Birmingham in less than 20 minutes along A4117.

Shrewsbury

The county seat of Shropshire, Shrewsbury (pronounced "SHROSE-bury") climbs a hill above a loop of the River Severn. As if this town of black-and-white half-timbered houses leaning over narrow lanes and alleys (called "shuts" because they were closed off at night to protect residents) weren't picturesque enough, the townsfolk have decided to bedeck every cultivatable square inch of the so-called "town of flowers" with flora.

The only way to get to know Shrewsbury, which is about 50 miles west of Birmingham, is to walk, beginning in the pedestrian quarter on Pride Hill and threading your way down toward the riverside gardens. You can follow one of the itineraries the tourist office hands out or, better yet, join one of the office's guided tours, offered daily in summer at 2:30 p.m. It's worth taking time out for a stop at **Rowley's House,** on Barker Street. The 16th-century warehouse and adjoining mansion, a testament to Shrewsbury's enormous wool wealth, serve as a local museum; the most interesting items here are the Roman finds. Admission is free; the house is open Easter–September, Tuesday–Saturday, 10 a.m.–5 p.m., Sunday, 10 a.m.–4 p.m.; October–Easter, Tuesday–Saturday, 10 a.m.–4 p.m.; phone (01743) 361-196.

The **Shrewsbury Tourist Information Centre** (top of the town on the Square; (01743) 281-200) is open from the end of May through September, Monday–Saturday, 10 a.m.–6 p.m., Sunday, 10 a.m.–4 p.m., and October–May, Monday–Saturday, 10 a.m.–5 p.m. Trains run from

Birmingham's New Street Station to Shrewsbury about every hour, and the trip takes about an hour; the round-trip fare is £10. By car, follow the M54 and A5; the trip takes less than an hour.

Stratford-upon-Avon

William Shakespeare happened to be born in this pleasant town on the River Avon in 1564, a fact that will greet you long before you disembark in the busy center. Despite the souvenir shops and an overabundance of Shakespearean nomenclature, Stratford holds its own against the onslaught of more than four million visitors a year. Quiet corners are easy to find; the town has a done a fine job of preserving its architectural treasures, many of which date from the Elizabethan era, when Stratford was already a prosperous market town; and the Shakespeare sights are extremely well done and expert at handling the crowds that come to admire them.

Planning Your Visit to Stratford-upon-Avon

The **Stratford-upon-Avon Tourist Information Centre** (Bridgefoot; (01789) 293-127; **www.shakespeare-country.co.uk**) provides information about sights and can book accommodations as well as seats at the Royal Shakespeare Theatre. The center is open April–October, Monday–Saturday, 9:30 a.m.–5:30 p.m., Sunday, 10:30 a.m.–4:30 p.m.; and November–March, Monday–Saturday, 9:30 a.m.–5 p.m., Sunday, 10 a.m.–3 p.m.

Arriving and Getting Oriented in Stratford-upon-Avon

Stratford is 37 miles southwest of Birmingham and 102 miles northwest of London. Trains run to Stratford about every hour from London's Paddington Station; the trip takes about two hours, and the round-trip fare is about £35. For information, call (08457) 484-950 or go to **www.railtrack.co.uk.**

By car, Stratford is about 45 minutes from Birmingham and under two hours from London on the M40. **National Express** buses leave London's Victoria Coach Station for Stratford about every two and a half hours throughout the day. The trip takes three hours and costs £19 round trip. Call (08705) 808-080 or go to **www.gobycoach.com.**

Hotels in Stratford-upon-Avon

Dukes Hotel *£69*

OVERALL ★★★ | QUALITY ★★★ | VALUE ★★★★

Payton Street, Stratford-upon-Avon, Warwickshire CV37 6UA; (01789) 269-300; fax (01789) 414-700

Location In the center of town, near Shakespeare's birthplace.

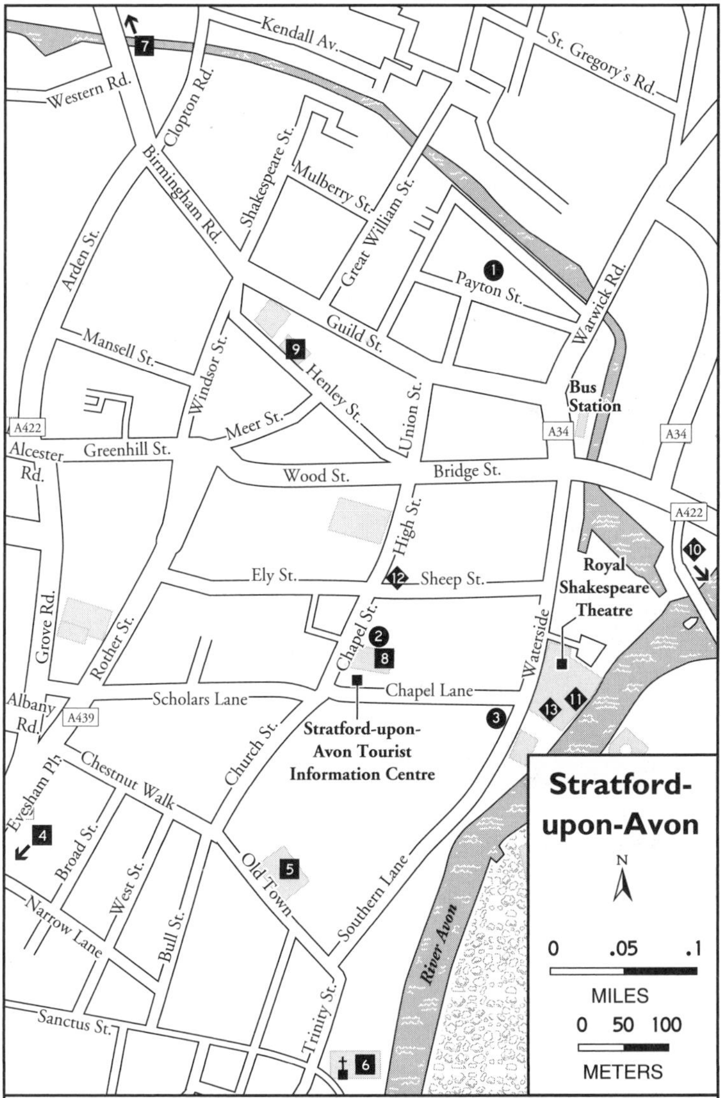

HOTELS

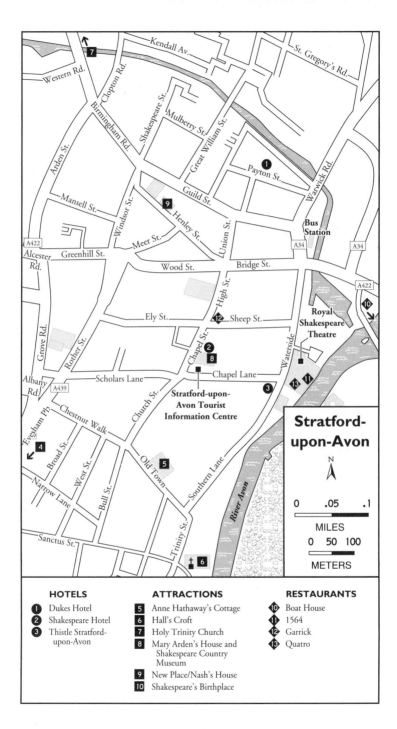

1 Dukes Hotel
2 Shakespeare Hotel
3 Thistle Stratford-upon-Avon

ATTRACTIONS

5 Anne Hathaway's Cottage
6 Hall's Croft
7 Holy Trinity Church
8 Mary Arden's House and Shakespeare Country Museum
9 New Place/Nash's House
10 Shakespeare's Birthplace

RESTAURANTS

10 Boat House
11 1564
12 Garrick
13 Quatro

Amenities & Services 22 rooms. Restaurant, large garden.

Elevator No.

Parking Free, on grounds.

Pricing Includes English breakfast.

Credit Cards V, MC, AMEX, D

Two Georgian town houses have been joined to create this pleasant, family-run hotel that has the feel of a relaxed but rather luxurious bed-and-breakfast, yet offers all the amenities—from a helpful desk staff to well-equipped private baths—of a full-service inn. Rooms have a comfy, country-house feel, and the rear garden next to the canal provides a welcome retreat from the crowds on the streets outside.

Shakespeare Hotel *£140–£165*

OVERALL ★★★★ | QUALITY ★★★ | VALUE ★★½

Chapel Street, Stratford-upon-Avon, Warwickshire CV37 6ER; (0870) 400-8182; info@shakespearehotel.net; www.shakespearehotel.net

Location In the center of town.

Amenities & Services 74 rooms. David Garrick Restaurant, Othello Bistro, lounge. Concierge service, CD players in rooms.

Elevator No.

Parking Nearby.

Pricing Includes English breakfast.

Credit Cards V, MC, AMEX, D

A fine Tudor building, full of rich paneling and centuries-old hearths, provides the perfect atmosphere for your visit to Stratford. The traditional atmosphere extends to the guest rooms, which are tucked under eaves and into various nooks and crannies and are furnished in a fairly non-surprising mix of faux period pieces that, if a bit conventional, provide comfortable surroundings, often beneath exposed beams. Service is attentive, and the desk staff in the stone-floored lobby will book theater tickets for you, a much-appreciated convenience.

Thistle Stratford-upon-Avon *£101–£115*

OVERALL ★★★ | QUALITY ★★★ | VALUE ★★

Waterside, Stratford-upon-Avon, Warwickshire CV37 6BA; (0870) 333-9146; fax (0870) 333-9246; stratforduponavon@thistle.co.uk; www.thistlehotels.com/stratforduponavon

Location Across the street from Royal Shakespeare Theatre.

Amenities & Services 63 rooms. Bards Restaurant, pleasant terrace; 24-hour room service; laundry/dry-cleaning service.

Elevator No.

Parking On site, £5 per day.

Pricing Includes full breakfast.

Credit Cards V, MC, AMEX, D

A brick, late-18th-century building with a modern extension and fronted by well-tended gardens houses this member of the Thistle chain. The main thing going for this hotel is its proximity to the theaters, though it also provides good service and comfortable, fairly predictable accommodation of the English country-house-look variety; guest rooms are on the smallish side, as are the bathrooms. Bards Restaurant downstairs offers a good menu of Continental cuisine—and begins serving dinner early, at 5:45 p.m., so you'll have plenty of time to enjoy a meal before walking across the street for a performance at the Royal Shakespeare or Swan theaters.

Exploring Stratford-upon-Avon

A walk through Stratford, with stops at the restored properties from Shakespeare's time, provides a satisfying look at the life of the bard and, more than that, richly evokes Elizabethan England. We recommend that you purchase a ticket from the Shakespeare Birthplace Trust for admission to five houses: **Shakespeare's Birthplace, Anne Hathaway's Cottage, New Place/Nash's House, Hall's Croft,** and **Mary Arden's House.** An inclusive ticket for admission to all five houses is £13 adults, £12 seniors and students, £6.50 children, and £29 families of up to two adults and three children. A ticket for admission to Shakespeare's Birthplace, New Place/Nash's House, and Hall's Croft is £9 adults, £8 seniors and students, £4.50 children, and £20 families of up to two adults and three children. Spend the extra money and buy the five-house ticket, because, in addition to Shakespeare's Birthplace, it includes two of the most interesting properties, Anne Hathaway's Cottage and Mary Arden's House, which are not included on the three-house ticket. We also suggest that for a complete day of sightseeing you arm yourself with a multiple-house ticket and a ticket for the circular bus tour (see "Tours of Stratford-upon-Avon," below).

You can purchase the house tickets from the Shakespeare Birthplace Trust, which is located in the **Shakespeare Centre** (Henley Street, next to Shakespeare's Birthplace; (01789) 201-813), which is open April–May, Monday–Saturday, 10 a.m.–5 p.m., and Sunday, 10:30 a.m.–5 p.m.; June–August, Monday–Saturday, 9 a.m.–5 p.m., and Sunday, 9:30 a.m.–5 p.m.; September–October, Monday–Saturday, 10 a.m.–5 p.m., and Sunday, 10:30 a.m.–5 p.m.; and November–March, Monday–Saturday, 10 a.m.–4 p.m., and Sunday, 10:30 a.m.–4 p.m.

In terms of the Shakespeare sights in and around Stratford, we recommend you visit them in the following order: Shakespeare's Birthplace, Anne Hathaway's Cottage, Mary Arden's House and Shakespeare Country Museum, Hall's Croft, and New Place/Nash's House.

Another stop in Stratford is **Holy Trinity Church,** where Shakespeare lies in front of the altar, next to his wife, Anne, his daughter, Susanna, and Susanna's husband, John Hall. The church is reached by a path from Trinity Street and is open Monday–Saturday, 8 a.m.–6 p.m., and Sunday, 2–5 p.m.

Tours of Stratford-upon-Avon

Open-top, double-decker **City Sightseeing** buses (phone (1708) 866-000; **www.city-sightseeing.com**) provide a handy, one-hour-long circular tour of town, allowing you to hop on and off as you wish to do so at the main sights: **Shakespeare's Birthplace, Anne Hathaway's Cottage, Mary Arden's House, New Place/Nash's House, Hall's Croft, the Royal Shakespeare Theatre, Holy Trinity Church,** the 15th-century **Grammar School,** and **Mary Arden's House** in Wilmcote. Tours originate at the Pen and Parchment Inn, next to the tourist information center on Bridgefoot.

Schedules vary, but in summer, buses run about every 15 minutes, 9:30 a.m.–5:30 p.m. Tour tickets, valid for 24 hours, cost £7.50 adults, £6 seniors and students, £3 children, and £18 families of up to two adults and four children; bus tickets do not include admission to the attractions. You can combine a bus tour with a boat trip on the Avon for £10 adults, £8.50 seniors and students, and £4.50 children.

For a relaxing look at Stratford from the water, consider **Bancroft Cruisers** (phone (01789) 269-669; **www.bancroftcruisers.co.uk**) for a half-hour trip from a landing stage by Moat House off Bridgefoot. Trips run throughout the day, daily, April–October. The fee is £3 adults and £2 children.

Attractions in Stratford-upon-Avon

Anne Hathaway's Cottage

Type of Attraction Childhood home of Shakespeare's wife

Location Shottery

Admission £5 adults; £4 seniors and students; £2 children ages 5–15; £12 families of up to two adults and three children

Hours
April–May: Monday–Saturday, 9:30 a.m.–5 p.m.; Sunday, 10 a.m.–5 p.m.; June–August: Monday–Saturday, 9 a.m.–5 p.m.; Sunday, 9:30 a.m.–5 p.m.; September–October: Monday–Saturday, 9:30 a.m.–5 p.m.; Sunday, 10 a.m.–5 p.m.; November–March: Monday–Saturday, 10 a.m.–4 p.m.; Sunday, 10 a.m.–4 p.m.

Phone (01789) 204-016

Website www.shakespeare.org.uk

When to Go Early or late, to enjoy the grounds in relative quiet

Special Comments Kids will probably enjoy seeing the interior of a thatched-roof cottage.

Overall Appeal by Age Group

Preschool —	Teens ★★★	Over 30 ★★★★
Grade school ★★★	Young Adults ★★★★	Seniors ★★★★

Author's Rating ★★★

How Much Time to Allow At least 30 minutes

Description & Comments This thatch-roofed cottage is the most appealing of the Shakespeare houses, probably because it seems so little disturbed; the Hathaway family lived here until 1892. This is where 18-year-old Will Shakespeare courted Anne, who was seven years his senior; a courting settle (a bench where courting couples sat) is among the 16th-century furnishings. The house is surrounded by an orchard and garden, where you might want to spend a little time.

Touring Tips The house, about a mile outside of town, is on the route of the circular City Sightseeing bus tour (see "Tours of Stratford-upon-Avon," above) or you can take a city bus from Bridge Street; better yet, walk out to the house on a well-marked path that cuts through pretty countryside.

Hall's Croft

Type of Attraction An elegant Tudor home

Location Old Town Street

Admission £3.50 adults; £3 seniors and students; £1.70 children ages 5–15; £9 families of up to two adults and three children

Hours April–May: daily, 11 a.m.–5 p.m.; June–August: Monday–Saturday, 9:30 a.m.–5 p.m.; Sunday, 10 a.m.–5 p.m.; September–October: daily, 11 a.m.–5 p.m.; November–March: daily, 11 a.m.–4 p.m.

Phone (01789) 204-016

Website www.shakespeare.org.uk

When to Go Anytime

Special Comments The house will be of special interest to visitors interested in historic furniture.

Overall Appeal by Age Group

Preschool —	Teens ★★	Over 30 ★★★
Grade school ★★	Young Adults ★★	Seniors ★★★

Author's Rating ★★½

How Much Time to Allow 30 minutes

Description & Comments You will come here not in the footsteps of the Bard but to see a refined Tudor residence. The house is believed to have been the home of Susanna, Shakespeare's elder daughter, and her husband, Dr. John Hall. The doctor's dispensary is on the ground floor and is filled with exhibits showing the state of medicine at the time. The rest of the house is magnificently furnished in fine, early-17th-century pieces.

Touring Tips Be sure to step into the walled garden.

Mary Arden's House and Shakespeare Country Museum

Type of Attraction The Tudor farm where Shakespeare's mother was born

Location Wilmcote

Admission £5.50 adults; £5 seniors and students; £2.50 children ages 5–15; £13.50 families of up to two adults and three children

Hours April–May: Monday–Saturday, 10 a.m.–5 p.m.; Sunday, 10:30 a.m.–5 p.m.; June–August: Monday–Saturday, 9 a.m.–5 p.m.; Sunday, 9:30 a.m.–5 p.m.; September–October: Monday–Saturday, 10 a.m.–5 p.m.; Sunday, 10 a.m.–5 p.m.; November–March: Monday–Saturday, 10 a.m.–4 p.m.; Sunday, 10:30 a.m.–4 p.m.

Phone (01789) 204-016

Website www.shakespeare.org.uk

When to Go Anytime

Special Comments This is a good place to let the kids unwind; even preschoolers will enjoy the many farm animals around the place, and sometimes there are falconry demonstrations; the Elizabethan farm implements are also popular with young visitors.

Overall Appeal by Age Group

Preschool ★★★	Teens ★★★★	Over 30 ★★★
Grade school ★★★★	Young Adults ★★★	Seniors ★★★

Author's Rating ★★★

How Much Time to Allow At least 1 hour to enjoy the grounds

Description & Comments Only in the year 2000 was it determined that this house, at Glebe Farm in outlying Wilmcote, was the house of Mary Arden, Shakespeare's mother. Until then, it had been believed that a house at adjoining Palmers Farm, a typical Tudor farmstead, deserved that distinction. Both houses are now part of the Countryside Museum and are filled with a fascinating collection of country furniture, some of which is surprisingly elegant. Most interesting are the grounds, which include a stone dovecote and other outbuildings, a pond, and fields that are ablaze with wildflowers in the spring.

Touring Tips Wilmcote is about three and a half miles north of Stratford; you can drive there on A34, and the museum is one of the stops on the City Sightseeing bus tour (see "Tours of Stratford-upon-Avon," above).

New Place/Nash's House

Type of Attraction Site of Shakespeare's last home

Location Chapel Street

Admission £3.50 adults; £3 seniors and students; £1.70 children ages 5–15; £9 families of up to two adults and three children

Hours April–May: daily, 11 a.m.–5 p.m.; June–August: Monday–Saturday, 9:30 a.m.–5 p.m.; Sunday, 10 a.m.–5 p.m.; September–October: daily, 11 a.m.–5 p.m.; November–March: daily, 11 a.m.–4 p.m.

Phone (01789) 204-016

Website www.shakespeare.org.uk

When to Go Anytime

Special Comments If you're running out of steam, this is probably the sight to miss, though the knot garden—in which four "knotts" separated by paths are planted with herbs and flowers—is intriguing.

Overall Appeal by Age Group

Preschool —	Teens ★★	Over 30 ★★
Grade school ★★	Young Adults ★★	Seniors ★★

Author's Rating ★★

How Much Time to Allow About 30 minutes

Description & Comments By 1597, Shakespeare was rich and famous, and he paid the then-astronomical sum of £60 for New Place, the finest home in Stratford. He died there in 1616, but the house was torn down in the mid-18th-century (supposedly the then-owner, Reverend Francis Gastrell, was tired of the visitors intruding upon his property to pay homage to the famous former inhabitant). What remains are the foundations, visible in a lovely garden that adjoins Nash House, a fine residence that was home to Thomas Nash, husband of Shakespeare's granddaughter Elizabeth Hall. Several rooms are devoted to a museum of local history.

Touring Tips If you come to this end of Stratford, step into the Grammar School, in the Guildhall across the street from New Place; young Will attended school there.

Shakespeare's Birthplace

Type of Attraction A half-timbered house where the Bard was born

Location Henley Street, next to Shakespeare Centre

Admission £6.50 adults; £5.50 seniors and students; £2.50 children ages 5–15; £15 families of up to two adults and three children

Hours April–May: Monday–Saturday, 10 a.m.–5 p.m.; Sunday, 10:30 a.m.–5 p.m.; June–August: Monday–Saturday, 9 a.m.–5 p.m.; Sunday, 9:30 a.m.–5 p.m.; September–October: Monday–Saturday, 10 a.m.–5 p.m.; Sunday, 10:30 a.m.–5 p.m.; November–March: Monday–Saturday, 10 a.m.–4 p.m.; Sunday, 10:30 a.m.–4 p.m.

Phone (01789) 204-016

Website www.shakespeare.org.uk

When to Go Early or late, as the house becomes very crowded

Special Comments Stairs may render parts of the house inaccessible to disabled visitors.

Overall Appeal by Age Group

Preschool —	Teens ★★★	Over 30 ★★★
Grade school ★★★	Young Adults ★★★	Seniors ★★★

Author's Rating ★★★

How Much Time to Allow About half an hour

Description & Comments The bard's birthplace is a busy place. A steady stream of visitors tromp through to pay homage, and the bustle of modern Stratford rattles the leaded windows. Even so, the two half-timbered houses—one was the shop of William's father, a glover and wool merchant—that constituted the Shakespeare residence are quite moving, filled with Elizabethan furnishings and memorabilia. Outside is a lovely garden.

Touring Tips To brush up on your Shakespeare before you set out to explore Stratford, spend some time looking over the well-done exhibition tracing the Bard's life and work.

Dining in Stratford-upon-Avon

Boathouse ★★★★

ASIAN/INTERNATIONAL | MODERATE–EXPENSIVE | QUALITY ★★★★ | VALUE ★★★

Swan's Nest Lane; (01789) 297-733

Reservations Recommended **Entrée Range** £6–£15; prix fixe menus, £19.95–£25 **Payment** V, MC, AMEX, D **Bar** Full service **Disabled Access** Yes

Hours Monday–Saturday, noon–2:30 p.m., 5:30–10:30 p.m.; Sunday, noon–2:30 p.m.

House Specialties Specials, such as duck and pheasant, in Thai preparations.

This Thai-inspired restaurant, decorated with exotic fabrics, carvings, and highly polished wood, overlooks the River Avon and provides an unusually pleasant setting for a good meal. Thai herbs and curries appear in fish and meat dishes, and the appetizers include spicy spring rolls and other traditional Thai dishes; you'll also find some delicate risottos and other European preparations.

1564 ★★★

CAFÉ | INEXPENSIVE | QUALITY ★★★ | VALUE ★★★

Royal Shakespeare Theatre; (01789) 403-415

Reservations Not necessary **Entrée Range** £4–£7 **Payment** V, MC, AMEX **Bar** Beer and wine **Disabled Access** Yes

Hours Daily, 10:30 a.m.–9:30 p.m. (or end of intermission)

House Specialties Salads, as well as pasta and other prepared dishes.

This stylish self-service restaurant (you won't be in Stratford for too long before you learn the significance of the name) is the place for a good-value meal while visiting the Royal Shakespeare Theatre or attending a performance. The selection is large, the food is nicely prepared, and the views across the River Avon are as pleasing from here as there are from the neighboring, more formal Quatro restaurant

Garrick ★★★★

PUB | INEXPENSIVE | QUALITY ★★★ | VALUE ★★★★

High Street; (01789) 292-186

Reservations Not necessary **Entrée Range** £6.95–£7.95 **Payment** V, MC **Bar** Full service **Disabled Access** Yes

Hours Monday–Saturday, 11 a.m.–11 p.m.; Sunday, noon–10:30 p.m.

House Specialties Sandwiches, fish and chips.

The heavily timbered nooks and crannies of this charming pub, named for the famous 18th-century Shakespearean actor, is just the place to soak up local atmosphere while enjoying a very decent meal at a good price. There's a wide choice of sandwiches and traditional favorites like meat pies and ploughmans, but the kitchen does a nice job with more elaborate fish and meat dishes as well.

Quatro ★★★★

MODERN BRITISH | EXPENSIVE | QUALITY ★★★★ | VALUE ★★★

Royal Shakespeare Theatre; (01789) 403-415

Reservations Recommended **Entrée Range** £13–£15 **Payment** V, MC, AMEX **Bar** Full service **Disabled Access** Yes

Hours Monday–Saturday, 5:45 p.m.–midnight; noon–2:30 p.m. on matinee days

House Specialties Traditional English lamb and beef dishes.

The Quatro is the new name for the Box Tree, a well-known restaurant in the Royal Shakespeare Theatre that has long been regarded as the best dining spot in Stratford. Quatro carries on the same tradition, providing excellent meals that draw on British and Continental influences served in an elegant, candlelit dining room overlooking the River Avon.

Entertainment and Nightlife in Stratford-upon-Avon

Not too surprisingly, the most appropriate way to spend an evening in Stratford is at the theater, and there are several options. The **Royal Shakespeare Theatre** is the home stage of the Royal Shakespeare Company, which mounts five productions between late March and January. Another excellent theater, the **Swan,** is a typical Jacobean playhouse resembling the Globe and is built in the shell of a Victorian theater destroyed by fire in the 1920s; the Swan stages works by Christopher Marlowe and other Shakespeare contemporaries. The **Other Place** puts on experimental productions.

All these theaters are operated by the Royal Shakespeare Company. To see a production at any of them, we strongly recommend that you book well in advance: For information on productions and to book tickets, call (0870) 609-1110, Monday–Saturday, 9 a.m.–8 p.m., or visit their website at **www.rsc.org.uk.** You can also write to the Royal Shakespeare Company Box Office at Waterside, Stratford-upon-Avon, Warwickshire CV37 6BB. You can buy advance tickets for performances at any of the theaters at the Royal Shakespeare Company Box Office, which is open Monday–Saturday, 9:30 a.m.–8 p.m. (to 6 p.m. on nonperformance days). The box office also sells a limited number of tickets the same day of the performances.

The Royal Shakespeare Theatre offers backstage tours most days, on a schedule that varies with rehearsals. Costs are £4 adults and £3 children ages 18 and younger, students, and seniors. Call (01789) 403-405 for times and other information.

Around Stratford-upon-Avon

Warwick

This medieval town on a rocky bluff above the River Avon eight miles north of Avon is most famous for its mighty **Warwick Castle.** The town itself, though, is a quaint and charming place, with crooked lanes that are overhung with half-timbered houses. **Lord Leycester Hospital** was established in 1571 by the favorite of Elizabeth I, Robert Dudley, Earl of Leicester, as a home for aged and disabled soldiers. These days, the half-timbered buildings, still home to black-capped ex-servicemen who show visitors around, lean photogenically against the town's **West Gate.** You can step through a tiny passageway into an inner, galleried courtyard and, off it, the Great Hall, Dining Hall, and candlelit chapel, then enjoy a cup of tea beneath the old beams of the Brethren's Kitchen. The hospital is open Tuesday–Sunday, 10 a.m.–4 p.m. (until 5 p.m. in summer); admission is £3.20 adults and £2.20 children. Robert Dudley is buried nearby in **St. Mary's Church,** which is topped by a beautiful tower and is where the 15th-century Beauchamp Chantry commemorates Richard Beauchamp, a powerful earl of Warwick. The church is open daily, 10 a.m.–6 p.m. (to 4:30 p.m. or so in winter).

Trains and buses run throughout the day from Stratford to Warwick, and the trip takes only about 15 minutes; check with the Stratford tourist office (phone (01789) 293-127) for schedules and fares. By car, Warwick is a quick jaunt northeast of Stratford on A46.

Warwick Castle

Type of Attraction Medieval fortress above the River Avon

Location Warwick

Admission March 1–May 2, September 8–February 28: £11.25 adults; £8 seniors; £8.50 students; £6.95 children; £32 families. May 3–September 7: £12.50 adults; £9 seniors; £9.40 students; £7.50 children; £34 families. Weekends and public holidays, May 3–September 7: £13.50 adults; £9.75 seniors; £10 students; £8 children; £36 families

Hours April–July and September: daily, 10 a.m.–6 p.m.; August: daily, 10 a.m.–6 p.m.; October–March: 10 a.m.–5 p.m.

Phone (0870) 442-2000

Website www.warwickcastle.co.uk

When to Go Early morning in summer, to avoid enormous crowds later in the day; best time is a winter's afternoon

Special Comments The castle hosts jousting matches, medieval fairs, and other events throughout the year; if you really want to get into the spirit of the place, you can partake of the Highwayman's Supper on Friday and Saturday evenings, when a five-course meal accompanied by singing is interrupted by the masked intruders (we suggest you save the £41 for a couple of nice meals elsewhere).

Overall Appeal by Age Group

Preschool ★★	Teens ★★★★	Over 30 ★★★
Grade school ★★★★	Young Adults ★★★★	Seniors ★★★

Author's Rating ★★

How Much Time to Allow At least 3 hours

Description & Comments Warwick Castle is one of the most popular attractions in England, but it's fairly low on our list of must-sees. The setting above the river is evocative, and the battlements, towers, private apartments, and gardens are impressive, but the place is filled to bursting (especially in the summer) with tourists, and the admission fees are close to thievery. The castle was founded by William the Conqueror in 1068 and added to many, many times over the ensuing centuries as it became a key link in the defenses of England. In 1601, James I gave the castle to Sir Fulke Greville, who converted much of the fortress into a luxurious palace—in keeping with a movement throughout England at the time to abandon the medieval fortress approach to domesticity in favor of more comfortable (but still fortified) dwellings.

In a quirky twist in the castle's history, in the 1970s, Madame Tussaud's bought the castle and its contents for a very hefty sum from the Earl of Warwick. These tourist wizards have shown remarkable restraint in redoing the place; they have populated the Private Apartments, the showiest part of the castle tour, with wax figures of an aristocratic crowd attending a Royal Weekend Party in 1898. You'll see a young Winston Churchill leafing through a book in the library, the Duke of York (later George V) smoking in the card room, and Daisy, Countess of Warwick, dressing for dinner. Your encounters with these and other notables are accompanied by a chatty sound track. The exhibit is a crowd pleaser, though we would rather enjoy the old rooms in silence and let our imaginations populate them. The Great Hall is filled with armor and provides beautiful river views, and paintings by Van Dyck, Rubens, and other masters hang in the Red Drawing and the Cedar Rooms. The dungeons are appropriately damp and gloomy.

Touring Tips *Do* take time to enjoy the grounds, which are spectacular; *do not* spend the extra £2.50 on the audio guide. The castle has several restaurants, but we suggest you wait to enjoy a meal or snack down below in Warwick.

Part Ten

Cambridge and East Anglia

East Anglia, tucked away in a corner of Britain that most people never have much need to go to, is a world removed from London and, for that matter, from other, busier parts of Britain, too. This is a land of rolling fields, skies full of fleecy clouds, meadows full of fleecy sheep, marshy fens, and quiet villages that haven't changed too much since their medieval marketplaces and half-timbered houses were erected. East Anglia is not, however, an unsophisticated backwater. One of the finest universities in the world is here, at **Cambridge,** as are a number of fine, proud towns, like **Bury St. Edmunds** and **Norwich,** that have played their proud parts in English history.

Not To Be Missed in Cambridge and East Anglia

- Fitzwilliam Museum at Cambridge (page 424)
- Ely Cathedral (page 428)
- Ruined abbey at Bury St. Edmunds (page 429)
- Norwich Cathedral (page 430)

Cambridge

Cambridge is linked to its famous **University of Cambridge** by reputation and geography. The colleges are scattered throughout the town, and the great centers of learning that have flourished here on the banks of the River Cam for seven centuries are often only a stone wall from the bustle of the busy streets. For us non-scholars, this proximity provides an opportunity to experience the great university up close, to admire the splendid architecture, and to enjoy a lively town life that is geared both to students and to the "townies" who, in greater and greater numbers, are choosing to live in this attractive and civilized place.

Planning Your Visit to Cambridge

The **Cambridge Tourist Information Centre** (Old Library on Wheeler Street; (01223) 322-640; **www.cambridge.gov.uk**) provides information

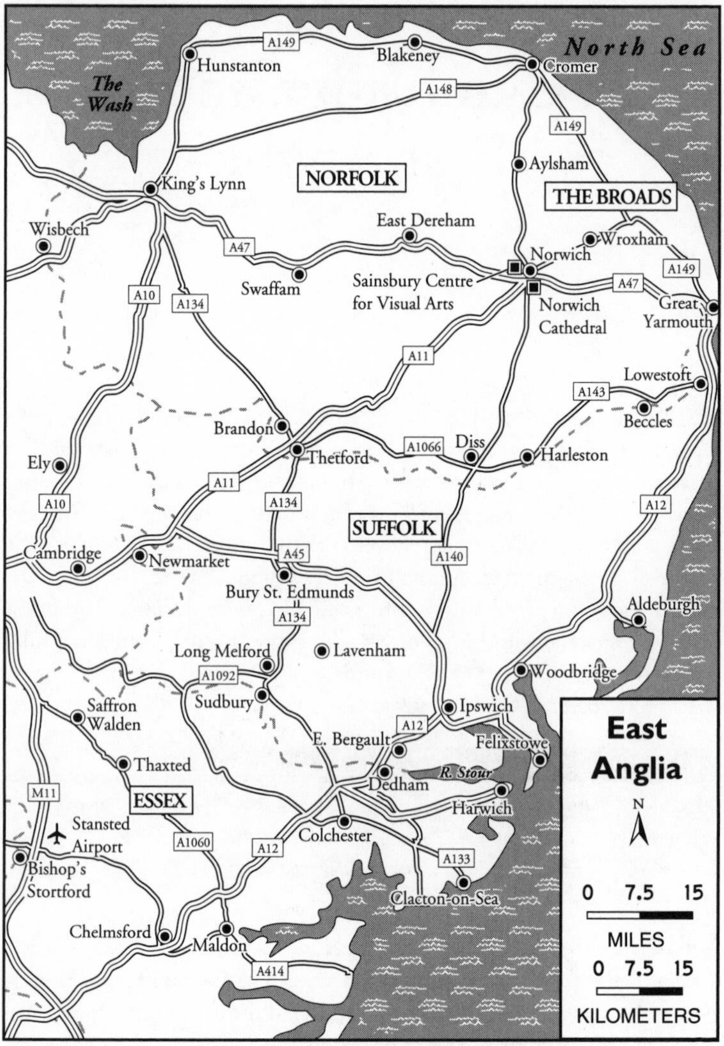

on visitor attractions, places to stay, what to see and do, where to dine and shop, and how to get around Cambridge and the surrounding area. The center is open Monday–Friday, 10 a.m.–5:30 p.m.; Saturday, 10 a.m.–5 p.m.; and Sunday, 11 a.m.–4 p.m.

Special Events in Cambridge

Cambridge hosts a full calendar of events. The **Charles Wells Folk Festival,** Europe's most celebrated folk extravaganza of its kind, takes place in late July and brings performers from around the world to Cambridge.

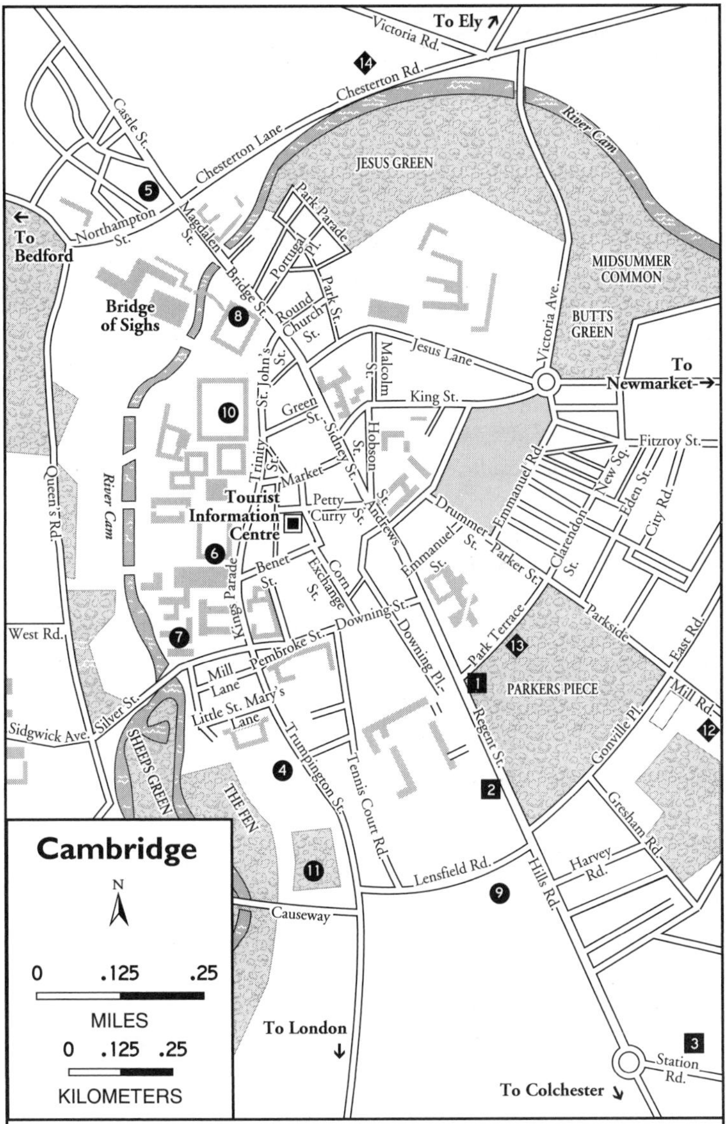

HOTELS

1 De Vere University Arms
2 Regent Hotel
3 Sleeperz

ATTRACTIONS

4 Fizwilliam Museum
5 Keetle Yard
6 King's College
7 Queen's College
8 St. John's College
9 Scott Polar Reseach Institute
10 Trinity College
11 University Botanic Gardens

RESTAURANTS

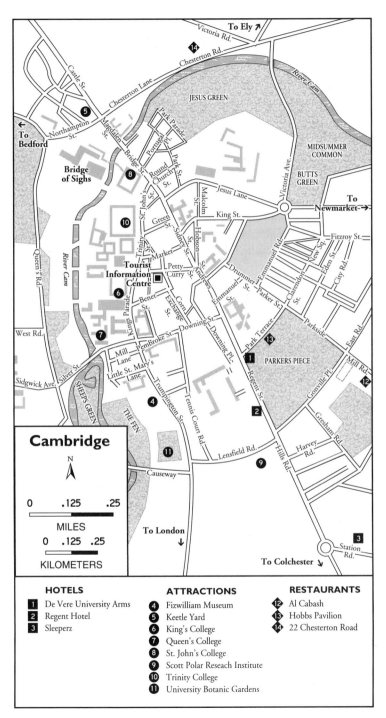

12 Al Cabash
13 Hobbs Pavilion
14 22 Chesterton Road

HOW HOTELS COMPARE

Hotel	Overall Rating	Quality Rating	Value Rating	Price
Cambridge				
De Vere University Arms	★★★★	★★★½	★★★	£95–£120
Regent Hotel	★★★	★★★	★★★★	£77–£96
Sleeperz	★★★	★★½	★★★★	£35–£45

For ticket information, call (01223) 357-851 or (01223) 457-245, or visit **www.cam-folkfest.co.uk.**

The **Cambridge Film Festival** is one of the United Kingdom's most highly respected showcases for international cinema; the fest includes new films and shorts as well as classics, documentaries, retrospectives, and revivals. For tickets and schedules, call (01223) 504-444 or visit **www.cambridgefilmfestival.org.uk.** The **Cambridge Summer Music Festival** brings classical music concerts to churches, university chapels, and other venues around town, daily, mid-July to mid-August. Call (01223) 892-945 or visit **www.cambridgesummermusic.com** for more information.

Arriving and Getting Oriented in Cambridge

Cambridge is just 50 miles north of London. Trains run about every half hour from London's King's Cross Station to Cambridge. The trip takes 45 minutes and costs about £15 round trip. For information, call (08457) 484-950 or go to **www.railtrack.co.uk.** The Cambridge train station is south of the city center, which is about a 15-minute walk away along Hills Road (which becomes Regent Street); there is a taxi stand at the station, and buses run into the center about every 15 minutes or so.

By car, the quickest route from London is M11, and the trip takes less than an hour. Parking in Cambridge is difficult, to say the least; most street parking is reserved for residents, and parking fines are steep. Try to get rid of your car as soon as possible. Centrally located car parks include **Lion Yard Car Park,** the **Grafton Centre Car Park,** the **Park Street Car Park,** and the **Queen Anne Terrace Car Park;** expect to pay £1.40 per hour, and about £12 for four or five hours. It's far less expensive to use the park-and-ride sites in outlying areas (well marked from entrances to the city); regular bus service connects these sites with the city center.

National Express buses leave London's Victoria Coach Station for Cambridge every half hour to hour. The round-trip fare is about £14.50.

IN CAMBRIDGE AND EAST ANGLIA

Hotel	Overall Rating	Quality Rating	Value Rating	Price
Bury St. Edmunds				
The Angel	★★★★	★★★★	★★★	£85–£119

Check the schedule carefully when buying a ticket because travel times vary from less than two hours for the direct trip to four and a half hours for trips with many stops. An advantage to taking the bus rather than the train is the central location of the Cambridge bus station, on Drummer Street at the edge of the city-center pedestrian zone. For more information, call (08705) 808-080 or go to **www.nationalexpress.com.**

Hotels in Cambridge

Cambridge has relatively few hotels, and very few moderately priced choices near the city center. Reserve well in advance of your visit.

De Vere University Arms — *£95–£120*

OVERALL ★★★★ | QUALITY ★★★½ | VALUE ★★★

Regent Street; (01223) 351-241; fax (01223) 273-037; dua.sales@devere-hotels.com; www.devereonline.co.uk

Location Near city center.

Amenities & Services 118 rooms. Scholars Restaurant, three bars. Off-site fitness center. Room service, porter, concierge.

Elevator Yes.

Parking On premises, £8.

Pricing Includes English breakfast.

Credit Cards V, MC, AMEX, D

Cambridge's landmark hotel is, for the most part, a handsome Victorian-era inn that overlooks Parker's Piece through large windows. To appreciate the graciousness and architectural merits of this hotel, though, you must overlook the unattractive extension that was attached to the Regency Street side in the 1970s and through which guests enter. The presence of this irksome annex is why you must request a room in the original wing, preferably overlooking Parker's Piece. If you manage to obtain one, you'll find yourself in airy, bright, high-ceilinged accommodations, nicely furnished with antique reproduction pieces.

HOW ATTRACTIONS COMPARE IN CAMBRIDGE AND EAST ANGLIA

Attraction	Comments	Author's Rating
Cambridge		
Cambridge Colleges	Historic colleges	★★★★
Fitzwilliam Museum	Treasure trove of art and archaeology	★★★★
Kettle's Yard	20th-century and contemporary art	★★★

Regent Hotel — *£77–£96*

OVERALL ★★★ | QUALITY ★★★ | VALUE ★★★★

41 Regent Street, Cambridge, Cambridgeshire CB2 1AB; (01233) 351-470; fax (01233) 566-562; reservations@regenthotel.co.uk; www.regenthotel.co.uk

Location Near the city center.

Amenities & Services 25 rooms. Bar, pleasant lounge.

Elevator Yes.

Parking In nearby car parks.

Pricing Includes Continental breakfast.

Credit Cards V, MC, AMEX

An elegant Georgian house at the edge of the downtown pedestrian zone is the atmospheric setting for this small and pleasant hotel, which has recently emerged from a cellar-to-roof refurbishment. Guest rooms are furnished in traditional style and, while not terribly exciting, are comfortable and well-equipped. The best are in the rear of the hotel, overlooking the greenery of Parker's Piece and delightfully quiet for the central location. Given the level of comfort, the charm of the surroundings, and the locale, the Regent offers one of the best lodging values in Cambridge.

Sleeperz — *£35–£45*

OVERALL ★★★ | QUALITY ★★½ | VALUE ★★★★

Station Road, Cambridge, Cambridgeshire CB1 2TZ; (01223) 304-050; fax (01223) 357-286; info@sleeperz.com; www.sleeperz.com

Location Across from the train station.

Amenities & Services 25 rooms.

Elevator No.

Parking In nearby car parks.

Pricing Includes Continental breakfast.

Credit Cards V, MC, AMEX, D

HOW RESTAURANTS COMPARE IN CAMBRIDGE AND EAST ANGLIA

Name	Cuisine	Overall	Quality	Value	Price
Cambridge					
22 Chesterton Road	British	★★★★	★★★★	★★★★	Mod
Al Casbah	Mediterranean	★★★	★★★	★★★★	Inexp
Hobbs Pavilion	Mediterranean	★★★	★★★	★★★	Mod

Who says a budget hotel has to be dreary? Sleeperz occupies a converted granary and lodges guests in cramped and spartan but stylish rooms that resemble the sleeping compartments on a train, consisting of not much more than bed and desk. Blond hardwood floors and white duvets provide a restful feel, and the baths (all with showers only) are quite commodious and well equipped. For a little more comfort, ask for one of the five double rooms on the ground floor, which come with a double bed (as opposed to the bunks in the twin rooms on other floors) and a little extra space.

Exploring Cambridge

The only way to see Cambridge is on foot, and you can get a nice sense of the city simply by walking down the city's main thoroughfare, King's Parade (which becomes Trumpington Street at the south end of the city center). Wherever you walk in Cambridge, be on your guard for young scholars zooming past you on bicycles—obviously, Cycling Safety 101 is not part of the Cambridge curriculum.

King's Parade leads through the main shopping precincts of Cambridge, and it passes the entrances to many of the colleges (see profiles below); since entrance times vary, check the signs at the porter's lodges at the entrance to each to see if you might enter upon the hallowed ground. We suggest you make a detour onto Trinity Lane into the precincts of **Trinity Hall** college, where you will get a nice view of the river and the **Backs,** as the green parkland behind the colleges on the River Cam is known. You should also take a look at Trinity College's **Wren Library,** designed by Sir Christopher Wren and open to the public Monday–Friday, noon–2 p.m., and Saturday, 10:30 a.m.–12:30 p.m.

As you continue south of King's Parade, the street changes its name to Trumpington and comes to the **Fitzwilliam Museum,** which houses the university's art collection (see profile below). Just beyond the museum, follow Lensfield Road to the **Scott Polar Research Institute,** founded in 1920 to commemorate Sir Robert Scott and his ill-fated team who died shortly after setting foot on the South Pole in 1912. Exhibits are filled with gear, photos, diaries, and other mementos; the institute is open Monday–Saturday, 2:30–4 p.m. Admission is free, and the phone number is (01223) 336-540. Back on Trumpington, continue just a little farther to the **University Botanic Garden,** where 40 acres are planted with exotic species and laced with rock gardens and ornate greenhouses; gardens open daily, March–September, 10 a.m.–6 p.m.; November–January, 10 a.m.–4 p.m.; February–October, 10 a.m.–5 p.m. Admission is £2, free on Wednesday mornings; phone (01223) 336-265.

Tours of Cambridge

A good way to see Cambridge is on one of the tours led by **Blue Badge Guides;** the tours always include at least a visit to King's College or another college, depending on whether or not they are open to visitors at that time, and admission fees are included in the cost of the tour. Tours depart from the Tourist Information Centre daily throughout the year at 1:30 p.m. and last two hours; there are additional tours April–October, daily at 11:30 a.m.; mid-June–September, Monday–Friday, 10:30 a.m.; and mid-June–mid-August, daily, 2:30 p.m. Tickets go on sale in the Tourist Information Centre 24 hours before departure, and since each tour is limited to 20 people, it's a good idea to pick up a ticket well in advance. For more information, contact the tourist office at (01223) 457-574 or e-mail tours@cambridge.gov.uk.

Open-top **City Sightseeing** (01709) 866-000; **www.guidefriday.com**) tour buses make a one-hour circuit of Cambridge, leaving from the train station every 15 to 30 minutes, 10 a.m.–4 p.m., and passing many of the colleges. Fares are £7.50 adults, £5.50 seniors and students, £3 children ages 5–15, and £18 for families of up to two adults and four children.

Attractions in Cambridge

Cambridge Colleges

Type of Attraction Historic colleges

Location Throughout Cambridge

Admission Varies from college to college

Hours Varies from college to college and may change seasonally.

Website www.cam.ac.uk; lists information about the university and its departments as well as general information for visitors

When to Go Depends on when various colleges are open

Special Comments If you want to visit colleges on your own (i.e. without a guided tour), it's important to check the university website or tourist information center for hours and admission policies.

Overall Appeal by Age Group

Preschool ★	Teens ★★	Over 30 ★★★★
Grade school ★★	Young Adults ★★	Seniors ★★★★

Author's Rating ★★★★

How Much Time to Allow Depends on how many colleges you plan to visit and how much time you plan to spend at each; guided walking tours last 2 hours

Description & Comments There are 31 colleges in Cambridge, though visitors are allowed into only some of them.

The aptly named **King's College** was founded by Henry VI in 1441 and can lay claim to having the university's most celebrated chapel, where the famous King's Chapel Choir sings evensong amid such architectural and artistic triumphs as a beautifully carved stone ceiling and Rubens's glorious *The Adoration of the Magi,* which hangs on the altar. Open during term time: Monday–Friday, 9.30 a.m.–3.30 p.m.; Saturday, 9:30 a.m.–3:15 p.m.; Sunday, 1:15–2:15 p.m., 5–5:30 p.m. Open out of term: Monday–Saturday, 9:30 a.m.–4:30 p.m.; Sunday, 10 a.m.–5 p.m. Admission is £4 adults, £3 children and students, free for children under age 12 if part of a family.

Queens' College, on Silver Street, is named after its two founders, Margaret of Anjou (wife of Henry VI) who founded the college in 1448, and Elizabeth Woodville, wife of Edward IV, who was actually responsible for seeing the brick buildings through to their completion in 1456. Erasmus lived here 1510–1513 in what is today known as the Erasmus Tower. The college's famous Mathematical Bridge leads to the Cloister Court; a famous story (alas, untrue) tells how students once took the bridge apart, only to find that no one could put it back together again without some serious re-engineering. Open June 22–September 28: daily, 10 a.m.–4:30 p.m.; admission £1.30. September 29–October 19: Monday–Friday, 1:45–4:30, Saturday and Sunday, 10 a.m.–4:30 p.m.; admission free. October 20–March 20: daily, 1:45–4:30 p.m.; admission free. March 22–April 17: Monday–Friday, 11 a.m.–3 p.m., Saturday and Sunday, 10 a.m.–4:30 p.m.; admission £1.30. April 18–April 21: daily, 10 a.m.–4:30 p.m.; admission £1.30. April 22–May 18: Monday–Friday, 11 a.m.–3 p.m., Saturday and Sunday, 10 a.m.–4:30 p.m.; admission £1.30.

St. John's College, on St. John's Street, was founded by Lady Margaret Beaufort, the mother of Henry VII, in 1511. One of the university's most famous works of architecture is the college's Bridge of Sighs, built in 1831 after the famous bridge in Venice and joining New Court, built in the 1820s, with the old part of the college. William Wordsworth is one famous alumnus of St. John's. Open March–October: daily, 10 a.m.–5:30 p.m.; £2 adults, £1.20 children.

Trinity College was founded in 1546 by Henry VIII, who died just weeks after doing so. It is the wealthiest and largest of the university's colleges. Its Great Court is the largest enclosed courtyard in Europe, and the Wren Library is one of Britain's finest buildings. Trinity's scholars have collected a total of 31 Nobel Prizes and include philosophers Ludwig Wittgenstein and Bertrand Russell, authors A. A. Milne and William Thackeray, composer Ralph Vaughan Williams, mathematician and physicist Sir Isaac Newton, poets Lord Byron and Tennyson, novelist Vladimir Nabokov, Indian Prime Ministers Jawaharlal Nehru and Rajiv Gandhi, and H. R. H. Prince Charles. Hours of admission vary, and you must check at the West Gate to see if the public is allowed to visit at any given time; admission is £2.

Touring Tips A guided tour will enhance your visit to the colleges considerably, and the fee is less than you will pay in individual admissions to the colleges.

Fitzwilliam Museum

Type of Attraction A treasure trove of art and archaeology

Location Trumpington Street

Admission Free

Hours Tuesday–Saturday, 10 a.m.–5 p.m.; Sunday, 2:15–5 p.m.

Phone (01223) 332-900

Website www.fitzmuseum.cam.ac.uk

When to Go Anytime, as the museum is rarely crowded

Special Comments A café on the museum's north lawn serves coffee, tea, and light refreshments.

Overall Appeal by Age Group

Preschool ★	Teens ★★	Over 30 ★★★
Grade school ★★	Young Adults ★★	Seniors ★★★

Author's Rating ★★★★

How Much Time to Allow At least 1 hour, possibly more

Description & Comments The Fitzwilliam, founded in 1816, is one of the principal art collections in Great Britain. Highlights of the museum include the antiquities, especially the stunning examples of Egyptian funerary equipment, funerary sculpture from Greece and Rome, and Greek painted pottery; manuscripts and printed books, especially the medieval illuminated manuscripts; and paintings, drawings, and prints, which include masterpieces by Titian, Veronese, Rubens, Van Dyck, Hals, Canaletto, Gainsborough, Hogarth, Constable, Monet, Degas, Renoir, Cezanne, and Picasso, as well as a fine collection of 20th-century miniatures, drawings, watercolors, and prints. The handsome building, with its acres of marble and mosaics, is itself a treasure.

Touring Tips There are guided tours on Sunday at 2:45 p.m.; group size is limited to 20, and tickets are £3.

Kettle's Yard

Type of Attraction A collection of 20th-century art and exhibits of contemporary art

Admission Free

Hours House: mid-April–late August, Tuesday–Sunday, 1:30–4:30 p.m.; late August–mid-April, Tuesday–Sunday, 2–4 p.m. Gallery: Tuesday–Sunday, 11:30 a.m.–5 p.m.

Phone (01223) 352-124

Website www.kettlesyard.co.uk

When to Go When both house and gallery are open.

Special Comments There is access for visitors with disabilities to the gallery and limited access to the house

Overall Appeal by Age Group

Preschool —	Teens ★★	Over 30 ★★★
Grade school ★	Young Adults ★★★	Seniors ★★★

Author's Rating ★★★

How Much Time to Allow About 1 hour

Description & Comments In 1966, Jim and Helen Ede bequeathed their home and collection of 20th-century art to the university. Since then, a gallery has been added to host rotating exhibits of contemporary works. While many of the shows are spectacular, the house, with its wonderful paintings, sculpture, and ceramics, is the real draw—try to come during the limited hours when it's open.

Touring Tips The museum sponsors Sunday morning "coffee concerts" in the winter and early spring; check the schedule when you visit.

Dining in Cambridge

Aunties is a venerable Cambridge tearoom at 1 St. Mary's Passage, just off Market Square; this popular gathering spot for students and townsfolk is open Monday–Friday, 9:30 a.m.–5:30 p.m., Saturday, 9:30 a.m.–6:30 p.m., and Sunday, 11 a.m.–5:30 p.m.; (01223) 315641.

Restaurants in Cambridge

Al Casbah ★★★

MEDITERRANEAN | INEXPENSIVE | QUALITY ★★★ | VALUE ★★★★

62 Mill Road; (01223) 579-500

Reservations Not necessary **Entrée Range** £6.50–£7.95 **Payment** V, MC, AMEX, D **Bar** Full service **Disabled Access** Yes

Hours Monday–Saturday, noon–3 p.m., 5:30–11 p.m.; Sunday, 5:30–11 p.m.

House Specialties A good selection of appetizers; brochettes.

This stretch of Mill Road is lined with appealing ethnic restaurants and spice shops, and Al Casbah is one of the most pleasant places to stop for a meal. The wood-floored, fabric-draped room is welcoming, and from the open kitchen emerges a nice variety of Algerian and other north African specialties.

Hobbs Pavilion ★★★

MEDITERRANEAN | MODERATE | QUALITY ★★★ | VALUE ★★★

Parker's Piece; (01223) 367-480

Reservations Not necessary **Entrée Range** £9–£13 **Payment** MC, V, AMEX, D **Bar** Full service **Disabled Access** Yes

Hours April 1–August 31: daily, 11 a.m.–11 p.m.; September 1–March 31: daily, noon–3 p.m., 6–10 p.m.

House Specialties Sandwiches at lunch; kebabs and fish specials in the evening.

A cricket pavilion on the edge of Parker's Piece houses this unusual, informal restaurant, where seating is on a terrace in good weather or in a paneled room decorated, not surprisingly, with cricket paraphernalia. The food is surprisingly accomplished for the casual surroundings, and the menu offers a wide variety of choices. For a good, inexpensive meal in Cambridge, Hobbs is hard to beat.

22 Chesterton Road ★★★★

MODERN BRITISH | MODERATE | QUALITY ★★★★ | VALUE ★★★★

22 Chesterton Road; (01223) 351-880

Reservations Recommended **Entrée Range** Prix fixe only, £24.95 **Payment** V, MC, AMEX, D **Bar** Extensive wine list **Disabled Access** Yes

Hours Tuesday–Saturday, 7–9:30 p.m.

House Specialties Menu changes every month; anything offered will be fresh and beautifully prepared.

The parlors of a modest Victorian home are the setting for this restaurant that over the past decade or so, in the capable hands of chef/owner David Carter, has become one of the finest in Cambridge and serves a changing menu that is always full of surprises. Traditional dishes often appear with French, Asian, and other eclectic influences and are always delicious. The service is impeccable, adding to the impression that a meal here is a very good value indeed.

Entertainment and Nightlife in Cambridge

The Cambridge Tourist Information Centre (Old Library on Wheeler Street; (01223) 322-640; **www.cambridge.gov.uk**) keeps listings of events around town and can book tickets for some.

Music and Theater

The world-famous **King's College Choir** owes its existence to King Henry VI, who wanted his glorious chapel filled with the daily singing of services. The boy's choir makes a daily show at evensong, when they file right across the quad before entering the chapel. Evensong is Tuesday–Saturday at 5:30 p.m. Sunday services are at 10:30 a.m. and 3:30 p.m. Call (01223) 331-443 for information.

The **Trinity College Music Society** presents 20 concerts each term, ranging from Renaissance to modern music, as well as performances of works by Gilbert and Sullivan. For schedules and ticket information, phone (01223) 304-922 or visit **www.tcms.org.uk.**

The **Corn Exchange** on Wheeler Street presents a wide range of entertainment, including music and theater. The theater has showcased such diverse programs as the City of London Sinfonia and *Joseph and the Amazing Technicolor Dreamcoat.* For events listings and tickets, call (01223) 357-851 or visit **www.cornex.co.uk.** Emma Thompson is one of many British actors who launched their careers at the **University Amateur Dramatics Club** on Park Street near Jesus Lane. The club stages two student productions nightly Tuesday through Saturday; it is closed in August and September. For information, call (01223) 503-333.

Clubs and Pubs

Cambridge clubs, which are relatively few in number, are open Monday–Saturday, about 9 p.m.–2 a.m.; cover charges are typically £2–£3.

Some popular spots known for a good mix of live music include **The Fez Club** (15 Market Passage; (01223) 519-224) and **The Junction** (Clifton Road; (01223) 511-511).

Pubs are far more numerous than clubs and are generally open from Monday to Saturday, noon–11 p.m., and Sunday, noon–10:30 p.m. The **Pickerel Inn** (30 Magdalene Street; (01223) 355-068) is on the tourist map as the oldest pub in Cambridge and has been serving pints for 600 years; there are plenty of old beams to prove the heritage. The second-oldest drinking spot in town is probably the **Eagle** (Benet Street; (01223) 505-020), a dark and atmospheric spot from 1600; don't be surprised if you see a lot of old geezers craning their necks toward the ceiling in the back room—it's famously emblazoned with the names of airmen who drank here during World War II. The **Anchor** (Silver Street; (01223) 353-554) has the advantage of a lovely setting beside the waters of the Cam, which can be enjoyed from a sunny terrace in good weather.

Shopping in Cambridge

The vendors of **Cambridge Market,** on Market Hill, do a lively business Monday–Saturday, 9 a.m.–6 p.m., selling everything from old clothing to rare books and local produce. Several tastefully designed shopping centers, housing the usual chain stores, are in the center of Cambridge, among them the **Grafton Centre** and **Lion's Yard.** You'll find a nice selection of independent shops on the lanes that lead off King's Parade and Market Hill. Some of the most interesting shops here are book dealers, including the **University of Cambridge Press Bookshop** (1 Trinity Street; (01223) 333-333), which claims to carry every title on the press's current list. **Heffers,** down the way at 13 Trinity Street (phone (01223) 568-582), is a superb general-interest bookstore with a huge selection (there are outlets in the Grafton Centre and on St. Andrews Street).

Exercise and Recreation in Cambridge

You can go native and hop on a bike from **Geoff's Bike Hire** (near the train station at 65 Devonshire Road; (01223) 365-629). Rates are £7 for a day, £4 for half a day; the shop supplies a free leaflet detailing rides in and around Cambridge. If you aren't put off by the distinct possibility of being dunked in the river in front of mirthful onlookers, you can try your hand at punting in a rental from **Scudamore's Backyards** (Granta Place; (01223) 359-750) or one of the other outfits along the Cam. Boats are usually for rent from 9 a.m. to 6 p.m., spring through summer, and you can expect to pay about £12 per hour. You can enjoy the experience without doing the work by hiring a chauffeured punt, which will cost about £40 an hour. A lovely way to enjoy the river while staying dry is walking the footpath from Cambridge to **Grantchester,** an outlying "village" (still surrounded by meadows) where the poet Rupert

Brooke lived while a student at Cambridge in the years just before World War I.

Around Cambridge

Ely

This compact town, 16 miles north of Cambridge, is built on high ground, a practicality made necessary by the fact that until recent decades Ely was surrounded by marshland. The marshes have been drained and Ely now rises above low-lying flatlands laced with canals known as the **Fens.**

You'll see the towers of the famous **Ely Cathedral** from miles away as you cross the flat landscape, and on arrival you'll discover a medieval masterpiece with an enormous lantern tower and a historical curiosity—in the elegant, stone-carved Lady Chapel, the statues are headless, having been defaced during the Reformation. The cathedral is open April–October, daily, 7 a.m.–7 p.m.; November–March, Monday–Saturday, 7:30 a.m.–6 p.m., Sunday, 7:30 a.m.–5 p.m. Admission is £4 adults, £3.50 seniors and students, free for children under age 16; call (01353) 667-735 for more information. Oliver Cromwell, the Puritan who rose to power during the British Civil Wars that briefly replaced the monarchy with a commonwealth, was from Ely, and his half-timbered house near the cathedral is now the **Cromwell Museum** honoring this powerful man. The museum is open April–September, daily, 10 a.m.–5:30 p.m.; October–March, Monday–Saturday, 10 a.m.–5 p.m., Sunday, 11:15 a.m.–4 p.m. Admission is £3.50 adults; £3 seniors, students, and children; and £8.50 families; phone (01353) 662-062.

Frequent train and **Cambus** service (phone (01223) 423-554) connect Cambridge and Ely. By car, follow the A10 north from Cambridge.

Newmarket

You'll catch on to what keeps this one-industry town in business as you pass the stud farms, stables, and meadows full of mares and foals on the outskirts. King Charles II put Newmarket, 12 miles northeast of Cambridge, on the map as the epicenter of British horse racing in the late 17th century, and these days the refined town supports two racecourses, the **Rowley** and the **July.** For a close look at the sport of kings, pay a visit to the **National Horseracing Museum;** better yet, join one of the museum's bus tours of surrounding stud farms. The museum is open July–August, daily, 10 a.m.–5 p.m.; September–October and April 15–June, Tuesday–Sunday, 11 a.m.–5 p.m. Admission is £4.50 adults, £3.50 seniors, £2.50 children, and £10 families of up to two adults and two children; call (01638) 667333 for information.

Frequent train and **Cambus** service (phone (01223) 423-554) connect Cambridge and Newmarket. By car, follow the A1304 northeast from Cambridge.

Bury St. Edmunds

This quiet, delightful market town, about 30 miles east of Cambridge, was once known to all decent Christians, many of whom made pilgrimages here to honor St. Edmund, a ninth-century king of East Anglia who was killed by the Danes when he refused to renounce his Christian faith. The Danes shot Edmund full of arrows, beheaded him, and threw the body in a wood; a wolf led the king's subjects to his body. The Bury St. Edmunds town crest depicts a wolf carrying a human head in its mouth.

A vast and important shrine was erected to honor Edmund, and it thrived until Henry VIII dissolved the monasteries. Towers, gates, and fragments of wall still stand in romantic ruin, surrounded by the **Abbey Botanical Gardens,** and two churches that were once enclosed within the abbey walls remain intact, **St. Mary's** and **St. James** (both churches are open 8 a.m.–dusk). Bury has been endowed with some fine later buildings, too, including a Victorian **Corn Exchange** in the center of town, and the **Athenaeum,** a Georgian assembly hall. You might notice the pleasant aroma of hops as you walk around town—Bury is home to the **Greene King Brewery,** and you can try a pint at the **Nutshell,** squeezed into a corner house at Abbeygate Street and the Traverse. This tiny room, with seats for only a few patrons, claims to be the world's smallest pub, and it's unlikely anyone who's ever tried to bend an elbow here would doubt the fact.

You can reach Bury St. Edmunds via frequent train and bus service from Cambridge; for bus information, contact **Cambus** at (01223) 423-554. By car, follow the A45 from Cambridge. Then, after walking around the town, make a circuit south from Bury to **Long Melford** and **Lavenham,** two beautiful and well-preserved villages chockablock with half-timbered buildings.

The Angel — *£85–£119*

OVERALL ★★★★ | QUALITY ★★★★ | VALUE ★★★

Angel Hill, Bury St. Edmunds, Suffolk IP33 1LT; (012847) 714-000; fax (012847) 714-001; sales@theangel.co.uk; www.theangel.co.uk

Location In the center of town, across from Abbey Gate.

Amenities & Services 66 rooms. Two restaurants, the Abbeygate and the Vaults, lounge with open fire.

Elevator Yes.

Parking Yes, in rear of hotel.

Pricing Includes full English breakfast.

Credit Cards V, MC, AMEX, D

This coaching inn has been receiving guests since the 15th century, and among them was Charles Dickens, who wrote part of *The Pickwick Papers* in a room now named in his honor. This and most of the other guest rooms are graced with high ceilings and generous proportions and are furnished traditionally but sensibly and comfortably. Ask for a room in the front of the house to enjoy the view over the square and the abbey ruins. The Angel is a good place if you want to enjoy British market-town life while visiting Cambridge and other nearby towns. It is also a good place to stop for tea or a drink in front of the hearth, or, for that matter, to enjoy a meal in the formal Abbeygate Restaurant or the Vaults Brasserie, occupying the ancient cellars.

Norwich

Aptly described by the 19th-century British author and linguist George Borrow as "a fine old city," Norwich was founded by the Saxons and laid waste to by the Normans. To their credit, though, the Normans erected what are still the town's two finest structures, **Norwich Cathedral** and **Norwich Castle,** and these rise above an attractive assemblage of medieval, Tudor, and more recent structures that line narrow lanes leading off the Market Place.

Norwich Cathedral is set in a beautiful close surrounded by restored medieval and Georgian houses. Before entering the church, stop outside the east end to pay tribute at the simple grave of Edith Clavell, a local nurse who was arrested and shot in Belgium during World War I for helping Allied soldiers escape. If you continue past the medieval infirmary, refectory, and other outbuildings, you'll come to a path that leads to the banks of the River Wensum and Pull's Ferry, a water gate built in the 15th century. When you step into the cathedral, you'll be confronted with a sea of Norman columns that support a fan-vaulted ceiling embellished with bosses of carved stone; mirrors are placed around the nave so you can admire the carvings, which depict biblical scenes, without craning your neck. The cloisters, surrounding an enormous greensward, are the largest in England. The cathedral is open daily, 7:30 a.m.–6 p.m., later in summer. Admission is free (donations are suggested); phone (01603) 218-321.

Though **Norwich Castle** was a Norman stronghold, it was refaced with Bath stone in the 19th century, making the walls and towers look more decorative than mighty. The views from the ramparts over the city and surrounding fields are wonderful, and a small museum houses a collection of paintings by the so-called Norwich school of painters. The castle is open Monday–Saturday, 10 a.m.–5 p.m., and Sunday, 2–5 p.m. Admission is £3; phone (01603) 223-624.

Another mandatory stop in Norwich is about three miles outside the city center: the **Sainsbury Centre for Visual Arts** on the campus of the University of East Anglia. Here, the Sainsbury family of the British supermarket fortune have built a remarkable modern gallery (designed by architect Norman Foster) and filled it with Art Nouveau paintings, as well as other 20th-century art by Francis Bacon and others, tribal art and other ethnographic pieces, and classical sculpture. The center is open Tuesday–Sunday, 11 a.m.–5 p.m., and admission is £2 adults, £1 children. Call (01603) 456-060 for more information. To reach the center, take buses 3, 4, 12, or 27 from Castle Meadow in the center of Norwich.

Norwich is 63 miles northeast of Cambridge. Trains run from Cambridge to Norwich about every half hour, and the trip takes about an hour; the round-trip fare is £15. By car, you can reach Norwich in just about an hour on the A11. The **Norwich Tourist Information Centre** (off Market Place ; (01603) 727-927) is open April–October, Monday–Saturday, 10 a.m.–6 p.m.; Sunday, 10:30 a.m.–4:30 p.m.; November–March, Monday–Saturday, 10 a.m.–5:30 p.m.

Part Eleven

York and Yorkshire

Most visitors will bring some sort of preconceived notion to Yorkshire. There are, of course, the rugged moors where Heathcliff brooded in *Wuthering Heights,* the green valleys that veterinarian author James Herriott describes in his appealing representations of English country life, even the gloomy graveyard on a hill above the sea in **Whitby** that allegedly inspired Bram Stoker's *Dracula.*

Whatever expectations you bring to Yorkshire, your journey up north will be well rewarded. At the center of this swath of northern England is the richly historic and remarkably attractive walled city of York. To the west are the deep, luxuriant river valleys of the **Yorkshire Dales,** and to the east and north are the rugged, heather-covered **Yorkshire Moors.** In these landscapes are literary shrines (notably, **Haworth,** where the Brontë sisters wrote their masterpieces); ruined abbeys (the most spectacular are those at **Bolton** and **Rievaulx**); isolated but lavish country houses (aside from a royal palace or two, **Castle Howard** may well be the grandest home in England); and charming towns and villages (our favorite is seaside Whitby). Given the riches that await you in Yorkshire, it would be a shame to come to England and not make the journey north. We suggest you make York your base and set out on easy day trips from there.

Not To Be Missed in York and Yorkshire

- York Minster, city walls and gates, medieval streets and lanes (page 445)
- Brontë pilgrimage to Haworth (page 457)
- Rievaulx Abbey (page 455)
- Castle Howard (page 453)
- Whitby (page 453)

York

York is a theatrical place, a dream come true for travelers in search of a romantic old European city of twisting and cobbled lanes, medieval towers,

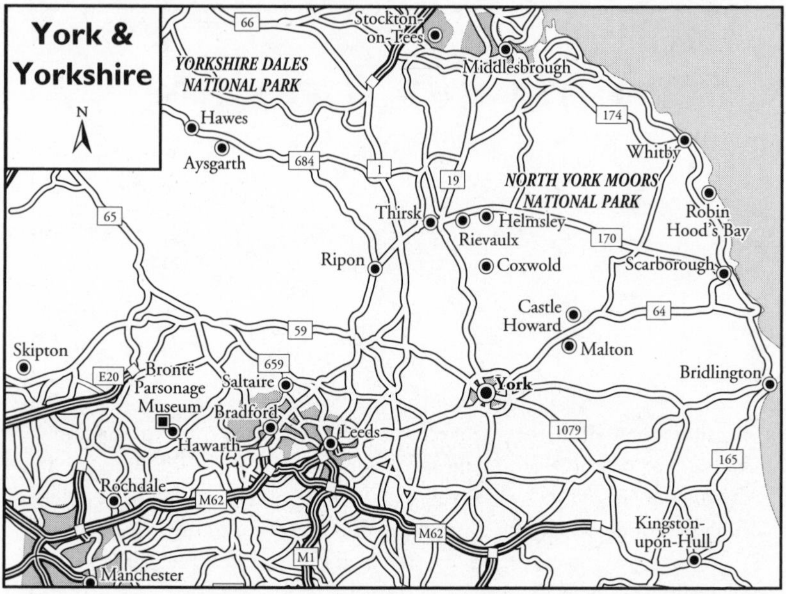

and mossy old stones. Roman York, Eboracum, was the capital for the legions who occupied northern Britain. The Saxons renamed the city Eofowic and made it capital of their kingdom of Northumbria. The Vikings arrived in the ninth century, and the newly named Jorvik became capital of Danelaw, as their holdings in northern and eastern Britain were known. After the Normans invaded England in 1066, York was soon thriving as a major port and center of government, one of the great medieval cities of Europe.

York wears this considerable mantle of history well. The city is largely medieval and remarkably intact, and museums and churches are brimming with artifacts of this long and storied past. Yet York is a thriving city, too, with a vibrant street life and a good-natured attitude toward the two million visitors who come north every year to enjoy one of England's most appealing cities.

Planning Your Visit to York

The **York Tourist Information Centre** has two offices in the city, one at the railway station and one on Exhibition Square in the center of the old city. Both are open Monday–Saturday, 9 a.m.–5 p.m., and Sunday, 10 a.m.–4 p.m.; the offices keep longer Sunday hours in summer—10 a.m.–5 p.m. at Exhibition Square, and 9:30 a.m.–4:30 p.m. at the railway station. Both offices provide an accommodation-booking service, sell tickets for events and sight-seeing tours, and supply maps and other visitors' information. For either office, call (01904) 621-756 or visit **www.visityork.org.**

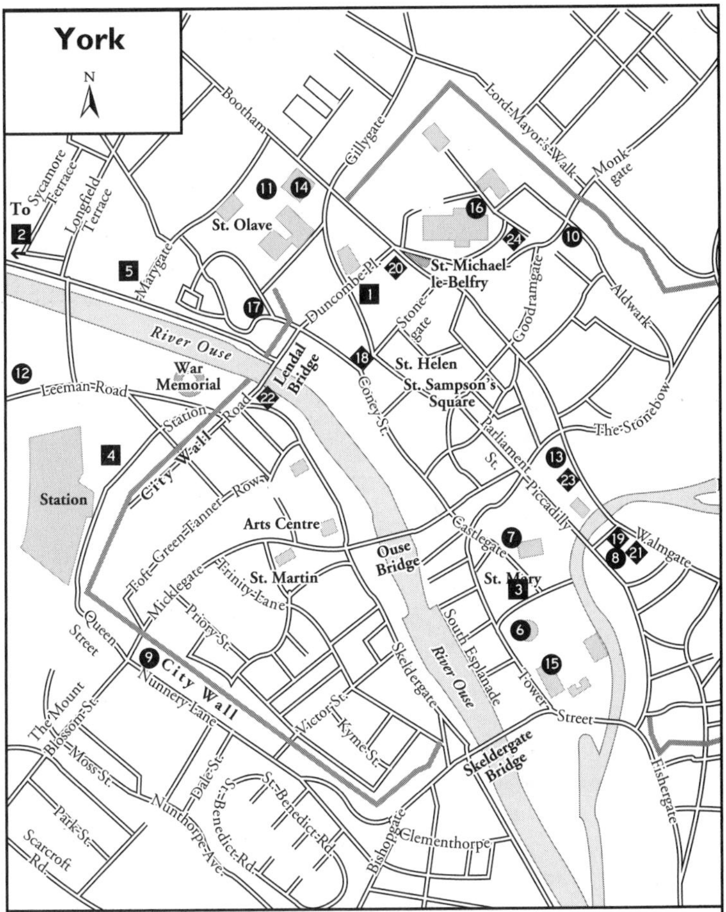

HOTELS

1 Dean Court
2 The Grange
3 Hilton York
4 Le Meridien York
5 Water's Edge

ATTRACTIONS

6 Clifford's tavern
7 Jorvik, the Viking City
8 Merchant Adventures Hall
9 Mickelgate Bar Museum
10 Monk Bar
11 Museum Gardens
12 National Railway Museum
13 The Shambles
14 York Art Gallery
15 York Castle Museum
16 York Minster
17 Yorkshire Museum

RESTAURANTS

18 Betty's Café Tea Rooms
19 Blue Bicycle
20 Cafe Concerto
21 Meltons, Too
22 Pizza Express
23 Rish
24 St. Williams Restaurant

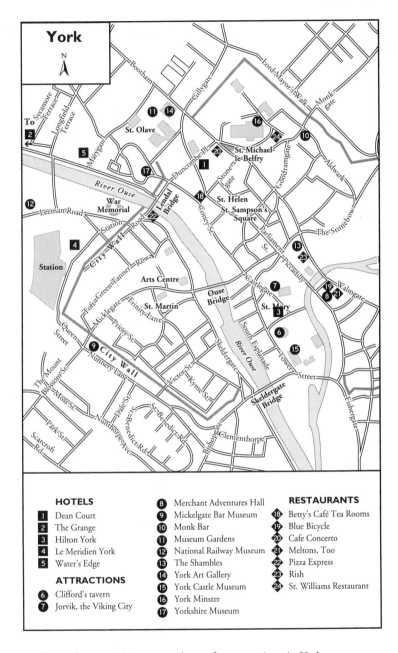

If you plan on visiting more than a few attractions in York, we recommend purchasing the **York Pass.** This handy card provides admission to some 30 attractions, including those you will probably want to see, including **Jorvik, the Viking City,** the **Merchant Adventurers' Hall,** the **National Railway Museum,** and such nearby places as **Castle Howard**

HOW HOTELS COMPARE

Hotel	Overall Rating	Quality Rating	Value Rating	Price
York				
The Grange	★★★★	★★★★	★★★	£135–£195
Le Méridien York	★★★½	★★★	★★★½	£80–£185
Water's Edge	★★★	★★★	★★★★	£50–£75

and **Eden Camp.** Costs are: one day, £18 adults, £13 children ages 5–15; two days, £26 adults, £18 children ages 5–15; three days, £33 adults, £25 children ages 5–15. Passes are available at the tourist offices; for more information, call (01664) 500-107 or visit **www.yorkpass.com.**

Special Events in York

During the **Jorvik Viking Festival** in February, hundreds of Viking and Saxon warriors take to the streets in a colorful reenactment of York's past, accompanied by long-ship races, demonstrations of Viking crafts, and other events. The **International Jazz Series** showcases leading musicians for a week in late May. The week-long **York Comedy Festival** in late June brings top British comedians to the city, and York's medieval churches, guildhalls, and other historic buildings provide the setting for the **York Early Music Festival** in early July. During the **St. Nicholas Fayre** in late November, market stalls spring up around the city selling crafts, food, and other seasonal goods. For information on these and other events in York, call (01904) 621-756 or visit **www.visityork.org.**

Arriving and Getting Oriented in York

York is 200 miles north of London. Trains run hourly, with half-hourly departures at peak travel times, from London's King's Cross Station to York. The trip takes only two hours and costs about £75 round trip. For information, call (08457) 484-950 or go to **www.railtrack.co.uk.** The York railway station is just beyond the city walls, about a ten-minute walk east of the city center along Station Road and Museum Street. City buses run from the station to locations around town, but most places in the center are within walking distance. There is a taxi rank outside the station (call (01904) 638-833 to summon a cab).

By car, the quickest route from London to York is via the busy M1, England's major north-south artery, then the A64. Allow at least four hours for the drive. Traffic on city-center streets is severely restricted Monday–Friday, 11 a.m.–4 p.m.; Saturday, 10:30 a.m.–4:30 p.m.; and Sunday, noon–4 p.m. The 19 car parks in and around the city center are

IN YORK AND YORKSHIRE

Hotel	Overall Rating	Quality Rating	Value Rating	Price
York (continued)				
Dean Court	★★★	★★★	★★½	£95–£149
Hilton York	★★★	★★½	★★	£109–£157

well marked along the routes into the city and provide short-term and long-term parking; expect to pay about £1.20 per hour or about £4.20 for half a day. The most convenient and inexpensive places to park are the city's **Park and Ride** facilities at the edge of the city center, at Askham Bar, Rawcliffe Bar, the Designer Outlet center, and Grimston Bar, all marked from approaches into the city. From all, buses run into the city center every ten minutes, 7 a.m.–8 p.m.; for more information, call (01904) 551-400.

National Express buses leave London's Victoria Coach Station for York every hour. The trip takes from five to six hours, making the train a much more attractive option; the round trip costs about £40. The bus station is near the railway station off Rougier Street. For more information, call (08705) 808-080 or go to **www.gobycoach.com.**

Hotels in York

There are a limited number of hotels in the old city of York, and these are often full in the summer and around Christmas, so reserve well in advance at these times. While York hotels tend to be expensive (on par with those in London), many offer specials that can bring prices down considerably, such as reduced rates on a third night and package rates for dinner, bed, and breakfast; ask when booking or check out the hotel websites. If you arrive in town without a room reservation, go right to the tourist office (see "Planning Your Visit to York," above), where the helpful staff provides an accommodation-booking service.

Dean Court — *£95–£149*

OVERALL ★★★ | QUALITY ★★★ | VALUE ★★½

Duncombe Place, York, North Yorkshire YO1 7EF; (01904) 625-082; fax (01904) 620-305; info@deancourt-york.co.uk; www.deancourt-york.co.uk

Location Across from York Minster.

Amenities & Services 39 rooms. Restaurant, café, pleasant lounges, room service.

Elevator Yes, to some rooms.

Parking In private car park, £10 per day.

Pricing Includes full English breakfast.

Credit Cards V, MC, AMEX

If you can't get your fill of views of York Minster, the Dean Court is the hotel for you. This older, well-kept hotel is directly across the street from the cathedral, in the heart of the medieval city. Location is what you pay for here, because the rooms, while perfectly comfortable, are a bit dowdy, and some tend to be cramped. We strongly recommend you request one of the superior or deluxe rooms with a view; room 61, with a bow window, is particularly charming, as is room 36, a large family room with a pull-out sofa and dramatic views through a corner window. Ask about the hotel's "Getaway Breaks," which offer room, dinner, and breakfast for two from £125—an especially good value.

The Grange — *£135–£195*

OVERALL ★★★★ | QUALITY ★★★★ | VALUE ★★★

1 Clifton, York, North Yorkshire Y030 6AA; (01904) 644-744; fax (01904) 612-453; info@grangehotel.co.uk; www.grangehotel.co.uk

Location On the edge of the city center, within walking distance of York Minster and the railway station.

Amenities & Services 32 rooms. Comfortable lounges with open fires; three restaurants: The Ivy, Dom Ruinart Seafood Bar, the Brasserie; ISDN lines in rooms, porter.

Elevator No.

Parking In private car park, free.

Pricing Includes full English breakfast; good-value bed, breakfast, and dinner rates available.

Credit Cards V, MC, AMEX

This spacious Regency town house has the air of a grand country home, and the décor enhances the feeling with old prints, deep armchairs next to ornate hearths, old carpets on the floors, and elegant draperies at the windows. The guest rooms, reached via a sweeping skylit staircase, are large and also traditionally furnished, with nice outlooks toward the old city and the parks and surrounding gardens; all have spacious, modern baths equipped with power showers. The Ivy restaurant wins awards for its French and modern British cuisine, and the Brasserie is a stylish, stone-floored and brick-walled room in the cellars serving informal fare. It's well worth looking into the hotel's special offers, including reduced rates for a third night's stay and special midwinter value breaks; call or check the hotel's website for updates.

Hilton York — *£109–£157*

OVERALL ★★★ | QUALITY ★★½ | VALUE ★★

1 Tower Street, York, North Yorkshire YO1 9WD; (01904) 648-111; fax (01904) 610-317; www.york.hilton.com

Location In old city, across from Clifford's tower and city walls.

Amenities & Services 130 rooms. Restaurant, bar, concierge, room service.

Elevator Yes.

Parking In hotel garage, £10 per night (often full; we recommend using the municipal car park across the street).

Pricing Full breakfast sometimes included, depending on room rate.

Credit Cards V, MC, AMEX, D

Location is the appeal of this modern hotel, which has the anonymous feel, as well as the conveniences, of a chain. Rooms are a bit cramped but comfortably furnished in standard hotel-issue pieces, and baths, likewise, are small but well equipped. Views from the front rooms over Clifford's tower, one of the city's medieval fortifications, are especially atmospheric at night in the glow of floodlights, and all of the city sights are within an easy walk.

Le Méridien York *£80–£185*

OVERALL ★★★½ | QUALITY ★★★ | VALUE ★★★½

Station Road, York, North Yorkshire YO24 1AA; (08000) 282840 in U.K., (800) 543-4300 in U.S.; www.lemeridien.com

Location Just outside the city walls near the railway station.

Amenities & Services 160 rooms. Restaurant, bar, indoor swimming pool, three acres of gardens, concierge, room service.

Elevator Yes.

Parking On grounds, free.

Pricing Includes buffet breakfast.

Credit Cards V, MC, AMEX, DC

This ornate, rambling Victorian railway hotel is now under the management of the French Méridien group. While retaining the grand staircases, paneled and frescoed public rooms, and all of the other architectural details of an era when attention to detail seemed to matter, the group has renovated the premises from the cellar pool and health club to the top-floor rooms under the sloping roofs. New décor schemes have infused musty, unimaginative guest rooms with style and modern amenities that include dramatic lighting, state-of-the-art baths, chic and comfortable furnishings, and fine French linens. Renovated rooms are the best value and most pleasant; insist on these rather than the older rooms. The hotel is set in extensive gardens, and rooms in front of the hotel (the ones you should request), have views of the Minster towers and other sights of the old town.

Water's Edge *£50–£75*

OVERALL ★★★ | QUALITY ★★★ | VALUE ★★★★

5 Earlsborough Terrace, Marygate, York, North Yorkshire YO30 7BQ; (01904) 644-625; fax (01904) 731-516; julie@watersedgeyork.co.uk; www.watersedgeyork.co.uk

Location In a neighborhood of Victorian row houses on the River Ouse, near the National Railway Museum.

Amenities & Services 5 rooms, all with private bath. The premises are nonsmoking. Comfortable lounge; color TV, hair dryers, and other in-room amenities not usually found in bed-and-breakfast establishments.

Elevator No.

Parking On street, free with permit from hotel.

Pricing Includes full English breakfast.

Credit Cards V, MC

A pretty garden at the water's edge is one of the many attractions of this attractive bed-and-breakfast, which is only a ten-minute walk from most of the city sights. Rooms are large, bright, and appealingly furnished in traditional style, and guests also enjoy the homey sitting room and lovely garden. Given the high quality of accommodation and the excellent location, this small establishment is a very good value.

Exploring York

Old York is compact, still contained within medieval walls built in the 14th century to replace the stockades and earthen fortifications the Vikings put up to protect the city. Within these walls is a warren of twisting streets that follow the paths of Roman thoroughfares and narrow medieval alleys known as "ginnels."

It's a pleasure to walk through old York, and you can easily reach all of the city's attractions on foot. You should also allow yourself the luxury of getting lost and ambling aimlessly; take time to admire medieval churches and half-timbered houses, as well as the shops and other signs of modern York, which, for all of its historic appeal, remains a prosperous and vital city.

A walkway runs along the top of the well-maintained walls, and four crenellated towers rise above the old city gates (or "bars") to the city. The tiny **Micklegate Bar Museum** records the pageantry that once accompanied the passage of kings and queens through its arch, the official royal entry to the city, and also houses casts of some of the traitors and other unfortunates whose heads were displayed from the tower. The museum is open February–October, daily, 9 a.m.–dusk, and December–February, Saturday and Sunday, 9 a.m.–dusk; admission is £2 adults, £1 seniors, and £.50 children; for information, call (01904) 634-436. **Monk Bar,** which retains its medieval wooden portcullis (last lowered in 1953), houses a small museum devoted to Richard III, the 15th-century Duke of York and King of England who is often accused of killing his young nephews to secure the throne. The museum is open March–October, daily, 9 a.m.–5 p.m., and November–February, daily, 9:30 a.m.–4 p.m.; admission is £2 adults, £1 seniors; for information, call (01904) 634-

191. **Clifford's Tower** is a small castle built atop a steep mound along the walls; in 1190, the city's Jewish population took refuge from an angry mob inside the then-wooden castle, which was burned to the ground; the tower is open April–June, daily, 10 a.m.–6 p.m.; July–August, daily, 9:30 a.m.–7 p.m.; and October–March, daily, 10 a.m.–4 p.m.; admission is £2.10 adults, £1.60 seniors, £1.10 children, and £5.30 families; for more information, call (01904) 646-940.

The most famous structure within the walls is **York Minster,** the city's vast Gothic cathedral. Surrounding the cathedral yard are the twisting lanes of the medieval city. Stonegate, one of the most atmospheric streets in York, leads directly out of Minster Yard and has been a busy thoroughfare since the Romans laid it out more than 2,000 years ago; a Norman house at 52A dates from the 12th century. The best preserved of the lanes is **the Shambles,** where the upper stories of half-timbered houses cast the old cobblestones in perpetual shadow; these days, coy boutiques have replaced the butcher shops that once lined the Shambles, and the much-photographed street seems more like a Ye Olde England tourist attraction than the real place it once was.

The 14th-century, half-timbered **Merchant Adventurers' Hall,** just south of the Shambles on Fossgate, is considered the best-preserved guildhall in Europe. Members of the Merchant Adventurers Guild dealt in imported goods, which, as evidenced by the size and rich detail of the hall, was a lucrative trade in medieval York. The ground floor (undercroft) houses the guild's chapel and the hospice where, as part of the guild charter, members provided food and shelter to the poor and infirm; upstairs is the Great Hall, with a soaring, beamed ceiling, and there's a lovely garden in the rear. It's open Easter–September 30, Monday–Saturday, 9 a.m.–5 p.m., and Sunday, noon–4 p.m., and October–Easter, Monday–Saturday, 9 a.m.–3 p.m.; admission is £2 adults, £1.70 seniors, £0.70 children, and £5 for families; for information, call (01904) 654-818.

The **Museum Gardens,** just west of York Minster on the banks of the River Ouse, provide an expanse of greenery that can be most welcome after a day spent dodging the summertime crowds in the narrow lanes of the city. Within the gardens are a medieval hospice as well as the Yorkshire Museum (see profile below) and the **York Art Gallery,** near the Tourist Information Centre on Exhibition Square. The Gallery is a small and often overlooked treasure that counts among its holdings Western European paintings spanning seven centuries, including masterpieces by Italian Renaissance masters Martino di Bartolommeo and Annibale Carracci, and an excellent collection of 20th-century studio pottery. The museum is open daily, 10 a.m.–5 p.m. (closed December 25 and 26) and admission is free; for more information, call (01904) 697-979.

Tours of York

In York, your choice of walking and sight-seeing tours is greater than it is in any other city outside of London. The York **Association of Voluntary Guides** offers free walking tours daily at 10:15 a.m. (additional tours at 2:15 p.m., April–September, and 6:45 p.m., June–August). The two-hour tours are an excellent introduction to the Roman, Viking, and medieval city, and include stops at York Minster and several other churches and monuments. Walks depart from in front of the Art Gallery in Exhibition Square, near the main Tourist Information Centre; you don't have to reserve, just show up. For more information, call (01904) 640-780 or visit **www.york.touristguides.btinternet.co.uk.**

The four-hour **Complete York Tour** (given March–October at 10 a.m.) includes a visit to Jorvik Viking Centre and stops for a drink along the way. The cost is £10 adults, £9.50 seniors and students, and £5 children ages 5–15. The walk departs from the tree at the west end of York Minster; you must call (01904) 706-643 to reserve a place. **York Walks** provide in-depth specialized tours that look at such aspects of the city as medieval alleyways, the walls, and Roman remnants. Walk prices vary but in general cost £5 adults and £4.50 children. All walks start at the Museum Garden Gates on Museum Street; you don't need to reserve. Check out itineraries and schedules at **www.yorkwalk.co.uk,** or call (01904) 622-303.

Guide Friday operates open-top bus tours that depart every 20 minutes throughout the year and take in all of the major sights in York. The complete circuit lasts about one hour, but you can hop on and off the bus as often as you wish throughout the day. The cost is £7.50 adults, £6 seniors and students, £2.50 children ages 5–15, and £17.50 families of up to two adults and two children. For more information, call (01904) 625-618. **York City Sightseeing** offers a similar tour and hop-on-and-off arrangement; call (01904) 692-505 for information.

For an unusual view of historic York from the water, take the 45-minute boat tour that **York Boat** offers daily, February 9–November 24. There are at least four tours a day along the River Ouse; the cost is £6 adults, £5.50 seniors and students, and £3 children ages 5–15. Boats leave from the landing stage at Lendal Bridge; for information, call (01904) 647-204 or go to **yorkboat.co.uk.**

York is said to be the most haunted city in Britain, and every evening the medieval streets are crowded with enthusiastic participants in **Ghost Walks.** These visits to places where ghost sightings have been reported typically last about an hour. Your chances of making a spectral sighting are slim, since it's unlikely a self-respecting ghost would choose to make an appearance in front of the hordes who join the walks. The tours are to be enjoyed for their entertainment value (the quality of which depends entirely on the storytelling skill of the tour guide), and they provide a nice way to enjoy the city at night. One of the most popular tours is the **Ghost Hunt of York,** which departs nightly at 7:30 p.m. from the Shambles, York's famous medieval street. Cost is £3 adults, £2 children. No reservations are necessary, and you pay the guide; call (01904) 608-700. The Tourist Information Centre furnishes brochures on this and other Ghost Walks.

Attractions in York

Jorvik, the Viking City

Type of Attraction Re-created Viking village with animatronic figures

Location Coppergate

Admission £7.20 adults; £6.10 seniors and students; £5.10 children ages 5–15; £21.95 families of up to two adults and two children; £26.50 families of up to two adults and three children

Hours November 4–March 30: daily, 10 a.m.–4 p.m;. March 31–November 3: daily, 10 a.m.–5 p.m.

Phone (01904) 543-403

Website www.vikingjorvik.com

When to Go The attraction is most crowded during school holidays and summer; go early in the morning or late in the afternoon to avoid crowds and a long wait for what amounts to a ten-minute ride.

Special Comments It's possible to book tickets by calling the number above or going to the Jorvik website, but this will add an additional fee to an already expensive experience.

Overall Appeal by Age Group

Preschool ★	Teens ★★★	Over 30 ★★
Grade school ★★★	Young Adults ★★★	Seniors ★★

Author's Rating ★★★

How Much Time to Allow 30 minutes

Description & Comments Jorvik, the Viking name for York, is a reconstruction of the city as it was during the Viking era, when Jorvik was a trading hub of some importance. The multisensory attraction was completed after 20 years of archaeological investigation and presents a meticulously re-created village with shops, stalls, houses, even an outdoor privy; the faces of the animatronic Vikings were created from Viking skulls. The show begins with a brief introduction that pretends to take visitors back in a time capsule. You then board four-passenger "time trains" that make a circuit of the village, as Viking voices (at least, we assume that's what the accents are intended to portray) provide a commentary. While archaeological authenticity lends some merit to the experience, Jorvik otherwise seems like an amusement park attraction; we can think of better ways to spend the substantial amount you'll have to lay out for the admission fee, and you can see Viking artifacts (along with remnants of York during the Roman period and other times) in the Yorkshire Museum.

HOW ATTRACTIONS COMPARE

Attraction	Comments	Author's Rating
York		
National Railway Museum	Historic English trains	★★★★
York Minster	Largest medieval Gothic church in England	★★★★
York Castle Museum	Museum of local life	★★★½
Jorvik, the Viking City	Re-created Viking village with animatronic figures	★★★
Yorkshire Museum	History of York and Yorkshire	★★
The North York Moors and Whitby		
Castle Howard	Largest and most historic manor house in Yorkshire	★★★

Touring Tips Plan on spending time in the small museum at the end of the "ride," where artifacts unearthed in York are on display and exhibits portray Viking ships and other facets of history.

National Railway Museum

Type of Attraction Museum displaying historic English trains

Location Leeman Road

Admission Free

Hours Daily, 10 a.m.–6 p.m.; closed December 24–26

Phone (01904) 621-261

Website www.nrm.org.uk

When to Go Anytime

Special Comments There is a café/restaurant in the museum, as well as a shop selling fascinating railroad-related items.

Overall Appeal by Age Group

Preschool ★★★	Teens ★★★	Over 30 ★★★★
Grade school ★★★★	Young Adults ★★★★	Seniors ★★★★

Author's Rating ★★★★

How Much Time to Allow About 2 hours

Description & Comments The extraordinary quality, meticulous restoration, and historic importance of the trains on view make this museum a pleasure to visit. The earliest trains, dating from the 1840s, look like stagecoaches on wheels. Several private train compartments used by British monarchs have been preserved, from Queen Victoria to Queen Elizabeth II. Children can climb up into the engineer's area in some of the trains. All told, there are 103 locomotives here and 177 other

IN YORK AND YORKSHIRE

Attraction	Comments	Author's Rating
The North York Moors and Whitby (continued)		
Rievaulx Abbey	Majestic ruins of 12th-century abbey	★★★
Eden Camp	Modern history museum in former prisoner-of-war camp	★★
Yorkshire Dales		
Bolton Priory	Historic priory and landscaped park on Devonshire estate	★★★
Haworth		
Brontë Parsonage Museum	Home of literary Brontë family and adjacent museum	★★★★

railway cars, as well as extensive collections of railroad posters and other paraphernalia and a new "works" wing where visitors can learn about signaling and other railroad technology and visit a workshop where trains are restored.

Touring Tips A well-done audio guide provides fascinating commentary and includes 60 tales of British railway lore.

York Minster

Type of Attraction Largest medieval Gothic church in England

Location Minster Yard

Admission Minster: free. Chapter House: £1. Undercroft/Crypt/Treasury: £3.80 adults, £1.50 children; Tower: £3 adults, £1 children

Hours *Cathedral and Chapter House:*
November–March, Monday–Saturday, 7 a.m.–6 p.m. Sunday, 1–6 p.m.
April, Monday–Saturday, 7 a.m.–6:30 p.m., Sunday, 1–6:30 p.m.
May, Monday–Saturday, 7 a.m.–7:30 p.m., Sunday, 1–7:30 p.m.
June–August, Monday–Saturday, 7 a.m.–8:30 p.m., Sunday 1–8:30 p.m.
September, Monday–Saturday, 7 a.m.–8 p.m.
October, Monday–Saturday, 7 a.m.–7 p.m., Sunday, 1–7 p.m.
Crypt/Undercroft/Tower: December–February, 10 a.m.–4:30 p.m., Sunday, 1–4:30 p.m.
March, Monday–Saturday, noon–6 p.m., Sunday, 1–6 p.m.
April and October, Monday–Saturday, 10 a.m.–5:30 p.m., Sunday, 1–5:30 p.m.
May and September, Monday–Saturday, 10 a.m.–6 p.m., Sunday, 1–6 p.m.
June–August, Monday–Saturday, 9:30 a.m.–6:30 p.m., Sunday, 1–6:30 p.m.
November, Monday–Saturday, 10 a.m.–4 p.m.

Phone (01904) 557-216

Website www.yorkminster.org

When to Go Anytime during daylight hours, so you can enjoy the stained-glass windows

Special Comments Your enjoyment of York Minster will be enhanced if you hear choral music in this great space. The 13th-century Chapter House is frequently used for concerts. In the cathedral, you can hear evensong daily at 5 p.m. (4 p.m. on Saturdays and Sundays). There is usually no sung service on Mondays during term time; call (01904) 557-200 to check whether the choir is singing on a particular day.

Overall Appeal by Age Group

Preschool ★	Teens ★★★	Over 30 ★★★★
Grade school ★★★	Young Adults ★★★	Seniors ★★★★

Author's Rating ★★★★

How Much Time to Allow About 30 minutes for the upper part of the cathedral, and another 20–30 minutes for the Crypt and Undercroft

Description & Comments Though earlier Roman and Christian structures stood on the site, the genesis of York Minster as it exists today dates back to 1220, when Archbishop Walter de Grey decided to build a cathedral to rival Canterbury in Kent. It took 250 years and countless masons and carpenters to complete the gigantic edifice that towers over the city of York. At 534 feet long, 249 feet at its widest point, and 90 feet high, it is the largest Gothic church in England. Building styles changed during the course of construction, so the Minster exhibits several different—but somehow harmonious—architectural modes. The transepts are in Early English style, the nave and beautiful octagonal Chapter House are from the Decorated period, and the choir and East End are of the later Perpendicular style. This amazing structure was finally consecrated in 1472, with its giant west towers still incomplete. Make a circuit around the exterior before entering, and you'll better appreciate the labor it took to create this place of worship. The North Transept and the South Transept, both begun in the 13th century, are the oldest parts of the present cathedral; the East End, completed in 1472, was one of the last parts of the cathedral to be built. York Minster's octagonal 13th-century Chapter House is particularly beautiful and something of an architectural marvel, having no central support to spread the weight of its domed roof. Carved stone canopies line the walls. The Crypt was the earliest part of the cathedral to be built. Excavation work in the Undercroft has revealed the foundations of a Roman fort and street and parts of the earlier Norman cathedral; this area has been turned into an intriguing walk through time.

Ornamental stonework, rich roof bosses, and the carved choir screen depicting the kings of England contribute to the greatness of this minster, but the stained glass is the most remarkable decorative element in the church. The Great West Window, its stained glass dating from 1338, is called the "Heart of Yorkshire." The South Transept contains a beautiful Rose Window, while the North Transept glows with the famous Five Sisters Window, dating from 1260. The Great East Window, dating from 1408, is the largest window of medieval stained glass in England.

Touring Tips The Treasurer's House in the Minster Yard is a small museum of 17th- and 18th-century period rooms; it is open to the public April–October, Saturday–Thursday, 10 a.m.–6 p.m.; admission is £3.70 adults, £2 seniors and children, and £9.50 families. For more information, call (01904) 624-247.

Yorkshire Museum

Type of Attraction Museum dedicated to the history of York and Yorkshire

Location Museum Gardens

Admission £4 adults; £2.50 children ages 5–15; £10 families of up to two adults and two children

Hours Daily, 10 a.m.–5 p.m.; closed December 25–26, January 1

Phone (01904) 551-800

Website www.yorkshiremuseum.org.uk

When to Go Anytime

Special Comments

Overall Appeal by Age Group

Preschool ★	Teens ★	Over 30 ★★
Grade school ★	Young Adults ★★	Seniors ★★★

Author's Rating ★★

How Much Time to Allow About 1 hour

Description & Comments There's plenty to see in this old-fashioned museum, but the sheer number of text panels, while useful, tends to slow one down along the way. Collections contain important artifacts from the entire 2,000-year history of York—Roman jewelry, Anglo-Saxon silver, and Viking swords and axes are all on display. One of the museum's most famous treasures is the 15th-century, sapphire-studded Middleham Jewel, found in North Yorkshire in 1985.

Touring Tips The museum, set among the picturesque ruins of St. Mary's Abbey, is surrounded by ten acres of strollable landscaped gardens. On the grounds you'll find a half-timbered, 15th-century hospital.

York Castle Museum

Type of Attraction Museum of local life

Location Clifford Street

Admission £6 adults; £3.50 seniors; £3.50 children; £16 families

Hours April–October: daily, 10 a.m.–5 p.m.; November–March: daily, 9:30 a.m.–4:30 p.m. Closed December 25–26.

Phone (01904) 650-333

Website www.yorkcastlemuseum.org.uk

When to Go Anytime; the museum does not get as crowded as some of York's other attractions

Special Comments The museum has a shop and snack bar and is accessible to visitors with disabilities.

Overall Appeal by Age Group

Preschool —	Teens ★★★★	Over 30 ★★★
Grade school ★★★★	Young Adults ★★★★	Seniors ★★★

Author's Rating ★★★½

HOW RESTAURANTS COMPARE

Name	Cuisine	Overall	Quality	Value	Price
York					
Blue Bicycle	British	★★★★	★★★★	★★★½	Mod
Rish	International	★★★★	★★★★	★★★	Mod
Betty's Café Tea Rooms	Café	★★★★	★★★	★★	Exp
Meltons, Too	Bar/Bistro	★★★	★★★	★★★★	Mod

How Much Time to Allow About 2 hours

Description & Comments A former prison now houses evocative displays that capture everyday life as it once transpired in York. At the core of the museum, and featured in the displays you'll want to spend the most time viewing, are artifacts collected by physician John Kirk, who between 1890 and 1920 amassed household objects, tradesmen's tools, shop displays, and other artifacts that he realized represented a fast-disappearing way of life. Most of Kirk's finds are displayed in reconstructed shops and workshops along Kirkgate, a facsimile of a typical York street from the end of the 19th century. Also of great interest are period rooms reflecting domestic tastes from the Georgian era through the 1950s.

Touring Tips For a kid-pleasing afternoon, combine a visit to the museum with a stop at nearby Clifford's Tower.

Restaurants in York

Betty's Café Tea Rooms ★★★★

CAFÉ | EXPENSIVE | QUALITY ★★★ | VALUE ★★

6–8 St. Helens Square; (01904) 659-142

Reservations Not necessary **Entrée Range** £4.50–£11 **Payment** V, MC, AMEX **Bar** No **Disabled Access** Yes

Hours Daily, 9 a.m.–9 p.m.

House Specialties Omelets; sandwiches; selections from the dessert trolley.

Betty's became a York institution almost as soon as it opened its doors in the late 1930s, and these days is such a favorite on the tourist trail that chances are you will have to line up for a seat in the mirrored Art Deco room decorated with hundreds of teapots. If you do decide to wait and pay the fairly high prices for a cup of tea, you will find a huge selection that includes brews made from the world's rarest leaves, as well as delicious sandwiches and sweets, all served with grace and style.

Blue Bicycle ★★★★

MODERN BRITISH | MODERATE | QUALITY ★★★★ | VALUE ★★★½

34 Fossgate; (01904) 673-990

IN YORK AND YORKSHIRE

Name	Cuisine	Overall	Quality	Value	Price
York					
Café Concerto	Bistro	★★★	★★★	★★★	Mod
St Williams Restaurant	Mediterranean/ British	★★★	★★★	★★★	Mod
Pizza Express	Pizza	★★★	★★	★★	Inexp

Reservations Recommended **Entrée Range** £11.95–£16.50 **Payment** V, MC, AMEX **Bar** Full service **Disabled Access** Yes, on ground floor

Hours Monday–Saturday, noon–2:30 p.m., 6–10 p.m., Sunday, noon–9 p.m.

House Specialties Any of the innovative seafood preparations.

A bistrolike atmosphere pervades this distinctive restaurant on the banks of the River Fosse, where the emphasis leans heavily to fish dishes as well as to innovative takes on such old standards as duck and lamb. Upstairs is a roomy dining room with bare floors and large windows overlooking the river; downstairs, the surroundings are loungelike, with sofas and curtained alcoves. A relaxed vibe and sense of fun pervade this restaurant, but it soon becomes clear that the kitchen is very serious about what it sends out to the dining rooms. The Blue Bicycle also runs the Blue Minelle, a coffee bar and patisserie just down the street at 13 Fossgate.

Café Concerto ★★★

BISTRO | MODERATE | QUALITY ★★★ | VALUE ★★★

21 High Petergate; (01904) 610-478

Reservations Not necessary **Entrée Range** £8.95–£11.95 **Payment** V, MC **Bar** Beer and wine **Disabled Access** Yes

Hours Daily, 10 a.m.–10 p.m.

House Specialties Salads; local specialties such as pork and leek sausages; desserts.

A pleasant, wood-floored café-bistro provides casual surroundings for an easygoing but satisfying meal, or just a cup of coffee or glass of wine. While the menu includes a good number of hearty main courses, it's also possible to eat lightly and order any of the starters (pasta, salads) as a main course. Café Concerto is a good spot for a meal before or after a visit to the Minster, which is just around the corner.

Meltons, Too ★★★

BAR/BISTRO | MODERATE | QUALITY ★★★ | VALUE ★★★★

25 Walmgate; (01904) 629-222

Reservations Not necessary **Entrée Range** £6.90–£11.90; sandwiches and salads, £3.50–£5.60 **Payment** V, MC **Bar** Full service **Disabled Access** Yes, on ground floor

Hours Monday–Saturday, 10:30 a.m.–11 p.m.; Sunday, 9:30 a.m.–10:30 p.m.

House Specialties Tapas; good selection of breakfast dishes; sandwiches and salads.

This popular, multifloored establishment can become fiercely busy in the evenings, when a young crowd packs in to enjoy the hip atmosphere and inexpensive food. In mornings and afternoons, though, Meltons Too, can be just the place to settle in with a newspaper or book and linger over a light meal and coffee or wine.

Pizza Express ★★★

PIZZA | INEXPENSIVE | QUALITY ★★ | VALUE ★★

River House, 17 Museum Street; (01904) 672-904

Reservations Not necessary **Entrée Range** £5–£9 **Payment** V, MC **Bar** Beer and wine **Disabled Access** Some stairs

Hours Daily, 11 a.m.–10 p.m.

House Specialties Salads; pizza margarita (with mozzarella and tomato) and other, simpler pizza concoctions.

The London-based Pizza Express chain has snapped up character-filled real estate in many British cities, but the surroundings here in York—the ornate, high-ceilinged rooms of a former gentleman's club—are hard to beat. The same, however, cannot be said of the pizza, so come here only if you want a quick, easy meal in exciting surroundings.

Rish ★★★★

INTERNATIONAL | MODERATE | QUALITY ★★★★ | VALUE ★★★

7 Fossgate; (01904) 622-688

Reservations Required on weekends, recommended at other times **Entrée Range** £10.95–£18; prix fixe lunch and pretheater menus, £11 for 2 courses, £14 for 3 courses **Payment** V, MC, AMEX **Bar** Full service **Disabled Access** Yes

Hours Daily:noon–2 p.m.,, 6–10 p.m.

House Specialties Thai hash; crispy belly pork; other Asian-influenced dishes.

An attractive Art Deco building on one of York's most charismatic streets houses this wonderful restaurant, where the cuisine and service are frequently recognized for excellence. In the chic, modern dining room, the emphasis is on making diners feel welcome and comfortable as they enjoy a blend of Asian and Continental preparations that are both surprising and satisfying. Given the atmosphere and the quality of the offerings, Rish is our first choice for a memorable meal in York.

St Williams Restaurant ★★★

MEDITERRANEAN/MODERN BRITISH | MODERATE | QUALITY ★★★ | VALUE ★★★

5 College Street; (01904) 634-830

Reservations Recommended for dinner **Entrée Range** £9.50–£14.95 **Payment** V, MC, AMEX **Bar** Full service **Disabled Access** Yes

Hours Daily: coffee, light lunch, and pastries, 10 a.m.–5 p.m.; dinner, 6–10 p.m.

House Specialties Evening specials, which usually include a selection of light fare as well as duck and other traditional dishes.

One of the more historically resonant places to dine in York is this medieval building of St. Williams College, part of the York Minster complex. In good weather, lunch and snacks are served outdoors on the sidewalk on a pedestrian-only street and in a courtyard, with the towers of the church looming nearby. At night, the beamed dining room is romantically candlelit.

Entertainment and Nightlife in York

York's most venerable venue for performing arts is the **Theatre Royal,** on St. Leonard's Place. Some of Britain's greatest actors have graced the stage of the 250-year-old theater, which presents drama as well as opera and dance. For information on performances, call (01904) 623-568 or visit **www.theatre-royal-york.co.uk.** The **York Grand Opera House** on Cumberland Street also hosts visiting dance, music, and theater companies, and it is York's major stop for road shows—the place to see Tap Dogs or the Ice Capades. For upcoming events and information, call (01904) 671-818.

York Minster is the evocative setting for frequent concerts, including splendid choral programs by the **York Chapter House Choir.** If your visit to York coincides with one of the choir's concerts, you should by all means try to attend one of these events when centuries-old stones resound with the sounds of heavenly voices. Tickets are usually about £8; for more information, call (01904) 644-194 or visit **www.chapterhousechoir.org.**

York's medieval streets are lined with historic pubs, and locals have strong opinions about which ones have become overly commercialized and which ones retain their old, local flavor. No one can doubt the authenticity of the **Blue Bell,** a tiny, atmospheric little place on Fossgate (phone (01904) 654-904) with an Edwardian interior and an admirable selection of beers and ales. **The Maltings** (Tanners Moat, near the railway station just below Lendal Bridge; (01904) 655-397) is another old York favorite, with an eclectic décor and a nice selection of ales, beers, and pub fare. The top award for old-time atmosphere must go to the **Roman Baths** (St. Sampson's Square; (01904) 620-455), which was a fairly run-of-the-mill drinking establishment until 1930, when an extensive Roman bath complex was discovered beneath the premises; patrons can now view a caldarium, steam bath, plunge pool, and other parts of the baths through a plate-glass window. These and other pubs in York are generally open Monday–Saturday, noon–11 p.m., and Sunday, noon–10:30 p.m.

Shopping in York

York's medieval buildings house any number of enticing shops, many selling items just waiting to be spirited away as a souvenir of this historic and atmospheric city. **Ken Spelman** (70 Micklegate; (01904) 624-414), in an old shop crowded with more than 40,000 titles, is one of the city's most respected purveyors of old and rare books. Shoppers eager to take a piece of old England home with them make their way to **The Miniature Scene** (42 Fossgate; (01904) 638-265), where shelves are packed with Lilliputian reproductions of villages, country houses, shops, pubs, and other typically British landmarks. Another British commodity is on hand, loose and in bags, at **Betty's Café Tea Rooms** (6–8 St. Helens Square; (01904) 659-142) and at the **Earl Grey Tea Rooms and Gift Shop** (13–14 The Shambles; (01904) 654-353). **Mulberry Hall,** in a timbered building on Stonegate (phone (01904) 620-736), specializes in all the big names in British china and crystal.

Around York

York is surrounded by glorious countryside, with the deep, lush river valleys and crags of the **Yorkshire Dales** lying to the west and the lonely moorlands stretching to the north. Against these dramatic backdrops are historic towns and villages, ruined abbeys, historic homes, and other sights that amply reward tearing yourself away from York for a day trip or two.

The North York Moors and Whitby

Much of the moorland north of York is protected as **North York Moors National Park.** In addition to the places we mention below, all of which are in the park or on its fringes, you will find miles of lonely walking trails and picnic spots. While the landscapes can be gloomy in the winter, they are beautiful in the summer when heather renders them a sea of purple. On its eastern borders, the park follows the rugged coastline, where small stone villages have earned their living from the sea for centuries. Inland, the moors are interspersed with small farms and grazing lands. For information on exploring the moors, stop in at one of the information centers of North York Moors National Park. In Helmsley, the information center is in the Old Vicarage, Bondgate, and is open March 1–October 31, daily, 9.30 a.m.–5.30 p.m., and November 1–February 28, Friday–Sunday, 10 a.m.–4 p.m.; for more information, call (01439) 770-173. In Malton, the center is at 58 Market Place; open March–October, Monday–Saturday, 9.30 a.m.–5.30 p.m.; November 1–mid-March, Monday–Wednesday, Friday, and Saturday, 10 a.m.–4 p.m.; during winter, center is closed for lunch daily except Monday and Saturday, 1–1:30 p.m. For more information, call (01653) 600-048.

To reach the park by car from York, follow A64 north to A169, the only major route that traverses the park. If you wish to see the moor and are not traveling by car, contact **Moorbus,** a network that operates buses between York and towns, villages, and visitors' centers within the park. Passes cost £3 and are valid for unlimited travel within a day. For timetables, routes, and other information, visit **www.moorbus.net.**

Walking on any of more than 2,000 miles of public footpaths is the best way to see the park. You might want to combine a day of walking with a trip on the **North Yorkshire Moors Steam Railway,** which chugs across the moors along 18 miles of track between the towns of **Grosmont** and **Pickering,** stopping at villages en route. Riders can get on and off the train as often as they like; since trails also connect the villages, it's possible to walk as far as you wish before reboarding the train. The line operates April–October, daily, with five to eight runs a day; the round-trip fare is £12 adults, £10.50 seniors, £6 children, and £26 families of up to two adults and two children. For more information, call (01751) 472-508 or visit **www.northyorkshiremoorsrailway.com.**

If you have time to visit only one of the many beautiful towns and villages in the park, make it **Whitby,** an ancient fishing port and smuggling village on the North Sea at the mouth of the River Esk. The town's maritime history dates back over a thousand years, and in the 19th century, Whitby was the main whaling port in northern England. Today, this lively resort town is an enjoyable place to spend a morning or afternoon. Stop in at the **Whitby Tourist Information Centre** (Langborne Road; (01947) 602-674) for a map and information on the town and nearby coastal and moorland attractions; the center is open May–September, daily, 9:30 a.m.–6 p.m., and October–April, daily, 10 a.m.–4:30 p.m. The **Whitby Tour,** an open-top bus tour that runs daily April–October, covers the main sights of the town and nearby coastline, but you can just as easily explore on your own; call (01947) 521-0202 for information on the tour.

The river divides Whitby into east and west sections. On the newer, west side of town are a few seaside amusement arcades and other typical seaside-town attractions, as well as a pier extending out into the turbulent North Sea. Whitby's most famous son, the 18th-century explorer and voyager Captain James Cook, is commemorated with a monument. The east side of town is older and more picturesque, with a pedestrian-only shopping street and narrow lanes and alleyways lined with former fishermen's cottages. A stone flight of 199 steps leads up to the parish church of **St. Mary,** one of the finest Anglo-Saxon churches in the country, and the ruins of **St. Hilda's Abbey.** The churchyard, with its acres of graves and tombstones spread along the cliffs overlooking the sea, reputedly inspired Bram Stoker to write the novel *Dracula.*

Castle Howard

Type of Attraction Largest and most historic manor house in Yorkshire

Location Malton, Yorkshire; 15 miles north of York, signposted from the A64; if traveling by public transportation, take the train to Malton, 5 miles from Castle Howard, and a taxi to Castle Howard from there

Admission £9 adults; £8 seniors and students; £6 children ages 4–16. Grounds only: £6 adults, £4 children ages 4–16

Hours February 14–November: daily, 11 a.m.–4:30 p.m.; grounds open at 10 a.m. year-round

Phone (01653) 648-333

Website www.castlehoward.co.uk

When to Go If you enjoy gardens, arrive when the gates open at 10 a.m. and spend some time exploring the grounds before they fill up with visitors.

Special Comments If Castle Howard seems familiar, you are not having a past-life experience in which you remember living here—the house became famous around the world when it was used in the BBC television series *Brideshead Revisited.* There are three restaurants on the grounds.

Overall Appeal by Age Group

Preschool ★★	Teens ★★	Over 30 ★★★
Grade school ★★	Young Adults ★★★	Seniors ★★★★

Author's Rating ★★★

How Much Time to Allow About 1 hour for the house and another hour or more for the grounds

Description & Comments Castle Howard, the home of the Howard family since the 17th century, is an enormous manor house set within a magnificent Yorkshire estate. Designed by Sir John Vanbrugh with help from Nicholas Hawksmoor, the house was built with a classical sense of proportion and ornamentation and is crowned by a massive cupola, providing the cumulative impression that this is not a home but a monumental structure. You're free to wander through the house at your own pace, consulting the sheets placed near the entrance to each room explaining the contents, or speaking with informative and chatty guides who are most willing to fill you in on the details. The Long Gallery is one of the most impressive rooms, but there are dozens of others that seem just as grand, all decorated with fine original furniture and a collection of paintings that includes masterful works by Tintoretto, Canaletto, Rubens, and Holbein. The "Brideshead Room" houses memorabilia from the television series *Brideshead Revisited.* The 1,000-acre park, its lakes and fountains set against the bare green backdrop of the Howardian Hills, has several different gardens. Vanbrugh's Temple of the Four Winds acts as a focal point in this carefully crafted classical landscape. The woodland garden contains many rare species of rhododendron, and the Rose Garden is a memorable adjunct to a summertime visit to Castle Howard.

Touring Tips Castle Howard and Eden Camp are only a few miles apart, so you can easily combine a visit to both.

Eden Camp

Type of Attraction Modern history museum in former prisoner-of-war camp

Location Malton, North Yorkshire, at the junction of A64 (York-Scarborough Road) and A169 (Malton-Pickering Road); 18 miles northeast of York, 14 miles east of Helmsley; if you are traveling by public transportation, take the train to Malton and a taxi to Eden Camp

Admission £3 adults; £2 seniors and children

Hours Daily, 10 a.m.–5 p.m. (last admission 4 p.m.); closed December 24–second Monday in January

Phone (01653) 697-777

Website www.edencamp.co.uk

When to Go Anytime

Special Comments Accessible to visitors with disabilities; some exhibits are embellished with startling special effects.

Overall Appeal by Age Group

Preschool ★	Teens ★★	Over 30 ★★★
Grade school ★★	Young Adults ★★	Seniors ★★★★

Author's Rating ★★

How Much Time to Allow About 2–3 hours

Description & Comments Eden Camp was established in 1942 as a prisoner-of-war camp; the first inmates, Italians captured in North Africa, built the 35 wooden huts that are used today to tell the story of Britain during World War II. Eden Camp uses everyday objects from the period, news clips, sound and light effects, mannequins dressed in period costume, and all manner of other dramatics to tell the story of the war in an evocative way. Some of the huts contain re-creations of life in Britain during the war years, and you see what people wore and how they lived. Other huts house simulations of the drama of bombings, fires, and other wartime dangers, and still others trace economic and political events that led to the war. The camp is continually adding new exhibits, among them a newspaper archive in which you can browse coverage of the time and a somewhat text-heavy but worthy look at other recent conflicts around the globe. All in all, the camp succeeds in its mission to portray Britain during the war years, and it provides a fascinating experience that is entertaining and informative both for those who lived through the war and for those to whom it's only a piece of history.

Touring Tips Mess Room, Canteen, and cinema bar provide food and drink.

Rievaulx Abbey

Type of Attraction Majestic ruins of a 12th-century Cistercian abbey

Location Rievaulx, 30 miles north of York, 1.25 miles west of Helmsley off B1257

Admission £3.60 adults; £2.70 seniors and students; £1.80 children ages 5–15

Hours March 29–July 16: daily, 10 a.m.–6 p.m.; July 17–August 31: daily, 9:30 a.m.–6 p.m.; September: daily, 10 a.m.–6 p.m.; October: daily, 10 a.m.–5 p.m.; November–March 28: daily, 10 a.m.–4 p.m.

Phone (01439) 798-228

When to Go Anytime, year-round, though grounds can be soggy in winter

Special Comments A free and informative audio guide is included in admission.

Overall Appeal by Age Group

Preschool ★	Teens ★	Over 30 ★★★
Grade school ★	Young Adults ★★	Seniors ★★★

Author's Rating ★★★

How Much Time to Allow About 1 hour

Description & Comments In the 12th century, at the invitation of the Archbishop of York, St. Bernard of Clairvaux sent a colony of monks from France to establish the first Cistercian monastery in England. The monks were presented with an estate in the valley of the small river Rie (from which the abbey derived its name), a lonely spot surrounded by forested hills. The community took possession of the ground in 1131 and within a very few years numbered 150 monks and 500 lay brethren and was the most celebrated monastery in England, making enormous sums of money from the wool trade. At the time of its suppression and confiscation by Henry VIII in the 16th century, this once-thriving religious community had only 23 members. The massive church, abbey, and monastic buildings that the Cistercians built and dedicated to the Blessed Virgin Mary stand today as magnificent and melancholy ruins. The first church, built around 1135, was based on the Mother House at Clairvaux and reflected the functional austerity of that time. Later, however, it was partially demolished and rebuilt in a far more elaborate style, with clustered columns, molded arches, and elegant lancet windows. The ruins of the church and the monastic outbuildings can be seen on the 15-acre site. Particularly beautiful is the monks' refectory, 124 feet long and 50 feet high, with many of its arcades and several of its graceful lancet windows still intact.

Touring Tips Walks in the surrounding hills provide wonderful views over the ruined abbey complex.

The Yorkshire Dales

West of York, some 700 miles of rolling farmland, moors, pastureland, and fertile river valleys are protected as **Yorkshire Dales National Park.** The **Dales Way** is one of scores of footpaths that crisscross the park; some of the most popular walking country is around **Malhamdale,** where the landscapes are etched with limestone formations, and at **Aysgarth,** where much-used paths follow a series of waterfalls.

You can stock up on walking maps and other information at any of the **Yorkshire Dales National Park Centres,** including branches at Hawes (phone (01969) 667-450) and Aysgarth Falls (phone (01969) 663-424); most centers are open April–October, daily, 9:30 a.m.–5 p.m., and November–March, Saturday and Sunday, 10 a.m.–4 p.m. For more information on the park, visit **www.yorkshiredales.org.**

To reach the Dales by car from York, follow A59 west to the southern edge of the park. It is difficult to reach much of the park by public transportation, although local buses serve many of the villages; for information, call (0113) 245-676.

Bolton Priory

Type of Attraction Historic priory and landscaped park on the estate of the Duke and Duchess of Devonshire

Location Skipton, North Yorkshire; 37 miles east of York; from the M6, follow the A59 at junction 31, 4 miles past Skipton, turn left onto the B6160, signposted "Bolton Abbey" at the roundabout

Admission £4 per vehicle

Hours Daily, year-round, 7:30 a.m.–dusk

Phone (01756) 718-009

Website www.boltonabbey.com

When to Go The grounds are prettiest April–September

Special Comments Electric wheelchairs are available for disabled visitors; there is a tearoom near the ruins.

Overall Appeal by Age Group

Preschool ★	Teens ★★	Over 30 ★★★
Grade school ★★	Young Adults ★★	Seniors ★★★

Author's Rating ★★★

How Much Time to Allow At least 1 hour, longer for a walk on the estate

Description & Comments Bolton Abbey extends along a six-mile stretch of the River Wharfe between Bolton and Barden bridges. Bolton has been an estate for about a thousand years and in the possession of the Dukes of Devonshire since the 1750s. It now comprises some 30,000 acres and remains a working estate. The romantic beauty of the landscape, which includes the ruins of Bolton Priory and more than 80 miles of moorland and riverside footpaths, has inspired painters and poets such as William Wordsworth, Joseph Turner, and Edwin Landseer. "Bolton," which means "an enclosure with a house," may refer to the original Saxon manor house on the estate. Today, the entire estate goes by the name Bolton Abbey, even though the religious house established here was actually a priory. The history of Bolton Priory, whose impressive ruins are what draw most visitors, dates back to the 12th century, when the Black Canons of the Order of St. Augustine established a monastic order at Bolton. The 800-year-old Priory Church stands among the ruins of the rest of the priory complex, dissolved under Henry VIII, and still serves the local community as a place of worship.

Touring Tips The estate includes miles of woodland and riverside paths, so in addition to visiting the priory, you have ample opportunity to explore the surrounding countryside. The admission ticket lets you park at any of the three estate car parks: Strid Wood, Sandholme (along the river), and Bolton Abbey Village (closest to the Priory).

Haworth

If it weren't for the Brontës—that famous trio of novelist sisters—it's doubtful that Haworth would be on any tourist's itinerary. But the continuing fascination with the lives and works of Charlotte *(Jane Eyre)*, Emily *(Wuthering Heights)*, and Anne *(The Tenant of Wildfell Hall)* ensures that this somewhat grim Yorkshire town, a former textile manufacturing village, will remain one of England's busiest literary shrines.

The main focus of pilgrimage is the **Brontë Parsonage Museum;** the town does not otherwise offer much of interest to the traveler. One exception is the **Keighley–Worth Valley Railway,** which runs historic steam trains between Haworth and Keighley, three miles south, and on to the town of Oxenhope. Service is on weekends year-round and daily in July and August; for more information, call (01535) 647-777 or visit **www.kwvr.co.uk.**

Arriving and Getting Oriented in Haworth

Haworth is about 45 miles west of York. The quickest and easiest way to make the trip from York is by car, on the A64 west to Leeds and the A6120 to Shipley, where you pick up the A650 to Keighley and the B6142 to Haworth.

Reaching Haworth by train from York means changing trains twice, at Leeds City Station for Keighley and at Keighley for the historic steam railway to Haworth. You can make the trip by train daily, June–July, and on Saturday and Sunday the rest of the year. Alternatively, you can travel by train to Keighley daily, with departures from York about every half hour, and take a taxi from there to Haworth. For more information, call (08457) 484-950 or go to **www.railtrack.co.uk.** The **Haworth Tourist Information Centre** (2–4 West Lane; (01535) 642-329) is open April–October, daily, 9:30 a.m.–5:30 p.m., and November–March, daily, 9:30 a.m.–5 p.m.

Brontë Parsonage Museum

Type of Attraction Home of the literary Brontë family and adjacent museum

Locatioiall Appeal by Age Group

Preschool ★	Teens ★★	Over 30 ★★★
Grade school ★	Young Adults ★★	Seniors ★★★

Author's Rating ★★★★

How Much Time to Allow About 1 hour

Description & Comments Built of dark brick and located just a few yards from the town cemetery, the late-18th-century parsonage where the Brontës spent most of their lives is not what you'd call appealing. Yet it was here that three sisters, Charlotte (1816–1855), Emily (1818–1848), and Anne (1820–1849) Brontë, wrote some of the most enduring classics of 19th-century English literature. Charlotte lived in this house with her father, the Reverend Patrick Brontë, after the deaths of her brother Branwell and her sisters Emily and Anne. The house retains the basic floor plan as the Brontës knew it and contains many pieces of original furniture and personal possessions of theirs. Display cases on the second floor contain a dress and other articles of clothing worn by Charlotte (a surprisingly small woman), as well as letters and personal effects. The museum, entered from the house, contains an amazing collection of Brontëiana, including the tiny handmade books in which the three girls and their brother Branwell wrote their earliest fantasy sagas; watercolors and pencil sketches by Charlotte; and even the collars worn by Emily's beloved dogs. All in all, this is one of the finest literary museums in the world.

Touring Tips After visiting the parsonage, you can visit the adjacent (and much altered) parish church where Emily and Charlotte are interred. Not far from the parsonage there are well-marked paths out onto the moors that figure so prominently in *Wuthering Heights* and *Jane Eyre*.

Saltaire

If you are driving from York to Haworth, consider making a stop at Saltaire, a specially built "model" Victorian industrial village about 35 miles west of York near the dreary town of Bradford. The 25-acre village was built by Sir Titus Salt between 1851 and 1876 to provide living quarters for the workers at his woolen mills. The textile trade was a huge business in this part of Yorkshire; in just one of Sir Salt's Saltaire mills, more than 3,000 people were employed to work at some 1,200 looms. But unlike other dreary mill towns, the streets of Saltaire are lined with neat brick row houses, detached houses of various sizes (the size reflected your standing in the mill hierarchy), shops, schools, churches, and neoclassical buildings with ornamental cast-iron railings and street lamps. The town has remained remarkably intact and is such a unique example of "advanced" town planning that in 2000 it was named a UNESCO World Heritage Site.

The best way to see Saltaire is by walking. One-hour guided walks depart year-round, Saturday at 2 p.m. and Sunday at 11 a.m. and 2 p.m., from the **Saltaire Tourist Information and Gift Centre** (2 Victoria Road; (01274) 774-993). The cost is £2.25 adults, £1.75 children. If you can't do one of the walks, the center sells maps of the town so you can explore on your own.

Salts Mill on Victoria Road, in use as a factory from 1856 to 1986, has been converted into an arts and cultural center and shops. The "1853 Gallery" houses a mishmash collection of works by David Hockney, who was born in nearby Bradford. On the second and third floors, more Hockneys and a collection of local pottery share gallery space with an arts-related bookshop and a restaurant/café. The complex is open daily; for information, call (01274) 531-163 or visit **www.saltsmill.org.uk.** Other buildings in the village have also been transformed into shops, restaurants, and pubs.

Part Twelve

The Lake District

The Lake District, or Lakeland as it's also called, or just "the Lakes," has been enchanting visitors for centuries. The poet William Wordsworth, who spent his entire life in the region, captured the essential appeal of the Lakes when he wrote in his *Guide through the District of the Lakes* that these landscapes of craggy mountains and still, mist-shrouded waters were to be treasured by "persons of good taste . . . [with] an eye to perceive and a heart to enjoy." The poet rambled and climbed through almost every square mile of this region wedged into a small corner of the northwest coast near the Scottish border, and he lobbied to protect his beloved landscapes as a national property. Almost exactly a hundred years after Wordsworth's death, in 1951, the British parliament established the **Lake District National Park,** which covers nearly 800 square miles.

The craggy, bracken-covered peaks of the Lake District are not particularly tall (none more than 3,000 feet), but they are dramatically beautiful nonetheless. They tower above moors (known as "fells" in the local parlance) laced with becks (mountain streams) and tarns (small lakes). In the gentle, wooded valleys beneath these mountain landscapes are the famous meres (lakes)—long, slender bodies of sparkling water that reflect the crags, forests, and meadows above them. Many visitors follow, quite literally, in Wordsworth's footsteps and explore the region on foot, and you should partake of this experience, too, while in the Lake District. You'll also want to visit any number of historic homes (including two where Wordsworth lived), explore the towns and small villages built of slate and stone that seem to blend into the landscape, and simply enjoy this part of the world that is both beautiful and quintessentially English.

Folks in the Lake District say that if you don't like the weather, just wait . . . it will change in a few minutes. Although the sun does frequently shine upon the Lake District, when it becomes the most beautiful place on earth, be prepared for rain (which the locals call "lake fill") in any season. Most walkers don't let the rain slow them down, and there's

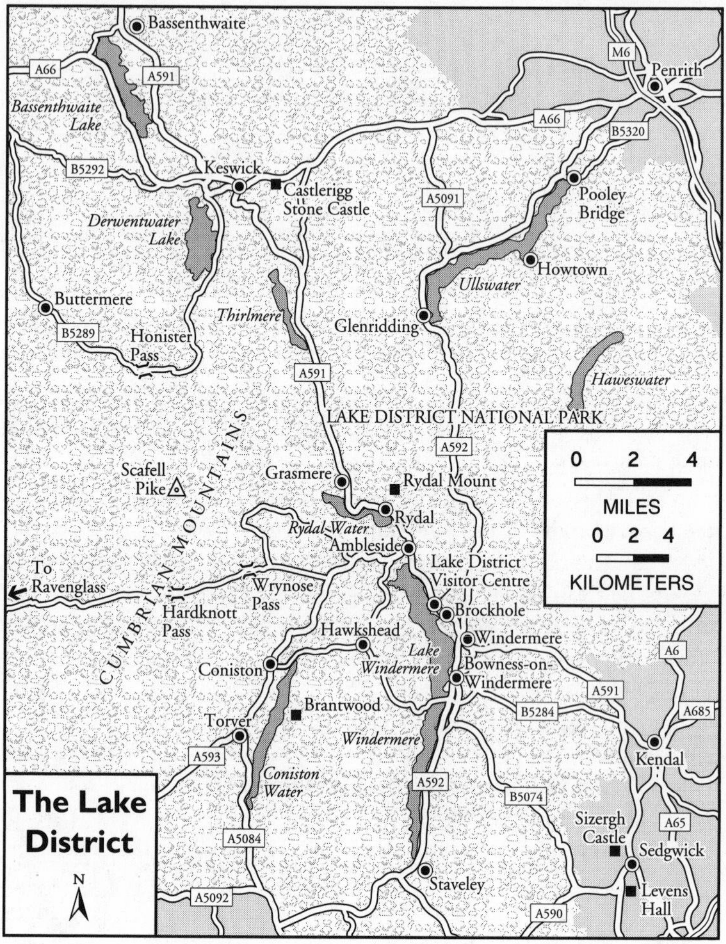

no small amount of beauty to the familiar sight of the mists that swirl across the surface of the lakes and around the peaks.

Not To Be Missed in the Lake District

- Beatrix Potter Gallery in Hawkshead (page 473)
- Castlerigg Stone Circle (page 478)
- Coniston (page 474)
- Grasmere (page 475)
- Cruise on Coniston Water (page 469)
- Lake Windermere (page 469)
- The Wordsworth Sights: Dove Cottage (page 476) and Rydal Mount (page 477)

Planning Your Visit to the Lake District

The **Lake District Visitor Centre** at Brockhole (phone (015394) 466-01; **www.lake-district.gov.uk**) is administered by the Lake District National Park Authority and is located in a mansion with terraced gardens on the shores of Lake Windermere, between Windermere and Ambleside on the A591. The center houses exhibits on the history, wildlife, geography, and people of the Lake District, and also provides extensive information on touring the region. The center is open April–October, daily, 10 a.m.–5 p.m., and on weekends in November, 10 a.m.–5 p.m. From the Visitor Centre's jetty, you can board a scenic circular cruise of Lake Windermere, with departures every hour between 9:45 a.m. and 4:45 p.m.; fees are £4.60 adults, £2.30 children, and £12.50 families of up to two adults and two children.

You will also find visitor centers in other Lake District towns and villages; see Windermere, Grasmere, Hawkshead, and Keswick, below.

Special Events in the Lake District

The Lake District celebrates the arrivl of spring in mid-March with a colorful **floral show** in Ambleside; for information, call (01539) 432-252. You can enjoy one of the region's most lavish **Guy Fawkes Day** fireworks displays in Cockermouth on or around November 9; call (01900) 822-634 for information.

Arriving and Getting Oriented in the Lake District

The Lake District is about 250 miles northwest of London. Trains run about every two hours throughout the day from London's Euston Station to the Oxenholme Lake District station, where you can change to a local train for Windermere, only 15 minutes away. The total trip takes about three and a half hours and costs about £90 round trip. For information, call (08457) 484-950 or go to **www.railtrack.co.uk.** The Windermere train station is in the center of town.

By car, the quickest route from London is the M1 and the M6 to Kendal, then A590 and A591 to Windermere. Allow at least five hours for the trip, as traffic on the M1 and M6, two of England's main arteries, is often heavy. If you're uneasy about hitting the British motorways, consider taking the train to Windermere and traveling by local bus from there; see "Getting around the Lake District," below.

National Express buses leave London's Victoria Coach Station for Windermere about every two hours, but the trip is long, from seven and a half to ten hours, making the train a much more appealing option. The

HOW HOTELS COMPARE

Hotel	Overall Rating	Quality Rating	Value Rating	Price
Linthwaite House Hotel	★★★★½	★★★★½	★★★★	£120–£231
Miller Howe	★★★★	★★★★	★★★	£170–£350
Wordsworth Hotel	★★★½	★★★½	★★½	£140–£160

round trip costs about £50. For more information, call (08705) 808-080 or go to **www.gobycoach.com.**

Hotels in the Lake District

The Lakes are a popular spot for summer holidays, so reserve well in advance if you are planning to visit June–August or on weekends in May and September. Rates vary considerably with season, and many hotels offer rooms at many different prices, depending on level of luxury and whether or not a room has amenities such as a terrace or a lake view. Also, many of the hotels in the region, including several of those we list here, have excellent dining rooms, and offer dinner, room, and breakfast packages that are well worth considering. These packages are often available at substantial discounts out of season; ask when booking or check the hotel websites.

Ivy House — *£98–£102*

OVERALL ★★★ | QUALITY ★★★ | VALUE ★★★★

Hawkshead, Cumbria LA22 0NS; (015394) 362-04; fax (015394) 361-71; david@ivyhousehotel.com; www.ivyhouse.com

Location In the village center.

Amenities & Services 11 rooms. Homey lounge with log fire.

Elevator No.

Parking Near hotel, free.

Pricing Includes dinner and full English breakfast.

Credit Cards V, MC, AMEX

If you are looking for small, charming accommodation in the Lake District, you won't do much better than this gracious Georgian house in Hawkshead, one of the prettiest villages in the region. Since the village is a good base for walks, you'll probably enjoy coming in from the surrounding hills to relax in the lounge, where drinks are served, then sitting down to a home-cooked meal (dinner is included in the rates). Six of the guest rooms are in the main house, and five are in a newer building across the street; all are furnished comfortably and simply and have mod-

IN THE LAKE DISTRICT

Hotel	Overall Rating	Quality Rating	Value Rating	Price
Ivy House	★★★	★★★	★★★★	£98–£102
Lindeth Howe	★★★	★★★	★★★½	£100–£180
Langdale Chase	★★★	★★★	★★★	£130–£190

ern baths; two have extra beds for children. The Ivy House is a good choice for travelers without cars, since Hawkshead is on the regional bus routes and all the village services are just outside the hotel door.

Langdale Chase *£130–£190*

OVERALL ★★★ | QUALITY ★★★ | VALUE ★★★

Windermere, Cumbria LA23 1LW; (01539) 432-201; fax (01539) 432-604; sales@langdalechase.co.uk; www.langdalechase.co.uk

Location On Lake Windermere, between Windermere and Ambleside.

Amenities & Services 27 rooms. Dining room, bar, two-story Great Hall paneled in 17th-century oak, extensive gardens and lakefront lawns.

Elevator No.

Parking On grounds, free.

Pricing Includes full breakfast.

Credit Cards V, MC, AMEX

This formidable, stone, 19th-century mansion, complete with a paneled and galleried Great Hall, sits on a hill above Lake Windermere. While the surroundings seem to be tailor-made as the setting of a television murder mystery, they also provide character-filled and quirky accommodation in one of the most scenic settings on the lake. Guest rooms are in the main house, in a bungalow set in the garden, and in a boat house. All the rooms are quite large, most overlook the lake, and they are furnished in a somewhat dowdy but comfortable style that invites relaxing. Service is attentive, and drinks and meals are available on the extensive terraces in good weather.

Lindeth Howe *£100–£180*

OVERALL ★★★ | QUALITY ★★★ | VALUE ★★★½

Longtail Hill, Windermere, Cumbria LA23 3JE; (015394) 457-59; fax (015394) 463-68; hotel@lindeth-howe.co.uk; www.lindeth-howe.co.uk

Location A mile south of Bowness-on-Windermere.

Amenities & Services 36 rooms. Dining room and bar, pleasant lounges, indoor swimming pool, free Internet access.

Elevator No.

Parking Free, on grounds.

Pricing Includes full English breakfast.

Credit Cards V, MC, AMEX

Beatrix Potter lived at Lindeth Howe from 1905 to 1913 and wrote several of her famous books here, including *Timmy Tiptoes* and *Pigling Bland.* Family photos and other Potter knickknacks decorate the halls and public rooms of this pleasant hotel, which has been tastefully expanded in recent years, and there's a collection of the author's books in the library. Even without the Peter Rabbit connection, Lindeth Howe would be an excellent choice for families, with amenities that include a swimming pool and extensive grounds, and a special high tea for youngsters. Family rooms are available, and many of the doubles are large enough to accommodate cots. All of the rooms are nicely done in a mix of country and modern pieces.

Linthwaite House Hotel *£120–£231*

OVERALL ★★★★½ | QUALITY ★★★★½ | VALUE ★★★★

Crook Road, Bowness-on-Windermere, Cumbria LA23 31A; (015394) 886-00; fax (015394) 886-01; admin@linthwaite.com; www.linthwaite.com

Location On a hillside above Lake Windermere, about a mile outside Bowness-on-Windermere.

Amenities & Services 26 rooms. Excellent restaurant. Several lounges, terraces, gardens, private tarn (lake), croquet lawn; in-room CD players and dataports.

Elevator No.

Parking Free, on grounds.

Pricing Includes full breakfast.

Credit Cards V, MC, AMEX

An air of informal refinement pervades this wonderful hotel, our favorite in the Lake District. A glowing hearth greets you at the door, comfortable lounges overlook the lake, and public areas and guest rooms alike manage to suggest luxury without a hint of pretension. Service, likewise, is attentive and friendly. Furnishings throughout forgo the typical country look for a chic mix of contemporary and traditional styles, with an emphasis on comfort; rooms are well-equipped with armchairs, reading lamps, ample storage, and other thoughtful touches, and all have new or newly refurbished bathrooms. All rooms have views of Lake Windermere, about a mile away, or the lovely, wooded grounds, and rooms in a new wing are especially large and comfortable. Room 16 is a luxurious double with such special touches as a walk-in closet and a small balcony. Many guests find it difficult to leave the grounds even for meals, which are served here in one of the region's best-regarded restaurants.

Miller Howe *£170–£350*

OVERALL ★★★★ | QUALITY ★★★★ | VALUE ★★★

Rayrigg Road, Windermere, Cumbria LA23 3JE; (015394) 425-36; fax (015394) 456-64; lakeview@millerhowe.com; www.millerhowe.com

Location On Lake Windermere, between Windermere and Bowness-on-Windermere.

Amenities & Services 13 rooms. Excellent restaurant, handsome lounges, conservatory, extensive lakeside gardens.

Elevator No.

Parking Free, on grounds.

Pricing Includes dinner and English breakfast.

Credit Cards V, MC, AMEX

Miller Howe has lost none of the cachet of the comfortable private home it once was. In fact, the intimacy of the surroundings and the warmth and professionalism of the service ensure that Miller Howe is the favorite of many regular visitors to the Lake District, and it is certainly one of the finest hotels in the region. Paintings, antiques, and other stylishly distinctive furnishings fill the lounges and the guest rooms, no two of which are alike. While we find the décor of the rooms to be a bit fussy and claustrophobic, this is not true of the outlooks—most rooms have balconies and command spectacular views of the lake and surrounding mountains. A cottage on the grounds has been converted to three luxurious suites that provide the ultimate Lake District lodging experience. Rates include dinner in the hotel restaurant, which is generally considered to be one of the two or three best in the Lake District.

Wordsworth Hotel *£140–£160*

OVERALL ★★★ | QUALITY ★★★½ | VALUE ★★½

Grasmere, Ambleside, Cumbria LA22 9SW; (01539) 435-592; fax (01539) 435-765; www.grasmere-hotels.co.uk

Location In the center of the village of Grasmere.

Amenities & Services 37 rooms. Restaurant and bar; several comfortable lounges with sofas and armchairs; conservatory; indoor swimming pool and small gym; attractive grounds; porter; 24-hour room service.

Elevator Yes.

Parking On grounds, free.

Pricing Includes full English breakfast.

Credit Cards V, MC, AMEX, D

The Wordsworth has the look and ambience of a country-house hotel, though it's right in the center of Grasmere, set away from the summertime crowds in shaded lawns and gardens that make the hotel seem like a rural retreat. In fact, the Wordsworth is an excellent choice for travelers without cars, because it is within an easy walk of shops and restaurants. While the hotel doesn't overlook the lake, the shoreline as well as mountain walks are just steps away. The traditionally furnished guest rooms are comfortable and welcoming, and guests also make themselves at home in the ground-floor lounges, which are well-equipped with deep sofas and armchairs. The hotel restaurant, the Prelude, is excellent, and an informal pub and bar, the Dove Olive Branch, adjoins the hotel.

Getting around the Lake District

The region is small and laced with a good network of roads, many of which are narrow and can be fiendishly congested in peak tourist season (July and August, which are good times *not* to visit the Lake District). In most towns and villages, you'll find municipal car parks where you "pay and display"; following the instructions on a pay machine, you'll pay for an allotted period of time (expect to pay about £0.50 per hour) and will be issued a receipt to be displayed in your car. Pay close attention to parking and other traffic signs because municipalities enforce strict rules (and heavy fines) to protect themselves from the onslaught of cars. If you want to rent a car specifically for a tour of the Lake District, you'll have the widest selection in Manchester, about 70 miles south (you can reach Manchester by train from London in about two and a half hours; see "Car Rentals," page 55, for information on rental cars in England).

With perhaps a little help from the tourist offices and some planning, you'll be able to get around the Lake District without a car quite handily. The local bus company, **Stagecoach,** serves Windermere, Grasmere, Hawkshead, Keswick, and other towns in the Lake District with fairly frequent service; you can pick up schedules at the tourist offices, or call (08706) 082-608. Fares vary depending on the destination, but expect to pay just over £1 for the trip from Windermere to Grasmere. If you're not traveling by car, you should plan on taking an organized day tour (see "Tours of the Lake District," below) so you can see the sights and remote areas that are difficult to reach by public transportation. For an effortless way to get around the Lake District, contact **Alistairs of Windermere** at (015394) 881-91 for information on hiring a private car and driver; the fee is £200 a day for up to four people.

Exploring the Lake District

You can see much of the Lake District in a couple of days, but this is a region that is meant to be savored. Without making elaborate arrangements, you can put on your walking shoes from even the busiest town and soon find yourself in beautiful countryside (but never too far from a village or country pub). We recommend that, to best enjoy the quintessentially English experience of a holiday in the Lakes, you settle in for at least three or four days. We also suggest renting a car for the visit, which makes getting around much easier. Spend one or two days driving from village to village and seeing the sights, then spend at least a day or two doing what most British visitors to the region do—enjoy a hearty breakfast, then take to the hills for a bracing walk.

A pleasant, introductory drive through the region might begin in **Windermere** and **Bowness-on-Windermere,** where you board a ferry to cross Lake Windermere to **Far Sawrey,** then continue to **Hawkshead.**

From here, route B5286 heads north through **Ambleside,** a pleasant tourist village at the head of Lake Windermere, and past the William Wordsworth houses, **Rydal Mount** and **Dove Cottage,** to Grasmere. The A591 leads north from **Grasmere** to **Keswick,** but we suggest you leave this busy road to drive through the forested western shore of the lake known as Thirlmere (signposted from the highway) then to **Castlerigg Stone Circle** before driving into Keswick.

Tours of the Lake District

You'll want to enjoy the scenery of the Lake District from the waters of one of the many lakes, and there are plenty of opportunities to do so on any number of lake cruises. Some of the most memorable cruises are those aboard the ***Gondola,*** a Victorian steam yacht that has been restored by the National Trust and sails on Coniston Water. You can lounge in one of the opulently upholstered salons and watch the spectacular scenery slip by. The *Gondola* operates from Coniston Pier, April 1–November 1, with sailings every hour, 11 a.m.– 4 p.m.; for current rates and more information, call (015394) 412-88.

You can make a circuit of three-mile-long Derwentwater on small boats operated by **Keswick Launch;** the lake, studded with small islands and surrounded by craggy peaks, is one of the prettiest in the Lake District. Cruises operate year-round, with departures every half hour, 10 a.m.–7 p.m., March 24–November 30, and every hour, 10:30 a.m. and 3:30 p.m., the rest of the year. Fares are £5.40 adults, £2 children under age 16, free for children under age five, £10.90 families of up to two adults and three children. For more information, call (017687) 772-63 or visit **www.keswick-launch.co.uk.**

Boat trips on Lake Windermere are available year-round. From the piers at Bowness-on-Windermere, ferries make regular trips to Waterhead (near Ambleside) on the north shore and Lakeside on the southern end. November 3–April 11, boats run roughly every hour in each direction, 10 a.m.–3:35 p.m.; April 12–November 2, cruises run roughly every half hour in each direction, 9 a.m.–6:30 p.m. Fares are £4.30 adults each way, £6.40 round trip; £2.60 children each way, £3.30 round trip; and £17.50 families. Sight-seeing cruises that steam around the lake's islands for 45 minutes are available year-round and cost £5 adults, £2.45 children, and £13 families. If you're staying around Lake Windermere, consider purchasing a **Freedom of the Lake** pass, which allows you to board a vessel anytime you want in a 24-hour period and costs £11.50 adults, £5.75 children, and £29 families. Contact **Windermere Lake Cruises** at (015395) 311-88 or **www.windermere-lakecruises.co.uk.**

One of the best-reputed of the many local companies that offer land tours of the region is **Mountain Goat** (Victoria Street, Windermere; (015394) 451-61; **www.mountain-goat.com**). The company offers a

HOW ATTRACTIONS COMPARE

Attraction	Comments	Author's Rating
Windermere and Bowness-on-Windermere		
Windermere Steamboat Centre	Collection of historic boats	★★★
The World of Beatrix Potter	Miniature tableaux created from Beatrix Potter stories	★★
Hawkshead		
Beatrix Potter Gallery	Original Beatrix Potter drawings	★★★
Hill Top	Beatrix Potter's home	★★★

variety of half-day and full-day tours that often combine boat cruises, drives through some of the more scenic mountain scenery, and stops at Rydal Mount and other local sights and villages; fees range from about £14 for half-day tours to about £23 for full-day tours.

Windermere and Bowness-on-Windermere

The adjoining towns of Windermere and Bowness-on-Windermere have long since lost their distinct boundaries, and they now merge into one another as the Lake District's major resort. Although there were fishing and farming villages here long before the mid-19th century, the arrival of the railroad put them on the map and ensured the popularity that they still enjoy. Both towns have long since surrendered any claim to quaintness, but they are relatively attractive, small-scale places with rows of Victorian houses and a few quiet back lanes to explore. The center of Windermere is about a mile from the lakeshore, while Bowness lies right beside the lake—which remains a remarkably beautiful sight no matter how many visitors are crowding its shores or boats are plying its waters. There is frequent bus service from the Windermere train station to Bowness, and it's an easy downhill walk from the center of Windermere on Lake Road into Bowness.

The long, narrow lake, 11 miles long and a mile and a half wide, is the largest in England and is surrounded by wooded hills that seem to beckon walkers (and many visitors heed the call; the tourist office in Windermere provides a list of nearby walks). The easiest way to get onto the waters of the lake is to board the **Windermere Ferry,** which has been shuttling passengers between Bowness and Far Sawrey on the western shore since Wordsworth rode it when he was a boy; these days, the boats also accommodate cars. Ferries depart about every 20 minutes throughout the day from Ferry Nab, south of the excursion-boat piers in Bow-

IN THE LAKE DISTRICT

Attraction	Comments	Author's Rating
Coniston		
Brantwood	Historic home and gardens of John Ruskin	★★★½
Grasmere		
Dove Cottage and Wordsworth and Grasmere Museum	Early home of William Wordsworth, local museum	★★★★
Rydal Mount	Later home of William Wordsworth	★★★

ness. Fares are £0.40 for passengers, £2 for cars; for information, call (01228) 606-744. The **Windermere Tourist Information Centre** (Victoria Street; (015394) 464-99) provides maps, information on local attractions and tours, and itineraries for walks in the surrounding hills; the center is open July–August, daily, 9 a.m.–7:30 p.m., and September–June, daily, 9 a.m.–6 p.m.

The World of Beatrix Potter

Type of Attraction Miniature tableaux created from Beatrix Potter stories

Location The Old Laundry, Bowness-on-Windermere

Admission £3.50 adults; £2 children

Hours Summer: daily, 10 a.m.–5:30 p.m. Winter: daily, 10 a.m.–4 p.m. Closed December 25 and January 1.

Phone (015394) 884-44

Website www.hop-skip-jump.com

When to Go Anytime, but crowds are thick in the summer months

Special Comments Your young traveling companions will probably enjoy having tea in the Tailor of Gloucester tearoom.

Overall Appeal by Age Group

Preschool ★★★	Teens ★	Over 30 ★
Grade school ★★★	Young Adults ★	Seniors ★

Author's Rating ★★

How Much Time to Allow 45 minutes to 1 hour

Description & Comments Since *The Tale of Peter Rabbit* was first published over a century ago, in 1902, children throughout the world have fallen in love with the stories and pictures created by Beatrix Potter. Scenes and characters from Potter's famous stories, all of which are set in the Lake District, are re-created in this popular attraction. Tableaux include Peter Rabbit eating radishes in Mr. McGregor's garden; Jemima Puddle-duck amongst the foxgloves; and the washerwoman, Mrs. Tiggy-winkle, bustling about in her kitchen. Beatrix Potter's life is chronicled in the "Hidden Beatrix Potter" presentation and video wall. If you grew up on Beatrix Potter stories, or your kids are familiar with them, chances are you'll find this miniature theme park charming. As with the other Potter-related attractions in the area, there is a strong commercial element at work here, as you'll notice when you enter the shop filled to bursting with Potter-inspired merchandise.

Touring Tips If you're on the trail of Beatrix Potter, or on the tail of Peter Rabbit, you can hop from this attraction over to the Beatrix Potter Gallery in Hawkshead to see her original drawings, and also visit her house in Hawkshead.

Windermere Steamboat Centre

Type of Attraction Collection of historic boats

Location Rayrigg Road, Windermere

Admission £3.40 adults; £2 children; £8.50 families

Hours March 16–October 27: daily, 10 a.m.–5 p.m.

Phone (015394) 455-65

Website www.steamboat.co.uk

When to Go Anytime

Special Comments Upon request, a guide will show you around the museum at no extra charge—we recommend you take advantage of this opportunity.

Overall Appeal by Age Group

Preschool ★	Teens ★★	Over 30 ★★
Grade school ★★	Young Adults ★★	Seniors ★★★

Author's Rating ★★★

How Much Time to Allow At least 1 hour

Description & Comments A fascinating collection of boats used on Lake Windermere over the past 150 years fills this small lakeside museum. The oldest craft is a steam launch from 1850, though displays chronicle the role the lakes have played in history from the time the Roman legions camped nearby. There are also exhibits on the history of boating and racing on the lake.

Touring Tips The Centre offers a daily, 50-minute cruise around Belle Isle, an island in Lake Windermere, in an Edwardian steam launch; call ahead to reserve. Cost for the cruise is £5 adults, £2.50 children.

Hawkshead

This attractive village of 17th- and 18th-century stone houses, about ten miles west of Windermere, is surrounded by enticing countryside, and, accordingly, is a popular base for walkers. The village itself is worthy of a leisurely stroll down its cobbled lanes, which have mercifully been closed to car traffic. You can wend your way to the **Beatrix Potter Gallery,** the town's primary attraction (see below), then to the **Old Grammar School,** founded in 1585. William Wordsworth attended school here between 1779 and 1787 and carved his name on a desk that can be seen in the ground-floor classroom. Upstairs, in the headmaster's study, there is an exhibition on the history of the school, its founder (Edwin Sandys, the Archbishop of York), and Wordsworth, its most famous pupil. The school is open somewhat sporadically, April–October, daily, 10 a.m.–4 p.m.; for information, call (015394) 356-47. The **Hawkshead Tourist Information Centre** (phone (015394) 365-25) is at the edge of the village next to the municipal car park; it is open June–August, daily, 9:30 a.m.–5:30 p.m., and September–May, Friday–Sunday, 10 a.m.–3:30 p.m.

The quickest way to reach Hawkshead from Windermere is to take the ferry from Bowness-on-Windermere to Far Sawrey (see "Windermere and Bowness-on-Windermere," above); the crossing spares you the drive around the shores of Lake Windermere.

Beatrix Potter Gallery

Type of Attraction Gallery devoted to original Beatrix Potter drawings

Location Main Street, Hawkshead

Admission £3 adults; £1.50 children ages 5–15; £7.50 families of up to two adults and two children

Hours March 24–October 29: Sunday–Thursday, 10:30 a.m.–4:30 p.m.

Phone (015394) 363-55

Website www.nationaltrust.org.uk

When to Go On weekdays in early mornings or late afternoons to avoid crowds

Special Comments The gallery space, which is accessible only by a steep staircase, is inaccessible to wheelchairs and is too small for baby carriages or baby carriers.

Overall Appeal by Age Group

Preschool ★★	Teens ★★	Over 30 ★★★
Grade school ★★★	Young Adults ★★	Seniors ★★★

Author's Rating ★★★

How Much Time to Allow About 30 minutes

Description & Comments This 17th-century building, once the office of William Heelis, Beatrix Potter's husband, displays an annually changing exhibition of original sketches and watercolors that Potter painted for her children's stories. The interior remains much the same as it was when Heelis worked here as a solicitor, and Potter fans may recognize the premises as Tabitha Twitchit's shop.

Touring Tips You may want to combine a visit to the Gallery with a stop at Hill Top, Beatrix Potter's nearby home, and also take time to stroll through this pleasant village.

Hill Top

Type of Attraction Beatrix Potter's home

Location Near Sawrey, Ambleside, on west side of Lake Windermere (2 miles south of Hawkshead)

Admission £4 adults; £2 children; £9.75 families of up to 2 adults and 2 children

Hours April–May and September–October: Saturday–Wednesday, 11 a.m.–4:30 p.m.; June–August: Saturday–Tuesday, 10:30 a.m.–5 p.m.

Phone (015394) 362-69

Website www.nationaltrust.org.uk

When to Go Early or late to avoid midday crush

Special Comments Hill Top has a timed-entry admission policy, which may keep you waiting in summer months. Windermere Lake Cruises (phone (015395) 311-88) runs a convenient boat and bus shuttle from Pier 3 at Bowness, connecting to a minibus at Hawkshead for Hill Top. Round-trip fares are £5.70 adults, £3.20 children. Between April and October, you can also take bus 505 or 506 from Windermere train station to Hill Top.

Overall Appeal by Age Group

Preschool ★★	Teens ★★	Over 30 ★★★
Grade school ★★★	Young Adults ★★	Seniors ★★★

Author's Rating ★★★

How Much Time to Allow About 30 minutes

Description & Comments Beatrix Potter was born in London but spent summer holidays in the Lake District with her family. The evocative landscapes had a profound effect on her, and the international success of *The Tale of Peter Rabbit* allowed her to buy this small, pretty, 17th-century stone house and move here permanently. Potter wrote and illustrated many of her famous children's tales in this cottage. She deeded her house and several parcels of land to the National Trust before she died in 1943, thus ensuring its preservation. The cottage has been left exactly as it was when she lived there, complete with her furniture, bone china, and garden. Because the house is so small, only a certain number of visitors are allowed in at any one time.

Touring Tips There are a restaurant and a shop on the grounds.

Coniston

This small village crouching beneath its famous peak, the **Old Man of Coniston,** is just three miles west of Hawkshead. The village is prettily located on one of the region's larger lakes, Coniston Water, and is a good base for walks in the surrounding hills. Just across the lake from the village is **Brantwood,** the home of another local man of letters, John Ruskin, who is buried in the village churchyard.

Brantwood

Type of Attraction Historic home and gardens of John Ruskin

Location Across Coniston Water from the village

Admission £4.75 adults; £3.50 students; £1 children; £10 families of up to two adults and three children. Ruskin's studio and grounds only: £3.

Hours Mid-March–mid-November: daily, 11 a.m.–5:30 p.m.; mid-November–mid-March: Wednesday–Sunday, 11 a.m.–4 p.m. Closed December 25–26.

Phone (015394) 413-96

Website www.brantwood.org.uk

When to Go Brantwood does not become as crowded as the Wordsworth sights, and, with its beautiful grounds, provides a good outing on a warm day.

Special Comments There is a pleasant restaurant on the grounds, as well as some attractions of special interest to children, including a bee house and Ruskin's coach and boat. Brantwood sometimes hosts chamber music concerts on Saturday evenings.

Overall Appeal by Age Group

Preschool —	Teens ★★★	Over 30 ★★★
Grade school ★★★	Young Adults ★★★	Seniors ★★★

Author's Rating ★★★½

How Much Time to Allow At least 2 hours to see the house and grounds

Description & Comments This lakeside manor was the home of poet, critic, social reformer, and artist John Ruskin from 1872 until his death in 1900. One of Ruskin's most quotable pearls was "There is no wealth but life," and one of the pleasures of touring the house and grounds is to see the degree to which this intelligent and cultivated man seemed to embrace this dictum. Ruskin's furnishings, books, and art collection fill the rooms of the mansion; the most enchanting items on view are Ruskin's own drawings and watercolors. Ruskin also laid out the gardens and plantings on the 250-acre estate, and the immaculately tended grounds are laced with tree-lined walks and herb, fern, and flower gardens.

Touring Tips The best way to approach the house is by water, and you can do so on boats from the pier in Coniston. These include the Victorian steam yacht *Gondola,* which stops at Brantwood during the summer, and the *Ruskin,* a launch that makes the crossing, weather permitting, year-round; the fare is £1.40 each way and includes a discount on admission fees to the house and grounds.

Grasmere

Grasmere, some eight miles north of Windermere and 18 miles north of Hawkshead, is famous as the place where the poet William Wordsworth spent most of his adult life, first in **Dove Cottage** and then at nearby **Rydal Mount.** The poet, along with his wife, two of his five children, and his sister, Dorothy, are buried in the churchyard of **St. Oswald,** Grasmere's parish church. Miraculously, Grasmere has avoided becoming a Wordsworth theme park (though it may seem that way if you visit on a crowded summer day), and its attractions go far beyond its famous poet. The small village retains a great deal of charm, and on a day when it is not too crowded and the rain is not coming down too hard, the place can be picture-perfect. The narrow lanes are lined with slate houses and pretty gardens, and at the edge of the village are the wooded shores of Lake Grasmere, one of the smallest but most appealing lakes in the region, backed by dramatic fells, or peaks. The **Grasmere Tourist Information Centre** (Red Bank Road; (015394) 352-45) is open April–October, daily, 9:30 a.m.–5:30 p.m., and November–March, Friday–Sunday, 10 a.m.–3:30 p.m.

Dove Cottage and Wordsworth and Grasmere Museum

Type of Attraction Early home of the poet William Wordsworth

Location On A591, a half mile south of Grasmere village

Admission £5 adults; £2.50 children ages 5–15; £12.50 families of up to two adults and two children

Hours Daily, 9:30 a.m.–5:30 p.m. (last tickets sold at 5 p.m.); closed December 24–26 and last three weeks in January

Phone (015394) 355-44

Website www.wordsworth.org.uk

When to Go Early or late to avoid the midday summer crowds; there are far fewer visitors from November through March

Special Comments Dove Cottage can only be seen on a guided tour; at peak times, you may have to wait up to an hour (there's a good bookstore in the ticket office, where you may pass the time). The cottage is not wheelchair accessible, but the museum is.

Overall Appeal by Age Group

Preschool ★	Teens ★★	Over 30 ★★★★
Grade school ★	Young Adults ★★	Seniors ★★★★

Author's Rating ★★★★

How Much Time to Allow About 20 minutes for the guided tour of Dove cottage, another hour for the museum (more if you're a Wordsworth fan)

Description & Comments From 1799 to 1808, Dove Cottage was the home of the poet William Wordsworth. He composed his greatest works while living in this small stone house built in the early 17th century. The house, with its whitewashed exterior festooned with climbing roses, honeysuckle, and scarlet beans, and its snug interior with oak-paneled hall and slate floors, remains much as it was when Wordsworth lived here with his wife, Mary, several children, and his sister Dorothy. Thomas De Quincey and Samuel Taylor Coleridge were frequent visitors. De Quincey moved in when the Wordsworths moved to the much larger Rydal Mount (see below). Much of the Wordsworths' life at Dove Cottage was centered around the orchard and garden, planted with wild thyme, columbine, and orchids. From the garden—like the house, kept as intact as possible—there are views of the valley, Lake Grasmere, and the surrounding hills that so inspired the poet: Loughrigg, Silver Howe, Easedale, Helm Crag, and Steel Fell.

Touring Tips The admission ticket to Dove Cottage also includes entry to the nearby Wordsworth and Grasmere Museum, which displays manuscripts, pictures, books, and memorabilia from the permanent collection of the Wordsworth Trust. Construction has just begun on a new museum site next to Dove Cottage, scheduled to open around 2005. If you're on the literary trail of Wordsworth, you can go from Dove Cottage to Rydal Mount, the poet's final home.

Rydal Mount

Type of Attraction Home of the poet William Wordsworth

Location Off A591, between Ambleside and Grasmere; 2.5 miles south of Grasmere, 1.5 miles north of Ambleside

Admission £4 adults; £1.25 children

Hours March–October: daily, 9:30 a.m.–5 p.m.; November–February: Wednesday–Monday, 10 a.m.–4 p.m. Closed January 10–31.

Phone (015394) 330-02

Website www.wordsworthlakes.co.uk

When to Go The garden is at its prettiest April–June; try to visit on a weekday, when the grounds and house are less likely to be crowded.

Special Comments Visitors are welcome to linger on the grounds, so you might want to consider bringing a book and relaxing here.

Overall Appeal by Age Group

Preschool ★	Teens ★	Over 30 ★★★
Grade school ★	Young Adults ★	Seniors ★★★

Author's Rating ★★★

How Much Time to Allow About 30 minutes

Description & Comments Rydal Mount, a large house on a hillside with views of the surrounding fells, the lake (Rydal Water), and Lake Windermere, was the home of William Wordsworth and his family between 1813 and 1850. Wordsworth, who was given the job of "Distributor of Stamps" and became England's Poet Laureate in 1847, died here on April 23, 1850, at the age of 80. Originally a small farm cottage built in the mid-16th century, Rydal Mount was later enlarged and improved upon. The dining room still contains the oak beams and flagstone floor of the original house, and in the "newer" portion of the house, you can see the drawing room, the bedrooms, and the poet's study in the attic. Portraits, personal possessions, and first editions of Wordsworth's work are on display. The gardens at Rydal Mount, designed by Wordsworth, have changed little in 150 years. In the spring, Dora's Garden, planted and named for a beloved daughter who predeceased him, becomes a field of daffodils and brings to mind Wordsworth's poem: "I wandered lonely as a cloud/That floats on high o'er Vales and Hills,/When all at once I saw a crowd,/A host of golden daffodils;/Beside the Lake, beneath the trees,/Fluttering and dancing in the breeze."

Touring Tips By combining visits to Rydal Mount and Dove Cottage, you will get a sense of how welcome the prosperity that allowed the poet to move to this larger, airier property must have been.

HOW RESTAURANTS COMPARE

Name	Cuisine	Overall	Quality	Value	Price
Miller Howe	British	★★★★½	★★★★½	★★★★	Exp
Linthwaite House	British	★★★★	★★★★	★★★★	Exp
Drunken Duck	Pub	★★★	★★★	★★★	Inexp

Keswick

Keswick, 11 miles north of Grasmere and 20 miles north of Windermere on the A591, is a busy regional market town that doubles as a lakeside resort. Its location on Derwentwater, one of the larger lakes, and its proximity to scenic peaks and marvelous walking trails attract weekend daytrippers year-round and outdoor-oriented holiday makers in the summer. Keswick is not particularly charming, though the old center of town close to the lake is quite attractive. One of the town's claims to fame is as the residence of two other poets of the Lake District, George Southey and Samuel Taylor Coleridge. Both men were close to William Wordsworth, and the three would often set off together on rambles through the fells.

The discovery of pure graphite near Keswick in the early 16th century launched the development of several industries, including pencil making. The history of the humble, low-tech implement is quite interesting and is nicely documented at the **Cumberland Pencil Museum** (Southey Lane; (01768) 736-26) open year-round, daily, 9:30 a.m.–4 p.m. The museum is administered by Derwent, one of the world's leading manufacturers of graphic and artists' pencils, and the products are available in a shop on the premises, which still serve as the company factory.

One of England's most fascinating and enigmatic prehistoric sites, **Castlerigg Stone Circle,** lies a mile-and-a-half east of Keswick, just off the A591 (follow the signs as you enter the outskirts of town). If you want to approach the site on foot, there's a marvelous walk through woods and fields that starts at the National Park Information Centre in town; if you're driving, you can park on the road across from the entrance to the site. Occupying a commanding location atop a hill, Castlerigg consists of 33 standing stones that form a circle around a rectangular enclosure. As with all prehistoric stone circles, no one can say definitively what this one was used for, but it was obviously a gathering place for local people thousands of years ago.

To stock up on information on Keswick and nearby attractions, stop in at the **National Park Information Centre** (in the Moot Hall on Market Square; (01768) 726-45; **www.keswick.org**). The center is an especially good source for information on the many walks in the mountains around

IN THE LAKE DISTRICT

Name	Cuisine	Overall	Quality	Value	Price
Travellers Rest	Pub	★★★	★★★	★★★	Inexp
Hole in t'Wall	Pub	★★★	★★½	★★★	Inexp

Keswick. The center is open April–September, daily, 9:30 a.m.–5:30 p.m., and October–March, daily, 9:30 a.m.–4:30 p.m.

Dining in the Lake District

Drunken Duck ★★★

PUB | INEXPENSIVE | QUALITY ★★★ | VALUE ★★★

Hamlet of Barnsgate, outside Hawkshead; (015394) 363-47

Reservations Not necessary **Entrée Range** £5.95–£13.95 **Payment** V, MC, AMEX **Bar** Full service **Disabled Access** Yes

Hours Monday–Saturday, 11:30 a.m.–11:30 p.m.; Sunday, noon–10:30 p.m.; full meals served noon–2:30 p.m., 6–9 p.m.

House Specialties Toasted open sandwiches; local fish and game.

This cozy, beamed pub in a stone village surrounded by walking country is the perfect place to settle in front of the fire for a pub lunch or evening meal, accompanied by a wide choice of ales and whiskies. Food and drink is served on a terrace in good weather.

Hole in t'Wall ★★★

PUB | INEXPENSIVE | QUALITY ★★½ | VALUE ★★★

Lowside, Bowness-on-Windermere; (015394) 434-88

Reservations Not necessary **Entrée Range** £5–£12 **Payment** V, MC **Bar** Full service **Disabled Access** Yes

Hours Monday–Saturday, 11 a.m.–11 p.m.; Sunday, noon–10:30 p.m.; full meals served noon–2:30 p.m., 6–9 p.m.

House Specialties Curries; meat pies; other homemade specials.

The official name of this 17th-century inn on a back street near the lake is the New Hall, but few locals would know the place by any other moniker than "Hole in t'Wall," which refers to the opening made to connect a blacksmith's shop and the original alehouse to create the present premises. Stone walls, darkened beams, and slate floors set the mood in an establishment that can even claim to have once housed Charles Dickens. If you want to soak in the atmosphere, come for lunch or an afternoon pint—at night, the place can get unbearably noisy and smoky.

Linthwaite House ★★★★

MODERN BRITISH | EXPENSIVE | QUALITY ★★★★ | VALUE ★★★★

Crook Road, Bowness-on-Windermere; (015394) 886-00

Reservations Recommended, required in summer **Entrée Range** prix fixe at dinner, £42 for 4-course meal **Payment** V, MC, AMEX **Bar** Full service **Disabled Access** Yes

Hours Lunch: daily, 12:30–1:30 p.m. Dinner: Sunday–Thursday, 7:15–9 p.m.

House Specialties Excellent seafood preparations; creative vegetarian dishes; local lamb and game.

The casual elegance that is the hallmark of the rest of this stunning hotel prevails in the intimately attractive, candlelit dining room. Service is attentive and always on the mark, and diners are encouraged to linger and savor each course, right through the delicious desserts. Sandwiches and other light fare are available throughout the day and can be enjoyed on the terrace in good weather or in front of a hearth in one of the hotel's appealing lounges.

Miller Howe ★★★★½

MODERN BRITISH | EXPENSIVE | QUALITY ★★★★½ | VALUE ★★★★

Rayrigg Road, Windermere; (015394) 425-36

Reservations Required **Entrée Range** Prix fixe: dinner, £39.50; lunch, £17.50; Sunday lunch, £19.95; tea, £9.99 **Payment** V, MC, AMEX **Bar** Full service **Disabled Access** Yes

Hours Monday–Saturday, 7–9:30 p.m.; Sunday, noon–2:30 p.m., 7–9:30 p.m.

House Specialties Seafood appetizers and main courses; any of the creative vegetarian choices; local cheeses.

The dining room of Miller Howe is, like the rest of the hotel, small and intimate, and diners are made to feel like they are guests in a private home. Dining in the airy, multileveled room overlooking Lake Windermere and the hotel's extensive gardens is an occasion, marked by exquisite service and what many fans claim is the finest cuisine in the Lake District.

Travellers Rest ★★★

PUB | INEXPENSIVE | QUALITY ★★★ | VALUE ★★★

On A591, just north of Grasmere; (015394) 356-04

Reservations Not necessary **Entrée Range** £3.95–£10.95 **Payment** V, MC, AMEX **Bar** Full service **Disabled Access** Yes

Hours Monday–Saturday, 11:30 a.m.–11 p.m.; Sunday, noon–10:30 p.m.; full meals served noon–2:30 p.m., 6–9 p.m.

House Specialties Soups; open sandwiches; homemade meat pies.

You can actually get away from Grasmere's summertime crowds at this charming 16th-century inn on the outskirts of the village. Aside from pub meals and a good selection of ales, the premises also serve an excellent afternoon tea, with home-made scones and breads.

Shopping in the Lake District

You might not leave the Lake District without a stuffed bunny or two (the Peter Rabbit connection) or a stash of Kendal Mint Cakes, mint concoctions that are so sugary Sir Edmund Hilary took some up Mount Everest with him (an early energy bar). Both items are readily available throughout the region; in fact, there are so many shops in the Lake District selling Peter Rabbit articles that you might soon become rather tired of the cute little fellow. For some serious Peter Rabbit shopping—stuffed and porcelain figurines, infant-sized T-shirts emblazoned with bunnies, toddler-resistant editions of the books—check out the shop at **The World of Beatrix Potter** (Bowness-on-Windermere; (015394) 884-44). If you find that you don't have the caps, rain slickers, woolen sweaters, and other gear that comes in handy on soggy Lake District walks, pay a visit to **Lakeland Sheepskin and Leather Centre** (Lake Road, Bowness-on-Windermere, (015394) 444-66; or Main Street, Hawkshead, (01539) 436-633). In Grasmere, the aroma of baking gingerbread will lead you to the **Gingerbread Shop** (phone (015394) 435-428), housed in the original village schoolhouse from 1660 in a corner of St. Oswald's Churchyard; the shop still uses a recipe concocted by Sarah Nelson in 1854.

Exercise and Recreation in the Lake District

Walking is the best way to enjoy the Lake District; in fact, the chance to walk is what brings many visitors to the region. Dozens of paths traverse the peaks and valleys, ranging in length from a few miles to as many as 60 and 70 miles on such routes as the **Cumbria Way** and the **Coast to Coast Walk.** It's easy to get into the hills from even the busiest towns and villages. In Windermere, for example, the relatively easy 2.5-mile round-trip trail from the tourist office to 784-foot-high Orrest Head provides memorable views of the lake, lakeshore villages, and surrounding hills.

All the tourist centers provide maps and other information for walks in the region, and shops are well stocked with maps and guidebooks to Lake District walks. We suggest you check out **www.lakedistrictwalks.com,** compiled by John Dawson; this Lake District resident and avid walker provides details and expert advice on some 40 walks in the region.

Among the many organizations that lead guided walks we highly recommend the experienced guides of **Keswick Rambles** (phone (017687) 712-92; **www.keswickrambles.ic24.net**); they lead walks of varying degrees of difficulty from the Moot Hall in Keswick into the spectacular countryside that surrounds the town. The organization leads a different walk every day, most starting at 10:15 a.m. and ending at 4 or 5 p.m., and provides bus transportation to paths that are not easily accessible from the center of town. To join a walk, you need only show up at the Moot Hall and pay a fee, £5 adults and £3 children. Local chapters of Britain's venerable Ramblers' Association (Second Floor, Camelford House, 87–90 Albert Embankment, London SE1 7TW; (0207) 339-8500; **www.ralakedistrict.uk**) offer some 800 guided walks a year in the Lake District, and nonmembers are welcome to participate. The Lake District National Park Authority also leads walks in the region; for more information, check with the Lake District Visitor Centre at Brockhole (between Windermere and Ambleside on the A591), call (015394) 466-01, or visit **www.lake-district.gov.uk.**

Around the Lake District

Hadrian's Wall

In the first century A.D., on the orders of the Roman emperor Hadrian, an enormous wall was built across northern England in what is today Northumbria. The purpose was to prevent the "barbarians" living in the north to invade Roman holdings in England (Britannia). Hadrian's Wall, one of the preeminent Roman monuments in England, stretches nearly 74 miles from Bowness on Solway in the west, through Newcastle-upon-Tyne, and eastward to Wallsend. There were forts all along the wall, manned by soldiers from throughout the empire, including Italy, Holland, Belgium, France, and Spain. After the Roman garrisons left England in the fourth century, the wall fell into disrepair. Whole sections were destroyed or carted away, the stone put to other uses.

By car, it is easy to visit this remnant of early Britain from the Lake District on a day's outing. A long stretch of the wall remains standing near the town of **Hexham,** about 70 miles north and east of Kendal via the M6 and A69. Plan on stopping first at the Roman Army Museum and Vindolanda, about 15 minutes apart along remaining portions of the wall; they provide an excellent overall introduction to the wall and England's Roman heritage.

The **Roman Army Museum** (phone (01697) 474-85) is situated beside **Walltown Crags,** one of the best preserved sections of the Wall, and you can walk along part of the ancient fortification. In the small museum, period reconstructions, life-size figures, Roman objects, and films offers insights into the garrisons—from their training to their everyday life here on the northern boundary of the Roman Empire—that served along Hadrian's Wall. **Vindolanda** (phone (01434) 344-277) is the site of a Roman fort and civilian settlement, just south of the Wall. Ongoing excavations continue to unearth artifacts and entire buildings, while the museum and gardens house life-size replicas of a temple, a house, a shop, and a section of the Wall, as well as excavated remains from the period of Roman occupation, including boots and shoes, jewelry, tools, locks, and textiles. Both museums are open March and October, daily, 10 a.m.–5 p.m.; April and September, daily, 10 a.m.–5:30 p.m.; May and June, daily, 10 a.m.–6 p.m., and July and August, daily, 10 a.m.–6 p.m.; last admission is half an hour before closing. Admission to the Roman Army Museum is £3.30 adults, £2.90 students and seniors, £2.20 children, and £9.50 families; admission to Vindolanda is £4.10 adults, £3.50 students and seniors, £2.90 children, and £12.50 families; combined admission to both sites is £6 adults, £5.20 students and seniors, £4.30 children, and £20 families. Guides at the museum will be happy to steer you to places in the area that provide the best views of the portions of the wall that remain intact. For more information on the Roman Army Museum and Vindolanda, visit **www.vindolanda.com.**

Index